The Undiscove

Studies in German Literature, Linguistics, and Culture

The Undiscover'd Country

W. G. Sebald and the Poetics of Travel

Edited by
Markus Zisselsberger

CAMDEN HOUSE
Rochester, New York

First published 2010 by Camden House
Transferred to digital printing 2012
Reprinted in paperback 2013

Camden House is an imprint of Boydell & Brewer Inc.
668 Mt. Hope Avenue, Rochester, NY 14620, USA
www.camden-house.com
and of Boydell & Brewer Limited
PO Box 9, Woodbridge, Suffolk IP12 3DF, UK
www.boydellandbrewer.com

Paperback ISBN-13: 978-1-57113-566-7
Paperback ISBN-10: 1-57113-566-9
Hardcover ISBN-13: 978-1-57113-465-3
Hardcover ISBN-10: 1-57113-465-4

Library of Congress Cataloging-in-Publication Data
The undiscover'd country: W. G. Sebald and the poetics of travel / edited by
Markus Zisselsberger
    p. cm. — (Studies in German literature, linguistics, and culture)
Includes bibliographical references and index.
ISBN-13: 978-1-57113-465-3 (hardback: alk. paper)
ISBN-10: 1-57113-465-4 (hardback : alk. paper)
    1. Sebald, Winfried Georg, 1944–2001—Criticism and interpretation.
2. Sebald, Winfried Georg, 1944–2001—Travel. 3. Travel in literature.
I. Zisselsberger, Markus. II. Title. III. Series.

PT2681.E18Z93 2010
833'.914—dc22

                                                          2010019979

This publication is printed on acid-free paper.
Printed in the United States of America.

"Die Kunst des Fliegens" by W. G. Sebald. Copyright © 1987 by W. G. Sebald,
used with permission of the Wylie Agency LLC.

Images from *Austerlitz.* Copyright © by W. G. Sebald,
used with permission of the Wylie Agency LLC.

Cover image: *Das Land des Lächelns* by Jan Peter Tripp.
Copyright © 1990 by Jan Peter Tripp. Reprinted with permission of the artist.

Contents

List of Illustrations   vii

Acknowledgments   ix

List of Abbreviations   xi

Introduction: *Fluchtträume/Traumfluchten.* Journeys to the
Undiscover'd Country   1
Markus Zisselsberger

Die Kunst des Fliegens   31
W. G. Sebald

I: Departures

1:   Peripatetic Liminality: Sebald and the Tradition of the
Literary Walk   37
Christian Moser

2:   W. G. Sebald: The Anti-Tourist   63
J. J. Long

3:   "A Wrong Turn of the Wheel": Sebald's Journeys
of (In)Attention   92
Carolin Duttlinger

II: Textual Excursions, Expeditions, and Adventures

4:   If You Come to a Spa: Displacing the Cure in
Schwindel. Gefühle. and *Austerlitz*   123
Martin Klebes

5:   *Campi deserti*: Polar Landscapes and the Limits of
Knowledge in Sebald and Ransmayr   142
James Martin

6:   "Eine Art Eingang zur Unterwelt": *Katabasis* in *Austerlitz*   161
Alan Itkin

III: Traveling Companions and Convergences

7: Convergence Insufficiency: On Seeing Passages between
W. G. Sebald and the "Travel Writer" Bruce Chatwin   189
Brad Prager

8: Tripping: On Sebald's "Stifter"   213
Neil Christian Pages

9: Adventure, Imprisonment, and Melancholy: *Heart of
Darkness* and *Die Ringe des Saturn*   247
Margaret Bruzelius

IV: Topographies and Theories

10: Mapping Historical Networks in *Die Ringe des Saturn*   277
Barbara Hui

11: Topographical Anxiety and Dysfunctional Systems:
Die Ausgewanderten and Freud's *Little Hans*   299
Dora Osborne

12: While the Hidden Horrors of History are Briefly Illuminated:
The Poetics of Wandering in *Austerlitz* and *Die Ringe
des Saturn*   322
Peter Arnds

Works Cited   345

Notes on the Contributors   371

Index   375

Illustrations

Fig. 1. Robert Walser and Adolf Wölfli practice flying with
paper planes. 30

Fig. 2. Robert Walser and Adolf Wölfli flying. 34

Fig. 3. A opens the drawer, video still from *L'année dernière
à Marienbad* (1961). 137

Fig. 4. Image of trash cans from W. G. Sebald's *Austerlitz*. 176

Fig. 5. Image of Austerlitz's mother from W. G. Sebald's
Austerlitz. 179

Fig. 6. Map of Suffolk showing the narrator's journey in
Die Ringe des Saturn. 281

Fig. 7. World map showing locations mentioned in *Die Ringe
des Saturn*. 282

Acknowledgments

THE IDEA FOR THIS VOLUME arose from a panel on "W. G. Sebald and the Poetics of Travel," held at the annual convention of the Modern Language Association in 2006. I am grateful to the participants — Peter Arnds, Christopher C. Gregory-Guider, and James Martin — for offering the initial intellectual impetus for this project through their intriguing panel papers. My gratitude also goes to John Zilcosky, who provided encouragement for this project in the early stages of its conception. I have had the pleasure and privilege of working with an outstanding group of scholars; I am grateful for their excellent contributions to this volume. I am indebted to Neil Christian Pages and Brad Prager for their generous editorial advice throughout the editing process. Both David Ellison and Sven Meyer read drafts of the introduction and made valuable suggestions for revision and improvement. I am particularly grateful to the Dean's Office at the University of Miami, which generously supported this project through the Faculty Publication Fund. Carsten Meier and Noah Iliinsky kindly assisted in the preparation of the images included in this volume. I would also like to thank the following individuals and institutions for granting the use of images and other copyrighted materials reproduced in the book: Jan Peter Tripp; StudioCanal; Bucknell University Press; Penguin Books Ltd.; and the Wylie Agency. Unfortunately, permission to publish Sebald's prose text "Die Kunst des Fliegens" in English translation could not be obtained. This project would not have been possible without the editorial work and support of Jim Walker, the Editorial Director at Camden House; I have benefited and learned a great deal from his advice and am very fortunate to have worked with him.

This volume is dedicated to Margarita, for being here — and to Elias, for arriving.

M. Z.

Abbreviations

A	Sebald, W. G. *Austerlitz*. Frankfurt am Main: Fischer, 2003. English edition: translated by Anthea Bell. New York: The Modern Library, 2001.
AN	Sebald, W. G. *After Nature*. Translated by Michael Hamburger. New York: The Modern Library, 2003.
BC	Shakespeare, Nicholas. *Bruce Chatwin: A Biography*. New York: Anchor Books, 2001.
BU	Sebald, W. G. *Die Beschreibung des Unglücks: Zur österreichischen Literatur von Stifter bis Handke*. Frankfurt am Main: Fischer, 1994.
CS	Sebald, W. G. *Campo Santo*. Edited by Sven Meyer. Frankfurt am Main: Fischer, 2006. English edition: translated by Anthea Bell. New York: Random House, 2005.
DA	Sebald, W. G. *Die Ausgewanderten*. Frankfurt am Main: Fischer, 1992.
E	Sebald, W. G. *The Emigrants*. Translated by Michael Hulse. New York: New Directions, 1997.
Gr	Kafka, Franz. "The Hunter Gracchus: Four Fragments." In *The Great Wall of China and Other Short Works*, translated and edited by Malcolm Pasley, 47–55. London: Penguin, 2002.
H	Conrad, Joseph. *Heart of Darkness with The Congo Diary*. Edited by Robert Hampson. New York: Penguin, 1995.
HB	Sebald, W. G. "Helle Bilder und dunkle: Zur Dialektik der Eschatologie bei Stifter und Handke." In *Die Beschreibung des Unglücks*, 165–86. Frankfurt am Main: Fischer, 1994.
KB	Jean Paul. *Dr. Katzenbergers Badereise*. In *Werke*, vol. 6, edited by Norbert Miller, 77–309. Munich: Hanser, 1963.
LG	Sebald, W. G. *Logis in einem Landhaus: Über Gottfried Keller, Johann Peter Hebel, Robert Walser und andere*. Frankfurt am Main: Fischer, 2003.

LH	Freud, Sigmund. *Analyse der Phobie eines fünfjährigen Knaben.* In Freud, *Gesammelte Werke* 7:241–377. In English, *Analysis of a Phobia in a Five-Year-Old Boy.* In Freud, *The Standard Edition* 10:3–149.
LL	Sebald, W. G. *Luftkrieg und Literatur.* Frankfurt am Main: Fischer, 2001.
MP	Deleuze, Gilles, and Félix Guattari. *A Thousand Plateaus: Capitalism and Schizophrenia.* Translated by Brian Massumi. Minneapolis: U of Minnesota P, 1987.
NB	Stifter, Adalbert. "Nachgelassenes Blatt." In *Gesammelte Werke in sechs Bänden* 6:583–87. Gütersloh: C. Bertelsmann, 1957.
NH	Sebald, W. G. *On the Natural History of Destruction.* Translated by Anthea Bell. New York: The Modern Library, 2004.
NN	Sebald, W. G. *Nach der Natur: Ein Elementargedicht.* Frankfurt am Main: Fischer, 1995.
OGD	Benjamin, Walter. *The Origin of German Tragic Drama.* Translated by John Osborne. London: Verso, 2003.
RO	Lacan, Jacques. *Le séminaire: Livre IV. La relation d'objet.* Edited by Jacques-Alain Miller. Paris: Seuil, 1994.
RS	Sebald, W. G. *Die Ringe des Saturn: Eine englische Wallfahrt.* Frankfurt am Main: Fischer, 2002. English edition: *The Rings of Saturn.* Translated by Michael Hulse. New York: New Directions, 1998.
SEF	Ransmayr, Christoph. *Die Schrecken des Eises und der Finsternis.* Frankfurt am Main: Fischer, 1987.
SG	Sebald, W. G. *Schwindel. Gefühle.* Frankfurt am Main: Fischer, 1994.
TID	Ransmayr, Christoph. *The Terrors of Ice and Darkness.* Translated by John E. Woods. New York: Grove, 1991.
UH	Sebald, W. G. *Unheimliche Heimat: Essays zur österreichischen Literatur.* Frankfurt am Main: Fischer, 1995.
UT	Benjamin, Walter. *Ursprung des deutschen Trauerspiels.* In *Gesammelte Schriften,* vol. 1, edited by Rolf Tiedemann and Hermann Schweppenhäuser, 203–430. Frankfurt am Main: Suhrkamp, 1991.
V	Sebald, W. G. *Vertigo.* Translated by Michael Hulse. New York: New Directions, 2000.
VS	Sebald, W. G. "Bis an den Rand der Natur: Versuch über Stifter." In *Die Beschreibung des Unglücks,* 15–37.

In-text references for works that have both German and English editions are given as follows:

(*A*, 20/35)	where the German and the English editions have the same abbreviation. The first page number refers to the German edition and the second to the English.
(*DA*, 20/*E*, 35)	where the German and English editions have different abbreviations.

Introduction: *Fluchtträume/ Traumfluchten.* Journeys to the Undiscover'd Country

Markus Zisselsberger

> *Ce voyage n'est que mon rêve —*
> *nous ne sommes jamais sortis*
> *de la chambre de nos pensées —*
> *et nous avons passé la vie*
> *sans la voir. Nous lisions.*
> — André Gide, *Le voyage d'Urien*

> [This voyage is but my dream,
> we never left the confines
> of the chamber of our thoughts, —
> and we passed through life
> without ever seeing it. We read.][1]

IN 1987 A SHORT PIECE OF PROSE FICTION with the title "Die Kunst des Fliegens" (The Art of Flying), written by the then relatively unknown German-language writer W. G. Sebald, appeared in a volume aptly titled *Träume* (Dreams).[2] In this text Sebald stages an exercise in travel as both a physical levitation and a trip of the imagination: an airplane descends toward an airport, and as it approaches, a familiar landscape of forests and meadows reveals itself to the narrating passenger. Then the landing gear is released, and the sound interrupts the narrator's silent contemplation of the panorama. The descent of the airplane toward the earth suddenly becomes an intrusion, a kind of inauthentic, "primitive" flight that is enabled only by the false promise of technology, which the narrator dismisses as "die Ausgeburten des Traums, die Schöpfung wiederholen zu können" (the figments of the dream of being able to repeat the act of creation; 134). The narrator counters this technological conquering of the air with an act of storytelling and thus with a flight of the imagination; indeed, in the next paragraph he takes the reader down to the ground and replaces observation with memory: the narrator is suddenly reminded of his first encounter with a ten-year-old child who occupies himself exclusively with constructing dinosaurs from paper and cardboard, which, given their enormous number, his mother can barely remove from the house. Readers familiar with Sebald's work, in particular with his melancholy lamentations of the gradual destruction of nature, may suspect that this exercise in *Basteln*, this childlike crafting, fascinates the narrator because to the child it is an end in itself and, unlike the teleology of machines, not directed at the conquering of nature.

The possibility that nature could be completely annihilated in and by a world of technology later seems to have become reality. Having landed, the narrator now becomes a typical Sebaldian traveler: a walker who traverses a seemingly futuristic, post-apocalyptic region that bears the marks of a natural history of destruction, one we know also from those ruined postwar landscapes that are characteristic of Sebald's later prose writing and central to his lectures on the air war and German literature. The narrator now walks through the airport facilities, which leave him with the impression "als habe die Zukunft schon angefangen" (135; that the future has already begun), and the figures who pass him seem like "die Vorhut eines neuen nomadischen Geschlechts" (135; the vanguard of a new nomadic race). Later, after a car ride through evening traffic, the narrator arrives at the residence of his hosts. Watching television, he hears a report about the survival chances following a nuclear catastrophe. As if this catastrophe has in fact taken place, he later sits in the garden where the isolation of the house leaves the impression that "wir seien die letzten organischen Lebewesen, die . . . letzten Repräsentanten einer untergegangenen Zivilisation" (136; we are the last organic creatures, the last representatives . . . of a perished civilization); the entire property feels like "ein[.] Schiff, das steuerlos und still auf den kaum wahrnehmbaren Wellen schwankt" (136; a ship rocking back and forth, rudderless and calm . . . on the barely perceptible waves), like an ark bearing the only survivors of a flood but perhaps with no promise of a new beginning — a time after nature, *nach der Natur*.

At this point in the prose piece, time has already begun to slow down — an effect typical of Sebald's mature writing style — and physical travel gradually turns into a journey of the mind in which the body is in stasis and only the imagination is in motion. The narrator lies awake in bed, listening attentively to the sounds of the night and appearing to be on the threshold to a trance-like state. Then he suddenly remembers a man named Peter Schawalder who once wrote a brief essay for him, in broken English and with the title, "An Unforgettable Dream," in which its author describes a dream of flying. The memory of this essay allows the narrator to conjure the possibility of escape and embark on a dream-induced flight. As if sharing Schawalder's desire to see "the world like a bird sees our world" (137), the narrator takes off, allowing himself to drift into a dreamlike state that also effects a self-miniaturization, that induces the self to achieve "eine schmerzlose Levitation" (137; a painless levitation). Having reached the "Rand des Bewußtseins" (138; edge of consciousness), the narrator himself becomes a body in flight; "herausgehoben aus der Welt" (138; lifted from the world), he descends anew. Rather than repeating the plane's approach, however, this flyer crosses the mysterious Sargasso Sea and passes over nameless regions until he lands in a field where man's relationship with nature appears intact and harmonious, reflected in the narrator's vision of lifting and embracing the children of a farmer and his wife who have been tending to the field.

In its movement from physical to imaginative flight, Sebald's "Die Kunst des Fliegens" is itself a kind of *Fluchttraum*, a dream of overcoming gravity and escaping the weight of melancholy through a certain type of *Leichtigkeit* (lightness). At the same time, the text also creates a series of *Traumfluchten* as imaginative dream-spaces, connections, and networks that open up in the shift of perspective and perception and transform the familiar into the unfamiliar. The landscape becomes an estranged territory: an "undiscover'd country." This brief exercise in levitational prose neither achieves the stylistic perfection of Sebald's subsequent prose writing, nor does it, in its prosaic *Leichtigkeit* and imaginative levitation,[3] recall the melancholy gravity of later texts like *Nach der Natur, Die Ausgewanderten, Die Ringe des Saturn*, and *Austerlitz*. It does, however, foreground many of the themes and aesthetic strategies that will emerge in Sebald's later texts and, more particularly, suggests the crucial role travel will play in his writings. In "Die Kunst des Fliegens," we already find traces of the generic combination of travelogue with biography; the representation of travel as an antidote to melancholy; the traversal of physical space as a means to arrest time;[4] and, more generally, travel as a structuring principle for a kind of narrative in which the distinction between real, imaginative, and textual travel becomes blurred.

Jo Catling, in an early article on Sebald titled "Gratwanderungen bis an den Rand der Natur: W. G. Sebald's Landscapes of Memory," identifies this movement through imaginary landscapes, where the distinction between fiction and reality becomes increasingly unclear, as one of the characteristics and "paradoxes" of Sebald's prose texts. "The most vividly evoked landscapes," she notes, "often seem to occur in dreams or imagination, or recollections or representations, rather than as descriptions of the actual place the narrator happens to be at a given time."[5] The traversal of these dream-like spaces — "collaged landscapes," as Christopher Gregory-Guider aptly calls them[6] — is, by extension, bound to movement and travel, in particular to *wandern* and walking, with, as Catling puts it, "the narrator walking through a landscape where place evokes past time, or conjures up visual images or dream sequences, leading by association to stories of other lives, and other Wanderer" (22). The landscapes constructed by Sebald's texts thus often lead, as Catling observes, "beyond the limits of perception, offering symbolic glimpses of a gateway to another world" (48).

Although at the time of the publication of "Die Kunst des Fliegens" Sebald was not yet well known as a prose writer, other writing projects dating from around the same time suggest that he was becoming increasingly interested in such "gateways," and in the insights resulting from travels not only across geographical but also metaphysical and psychological thresholds. Two years earlier, when he was still actively working as a literary scholar and critic, Sebald had published *Die Beschreibung des Unglücks* (The Description of Calamity, 1985), a collection of essays with readings of texts by Austrian writers from a psychological perspective. In the foreword to the collection Sebald suggests that what distinguishes the work of Austrian writers is their particular interest in various forms of "Grenzübergänge" (border crossings) that are psychological, metaphysical, but also disciplinary in nature. Austrian literature, as Sebald notes in the preface, blurs the boundaries between *Wissenschaft* (science) and literary writing and, in doing so, actually succeeds in offering insights into the human psyche that are potentially more illuminating than those offered by the discipline of psychology (*BU*, 9). Thus, in his essay on Peter Handke's novel, *Die Angst des Tormanns beim Elfmeter*, Sebald credits the writer with offering a picture of the nature of schizophrenia that not only "diagnoses" the "Grenzüberschreitung" (crossing of the threshold) between normal and pathological states but actually "sie mit- und nachvollzieh[t]" (reenacts and reconstructs it).[7] Because Handke's literary *Krankheitsbild* is ultimately grounded in empathy rather than in the scientific identification of symptoms, it proves more suitable than psychology for highlighting the "emotionale Entfremdung" (emotional estrangement) from which the schizophrenic subject suffers (*BU*, 116). In one of Sebald's essays on Kafka, "Das unentdeckte Land: Zur Motivstruktur in Kafka's *Schloss*" ("The Undiscover'd Country: The Death Motif in Kafka's *Castle*"), on the other hand, travel is metaphysical rather than psychological. In the story of K.'s futile attempts to reach the castle, Sebald argues, Kafka's novel-fragment stages a journey into a realm in which the subject is displaced from his own history and rendered permanently homeless.[8] The "undiscover'd country" — a reference to Shakespeare's Hamlet with which Sebald concludes the essay — here figures as a seductive landscape of death in which the subject — falsely — hopes to overcome the "Unglück" (calamity; misfortune) of homelessness.

The kinds of *Schwellenerfahrungen* — liminal experiences — thematized in the essays on Handke and Kafka, and in *Die Beschreibung des Unglücks* more generally — pathological states of estrangement and metaphysical displacement — are, however, not only a reflection of Sebald's interests as a reader of Austrian literature but also reminders of his own *Grenzübergänge*, in particular, his gradual turn away from scholarly oriented work to essayistic and prose writing. Indeed, in the mid-1980s Sebald also published, in the Austrian literary journal *manuskripte*, the three individual poems that would later appear together as *Nach der Natur: Ein Elementargedicht* (*After Nature*, 1989). Each of the three poems deals with the biography and journeys, the *Lebenswege*, as well as the extreme experiences of a male subject: in "Und blieb ich am äussersten Meer" (And if I remained at the outermost sea), the middle section of *Nach der Natur* but the first poem to be published, Sebald reconstructs Georg Wilhelm Steller's experiences in Vitus Bering's polar expedition; "Wie der Schnee auf den Alpen" (. . . As the snow on the Alps) retraces the life and extremistic art of the painter Matthias Grünewald; and the autobiographical "Die dunckle Nacht fahrt aus" (Dark Night Sallies Forth) stages a symbolic passage from childhood in which the autobiographical subject seems to have crossed a threshold into a world of catastrophe and into an imagination of disaster.[9] It is this latter crossing that deserves particular attention in the context of travel in Sebald's writing, because it may well be that this is where Sebald reconstructs the moment in which he, as a child, "discover'd" the heretofore unknown "country" of destruction:

> . . . bin ich,
> dem anderwärts furchtbaren Zeitlauf zum Trotz,
> am Nordrand der Alpen, wie mir heut scheint,
> aufgewachsen ohne einen Begriff der Zerstörung.
> Aber daß ich vielfach auf der Straße gestürzt
> und mit einbandagierten Händen oft im Fenster
> bei den Fuchsienstauden gesessen bin,
> auf das Nachlassen der Schmerzen gewartet
> und stundenlang nichts als hinausgeschaut habe,
> brachte mich früh auf die Vorstellung
> von einer lautlosen Katastrophe, die sich
> ohne ein Aufhebens vor dem Betrachter vollzieht.
> Über das, was ich mir damals ersonnen,
> als ich in den Krautgarten hinabsah,
> in dem die Klosterfrauen mit ihren weißen
> gestärkten Hauben so langsam sich
> zwischen den Beeten bewegten,
> als seien sie vor einem Augenblick
> noch Raupen gewesen, über das
> bin ich immer noch nicht hinaus.

> [. . . I grew up,
> despite the dreadful course
> of events elsewhere, on the northern
> edge of the Alps, so it seems
> to me now, without any
> idea of destruction. But the habit
> of often falling down in the street and

often sitting with bandaged hands
by the open window between the potted
fuchsias, waiting for the
pain to subside and for hours
doing nothing but looking out,
early on induced me to imagine
a silent catastrophe that occurs
almost unperceived.
What I thought up at the time,
while gazing down into the herb garden
in which the nuns under their white
starched hoods moved so slowly
between the beds as though a moment ago
they had still been caterpillars, this
I have never gotten over. (NN, 76–77/AN, 89)]

This scene seems to represent the origins of Sebald's writing project insofar as the narrator reconstructs in memory the moment when the world first appeared to him as marked by permanent destruction. The scene, however, leaves undetermined the exact nature of this "nicht näher identifizierbaren Katastrophe" (the scarcely identifiable disaster; NN, 77/AN, 89) and further does not identify a specific event that could explain the emergence of such a worldview. All we learn is that the narrator recalls a moment of wounding and of feeling a pain resulting from a fall in the street, but "die Vorstellung von einer lautlosen Katastrophe" ([the idea of] a silent catastrophe; NN, 77/AN, 89; trans. modified) appears to result purely from the child's imagination, from what he has "ersonnen" (thought up) while sitting motionlessness in front of the window, engaged in a *stundenlanges Hinausschauen*, a seeing that seems to have no particular object.

The scene, then, stages a possibly psychological or metaphysical border-crossing in a moment of stasis, and ultimately points to a paradox that generally characterizes Sebald's later prose texts on several levels: his narrators and protagonists are all avid travelers but the narratives themselves, in their high level of self-reflexivity, in the way they draw attention to their own status as fictional constructions, and in their creation of memorial spaces in which time slows down or is even suspended, tend strangely toward stasis. Moreover, Sebald's narrators share a profoundly melancholy worldview, in which history takes on a metaphysical quality and often tends to appear, *a priori*, as a natural history of destruction. Thus one might ask whether the border-crossing in *Nach der Natur* from the "physical" world into an imagination of disaster is not in fact Sebald's "original" journey. And is it not that Sebald, after this journey, never truly "travels" again because he has arrived in a "country" in which all landscapes bear the same traces of destruction? In other words, is it really a matter of discovering unknown regions in and through literary writing? Or does the "undiscover'd country" not rather designate a melancholy space, a realm of irrecoverable loss that at one point had become all too familiar to Sebald and that he tries to render strange in literature only to find ways of escaping it, to find a way "darüber hinaus," to "get over it" — to fly over and beyond it, so to speak, as he does in "Die Kunst des Fliegens"? These questions suggest that travel in Sebald's writing may well be a hidden nexus that deserves more careful examination. The essays in this collection seek to offer responses to that suggestion by taking up the question of travel, both as a theme and trope, as a fruitful way to investigate the aesthetic and imaginative border-crossings that characterize Sebald's work, both his writing as a literary scholar and his prose fiction works.

Experiences of travel, the traversing of landscapes, and visits to particular places are also crucial dimensions of the texts which eventually made Sebald famous. *Schwindel. Gefühle.* (*Vertigo*, 1990) recounts the travels of Stendhal and retraces Kafka's footsteps during his travels through Austria and Italy. *Die Ausgewanderten: Vier lange Erzählungen* (*The Emigrants*, 1992), the first of Sebald's prose fiction works to appear in English translation, presents the life-stories of four émigrés and reconstructs their experiences of exile, displacement, and homelessness. *Die Ringe des Saturn: Eine englische Wallfahrt* (*The Rings of Saturn*, 1995), the recounting of a walking tour along the Suffolk coast, is interspersed with the narrator's meandering reflections on subjects ranging from the individual life stories of figures such as Joseph Conrad and Roger Casement to the philosophy of Sir Thomas Browne and the histories of colonialism.[10] *Austerlitz* (2001) follows the narrator's repeated encounters with the protagonist at various European locales across several decades, and gradually reveals, through the mediation of the nameless German narrator, the story of Austerlitz's escape from Nazi-occupied Europe on a *Kindertransport*, the memory of his childhood in Wales, the discovery of his true identity, and the story of his travels across Europe in an attempt to find traces of his parents.

To relate the story of Austerlitz, Sebald uses travel both as an aesthetic strategy to stage the narrator's encounters with the protagonist and as a reflection of the latter's inability to come to terms with his experience of exile and dislocation. The narrator's travels are the basis for his accompaniment and empathetic listening through which Austerlitz's story gradually emerges. For Austerlitz, on the other hand, traveling indicates his sense of isolation and homelessness, which sends him on a series of solitary "Nachtwanderungen durch London" (nocturnal wanderings through London; *A*, 186/126). This "einsame Gehen" (walking alone; *A*, 186/126) eventually takes Austerlitz to the Liverpool Street train station, where the memory of his arrival on a *Kindertransport* begins to return to him. The return of his memory initiates a compulsive search for traces of his parents, a process in which travel becomes a kind of *Nachgehen*, an investigative peripatetic pursuit that may promise redemption and healing but ultimately disappoints this hope.[11]

The experience of emigration and the persistent consequences of a loss of *Heimat* Sebald had already explored in detail in *Unheimliche Heimat* (Uncanny Homeland, 1991), his second collection of essays on Austrian writers. The essays in that volume are concerned with the writing subject's relationship to place and *Heimat* and with the geographical, psychological, and aesthetic border-crossings that Sebald had already recognized as constitutive features of Austrian literature in *Die Beschreibung des Unglücks*.[12] Travel and travel writers are also the subject of several of Sebald's other literary essays, such as those on Bruce Chatwin and Franz Kafka, as well as on Robert Walser and Jean-Jacques Rousseau, the latter two included in the collection *Logis in einem Landhaus* (Lodging in a Country-House, 1998).

However, it is not only Sebald's work as a literary scholar and critic that suggests the multivalent and complex position of "travel" as a theme. Two recent posthumous publications of Sebald's poetry and prose also serve as a reminder of the prominence of travel in his oeuvre. As the title of the collection of poems, *Über das Land und das Wasser* (Across Land and Water, 2008) suggests, much of Sebald's poetry thematizes the experience of travel and landscape.[13] Indeed, as Sven Meyer observes, many of the poems, and in particular the ones published shortly before his death, are "Reisenotizen" (travel notes) consisting of material gathered during Sebald's journeys.[14] The poem "Walzertraum" ("Waltz Dream"), accompanied by an image of Jan Peter Tripp's painting, "Das Land des Lächelns" (The Land of Smiling), at first glance appears to be Sebald's most beautiful description of the "undiscover'd country," of the nether realm frequently invoked elsewhere in his writing:

An der Grenzstation
angelangt ist jetzt
endlich der Reisende

Ein Zöllner hat ihm
die Schuhbänder gelöst
die Schuhe ausgezogen

Auf den gehobelten Brettern
des Bodens herrenlos
steht das Gepäck

Das schweinslederene Köfferchen
ist aufgegangen, die arme
Seele entflogen.[15]

[At the customs station
at last
the traveler has arrived

A customs official undid
his shoe laces
removed his shoes

Abandoned on the ground
on top of the planed wood
the luggage

The little pigskin suitcase
has opened, the poor
soul taken off.]

Like an ekphrastic description of Tripp's painting, the poem presents an image that shows a man lying motionless on a table, under which we see his suitcases. The man's motionless state is strangely reminiscent of the narrator's sleep- and dreamlike condition at the end of "Die Kunst des Fliegens." Sebald's conjecture, that "die arme Seele [ist] entflogen" (the poor soul has taken off) from the open suitcase indicates that the scene is indeed another exercise in levitation. Here, however, it is not a willful state of trance that is deliberately induced by the narrator himself; nor is it a flight of the imagination that offers new perspectives. This spirit is not joyfully "herausgehoben aus der Welt" as in "Die Kunst des Fliegens" (138). Rather, it is "*ent*flogen"; it has escaped, and what is left is a material human corpus potentially subject to anatomical violation. If the poem is supposed to offer a kind of *Fluchttraum*, the final destination of this flight remains unclear. The title — "Ein Walzertraum" — alludes to an Oscar Straus operetta that ends in the happy reconciliation of a married couple. It may therefore suggest earthly delights and harmony. Such a hope, however, is contradicted by Tripp's painting, whose title refers to Franz Lehár's operetta, *Das Land des Lächelns*, which also deals with a romantic relationship (this one between a Viennese princess and her Chinese prince). That relationship, however, ends in separation because the princess cannot adjust to the Chinese culture of her spouse, thus pointing to a condition of estrangement and homelessness. Hence, when the narrator of Sebald's poem concludes with the speculation that despite — or because of — an anatomical intervention that has rendered the body "ausgehöhlt und gewichtlos" (hollow and weightless), the latter may already be on its way "in das Land das / man nur barfuß betreten darf" (the land one may enter only barefooted), we are left to wonder what kind of "undiscover'd country" this land may represent.

Such ventures into symbolic realms that tend to blend real topographies with landscapes of the mind notwithstanding, many of Sebald's poems are based on impressions and observations gathered during actual travels. They offer a series of *Momentaufnahmen*, travel snap-shots, which the aesthetic form of Sebald's prose poetry tends to accommodate rather easily. Once Sebald turned to prose narratives, however, he more actively explored the viability of using forms of travel writing as a means to translate travel experiences aesthetically. His unfinished "Corsica project" is an example. This posthumously published work comprises two fragmented versions that were included in the catalogue accompanying the Sebald exhibition at the Deutsches Literaturarchiv in Marbach in 2008.[16] The project was based ostensibly on Sebald's trip to Corsica in September 1995, thus falling between the completion of *Die Ringe des Saturn* and the project that would become *Austerlitz*, with the latter containing many of the themes and motifs from the Corsica texts. As the title of the manuscript suggests — "*Aufzeichnungen aus Korsika: Zur Natur & Menschenkunde*" (Notes from Corsica: On Natural History & Anthropology) — Sebald was engaged in the writing of an ethnographical and anthropological history of the island, first within the framework of the travel diary, a form he later abandoned for the longer second version, for which he chose a hybrid and more open-ended combination of essay, travelogue, and biography that Ulrich von Bülow also describes as a kind of "essayistisches Reisebuch" (essayistic travelogue).[17] The two Corsica fragments thus provide evidence of Sebald's exploration of the various possibilities of translating travel experiences into an aesthetic form that would accommodate the blending of physical, imaginative, and textual "travels."

Such experiments, though, are hardly limited to Sebald's work as a writer and literary critic. Experiences related to travel and to place shaped Sebald's personal life and extend all the way back to his frequently invoked origins and the "journeys" that followed what he described as his "freiwillige Expatriierung" (voluntary expatriation).[18] Born in 1944 in Wertach, a small village in Southern Germany, Sebald left his home country in 1966 to work and study in Manchester, England. Following intermittent stays in Switzerland, where he worked as a schoolteacher, and Munich, where he lectured for the Goethe Institut, he moved back to England, where he would live in Norwich and teach as a professor of German and European literature at the University of East Anglia for over thirty years. Even though England remained his chosen place of residence until the end of his life, he never considered it his "home." Nonetheless, though he was at times drawn back to Germany, his relationship to the country of his origins remained fundamentally ambivalent, marked, one the one hand, by disdain for the failure of Germans to actively confront their own violent past. On the other hand, Sebald nevertheless had a strange sense that he remained the child of the destruction of German cities during the Allied aerial bombings and that the postmemory of the landscapes of ruin had somehow become a kind of *Heimat,* as he would note in *Luftkrieg und Literatur* ("Air War and Literature," 1999; *LL,* 76/*NH,* 71).

As a result, when Sebald began to emerge as a German-language prose writer in the late 1990s, his words came, strangely enough, from abroad and from the periphery. Like other readers and critics, German writer Daniel Kehlmann has observed, here in remarks made on the occasion of the opening of the Sebald exhibition at the *Literaturhaus* in Stuttgart in 2008, that the "peripheral" dimensions of Sebald's writing project are crucial for understanding both his literary greatness and his rather reserved reception in Germany itself. Sebald's achievements as a writer — which, according to Kehlmann, put him in line with Thomas Mann, Franz Kafka, and Joseph Roth — are linked to his ability to approach the catastrophes of twentieth-century history from the margins and in a literary language that conveys the horrors of individual suffering without appropriating or mitigating them.[19] The peripheral, however, is not only a fitting description of the narrative perspectives found in Sebald's prose texts but also a reminder of the fact that he lived and wrote in the United Kingdom and was not a presence in the German *Kulturbetrieb*, the culture industry. That absence, Kehlmann notes, ultimately explains the rather reserved and delayed reception of Sebald's writing in Germany, particularly in contrast to Sebald's renown in the English-speaking world: "Das Problem war einfach: Sebald war nicht da, er war in Norwich" (The problem was simple: Sebald was not there, he was in Norwich).[20] The belated emergence of Sebald on the literary scene of the country of his birth, then, seems to have marked the return of the kind of storyteller — or rather story*writer* — who, as Benjamin notes, "von weither kommt" — who has come from afar and whose experiences of travel and border-crossings form the basis of his ability to tell and write stories.[21]

In fact Sebald once described his departure from Germany as the premise for his discovery of the kind of life stories that would become the stuff of *Die Ausgewanderten*. In a conversation with Michael Silverblatt, he explained, "I would never have encountered these witnesses if I hadn't left my native country at the age of twenty, because the people who could tell you the truth, or something at least approximating the truth, did not exist in that country anymore. But one could find them in Manchester and in Leeds or in North London."[22] It is perhaps because of the discoveries that his border-crossings and "expatriate experience" afforded him that Sebald often mobilized tropes of travel to describe the ideas and methods that informed his writing. In an interview with Joe Cuomo, for example, he commented on his dislike of "doing things systematically," and his preference for working in a "random, haphazard fashion," which he also compared to the instinctual searches of a dog: "If you look at a dog following the advice of his nose, he traverses a patch of land in a completely unplottable manner. And he always finds what he's looking for."[23]

These instinctual investigations often led Sebald to "patches of land" in which he encountered traces of the kind of life stories he would then try to reconstruct in his prose texts, in a manner in which biographies are intimately connected to descriptions of place. Indeed, following the traces of past lives for Sebald ultimately amounted to the traversal of space. Asked by Eleanor Wachtel if he would consider himself as a type of "ghost hunter," Sebald responded by commenting on the "odd presence" the dead had for him and characterized his pursuits as the "occup[ation] of this person's territory," as a journey through a personal and cultural space in order "to look around there and to feel, after a while, quite at home."[24] The description of an individual's life in terms of a "territory" may seem an odd choice, but it is certainly not surprising, given that Sebald's reconstruction of life stories is intimately connected to the description and photographic reproduction of the places his subjects have traversed in their diverse experiences of emigration, exile, and displacement.[25]

Nevertheless, his statement, however metaphorical, that pursuing the traces of the dead amounted to the "occupation" of personal space in which the "hunter" may also come to feel "quite at home" suggests a potentially invasive transgression on the part of the writer. Such transgressions are not unproblematic in the context of Sebald's work, for example, in *Die Ausgewanderten,* but more particularly in *Austerlitz.* In the latter, the reconstruction of the protagonist's story rests on the narrator's mediation and tends to blur the distinction between his voice and that of the protagonist. Thus Sebald's recourse to the tropes of travel to describe his writing project points also to the ethical tensions inherent in his work and raises questions about the place of travel in his aesthetics, questions that suggest the need for caution in uncritically appropriating Sebald's own tropes to conceptualize his work in terms of a "poetics of travel." The complex issues behind Sebald's own statements are further illustrated in his response to Michael Silverblatt's suggestion that his texts in part work toward "revelations":

> Well, I suppose if there is such a thing as a revelation, if there can be a moment in a text which is surrounded by something like *claritas, veritas,* and the other facets that qualify epiphanies, then it can be achieved only by actually going to certain places, by looking, by expending great amounts of time in actually exposing oneself to places that no one else goes to.[26]

The main problem with Sebald's descriptions of his aesthetics in numerous interviews is that they are often just as stylized, indeed, seductively "poetic" as his prose texts. In this way they tend to conceal the actual complexities of his methods as reflected in his writing. Sebald's statement above suggests that prose fiction can and must produce a certain degree of "truth" (*veritas*) and "lucidity" (*claritas*), and that it can do so only if one visits certain places *and* experiences them in a *certain* way. This proposition implies a complex relationship between literary writing and travel. It also calls for a traveler who is endowed with a privileged capacity for perception. For once, Sebald seems to say that actual, physical travel can serve as the basis for the *textual* effects through which literature produces "truth." But this effect requires the *translation* of that experience into fiction, an aspect which Sebald left uncommented here. In addition, he emphasized that the places must be carefully chosen from among those that "no one else goes to." This demand for solitary travel implies an anti-touristic itinerary by a "cultured" traveler who seeks out places on the periphery and is capable of experiencing and looking at them other than in terms of sightseeing. But what lends such sites their particularity, and what might it mean to "expose oneself" to them?

In his conversation with Silverblatt, Sebald named the fortress at Breendonk, which the narrator visits in the opening pages of *Austerlitz,* as an example of such a particular site and explained: "I had read about Breendonk before, in connection with Jean Améry. But the difference is staggering, you know — whether you've just read about it or whether you actually go and spend several days in and around there to see what these things are actually like" (85–86) The particularity of Breendonk as a place worth visiting derives in part then from the textually mediated knowledge of another individual's singular experience at the same site — in this case Améry's experience of incarceration and torture. From Sebald's statement we may surmise that it was this reading experience that motivated him to see Breendonk with his own eyes. Elsewhere Sebald attributed the particularity of Breendonk to its status as a "liminal" site which, contrary to places such as the extermination camps of Treblinka and Auschwitz, still allows the visitor to "imagine" — *vorstellen* — what transpired there:

> Ich wusste von Anfang an, dass man sich an einem solchen Ort [wie Treblinka oder Auschwitz] diese Geschichte nicht vorstellen kann. Breendonk liegt irgendwo in der grauen Zone dazwischen, als ein kleines Auffanglager, ein überschaubarer Ort, der es einem gerade noch erlaubt, sich die Sache vorzustellen. Dort kann man sich das also vorstellen, obwohl es natürlich grauenvoll ist, wenn man in diese finsteren Gänge hineingeht — so ist es doch! Ein Ort, an dem man sich gerade noch — als Forscher in diesem Fall — ausdenken kann, wie es vielleicht war.[27]

> [I knew from the outset that one cannot grasp, cannot imagine history at a place like that [Treblinka or Auschwitz]. Breendonk is located somewhere in-between, in the gray zone, as a small detention center, a place that can be grasped, that allows one, barely, to imagine the things that went on. There, after all, you can imagine it, although it's of course horrifying, when one enters these dark hallways — that's how it is! A place where one — in my case, as a researcher — just barely can still imagine how it perhaps was.]

Sebald suggests that because the fortress Breendonk was not one the infamous sites used specifically for the systematic extermination of millions of human beings, it figures as a "gray zone" that one can visit to somehow get a sense of *Geschichte* without being overwhelmed by it. At places like Treblinka or Auschwitz, on the other hand, one would be directly confronted with these "things that went on" (*die Sache*). Such a confrontation would impair the visitor's understanding (*Vorstellung*) of this aspect of history, which Sebald evidently considers unimaginable and unrepresentable (*nicht vorstellen kann*). The "dimensions" of these sites and of the events that transpired there are simply, as Sebald explains, "unfassbar," ungraspable, while Breendonk remains "überschaubar," graspable by human vision.

Sebald's statement, however, is marked by inconsistencies, and both his tentative tone and rhetoric suggest that the relationship between *Ort* and *Geschichte*, between place and history, is not as clear-cut as his explanation may at first suggest. For once, Sebald claims that he knew "from the outset" that one cannot imagine history at places like Treblinka and Auschwitz. As he himself notes, however, he ostensibly never visited these sites: "Ich habe mich immer davor gehütet, an solche Orte zu fahren" (I have always been careful not to visit such places).[28] His judgment about the unsuitability of such places as a traveler's and, more particularly, a "researcher's" — a *Forschers* — destination thus seems to rest on presumption rather than actual previous travel experiences.

There is a tension, then, between the insights resulting from physical travel experiences and imaginative conjecture, a tension also reflected in Sebald's switch from "vorstellen" (to understand, to represent, to imagine) to "ausdenken" in his statement. Like "vorstellen," "ausdenken" involves the work of the imagination but, unlike the former, more specifically entails invention. Thus, Sebald's last sentence is not simply a reaffirmation of his previous claim that Breendonk is a "place that can be grasped, which allows one, barely, to imagine the affairs"; instead, the statement also suggests the need for a creative investment on behalf of the investigating visitor and thus, by extension, points to the imaginative and aesthetic interventions of the prose fiction writer.[29]

This implied need for the writer's creative work in the encounter with the material remnants of history brings us back, then, to the previous question of how travel experiences can be *translated* into fiction. More particularly, it raises the question, so important for Sebald's writing, of how a real, material history of human suffering that took place at specific geographical sites can be represented in the imaginative space created by literary writing.

Sebald's "translation" of his visit to Breendonk into the fiction of *Austerlitz* highlights the complexity of this question. Critics have often noted the similarities between Sebald and the narrator of *Austerlitz*, but the fictionalized visit to Breendonk actually points to a fundamental difference between them: while Sebald had explained his actual journey to the fortress as motivated by his prior reading of Améry, the narrator "discovers" the site by chance, hearing about it from Austerlitz during their first encounter and learning more about it from a newspaper article the morning after. Thus, the text constructs the subsequent experience of traveling to Breendonk as the product of a contingent event. Indeed, the initial premise of learning about it through Améry is turned into its opposite: traversing the hallways of Breendonk, the narrator explicitly denies knowing anything about the interrogations that took place in the fortress because, as he claims, he read Améry's account only *after* his visit (*A*, 42–43/26). In the fictionalization of this visit, then, it seems to have been important to Sebald to construct a travel experience, a moment of sight-seeing unmediated by the textual memory of reading the testimony by a victim and eye-witness.[30]

The narrator's description of his walk through Breendonk, on the other hand, stages a complex exploration of the representational problems Sebald had pointed to in the interview. In fact, the narrator's peripatetic approach to the site reads like an attempt at relating the fortress' significance as a liminal place, its location in a "gray zone, in-between" where the history of human suffering is both "there" and "not there," where it eludes the traveler's *Vorstellungskraft*, his power of imagination and understanding, as soon as it announces itself. From the outside the structure indeed appears as if it were "outside" history in general. It "wuchs," as the narrator observes, "so weit über meine Begriffe hinaus, daß ich sie zuletzt mit keiner mir bekannten Ausformung der menschlichen Zivilisation, nicht einmal mit den stummen Relikten unserer Vor- und Frühgeschichte in irgendeinen Zusammenhang bringen konnte" (so far exceed[ed] my comprehension that in the end I found myself unable to connect it with anything shaped by human civilization, or even with the silent relics of our prehistory and early history; *A*, 34/20). Similarly, once the narrator enters the fortress, he describes the experiences of those who suffered as "undenkbar" (unthinkable, unimaginable; *A*, 37/22).[31] What is *vorstellbar* (imaginable) to the narrator is ultimately only the presence of the perpetrators, the members of the SS responsible for the events at Breendonk. The experience of the victims, on the other hand, though briefly illuminated, seems to quickly dissolve in the darkness from which it emerged. In the narrator's travel through the fortress Sebald thus constructs an experience of place in which the individual experience of human suffering is invoked but also, in its essence and singularity, rendered inaccessible. That simultaneity, it seems, is the moment of *veritas* and *claritas* experienced here and is reflected in what the narrator describes as his fading memory of Breendonk:

Selbst jetzt, wo ich mich mühe, mich zu erinnern, . . . löst sich das Dunkel nicht auf, sondern verdichtet sich bei dem Gedanken, wie wenig wir festhalten können, was alles und wieviel ständig in Vergessenheit gerät, mit jedem ausgelöschten Leben, wie die Welt sich sozusagen von selber ausleert, indem die Geschichten, die an den ungezählten Orten haften, welche selbst keine Fähigkeit zur Erinnerung haben, von niemandem je gehört, aufgezeichnet oder weitererzählt werden.

[Even now when I try to remember . . ., the darkness does not lift but becomes yet heavier as I think how little we can hold in mind, how everything is constantly lapsing into oblivion with every extinguished life, how the world is, as it were, draining itself, in that the history of countless places and objects which themselves have no power of memory is never heard, never described or passed on. (*A*, 38–39/23–24)]

The very possibility of "experiencing" such places, Sebald once noted, depends one's one ability to avoid the itineraries and travel habits of tourists. Thus he explained that another reason for avoiding places like Treblinka and Auschwitz is the fact that traveling to them, "zu einer Art von Massentourismus geworden ist" (has become a kind of mass tourism).[32] Sebald stressed that he disliked the kind of "modern" tourist travel that, enabled by the prostheses of technology and the travel habits of a globalized world, allowed for travel "everywhere" and thus undermined the individual's ability to develop a meaningful relationship to a place. He noted in a conversation with Arthur Lubow, for example: "That is what is so awful about modern life — we never return. . . . One year we go to India and the next year to Peru and the next to Greenland. Because now you can go everywhere. I would much rather have half a dozen places that meant something to me than to say, at the end of my life, 'I have been practically everywhere.' The first visit doesn't reveal very much at all."[33]

Sebald's desire for a kind of travel that would result in a repeated return to places to which the self is — or eventually becomes — bound in a meaningful relationship suggests a harmonious, intact relationship between the traveler and the world. Ironically, Sebald's prose writing renders such harmony problematic if not impossible, since for his protagonists "travel" hardly ever leads to unique and meaningful experiences at and of places. Instead, his characters experience exile and dislocation in a way that usually makes any identificatory relationship to places impossible. Similarly, his narrators, in their melancholy worldview, perceive the landscapes they traverse for the most part only as emblems of a natural history of catastrophe.

The very idea of traveling to particular sites and reaching actual destinations is further complicated in Sebald's writing because his narratives are, as Ulrich von Bülow notes, "rückwärtsgebunden," focused backwards, bound to and up in the past. Sebald's travelers have "aufgegeben . . ., bestimmte Ziele zu verfolgen [und] [w]o sich dennoch Handlungszusammenhänge andeuten, werden sie vom Erzähler sofort durch Abschweifungen, Erinnerungen und Assoziationen in den Hintergund gedrängt" (have given up the pursuit of specific destinations and goals. At places at which storylines still seem to suggest themselves, the narrator immediately relegates them to the background through recourse to digressions, memories, and associations).[34] Even where actual travels provide the narrative with its initial impetus, the text quickly gives way to digressive reflections. Finally, Sebald's criticism of modern travel suggests that an "authentic" form of travel would be able to avoid the kind of superficial "experience" and appropriation of places that has been historically and culturally attributed to the phenomenon of tourism. The claim to "authentic" travel, however, rests on the premise that the traveler who deviates from the tourist's itinerary and way of (sight)seeing is able to discover something new and original, a notion frequently put into question by the wanderings of Sebald's narrators, who "discover" the familiar in places where they had hoped to find an "undiscover'd country."

The invocation of an "undiscover'd country" with the name of W. G. Sebald, as in the title of the present collection, may therefore seem to be a contradiction, and not only because of his narrators' apparent inability to escape the familiar. After all, Sebald's writings continue to enjoy immense popularity among a broad and international readership. Expressions of fascination and a sense of discovery were characteristic especially for the initial reception of Sebald's work, in particular in Britain and the United States, and enthusiastic reviews by literary critics suggested that his books were the unknown promised land of a new kind of literary writing. This "land" has since been populated at a rapid pace by an astonishing body of scholarship that in all likelihood will continue to grow fairly rapidly in the coming years.[35] In particular, the ethics and aesthetics of memory, intertexuality, text-image relationships and the use of photographs, as well as the aesthetic principles informing Sebald's writing, have proved to be of continuing interest and consistently draw the scholarly attention of readers.[36] In this context travel, both as a theme and a structural principle, has generally been recognized as a central component of Sebald's texts, which critics have described as "travelogues" or at least as "travel narratives of one kind or another."[37] Richard Bates, for example, views Sebald's narratives as inherently peripatetic in nature and stresses that in his texts "travel is not just an add-on feature: it is the permanent, yet constantly evolving fabric, not just of the characters who inhabit the text, but the *textus* itself."[38] David Darby has observed that "movement through landscape is essential to the processes of memory enacted in Sebald's writing" and that "the discussion of his books under the rubric of travel writing . . . suggests numerous possible interpretative paths through the spaces and times invoked in Sebald's work."[39]

These interpretative paths have to some extent been pursued by scholarly readers like Bianca Theisen and John Zilcosky, who were the first to offer sustained, historicized examinations of Sebald's relationship to various travel and travel-writing traditions.[40] Theisen shows that Sebald's texts make use of the motifs and stylistic elements of various genres of travel writing and in this way "map[.] a cultural history of travel and travel writing."[41] Their appearance as "travelogues," however, also derives in large part from the integration of extra-textual and pseudo-documentary material that lends the texts the frequently observed "reality effect" and appears to provide factual evidence for the narrators' journeys. This reality-effect, in turn, tends to distract from the fact that Sebald's travels are highly "textualized" insofar as they engage with the literary works of writers like Kafka, Stendhal, and Conrad, and repeat the travels recounted therein. This form of "armchair travel," consisting of a "poetic flight to the library or the archive," consequently results in the paradox that what appears to be unfamiliar territory is in fact familiar," and that "the search for a terra incognita . . ., for an authentic perception of the foreign or for unmediated experience has to resort to a textualized world."[42] Zilcosky, too, views Sebald largely as a "textual traveler," but unlike Theisen, who counts his work as part of "postmodern literature's experiments with the travelogue,"[43] he views Sebald as a modernist who rewrites "travel writing's master trope: the fear of getting lost and the desire to find one's way."[44] Rather than losing their way only to return home in the end, Sebald's narrators never leave the realm of the familiar and thus remain in a state of stasis even while engaged in travel. That Zilcosky subsequently revised this thesis, suggesting that in his writing of *Austerlitz* Sebald returned to a more traditional paradigm based on departure and a return home, highlights both the fluidity inherent in the trope of "travel" itself and Sebald's complex aesthetic appropriation of the trope, but also the difficulty of pinpointing it as the basis for a "poetics."[45]

In addition to being a thematic focus of Sebald's work, travel also serves as a structuring principle that fulfills a multiplicity of functions and organizes the hybrid components of his texts. Several critics have drawn attention to the fact that the inherent hybridity of the travelogue as a genre, in particular, in its recourse to other genres like the essay or the reportage, may in fact have served as a kind of structural model for Sebald's writing. Whatever one may say about the mixing of genres in Sebald's writing, "their hybridity has been antedated by the travelogue," Theisen argues.[46] Similarly, Massimo Leone has observed that

> the narrative structure of the travelogue provides Sebald with an extremely flexible and nevertheless coherent device for the organization of extremely multifarious material. The extraordinary mélange of genres (autobiography, biography, apologue, fiction, essay), which characterizes Sebald's text, would probably appear chaotic without the thread of travel.[47]

According to Leone, the presence of travel on a structural level also may account for the "vertiginous reception" of Sebald's work: his texts seem to "trigger the desire to travel with him," as "he obliges the reader to follow him while he rapidly scales between different (and often remote) levels of enunciation, between different planes of his interior narrative prose."[48] Deane Blackler's reading of Sebald implicitly supports this argument but also takes it one step further, suggesting that his texts demand a "disobedient" and "adventurous" reader, one who is willing to "travel beyond the textual boundary," follow the trajectories suggested by the reader's own imaginative response to the text, and "pursue a solitary subjective itinerary."[49]

Although Leone warns against "empathetically" motivated readings of Sebald — an approach that he attributes to the seductiveness of Sebald's "literary charisma" and the wish to become his travel companion — some readers have felt an urge to "search" for him and the textual and visual landscapes in his texts. Actually, a more curious aspect of the reception of Sebald is not only that the demands his texts make upon the reader have been described and conceptualized in terms of "travel," but that his texts have literally induced in readers a desire to travel in Sebald's footsteps, thus turning his work into a peculiar kind of *Reiseführer* or travel guide. The editors of *Searching for Sebald*, a collection of critical essays and artwork about photography and the visual in Sebald's writing, made travel to the sites of *Die Ringe des Saturn* and the on-site pursuit of Sebald's images an integral part of their project.[50] In addition, the book was made available as part of a limited number of "traveling suitcases" each of which contained original art by contributors to the collection.[51] In 2005, the city of Wertach, Sebald's German birthplace, set up a "Sebald-Weg" that allows visitors to retrace the narrator's steps upon his return to his home town in "Il ritorno in patria," the fourth narrative of *Schwindel. Gefühle.*, quotations from which are engraved on several steles erected along the way.[52] More recently the British writer Will Stone visited Terezin in the Czech Republic and Breendonk in Belgium, two sites that figure prominently in *Austerlitz*. The motivation for this journey ostensibly came from what Stone perceived to be parallels between his experiences of visiting these locations, both before and after reading Sebald's works, and those recounted in Sebald's texts, "resulting in a kind of uncanny merging and subsequent blurring of events which defies explanation."[53] The results of such journeys in search of Sebald are, at best, mixed. While the travels of the ICI Research Team, the editors of *Searching for Sebald*, yielded valuable insights into Sebald's use and manipulation of visual material, Stone's retracing of Sebald's steps, initiated by a mysterious sense of uncanny resemblances and thus following the trajectories of the kind of "adventure" suggested by Blackler, tend to give us the account of a subjective, indeed "literary" experience of reading and traveling with Sebald. Nonetheless, such accounts leave unanswered the question as to what insights about his work the reader is supposed to gain.

While not dismissing these kinds of more subjectively motivated, literal retracings of Sebald's journeys, the contributions in this collection aim to illuminate Sebald's engagement with travel from multivalent critical perspectives. The collection opens with the previously unpublished text with which I began the introduction, namely Sebald's little-known prose piece, "Die Kunst des Fliegens." The text is framed by two paintings by the artist Jan Peter Tripp that "document" an encounter between the writer Robert Walser and the poet and painter Adolf Wölfli and their attempt at learning to fly — an exercise in overcoming gravity in which, much like in Sebald's "Kunst des Fliegens," physical levitation and imaginative flight become inseparable.[54] The essays that follow contextualize Sebald's writing within the larger framework of travel literature. They are followed by an examination of particular forms of travel and of Sebald's relationship to specific "traveling" companions. The collection closes with a group of essays that explores the significance of space and topography in his writing.

The first section of the anthology begins with Christian Moser's examination of walking in Sebald's oeuvre. Moser proposes that the narrator's peripatetic tracing of destruction in *Die Ringe des Saturn* constitutes a rewriting of the Romantic and Enlightenment tradition of the literary walk. He shows that Sebald deviates from this tradition by revealing the continuity between nature and culture, and between the freedom and autonomy of the walker as illusions; instead, Sebald favors the liminal and discontinuous and the insights afforded by the combination of an "animal-like crawl" with a view from the edge. *Die Ringe des Saturn* thus develops a "double perspective" that combines peripatetic pursuits with a perspective from the margins and makes walking the basis for a unique mode of perception. J. J. Long, on the other hand, situates Sebald's travel narratives in a history of travel writing marked by the dichotomy between authentic travel and tourism. Sebald's narrators seek to establish themselves as cultured "anti-tourists" with authentic travel experiences and privileged access to the histories and life-stories inscribed in the landscapes of modern European culture. To this end Long argues that the texts employ various "anti-touristic" strategies, on the narrative level, as well as anti-touristic performances through the insertion and appropriation of tourist photography. Long demonstrates that the narrators' search for the authentic and new ultimately fails on both the narrative and the visual level, insofar as Sebald's texts cannot escape the contradictions inherent in anti-tourism: in their attempts to authenticate their travels and distinguish them from tourism they necessarily revert to strategies deeply embedded in the tourist paradigm itself, thus complicating any claim to authenticity. Carolin Duttlinger reads both *Schwindel. Gefühle.* and *Die Ringe des Saturn* as travelogues that thematize the insights afforded by various states of *Aufmerksamkeit* (attention, attentiveness). Through a discussion of Adorno's critique of modernity, Duttlinger is able to argue that Sebald's narrators aim to counter the numbing effect of modern transport systems with a heightened and renewed sensitivity that rests on the traveler's ability to allow mind and body to meander. Yet *Aufmerksamkeit* proves inseparable from inattention and distraction, showing that the potentially liberating effect of attentiveness is also destabilizing and restrictive. Duttlinger demonstrates that this binary is thematized in Kafka's story of the hunter Gracchus, which takes on a self-reflexive significance for the problematic of attentiveness in Sebald's writing.

Particular types of journeys — in this case, spa travel, the polar expedition, and the epic journey to the underworld — are the focus of the contributions in the second part of the collection. Martin Klebes examines the trope of the *Badereise* or spa travel and its relationship to intertextuality in *Schwindel. Gefühle.* and *Austerlitz.* Spa travels in Sebald's texts do not serve a healing and recuperative function designed to help the subject restore an original unity but instead make conspicuous the fundamentally split nature of the modern subject. By investigating Sebald's intertextual engagement with the work of Jean Paul and Kafka, and Alain Resnais's film *Last Year at Marienbad*, Klebes shows that this split is not a reflection of the subject's psychological constitution but rather an inscription on the level of textuality. The trope of spa travel in this way emerges as a defining feature of the intertextuality of Sebald's texts, in which subjectivity remains inaccessible behind the play of language. James Martin's chapter traces the affinities between the arctic landscapes and polar expeditions in Sebald's prose poem *Nach der Natur* and those in Austrian writer Christoph Ransmayr's novel, *Die Schrecken des Eises und der Finsternis.* In the work of both writers the polar expedition figures as a voyage to a landscape that exposes the traveler to a limit experience in threatening his survival and functions as a trope for the subject's inability to conceptualize this experience within a framework of knowledge. Sebald and Ransmayr, Martin contends, underscore this epistemological crisis by revealing travel experiences as always already textually mediated, a strategy that Martin suggests is one of the key aspects of "postmodern intertextuality." In a further investigation of intertextual presences, Alan Itkin turns to the significance of classical journeys for Sebald's writing. Arguing for an intertextual connection bewteen *The Odyssey* and *Austerlitz*, Itkin suggests that Sebald both appropriates and rewrites *katabasis*, the epic journey to the underworld, to articulate a particular philosophy of history. *Katabasis*, he maintains, is not merely a particular trope for the relationship between past and present; it also entails a conception of history as destiny. Thus Itkin argues that in mobilizing *katabasis* for the writing of *Austerlitz*, Sebald advances a theory of history that postulates a continuity between the era of bourgeois expansionism and colonialism and the Holocaust, suggesting that German National Socialism is in part the product of the "destiny" of modernity.

Each of the essays in the third section investigates Sebald's relationship to other writing travelers and to writers whose work accompanies Sebald's prose writing and literary criticism more generally. Brad Prager explores the affinities between Sebald's work and that of English author

Bruce Chatwin and analyzes each author's respective status as a "travel writer." Focusing on Sebald's essay on Chatwin, Prager detects various "convergences" in the prose writing of each and argues that both writers' relationship to travel was ambivalent: while Chatwin tried to negotiate the need to travel with the desire to be at home, Sebald complicated this dichotomy, suggesting instead that travel and homecoming are essentially illusions. The problematic relationship between "here" and "there" is thematized by both Sebald and Chatwin in the contrasting activities of traveling and collecting. By examining Sebald's approaches — *Annäherungen* — to Chatwin, Prager's contribution also provides insights into Sebald's idiosyncratic work as a reader and literary critic. Neil Christian Pages, too, turns his attention to Sebald's work as a reader. In Pages's contribution, "travel" functions as a trope for the readerly relationship between Sebald and Adalbert Stifter and for the way in which Stifter's words and images find their way into Sebald's literary imagination. Focusing on Sebald's literary essays on Stifter's life and work, Pages argues that rather than functioning as on object of scholarly analysis, Stifter's life and work become the basis for the story of a reading experience in which Sebald seeks to communicate what he has learned from Stifter about the writing of his own story. From Sebald's engagement with Stifter the article thus sketches a "poetics of reading" in which the intertextual presence of Stifter in Sebald's writing is conceptualized not as mere influence and appropriation but as a form of "illumination" and "transmigration." Margaret Bruzelius offers a comparative study of Joseph Conrad's *Heart of Darkness* and *Die Ringe des Saturn* and argues that the travels in both texts are modeled on the plot elements and conventions of the adventure or romance novel. Both texts offer first-hand person accounts of travel experiences based on an act of story-telling that self-reflexively draws attention to its literary status and, by extension, exposes the experience it seeks to convey as fictionalized. Adopting the conventions of the adventure novel in an age of calamity and drawing attention to the constructedness of their stories, both Conrad and Sebald suggest that storytelling no longer possesses a redemptive quality.

The contributions that make up the final section turn to space and place in Sebald's writing and offer more theory-oriented approaches to reading Sebald. In her reading of space and spatiality in *Die Ringe des Saturn*, Barbara Hui proposes that the text's representation of space rests on the combination of a postmodern perspective with a seventeenth-century worldview. The former takes on the "logic of the network" in which local places are always intertwined with global histories; the latter derives from Sebald's engagement with the philosophy of Sir Thomas Browne and offers a cosmological and mystical view of history. The narrative complexity of *Die Ringe des Saturn* hence rests on a combination of two different conceptions of space that bring together rationalist and mystical views of history. Dora Osborne offers a psychoanalytically framed reading of topographical and transportational systems in *Die Ausgewanderten*, bringing Sebald into conversation with the work of Lacan, Deleuze and Guattari, and Freud. To this end, she suggests that Sebald's text shares important affinities with Freud's case study of Little Hans, which provides a viable background against which to conceptualize the emigrants' experiences of displacement in a mechanized, industrialized environment and their inscription in the networks, resemblances, and systems of signification characteristic of Sebald's narratives. Osborne ultimately detects an ambivalent and "unresolved" engagement with psychoanalysis in *Die Ausgewanderten*, one that oscillates between Freud's genealogical model of oedipal and familial origins, and a deconstructive, anti-oedipal model of Deleuzian becomings. In the final contribution, Peter Arnds frames Sebald's poetics of wandering in philosophical terms, suggesting that the trope of travel in his writing revolves around a series of binaries typical of modernity, including those between dwelling and migration, reason and madness, and memory and forgetting. These dichotomies, Arnds contends, are best understood if examined through the lens of the philosophies and cultural theories of Heidegger, Nietzsche, and Deleuze and Guattari, which suggest that travel in Sebald's work is inscribed in a tension between arborescence, the Apollonian, and *lethe* as tropes of non-movement, concealment, and forgetting on the one hand, and, on the other hand, the rhizome, Dionysus, and *aletheia*. In this reading, wandering emerges as an ambivalent movement through landscapes of destruction that carries with it the potential to "briefly illuminate" the horrors of history but also reveals the absurdity of any notion of history as progress.

Commenting on travel in Sebald's texts, Leone has noted that the reader who feels compelled to travel with Sebald at one point encounters the fundamental paradox that Sebald's "travels" are premised on solitude and thus on a "model" that excludes emulation and companionship as such. However, Leone adds that "the impossibility of physical companionship does not exclude the opportunity for theoretical friendship," proposing that critically investigating the narrative strategies that underlie Sebald's travels rather than letting oneself be guided by "aesthetic fascination" may provide more valuable insights into the significance of travel in his writing.[55] By bringing together a diverse range of voices, the collection seeks to offer such insights while, at the same time, exploring what a "theoretical friendship" and continued critical accompaniment of Sebald may look like.

Notes

1 André Gide, *Urien's Voyage*, trans. Wade Baskin (New York: Philosophical Library, 1964), 93.

² W. G. Sebald, "Die Kunst des Fliegens," in *Träume: Literaturalmanach, 1987,* ed. Jochen Jung (Salzburg: Residenz Verlag, 1987), 134–38. I would like to thank the Wylie Agency for permission to quote and translate from this text. All translations in this chapter are my own unless otherwise credited.

³ For more on Sebald's art of levitation, see Ben Hutchinson, "Die Leichtigkeit der Schwermut: W. G. Sebalds 'Kunst der Levitation,'" *Jahrbuch der deutschen Schillergesellschaft* 50 (2006): 458–77, as well as the expanded chapter version with the same title in Hutchinson's monograph, *W. G. Sebald — Die dialektische Imagination* (Berlin: Walter de Gruyter, 2009), 145–66.

⁴ For more on the arresting of time and temporality more generally in Sebald, see Amir Eshel, "Against the Power of Time: The Poetics of Suspension in W. G. Sebald's *Austerlitz,*" *New German Critique* 88 (Winter 2003): 71–96, and Heike Polster, *The Aesthetics of Passage: The Imag(in)ed Experience of Time in Thomas Lehr, W. G. Sebald, and Peter Handke* (Würzburg: Königshausen & Neumann, 2009). Leone views Sebald as a "vertiginous travel literature writer" whose journeys work toward not only the suspension of time but also the "annihilation of space and movement through space and movement themselves." Leone, "Literature, Travel, and Vertigo," in *Cross-Cultural Travel: Papers from the Royal Irish Academy Symposium on Literature and Travel,* ed. Jane Conroy (New York: Lang, 2003), 513–22; here 515.

⁵ Jo Catling, "Gratwanderungen bis an den Rand der Natur: W. G. Sebald's Landscapes of Memory," in *The Anatomist of Melancholy: Essays in Memory of W. G. Sebald,* ed. Rüdiger Görner (Munich: iudicium, 2003), 19–50; here 28–29. Massimo Leone notes that "Sebald's travelogues almost immediately plunge into a sort of day-dream," while David Darby speaks of the construction of space in Sebald's writing as "the making of a landscape in the imagination." See Massimo Leone, "Textual Wanderings: A Vertiginous Reading of W. G. Sebald," in *W. G. Sebald: A Critical Companion,* ed. J. J. Long and Anne Whitehead (Seattle: U of Washington P, 2004), 89–101; here 96; and David Darby, "Landscape and Memory: Sebald's Redemption of History," in *W. G. Sebald: History — Memory — Trauma,* ed. Scott Denham and Mark McCulloh (Berlin: Walter de Gruyter, 2006), 265–77; here 266.

⁶ Christopher C. Gregory-Guider, "The 'Sixth Emigrant': Traveling Places in the Works of W. G. Sebald," *Contemporary Literature* 46.3 (2005): 422–49; here 424 and passim.

⁷ W. G. Sebald, "Unterm Spiegel des Wassers: Peter Handkes Erzählung von der Angst des Tormanns," in *BU,* 115–30; here 115–16. Originally published under the same title in *Austriaca* 16 (1983): 43–56. Neil Christian Pages offers an insightful reading of this essay and the pathological in Sebald in his article "Crossing Borders: Sebald, Handke, and the Pathological Vision," *Modern Austrian Literature* 40.4 (2007): 61–92.

⁸ *BU,* 78–92. Both a German and a slightly amended English version of this essay were published in 1972 as "Thanatos: Zur Motivstruktur in Kafkas *Schloß,*" *Literatur und Kritik* 66/67 (1972): 399–411, and "The Undiscover'd Country: The Death Motif in Kafka's *Castle,*" *Journal of European Studies* 2 (1972): 22–34. On Sebald's reading of Kafka, see Brad Prager, "Sebald's Kafka," in Denham and

McCulloh, *W. G. Sebald: History, Memory, Trauma*, 105–26, as well as Zisselsberger, "Melancholy Longings: Sebald, Benjamin, and the Image of Kafka," in *Searching for Sebald: Photography after W. G. Sebald*, ed. Lise Patt (Los Angeles: Institute of Cultural Inquiry, 2007), 280–301.

[9] W. G. Sebald, "Und blieb ich am äussersten Meer," *manuskripte* 85 (1984): 23–27; "Wie der Schnee auf den Alpen," *manuskripte* 92 (1986): 26–31; and "Die dunckle Nacht fahrt aus," *manuskripte* 95 (1987): 12–18.

[10] In the case of *Die Ringe des Saturn* it is likely that the conception of the text was strongly influenced by Sebald's reading of Claudio Magris's famous travel book, *Danubio* (Milan: Garzanti, 1986), which Sebald had reviewed and which, as Mark McCulloh has noted, "anticipated Sebald's in form and content." McCulloh, "Destruction and Transcendence in W. G. Sebald," *Philosophy and Literature* 30 (2006): 395–409; here 405. Sebald reviewed Heinz Georg-Held's German translation of Magris's book (*Donau — Biographie eines Flusses*) in *Austrian Studies* 1 (1990): 183–84.

[11] For a discussion of the notion of *Nachgehen* as a trope for Sebald's investigative pursuits, see Carsten Strathausen, "Going Nowhere: Sebald's Rhizomatic Travels," in Patt, *Searching for Sebald*, 472–92.

[12] For more on Sebald's relationship to Austrian literature, see the special issue of the journal *Modern Austrian Literature*, ed. Zisselsberger, 40.4 (2007); on the notion of *Heimat* and place in Sebald's writing, see Gisela Ecker, "*Heimat* oder die Grenzen der Bastelei," in *W. G. Sebald: Politische Archäologie und melancholische Bastelei*, ed. Michael Niehaus and Claudia Öhlschläger (Berlin: Erich Schmidt, 2006), 77–88.

[13] W. G. Sebald, *Über das Land und das Wasser: Ausgewählte Gedichte, 1964–2001*, ed. Sven Meyer (Munich: Hanser, 2008).

[14] Sven Meyer, "*Portrait ohne Absicht:* Der Lyriker W. G. Sebald. Nachwort," in Sebald, *Über das Land und das Wasser*, 105–12; here 109.

[15] Sebald, "Walzertraum," in *Über das Land und das Wasser*, 75. English translation included with permission of Penguin Books Ltd.

[16] "'Aufzeichnungen aus Korsika: Zur Natur- & Menschenkunde,' von W. G. Sebald," aus dem Nachlass herausgegeben von Ulrich von Bülow, in *Wandernde Schatten: W. G. Sebalds Unterwelt*, Marbacher Katalog, ed. Ulrich von Bülow, Heike Gfrereis, and Ellen Strittmatter (Marbach: Deutsche Schillergesellschaft, 2008), 129–58 (first version); 159–210 (second version). Parts of this project had been published or prepared for publication by Sebald and were included in the posthumously published *Campo Santo* under the titles "Kleine Excursion nach Ajaccio" (1996); "Campo Santo" (unpublished manuscript from the literary estate); "Die Alpen im Meer" (2001); and "La cour de l'ancienne école" (1997).

[17] Ulrich von Bülow, "Sebalds Korsika-Projekt," in von Bülow, Gfrereis, and Strittmatter, *Wandernde Schatten*, 210.

[18] Jean-Pierre Rondas, "'So wie ein Hund, der den Löffel vergisst': Ein Gespräch mit W. G. Sebald über *Austerlitz*," in *Literatur im Krebsgang: Totenbeschwörung und memoria in der deutschsprachigen Literatur nach 1989*, ed. Arne De Winde and Anke Gilleir (Amsterdam: Rodopi, 2008), 351–63; here 354. For a discussion of

the different meanings of "Expatriierung" and "expatriation" in German and English as well as Sebald's status as an "expatriate" writer, see Gerhard Fischer, "W. G. Sebald's Expatriate Experience and His Literary Beginnings," introduction to *W. G. Sebald: Schreiben ex patria*, ed. Gerhard Fischer (Amsterdam: Rodopi, 2009), 15–25.

[19] Tim Schleider, "Vom Glänzen der Heringe, vom Zucken der Leiber. Der Bestsellerautor Daniel Kehlmann ist in Stuttgart — und spricht über einen zutiefst bewunderten Kollegen: W. G. Sebald," *Stuttgarter Zeitung*, 24 Sept. 2008, Kultur, 26. Kehlmann notes: "Sebald hat über den Holocaust geschrieben, ohne das Wort Holocaust zu benutzen. Diese Methode des Indirekten, des unter der Oberfläche Miterzählten — das ist seine Leistung" (Sebald has written about the Holocaust without using the word Holocaust. This method of indirectness, of stories that are told and emerge from beneath the surface — that's his achievement).

[20] Kehlmann, quoted in Schleider, "Vom Glänzen der Heringe": "Das Problem war einfach Sebald war nicht da, er war in Norwich. Die deutschen Autoren und die Kritiker treffen sich ständig untereinander. Die ganze literarische Szene funktioniert weitgehend über Bekanntschaften. Und Sebald lebte als Hochschulprofessor in England. Er stand außen vor" (The problem was simple: Sebald was not there, he was in Norwich. German authors and critics constantly interact with each other. The entire literary scene operates largely through personal connections. And Sebald lived as a university professor in England. He was on the outside). For Fischer, it is ultimately this absence and view from the margins that makes Sebald a writer with a unique perspective, "a *Zaungast* observing the literary party at home from the marginal position of an expatriate outsider who sees more and knows more because his horizon has considerably widened on account of his life experiences in two home countries (Fischer, "W. G. Sebald's Expatriate Experience," 23).

[21] Walter Benjamin, "Der Erzähler: Betrachtungen zum Werk Nikolai Lesskows," in *Illuminationen* (Frankfurt am Main: Suhrkamp, 1977), 385–410; here 386; "The Storyteller: Reflections on the Works of Nikolai Leskov," in *Illuminations*, ed. Hannah Arendt, trans. Harry Zohn (New York: Schocken, 1969), 83–110; here 84. For a discussion of the significance of Benjamin's essay for Sebald's aesthetics, see the chapter "Ezähltechnik I: 'Seemann' oder "Ackermann'?" in Hutchinson's *W. G. Sebald — Die dialektische Imagination*, 35–56.

[22] Michael Silverblatt, "A Poem of an Invisible Subject (interview)," in *The Emergence of Memory: Conversations with W. G. Sebald*, ed. Lynne Sharon Schwartz (New York: Seven Stories, 2007), 85.

[23] Joe Cuomo, "A Conversation with W. G. Sebald," in Schwartz, *The Emergence of Memory*, 93–118; here 96. Originally published as "The Meaning of Coincidence: An Interview with the Writer W. G. Sebald," *New Yorker*, 3 Sept. 2001, online edition, based on an interview on 13 Mar. 2001.

[24] Eleanor Wachtel, "Ghost Hunter (interview)," in Schwartz, *The Emergence of Memory*, 37–62; here 42.

[25] Christopher C. Gregory-Guider suggests that Sebald reconstructs the stories of his subjects by linking their experiences to the places they have traversed. This

method, Gregory-Guider argues, qualifies his work as a form of "autobiogeography," a particular genre in the field of life-writing. See his "Memorial Sights/Sites: Sebald, Photography, and the Art of Autobiogeography in *The Emigrants*," in Patt, *Searching for Sebald*, 516–41.

[26] Silverblatt, "A Poem of an Invisible Subject," 85.

[27] Rondas, "'So wie ein Hund, der den Löffel vergisst,'" 355.

[28] Rondas, "'So wie ein Hund, der den Löffel vergisst,'" 355.

[29] This question would also require a closer examination of the relationship between travel and Sebald's understanding and use of photography, in particular because Sebald attributed to photographs an imaginative potential that he also described in peripatetic terms. In an interview with Christian Scholz he noted: "Immer ist mir dabei aufgefallen, dass von diesen Bildern ein ungeheurer Appell ausgeht; eine Forderung an den Beschauer, zu erzählen oder sich vorzustellen, was man, *von diesen Bildern ausgehend*, erzählen könnte. . . . Beim Schreiben erkennt man Möglichkeiten, *von den Bildern erzählend auszugehen*, in diese Bilder erzählend *hineinzugehen*, diese Bilder statt einer Textpassage zu subplantieren und so fort" (my italics; I've always noticed then that an enormous appeal emanates from these images; a demand on the viewer to tell stories or to imagine what one could tell, by starting with these pictures. . . . When writing you recognize possibilities to start by telling stories about the images, to walk into these images through the telling of stories, to implant these images into a text-passage, and so on). Christian Scholz, "'Aber das Geschriebene ist ja kein wahres Dokument': Ein Gespräch mit dem Schriftsteller W. G. Sebald über Literatur und Photographie," *Neue Züricher Zeitung*, 26 Feb. 2000. 77; in English, "'But the Written Word is Not a True Document': A Conversation on Literature and Photography with the Writer W. G. Sebald," trans. Markus Zisselsberger, in Patt, *Searching for Sebald*, 104.

[30] For a reading of Sebald's relationship to Jean Améry and the narrator's retracing of the latter's steps in *Austerlitz*, see Zisselsberger, "Towards an Extension of Memory: W. G. Sebald Reads Jean Améry," in *Trajectories of Memory: Representations of the Holocaust in History and the Arts*, ed. Christina Guenther and Beth Griech-Polelle (Newcastle-upon-Tyne, UK: Cambridge Scholars, 2008), 191–223.

[31] Sebald uses "undenkbar" twice, which Anthea Bell translates as "could not imagine" and "it was impossible to picture" (*A*, 22).

[32] Rondas, "'So wie ein Hund, der den Löffel vergisst,'" 355.

[33] Arthur Lubow, "Crossing Boundaries," in Schwartz, *The Emergence of Memory*, 159–73; here 167.

[34] Von Bülow, "Sebalds Korsika-Projekt," 214. This assessment is shared by Strathausen, who similarly notes that Sebald's texts "never really arrive anywhere, but continue to wander aimlessly in an infinitely expanding, labyrinthine space that defies traditional topography." Strathausen, "Going Nowhere: Sebald's Rhizomatic Travels," 472.

[35] For detailed reviews and overviews of more recent scholarship, see Richard Sheppard, "'Woods, trees and the spaces in between': A Report on Work Published on W. G. Sebald, 2005–2008," *Journal of European Studies* 39.1 (2009): 79–128;

Markus Zisselsberger, "A Persistent Fascination: Recent Scholarship on the Work of W. G. Sebald," *Monatshefte* 101.1 (Spring 2009): 88–105; J. J. Long, "A Bibliographical Essay on Current Research," in *W. G. Sebald and the Writing of History*, ed. Anne Fuchs and J. J. Long (Würzburg: Königshausen & Neumann, 2007), 11–30; and Lynn Wolff, "'Das metaphysische Unterfutter der Realität': Recent Publications and Trends in W. G. Sebald Research," *Monatshefte* 99.1 (2007): 78–101.

[36] Recent monographs include Ben Hutchinson, *Die dialektische Imagination*; Bettina Mosbach, *Figurationen der Katastrophe: Ästhetische Verfahren in W. G. Sebalds* Die Ringe des Saturn *und* Austerlitz (Bielefeld: Aisthesis Verlag, 2008); J. J. Long, *W. G. Sebald: Image, Archive, Modernity* (New York: Columbia UP, 2007); Deane Blackler, *Reading W. G. Sebald: Adventure and Disobedience* (Rochester, NY: Camden House, 2007); and Claudia Öhlschläger, *Beschädigtes Leben. Erzählte Risse: W. G. Sebalds poetische Ordnung des Unglücks* (Freiburg: Rombach, 2006). Jo Catling and Richard Hibbitt are currently editing *Saturn's Moons: A W. G. Sebald Handbook*, to be published by Legenda in 2010.

[37] Martin Klebes, "Infinite Journey: From Kafka to Sebald," in Long and Whitehead, *A Critical Companion*, 123–39; here 128.

[38] Richard Bates, "The Loneliness of the Long-Distance Narrator: The Inscription of Travel in Proust and W. G. Sebald," 511.

[39] Darby, "Landscape and Memory," 265.

[40] For a detailed and recent discussion of the problem of defining the features of "travel writing," see John Zilcosky, "Writing Travel," introduction to *Writing Travel: The Poetics and Politics of the Modern Journey*, ed. John Zilcosky (Toronto: U of Toronto P, 2008), 3–24.

[41] Bianca Theisen, "Prose of the World: W. G. Sebald's Literary Travels," *Germanic Review* 79.3 (Summer 2004): 163–79; here 163.

[42] Theisen, "Prose of the World," 164.

[43] Theisen, "Prose of the World," 167.

[44] John Zilcosky, "Sebald's Uncanny Travels: The Impossibility of Getting Lost," in Long and Whitehead, *A Critical Companion*, 102–20; here 102.

[45] Zilcosky, "Lost and Found: Disorientation, Nostalgia, and Holocaust Melodrama in Sebald's *Austerlitz*," *MLN* 121.3 (2006): 679–98. In his introduction to *Writing Travel* Zilcosky also speaks of Sebald as a "postmodern travel writer" (9). For a convincing argument for Sebald as a postmodern traveler, see also Carsten Strathausen, "Going Nowhere: Sebald's Rhizomatic Travels."

[46] Theisen, "Prose of the World," 165.

[47] Leone, "Textual Wanderings," 100.

[48] Leone, "Textual Wanderings," 90 and 94–95.

[49] Deane Blackler, *Reading W. G. Sebald: Adventure and Disobedience*, 23, 17, and passim.

[50] ICI Research Team, "A Truth That Lies Elsewhere," in Patt, *Searching for Sebald*, 492–509.

51 For a description and images of these suitcases, see http://www.culturalinquiry. org/ordersuitcase.html (accessed 15 Dec. 2009).

52 Daniel Stender, "Wandern im Zitat. Unheimliche Heimat Allgäu: In W. G. Sebalds Geburtsort Wertach führt ein Wanderweg durch Szenen seiner Romane und Erzählungen," *Frankfurter Allgemeine Sontagszeitung* 2 (17 Jan. 2010), Reise, V3.

53 Will Stone, "At Risk of Interment: W. G. Sebald in Terezin and Breendonk," *Vertigo* 40.3 (Summer 2009): 67.

54 Jan Peter Tripp, "Die Waldauer Begegnung," in *Centrales & Occasionelles* (Offenburg: Schwarzwaldverlag, 2001), 98–106.

55 Leone, "Textual Wanderings," 90.

Fig. 1. Illustration and accompanying text © *Jan Peter Tripp, from "Die Waldauer Begegnung," in Tripp,* Centrales & Occasionelles *(Offenburg: Schwarzwaldverlag, 2001). Image II, page 101: Robert Walser and Adolf Wölfli practice flying with paper planes. Text, page 98: "In den ersten Frühlingstagen, in Parallelaktion also zur äußeren Natur, beschlossen der Schriftsteller Robert Walser und Adolf Wölfli, der Malerdichter, ein kühnes Projekt, den 'freien Flug ohne Inanspruchnahme jeglichen Hilfsmittels.'"*

Die Kunst des Fliegens

W. G. Sebald

Mit ungeheurer Schwerfälligkeit arbeitet sich die Maschine aus der Höhe herunter. Die Oberfläche der Erde gibt sich zu erkennen. Das ist die Burgundische Pforte, das ist das Basler Land, das sind die Schatten- und Sonnenflecken, grün, hell und dunkel, die Waldungen, Wiesen und Apfelbäume. Und da ist das Aaaretal mit seinen grauweißen, immer weiter in- und auseinanderwachsenden Ansiedlungen. Straßenzüge, Eisenbahnlinien, Hochspannungsleitungen, Rauchfahnen. Krachend und schütternd schiebt sich unter mir jetzt das Fahrwerk heraus. Nichts Primitiveres gibt es als die Technik, als die Ausgeburten des Traums, die Schöpfung wiederholen zu können.

Christopher Sandbach war zehn Jahre alt, als ich ihn kennenlernte. Er lebte in Stockport in Cheshire mit seinen Eltern am Ende einer Häuserzeile, hinter der sich ein ungeheures, aus Millionen von Ziegeln erbautes Viadukt erhob. Seit seinem dritten Lebensjahr hatte er sich geweigert, eine warme Mahlzeit oder irgend etwas Gekochtes zu sich zu nehmen. Er ernährte sich von Keksen und Sandwiches und beschäftigte sich ausschließlich mit der Konstruktion von Sauriern aus Papier und Karton. Einige dieser Viecher wurden größer als er selbst. Sie bevölkerten bereits sämtliche Räume des Hauses, da es Christophers Mutter nicht gelang, sie schnell genug wieder beiseite zu schaffen. Christopher kümmerte sich nicht um das Schicksal seiner Kreaturen. Allzusehr war er, wie der Glanz seiner myopischen Augen verriet, in das Geheimnis ihrer Herstellung versunken.

Immer kleiner wird der durch das Bullauge wahrnehmbare Ausschnitt der Welt. Ein Zittern läuft durch die silberne, mit kleinen Metallflecken vielfach ausgebesserte Tragfläche. Wie erstarrt sitzen die Passagiere an Bord. Draußen, auf einem Feldweg entlang der Einflugschneise, steht eine bunte Schar Kinder mit ihren Fahrrädern. Einige winken, einige halten nur die Hand über die Augen.

Die unverhältnismäßig großzügige Anlage des Flughafens Kloten macht auch diesmal auf mich den Eindruck, als habe die Zukunft schon angefangen und als seien die Menschen, die da in oft weit auseinandergezogenen Gruppen die riesigen vollklimatisierten Hallen durchqueren, die Vorhut eines neuen nomadischen Geschlechts. Ein eigenartig zielstrebiges Gehabe zeichnet sie aus. Alle sind sie leicht vornübergebeugt wie die seit Jahrhunderten auf ihr Ende zustürzenden Figuren der Wiener Genesis.

Erst die Kontrollschleusen zwingen wieder zu einer verhalteneren Gangart. Nur kein Zeichen der Panik. Die Resozialisierung beginnt. Der Zollbeamte Wengi würdigt mich eines abgründigen Blicks, der mich ähnlich berührt wie gleich darauf in der Enge des Fahrstuhlgehäuses die gesenkten Lider meiner anscheinend schwergeprüften Mitreisenden. Dann das Hallen des Parkhauses, einzelne erhobene Stimmen, Türenschlagen und Ausfahrt. Draußen weht eine linde Luft. Sanft hügelan, hügelab und in weiten Bögen treiben wir im Strom des abendlichen Verkehrs über die Autobahnen der Stadt, westwärts, wo am Himmel über einem goldenen Streifen am Horizont noch ein orange- und purpurrotes Schauspiel zu sehen ist. Ein tiefes Glücksgefühl erfaßt mich, nicht anders als sei ich nun wieder eingekehrt in die Natur.

Als wir die Wohnung meiner Gastgeber betreten, läuft gerade die Tagesschau. Die Nachrichtensprecherin entbietet mir mit sphinxhaftem Lächeln den englischen Gruß. Wenn ich einen Hut aufhätte, müßte ich ihn jetzt abnehmen, denke ich mir. Doch da übergibt sie schon, die schöne Illusion zerstörend, das Wort an einen verdächtig zivilistisch aussehenden Herrn, der anhand einer Karte erläutert, daß im Umkreis der Kraftwerke Leibstadt, Beznau, Gösgen und Mühleberg je zirka 800 000 Menschen leben. Dies sei jedoch, fügt er hinzu, insofern nicht weiter beunruhigend, als in der Schweiz das Schutzkellersystem in zügigem Ausbau begriffen sei. Man werde sich also gegebenenfalls zurückziehen und, wie er sich ausdrückt, „Zeit gewinnen" können, bis von den Behörden Anweisungen betreffend ein der Lage entsprechendes Verhalten ergingen.

Später, es ist nun fast schon ganz finster geworden, sitzen wir bei einer Flasche Williams auf dem Rasenstück des Vorgartens der etwa um 1900 erbauten kleinen Villa, deren Hochparterre meine Gastgeber bewohnen. Die übrigen Mietparteien sind in die Ferien gefahren, und da dieses Haus, vielleicht aufgrund eines Planungsfehlers, tatsächlich als einziges Wohnhaus zwischen lauter Büro- und Industriegebäuden übriggeblieben und also außer uns nirgends eine menschliche Seele zu sehen ist, dünkt es mich, wie wir da im Widerschein des Windlichts mit flackernden Gesichtern einander gegenübersitzen, wir seien die letzten organischen Lebewesen, die durch irgendeinen abstrusen Zufall verschont gebliebenen letzten Repräsentanten einer untergegangenen Zivilisation, von der einzig noch die obersten Stockwerke der höchsten Gebäude aus dem Wasser ragten. Das Grundstück aber erscheint mir als das Deck und die Villa als die Decksaufbauten eines Schiffs, das steuerlos und still auf den kaum wahrnehmbaren Wellen schwankt.

Nach Mitternacht liege ich wach, ein fortwährendes graues Rauschen im Ohr. Es ist der flache Atem der Ventilatoren auf dem Dach des Bürogebäudes von nebenan. Ein Luftzug bewegt die weißen Vorhänge.

Im Videorecorder leuchtet das ewige Licht. Der elektrische Strom geht durch meine Glieder. Alle Viertelstunden schlägt, seltsamer Anachronismus, irgendwo eine Turmuhr, und ich zähle: „Eins, eins, eins und eins." Viermal hat die Turmuhr „ein Uhr" geschlagen. Ist sie verrückt geworden, ist das die Gespensterstunde der Zahlen oder das Ende der Zeit?

Peter Schwalder fällt mir ein und der Aufsatz mit der Überschrift, „An Unforgettable Dream," den er vor nunmehr bald zwanzig Jahren, als ich noch Schullehrer gewesen bin in der Schweiz, in ebenso fehlerhaftem wie wundervollem Englisch für mich verfaßt hat. „Last night," schrieb Schawalder, „I had a wonderful dream. I dreamt I should can fly. I climbed on to the roof of our house, swang my arms, swang my feet and rose myself highly in the sky. I flew across our house, our garden. Higher and higher. And the village was always less and less. There were stars in the black sky and the watch tower showed twelve o'clock. I knew I should go back, but I was not tired. Below me I looked a little lake. A boat sailed across the lake. Nobody was in the boat. I saw the world like a bird sees our world. A train drove through the night. I saw the lights until he dispaired [*sic*] behind a hill. At last I saw again my village. I sat down on the roof and said to me: 'Of this moment you will be free.'"

Draußen schreit eine Amsel. Lang wart ich auf eine Antwort. Aber kein Laut, kein Flügelschlag, nichts. Ganz winzig komm ich mir vor, wie ein Maikäfer in einer Pappschachtel, horchend auf die Verlockungen einer verlorenen Welt, auf ein Rascheln bloß in den Blättern. Dann rührt Alba, die Dämmerung, an die Dächer. Die lilafarbene Siemensleuchtschrift erlischt, und endlich breitet die Müdigkeit ihr stillendes Gift in meinen Adern aus. Wie es die letzten Verästelungen erreicht, spüre ich eine Erleichterung des Körpers, ein Schwebezustand tritt ein, eine schmerzlose Levitation. Spinnen ziehen ein Netz über mein Gesicht. Alma quies optata veni, nam sic sine vita vivere tam suave est quam sine morte moriri. So oder so ähnlich. Zum Andenken an den Autor dieser Zeilen. Der Maiboum hieß, glaub ich.

Jetzt bin ich am Rand des Bewußtseins. Bilder kommen herein wie Wasser über ein Wehr. Herausgehoben aus der Welt, schweb ich im Auge des Sturms hoch über der Erde. Ich sehe die Sargasso-See, Fischzüge, rostfarbene Algenwälder in der Strömung. Meilenweit unter mir die weiße Zeile eines Strands, der sich zum Horizont hinaufkrümmt. Wolkenbänke türmen sich vor mir auf. Lange Zeit sehe ich nichts mehr als die Schwaden des Nebels. Dann liegt die Landebahn unter mir. Ein teils schwarzes, teil lindgrünes Marschland. Ich sehe eine mir bekannte Gärtnerfamilie, die auf dem Land mit dem Ernten von Kopfsalat beschäftigt ist. Überall liegt der Kopfsalat herum. Nie hätte ich mir träumen lassen, daß es soviel Kopfsalat gibt. Den linken Handrücken in das steife Kreuz gestützt, haben der Gärtner und seine Frau sich aufgerichtet und schauen, die rechte Hand über die Augen gelegt, in den Himmel hinauf, aus dem ich, heftig gegen die Luft anrudernd, herunterkomme. Im Aufsetzen auf dem Boden ergreift mich ein Schwindelgefühl. Schon laufen die Gärtnerskinder auf mich zu, und ich hebe sie auf, eins nach dem anderen.

Fig. 2. Illustration and accompanying text © Jan Peter Tripp, from "Die Waldauer Begegnung," in Tripp, Centrales & Occasionelles *(Offenburg: Schwarzwaldverlag, 2001). Image X, page 106: Robert Walser and Adolf Wölfli flying. Text, page 98: "Die Bewegungen ihrer verhältnismäßig kurzen, stumpfen Flügel sollen von so ungeheurer Geschwindigkeit gewesen sein, daß sie darin dem Kolibri glichen, dessen Flügelschlag auch nur mit äußerster Anstrengung vom menschlichen Auge erfaßt werden kann."*

I: Departures

1: Peripatetic Liminality: Sebald and the Tradition of the Literary Walk

Christian Moser

Sebald and the Peripatetic Mode of Traveling

W. G. SEBALD'S TRAVELOGUE *Die Ringe des Saturn*, which depicts a walking tour of several days' duration through the coastal region of East Anglia, significantly bears the subtitle *Eine englische Wallfahrt — An English Pilgrimage*.[1] In more than one respect, the subtitle hints at the outdated mode of traveling that the protagonist has chosen for his tour. First of all, it marks a gesture of distinction — distinction from the dominating travel-form of mass tourism. Sebald seems to evoke an opposition between the pilgrimage, on the one hand, devoted to worship, asceticism, and repentance, and tourism, on the other, which aims at entertainment and diversion. Whereas the pilgrim seriously contemplates the objects of adoration, the monuments and relics of the history of suffering and salvation, in order to tap a mine of spiritual meaning, the tourist is given to the fugitive consumption of commercialized sights and souvenirs — superficial signifiers that refer to nothing substantial beyond their own semiotic status as touristic "markers."[2]

To be sure, the relics into which Sebald's pilgrim becomes absorbed are no longer part of an overarching salvific structure devised by a Christian God; they do not attest to salvation, but, on the contrary, to the omnipresence of destruction.[3] The wanderer presented in *Die Ringe des Saturn* searches for the traces of a silent catastrophe that constitutes the obverse of modernity and its history of progress. Therefore the old-fashioned practices of traveling such as pilgrimage and wandering interest Sebald to the extent that they cultivate a certain mode of perception. This mode of perception is tied to a specific type of movement: the movement of walking. Like the medieval pilgrim or the romantic wanderer, the protagonist of *Die Ringe des Saturn* travels through East Anglia on foot. As far as possible, he disclaims the use of modern means of transportation, hoping thereby to experience the country in a different, more intensive way than ordinary travelers.

This hope is articulated by Sebald's protagonist on the occasion of the
first stop in his itinerary. Nowadays tourists are wont to visit the country
seat of Somerleyton Hall by car. A smooth road leads them directly up to
the main gate and front of the old manor house. Sebald's protagonist, by
contrast, approaches the place in two stages: first he takes the train —
"[einen] alten, bis an die Fensterscheiben hinauf mit Ruß und Öl ver-
schmierten Dieseltriebwagen" (one of the old diesel trains, grimed with oil
and soot; *RS,* 41/29) — then he alights at a station no longer in general
use, in order to proceed to the estate as a pedestrian. He has to climb its
wall "gleich einem Strauchdieb" (like some interloper) and struggle
through the thicket before reaching the back of the country house (*RS,*
44/32). Instead of passively following an already existing road, Sebald's
protagonist must force his own way through a sort of no-man's-land, an
area of waste and wilderness. This strange mode of approach is matched by
the eccentric perspective from which Somerleyton Hall is viewed by the
interloper. He perceives what ordinary visitors tend to overlook: a solitary
Chinese quail, for example, who, "offenbar in einem Zustand der Demenz"
(evidently in a state of dementia), runs to and fro along the edge of its cage
(*RS,* 50/36); an old gardener who intercepts the walker during his stroll
in the overgrown park and informs him about the role that Somerleyton
Hall played in the bombing raids against German cities in 1944 and 1945
(*RS,* 52–53/38–39); and the rear view of the manor, usually concealed
from visitors, which, arising out of the exuberant thicket, suddenly dis-
closes itself to the pedestrian, thus forcing him to acknowledge the fact
that the estate is nearing the brink of dissolution ("dem Rand der
Auflösung sich näher[nd]"; *RS,* 50/36). To conclude: whereas the ordinary tourist, abruptly transported by car from the twentieth century into a
distant past, relishes Somerleyton Hall as a curious remnant of bygone
times, the pedestrian who must transgress a liminal space of waste and
wilderness before reaching his goal is enabled to place the estate within the
historical framework of creaturely suffering, martial violence, and dissolution. His point of view removes Somerleyton Hall from the "Zirkulation"
(circulation; *RS,* 48/35, my translation) of marketable goods: it transforms the touristic marker into a historic signifier, an allegory of destruction. At least, this seems to be the pretension that Sebald connects to his
special way of traveling.

Thus there is a link between the peripatetic mode of movement and
Sebald's attempt to recover the repressed and marginalized contents of
history, but this link — it seems to me — has not yet been sufficiently
recognized. Why does Sebald choose to *walk* his way through East Anglia?
And why, of all things, does he choose the coastal region of Suffolk as the
locale of his wanderings? If these questions are raised at all, they are quickly
dismissed with reference to the remark that Sebald places at the beginning
of his travelogue: there he claims to have undertaken his journey "in der

Hoffnung, der nach dem Abschluß einer größeren Arbeit in mir sich ausbreitenden Leere entkommen zu können" (in the hope of dispelling the
emptiness that had taken hold of me after the completion of a long stint
of work; *RS*, 11/3). The pedestrian tour seems to be conceived as a
therapy against a developing onslaught of melancholy, to which the planet
Saturn, mentioned conspicuously in the book's title, alludes as well.[4] As a
matter of fact, traveling and — more specifically — pedestrian travel
belong to the arsenal of remedies that are traditionally prescribed for the
pernicious impact of black bile. Both Marsilio Ficino in his *De vita* and
Robert Burton in his *Anatomy of Melancholy* recommend the "*deambulatio per amœna loca*" (walk in pleasant places) as an effective cure for the
spleen.[5] Nevertheless, the reference to the traditional discourse of melancholy does not suffice to explain Sebald's predilection for the peripatetic
mode. First, as a cure for melancholy, the journey along the East Anglian
coastline seems to be ill-conceived. If Sebald's intention is to dispel an
inner emptiness, why does he choose, as the site for his *deambulatio*, a
landscape that is characterized, as the narrator frequently asserts, by its
monotony and desolation? The coastal region of East Anglia may have its
charms, but it certainly is no *locus amoenus*. It is more apt to produce
melancholy than to cure it.

Second, the reference to melancholy cannot account for the fact that
Sebald continuously devotes his attention to the different modes of travel
and movement — not only in *Die Ringe des Saturn* but in virtually all of
his writings. *How* individuals move through space is a matter of considerable importance to him. He is particularly interested in the influence that
the diverse means of transportation exert on the perceptive and cognitive
behavior of the traveler. Three modes of travel are repeatedly discussed in
his works: going by train — this means of transportation plays a major role
in the novel *Austerlitz*; it is associated with the scientific paradigm of the
network and the Freudian concept of the neuronal "track" ("Bahnung");
flying (either by airplane or by balloon) — Sebald connects this type of
transportation with the totalizing viewpoint of the panorama; and the
slow, precarious and earth-bound movement of walking. Sebald's attitude
toward train journeys and flying have been thoroughly dealt with by Todd
Presner and Claudia Öhlschläger respectively;[6] therefore, in what follows,
I will concentrate on the significance of walking — with occasional comparative side-glances toward the other modes of movement, for the sake of
clarity.

A cursory view through Sebald's writings quickly reveals the extraordinary importance that the author attributes to the peripatetic mode of
traveling. The protagonist of "All'estero," the longest of the stories collected in the volume *Schwindel. Gefühle.*, is presented as aimlessly walking
through the cities of Vienna and Milano, thus inducing the feeling of
vertigo mentioned in the title of the book. In "Il ritorno in patria," con-

tained in the same volume of stories, the narrator describes how, after an absence of more than thirty years, he returns to his native village in the Bavarian Allgäu region. He returns as a peripatetic, for, approaching the Allgäu from the south via Tyrol, he descends from the bus at the Oberjoch customs post, in order to cross the border on foot. As in the case of Somerleyton Hall, the problematic experience of homecoming is mediated by walking through a "Niemandsland" (a no-man's-land; *SG*, 193/*V*, 177), a liminal zone. The protagonist of the story "Paul Bereyter," published in the volume titled *Die Ausgewanderten*, is an indefatigable walker and climber of mountains; this is also true of Dr. Henry Selwyn, the main character of the opening story in the same volume. Thus Sebald establishes a link between emigration and peripatetic movement. In *Austerlitz*, the protagonist, who is involved in uncovering the deeply buried and traumatic past of Nazi persecution to which his family fell victim, undertakes long nightly walks through the city of London. Later he deliberately approaches the former concentration camp of Theresienstadt, where his mother was imprisoned, on foot (*A*, 271/186); the same applies to the narrator, who, on the occasion of his second visit to the concentration camp of Breendonk, decides to walk the final ten kilometers to his destination (*A*, 417/411). Hence the confrontation with a troublesome past is mediated by the peripatetic movement through space. Finally, two of the essays contained in the collection *Logis in einem Landhaus* explicitly treat the correlation between walking and writing and are devoted to prominent literary peripatetics, Jean-Jacques Rousseau and Robert Walser.[7]

This survey is far from complete, but it attests to the fact that the motif of walking holds a privileged position in Sebald's oeuvre. Furthermore, it gives rise to the suspicion that the author deliberately attempts to place his work in a preexisting tradition of the literary walk. Thus Sebald's endeavor to oppose the officious history of modern progress and enlightenment by an archeology of the particular, the marginal, and the incommensurable is related to the cultural practice of walking and its literary representation.[8] In order to elucidate this relation, I propose to proceed in three steps. First, I would like to sketch the tradition that Sebald evokes in *Die Ringe des Saturn* — the tradition of the literary walk as it evolved in the late eighteenth and early nineteenth centuries.[9] Second, I intend to show which elements he adopts from this tradition and which he rejects in order to develop his own variant of peripatetic writing. Last, I want to point out the cognitive and anthropological implications inherent in Sebald's conception of walking. For in revising the Romantic and Enlightenment modes of the literary walk, he establishes a connection to an older way of thinking about the relationship between man and nature. In *Die Ringe des Saturn* this alternative way is indicated by the name of Sir Thomas Browne.

The Tradition of the Literary Walk

In his pedagogical novel *Emile ou de l'éducation* (1762), Jean-Jacques Rousseau characterizes the advantages of pedestrian travel as follows:

> Nous [Emile and his mentor] ne voyageons donc point en courriers mais en voyageurs. Nous ne songeons pas seulement aux deux termes mais à l'intervalle qui les sépare. Le voyage même est un plaisir pour nous. . . . Je ne conçois qu'une maniére de voyager plus agréable que d'aller à cheval; c'est d'aller à pied. . . . Par tout où je me plais, j'y reste. A l'instant que je m'ennuye, je m'en vais. Je ne dépends ni des chevaux ni du postillon. Je n'ai pas besoin de choisir des chemins tout faits, des routes comodes, je passe par tout où un homme peut passer; je vois tout ce qu'un homme peut voir et ne dépendant que de moi-même je joüis de toute la liberté dont un homme peut joüir.[10]

> [We (Emile and his mentor) do not travel as express messengers but as travelers. We do not only think of the extreme points of our journey, but also of the space in between which separates them. . . . There is only one mode of traveling more agreeable than riding on horseback, namely walking. . . . Wherever it pleases me, I can stop. As soon as I am satisfied, I walk on. I depend neither on horses nor on the postillion. I have no need of beaten tracks or smooth roads; I walk wherever a man can walk; I see whatever a man can see; and since I depend on nobody but myself, I enjoy whatever freedom a man can enjoy.]

Rousseau talks about pedestrian travel in general, but the paradigm for this mode of traveling unmistakably is the innovative bourgeois practice of the *promenade* (*Spaziergang*). Whereas the aristocratic *promenade* takes place in a public (and mostly urban) space and serves as a stage for displaying the insignia of a superior social station, the bourgeois *promeneur* is essentially a solitary walker — he walks alone or in the company of family members and intimate friends.[11] His movement may possess a destination, but his aim is not to arrive there as quickly as possible. On the contrary, the peripatetic movement becomes an end in itself; it is divested of its pragmatic purposes.[12] Paradoxically, the evolution of the bourgeois *promenade* is correlated to the development of innovative means of transport such as fast long-distance mail-coach services or networks of railway connections. The *promeneur* deliberately chooses a slow mode of movement that brings him into immediate contact with the environment. Rousseau, for example, refuses to be transported through the landscape in a closed box like an article of commerce.[13]

The point of pedestrian travel is to leave the closed spaces of urban civilization behind and to step out — at least temporarily — into the openness of nature. The *promeneur* discovers the value of the spaces that lie in between the point of departure and the destination — and he discovers these spaces as a realm of *openness*. They no longer constitute a mere transit zone. Stepping out into the open is a symbolic act: the bourgeois *promeneur* turns his back on the alienating conditions of civil society and experiences himself as an autonomous subject who is able to stand (and to walk) on his own feet.[14] It is no coincidence that the proponents of enlightenment philosophy are fond of metaphors of walking. Thus Immanuel Kant, in his famous attempt to answer the question "Was ist Aufklärung?" (What is enlightenment?), offers the following definition: "Aufklärung ist der *Ausgang* des Menschen aus seiner selbst verschuldeten Unmündigkeit," the walking (or stepping) out of self-imposed minority.[15]

Freedom and autonomy are the key-concepts of the bourgeois "ideology of walking," which, according to the critic Anne D. Wallace, emerged in the eighteenth century and has exerted its influence for more than 200 years.[16] However, this ideology is marked by blatant contradictions. On the one hand, the *promeneur* manifests his freedom by establishing an immediate relationship to the environment. He wishes to shed the instruments and media that facilitate and accelerate his movement but bar his access to the objects of nature and falsify his perception of them. The *promeneur* claims to possess an undistorted view of things as they are in their "natural" setting. The German peripatetic Johann Gottfried Seume succinctly summarizes this claim to cognitive superiority: "Wer geht, sieht im Durchschnitt anthropologisch und kosmisch mehr, als wer fährt. . . . So wie man im Wagen sitzt, hat man sich sogleich einige Grade von der ursprünglichen Humanität entfernt" (He who walks gains a deeper insight into anthropological and cosmological matters than he who rides. . . . As soon as you sit in a coach you are removed by several degrees from humanity in its original state).[17] The walker condescends to move on the same level as his fellow beings. Therefore he is able to gain intimate knowledge about their affairs. While he cannot oversee matters from a superior position, he replaces this overview with a penetrating insight that is sensitive to human suffering and to the effects of political inequality. With both feet securely on firm ground, the walker gains a realistic picture of the conditions that dominate people's lives.

On the other hand, the freedom realized by the walker in his immediate interaction *with* nature is, at the same time, a freedom *from* nature. According to Rousseau, the *promeneur* possesses the license to dream. As a *rêveur* he no longer moves on the same level as the objects around him; rather, he utilizes them as a spring-board for his imagination that is allowed to roam freely. In *Emile*, Rousseau presents a pedestrian who applies himself to the precise observation of nature and its immutable laws. In his *Confessions*, however, he describes himself as a walker who instrumentalizes nature as building material for his imaginative dream constructions. The *promeneur* no longer moves through a tangible landscape but in a land of fantasy ("dans le pays des chiméres").[18] A similar flight of the imagination is staged by Friedrich Schiller in his famous elegy *Der Spaziergang* (The Walk).[19] The poem's protagonist is a walker who flees from the prison of his study ("des Zimmers Gefängnis"; *S,* 7) in order to find regeneration in the intercourse with nature. His way leads him into the mountains. As he ascends, an immense vista opens up before him: "Unabsehbar ergießt sich vor meinen Blicken die Ferne" (the distance extends immeasurably before my eyes; *S,* 29). This view from above sets in motion a philosophical reverie. The external seeing that surmounts great spatial distances is transformed into an internal vision that bridges temporal gaps equally vast. The walker's imagination paints a panoramic view of human history — beginning with the earliest glimmerings of reason and culture in archaic times down to the corruptions of a degenerate civilization as it becomes manifest in the *terreur* of the French Revolution. The overview, given up by Seume in favor of a penetrating insight, seems to be rehabilitated by Schiller's elegy.

Significantly, however, such scenarios of flight (Schiller mentions the eagle hovering in mid-air; *S,* 182) and of panoramic seeing are problematized in peripatetic literature itself. They are denounced as errors, as a form of errancy, a wrong way of walking or a walk along wrong ways. At a certain point in his wanderings Schiller's *promeneur* awakens from his dream and realizes that he has lost his way: "Aber wo bin ich? Es birgt sich der Pfad" (But where am I? The trail conceals itself; *S,* 173). At this point his reverie has developed into a nightmare — the nightmare of a civilization running amok against itself in the excesses of the *ancien régime* and the French Revolution. The elegy thus implicitly admonishes the walker to stick to a suitable terrain. The view from above is criticized as a form of hubris and alienation — in terms of politics as well as aesthetics.

The aesthetic critique of the view from above was initiated in the eighteenth century by the writers who developed the innovative theory of the picturesque.[20] In his *Essays on Picturesque Beauty; on Picturesque Travel; and on Sketching Landscape* (1794), for example, the English aesthetician William Gilpin criticizes the gentleman who abuses art for the sake of self-aggrandizement. He imagines a landowner who leads an artist to the highest point of his estate — "the point of amplest prospect" — and gives him the following direction: "Take thy stand / Just here [. . .] and paint me *all* thou seest." The work of art that results from this direction, however, is "but a painted survey, a mere map."[21] According to Gilpin, the penchant for prospects betrays a possessive attitude that tends to reify nature. Therefore he considers it necessary to replace the static, immobilizing view from above with the mobile and limited perspective of the walker, who moves in a horizontal direction. The view from above turns pictures into maps.[22] To speak with the French theoretician Michel de Certeau, it ossifies the peripatetic *parcours* into a rigid *carte* and transforms the spectator into a surveyor who strives to subdue nature instead of using it as a source of regeneration.[23]

Thus the ideology of walking devises strategies to discipline and contain the walker's movements. The *promeneur* is admonished not to take a station *above* his fellow human beings. But attempts are also made to keep him from straying too far *beyond* the confines of society, from extravagating horizontally, so to speak, from losing himself in the unlimited openness of nature. The walk is conceived of as a form of regeneration — albeit as one that is limited both in temporal and in spatial terms. In the *Confessions*, Rousseau describes certain pedestrian excursions that he undertook as an adolescent in the environment of his hometown, Geneva. His thoughts far off in a world of reverie, the young peripatetic was wont to lose all sense of time and place, with the result that one day, when returning from his excursion and finding that the city gates were already closed, he decided to leave his hometown and to try his luck abroad. Thus, the autobiographer comments, a limited walk turned into a lifelong vagabondage.[24] To prevent this kind of aberration, the German philosopher Karl Gottlob Schelle, author of *Die Spatziergänge oder Die Kunst spatzieren zu gehen* (Promenades or the Art of Walking, 1802), proposes an ingenious expedient: instead of strolling *beyond* the city walls, the walker should move precisely *on* the city walls. According to Schelle, walking along the circular path of the city walls allows the peripatetic to wander aimlessly in the face of nature without incurring the danger of getting lost.[25] By moving in the liminal space between the country and the city, the walker experiences the openness of nature but remains safely bound to an orbit that is centered in urban civilization. In Schelle's view the inner disposition of the walker who sticks to this liminal path corresponds to his outer station: he enjoys "ein freyes Spiel der Gemüthskräfte" (the free play of his mental faculties) — reason and sensuality are in a state of harmony.[26]

By restricting his movements to the liminal space between nature and culture, Schelle wishes to safeguard the walker against the dangers of vagary. Once again it is Rousseau who manages to expose the shortcomings of this narrow-minded bourgeois conception. Rousseau describes the zone of transition between the city and the country not as the walker's safe haven but as a place where dangerous accidents and traumatic breaks are especially likely to occur. Correspondingly, this liminal space does not effect a harmonious reconciliation between nature and culture; on the contrary, it marks the scene where they play out their irreconcilable opposition. In the second piece of his *Les rêveries du promeneur solitaire*, one of the highlights of peripatetic literature, Rousseau depicts a walk that leads him from the city center of Paris to its rural outskirts in Ménilmontant. Here, on the outer edge of the great city, he is run down by a giant mastiff accompanying a speeding coach that belongs to a great nobleman. Knocked out by aristocratic ruthlessness *and* by an animal nature breaking free from civil repression, Rousseau experiences the liminal zone as a place where the extremes of nature and culture meet in a violent confrontation that threatens to dismember the peripatetic subject. In the *Rêveries*, the liminal sphere takes on an ambiguous and ominous look, after all.

Walking vs. Flying: View from Above vs. View from the Edge

Before I lose myself in some liminal no man's land, let me return from this longish excursion into the tradition of peripatetic literature to the writings of W. G. Sebald. How does Sebald relate to this tradition? At first sight, one gains the impression that there are quite a few points of contact and that Sebald follows rather closely on the heels of his peripatetic predecessors. A more thorough inspection, however, reveals that the relation is a broken one, and that this brokenness is reflected by the figurations of the crack, the fissure, and the incision that frequently recur in *Die Ringe des Saturn*.

To start with one of the main characteristics of the literary walk: the devaluation of the point of departure and the destination; the tendency to see the act of walking as an end in itself. This feature of the *promenade* is most graphically illustrated by the circular course that Schelle advocates in his *Die Spaziergänge oder Die Kunst spatzieren zu gehen*: ideally, walking is a movement on the brink of nature that revolves around itself at the same time that it rotates around a stable center of "reason" or "culture." On his pedestrian excursion to Somerleyton Hall, Sebald significantly refuses to make such a circular movement: "Wer . . . wie ich . . . nicht . . . die halbe Domäne umrunden will, [muß] gleich einem Strauchdieb über die Mauer klettern und sich durch das Dickicht kämpfen, ehe er den Park erreicht" (If, like me, one has no desire to walk all the way around the estate, one has to climb the wall like some interloper and struggle through the thicket before reaching the park; *RS*, 44/32; trans. modified). Contrary to "d[as] zahlende[.] Publikum . . . im eigenen Automobil" (the paying public with their automobiles; *RS*, 44/31), Sebald forces his way in like a thief. He does not pay; he falls out of the general circulation of cars, money and goods. Sebald's walker is a "supernumerary"; he penetrates the inside (in order to procure "insight" — like his predecessor Seume), but on the inside he remains an outsider, an alien body within the organism through which the bloodstream of capital pulsates. He brings to bear an eccentric perspective, which enables him to see the fissures and breaks that run through this organism. Formerly, the narrator declares, the estate was celebrated for being seamlessly integrated into its natural environment:

> 1852 schon . . . finden sich . . . die überschwenglichsten Berichte von dem neuerstandenen Somerleyton, dessen besonderer Ruhm anscheinend darin bestand, daß sich die Übergänge zwischen Interieur und Außenwelt so gut wie unmerklich vollzogen. Die Besucher vermochten kaum zu sagen, wo das Naturgegebene auf- hörte und das Kunsthandwerk anfing.

> [As early as 1852, . . . periodicals were running the most effusive reports on Somerleyton. In particular, it was famed for the scarcely perceptible transitions from interiors to exterior; those who visited were barely able to tell where the natural ended and the man-made began. (*RS*, 46/33)]

Sebald's walker exposes this continuity between nature and culture as an illusion. He notices that the buildings are in a state of decay, while the sur- rounding gardens are "auf dem Höhepunkt ihrer Evolution" (at their evolutionary peak; *RS*, 51/37). The peripatetic realizes the simultaneity of diverse stages of evolution. Evolution is no continuous process but is marked by discontinuity, by the superimposition of heterogeneous strata of time. Thus the tourists who frequent Somerleyton Hall appear to be humans and animals at the same time. Their humanity is superimposed on their animality — they remind the walker of "verkleidete Hunde oder Seehunde im Zirkus" (dressed up circus dogs or seals; *RS*, 44/32). From this alienating perspective, Somerleyton Hall ceases to be part of the mod- ern network of traffic and communication; rather, it seems to be situated "an einem sehr weit abgelegenen, quasi extraterritorialen Ort, an der Küste des Nordmeers" (in some kind of no-man's-land, on the shores of the Arctic Ocean; *RS*, 49/36), an *ultima Thule*, so to speak. The estate is transferred to the extreme limits of the earth, which no longer has the modern appearance of a globe but seems to be a premodern disk. The earth as Sebald's walker sees it still possesses sharply cut edges.[27] Instead of circulating around the globe, he advances toward limits that abut on emptiness.

In his attempt to turn the peripatetic into a bourgeois art, Schelle defines walking as a circular and liminal movement that is based on the continuity between nature and culture. Sebald, by contrast, discards the circular, disrupts the continuous, and exalts the liminal. But what about the second characteristic of the literary walk, its connection to the free- dom of the autonomous subject? In the Somerleyton episode Sebald seems to oppose the tourist who moves along beaten tracks to the walker who must find or even invent his own way. Apparently, therefore, he revives the notion of unbounded freedom that is associated with the enlightenment walker and the Romantic wanderer. As a matter of fact, on the very first page of his travelogue Sebald recalls "die schöne Freizügigkeit" (the beautiful freedom of movement; *RS*, 11/3; trans. modified) that he experienced during his walking tour through East Anglia: "selten habe ich mich so ungebunden gefühlt wie damals bei dem stunden- und tagelangen Dahinwandern durch die teilweise nur spärlich besiedelten Landstriche hinter dem Ufer des Meers" (I have seldom felt so carefree as I did then, walking for hours in the day through the thinly populated countryside that stretches inland from the coast; *RS* 11/3). But Sebald is quick to qualify the feeling of independence that he attributes to the walker. His freedom of movement is balanced by "das lähmende Grauen" (the paralyzing horror; *RS*, 11/3) that comes over him when he is confronted with the traces of destruction — a destruction that even in remote East Anglia is noticeable everywhere. In chapter 8 of *Die Ringe des Saturn* Sebald again points to the ambivalent status of the walker, who seems to be poised between unfettered mobility and inhibiting paralysis: the wanderer who roams through the deserted island of Orfordness "als ginge ich durch ein unentdecktes Land" (as if I were passing through an undiscovered country) feels "zugleich vollkommen befreit und maßlos bedrückt" (at the same time, utterly liberated and deeply despondent; *RS*, 279/234). Thus the unbounded freedom of the walker is no more than an illusion. The individual who believes he is moving around freely and according to his own will is in fact subject to some latent compulsion. Even when he sets foot on seemingly undiscovered land, he is following some hidden tracks.[28]

This is made poignantly clear in the opening pages of the story "All'estero" in *Schwindel. Gefühle*. The narrator reports how he traveled to Vienna, "in der Hoffnung, durch eine Ortsveränderung über eine besonders ungute Zeit hinwegzukommen" (hoping that a change of place would help me get over a particularly difficult period; *SG*, 39/*V*, 33). In Vienna he fills his days with nothing else but rambling aimlessly and without purpose through the streets of the city. Later, when he looks at the map, he finds to his astonishment that none of his journeys has taken him "über einen genau umrissenen, sichel- bis halbmondförmigen Bereich hinaus" (beyond a precisely defined sickle- or crescent-shaped area; *SG*, 39/*V*, 33). It turns out that his wanderings were not aimless at all; in fact, they were predetermined by some plan that was unconsciously carried out by the walker. Without knowing, he had moved in certain tracks — written tracks or tracks of writing, as he subsequently realizes, for he remembers that in the course of his ramblings he had followed people who had reminded him of acquaintances, of the Italian poet Dante, for example, famous for his peripatetic expedition into Hell. Thus the persons followed by the city walker are literary and peripatetic predecessors — "Vor-Gänger" in the literal and the figurative sense of the word.[29] For Sebald, every walk, even the seemingly unconditional walk into the openness of nature, constitutes an act of succession — a "Nach-Gang" or "Nach-Folge," the pursuance of a preexisting track. The task of the literary walker is to uncover and decipher this hidden track, which, more often than not, is buried in the landscape like an invisible wound.

But how exactly does this deciphering function? Is it enough simply to follow the track? The example from "All'estero" suggests that there is more to it than walking and suspending one's determinate will. The hidden order that lies behind the peripatetic movement becomes visible retroactively — only *after* the walker has consulted a map. It is the map that allows Sebald to decode the "writing" of his steps. Within the opposition, established by Gilpin and de Certeau, between *parcours* and *carte*, Sebald seems to switch places and change to the side of the *carte*. Insight gives way to overview, walking, so it appears, to a sort of flying. Indeed, in *Die Ringe des Saturn*, Sebald seems to be in favor of supplementing the limited perspective of the peripatetic by the totalizing viewpoint of the flyer. In chapter 1 he refers to a predecessor who is of considerable importance to his project of deciphering the traces of creaturely suffering, the seventeenth-century physician and writer Sir Thomas Browne. According to Sebald, Browne sought to look upon earthly existence

> vom Standpunkt eines Außenseiters, ja man könnte sagen, mit dem Auge des Schöpfers. . . . selbst den heutigen Leser [ergreift] noch ein Gefühl der Levitation. Je mehr die Entfernung wächst, desto klarer wird die Sicht. Mit der größtmöglichen Deutlichkeit erblickt man die winzigsten Details.

> [with the eye of an outsider, one might even say of the creator. . . . even today the reader is overcome by a sense of levitation. The greater the distance, the clearer the view: one sees the tiniest of details with the utmost clarity. (*RS*, 29–30/18–19).]

Thus Browne marks the ideal of a mode of representation that combines the myopic vision of the walker with the totalizing perspective of the cosmic flyer.[30] To put it in the words that Sebald uses with regard to another of his predecessors, the writer Johann Peter Hebel, this mode of representation effects a paradoxical synthesis of "Mitleidenschaft und Indifferenz" (sympathy and indifference).[31]

Consequently the question arises: did Sebald intend to follow the ideal associated with Browne and Hebel in *Die Ringe des Saturn*? Does he attempt a combination of the walker's and the flyer's perspectives? I already indicated that Sebald's relation to his predecessors tends to be a broken one, and this also holds true for the question under consideration. In following Browne and Hebel, Sebald deviates from them. Ultimately he abandons the idea of uniting flight with walking,[32] striving to expand the peripatetic's perceptive apparatus by different means instead. He disclaims the totalizing viewpoint of the flyer frequently in *Die Ringe des Saturn*. One example can be found in the immediate context of Sebald's praise of Thomas Browne. The physician Browne comes into his mind during a stay in a Norwich hospital, where he was taken exactly one year after his walking tour through East Anglia, "in einem Zustand nahezu gänzlicher Unbeweglichkeit" (in a state of almost total immobility; *RS,* 12/3). Since the space that the walker passes through is not simply a given but is constituted by his peripatetic practice,[33] to him, the total loss of mobility equals the loss of the world, which seems to be "zusammengeschrumpft auf einen einzigen blinden und tauben Punkt" (shrunk . . . to a single, blind, insensate spot; *RS,* 12/4). He perceives the world, so to speak, from an immense, extraterrestrial distance. In order to reestablish his relation to the world the narrator leaves his bed and crawls "auf allen vieren" (on all fours) to the window of the hospital room, from where, "in der krampfhaften Haltung eines Wesens, das sich zum erstenmal von der ebenen Erde erhoben hat" (in the tortured posture of a creature that has raised itself erect for the first time), he gazes at the city below (*RS,* 13/5). Although this is his hometown, Norwich seems like an utterly alien place ("vollkommen fremd") to him (*RS,* 13/5). Thus, like Browne, the narrator occupies an alienating outsider's position. However, whereas Browne's narrator is a cosmic flyer who levitates into spiritual heights, Sebald's narrator is a creature that has just taken the precarious step from crawling to walking on the evolutionary ladder. This creature is especially susceptible to the forces of gravity and remains under the spell of the horizontal. It moves in the liminal sphere between the animal and the human, nature and culture. Sebald advocates a mode of walking that does not disavow its kinship to the animal crawl. Thus he rejects the pathos of "erectness" and "uprightness" articulated by the peripatetic literature of the enlightenment, and he rejects the perspectives of overview and penetrating insight connected to this posture.

In Sebald's opinion the totalizing perspective of the cosmic flyer is related to a certain mode of experiencing and representing history. He clarifies this relation in chapter 5 of *Die Ringe des Saturn,* where the narrator dwells on his memories of a tour through Belgium and a walk across the battlefield of Waterloo. His excursion also included a visit to the Waterloo Panorama,

> das in einer mächtigen Kuppelrotunde untergebrachte Panorama, in dem man von einer im Zentrum sich erhebenden Aussichtsplattform die Schlacht . . . in alle Himmelsrichtungen übersehen kann. Man befindet sich sozusagen am imaginären Mittelpunkt der Ereignisse.
>
> [housed in an immense domed rotunda, where from a raised platform in the middle one can view the battle . . . in every direction. It is like being at the imaginary centre of events. (*RS* 151/124; trans. modified)]

The viewer of the panorama is thus situated in a position both above the action and in the middle of it. As in the case of Browne or Hebel, the distance produced by elevation does not prevent the spectator from closely observing particulars. He gains an overview of the battle and perceives the details of suffering — rendered especially "lifelike" by means of plastic representation — at the same time.[34] Significantly, however, the narrator condemns this way of seeing as inadequate. The Waterloo Panorama is turned into the paradigm of a deceptive mode of historical representation:

> Das also, denkt man, indem man langsam im Kreis geht, ist die Kunst der Repräsentation der Geschichte. Sie beruht auf einer Fälschung der Perspektive. Wir, die Überlebenden, sehen alles von oben herunter, sehen alles zugleich, und wissen dennoch nicht, wie es war.

> [This then, I thought, as I looked round about me, is the representation of history. It requires the falsification of perspective. We, the survivors, see everything from above, see everything at once, and still we do not know how it was. (*RS*, 151–52/125)]

Sebald discards the view from an elevated and central position because "ein deutliches Bild ergab sich nicht" (no clear picture emerged; *RS*, 153/126). Paradoxically, in order to gain a sense of "how it was" and to produce a "clear picture," the spectator must close his eyes. Having shut his eyes, he achieves a momentary vision — he sees "eine Kanonenkugel, die auf schräger Bahn eine Reihe von Pappeln durchquerte, daß die grünen Zweige zerfetzt durch die Luft flogen" (a cannonball smash through a row of poplars at an angle, sending the green branches flying in tatters; *RS*, 153/126). The static and totalizing panorama of history is substituted by a flash of the imagination that exposes a minute but dynamic particular. This particular is not a mimetic representation of reality but, on the contrary, irritates mimesis. The trees torn to tatters by the cannonball reiterate the panorama's "Bühnenlandschaft" (landscaped proscenium) that contains "Baumstümpfe[.] und Strauchwerk" (tree stumps and undergrowth; *RS*, 151/124). In its oblique trajectory ("auf schräger Bahn"), the cannonball cuts through the panoramic representation like a knife. By diametrically cutting the picture in two, a clear(er) picture of history is produced *in* the cleft that disrupts its "factual" or "realistic" mode of representation. For the vision of the cannonball is immediately followed by a second vision, equally fugitive — the vision of Fabrizio, the protagonist of Stendhal's novel *La chartreuse de Parme*, "in der Schlacht herumirren[d]" (wandering about the battlefield; *RS*, 153/126). The central position held by the viewer of the panorama is "imaginary," but the alternative standpoint linked to an inner vision is no less so — it is induced by a work of fiction. Moreover, this alternative standpoint is associated with the horizontal movement of walking, namely Fabrizio's aimless wandering across the battlefield.

Thus Sebald rejects the view from above and indicates the possibility of an alternative. This alternative is further developed in his discussion of Rembrandt's famous painting *The Anatomy Lesson*.[35] According to Sebald, the Waterloo Panorama is a paradigm of the falsification of perspective; Rembrandt's painting, by contrast, is a paradigm of its rectification. Significantly, the subject of the painting is an act of cutting, the incision and dissection of a human body. But the painting is also, in a self-referential turn, about the act of seeing. It articulates the interrelation between seeing and cutting. The painting features a group of surgeons who are staring at an open anatomical atlas. The atlas, placed on the right-hand edge of the painting, contains a totalizing overview of the human body, a *map* of the body considered as a Cartesian *res extensa*. By looking at the map, the surgeons "overlook" (in both senses of the term) the body that is being dissected. They enact a kind of seeing that maps and reifies the body at the same time that it strives to conceal the act of violence involved in it. In Sebald's opinion, Rembrandt attempts to rectify this kind of seeing that renders the suffering body invisible. At first sight, it seems as if he effects the rectification of perspective by a simple play of substitutions: the map, which is of central importance to the surgeons, is placed at the painting's margin, whereas the victim's body, which is marginal to them, is transferred to the painting's center. However, in order to induce an alternative practice of seeing — a marginal seeing, a seeing from the edge — it is not sufficient simply to reverse positions. Such a reversal would remain locked within the conventions of mimetic representation and the visual practice of "overlooking" that Rembrandt, according to Sebald, is striving to combat. Sebald is at great pains to point out "daß die vielgerühmte Wirklichkeitsnähe des Rembrandtschen Bildes sich bei genauerem Zusehen als eine nur scheinbare erweist" (the much-admired verisimilitude of Rembrandt's picture proves on closer examination to be more apparent than real; *RS*, 26/16). At the center of his picture — "genau in seinem Bedeutungszentrum, dort, wo die Einschnitte schon gemacht sind" (at the exact centre point of its meaning, where the incisions have already been made) — Rembrandt does not place a realistic representation of the victim's body, but "die krasseste Fehlkonstruktion" (a crass misrepresentation; *RS*, 27/16–17, trans. modified). The hand that is being dissected is

anatomisch gänzlich verkehrt. Die offengelegten Sehnen, die, nach der Stellung des Daumens, die der Handfläche der Linken sein sollten, sind die des Rückens der Rechten. Es handelt sich also um eine rein schulmäßige, offenbar ohne weiteres dem anatomischen Atlas entnommene Aufsetzung.

[anatomically the wrong way round: the exposed tendons, which ought to be those of the left palm, given the position of the thumb, are in fact those of the back of the right hand. In other words, what we are faced with is a transposition taken from the anatomical atlas. (*RS*, 27/16)][36]

In order to make visible what is overlooked and concealed by the representatives of modern science, and in order to replace the view from above with a view from the edge, Rembrandt, according to Sebald, does not content himself with showing the suffering body. He refrains from merely visualizing the bodily wounds and cuts that are excluded from the anatomical atlas and its cartographic mode of representation. Instead he cuts up the atlas, he clips out one of its illustrations and superimposes the clip on the site of the bodily cut which, in itself, cannot be shown. The body is represented by means of a disfiguring misrepresentation; the seeing is rectified by means of falsifying the appearance of things. According to Sebald, *The Anatomy Lesson* is not a mimetic representation of reality but a work of montage that implies making a slash in the anatomical atlas.

Rembrandt carries out an elaborate strategy of indirect representation in order to make the suffering body visible. Sebald approves of this strategy, but he does not seem to entertain any extravagant hopes concerning its effectiveness: "Und doch ist es fraglich, ob diesen Leib je in Wahrheit einer gesehen hat" (And yet it is debatable whether anyone ever really saw that body), he concedes (*RS*, 23/13). What then allows him to see it? Why is he able to reveal Rembrandt's strategy; why does he not belong to the vast majority of those who "overlook" the scandalous cut and its (mis-) representation? In chapter 4 of *Die Ringe des Saturn* the narrator makes it clear that his insight into Rembrandt's representational strategies is due not to his particular perceptive capacity but to a combination of extraordinary circumstances. Allegedly, a day before visiting the Mauritshuis in order to study *The Anatomy Lesson*, he narrowly escaped being slashed by a man who was running through the streets of The Hague with a kitchen knife. This incident prepared him to see *The Anatomy Lesson* differently — and it prepared him in two ways: First, it enabled him to identify intimately with the victim of the dissection represented in the picture. He was drawn into the picture; he no longer looked at it from the outside but entered a liminal sphere that mediated between his experience and the one expressed by Rembrandt. Consequently, the narrator received the impression of being "angegriffen" (assailed; *RS*, 102/82; trans. modified) by the work of art — as if the picture itself were trying to slash him. Second, the fact that he was "in [e]inem übernächtigten Zustand" (worn out) as a result of the incident and unable "irgendeinen Gedanken zu fassen" (to harness [his] thoughts; *RS*, 102/82; trans. modified), meant that he submitted the picture to a strangely distracted kind of seeing.[37] He was unable to concentrate, to centralize his viewpoint and to see the painting as an integral whole. Rather, his eyes wandered randomly across the canvas, thus opening up the possibility of being diverted by singularities and incongruities, such as the misrepresentation of the dissected hand.[38] Because of fortuitous circumstances, the concentrated "overview" from the outside gave way to a distracted, digressive movement of the eyes, a view from a standpoint on the margin between the onlooker's world and the world represented in the picture.

Peripatetic Liminality

Sebald thus develops an alternative to the panoramic perspective — a view from the edge instead of the view from above.[39] At the same time, he proposes an alternative to the Enlightenment and Romantic modes of the peripatetic — an animal-like crawl instead of the erect posture of the autonomous subject. The question remains as to whether these alternatives are put together in *Die Ringe des Saturn*. Does Sebald attempt to combine the practice of "seeing from the edge" with the practice of "walking under the spell of the horizontal," and if so, how is this combination effected? An obvious answer to this question would be: by walking along edges and margins. Indeed, Sebald's choice of the East Anglian coast as the locale of his walking tour seems to be motivated by his predilection for the liminal and the marginal. Suffolk constitutes the Eastern periphery of the British Isles. Sebald's walker roams through the heath- and marshlands that verge directly on the sea — the transitional zone between land and water, the solid and the fluid.[40] In this liminal sphere he attends to marginal objects that are half-forgotten or have nearly disappeared, such as the ruined city of Dunwich, which is almost completely buried in the sands, and he explores the spaces of transition between form and formlessness, life and death, animality and humanity.[41] From here he turns back his view and casts it on the ordinary world — in order to submit it to an alienating gaze, but also in order to establish a new form of intimacy, to gain an insider's knowledge. Not the view from above but the view from the edge allows the walker to establish the double perspective that Sebald initially attributed to Browne and Hebel. To conclude my analysis, I would like to interpret two episodes from *Die Ringe des Saturn* that exemplify the operation of this double perspective.

In chapter 3 a walker is presented who moves along the steep cliffs of Covehithe. The trail he follows is situated in immediate proximity to the precipice — to where the land breaks away into the sea. Suddenly the walker realizes that the sand martins who are swarming around him have dug their nesting holes into the topmost layer of clay and that consequently he is standing on perforated ground that might give way at any moment (*RS*, 87/68). But instead of leaving this fragile and dangerous edge as quickly as possible, the walker forces himself to remain. Moreover, he deliberately intensifies the feeling of insecurity that takes hold of him in the liminal sphere:

Demungeachtet legte ich . . . so weit es ging den Kopf in den Nacken, richtete den Blick an den Zenit hinauf, ließ ihn herabgleiten an der Himmelskugel und zog ihn dann vom Horizont her über das Wasser herein bis an den . . . unter mir sich befindenden schmalen Strand.

[I laid back my head as far as I could, . . . fixed my eyes on the zenith, lowered my gaze and let it glide down the celestial globe till it met the horizon, and then drew it in across the water, to the narrow strip of beach . . . below. (*RS*, 87–88/68; trans. modified)]

What is particularly striking about this passage is the occurrence of the archaic term "celestial globe" ("Himmelskugel"). It refers to the premodern worldview held by Sebald's wanderer. As Albrecht Koschorke points out in his *Die Geschichte des Horizonts*, in the premodern world the horizon still constitutes a limit or a threshold in the full sense of the term. The horizon marks the border to the totally unknown, the radically other.[42] In order to transgress this limit, the individual must undergo an elaborate *rite de passage*. The strange ritual of seeing performed by Sebald's walker *is* such a *rite de passage*. Although he is standing on top of the cliff, he does not simply look down or around from above. What he does instead is to *crawl* with his eyes along the edges of the sky. His eyes wander out into the extremities of nothingness and return from there to see what lies in the space *between*, in the "narrow strip of beach."

The immediate effect of this peculiar ocular exercise is "[ein] in mir aufsteigende[s] Schwindelgefühl" (a mounting sense of dizziness; *RS*, 88/68) to which the walker succumbs. He is attacked by the forces of gravity; he can no longer stand (or walk) firmly on his legs. Instead of taking what he sees into ocular possession (as Gilpin's gentleman does), he loses control of his mental and physical faculties; he is dispossessed of his reason and stands in danger of regressing to a primitive state. All this, however, is a necessary precondition of a different way of perceiving reality. In the liminal space between the cliff and the ocean the walker sees a human couple who are making love on the beach. But he does not recognize them as two distinct human beings. Viewing them from the perspective of extreme liminality, he identifies them as "eine[.] große[.], ans Land geworfene[.] Molluske . . ., scheinbar ein Leib, ein von weit draußen hereingetriebenes, vielgliedriges, doppelköpfiges Seeungeheuer" (some great mollusk washed ashore, . . . to all appearances a single being, a many limbed, two-headed monster that had drifted in from far out the sea; *RS*, 88/68). The walker perceives an amphibian creature that is attempting to take the evolutionary step from the sea to the land. Thus his liminal viewpoint serves to defamiliarize the familiar — it points to the atavistic, brutish and violent elements inherent in the human act of love. An archaic past is superimposed on the present. But the walker does not only observe this superimposition from afar. He himself suffers from it; he undergoes a transformation in his own body: "Voller Bestürzung richtete ich mich wieder auf, so unsicher, als erhöbe ich mich zum erstenmal in meinem Leben von der Erde" (Filled with consternation, I stood up once more, shaking as if it were the first time in my life that I had got to my feet; *RS*, 88/68). The walker identifies with the monster and thus reenacts the process of alienating regression. He gains an insider's experience of what he sees: he himself becomes alien.

Significantly, the wanderer's perception of the lovers possesses a visionary, flash-like quality. In the end, he cannot tell "ob ich das blasse Seeungeheuer am Fuß der Klippe von Covehithe nun in Wirklichkeit oder bloß in meiner Einbildung gesehen hatte" (whether I had really seen the pale sea monster at the foot of the Covehithe cliffs or whether I had imagined it; *RS*, 89/69). The monster's referential status is indeterminable. Possibly it constitutes a montage put into effect by the imagination, an image cut out of its original context and pasted onto the canvas of the beach — like the hand in Rembrandt's picture. Therefore, the liminal space of the beach does not constitute a zone of transitional continuity between nature and culture, but a place of rupture and discontinuity, where the walker is abruptly transposed into an archaic state and suffers from a fall or *Rückfall*.

Consequently, the empathy that connects the walker to the objects of his vision should not be interpreted as a means of effecting a reconciliation of nature and culture. However tempting it might be to relate the merging of the two lovers into a single being to the walker's empathy that enables him to merge with the objects of his perception, and thus to classify Sebald as a descendant of the romantic wanderer who aspires to become one with nature, such a reading is mistaken. After all, the single being is characterized as a monster, and its perception does not cause a jubilatory feeling of oneness or wholeness, but horror and "consternation." The merging with the other, in Sebald, is always accompanied by a traumatic break, an experience of division. This can be illustrated by an episode in chapter 8, where Sebald describes his ramblings through Orfordness. Orfordness is an ambiguous, liminal place. It is a spit of land — neither a real island nor really a piece of the continent, but something in-between. Walking across Orfordness, Sebald experiences a shocking encounter:

Mit jedem Schritt, den ich tat, wurde die Leere in mir und die Leere um mich herum größer und die Stille tiefer. Wahrscheinlich durchfuhr mich deshalb ein . . . nahezu tödlicher Schrecken, als unmittelbar vor meinen Füßen ein Hase, der sich verborgen gehalten hatte zwischen den Grasbüscheln am Wegrand, auf und davon schoß. . . . Mit unverminderter, ja mit einer über mein Begriffsvermögen gehenden Deutlichkeit sehe ich nach wie vor, was in diesem . . . Schreckensmoment sich ereignete. Ich sehe . . . den Hasen, wie er hervorspringt aus seinem Versteck, mit zurückgelegten Ohren und

einem vor Entsetzen starren, irgendwie gespaltenen, seltsam menschlichen Gesicht, und ich sehe, in seinem im Fliehen rückwärtsge-
wandten, vor Furcht fast aus dem Kopf sich herausdrehenden Auge,
mich selber, eins geworden mit ihm.

[With each step that I took, the emptiness within and the emptiness
without grew ever greater and the silence more profound. Perhaps
that was why I was frightened almost to death when a hare that had
been hiding in the tufts of grass by the wayside started up, right at my
feet. . . . I still see what occurred in that one tremulous instant with
an undiminished clarity. . . . I see the hare leaping out of its hiding-
place, with its ears laid back and a curiously human expression on its
face that was rigid with terror and strangely divided; and in its eyes,
turning to look back as it fled and almost popping out of its head with
fright, I see myself, become one with it. (*RS,* 279–80/234–35)]

The walker identifies with the hare; he sees himself in the terrified animal.
Here it is not the beast that is superimposed on the human, but the human
who is superimposed on the beast. The hare looks strangely human. What
makes it look human is a cleft inscribed (or incised) into its face. It is
caused by the human interloper who penetrates the hare's habitat and ter-
rifies the poor creature. The walker cuts into the face of nature.
Involuntarily, he commits an act of violence, splitting the hare and turning
it into a hybrid creature, half human and half animal. This division is the
precondition of the walker's total identification with the creature.[43]
Paradoxically, in order to become one with it, he must split it; in order to
feel its suffering, he must make it suffer; in order to transgress the limit
between nature and culture, he must draw a sharp line between them. The
walker's double vision of empathy and alienation is irreducibly connected
to violent acts of penetration and incision.

It is possible to read the episode of Sebald's encounter with the hare
as a rewriting of Rousseau's second *Promenade.* Both Sebald and Rousseau
characterize the liminal zone between nature and culture as dangerous —
as a space where traumatic breaks are likely to occur. In Rousseau's view,
however, this zone still harbors the chance of regeneration. He is knocked
out by the mastiff, but he experiences his awakening from the state of
unconsciousness as a kind of rebirth: he does not know where or who he
is, and his memory seems to be effaced — like an innocent child of nature,
he enjoys an undivided moment of sheer presence, a "sentiment de
l'existence." For Sebald, by contrast, the traumatic encounter does not
lead to the experience of innocence and plenitude, however illusionary it
may be, but perpetuates a relationship of guilt. In the liminal zone,
Sebald's walking subject is confronted with his own divided nature, which
he inflicts on the other. He experiences his self as hopelessly split; he realizes that, in order to become one with the other, he must alienate himself
both from himself and from the other.

To unify by means of dividing, by means of producing a deep incision: in this respect Sebald seems to subscribe to the skeptical anthropological view held by his predecessor Thomas Browne. Browne defines man as a microcosm — "that amphibious piece between a corporal and spiritual essence; that middle form that links those two together."[44] Paradoxically, however, man can fulfill the task of linking the two together only by means of keeping them separate. In man the two extreme ends of creation are not harmoniously united but diametrically opposed. I quote again from the *Religio medici*: "Thus is man that great and true amphibium whose nature is disposed to live, not only like other creatures in divers elements, but in divided and distinguished worlds."[45] Man as a microcosm is not one world but two worlds, and he holds the great world, the macrocosm, together by keeping these worlds divided, in a state of violent and irreconcilable conflict.

Notes

Earlier versions of this paper were presented on the occasion of the conference "W. G. Sebald and the European Tradition" at the University of East Anglia, Norwich, in June 2007 and at Deutsches Haus, Columbia University, New York, in October 2007. I am grateful to Dorothea von Mücke, Kelly Barry, and Stefan Andriopoulos for their helpful critique and suggestions.

[1] In the English translation by Michael Hulse, published in 1998 as a New Direction Book (New York), the subtitle *An English Pilgrimage* appears in the Library of Congress Cataloging-in-Publication Data, but, for inscrutable reasons, it is not featured on the title page.

[2] For the touristic sight as a "marker" — a sign that refers to itself as a "sight" — see Jonathan Culler, "The Semiotics of Tourism," in *Framing the Sign: Criticism and Its Institutions* (Oxford: Oxford UP, 1988), 153–67.

[3] Concerning "Sebalds Arbeit an der Darstellung der 'Wirklichkeit der Zerstörung,'" see Gerhard Neumann, "'lange bis zum Zerspringen festgehaltene Augenblicke': W. G. Sebald liest aus seinem Buch *Die Ringe des Saturn*," *Jahrbuch der Bayerischen Akademie der Schönen Künste* 13 (1999): 553–67; here 561–65.

[4] For interpretations that place *Die Ringe des Saturn* within the tradition of melancholy see Markus R. Weber, "W. G. Sebald," in *Kritisches Lexikon zur deutschsprachigen Gegenwartsliteratur*, vol. 10, ed. Heinz Ludwig Arnold (Munich: Text + Kritik, 1978-), 54. Nachlieferung 1996, 6; Thomas Kastura, "Geheimnisvolle Fähigkeit zur Transmigration: W. G. Sebalds interkulturelle Wallfahrten in die Leere," *Arcadia* 31.1/2 (1996): 197–216; here 207–8; Claudia Albes, "Die Erkundung der Leere: Anmerkungen zu W. G. Sebalds 'englischer Wallfahrt' *Die Ringe des Saturn*," *Jahrbuch der Deutschen Schillergesellschaft* 46 (2002): 279–305; here 285–87; Eluned Summers-Bremner, "Reading, Walking, Mourning: W. G. Sebald's Peripatetic Fictions," *Journal of Narrative Theory* 34 (2004): 304–34; here 308–9.

[5] Robert Burton, *The Anatomy of Melancholy*, ed. Holbrook Jackson (London: Dent, 1972), 2:74; Marsilio Ficino, *Three Books on Life*: A Critical Edition and Translation with Introduction and Notes by Carol V. Kaske and John R. Clark (Binghamton, NY: Center for Medieval and Early Renaissance Studies, 1989), 134–35.

[6] Todd Presner, *Mobile Modernity: Germans, Jews, Trains* (New York: Columbia UP, 2007), 233–83; Claudia Öhlschläger, "'Die Bahn des korsischen Kometen': Zur Dimension 'Napoleon' in W. G. Sebalds literarischem Netzwerk," in *Topographien der Literatur: Deutsche Literatur im transnationalen Kontext*, ed. Hartmut Böhme (Stuttgart: Metzler, 2005), 536–58.

[7] W. G. Sebald, "J'aurais voulu que ce lac eût été l'Océan: Anläßlich eines Besuchs auf der St. Petersinsel," in *LG*, 43–74; "Le promeneur solitaire: Zur Erinnerung an Robert Walser," in *LG*, 127–68.

[8] On the connection between Sebald's alternative form of historiography and his notion of travel see Bianca Theisen, "Prose of the World: W. G. Sebald's Literary Travels," *Germanic Review* 79.3 (2004): 169–70.

[9] For a survey of the cultural and literary history of the walk see Christian Moser and Helmut J. Schneider, "Einleitung: Zur Kulturgeschichte und Poetik des Spaziergangs," in *Kopflandschaften–Landschaftsgänge: Kulturgeschichte und Poetik des Spaziergangs*, ed. Axel Gellhaus, Christian Moser, and Helmut J. Schneider (Cologne: Böhlau, 2007), 7–27.

[10] Jean-Jacques Rousseau, *Emile ou de l'éducation*, in J.-J. Rousseau, *Œuvres complètes*. Edition publiée sous la direction de Bernard Gagnebin et Marcel Raymond, vol. 4 (Paris: Gallimard, 1959–95), 771–72. All English translations in this chapter are my own except where otherwise credited.

[11] On the differences between the aristocratic and the bourgeois *promenade* see Katharina Oxenius, *Vom Promenieren zum Spazieren: Zur Kulturgeschichte des Pariser Parks* (Tübingen: Tübinger Vereinigung für Volkskunde, 1992); Gudrun M. König, *Eine Kulturgeschichte des Spazierganges: Spuren einer bürgerlichen Praktik, 1780–1850* (Cologne: Böhlau, 1996), 26–27.

[12] Cf. Christian Moser and Helmut Schneider, "Einleitung," 8–9; Helmut J. Schneider, "Selbsterfahrung zu Fuß: Spaziergang und Wanderung als poetische und geschichtsphilosophische Reflexionsfigur im Zeitalter Rousseaus," in *Rousseauismus: Naturevangelium und Literatur*, ed. Jürgen Söring and Peter Gasser (Frankfurt am Main: Lang, 1999), 133–54; here 135.

[13] Cf. Rousseau, *Emile*, 771: "Nous ne le [le voyage] faisons point tristement assis et comme emprisonés dans une petite cage bien fermée."

[14] Schneider, "Selbsterfahrung zu Fuß," 36.

[15] Immanuel Kant, "Beantwortung der Frage: Was ist Aufklärung?" in *Werke in zehn Bänden*, ed. Wilhelm Weischedel, vol. 9 (Darmstadt: Wissenschaftliche Buchgesellschaft, 1964), 51–61; here 53 (my italics).

[16] Anne D. Wallace, *Walking, Literature, and English Culture: The Origins and Uses of the Peripatetic in the Nineteenth Century* (Oxford: Oxford UP, 1993), 166–99.

[17] Johann Gottfried Seume, *Mein Sommer 1805: Reisejournal*, in *Prosaschriften*, with an introduction by Werner Kraft (Darmstadt: Wissenschaftliche Buchgesellschaft, 1974), 638–39.

[18] Rousseau, *Les Confessions*, in *Œuvres complètes* 1:163.

[19] Friedrich Schiller, "Der Spaziergang," in *Sämtliche Werke*, ed. Gerhard Fricke and Herbert G. Göpfert, vol. 1 (Munich: Hanser, 1987), 228–34. Subsequent references to this work are cited in the text using the abbreviation *S* and verse number. For a recent and very stimulating interpretation of Schiller's elegy see Kenneth S. Calhoon, "Der virtuelle Bogen: Abgrund und Brücke in Friedrich Schillers *Der Spaziergang*," in Moser and Schneider, *Kopflandschaften*, 147–60.

[20] For connections between peripatetic practice and the theory of the picturesque and for the critique of the "cavalier perspective" as it is articulated in (pre-) Romantic poetry see Wallace, *Walking, Literature, and English Culture*, 17–66; and Robin Jarvis, *Romantic Writing and Pedestrian Travel* (London: Macmillan, 1997), 62–88.

[21] William Gilpin, *Three Essays on Picturesque Beauty; on Picturesque Travel; and on Sketching Landscape: to which is added a Poem, on Landscape Painting* (London: R. Blamire, 1794), 106–7.

[22] "Everything which offers a *picture*, when viewed from a station nearly horizontal, becomes a mere *map* to an eye placed at an elevation . . . above it." Thomas De Quincey, *Autobiography from 1785–1803*, vol. 1 of *Collected Works*, ed. David Masson (Edinburgh: Adam & Charles Black, 1889), 184. On the opposition between map and picture and its tradition in literature and art see Christian Moser, "Map vs. Picture: Techniken der Visualisierung in der englischen Großstadtliteratur des frühen 19. Jahrhunderts," in *Visual Culture*, ed. Monika Schmitz-Emans and Gertrud Lehnert (Heidelberg: Synchron, 2008), 151–65.

[23] Michel de Certeau, *Kunst des Handelns*, trans. Ronald Vouillé (Berlin: Merve, 1988), 179–82.

[24] Rousseau, *Les Confessions*, 43–44.

[25] K. G. Schelle, *Die Spatziergänge oder die Kunst spatzieren zu gehen*, ed. Markus Fauser (Leipzig: 1802; repr., Hildesheim: Olms, 1990), 87 and 91.

[26] Schelle, *Die Spatziergänge*, 52.

[27] On the significance of margins and edges in archaic geography cf. James S. Romm, *The Edges of the Earth in Ancient Thought: Geography, Exploration, and Fiction* (Princeton, NJ: Princeton UP, 1992), 9–44.

[28] Hence the narrator's "*inability* to lose his way," as John Zilcosky has put it. See John Zilcosky, "Sebald's Uncanny Travels: The Impossibility of Getting Lost," in *W. G. Sebald — A Critical Companion*, ed. J. J. Long and Anne Whitehead (Seattle: U of Washington P, 2004), 104.

[29] On the significance of the "Vorgänger" in the context of Sebald's peripatetic literature see also Albes, "Die Erkundung der Leere," 282–85.

[30] In Browne the view from above relates to a specific type of meditation whose origins lie in Stoic philosophy. For the view from above as a stoic technique of meditation and for its adaptation in early modernity see Jörg Dünne, "Karto-

graphische Meditation: Mediendispositiv und Selbstpraxis in der Frühen Neuzeit," in *Automedialität: Subjektkonstitution in Schrift, Bild und neuen Medien*, ed. Jörg Dünne and Christian Moser (Munich: Fink, 2008), 331–51. On the relationship between Browne's *Religio medici* and stoic technologies of the self see Christian Moser, "'The humour of my irregular self': Sir Thomas Brownes *Religio Medici* — ein Bekenntnis unter Vorbehalt," in *Autobiographisches Schreiben und philosophische Selbstsorge*, ed. Maria Moog-Grünewald (Heidelberg: Winter, 2004), 73–94.

[31] W. G. Sebald, "Es steht ein Komet am Himmel: Kalenderbeitrag zu Ehren des rheinischen Hausfreunds," in *LG*, 20.

[32] Öhlschläger ("'Die Bahn des korsischen Kometen,'" 546–50) draws similar conclusions in her analysis of Sebald's historiographical method.

[33] On walking as a (deviant) cultural practice that constitutes a certain kind of space see de Certeau, *Kunst des Handelns*, 179–97.

[34] In its foreground, the panorama features "lifesize horses, and cutdown infantrymen, hussars and chevaux-légers, eyes rolling in pain or already extinguished" (*RS*, 124).

[35] Sebald employs Rembrandt's painting as a paradigm for the representation of bodily suffering as early as 1986 in an essay on Peter Weiss. Cf. W. G. Sebald, "Die Zerknirschung des Herzens: Über Erinnerung und Grausamkeit im Werk von Peter Weiss," in *CS*, 128–48; here 134–35; in English, "The Remorse of the Heart: On Memory and Cruelty in the Work of Peter Weiss," in *NH*, 169–91; here 177–78. For a detailed discussion of Sebald's analysis of Rembrandt, see Christian Moser, "Anatomie der Folter: Zur Darstellung des gepeinigten Leibes in den Texten W. G. Sebalds," in *Marter — Martyrium: Ethische und ästhetische Dimensionen der Folter*, ed. Volker Dörr, Jürgen Nelles, and Hans-Joachim Pieper (Bonn: Denkmal, 2009), 207–26. As Muriel Pic points out, Sebald's interpretation of Rembrandt's painting is strongly indebted to Francis Barker's analysis of *The Anatomy Lesson* in his *The Tremulous Private Body*, which Sebald possessed in his private library. Cf. Muriel Pic, "Sebald's Anatomy Lesson: About Three Images — Documents from *On the Natural History of Destruction, The Rings of Saturn* and *Austerlitz*," *Colloquy: text theory critique* 9 (May 2005): 6–15, esp. 11 and 15. For Barker's interpretation of Rembrandt's *The Anatomy Lesson* see Francis Barker, *The Tremulous Private Body: Essays on Subjection* (London: Methuen, 1984), 73–85.

[36] Cf. Barker, *The Tremulous Private Body*, 79. Barker, on his part, draws this observation from the iconological study of the art historian William S. Heckscher, *Rembrandt's Anatomy of Dr. Nicolaas Tulp: An Iconological Study* (New York: New York UP, 1958), 66.

[37] In his attempt to relate the experience of shock to a distracted mode of perceiving the work of art, Sebald is indebted to Walter Benjamin. On the relation between shock, distraction, and the perception of art see Walter Benjamin, "Das Kunstwerk im Zeitalter seiner technischen Reproduzierbarkeit," in *Gesammelte Schriften*, vol. 1.2, ed. Rolf Tiedemann and Hermann Schweppenhäuser (Frankfurt am Main: Suhrkamp, 1980), 501–5.

38 What attracts Sebald to Thomas Browne is not his ability to "levitate," to look at the world from an outsider's detached position in order to uncover hidden geometrical structures, such as the quincunx described in *The Garden of Cyrus*, but, on the contrary, his propensity to be *distracted* from this geometrical point of view: "Auch Thomas Browne ist von der Erforschung der isomorphen Linie der Quincunx-Signatur immer wieder *abgelenkt* worden durch das neugierige Verfolgen singulärer Phänomene und die Arbeit an einer umfassenden Pathologie" (Thomas Browne too often was *distracted* from his investigations into the isomorphic line of the quincunx by singular phenomena that fired his curiosity, and by work on a comprehensive pathology; *RS* 33/22; my italics).

39 In an essay dealing with the literary representation of disaster and total destruction, Sebald contends "daß eine 'Beschreibung' der Katastrophe eher von ihrem Rand her als aus ihrem Zentrum heraus möglich ist" (that a "description" of catastrophe is more likely possible from its periphery than from its center). Cf. W. G. Sebald, "Zwischen Geschichte und Naturgeschichte: Über die literarische Beschreibung totaler Zerstörung" (in English, "Between History and Natural History: On the Literary Description of Total Destruction," in *CS*, 82/78).

40 This predilection for the swamp and the marshy land of coastal regions connects Sebald's travelogue to the peripatetic texts of the American transcendentalist Henry David Thoreau, especially his famous essay *Walking*, in which he praises the primeval swamps of America, and his travel book *Cape Cod*, in which he describes a journey on foot along the coast of Cape Cod. On Thoreau as a peripatetic see Michaela Keck, *Walking in the Wilderness: The Peripatetic Tradition in Nineteenth-Century American Literature and Painting* (Heidelberg: Winter, 2006).

41 According to the Scottish anthropologist Victor Turner, the concept of liminality refers to interstructural situations within society as they are often codified in *rites de passages*. The state of liminality is characterized by its ambiguity: "Liminal entities are neither here nor there; they are betwixt and between the positions assigned and arrayed by law, custom, convention, and ceremonial. As such, their ambiguous and indeterminate attributes are expressed by a rich variety of symbols in the many societies that ritualize social and cultural transitions." Cf. Victor Turner, *The Ritual Process: Structure and Anti-Structure* (New York: Aldine de Gruyter, 1969), 95. Sebald, however, seems to be less interested in the liminal situations that exist between different states *within* society than in the transitory spheres on the verge of human society and its other: nature, animality, destruction, death.

42 Albrecht Koschorke, *Die Geschichte des Horizonts: Grenze und Grenzüberschreitung in literarischen Landschaftsbildern* (Frankfurt am Main: Suhrkamp, 1990), 14. According to Koschorke, the horizon is deprived of its function as a limit or a threshold in modern times. The "open horizon" becomes a figure of the infinite and the illimitable (22 and 36).

43 One of the photographs that illustrate the story "All'estero" is a passport photo of Sebald. The photo is vertically split in two by a thick black line (*SG*, 129/*V*, 114). — In an essay devoted to the schizophrenic writer Ernst Herbeck, Sebald

points out that the motif of the hare frequently recurs in Herbeck's poetry. Following Gisela Steinlechner, Sebald interprets the hare "als das von Herbeck selbst entdeckte Emblem seiner Spaltung" (as the symbol upon which Herbeck himself fixed for his divided personality; *CS*, 177/132): Herbeck identifies with the hare and adopts it as his totem because it emblematizes the division that constitutes his personality. With reference to the French anthropologist Claude Lévi-Strauss, Sebald remarks that the harelip plays a major role in the mythology of native Americans: "Es ist diese Zweiheit in einem, die den Hasen mit seinem gespaltenen Gesicht zu einer allerhöchsten Gottheit macht, zu einem Vermittler zwischen Himmel und Erde" (This duality in one person makes the hare, with its split face, one of the highest deities, mediating between heaven and earth). Cf. W. G. Sebald, "Des Häschens Kind, der kleine Has: Über das Totemtier des Lyrikers Ernst Herbeck"; in English, "Des Häschens Kind, der kleine Has [The Little Hare, Child of the Hare]: On the Poet Ernst Herbeck's Totem Animal," in *CS*, 177/132.

[44] Sir Thomas Browne, *Religio Medici, Hydrotaphia and The Gardens of Cyrus*, ed. R. H. A. Robbins (Oxford: Oxford UP, 1982), 36.

[45] Browne, *Religio Medici*, 37.

2: W. G. Sebald: The Anti-Tourist

J. J. Long

As HE ARRIVES IN MIDDLETON to visit his friend Michael Hamburger, the narrator of W. G. Sebald's *Die Ringe des Saturn* muses on his position, conveying his own sense of displacement while also reflecting on the effect his appearance might have on the local rural populace:

> Weder auf der Dorfstraße noch in den Gärten war jemand zu sehen, die Häuser machten einen abweisenden Eindruck, und ich kam mir vor, mit dem Hut in der Hand und dem Rucksack über der Schulter, wie ein fahrender Geselle aus einem vergangenen Jahrhundert, so fehl am Platz, daß es mich gar nicht gewundert hätte, wenn auf einmal eine Schar Gassenbuben hinter mir her gesprungen oder einer der Hausbesitzer von Middleton über seine Schwelle getreten wäre, um mir ein "Schau, daß du weiterkommst!" zuzurufen. Schließlich zieht jeder Fußreisende, auch heute noch, ja gerade heute und vor allem, wenn er nicht dem gängigen Bild des Freizeitwanderers entspricht, sogleich den Verdacht der Ortsansässigen auf sich.

> [Neither in the village street nor in the gardens was there a soul in sight, the houses gave an unwelcoming impression and, with my hat in my hand and my rucksack over my shoulder, I felt like a journeyman in a century gone by, so out of place that I should not have been surprised if a band of street urchins had come skipping after me or one of Middleton's householders had stepped out upon his threshold to tell me to be on my way. After all, every foot traveler incurs the suspicion of the locals, especially if he does not fit the image of a local rambler. (*RS*, 208–9/175)]

Entering territory that is not merely devoid of human inhabitants but also unwelcoming in appearance, the narrator imagines himself a traveling journeyman of yore, unjustly pursued by hostile locals. This hostility, he claims, is a product of his failure to match the conventional image of the hiker or rambler. It is this final comment that is the crux of the above passage, for what the narrator seeks fundamentally to do here is to establish himself as a "traveler" and to differentiate himself from a "Freizeitwanderer" — in other words, a tourist. In this chapter, I seek to understand Sebald's mobilization of the tourist-traveler distinction, firstly through a historicized examination of the tropes and strategies by means of which the dichotomy is upheld, and secondly through an exploration of the ways in which Sebald's narrators negotiate their status as travelers, not only in the verbal narrative, but also in the texts' photographic discourse.

Travel, Tourism, Anti-Tourism

> *Everyone would like to travel with Sebald, because Sebald travels alone.*
>
> — Massimo Leone

In his invocation of the distinction between traveler and tourist, Sebald reproduces a dichotomy that has been deeply ingrained in Western travel discourse for over two centuries. As James Buzard notes in his classic study *The Beaten Track*, the distinction between "tourism" and "travel" can be traced back as far as the late eighteenth century, and was fully developed in its modern form by 1842. Though rarely used with precision, the word "tourist" is recurrently employed as a derogatory term implying certain predictable behaviors, character profiles, and class affiliations. The tourist, Buzard writes, is conventionally seen as a "dupe of fashion, following blindly where authentic travelers have gone with open eyes and free spirits." While the traveler is the intrepid collector of unique and authentic experiences, the tourist is nothing but the pampered unit of a leisure industry.[1] A pervasive characteristic of the tourist-traveler binary is that it is internal to the system of tourism itself. Hans Magnus Enzensberger, in an essay that foreshadows much recent sociological and anthropological accounts of tourism, noted as early as 1958 that criticism of tourists most often comes from people who are themselves tourists, and many later commentators have reiterated this insight.[2]

The tourism-travel binary can be explained by tourism's status as a product and consequence of modernity, and specifically through the changing functions of travel within the modernizing states of post-Napoleonic Europe.[3] As more and more people's lives became dominated by workplace discipline and increasing subjection to the demands of the industrial economy, liberal ideology developed an account of culture that saw it as a compensatory realm where the individual can, as Buzard puts it, "find inner redress for the sacrifices of living in a modern industrial society." In this sense, travel is a form of culture that facilitates liberation from domestic social life and the self defined thereby. According to the binary logic that pits a stunted workaday self against the authentic self-realization facilitated by travel, the "tourist" is someone who fails to employ the objects of culture in an effective process of acculturation: the tourist is characterized by lapses of taste and a disdain for things foreign that causes him to carry round with him the trappings of the very modernity from which the traveler flees.[4] One consequence of this is that tourism developed more or less simultaneously with "anti-tourism," a term coined by Dean MacCannell[5] and developed by Buzard as a central analytic category. Buzard defines anti-tourism as a "symbolic economy in which travelers and writers displayed marks of originality and 'authenticity' in an attempt to win credit for acculturation."[6] I shall thus argue in this essay that the discourse of travel and anti-tourism in Sebald has to be understood as part of his wider engagement with modernity that I have discussed elsewhere.[7]

Notions of acculturation and authenticity are of central significance for an understanding of travel and tourism in Sebald's travel narratives. The former term, clearly, is one of the primary motives for travel in much of Sebald's work, as his narrators journey to the cultural centers of Europe in order to visit particular buildings or view specific works of art. What his narrators often find, however, is that someone — most often a writer — has been there before them. This problematizes the second term, authenticity. For the authentic, it would seem, is belied by the very notion of acculturation, since this latter term implies the acquisition of knowledge and competencies that possess currency within a system of shared values. This, however, assumes a narrow definition of acculturation. Raymond Williams's discussion of the word "culture" elaborates three broad categories that will help to establish what is at stake in the relationship between acculturation and authenticity. The first category of usage, Williams writes, concerns "a general process of intellectual, spiritual and aesthetic development"; the second indicates "a particular way of life, whether of a people, a period, or a group." Thirdly, Williams notes, there is the noun designating "the works and practices of intellectual and especially artistic creativity."[8] Williams's definitions ultimately shake down into two fundamental understandings of "culture": the aesthetic object and its role in personal acculturation on the one hand, and a more generalized, anthropological understanding of culture as a group's "whole way of life" on the other. Buzard argues that modern tourism and anti-tourism are in part a quest for both of these meanings.[9] But with reference to Sebald, we can actually be more specific about the ways in which these two understandings of culture function. If the aesthetic object is publicly accessible and institutionally framed, its ability to produce the authenticity required by the traveler is profoundly compromised, as Sebald's narrators realize when they acknowledge their own "belatedness." This calls for compensatory measures by means of which authenticity can be renegotiated. On the one hand, Sebald's narrators frequently foreground their heightened aesthetic sensibility, which elevates them above the mere "tourist." On the other, they persistently seek out "culture" in the anthropological sense, claiming to have gained access to the "back region" where authentic life goes on independently of the tourist infrastructure.[10] By means of these twin strategies, which often, as we will see, operate side by side or overlap, Sebald's texts seek to negotiate between travel and tourism, acculturation and authenticity. While all of Sebald's works deal to a greater or lesser extent with travel, the texts that are explicitly concerned with the travel-tourism problematic are "All'estero" from *Schwindel. Gefühle.*, "Ambros Adelwarth" and "Max Aurach" from *Die Ausgewanderten*, and *Die Ringe des Saturn*. I concentrate on these texts in this essay.

Critics have not been slow to recognize the centrality of travel to Sebald's oeuvre.[11] Of particular interest are studies by John Zilcosky and Bianca Theisen, who have explicitly linked Sebald not only with the thematics of travel but also with the history and conventions of travel *writing*. John Zilcosky argues persuasively that Sebald reverses travel writing's master trope — according to which travelers get lost in order, ultimately, to find their way home — by demonstrating the uncanny *inability* to get lost and the troubling ubiquity of home. Bianca Theisen, meanwhile, asserts that in the eighteenth century a shift took place in the genre of travel writing. Having hitherto been a largely object-orientated account providing information about foreign countries and journeys, travel writing became a more clearly "fictional," subject-orientated genre. This, she claims, was made possible by improved infrastructure and consequent improved safety. Travel literature no longer needed to be bearer of information but was free to couch travel experiences in personal reflections and awareness of a world mediated by literature.[12] This supports Theisen's claim that Sebald's narrator admits to a kind of "armchair travel that escapes from the standardized perception of a highly marked cultural territory through a poetic flight to the library or archive." The search for pristine and unmediated *terra incognita* is possible only through resort to a textualized world.[13] Theisen's sketch of the historical development of travel writing oversimplifies what is in fact a much more complex development. But her point concerning the ineluctably mediated nature of travel experience in Sebald is apposite, and a more nuanced account of travel writing will help us to grasp what is at stake in Sebald's transformations of the travel genre.

The first point to note is that the kind of subjective, expressive travel writing that Theisen sees as characteristic of the last two-and-a-half centuries actually has a much longer history that goes at least as far back as early modern accounts of European encounters with the Americas, which repeatedly stress the experience of wonder.[14] Second, what Theisen sees as a kind of emancipation of travel writing from the necessity to provide information ignores the fact that much travel writing of the eighteenth century is in fact hybrid in nature, purporting to be the account of the author's travels while simultaneously including advice and practical information for the traveler.[15] Furthermore, if a specifically subjective mode of travel writing did emerge in the eighteenth century, it by no means displaced the "objective" mode. Mary Louise Pratt has shown that in eighteenth-century narrative accounts of Northern Europeans' travels in Africa the frontier is coded in terms of either science or sentiment, both being, ultimately, complementary discourses that "stake out the parameters of emergent bourgeois hegemony" and provide competing but ideologically congruent rhetorical models for constructing a non-interventionist European presence in Africa.[16] Moving closer to home, we can see an analogous bifurcation in travel writing inaugurated by the increasingly bureaucratic administration of tourism over the course of the nineteenth century. On the one hand, practical information soon came to be codified in the formulaic handbooks of Murray, Black, and Baedeker. On the other hand, we see the emergence of the subject-orientated genre noted by Theisen. As in the case of science and sentiment, however, this ostensible bifurcation concealed a deeper affinity between these two modes of writing. One of the salient differences between say, Murray or Baedeker on the one hand and earlier "informative" travel books — such as Europe's most widely read travel book at the turn of the eighteenth century, Heinrich August Ottokar Reichard's *Guide des Voyageurs* — on the other is that while Reichard limits himself to a sober and practical enumeration of the shortest routes, places to stay, prices, and local regulations, Murray and Baedeker recommended the most picturesque routes and laid down prescriptions concerning what the tourist was supposed to *see*.[17] The fundamental role of the tourist bibles of the nineteenth century, then, was to mediate a normative and predictable cultural experience. It was against such an experience that "travelers" sought to rebel, and one way they did so was to cultivate anti-touristic behavior with reference to the models provided by the travel writing of Mme de Staël, Goethe, Rousseau, and Bulwer-Lytton. "Scenes, situations and characters from these texts," writes Buzard, "became the appropriatable [*sic*], exchangeable markers in a cultural economy in which 'travelers' competed for preeminence by displaying their imaginative capacities and by attacking the always available enemy, the lowly tourist."[18] This involved would-be anti-tourists in a profound contradiction, namely that in order to be individual, they were obliged to repeat the gestures of those who had gone before. The "imaginative capacities" displayed by anti-tourists were themselves highly mediated affective responses. As such they were easily appropriated by the very tourist industry to which they seemed to offer an antidote: the guides issued by Baedeker and Murray were, increasingly, liberally sprinkled with quotations from literature, and Murray even published a portable edition of Byron, designed as a companion volume to his travel handbooks and as a guide to sentiment.[19]

From an early point in its history, then, the commercial enterprise that was tourism proved adept at absorbing and effectively reselling the gestures of anti-tourism.[20] Recourse to existing representations no longer functioned as a secure anti-tourist strategy, since it led ultimately to a sense of belated repetition. Sebald's narrators experience this whenever they follow in the footsteps of other writers. To give just one example: in "All'estero" the narrator is haunted by visions of Dante, seeks to understand Venice with the aid of Casanova's autobiographical writings and Grillparzer's diaries, and discovers traces of Kafka in even the least "cultural" of locations, such as the urinals at Desenzano station. Even the ultimate anti-tourist ploy — the expression of immense disappointment at the failure of a place to live up to its textually mediated reputation — turns out to be a repetition of Grillparzer's *Tagebuch auf der Reise nach Italien*. "Wie er," writes the narrator, "finde ich an nichts Gefallen, bin von allen Sehenswürdigkeiten enttäuscht und wäre, wie ich oft meine, viel besser bei meinen Landkarten und Fahrplänen zu Hause geblieben" (Nothing pleases me, any more than it did him; the sights I find infinitely disappointing, one and all; and I sometimes think that I would have done far better to have stayed at home with my maps and timetables; *SG*, 62/*V*, 53–54).[21] There is a sense here that the world has become so thoroughly textually mediated that the baldest of representations — the very maps and railway timetables that both facilitated and were facilitated by tourism — are ultimately preferable to the attempt to experience authenticity through travel. But the narrators travel nevertheless. The rhetoric of anti-tourism is sustained throughout by a variety of strategies designed to distinguish the texts' narrators from the mass of tourists and to individuate them as bearers of an authentic experience of culture. But as we shall see in the following analysis, they remain entangled in the contradictions outlined above, namely the problem of experiencing authenticity through acculturation.

Throughout *Schwindel. Gefühle.*, the narrator is at pains to stress his individuality vis-à-vis the undifferentiated hordes of tourists that he occasionally encounters. When he visits the amphitheatre on the Piazza Bra in Verona, he observes from the very highest seats a group of tourists in the orchestra who, he claims, have no interest whatsoever in the guide's comments on the architecture of the theater. The narrator, on the other hand, benefits from the acoustics of the theater, which allow him to hear the guide's words more clearly than the group for which they are intended. The narrator, as lone individual, thus claims to have privileged access to culture, while denigrating the tourist group as a "Kinderschar" (pack of children; *SG*, 83/*V*, 72). Not only are tourists repeatedly characterized as a "Schar" — throng or horde — in Sebald's writings,[22] but the compound "Kinderschar" represents a moment of infantilization that effectively robs the tourists of full subjectivity. Furthermore, they are described as "Ausflügler" (excursionists) — not even proper tourists, but merely daytrippers, a class of tourist that has long occupied the lowest position in the traveler-tourist hierarchy, being *even worse* than tourists (*SG*, 82/*V*, 71).[23] In Limone the narrator rows out onto Lake Garda as night falls, and the din from the town's various bars and clubs — in other words, the noise produced by tourists — reaches him dimly, constituting merely "eine geringe Störung" that does not really impinge on his contemplation of the mountains above the resort (a negligible disturbance; *SG*, 105/*V*, 92). In describing these mountains, the narrator writes of the "Gewaltigkeit der ungeheuren, schweigenden Schattenwand, die hinter dem zitternden Lichterhäufchen des Ortes so steil und hoch aufragte, daß ich meinte, sie neige sich mir entgegen und könne, im nächsten Augenblick, in den See hineinstürzen" (the huge bulk of the mountain that towered so high and steep above the quivering lights of the town that I thought it was inclining towards me and might tumble into the lake the very next moment; *SG*, 105/*V*, 92). The ability to appreciate the vast scale and potential violence of a geological formation that dwarfs the diminutive "Lichterhäufchen" (lights) of the town testifies to a refined sensibility that is schooled in the aesthetics of the sublime. This ability contrasts strongly with the faceless mass of other tourists, who appear as "das ganze Ferienvolk" (holidaymakers) and "eine einzige buntfarbene Menschenmenge" (a gaudy crowd; *SG*, 106/*V*, 93). Indeed, the narrator expresses embarrassment that most of the drunk and noisy tourists are his fellow-countrymen, and hurries off to bed, placing physical as well as ideological distance between himself and them. The number of examples could be expanded here to include Salvatore's denunciation of festival-goers who have lost all sense of theatricality (*SG*, 148–49/*V*, 132–33), or the narrator's managing to gain access to the Biblioteca Civica in Verona despite the fact that it is closed for the holiday season and hence off-limits for the common run of tourists (*SG*, 132–33/*V*, 117). What we witness here, of course, is the search for a "back region," an example of genuine indigenous culture.

The same agenda can be seen in *Die Ausgewanderten* at the point where the narrator enters the Bad Kissingen salina despite its being closed for repairs (*DA*, 342/*E*, 227). During his sojourn in Bad Kissingen the narrator contrasts himself to the "Volk der Alten" (translated as "elderly people" but in meaning something more akin to "aged race"; *DA*, 330/*E*, 220) who constitute the town's temporary residents, but it is predominantly a group of Japanese tourists in Deauville who are the object of the narrator's anti-touristic critique. The service personnel of the Hotel Normandy treat their Japanese guests with a level of studied politeness that borders on disdain (*DA*, 175–76/*E*, 119), and this disdain is implicitly shared by the narrator when he writes that the tourists "durch das genau vorgegebene Tagesprogramm gelenkt werden" (are steered through the minutely prescribed daily routine; *DA*, 176/*E*, 119). Earlier in the story the narrator expresses uncertainty regarding his own expectations of Deauville but mentions vague expectations of a "Rest von Vergangenheit, grüne Alleen, Strandpromenaden oder gar ein mondänes oder demi-mondänes Publikum" (some remnant of the past, green avenues, beach promenades, or even a stylish or scandalous clientele; *DA*, 171/*E*, 116). In other words, he is in search of the exotic, of distant times and places.

His comments on the Hotel Normandy, which, he claims, gives one the feeling of residing not in an international hotel but in a French gastronomic pavilion built for a world trade fair just outside Osaka, hint at the tendency of package holidays to minimize precisely the experience of cultural difference that the narrator seeks. The tourist world he encounters in the Normandy is thoroughly commodified. Every three days the current group of Japanese tourists is replaced by another,

> die jeweils . . . direkt vom Flughafen Charles de Gaulle in klimatisierten Autocars nach Deauville gebracht wurden, der nach Las Vegas und Atlantic City dritten Station einer Globusglücksreise, die über Wien, Budapest und Macao wieder nach Tokio zurückführte.

> [brought direct, in air conditioned coaches, from Charles de Gaulle airport to Deauville, the third call (after Las Vegas and Atlantic City) in a global gambling tour that took them on, back to Tokyo, via Vienna, Budapest and Macao. (*DA*, 176/*E*, 119–20)]

The problem of belatedness arises again, as this debased form of tourism is sharply contrasted with the romantic gambling travels of Adelwarth and Cosmo.

In order to resist recuperation by the leisure industry, the narrator employs two basic techniques. The first is to conjure up Deauville not as it is but as it was in its interwar heyday in a way that offers imaginary compensation for the town's current tawdry state (*DA*, 177–78/*E*, 120–21). But this involves him in precisely the contradictions of belatedness addressed above: his access to "authentic" experience is derived from textual mediations, such as Adelwarth's agenda. The other technique he uses is to seek authentic cultural experience at the margins of the industrial complex known as tourism. He does this by sneaking into the old gambling hall of the casino and listening to a wedding singer and her backing group rehearsing songs from the 1960s. The singer's breathy, child-like voice, her strong French accent, and her tendency to drift into wonderful humming whenever she forgets the words of the English songs prompt the narrator to sit down and listen. And though he dismisses the sentimentality of it all with the comment "Die reine Rührseligkeit" ("pure sentimentality"; *DA*, 179; unaccountably omitted from the English translation), the episode is nevertheless cast in clear opposition to the experiences of the Japanese tourists, whose itinerary merely shuttles them from the dining room to the gambling hall and back again. Sitting unseen at the back of a hall decked out for a wedding reception, the narrator implies that he has attained, once again, the yearned-for back region and gained knowledge of local culture that is not vouchsafed to the Japanese tourists.

Much of the Somerleyton Hall episode in *Die Ringe des Saturn* similarly consists of anti-touristic performances that are explicitly defined in opposition to the tourists who throng the house and its gardens. Whereas the "paying public" arrives by car and enters the grounds by the main entrance, the narrator arrives in an exceptionally uncomfortable train, scales the perimeter wall, and struggles through the undergrowth.[24] He mocks the miniature railway — the word "Miniaturbähnchen" (miniature train), with its entirely unnecessary diminutive suffix, betokening a literal and figurative belittling — and denigrates its passengers by comparing them to costumed dogs or trained seals (RS, 44/32). While the narrator walks through the designated rooms with an undifferentiated "Besucherschar," his remarks on its interior nevertheless display a level of discriminating attention that is implicitly not granted to the faceless mass of other visitors, who tarry here and there in random fashion ("da und dort ein wenig verweilenden Besucherschar"; throng of visitors who occasionally lingered here or there; RS, 49/36). So, for example, he can comment on the lurid style of "einige wahrscheinlich irgendwann zwischen 1920 und 1960 von einem mit dem Modernismus in Berührung gekommenen Kunstmaler angefertigte Familienporträts" (a number of family portraits painted perhaps some time between 1920 and 1960 by an artist not untouched by Modernism; RS, 49/35–36) and testify to a profound sense of temporal and spatial disorientation occasioned by the myriad artifacts from different times and places that now find themselves in strange juxtaposition in Somerleyton Hall. This represents, in miniature, the classic anti-touristic desire to diverge from tourism's beaten track, an aspect of Sebald's work on which Zilcosky has commented.[25] Indeed, those beaten tracks that do feature in Die Ringe des Saturn are almost all — to extend the metaphor — overgrown. Despite the fact that the narrator's pilgrimage takes place in August, in other words at the height of the holiday season, the down-at-heel resort town of Lowestoft is deserted, and the armor-plated fish from the deep-freeze that he is served for dinner at the Victoria Hotel suggests not merely that he is the only guest but that trade has been slack for some time (RS, 57–58/43). The episode is mirrored in the lengthy narrative of the Ashbury's guest house at the foot of the Slieve Bloom Mountains in Ireland, which is set up as a bed-and-breakfast establishment but fails to attract a guest for a decade, until the narrator's serendipitous arrival (RS, 247–64, esp. 262/208–21).

These various anti-tourist strategies, by means of which the narrators seek to distinguish themselves from mere "tourists" by foregrounding their superior aesthetic sensibilities or claiming to have attained the "back region," are underscored by the narratological dimensions of the texts. The first-person form allows the various "Scharen," "Heere," and "Völker" (throngs, hordes, races) of tourists to be not only dis-individualized but entirely denied interiority. This in turn foregrounds, at the level of narrative technique, the difference between the mute hordes of anonymous tourists and the rich unfolding of the narrators' consciousness that takes place within the pages of the text — particularly in Die Ringe des Saturn.

The characters to which a degree of autonomous subjectivity is granted in Sebald's texts tend to be the locals he encounters. We have seen above that the narrators are on occasion regarded with deep suspicion by the indigenous inhabitants of the places he visits and the employees of the service industries, not to mention the parents of the twin Kafka-look-alikes (*SG*, 102–3/*V*, 89–90). The flip side of the narrators' anti-tourist encounters is the spontaneous conversations into which they occasionally enter and which bespeak the narrators' privileged status compared with other tourists. Luciana, the wife of the hotel owner in Limone, demonstrates an uncommon degree of solicitude in ministering to the narrator's needs as he writes, and the encounter ends on a note of (admittedly insipid) eroticism (*SG*, 107–12/*V*, 94–98). The Turkish pleasure-boat pilot in *Die Ausgewanderten* divagates on the dangers of stupidity and meets with the narrator's complete understanding. "Es käme selten vor," she says, "daß man könne mit einem Fahrgast ein Gespräch führen, und noch dazu ein verständiges" (She rarely had the opportunity to talk to a passenger, she said, let alone one with a bit of sense; *DA*, 340/*E*, 227). The conversations with Malacchio (*SG*, 69–72/*V*, 60–63) and Salvatore Altamura (*SG*, 143–48/*V*, 127–32) in *Schwindel. Gefühle.*, or with William Hazel (*RS*, 52–55/38–40), Cornelis de Jong (*RS*, 229–31/193–95), and the Ashburys (*RS*, 251–64/208–21) in *Die Ringe des Saturn* are all part of the discourse of travel (as opposed to tourism): the narrator is the one who manages to overcome the superficialities of the tourist industry in order to arrive at an authentic experience of interpersonal connection — the so-called "back region" that the modern traveler allegedly seeks. The narrator's anti-touristic performance, then, is predicated on the narrative control of who speaks and who does not.

When Sebald's narrators undertake "typical" tourist activities, which they frequently do, further strategies of distinction come into play. The first is an insistence on the difficulties and discomforts of foreign travel. When visiting The Hague in order to view Rembrandt's *Anatomy Lesson* in the Mauritshuis, the narrator stays in a hotel that is a "selbst den bescheidensten Reisenden sogleich mit einem Gefühl der tiefsten Niedergeschlagenheit erfüllend[es] Etablissement[]" (this establishment, which would deeply have depressed even the humblest of travelers; *RS*, 99/*RS*, 80). On the perilous city streets themselves, which are populated mainly by pimps and drug-dealers, he witnesses, at uncomfortably close quarters, a knife-wielding chef pursuing his terrified victim, after which the narrator experiences "eine ungute, schwere Nacht" (a restless, difficult night. The adjective "ungut" is a particular Sebald favorite.) The following morning he is "in einer ziemlich schlechten Verfassung" (not in the best of states; *RS*, 102/82) as he stands before the painting he had come especially to see. As the infrastructure of tourism developed and the ease and safety of travel increased over the course of the nineteenth century, so commentators lamented the lack of *travail* in modern transport: one no longer had to work for the pleasures of travel.[26] Correspondingly, nineteenth-century travel writers frequently foreground the rigors and hardships of travel in order to establish their anti-touristic credentials. Sebald's evocation of the hardships he endured in The Hague, a hostile urban environment to which his miserable hotel fails to offer an antidote, is a belated example of this trend. The same assertions of hardship frequently occur in "All'estero": the arduous and frenetic process of purchasing a coffee at the station café in Venice (*SG*, 76–79/*V*, 66–68), the dismal experience of eating a pizza in the Pizzeria Verona (*SG*, 88–89/*V*, 76–78), the loss of his passport in Limone (*SG*, 112–17/*V*, 98–103), the attempted mugging or kidnapping in Milan (*SG*, 123–24/*V*, 109), the Hotel Boston for which the typically Sebaldian epithet "ungut" is employed (*SG*, 124/*V*, 109), and the appalling volume of traffic (*SG*, 130/*V*, 115).

A second anti-touristic strategy employed by Sebald's narrators is the self-conscious refusal to conform to tourist behavior. There are moments in *Die Ringe des Saturn*, for example, when the narrator explicitly deviates from the tourist path as demarcated by his map or physical barriers in the landscape. He asserts his willingness to ignore the map and strike out randomly across fields when the paths are overgrown or ploughed up and hence no longer discernible (*RS*, 296/249–50) and happily leaves a clifftop path by stepping over an electric fence in an act of willful trespass (*RS*, 85/66). It is in "All'estero," however, that anti-tourist behavior is most conspicuous. The narrator initially follows a typical tourist itinerary by visiting Vienna. While there, however, he eschews any kind of sightseeing activity: "Ich habe mir in den zirka zehn Tagen, die ich damals in Wien zugebracht habe, nichts angesehen," he writes (In the ten days or so that I spent in Vienna I visited none of the sights; *SG*, 42/*V*, 36). Instead, he pursues "end- und ziellose Wege" (wanders without aim or purpose; *SG*, 39/*V*, 33), walks "planlos, bis in die Nacht hinein" (aimlessly . . . until well into the night; *SG*, 41/*V*, 35). He cannot bring himself to board a tram that would take him to some of Vienna's recreational destinations, such as Schönbrunn, the Fasangarten, or the Dorotheerwald (*SG*, 40/*V*, 34), and the only buildings he enters are cafés and restaurants. Eventually he even gives up visiting these, preferring to eat at street stands or to munch a takeaway on the hoof (*SG*, 40, 43/*V*, 34, 36). The activities of walking and sitting on park benches begin to effect certain changes: the signs of "staubiger Abgerissenheit" (translated as "woeful state" but better rendered as "dusty shabbiness"; *SG*, 43/*V*, 36) begin to appear, and he starts carrying around a plastic bag filled with various objects from which he becomes inseparable. Although he starts out as a tourist, then, the narrator's anti-touristic performances are so successful that he gradually metamorphoses into a vagrant and is only cured from this condition when he decides to visit Ernst Herbeck and then travel to Venice on the night train.

This is the point, however, at which the narrator is realigned with tourist discourse. For one of the means by which tourists have typically long sought acculturation is visiting famous writers and the locations associated with them: birthplaces, homes, and graves. If the low-key and highly private visits to the homes of Herbeck (*SG*, 44–52/*V*, 38–45) and Michael Hamburger (*RS*, 208–26/175–90) appear to be greatly attenuated versions of the pious visits paid, for example, to Goethe or Wordsworth in the early years of the nineteenth century, they nevertheless partake of the same discourse of acculturation-through-tourism. The desire for acculturation, for the acquisition and display of cultural competence, is, of course, one of the primary motivations governing the narrator's travels, particularly in *Schwindel. Gefühle.* and *Die Ringe des Saturn.* This accounts for the numerous visits to museums and galleries and the correspondingly large quantity of ekphrastic description and art criticism in both books.

Sebald's essay on the paintings of Jan Peter Tripp spells out explicitly what is at stake, for Sebald, in looking at paintings:

> Das Andenken ist im Grunde nichts anderes als ein Zitat. Und das in einen Text (oder in ein Bild) einmontierte Zitat zwingt uns, wie Eco schreibt, zur Durchsicht unserer Kenntnisse anderer Texte und Bilder und unserer Kenntnisse der Welt. Das wiederum erfordert Zeit. Indem wir sie aufwenden, treten wir ein in die erzählte Zeit und in die Zeit der Kultur. (*LG*, 184)

> [The souvenir is basically nothing but a quotation. And the quotation inserted into a text (or a picture) forces us, as Eco says, to search through our knowledge of other texts and images and our knowledge of the world. That in turn requires time. By spending our time on such things, we enter into the time of narrative and the time of culture.]

Acculturation, on this model, is a fundamentally intertextual operation, whereby full access to culture — the ability to enter the "Zeit der Kultur" (time of culture) — can be gained only by plumbing our own memory and cultural repertoire. In what is so far the only article on Sebald and painting, Anne Fuchs discusses this passage and argues that immersion in the "Zeit der Kultur" runs counter to the demands for rationality and efficiency that are characteristic of modernity.[27] Conversely, however, modernity itself — as we saw in the opening section of this essay — licenses precisely this kind of cultural immersion in the service of a self-realization that compensates for the alienation that results from capitalist production. Furthermore, as Tony Bennett has argued at length in *The Birth of the Museum*, the museum in its current form was largely the product of the nineteenth century and was explicitly designed to exert a degree of disciplinary control over, and a civilizing influence on, the urban populace.[28] So the claim that immersing oneself in the "Zeit der Kultur" is a means of resisting the imperatives of modernity is true only in a qualified sense. When allied to travel, the contemplation of art is in fact a highly codified practice that exists in an uneasy relationship with tourism. It is facilitated by, but also seeks to differentiate itself from, those aspects of tourism that are the most indebted to industrial modernity: a developed transport infrastructure, a highly advanced hospitality industry, and the state funding of museums.

There is, then, ultimately no escape from the contradictions inherent in anti-tourism, for the more the narrators seek to establish their difference from the tourists in whose company they ineluctably find themselves, the more they end up having recourse to activities and representational strategies that have long been part of the anti-tourist's repertoire and can thus stake no claim to originality or authenticity. In recognition of this, perhaps, the narrators wage anti-tourist warfare on another front, namely within the photographic discourse of the texts, which themselves come to function as anti-tourist performances that compensate, at the level of representation, for the failure of anti-tourism in actuality.

Topography, Photography

> *The Picture Postcard enables the most indolent man to explore the wilds of Switzerland or Margate without perturbation. Nobody need fear that there is any spot on the earth which is not depicted on this wonderful oblong. The photographer has photographed everything between the poles. He has snap-shotted the earth.*
> — James Douglas, 1907

The activity of collecting images, as Dean MacCannell and many others after him have argued, is a fundamental feature of modern tourism.[29] Taking photographs as an aide-mémoire during his travels was a significant component of Sebald's own writing process, as he confided to Christian Scholz in an interview.[30] In his writings, photographs are frequently deployed as mementos of travel, and the acquisition of souvenirs, especially photographic souvenirs, constitutes one of the salient ways in which Sebald's narrators demonstrate their inescapable involvement within the very structures of tourism they seek to resist. Walter Benjamin was famously scathing in his critique of the souvenir:

Das Andenken ist die säkularisierte Reliquie.
Das Andenken ist das Komplement des "Erlebnisses." In ihm hat die zunehmende Selbstentfremdung des Menschen, der seine Vergangenheit als tote Habe inventarisiert, sich niedergeschlagen. . . . Die Reliquie kommt von der Leiche, das Andenken von der

abgestorbenen Erfahrung her, welche sich, euphemistisch, Erlebnis nennt.[31]

[The souvenir is a secularized relic.
The Souvenir is the complement of the *Erlebnis*. In it is deposited the increasing self-alienation of the person who inventories his past as dead possessions. . . . The relic comes from the corpse, the souvenir from the atrophied *Erfahrung* which, euphemistically, calls itself *Erlebnis*.[32]]

Elsewhere I have explored Benjamin's account of the souvenir in relation to the question of experience and memory in Sebald's work.[33] What interests me here is less memory than the question of the souvenir's function within the rhetoric of tourism and anti-tourism with which, as we have seen above, Sebald's works are intensively concerned. I have argued above that Sebald's texts narrate a series of anti-touristic performances that are designed to negotiate the distinction between tourist and traveler and to place the narrator firmly in the latter camp as one who possesses cultural competence and gains access to authentic experiences of travel that are withheld from the common throng of tourists. In this section I would like to pursue this argument further, looking at the ways in which the texts not only narrate but themselves *constitute* anti-touristic performances in their appropriation and transformation of tourist photography.

The paradigmatic form of the tourist photograph is the picture postcard, reproductions of which can be found in all of Sebald's prose narratives. The postcard enjoyed immense popularity from its earliest days. First introduced in Austria in 1869, it rapidly spread to the United Kingdom, other countries in Europe, and the United States. Austrian sales of postcards reached one-and-a-half million within a month of their first issue, while seventy-six million were used in Britain in the first year.[34] These were not, however, strictly speaking picture postcards as we would understand the term. Indeed, demand for picture postcards was sluggish until producers found ways of relating the postcard directly to the twin activities of tourism and collecting.[35] The Parisian Exposition Universelle of 1889 gave a huge impetus to the sales of picture postcards. The central attraction of that exhibition was the newly constructed Eiffel Tower, and the newspaper *Le Figaro* had the enterprising idea of printing a postcard with a lithographed image of the tower that could be purchased and posted from the top of the tower itself. The stunt was an immense success and spawned numerous imitations.[36] By 1895, postcards bearing the legend "Gruß aus . . ." or "Greetings from . . ." were highly popular and by the end of the nineteenth century were available "almost all over the world," as Frank Staff puts it.[37] By the turn of the nineteenth century, buying and sending postcards from the places one visited while traveling was a Europe-wide craze. It was especially evident in Germany. Here is G. R. Sims, writing in *The Referee* in 1900 after a summer holiday on the Rhine:

> Postcards in Germany were on sale in cigar shops, libraries, chemists and fruit stalls, or arranged in stands on restaurant tables, in the halls of hotels, railway stations, and hawked at landing stages for steamers. . . . You enter the railway station, and everybody on the platform has a pencil in one hand and a postcard in the other. In the train it is the same thing. Your fellow travelers never speak. They have little piles of picture postcards on the seat beside them, and they write continuously.[38]

Similar comments were made in an article in the *Standard*, published in August of the previous year: "The traveling Teuton['s] . . . first care on reaching some place of note is to lay in a stock [of postcards] and alternate the sipping of beer with the writing of postcards. Sometimes he may be seen conscientiously devoting to this task the hours of a railway journey."[39] The mildly xenophobic humor of these passages should not blind us to their significant implications. It is not merely that by the end of the nineteenth century writing postcards from the places one visited was an essential component of tourism; it is also the fact that acquiring and sending postcards had taken on a dynamic of its own, substituting, in the eyes of some observers at least, for any kind of genuine engagement with the experience of travel. Contemporary commentators drew attention to the increasingly mediated nature of the tourist experience. In the article by G. R. Sims, quoted above, the author also writes of his experience at the summit of the Rigi, a vantage point that offers some of Switzerland's most spectacular views: "I believe that the entire party had come up, not for the sake of the experience of the scenery, but to write postcards and post them at the top."[40] Carline notes that postcards became a necessity for the "flying visitor," and that jokes about Americans "doing" Oxford in half an hour existed even then. The most pessimistic diagnosis of the effects of postcards on the experience of travel, however, are to be found in the article by James Douglas from which the epigraph to this section is taken. Later in the same paragraph, he writes:

> Every pimple on the earth's skin has been photographed, and wherever the human eye roves or roams it detects the self-conscious air of the reproduced. The aspect of novelty has been filched from the visible world. The earth is eye-worn. It is impossible to find anything that has not been frayed to a frazzle by photographers.[41]

What we find in this passage is a radicalized, photographic version of the anti-tourist's dilemma: the search for the new and the authentic, the desire to leave the beaten track, is inevitably thwarted in a world where reality is always already photographically mediated.

This insight is echoed by more recent commentators.[42] MacCannell argues that mechanical reproduction is one of the phases in the process of sacralization, which is key to the establishment of a tourist site as different from other, similar objects and worthy of preservation. Mechanically reproduced images or effigies of the site, he argues, are "most responsible for setting the tourist in motion on his journey to find the true object."[43] In other words, photographic and other forms of mediation are necessary stimulants of tourist desire. The problem is, of course, that the desire for "the true object" is paradoxically thwarted in advance by the intensive mediation responsible for stimulating that desire in the first place, a problem addressed in Vilém Flusser's flippantly cynical account of postcards:

> Es gibt Sehenswürdigkeiten. Das sind Sachen und Sachverhalte, die nach Ansicht einiger Reiseführer (und Führer überhaupt) würdig sind, gesehen zu werden. Alles übrige ist laut dem Prinzip des ausgeschlossenen Dritten nicht wert, auch nur mit dem Blick gestreift zu werden. "X ist entweder sehenswürdig oder nicht. Es gibt kein Drittes." . . . Diese Ansicht der Führer betreffs der Ansehnlichkeit von Sachen und Sachverhalten schlägt sich auf Karten nieder. Sie heißen Ansichtskarten. . . . Abbilder sind verführerischer als Gedankenbilder weil sie (im Unterschied zu Straßenkarten) ihre Empfänger auch ohne intellektuelle Bemühung orientieren. . . . Daher ist es angebracht, in einen Papier- oder Tabakladen zu gehen, ohne vorher rechts und links zu sehen, wenn man in eine fremde Stadt kommt. Im Laden kann man Ansichtskarten kaufen, und hätte man sich vorher umgeschaut, dann wäre man Gefahr gelaufen, Unwürdiges zu sehen.[44]

> [There are sights. These are things and situations, which in the opinion of certain travel guides (*Reiseführer*) and leaders (*Führer*) in general[45] are worth seeing. Everything else is not worth even a passing glance, in line with the logic of the excluded third. "X is either worth seeing or not. There is no third term." . . . This opinion of guides (*Führer*) concerning the visual appeal of things and situations manifests itself on things called postcards. . . . Concrete images are more seductive than mental images because (in contrast to street maps) they can even orientate the viewer without intellectual effort. . . . It is therefore appropriate to go into a newsagent's or tobacconist's without so much as a glance to the left or right as soon as one arrives in a strange city. In the shop one can buy postcards, and if one had looked round beforehand one would have run the risk of seeing something that isn't worth seeing.]

On this model, postcards produce pervasive disciplinary effects that reduce all travel to the passive consumption of a series of narrow, prescribed, and normative visual experiences.[46]

I dwell on these matters in order to show that Sebald's texts engage not only with two centuries of travel writing but also with a century-long history of tourist photography. In one brief but telling episode we witness an engagement with travel, postcard collecting, and the construction of tourist sights that contains, *in nuce*, many of the issues addressed above. In "Il ritorno in patria," the narrator frequently visits the landlady of the Engelwirt, Rosina Zobel, and leafs through the three large folio volumes that contain her collection of several hundred postcards (*SG*, 213–14/*V*, 196). The collection, we learn, had been put together by her husband in the years before their marriage, when he had used up most of his large inheritance on global travel (*SG*, 214–15/*V*, 197), and shows a large number of cities in Germany, Austria, Switzerland, Bohemia, Italy, and the Far East. In Sebald's narrative the salient aspect of these photographs is their capacity to reduce everything to universal equivalence. Going through the album involves nothing more than the narrator's pointing at each picture and Rosina's supplying the name of the city depicted. This generates a list: "Chur, Bregenz, Innsbruck, Altaussee, Hallstadt, Salzburg, Vienna, Pilsen, Marienbad, Bad Kissingen, Würzburg, Bad Homburg, und Frankfurt am Main" (*SG*, 213–14/*V*, 196). Severed from their referents, the photographs lack all geographical and biographical contextualization. All that remains is equivalence. Not only is the experience of place mediated by the image, but all places lose their geographical specificity and subjective significance once they are mass-produced in postcard format, enter the space of commodity circulation, and are enshrined within the pages of the album. The postcard transforms space into spectacle by means of a twofold process. First, space becomes abstract, reduced to a series of images that are now linked to other images within the album rather than to their referents. Second, these images mediate a specific version or vision of the world to the viewing subject. The postcard establishes a hierarchy of spaces by excluding from representation those places that are not worthy of being seen/photographed, and decreeing in advance how those spaces that are represented are to be both seen and remembered. The viewing subject is thereby positioned within a set of representational conventions and becomes a product of the regime of spectacle.

Historians of the postcard have not been slow to recognize that postcards do not always and necessarily function in this way. Crouch and Lübbren note that the visual culture of tourism needs to be seen as fulfilling a multiplicity of functions in the subjective engagement with place, and cannot be reduced to the kind of disciplinary model of mediation discussed above.[47] In a similar vein, Christraud Geary and Virginia-Lee Webb note that the act of writing and mailing a postcard transforms mass-produced artifact into object of social interaction and communication.[48] Furthermore, the way in which postcards have conventionally circulated embeds them in the economy of the gift, establishing networks of social obligation that do

not fully coincide with the postcard's other functions as a circulating commodity and a mode of spectacular mediation. Common to these approaches
is their emphasis on what people *do with* photographs, on the function of
postcards within the "practice of everyday life." Paying attention to the
ways in which Sebald uses postcards as material objects in his texts will
allow us to explore the anti-touristic strategies that dominate not only the
narrated content of his texts but also their very form. In what follows
I investigate three salient techniques that Sebald uses in order to subvert
the conventional, mediating role of tourist photography: disorientation,
defacement, and the anti-aesthetic.

As the narrator leaves the Giardino Giusti in "All'estero," he writes:
"Ich . . . warf einen letzten Blick zurück auf den Garten" (I cast one last
glance back at the garden; *SG,* 81/*V,* 70–71). At this point a postcard of
the entrance to the garden is inserted in the text. The implication is that
the view represented in the image corresponds to the view of the narrator
as he passes through the gates. But a moment of disorientation occurs,
because even a cursory glance at the postcard shows that it has been taken
not from eye-level but from some distance above the ground and hence
cannot represent the vista seen by the narrator. The perspective is analogous to that of Ruisdael's *View of Harlem with Bleaching Fields,* which
Sebald describes as being painted from "einem künstlichen, ein Stück über
der Welt imaginierten Punkt" (an imaginary position some distance above
the earth; *RS,* 103/83). The fundamental difference, of course, is that a
photograph cannot possibly be taken from an imaginary point, and in fact
there is a building opposite the entrance to the Giardino Giusti from
whose upper stories the image must have been taken. But this information
relies on contextual knowledge and cannot be read out of the image itself.
As a consequence, the photograph offers the spectator no stable viewing
position within the world it represents; the view itself is strangely dis-
embodied, and the space of the image resistant to imaginative habitation.
There is thus a double disorientation going on here. First, the image
purports to be a record of what the narrator sees but cannot possibly be
so; and second, the point from which it has been taken is not identifiable
in or continuous with the represented world, severing the image from lived
bodily experience and rendering it mildly unsettling.[49] Ultimately, Sebald's
text foregrounds the fact that this most conventional of postcards turns
out to be a curious specimen that portrays a tourist sight — a
Sehenswürdigkeit — but in a way that no tourist is ever likely to see it,
which in turn calls into question facile assumptions about the functioning
of visual culture in the production of the tourist gaze.[50]

The unsettling effect of the Giardino Giusti postcard is largely a function not merely of the perspective from which it is taken but of the layout
of *Schwindel. Gefühle.* Lisa Patt notes that Sebald played a major role in
determining the precise layout of his texts, thereby controlling text-image

relations to an intimate degree.[51] She also shows that Sebald's interventions went much further than this, however, and included various forms of image manipulation. In the course of a report detailing a research visit by members of the Institute of Cultural Inquiry, Los Angeles, to Suffolk — a report that itself contains a fascinating photographic collage — Patt and her team discovered that the grainy quality of some images in *Die Ringe des Saturn* is a product not of inadequate photographic technology but of the Xerox machine. Of particular interest in the present context is the fact that at least two are postcards that have been subjected to repeated photocopying. The first is the image of Somerleyton Hall that is framed by the words "ein gleichsam mit dem Lebensstrom unserer Erde pulsierendes, ungeheuer helles Licht" (an immense brightness that pulsated like the current of life that runs through the earth; *RS*, 47/34), the image being inserted between "pulsierendes" and "ungeheuer" in the German original and thereby ostensibly illustrating the text. The crude image appears to depict the house by night, its gaslights producing a halo of illumination that contrasts sharply with the surrounding blackness. What emerges in the Institute's report, however, is that the image in Sebald's text is in fact based on a postcard of a nineteenth-century watercolour painting of the house.[52] The painting now hangs in Somerleyton Hall. Like the buildings themselves, paintings of country houses fulfilled the function of self-presentation, a means of displaying social prestige.[53] Hung on the walls of houses, they served as a reminder to those inside of what they could not see: the exterior of the house that contained them. Such paintings thereby ensured the continuity of spectacle between inside and outside, while also, in their choice of perspective, showing the house as the owners wished it to be seen. This double moment of mediation is, as we have seen, also a characteristic of the postcard. In the case of Somerleyton Hall, the mechanical reproduction of the image in postcard format, and its subsequent entry into multiple spaces of circulation and exchange, ensure that the moment of spectacular mediation becomes endlessly repeatable. This consideration returns us to the theme of the first section of this essay, namely the tendency of tourism to produce normative and predictable cultural experiences.

Sebald's defacement of the postcard of the watercolor of the house has to be understood in this light. "Two swipes of a bright light against a glass bed, and a gum eraser," sufficed, so Patt and her team tell us, to "sweep a pile of iron dust in the exact configuration Sebald had when he conjured his 'most wonderful sight of all.'"[54] Two things stand out from this statement. The first is that the image reproduced in *Die Ringe des Saturn* is the result of an artisanal process involving not only a mechanical aid (the photocopier), but the artist's hand. The second is that the image is "his" (that is, Sebald's or perhaps more properly the narrator's) "wonderful sight." In other words, it is a purely subjective vision that can be traced back neither to an "original" representation nor to an empirical phenomenon. Somerleyton Hall never looked like this, nor has it ever been represented like this outside the pages of *Die Ringe des Saturn*. Far from fulfilling the conventional functions of the postcard, then, the defaced image is the result of an anti-tourist performance that installs the subjective vision of the narrator in place of the mechanically reproduced "view." Like the numerous passages in which Sebald's narrators seek to stress their difference from mere tourists, the manipulations performed on the Somerleyton Hall postcard serve to underscore the narrator's distinction as one whose refined aesthetic sensibilities and historical imagination give him privileged access to *and the ability to represent* a cultural past that is invisible to ordinary eyes.

A similar process is at work in the image of the Somerleyton maze (*RS*, 206/173). This, too, is based on a postcard — a photographic one this time, which depicts not only the maze but also the extensive grounds of Somerleyton Hall and, in the top left corner, the house itself. Patt and her team claim that Sebald cut the maze from the postcard, to give a strange-shaped, quasi-circular vignette, and then photocopied it with the lid of the copier raised in order to produce the black rectangular background. The white line around the vignette, they argue, is the shadow produced by the cut-out.[55] Again, then, Patt's valuable detective work exposes traces of the author's hand. More significantly, though, the image is incorporated into the text to illustrate a dream in which the narrator finds himself on Dunwich Heath, but looking down from the Chinese pavilion in the center of the Somerleyton maze onto that maze itself. In the dream, the narrator knows with absolute certainty that it represents "einen Querschnitt durch [sein] Gehirn" (a cross-section of my brain; *RS*, 206/173). What starts out as a postcard, then, becomes, through the process of manipulation, an image of the narrator's brain, thereby once more demonstrating a profoundly subjective appropriation of tourism's visual culture that utterly subverts the normative mediating functions that critics from Sims to Flusser have attributed to postcards.

The third anti-tourist strategy employed by Sebald in his engagement with the photography of place is his adoption of anti-aesthetic modes of representation, particularly but not exclusively in those photographs that are attributable to the narrators themselves. Many commentators have noted the poor aesthetic quality of the images reproduced in his texts, and for Sebald himself, aesthetics were at best a secondary concern.[56] Despite numerous studies of photography in his work, this aspect of Sebald's texts has not been fully thematized. It is, I think, best understood in terms of the anti-touristic agenda evinced by Sebald's narrators both in their travels and in the deployment of photographs discussed above.

In general, topographical photography in Sebald concentrates on things that would in no sense qualify as tourist sights.[57] Furthermore, those photographs that represent potential tourist attractions are of exceptionally poor quality when judged according to conventional criteria concerning composition, focus, contrast, and so on. The unfocused image of Summerhill in Ireland sits obliquely across the page, is not properly centered, and is so under-exposed as to obscure all but the crudest of detail (*RS*, 258/216). The photograph of the quirky Bawdsey Estate is reproduced in such as way as to heighten contrast, producing a curious effect of simultaneous underexposure and overexposure and, once again, obscuring architectural detail (*RS*, 267/224). This is in all probability another product of the Xerox machine.

These anti-aesthetic photographs offer a twofold resistance to the economy of the *Sehenswürdigkeit* discussed above. In the first place, the images depict structures that are peripheral to conventional tourist itineraries.[58] In the second place, the images refuse the pleasures and satisfactions of aesthetics, which could have compensated for the perceived insignificance of the photographed objects themselves. The unattractive representation of the unimportant represents an attempt, on Sebald's part, to resist the economy of the spectacle and the normative protocols of viewing that it implies.

These exclusively visual techniques go hand in hand with an anti-tourist strategy that, as we have seen throughout this essay, is central to Sebald's work, namely the emphasis on the subjective experience of place that sets the genuine traveler apart from the tourist. The value of Sebald's topographical photographs derives not from their *Sehenswürdigkeit* but from their role within Sebald's wider attempts to reinvest space with the very subjective significance that it loses once it becomes appropriated by the tourist industry and enters the space of commodity circulation in the form of tourism's visual culture. Many commentators have discussed the representation of space in Sebald's work, most of them basing their analyses on questions of cultural and individual memory, history, and metaphysics.[59] What I wish to emphasize here is that Sebald's narrators' desire to find the invisible within the visible — evidence of a historical metaphysics or traces of the past within the physical landscape — not only forms part of the discourse of history and memory but is also central to Sebald's engagement with travel and tourism.

A few salient examples will suffice to demonstrate what is at stake in Sebald's topographical photography. Rather than being dismissed as the monstrosity it undoubtedly is, the breeze-block building in Klosterneuburg produces in the narrator an impression of serious crime (*SG*, 51/*V*, 43–44) — the phrase "machte *auf mich* den Eindruck eines schweren Verbrechens" (Looking at it was like witnessing a hideous crime; my emphasis) clearly signaling the subjective moment here. The photograph of the Pizzeria Verona (*SG*, 142/*V*, 126) takes on uncanny resonances, not only because of the name of the owner (Carlo Cadavero) and the narrator's fear of being pursued in 1980, but because of the refusal of the photographer, who occupies the shop next door, to photograph the building. While nothing is stated, an ill-defined sense of threat permeates the episode. In "Max Aurach," the narrator's peregrinations around Manchester take him into the northern suburbs and allow him to witness the otherwise invisible life of working-class children playing on the wasteland that was once the site of the city's Jewish quarter (*DA*, 232/*E*, 157), and to discover the disused warehouses along the former Ship Canal (*DA*, 235/*E*, 159). The Jewish cemetery in Bad Kissingen, to which the narrator can gain access only by scaling the wall, is represented in four photographs that testify to his ability to seek out the neglected treasures of a well-known spa resort (*DA*, 333–36/*E*, 222–25). What is more, the narrator confesses to the profound subjective impact this cemetery has when he states that Friederike Halbleib's grave evokes in him a sense of insuperable personal loss. It is in *Die Ringe des Saturn*, however, that the narrator's subjective investment in place is most pronounced. The photographs of Lowestoft (*RS*, 55, 59, 60/41, 44, 48), the empty expanse of the Blyth (*RS*, 166/137), and, supremely, the abandoned research facility at Orfordness (*RS*, 280–82/135–36) once more show that that narrator can access the "back regions," those areas of authentic cultural experience that other tourists seek but do not find. The line of fishermen on the beach, who remind the narrator of "die letzten Überreste eines wandernden Volkes" (the last stragglers of some nomadic people, *RS* 68/51), is the first of several images that mingle fantasies of nomadism and post-apocalyptic survival (see also *RS*, 105, 273, 282/85, 229, and 237), and taken together they signal the narrator's ability to project quasi-mythical significance into the disenchanted world. The image of the sailing boat is evidence of the strange sensation of stasis that the narrator experiences by dint of his and the boat's moving at an identical pace (*RS*, 84/65–66) — a peculiar and irreducibly unique experience. John Urry argues that tourist photography is governed by a circular logic: "What is sought for in a holiday is a set of photographic images, which have already been seen in tour company brochures or on TV programs."[60] Rather than merely confirming that he has seen what the tourist industry has already constructed as a "sight," the photographs in Sebald's books seek to do precisely the opposite, constructing an alternative topography that revalorizes the peripheral, the ostensibly uninteresting, and the anti-aesthetic in order to foreground the radically subjective experience of place that characterizes "travel."

The problem for Sebald is that the matter is not as straightforward as Urry implies. Caren Kaplan, for example, points out that tourism "insists upon proof of the authentic," and photography constitutes one component of a more widespread "technology of documenting the 'real.' When tourists believe that they have attained the 'back' region," she adds, "the need for proof is especially pressing."[61] On this reading, the quantitative predominance of photographs whose function is to document the narrator's visits to peripheral places, and the grainy nature of the photographs themselves, begin to appear not as a sovereign assertion of a subjective experience of place, but a symptom of a certain anxiety about the very possibility of authentic travel experience. Thus while at one level the photographic discourse of Sebald's texts resists the tourist gaze by refusing to participate in the economy of spectacle, there is a sense in which it is reinscribed into touristic discourse at another level, namely that of the ideology of authenticity.

Epilogue

I have argued above that Sebald's travel narratives have to be seen in the light of a long history of travel writing that strives to maintain the distinction between the traveler and the tourist. Sebald's prose texts repeatedly narrate what I, following James Buzard, have termed "anti-tourist" strategies in order to assert the narrators' privileged status as bearers of culture, and the authenticity of their travel experiences. I have also shown, however, that the search for authentic experience involves Sebald's narrators in various contradictions, since their taste and acculturation can be demonstrated only with reference to their own literary forebears. The very possession of cultural competence leads necessarily to a sense of belatedness, as the traveler is condemned to follow in the footsteps of the writers who preceded him. Perhaps in recognition of this situation, Sebald's narrators pursue the traveler-tourist distinction at the level of the text through their incorporation of numerous photographs that resist the tourist paradigm as exemplified, supremely, by the picture postcard. But even here there is the sense that, since modern tourism is predicated on the ideology of the authentic, Sebald's narrators are persistently at pains to provide photographic evidence that will authenticate even the most anti-touristic of their experiences, and in so doing they unwittingly reinscribe themselves within the very tourist paradigm they seek to resist. It should be noted that this is not a contingent failing on the part of Sebald's narrators but a structural function of tourism itself. For as we have seen, the tourist-traveler distinction is in fact internal to the logic of tourism, and by insisting on the opposition one therefore betrays one's entanglement within the very structures one wishes to evade.

Bearing this in mind, I would like to end with a brief consideration of the wider function of Sebald's texts — and particularly his photographs — in the context of literary tourism. As both Ian Ousby and, latterly, Nicola J. Watson have shown, the nineteenth century witnessed an increasing preoccupation with the birthplaces, homes, and graves of famous writers, as well as the cities and landscapes within which their works are set.[62]

What is interesting in Sebald's case is that the works of a writer who has himself been seen — by Susan Sontag among others — as first and foremost a travel writer should also have stimulated tourist activity.[63] Sebald tourism might yet be the preserve of a relatively small number of interested readers, but anecdotal evidence suggests that many readers — professional and amateur alike — have sought to visit the places described in Sebald's narratives — mainly Suffolk, but also to Wertach and, in my case at least, Lake Vyrwny in mid-Wales. The research trip by members of the Institute of Cultural Inquiry can clearly be seen as tourism, and a recent call for contributions to a Sebald conference at the University of East Anglia offered "an opportunity to retrace some of Sebald's steps around the East Anglian countryside." The phenomenon of *Sebaldtourismus* throws a new light on the photographs in Sebald's texts. The book, after all, is a commodity form like any other, and although the intratextual use of photographs in Sebald's works seeks to combat spectacle, we have seen that the images are ineluctably turned into images of tourist sights as soon as one works outwards from the book to the world. Once one has read Sebald, one's experience of the places he depicts in his photographs is necessarily mediated, and one's view of, for example, the pagoda-like structures of Orfordness or the Jewish cemetery at Bad Kissingen forever in part predetermined by prior acquaintance with the *Die Ringe des Saturn* or *Die Ausgewanderten*. In this sense, Sebald's photographs contribute to the process of "unlosing lost places," according to which places deemed "lost" (that is, not widely accessible and/or visible) are returned to terra cognita by means of the circulation of images.[64] The iconology of unlost places relies on the complete absence of people, an aspect of the images' rhetoric that allows us, as observers, to "enter into the negative space of the lost and fill it with our own sense of order."[65] This is, of course, precisely the way in which Sebald's photographs of empty landscapes address the viewer. And while this may create an illusion of authenticity or uniqueness, the continual production of the unlost is a central strategy of the tourist industry, which needs to be seen to provide unlimited access to places of escape — the "back regions" I have mentioned above.[66] By participating in this production of the unlost, by producing effects in the world, Sebald's photographs thus end up participating in the very regime of spectacle that they ostensibly oppose.[67]

Notes

[1] James Buzard, *The Beaten Track: European Tourism, Literature, and the Ways to "Culture," 1800–1918* (Oxford: Oxford UP, 1993), 1 and 2–5. A similar point is made by Ian Ousby, *The Englishman's England: Taste, Travel, and the Rise of Tourism* (Cambridge: Cambridge UP, 1990), 14.

[2] Hans Magnus Enzensberger, "Eine Theorie des Tourismus," in *Einzelheiten I* (Frankfurt am Main: Suhrkamp, 1962), 179–205; here 183. The essay was first published in the cultural periodical *Merkur* in 1958. See also Jonathan Culler, "Semiotics of Tourism," in *Framing the Sign: Criticism and Its Institutions* (Oxford: Oxford UP, 1988), 153–67; here 154; and Ousby, *Englishman's England*, 133.

[3] On tourism's status as a product of industrial modernity, see for example, John Urry, *The Tourist Gaze*, 2nd ed. (London: Sage, 2002), 5; and Enzensberger, "Tourismus," 191.

[4] Buzard, *Beaten Track*, 8.

[5] Dean MacCannell, *The Tourist: A New Theory of the Leisure Class* (1976; repr., New York: Schocken, 1989).

[6] Buzard, *Beaten Track*, 6; see also esp. 80–154.

[7] See J. J. Long, *W. G. Sebald: Image, Archive, Modernity* (New York: Columbia UP, 2007).

[8] Raymond Williams, *Keywords: A Vocabulary of Culture and Society* (New York: Oxford UP, 1976), 68. Quoted in Buzard, *Beaten Track*, 7.

[9] Buzard, *Beaten Track*, 7.

[10] On the "back region," see MacCannell, *The Tourist*, 92–96.

[11] Zilcosky, "Sebald's Uncanny Travels: The Impossibility of Getting Lost," in *W. G. Sebald: A Critical Companion*, ed. J. J. Long and Anne Whitehead (Edinburgh: Edinburgh UP, 2004), 102–20. Christopher C. Gregory-Guider's article "The 'Sixth Emigrant': Traveling Places in the Works of W. G. Sebald," *Contemporary Literature* 46 (2005): 422–49; and John Wylie's "The Spectral Geographies of W. G. Sebald," *Cultural Geographies* 14 (2007): 171–88, focus on the "psychogeographical" aspects of travel and displacement, while Massimo Leone's "Textual Wanderings" links travel to Sebald's narrators' attempts, through the experience of vertigo, to uncover a hidden meaning behind phenomena. The central claim of Eluned Summers-Bremner's meandering study "Reading, Walking, Mourning: W. G. Sebald's Peripatetic Fictions," *Journal of Narrative Theory* 34 (2004): 304–34, seems to be that Sebald's texts involve a "rewalking of German history" that rehabilitates an activity that had become ideologically debased in Nazism.

[12] Bianca Theisen, "Prose of the World: W. G. Sebald's Literary Travels," *Germanic Review* 79.3 (Summer 2004): 163–79; here 166.

[13] Theisen, "Prose of the World," 164.

[14] See Stephen Greenblatt, *Marvelous Possessions: The Wonder of the New World* (Chicago: U of Chicago P, 1991).

[15] Ousby, *The Englishman's England*, 12–13.

[16] Mary Louise Pratt, *Imperial Eyes: Travel Writing and Transculturation* (Abingdon, UK: Routledge, 1992), 78.

[17] Enzensberger, "Tourismus," 188.

[18] Buzard, *Beaten Track*, 114.

[19] Buzard, *Beaten Track*, 119–20.

[20] John Urry claims that the commercial marketing of "travel" (as opposed to tourism) is a recent development, but as I suggest here, it has in fact always been an integral part of the tourist industry. Urry, *Tourist Gaze*, 86.

[21] Sebald's paraphrase of Grillparzer is highly one-sided. In the *Tagebuch* Grillparzer begins by expressing disappointment: "Man hat oft den ersten Anblick von Venedig als so wunderbar beschrieben, ich habe es kaum so gefunden. . . . Der erste Eindruck, den Venedig auf mich machte, war befremdend, einengend, unangenehm" (The first view of Venice has often been described as quite wonderful, but that was hardly my impression. The first impression that Venice made on me was disconcerting, constricting, unpleasant). But he goes on to revise this opinion, concluding with the comment: "für einen, der ein Gemüt hat, gibt es keinen zweiten Ort wie Venedig" (For any person of feeling, there's nowhere quite like Venice). Grillparzer, *Tagebuch auf der Reise nach Italien*, in *Sämtliche Werke: Ausgewählte Briefe, Gespräche, Berichte*, ed. Peter Frank and Karl Pörnbacher (Munich: Hanser, 1965), 4:275–349; here 283 and 285. All translations are my own unless otherwise credited.

[22] See for example, *SG*, 148, "Scharenweise" (Crowds [of festival-goers]; *V*, 132), and the discussion of *Die Ringe des Saturn*, below. Cf. also the description of tourists in front of Venice station as "ein wahres Heer von Touristen" (a veritable army of backpackers) and "ungezählte junge Männer und Frauen" (countless young men and women; *SG*, 94/*V*, 82).

[23] See Ousby, *Englishman's England*, 148–49 for the denigration of trippers in the nineteenth century, and John Taylor, *A Dream of England: Landscape, Photography and the Tourist's Imagination* (Manchester: Manchester UP, 1994), 14, for a recent and uncritical reinscription of the hierarchy.

[24] Cf. his climbing over the wall of the Jewish cemetery in Bad Kissingen in *Die Ausgewanderten* (*DA*, 334/*E*, 222–23).

[25] Zilcosky, "Uncanny Travels," 105.

[26] Buzard, *Beaten Track*, 33–34. Theisen, too, notes the importance of what she misspells as "*travaille*" for Sebald's travelers ("Prose of the World," 174).

[27] Anne Fuchs, "W. G. Sebald's Painters: The Function of Fine Art in his Prose Works," *Modern Language Review* 101 (2006): 167–83; here 174.

[28] Tony Bennett, *The Birth of the Museum: History, Theory, Politics* (London: Routledge, 1995), esp. chapters 1–3.

[29] Dean MacCannell, *The Tourist*, 42. John Urry's book *The Tourist Gaze* expands MacCannell's insights, claiming that the entire infrastructure of tourism is designed primarily to mediate visual experience.

[30] Christian Scholz, "Aber das Geschriebene ist ja kein wahres Dokument," *Neue Zürcher Zeitung*, 26–27 Feb. 2000. Published in English as "'But the Written Word Is Not a True Document': A Conversation with W. G. Sebald on Literature and Photography," trans. Markus Zisselsberger, in *Searching for Sebald: Photography after W. G. Sebald*, ed. Lise Patt (Los Angeles: Institute of Cultural Inquiry, 2007), 104–9.

[31] Walter Benjamin, *Charles Baudelaire: Ein Lyriker im Zeitalter des Hochkapitalismus* (Frankfurt am Main: Suhrkamp, 1980), 177.

[32] *Erfahrung* and *Erlebnis* are both translated as "experience," but Benjamin famously differentiated them: *Erfahrung*, continuous with past and future and containing elements of both the past and the future in itself, is, according to Benjamin, progressively eroded in modernity, and experience breaks down into isolated and singular moments or events (*Erlebnis*). As the complement of the *Erlebnis*, then, the souvenir is fragmentary, incomplete, and severed from any putative experiential totality.

[33] See J. J. Long, *Image, Archive, Modernity*, 98–99.

[34] See Richard Carline, *Pictures in the Post: The Story of the Picture Postcard and Its Place in the History of Popular Art* (London: Gordon Fraser, 1971), 37. As Frank Staff shows, the birth of the postcard was a more protracted affair than the above summary suggests, with evidence suggesting that unofficial postal cards were in circulation in Britain in the 1850s, in the United States by 1861, and in France, Switzerland, and the German territories later in the 1860s. See Staff, *The Picture Postcard and its Origins*, 2nd ed. (London: Lutterworth, 1979), 45–46.

[35] Carline, *Pictures in the Post*, 43; Staff, *Picture Postcard*, 63.

[36] Carline, *Pictures in the Post*, 43–44.

[37] Staff, *Picture Postcard*, 57.

[38] Quoted in Carline, *Pictures in the Post*, 64.

[39] Quoted in Staff, *Picture Postcard*, 60.

[40] Quoted in Carline, *Pictures in the Post*, 44.

[41] James Douglas, writing in 1907. Quoted without source in Frank Staff, *The Picture Postcard and its Origins*, 2nd ed. (London: Lutterworth, 1979), 79.

[42] In addition to the other theorists quoted in this paragraph, see M. Christine Boyer, *The City of Collective Memory: Its Historical Imagery and Architectural Entertainments* (Cambridge, MA: MIT Press, 1994), 138.

[43] MacCannell, *The Tourist*, 44–45.

[44] Vilém Flusser, "Ansichtskarten," in *Standpunkte: Texte zur Fotografie* (Göttingen: European Photography, 1998), 195–97; here 195.

[45] Flusser puns on the words "Führer" (leader, and in particular Hitler) and "Reiseführer" (travel guide). The pun cannot be translated, but in Flusser's essay it underscores the quasi-dictatorial power of travel guides.

[46] It is worth noting in this context that postcard production evinced a high level of centralization and conventionality from a relatively early stage in its history. See Howard Woody, "International Postcards: Their History, Production and Distribution (circa 1895–1915)," in *Delivering Views: Distant Cultures in Early Postcards*, ed. Christraud M. Geary and Virginia-Lee Webb (Washington: Smithsonian Institution P, 1998), 13–45.

[47] David Crouch and Nina Lübbren, "Introduction," in *Visual Culture and Tourism*, ed. Crouch and Lübbren (Oxford: Berg, 2003), 1–20; here 11.

[48] Christraud M. Geary and Virginia-Lee Webb, "Introduction: Views on Postcards," in Geary and Webb, *Delivering Views: Distant Cultures in Early Postcards*, 1–12; here 4.

[49] I say "mildly" because this image actually reproduces a naturalized convention of much architectural photography which, through endless repetition, has ceased to exert a strongly disorientating effect.

[50] By comparison, the postcards in *Die Ausgewanderten* of the Hotel Eden in Monteux (*DA*, 113/*E*, 78), the Heliopolis Casino (*DA*, 140/*E*, 96), and the Banff Springs Hotel (*DA*, 142/*E*, 98) are significantly less problematic in terms of text-image relations and spectator position.

[51] See Lise Patt, "Searching for Sebald: What I Know for Sure," in *Searching for Sebald*, 17–101; here 39–43 and *passim*.

[52] The original postcards of Somerleyton Hall are reproduced in ICI Research Team, "A Truth That Lies Elsewhere," in *Searching for Sebald*, 492–509; here 502–3.

[53] On this function of country houses and the tourist industry that grew up around them, see chapter 2 of Ousby, *Englishman's England*, 44–71.

[54] ICI Research Team, "A Truth That Lies Elsewhere," 506.

[55] ICI Research Team, "A Truth That Lies Elsewhere," 506.

[56] See Sebald's fascinating interview with Christian Scholz, "Aber das Geschriebene ist ja kein wahres Dokument."

[57] See in particular the images on the following pages: *SG*, 49, 51, 142/*V*, 42, 44, 126; *DA*, 116, 128, 173, 174, 232, 235, 247, 250, 313, 332, 341, 343, 345, 347, 348, 353/*E*, 80, 87, 117, 118, 158, 159, 167, 168, 209, 221, 228, 229, 231, 232, 233, 235; and *RS*, 42, 55, 59, 60, 67, 84, 89, 100, 113, 165, 166, 187, 189, 268, 272, 274, 280, 281, 282, 315/*RS* 30, 44, 51, 65, 81, 91, 137, 138, 155, 157, 225, 228, 230, 235, 236, 265. It is worth noting that some images do, of course, possess a degree of aesthetic or touristic value, such as the image of Lower Manhattan tenements with the Brooklyn Bridge looming out of the morning haze (*DA*, 122/*E*, 84) or Southwold lighthouse (*RS*, 93/75). Quantitatively, however, the texts are swamped by the anti-touristic images I discuss in the main body of this article. It should also be pointed out that the texts that I do not deal with explicitly here contain many anti-aesthetic images of place. Some examples include the cemetery and various views of Prior's Gate and its gardens in "Henry Selwyn," and, supremely, the photographs of glass roofs, fortresses, Parisian streets, Brussels rooftops, and so on in *Austerlitz*. I do not discuss them here because the nature of travel — and consequently also the function of topographical photography — is different in those narratives than in "All'estero," "Ambros Adelwarth," "Max Aurach," and *Die Ringe des Saturn*.

[58] As Anne Fuchs has demonstrated at length, one of Sebald's achievements is to highlight the significance of the marginal for an understanding of history and a more adequate approach to cultural memory than that facilitated by official memory culture. See Fuchs, *Die Schmerzensspuren der Geschichte: Zur Poetik der Erinnerung in W. G. Sebalds Prosa* (Cologne: Böhlau, 2004), 69, 183 and *passim*. On the role of the periphery in Sebald's work, see also Claudia Albes, "Die Erkundung der Leere: Anmerkungen zu W. G. Sebalds 'englischer Wallfahrt' *Die*

Ringe des Saturn," *Jahrbuch der deutschen Schillergesellschaft* 46 (2002): 279–305.

[59] See, for example, Fuchs, *Schmerzensspuren der Geschichte*; Christopher C. Gregory-Guider, "The 'Sixth Emigrant'"; and Jo Catling, "Gratwanderungen bis an den Rand der Natur: W. G. Sebald's Landscapes of Memory," in *The Anatomist of Melancholy: Essays in Memory of W. G. Sebald*, ed. Rüdiger Görner (Munich: iudicium, 2003), 19–50. Christina Kraenzle has offered a reading of the topographical photography in *Die Ringe des Saturn* that summarizes the myriad functions of photography in that text. Her main point seems to be that the photographs are part of a discourse, at once historical and metaphysical, that reads landscape for visible traces of the invisible. See Kraenzle, "Picturing Place: Travel, Photography, and Imaginative Geography in W. G. Sebald's *Rings of Saturn*," in Patt, *Searching for Sebald*, 126–45. Thomas von Steinaecker's lengthy discussion of Sebald and photography in *Literarische Foto-Texte: Zur Funktion der Fotografien in den Texten Rolf Dieter Brinkmanns, Alexander Kluges und W. G. Sebalds* (Bielefeld: transcript, 2007), 248–312, notes the prevalence of images of place in Sebald's work. But Steinaecker can understand photography only in terms of thematic allegory, making his discussion repetitive, reductive, and ultimately ahistorical. He concentrates almost exclusively on the content of the images. As Silke Horstkotte and Lise Patt have argued, however, any account of photography in Sebald's work has to be attentive to their status not only as representations but also as material objects. See Silke Horstkotte, *Nachbilder: Zur Funktion von Fotografien in der deutschen Gedächtnisliteratur, Habilitationsschrift*, University of Leipzig, 2007, chaps. 4, 5 and 7; and Lise Patt, "Searching for Sebald," 17–101.

[60] Urry, *Tourist Gaze*, 129.

[61] Caren Kaplan, *Questions of Travel: Postmodern Discourses of Displacement* (Durham, NC: Duke UP, 1996), 61.

[62] Ousby, *The Englishman's England*, 17–43; Nicola J. Watson, *Literary Tourism: Readers and Places in Romantic and Victorian Britain* (Basingstoke, UK: Palgrave, 2006).

[63] See Susan Sontag, "A Mind in Mourning," in *Where the Stress Falls* (London: Cape, 2002), 43. Also quoted in Zilcosky, "Sebald's Uncanny Travels," 102.

[64] See Roger Balm and Briavel Holcomb, "Unlosing Lost Places: Image Making, Tourism and the Return to Terra Cognita," in Crouch and Lübbren, *Visual Culture and Tourism*, 157–74.

[65] Balm and Holcomb, "Unlosing Lost Places, 164.

[66] Balm and Holcomb, "Unlosing Lost Places, 171.

[67] I would like to thank the Leverhulme Trust for supporting the research and writing of this chapter.

3: "A Wrong Turn of the Wheel": Sebald's Journeys of (In)Attention

Carolin Duttlinger

HABIT AND ROUTINE ARE ESSENTIAL FEATURES of modern life, enabling us to function in an increasingly complex world.[1] At the same time, however, such forms of behavior have been criticized as posing a threat to autonomy, authentic experience, and self-fulfillment. Citing Marx, Walter Benjamin highlights the monotony of the modern workplace, which subjects the worker to a "Dressur der Maschine" (dressage of the machine), numbing him against any more immediate experiences.[2] Max Horkheimer and Theodor W. Adorno discern a similar effect in the standardized products of the culture industry, which extend the dressage of the workplace into our free time.[3] Given this ubiquity of disciplinary determination, travel seems to offer a rare opportunity for respite and escape. For Thomas Mann's narrator in *Der Zauberberg* (*The Magic Mountain*, 1924), travel has an invigorating effect not only on the body, "welcher Gefahr lief und schon im Begriffe war, im ungegliederten Einerlei der Lebensführung sich zu verwöhnen, zu erschlaffen und abzustumpfen" (which had been in danger, or indeed in the process, of becoming vitiated, slowed down, numbed by the unstructured monotony of daily life)[4] — but also on the mind. Mann's protagonist Hans Castorp has to learn "ohnehin Angeschautes genauer zu bemerken und Neues mit jugendlicher Empfänglichkeit in sich aufzunehmen" (to look at faces and facts more closely and to absorb new ones with youthful receptivity).[5]

Travel thus offers a training ground for attention. New environments force the traveler to abandon habitual modes of perception, enabling her to emerge from the fog of *Gewohnheit* (habit) with heightened alertness. This change is implied in the German word for attention: *Aufmerksamkeit* implies less a permanent, unwavering state of concentration than a process of *becoming aware*, a renewed, rekindled attention. It is this dynamic *Aufmerksamkeit* that underpins Sebald's travel writings, but just as such moments of alertness can be unpredictable and at times even startling, the role of attention in Sebald's narratives is far from stable. As his works illustrate, travel can have an intensifying, invigorating and even liberating effect, bringing previously overlooked details of reality into focus. That said, this renewed attentiveness can also have an unsettling, destabilizing effect. The traveler's heightened receptivity can divert him from his chosen path, leading him to lose sight of the "bigger picture." In Sebald's travelogues, *Aufmerksamkeit* is precariously linked to *Unaufmerksamkeit*; indeed, they are two sides of the same coin.

Sebald is not the first to pick up on this dynamic. The unstable nature of *Aufmerksamkeit* is a central concern of the tourist industry, whose many products are designed to curb and channel the traveler's potentially wayward attention. Guidebooks and itineraries, maps, plaques, and organized tours serve to discipline the traveler's physical and mental movements; they reduce the range of encountered impressions to a number of select highlights or *Sehenswürdigkeiten*, thereby turning travel into a uniform, predictable, and "manageable" experience.[6] Another feature that contributes to this effect is modern transport technology. As Wolfgang Schivelbusch argues, "The industrial revolution, in the production of goods as well as in travel, destroyed what one might call the 'esthetic freedom' of the preindustrial subject," as the relationship between the traveler and the surrounding (natural) world becomes increasingly mediated.[7] Ultimately, then, the modern traveler finds herself confronted with the same structures of determination that govern her day-to-day life.[8]

Sebald's writings are both a critique of and a reaction against this situation. The anaesthetizing effect of train travel is a recurring theme in his texts, as is the destructive impact of modern transport on the natural environment. A train journey through Germany, which is undertaken by the narrator of *Schwindel. Gefühle.* highlights both aspects:

> tags darauf also saß ich . . . im Express nach Hoek van Holland und fuhr durch das mir von jeher unbegreifliche, bis auf den letzten Winkel aufgeräumte und begradigte deutsche Land. Auf eine ungute Art befriedet und betäubt schien mir alles, und das Gefühl der Betäubung erfaßte bald auch mich. . . . Eigenartig berührte mich beim Hinausschauen auf einmal, daß fast nirgends ein Mensch zu erblicken war, wenn auch über die nassen Landstraßen genügend in dichte Sprühwolken gehüllte Fahrzeuge brausten.

> [The following day . . . I sat in the Hook of Holland express traveling through the German countryside, which has always been alien to me, straightened out and tidied up as it is to the last square inch and corner. Everything appeared to be appeased and numbed in some sinister way, and this sense of numbness soon came over me also. . . . As I looked out, it made me uneasy that not a soul was to be seen anywhere, though enough vehicles were speeding along the wet roads veiled in dense mists of spray. (*SG,* 276–77/*V,* 253–54)]

Transport technology streamlines not only the natural world but also the traveler's mental state; the clinically ordered landscape seen from the train carriage produces a sense of numbness in the spectator. Modern transport does not enable a greater intensity of experience; on the contrary, it shields the travelers from any contact with the outside world and indeed with each other, as is illustrated by the passengers on a London train, "die . . . mit blind bewegungslosen Augen auf die Vorhöfe der Metropole hinausstarrten" (who . . . were staring out at the desolate forecourts of the metropolis with fixed unseeing eyes; *SG,* 285/*V,* 260).

Time and again Sebald's texts highlight the dehumanizing effect of modern travel, which entraps the individual both physically and mentally. Looking out of the train window, the narrator of *Schwindel. Gefühle.* gets the impression "als habe unsere Art bereits einer anderen Platz gemacht oder als lebten wir doch zumindest in einer Form der Gefangenschaft" (as if mankind had already made way for another species, or at least was living in some form of captivity; *SG,* 277/*V,* 254; trans. modified). Here Sebald echoes Adorno's *Minima Moralia* (1951),[9] in which the American highway epitomizes an alienated, oblivious existence:

> Der Mangel der amerikanischen Landschaft ist nicht sowohl, wie die romantische Illusion es möchte, die Absenz historischer Erinnerungen, als daß in ihr die Hand keine Spur hinterlassen hat. Das bezieht sich . . . vor allem auf die Straßen. Diese sind allemal unvermittelt in die Landschaft gesprengt, und je glatter und breiter sie gelungen sind, um so beziehungsloser und gewalttätiger steht ihre schimmernde Bahn gegen die allzu wild verwachsene Umgebung. Sie tragen keinen Ausdruck. . . . Dem entspricht die Weise ihrer Wahrnehmung. Denn was das eilende Auge bloß im Auto gesehen hat, kann es nicht behalten, und es versinkt so spurlos, wie ihm selber die Spuren abgehen.

> [The shortcoming of the American landscape is not so much, as romantic illusion would have it, the absence of historical memories, as that it bears no traces of the human hand. This applies . . . above all to the roads. These are always inserted directly in the landscape, and the more impressively smooth and broad they are, the more unrelated and violent their gleaming track appears against its wild, overgrown surroundings. They are expressionless. . . . And it [the landscape] is perceived in a corresponding way. For what the hurrying eye has seen merely from the car it cannot retain, and the vanishing landscape leaves no more traces behind than it bears upon itself.][10]

Like the train passenger, the individual traveling on the highway is encased in an "armor" of technology that prevents any direct contact with the natural world. The sights encountered from the car cannot be mentally processed and hence do not leave a permanent trace in the viewer's mind. Indeed, this notion of the trace connects the mental and the physical aspects of traveling; when traveling by car or train, the traveler no longer leaves a direct trace in the landscape as the signature of an immediate, bodily encounter. In his critique of the American highway, Adorno thus implicitly gestures back to more traditional modes of travel, in particular to the journey on foot; while the roads cutting across the country emblematize man's supremacy over nature, the footprints that are gradually imprinted onto the landscape speak of a closer, non-dominating relationship with the natural world.

For Sebald, as for Adorno, then, traveling becomes a test case for the physical and psychological pitfalls of technological progress, and this realization in turn serves as the platform for alternative narrative practices. Sebald's narrators set themselves apart from the anaesthetized modern traveler. They usually travel alone and avoid fixed itineraries; destinations emerge as "a contingent by-product" of this form of traveling, "not its *telos*";[11] most importantly, the meandering nature of their travels is a reflection of an inner disposition. The *Aufmerksamkeit* of Sebald's travelers is "undisciplined" and unpredictable, and it readily tips over into absent-mindedness, fixation, or trance. This instability yields unexpected insights — moments of intense pleasure but also of profound sadness. Sebald's travelogues are journeys of the body as much as the mind, and in their meandering nature they chart the profound ambivalence of human attention — a faculty able to liberate but also to restrict. I will explore this ambiguity in two of Sebald's travelogues. Both *Schwindel. Gefühle.* and *Die Ringe des Saturn* are concerned with the interplay between attention and distraction and its impact on the traveler's experience, but they present this issue from rather different perspectives. While *Schwindel. Gefühle.* features moments of spellbinding intensity that disrupt habitual experience, in *Die Ringe des Saturn* such spontaneous attention is cast in a more negative light, as the mobility of this stance is increasingly subject to restrictions, both external and internal. In both texts Franz Kafka's (travel) writings act as a reference point, underlining the shifts as well as continuities in Sebald's discourse on attention.

Distractions and Diversions: "Der Jäger Gracchus"

Schwindel. Gefühle. is Sebald's first travelogue, a text whose clearly delineated four-part structure hides a complex network of recurring themes and allusions. The travels of the first-person narrator, which are described in sections 2 and 4, seem to follow an established narrative pattern: the journey into the unknown, "All'estero," is followed by the return home, "Il ritorno in patria." As is suggested by these Italian headings inserted into the German text, however, this process is less straightforward than it might at first seem; indeed, the distinction between home and away, between the familiar and foreign is continually blurred in Sebald's texts. The trip to Austria and Italy, though at times disorienting, is punctuated with uncanny moments of recognition,[12] while the journey to his home town leads the narrator into the alien and uncanny terrain of his childhood. Both "at home" and "abroad," the experience of traveling is shaped by the traveler's mental state, by moments of alertness or sudden distraction, which lead him in unexpected directions.

The associative nature of these travels is enforced by the narrative structure. The journeys of the first-person narrator are disrupted both temporally — by a gap of seven years that separates his two trips to Italy — and (inter)textually. The volume opens not with the narrator's own travels but with those of Henri Beyle, aka Stendhal, and the narrator's two trips to Italy and his subsequent visit to his childhood town W. are separated by the third chapter, "Dr. K.s Badereise nach Riva" (Dr. K. Takes the Waters at Riva), which reconstructs a journey undertaken by Franz Kafka. The travels of Sebald's narrator are connected to those of his literary predecessors both textually and psychologically and have to be read through the lens of their experiences. These connections take many forms; one such linking device is a travelogue which makes various ghostly appearances throughout *Schwindel. Gefühle.*, but which is only explicitly introduced in the third section: Kafka's fragment "Der Jäger Gracchus" (The Hunter Gracchus, 1917), which takes on a self-reflexive significance for Sebald's text. It tells the story of an uprooted traveler whose predicament chimes with that of Sebald's narrator; in particular, it foregrounds the precarious interplay between *Aufmerksamkeit* and *Unaufmerksamkeit* that has far-reaching consequences for Gracchus's journey and also for that of Sebald's narrator. These two stances do not have a fixed value in Kafka's texts but are explored in their dialectical interplay.

Kafka's Gracchus, who features in several loosely connected fragments, is an unconventional, archaic traveler. He journeys the world not by train or car but on the more somber vehicle of a death boat. This vessel was to convey the dead hunter to the underworld, but this clearly defined itinerary turns into a never-ending journey suspended between life and death. In Kafka's text, Gracchus's boat lays anchor in Riva, where he tells his story to the town's mayor. This story revolves around the thorny issue of attention, but attention is also thematized in the frame narrative depicting his arrival.

After Gracchus's death boat has arrived in the harbor, two men emerge carrying a bier "auf der unter einem großen blumengemusterten gefransten Seidentuch offenbar ein Mensch lag" (draped with a great tasselled cloth of flower-patterned silk, beneath which there evidently lay a man).[13] The detailed description of the silk cloth draws our attention to the burden that is hidden beneath. Curiously, however, this arrival does not spark any interest among the local men, women, and children, who are engaged in various mundane activities: "Auf dem Quai kümmerte sich niemand um die Ankömmlinge, selbst als sie die Bahre niederstellten, um auf den Bootsführer zu warten, der noch an den Seilen arbeitete, trat niemand heran, niemand richtete eine Frage an sie, niemand sah sie genauer an"

(Nobody on the quay troubled about the newcomers; even when they [the two men] lowered the bier to wait for the boatman, who was still busy with the ropes, nobody approached, nobody asked them a question, nobody gave them a closer look; *Gr*, 306/47). The four-fold repetition of "niemand" places particular emphasis on the indifference displayed by the inhabitants of Riva, which is at odds with the eerie scene unfolding in front of them.[14]

The people of Riva are, it seems, too wrapped up in their daily routines to be stirred up even by this strange arrival. Another character displays a very different behavior. The mayor, who has arrived to welcome the strange party, takes in his surroundings in great detail:

> Er blickte aufmerksam umher, alles bekümmerte ihn, der Anblick von Unrat in einem Winkel ließ ihn das Gesicht verzerren. Auf den Stufen des Denkmals lagen Obstschalen, er schob sie im Vorbeigehen mit seinem Stock hinunter.

> [He looked round attentively, everything disturbed him; the sight of some rubbish in a corner made him grimace, fruit skins were lying on the steps of the monument and he swept them off in passing with his cane. (*Gr*, 307/48; trans. modified)]

The mayor is attentive to his environment, but this does not prevent him from welcoming the new arrival; as Kafka's text implies, day-to-day attention is essential in preparing us for the encounter with the unusual, the uncanny or the exotic.

The opening, therefore, sets up a contrast between attention and indifference, and this opposition also recurs in Gracchus's story. Gracchus spent his life in the Black Forest, unwilling to explore unknown terrain,[15] and after his death is keen to complete his final journey without detours or diversions:

> Alles ging der Ordnung nach. Ich verfolgte, stürzte ab, verblutete in einer Schlucht, war tot und diese Barke sollte mich ins Jenseits tragen. Ich erinnere mich noch wie fröhlich ich mich hier auf der Pritsche ausstreckte zum erstenmal, niemals hatten die Berge solchen Gesang von mir gehört, wie diese vier damals noch dämmerigen Wände.

> [Everything happened in good order. I gave chase, I fell, I bled to death in a ravine, I was dead, and this bark was supposed to convey me to the next world. I can still remember how cheerfully I stretched myself out on this board for the first time; never had the mountains heard such song from me as was heard then by these four still shadowy walls. (*Gr*, 312/51)]

Gracchus, then, is a reluctant traveler, and his endless journey marks a sharp break with his previous existence: "so reise ich, der nur in seinen Bergen leben wollte, nach meinem Tode durch alle Länder der Erde" (So

I, who asked for nothing better than to live among my mountains, travel after my death through all the lands of the earth; *Gr*, 309/49). This changed situation does not, however, whet Gracchus's appetite for travel. Lying in his cabin, he takes in none of the sights passed by the vessel.[16] Despite his archaic mode of transport, Gracchus is the embodiment of the modern, efficient traveler who does not undertake his journey as an end in itself but views it as an intermediary stage on the way to his chosen destination. In this respect, he is reminiscent of those anaesthetized travelers who feature in Sebald's texts and whose irresponsiveness lends them an eerily lifeless character.[17]

The helmsman who is to take Gracchus to his destination is a very different traveler. While the hunter during his lifetime only had eyes for his prey, the helmsman is highly receptive to the beauty of the Black Forest — so receptive, as it turns out, that he gets distracted from his task and leads the ship off course.[18] As Gracchus explains:

> Mein Todeskahn verfehlte die Fahrt, eine falsche Drehung des Steuers, ein Augenblick der Unaufmerksamkeit des Führers, eine Ablenkung durch meine wunderschöne Heimat, ich weiß nicht, was es war, nur das weiß ich, daß ich auf der Erde blieb und daß mein Kahn seither die irdischen Gewässer befährt.

> [My death boat went off course; a wrong turn of the wheel, a moment's inattention on the part of the helmsman, the distraction of my beautiful native country, I cannot tell you what it was; I only know this, that I remained on earth and that ever since my boat has been sailing earthly waters. (*Gr*, 309/49; trans. modified)]

Just as the indifference of the Riva citizens contrasts with the attention of the mayor, a similar opposition underpins Gracchus's relationship to his helmsman. Here, however, the relationship between attention and inattention is more complex, for it is the helmsman's very receptiveness that makes him prone to "Unaufmerksamkeit." His case illustrates a more general psychological dynamic: attention is inextricably bound up with inattention, as the focus on one particular impression forecloses more general considerations. Within Kafka's story, this effect is given a distinctly negative slant by Gracchus, who blames the helmsman's distractible disposition for his own predicament. That said, the helmsman's slip can also be read in a different, more positive light. His mobile attention makes him receptive to the beauty of nature, yielding a moment of pleasure that counteracts the numbing effects of habit and routine.

If Gracchus is the embodiment of the modern, pragmatic traveler keen to arrive at his destination without detours or delays,[19] then his helmsman's disposition is, as we shall see, more akin to that of Sebald's narrators. His mental response is not predetermined by a fixed itinerary but leaves room for spontaneity. He is open to the beauty of nature — an experience increasingly eroded by modern life. Most importantly, however, his distraction disrupts a journey whose destination is not only fixed but definitive. At the heart of Kafka's narrative lies an epic struggle: against time, and therefore against death as the inevitable destination of our lives. The helmsman's absorption offers not just a momentary but a permanent escape from this teleology. As Alexander Honold notes, narrative is "an emergency break which postpones the arrival of the future: narrative is a means of gaining time."[20] The epitome of this postponement strategy is Scheherazade in the *Arabian Nights*, and Walter Benjamin draws an analogy between her stories and Kafka's: "In den Geschichten, die wir von ihm [Kafka] haben, gewinnt die Epik die Bedeutung wieder, die sie im Mund Scheherazades hat: das Kommende hinauszuschieben" (In the stories which Kafka left us, narrative art regains the significance it had in the mouth of Scheherazade: its ability to postpone the future).[21]

The helmsman's (in)attention in this way creates a diversion that in turn gives birth to Gracchus's story; thus, divertible attention lies at the heart of travel as well as narrative. This statement is as applicable to Kafka as it is to Sebald. One of the key features of his travelogues is their associative, meandering structure, which in turn requires a mobile alertness of the reader. However, Sebald's texts also display some of the same ambiguities that lie at the heart of Kafka's story. Gracchus's endless journey offers an escape from the teleology of death, but it also traps the travelers in limbo, giving rise to an endless journey. As I shall argue, Sebald's travelers experience a similar mixture of liberation and entrapment.

Schwindel. Gefühle.: Revelation and Displacement

The "Gracchus" story has many resonances within *Schwindel. Gefühle.*, not least regarding the traveler's mental disposition. The first-person narrator displays features of both Gracchus and his helmsman, as his mental stance oscillates between indifference and heightened sensitivity. He embarks on an extensive journey, from Austria to Italy and then back to Britain via Germany, yet he does not derive much pleasure from his travels, nor does he visit the conventional tourist sites. This lack of engagement is accompanied by a mental state verging on trance. At the start of the second section, "All'estero," the narrator spends ten days in Vienna, ceaselessly walking through the city without taking any interest in his surroundings: "Ich habe mir in den zirka zehn Tagen, die ich damals in Wien zugebracht habe, nichts angesehen, bin, außer in Kaffeehäuser und Gastwirtschaften, nirgends hineingegangen und habe, außer mit Kellnern und Serviererinnen, mit niemandem ein Wort gewechselt" (In the ten days or so that I spent in Vienna I visited none of the sights and spoke not a word to a soul except for waiters and waitresses; *SG*, 42/*V*, 36). The narrator's aimless wanderings are reminiscent of Gracchus, the reluctant traveler, who does not show an interest in the places he passes.

When in Venice, Sebald's narrator declares himself "von allen Sehenswürdigkeiten maßlos enttäuscht" (immeasurably disappointed by all the sights; *SG, 62/V,* 53–54; trans. modified) and, after a brief exploration of the city, remains in his hotel room for several days, lying on his bed almost motionless, "mit meinem teils immer weitere Kreise, teils immer engere Kreise ziehenden Nachdenken beschäftigt, und bisweilen auch umfangen von einer vollkommenen Leere" (preoccupied as I was with . . . the ever widening and contracting circles of my thoughts, and sporadically enveloped by a sense of utter emptiness; *SG, 74/V,* 65; trans. modified). As he becomes increasingly cold, the narrator begins to feel "wie ein Bestatteter oder doch zumindest wie ein Aufgebahrter" (as if I had already been interred or laid out for burial; *SG, 75/V,* 65), and he imagines travelling on a boat across the laguna.

The parallels between *Schwindel. Gefühle.* and Kafka's "Gracchus" fragment become even more pronounced in the final section, "Il ritorno in patria," which immediately follows the detailed recounting of Kafka's story at the end of the third part.[22] Here the narrator's journey ostensibly comes to an end as he visits the town of W. in the Bavarian Alps, where he had spent his early childhood. However, this topos of return indicated by the title is undermined on various levels. Even once the narrator has arrived in W., he is only tentatively rooted in the here and now; his narrative is shot through with reminiscences that divert his and the reader's attention, lending the text a vertiginous character. Whereas Gracchus leaves his *Heimat* for good, the narrator returns home; this home, however, is both familiar and strange in a way that prevents the experience of homecoming from providing a sense of narrative closure.

This already becomes clear on his journey to W. In Innsbruck the narrator boards a bus which is to take him across the border to the ominous-sounding destination of Schattenwald. The bus departs in the pouring rain, but then the weather suddenly changes:

> Die Sonne trat hervor, die ganze Landschaft erglänzte, die Tirolerinnen verstummten eine nach der anderen und schauten bloß noch hinaus auf das, was da draußen vorbeizog wie ein Wunder. Mir selber erging es ganz ähnlich. Die frisch gefirnißte Gegend . . ., die dampfenden Wälder, das blaue Himmelsgewölbe, es war für mich, der ich aus dem Süden heraufkam und die Tiroler Dunkelheit ein paar Stunden bloß hatte aushalten müssen, eine Offenbarung.

> [The sun came out, the entire landscape was radiant, and the Tyrolean women fell silent one after the other and simply looked out at the miracle passing by. I felt much the same myself. The countryside seemed freshly varnished . . . and the steaming forests and blue skies

above, though I had come up from the south and had had to endure the Tyrolean darkness for only a couple of hours, were like a revelation even to me. (*SG*, 191/*V*, 175)]

The sun lends the mountain scenery an epiphanic character, arresting the attention of the narrator and his fellow travelers. The intensity of this experience, which the narrator calls a "revelation," is owed in no small part to the mode of transport. Compared to the train journey and its anaesthetizing effect, the drive along the winding mountain road happens at a slower pace, offering a leisurely and continually changing view of the scenery. Once again, the mode of travel and the traveler's mental stance are closely linked. The narrator in particular is shaken out of his previous daze, but his attention does not fix on the present; rather, the panorama brings back memories of a childhood trip into this region, one made in an even less efficient vehicle:[23]

> An einer Wegkehre sah ich aus dem sich drehenden Autobus in die Tiefe hinunter und erblickte die dunkeltürkisgrünen Flächen des Fernstein-Sees und des Samaranger Sees, die mir schon in der Kindheit, als wir mit dem 170er Diesel des Schofförs Göhl den ersten Ausflug ins Tirol machten, wie der Inbegriff aller erdenklichen Schönheit vorgekommen waren.

> [At a hairpin bend I looked out of the turning bus down into the depths below and could see the dark turquoise green surfaces of the Fernstein and Samaranger lakes, which, even when I was a child, on our first excursions into the Tyrol, had seemed to me the essence of all conceivable beauty. (*SG*, 192–93/*V*, 176; trans. modified)]

Although these journeys are undertaken by bus or car rather than boat, the narrator's experience echoes that of the helmsman who is so captivated by Gracchus's *Heimat*, the equally mountainous Black Forest. This similarity even extends into linguistic details; the word "dunkeltürkisgrün" (dark turquoise green) used to characterize the Alpine lakes echoes Sebald's description of Gracchus's "wunderschöne dunkelgrüne Heimat" (the beauty of the huntsman's dark green country; *SG*, 180/*V*, 165), a color adjective that is not in fact used in Kafka's original story (*Gr*, 309/49). Its addition in Sebald's recounting of Kafka's story establishes a close link between the landscape as seen by the helmsman and the narrator's view of the Alps.[24] Both travelers, then, experience the beauty of nature from a perspective that has not been numbed by habit and indifference. In the case of the narrator, this sensitivity is that of the traveler returning home, but also that of the child who sees his surroundings with fresh eyes;[25] in Kafka's story, it is that of the helmsman, a traveler whose somber mission perhaps makes him all the more sensitive to the beauty that surrounds him. In both texts, then, the impression made by the beautiful landscape is heightened by a sense of distance, a lack of familiarity.[26] The helmsman responds to a *Heimat* that is really that of his passenger, whereas the scenery that unfolds beneath Sebald's narrator is situated abroad, across the Austrian border, and hence at a short but significant distance from his German home.

Even though Sebald's narrator, unlike Kafka's hapless helmsman, does not actually get lost as a result of his captivation, the theme of displacement nonetheless underpins this episode. Dwelling on the Alpine panorama, the narrator notices a dozen hens "mitten in einem grünen Feld, die sich, obschon es doch noch gar nicht lang zu regnen aufgehört hatte, ein für die winzigen weißen Tiere, wie mir schien, endloses Stück von dem Haus entfernt hatten, zu dem sie gehörten" (right out in the middle of a green field; even though it had only recently stopped raining, these tiny white animals were, it seemed to me, an endless distance away from the house to which they belonged; *SG*, 192/*V*, 175–76 and my translation).[27] The beautiful mountain scenery that so enraptured the narrator turns into a site of disorientation and loss, the backdrop for a journey into the unknown. In the text this journey is projected onto the animals, but the suddenly altered mood reflects the narrator's own sense of displacement with regard to his former *Heimat* and childhood, a feeling that grows stronger the nearer he gets to his former home town. At the same time, the shift from the Alpine panorama to the view of the hens at an "endless" distance from home is also reminiscent of Kafka's "Jäger Gracchus," where the spellbinding beauty of the Black Forest gives rise to an equally endless journey.

In this respect *Schwindel. Gefühle.* builds on the link between captivation and disorientation that underlies Kafka's story, suggesting that to be spellbound by natural beauty, and more specifically by the beautiful *Heimat*, can lead to a sense of alienation and displacement. The sight of the hens prefigures the narrator's own experience, for soon the mountain panorama gives way to a sense of claustrophobia. Having disembarked from the coach at the German border, he sets off to walk the remaining distance to W. through a gloomy forest shrouded in snow. Although he does not physically lose his way, he feels uneasy during his walk down into the forest, which is reminiscent of a walk through the underworld:

> In zunehmendem Maße verspürte ich ein Gefühl der Beklemmung in meiner Brust, und es war mir auch, als ob es, je weiter ich hinunterkam, desto kälter und finsterer werde.

> [Increasingly a sense of trepidation oppressed me, and it seemed as if the further down I walked, the colder and gloomier it became. (*SG*, 194/*V*, 178)]

However, it is only when he seeks refuge from the snow in a small chapel that this sense of disorientation becomes fully apparent:

Draußen vor dem winzigen Fenster trieben die Schneeflocken vorbei,
und bald kam es mir vor, als befände ich mich in einem Kahn auf der
Fahrt und überquerte ein großes Wasser. Der feuchte Kalkgeruch
verwandelte sich in Seeluft; ich spürte den Zug des Fahrtwindes an
der Stirn und das Schwanken des Bodens unter meinen Füßen und
überließ mich der Vorstellung einer Schiffsreise aus dem überschwemm-
ten Gebirge hinaus.

[Outside, snowflakes were drifting past the small window, and presently it seemed to me as if I were on a boat on a voyage, crossing vast
waters. The moist smell of lime became sea air; I could feel the spray
on my forehead and the boards swaying beneath my feet, and I imagined myself sailing in this ship out of the flooded mountains. (*SG*,
195/*V*, 179)]

As during the narrator's earlier stay in Venice, his journey merges with
that of Kafka's hunter, who is conveyed out of the Black Forest on his
bark. This intertextual reference offers an escape from the oppressive
present, but it also highlights the traveler's disempowerment, his sense of
being passively swept along. For the narrator, however, this sentiment is
associated not with distant countries but with home, the place of his childhood, which evokes the memories of mysterious events and uncanny
encounters.

Following the brief epiphany on the bus, then, the narrator descends
into a state of absent-mindedness; when he checks into the Engelwirt
hotel, where he had lived with his parents as a child, the receptionist scrutinizes him "mit unverhohlener Mißbilligung . . ., sei es wegen meiner von
der langen Wanderung in Mitleidenschaft gezogenen Erscheinung, sei es
wegen meiner ihr unerklärlichen Geistesabwesenheit" (with open disap-
proval, perhaps on account of my outward appearance, which was none the
better for my long walk, or because I betrayed an absent-mindedness that
must have been unaccountable to her; *SG*, 208/*V*, 191). This absent-
mindedness is to stay with the narrator during his stay in W. — a stay shot
through with memories and intermingled with literary references.[28] As in
Kafka's "Gracchus" story, then, *Heimat* is the true source of displacement,
a *Heimat* which, as the narrator remarks, was "weiter für mich in der
Fremde als jeder andere denkbare Ort" (more remote from me than any
other place I could conceive of; *SG*, 202/*V*, 185).

Die Ringe des Saturn: Evenly Suspended Attention

The exploration of attention and distraction as key components of the
travel experience is continued in *Die Ringe des Saturn*. Like his counterpart in *Schwindel. Gefühle.*, the narrator of Sebald's third prose text oscil-

lates between trance and alertness. Indeed, "Der Jäger Gracchus" recurs as an intertextual reference point, alongside another Kafka text that highlights the precarious role of attention.

The subtitle of the German original refers to a very particular type of journey. *Eine englische Wallfahrt* (An English pilgrimage) associates the narrator's travels with a particular religious tradition. Pilgrimages, visits to sites of religious importance, are "undertaken as a testament to religious devotion";[29] they are motivated by the belief that the sacred events of the past have left a trace that is still discernible in the present — an approach that closely resembles the intertwining of past and present in Sebald's texts, what Eric Santner calls their "spectral materialism."[30] This encounter with the past requires a particular mental state, a meditative stillness that shuts out the distractions of ordinary life.[31] Indeed, such contemplation is not only required upon arrival at the destination but is meant to inform the entire journey, for the walk, especially when physically challenging, is itself an act of devotion, as well as an opportunity for introspection and reflection.

Sebald's travelogue resembles the model of the pilgrimage but also diverges from it in important respects. His journey along the Suffolk coast harbors a spiritual dimension that is encapsulated not least in the text's illustrations. *Die Ringe des Saturn* contains many photographs of the sea recorded from the beach;[32] these images hint at "a space of emptiness or the unknown,"[33] thereby gesturing toward a crossing over from the material world into a transcendent realm.[34] These views offer moments of restful contemplation for the narrator as for the reader, but they are contained within a narrative that challenges this contemplative model.

Unlike pilgrims, "who set their hearts at reaching a destination," consciously resisting distractions or diversions,[35] the narrator pursues his walk along the Suffolk coast without a clear goal in mind. His meandering journey differs from the streamlined itineraries of modern travel, and this lack of a clear destination in turn reflects an unfocused inner disposition.[36] When the narrator gets lost in the heath of Dunwich, for instance, his disorientation is only partially caused by external factors such as the blank signposts that so disconcertingly line the paths. In fact, he enters the heath "in die unablässig in meinem Kopf sich drehenden Gedanken verloren und wie betäubt von dem wahnsinnigen Blühen" (lost in the thoughts that went round in my head incessantly, and numbed by this crazed flowering; *RS*, 204/171) and describes his growing confusion as the product of his "achtlosen Dahingehens" (careless walking; *RS*, 204).[37] The narrator's absent-mindedness reflects his subliminal resistance to predetermined routes;[38] however, this mental stance is not just liberating but also creates a sense of entrapment.

In various ways, then, Sebald's narrator recalls Gracchus's helmsman. His lack of focused attention leads him astray, but by doing so it also enables him to experience his surroundings in a new, intensified way. This intensity is not simply rooted in the here and now but draws links between the present and the past, between the locations visited and other times and places. Thus each section of his Suffolk walk gives rise to a lengthy excursus during which the main journey is interrupted in favor of temporally or spatially remote events. This narrative technique reflects a particular mental disposition — a form of mobile attention that is able to pick up on details that would often be overlooked by a more "focused" state of mind. In this respect, the meandering, digressive nature of the narrative reflects the protagonist's equally unstable mental state.[39]

At various points in the text the narrator succumbs to a state of trance, but while this can, as in the heath of Dunwich, lead to disorientation, it can also have an intensifying, productive effect. A TV documentary about the Irish revolutionary Roger Casement has a profound effect on the narrator, even though he is barely conscious:

> Obschon die Bilder dieses . . . Films mich sogleich in ihren Bann schlugen, bin ich in dem grünen Samtfauteil, den ich vor den Fernseher gerückt hatte, bald schon in einen tiefen Schlaf gesunken. Zwar hörte ich durch mein allmählich sich auflösendes Bewußtsein hindurch mit der größten Klarheit jedes der vom Erzähler der Geschichte Casements gesprochenen und, so war es mir vorgekommen, eigens für mich bestimmten Worte, aber verstehen konnte ich sie nicht.

> [The images in this film . . . immediately captivated me; but nonetheless, I fell asleep in the green velvet armchair I had pulled up to the television. As my waking consciousness ebbed away, I could still hear every word of the narrator's account of Casement with singular clarity, but was unable to grasp their meaning. (*RS*, 125–26/103)]

The narrator's almost hypnotic fascination gives way to sleep, and yet sleep does not undermine the lasting impression left by the program; indeed, this effect is skillfully reflected within the narrative, which initially abandons Casement's story in favor of Konrad Korzeniowski's (who later became known as Joseph Conrad), only to return to it at the end of the chapter.

The narrator's ability to keep listening even while asleep takes the affinity between *Aufmerksamkeit* and *Unaufmerksamkeit* to a new level. As in *Schwindel. Gefühle.*, moreover, this dynamic is underpinned by a reference to Kafka. As he falls asleep, Sebald's narrator thinks to himself: "Klappere, Mühle, klappere . . ., du klapperst nur für mich" (*RS*, 126; Clack away, little mill, clack away . . ., you're clacking just for me).[40] This cryptic remark links the experience of Sebald's traveling narrator to that of a literary predecessor, namely to K. in Kafka's *Das Schloß* (*The Castle*).[41] Toward the end of the novel, K. accidentally walks in on the secretary

Bürgel in the middle of the night. This encounter, the result of K.'s reduced alertness, has potentially life-changing implications for K. As Bürgel explains, when a secretary is stirred from his sleep and hence caught off guard, he will grant the visitor any wish, even if it violates existing regulations (*S, 422–23/239*).

This nocturnal encounter with Bürgel presents a unique opportunity for K., but just as this opportunity arises from a lack of alertness, it is lost for the same reason. Overcome by an overwhelming tiredness, K. cannot stay awake during the secretary's explanations; he falls asleep and in the end leaves Bürgel without having asked his wish. That said, K.'s is not an ordinary sleep, as it sharpens rather than numbs his awareness. In this state, "er hörte Bürgels Worte vielleicht besser als während des frühern totmüden Wachens, Wort für Wort schlug an sein Ohr, aber das lästige Bewußtsein war geschwunden, er fühlte sich frei" (he could hear Bürgel's words if anything better than before, when he had been awake but deadtired, word upon word struck his ear, but the burden of consciousness had disappeared, he felt free; *S, 415/235*). Here, the opposition between attention and inattention is transformed into a synthesis that combines a sharpened awareness with a sense of freedom from the constraints associated with more conventional, disciplinary forms of alertness. This is reflected in K.'s thought, "Klappere Mühle klappere . . ., du klapperst nur für mich" (*S, 419/237*), which treats Bürgel's words as a soothingly monotonous though still discernible background noise.

This carefree state is not, of course, without drawbacks. Neither K.'s free-floating attention nor the helmsman's redirected alertness yield concrete results for the characters; on the contrary, their response prolongs a (textual) journey which would otherwise have been concluded. In this respect, however, the (in)attention displayed by both characters is an essential plot device as it opens up new storylines or perspectives without curtailing the course of the narrative.

By citing K.'s dreamy remark in *Die Ringe des Saturn*, Sebald once again draws on Kafka's writings, importing this later and more openly dialectical model of (in)attention into his own travelogue. While in *Schwindel. Gefühle.* Gracchus and his helmsman embodied two conflicting stances — indifference versus a mobile, distractible attention — in *Die Ringe des Saturn* this balance appears to be tipped toward a trance that does not preclude continued awareness. Unlike for K., moreover, this approach yields tangible results for Sebald's narrator, whose interest in Casement's life is enforced, rather than curtailed, by his semi-conscious state. Although the next morning he has forgotten large parts of the program, individual details stand out all the more vividly,[42] motivating him to reconstruct Casement's story from various sources. In this respect the Casement episode illustrates a more general feature of Sebald's travelogues, whereby a conventionally linear storyline is replaced by a dream-like, associative narrative in which individual episodes stand out for their epiphanic clarity. The semi-detached state in which the narrator often encounters the world might preclude conventional concentration but enables him to unearth previously unnoticed details and connections.

In this respect, however, Sebald's approach is modeled not only on Kafka but also on another modernist writer concerned with attention and its ambiguities. The mixture of alertness and distraction displayed by both Sebald's and Kafka's protagonists is reminiscent of Freud's talking cure, a setup that is, like Kafka's Bürgel episode, based on a particular dynamic between narrator and listener. In "Ratschläge für den Arzt bei der psychoanalytischen Behandlung" (Recommendations to Physicians Practicing Psycho-Analysis, 1912), Freud argues that in order to be fully receptive to the patient's utterances, the analyst must not enter the cure with preconceived expectations: "folgt man bei der Auswahl seinen Erwartungen, so ist man in Gefahr, niemals etwas anderes zu finden, als was man bereits weiß" (if he follows his expectations he is in danger of never finding anything but what he already knows).[43] The only way out of this delimiting, self-perpetuating dynamic is to abandon any prior expectations, and therefore any form of directed alertness. Freud coins the term "gleichschwebende Aufmerksamkeit" (evenly-suspended attention; 377/112) to describe this stance, advocating a form of attention whose lack of deliberate focus borders on absent-mindedness.

Like Kafka, Freud is concerned with mental states that fruitfully undermine rigid distinctions between attention and inattention, and Sebald's traveling narrators put his model into practice. Thus *Die Ringe des Saturn* is full of chance discoveries that are made when the narrator is walking, watching, or reading.[44] In many cases the narrator does not look out for particular topics or pieces of information but is captivated by small, seemingly marginal details that give rise to lengthy explorations. Just as the narrator's interest in Roger Casement is first sparked by the TV documentary he watches while half asleep, he comes across a photographic history of the First World War while distractedly leafing through an old logbook in the Southwold Sailors' Reading Room (*RS*, 116/93–94). This discovery is followed by a second one; later in the same day the narrator is sitting alone in the restaurant of the Crown Hotel, listening to the hypnotic sound of an old grandfather clock:

> Der Perpendikel bewegte sich gleichmäßig hin und her, Ruck für Ruck ging der große Zeiger durch seine Runde, und ich fühlte mich eine Weile schon wie im ewigen Frieden, als ich, bei meiner eher achtlosen Durchsicht der Wochenendausgabe des *Independent* auf einen langen Artikel stieß, der in unmittelbarem Zusammenhang stand mit den Balkanbildern, die ich am Morgen im Reading Room angeschaut hatte.

[The cogwheels gripped, the pendulum swung from side to side, and
the big hand, bit by bit, in tiny jerks, went round. For some time I
had been feeling a sense of eternal peace when, leafing through the
Independent on Sunday, I came across an article that was related to
the Balkan pictures I had seen in the Reading Room that morning.
(*RS*, 119/96)]

As in the case of Casement, the events thus unearthed become the subject
of yet another narrative digression, which opens up the narrator's own
journey toward other times and places, or indeed into the realm of the
imagination. This digressive narrative structure is not without challenges.
Like Kafka's K., who is lulled into a semi-conscious state by Bürgel's
lengthy elaborations, Sebald's reader finds herself in a similar situation
when trying to follow the meandering and at times almost unnoticeable
turns of Sebald's texts. As his narratives switch between different places,
(sub-)plots, and contexts, they produce "a split attention, a kind of distraction in both the narrator and the reader."[45] Essential details are hidden in
lengthy excursi, requiring the reader to adopt a non-directed openness of
the kind which is also displayed by the protagonists.

The effect of this narrative technique is not necessarily a pleasant one
for either protagonist or reader. Indeed, the sense of disorientation that
can be induced by Sebald's digressions is aptly captured in a passage that
links *Die Ringe des Saturn* to an earlier travelogue. Before falling asleep in
his room at an inn in Woodbridge, the narrator feels "als läge ich in einer
Kajüte auf einem Schiff, als befänden wir uns auf hoher See, als höbe das
ganze Haus sich auf den Kamm einer Welle, als zitterte es dort ein wenig
und senkte sich dann mit einem Seufzer in die Tiefe hinab" (as if I were in
a cabin aboard a ship on the high seas, as if the whole building were rising
on the swell of a wave, shuddering a little on the crest, and then, with a
sigh, subsiding into the depths; *RS*, 247/208). This description takes us
back to Gracchus trapped on his boat, but also to the narrator of
Schwindel. Gefühle., who at various points feels similarly afloat. The recurrence of this boat image in *Die Ringe des Saturn* implies that this narrator
is no more in charge of his — physical as well as mental — journey than
his predecessors; he, too, is subject to chance discoveries and encounters,
but most importantly to his own (in)attention, which leads him from one
place to the next, and from the present into the past, without clear breaks
or transitions.

Contemplation: The Stalled Journey

Sebald's narrative, then, is as meandering as his protagonist's Suffolk walk.
Key discoveries are made in a state of absent-mindedness and are recounted
in a manner that produces a similar state in the reader. That said, while the

narrative structure is highly associative, the discoveries made by the narrator in his state of suspended (in)attention are remarkably similar in their mood and focus. Thus the Balkan photographs that the narrator comes across by chance at the Crown Hotel document the horrific genocide carried out by Croats in Bosnia during the Second World War with the approval of the Nazis, while Roger Casement's life, first encountered by the narrator while half asleep, ends with his execution for treason. To illustrate how Casement became the subject of a homophobic witch-hunt during his trial, Sebald reproduces an excerpt from his so-called *Black Diaries*, which chronicle Casement's homosexual encounters. The double page reproduced in *Die Ringe des Saturn* does not, however, detail the effects of sexual debauchery but describes symptoms that Casement developed as a result of dysentery. As J. J. Long has argued, the inclusion of this extract demonstrates the alignment of Sebald's narrator with "a medical-judicial apparatus";[46] what is more, it illustrates a more general pattern underlying the travelogue. Wherever he turns, the narrator finds examples of persecution, death, and destruction, even where the evidence does not fully support such narratives. Ultimately, then, his attention is less open and unpremeditated than stipulated by Freud, and his discoveries follow preexisting patterns and expectations.

The narrator reflects on this narrative *Wiederholungszwang* (repetition compulsion) at the beginning of the narrative. Looking back at his Suffolk journey, he remembers the underlying sense of freedom, remarking that "selten habe ich mich so ungebunden gefühlt wie damals bei dem stunden- und tagelangen Dahinwandern durch die teilweise nur spärlich besiedelten Landstriche hinter dem Ufer des Meers" (I have seldom felt so carefree as I did then, walking for hours in the day through the thinly populated countryside that stretches inland from the coast; *RS*, 11/3; trans. modified). The narrator's "Dahinwandern," his casual, non-directed walking, is the spatial equivalent of a mobile, wandering mind attracted by seemingly random details. As it turns out, however, this "schöne Freizügigkeit" (unaccustomed or, literally, beautiful sense of freedom) is curbed by a different sentiment, namely "das lähmende Grauen, das mich verschiedentlich überfallen hatte angesichts der selbst in dieser entlegenen Gegend bis weit in die Vergangenheit zurückgehenden Spuren der Zerstörung" (the paralyzing horror that had come over me at various times when confronted with the traces of destruction, reaching far back into the past, that were evident even in that remote place; *RS*, 11/3). Movement turns into (physical as well as mental) paralysis in the face of a destruction that the narrator sees wherever he turns. In the end the narrator finds himself in a hospital "in einem Zustand nahezu gänzlicher Unbeweglichkeit" (in a state of almost complete immobility; *RS*, 12/3). This physical state is the expression of a mental, as well as narrative, process whereby the spontaneous movement of his journey is stalled by a sense of uniformity and repetition.

This tendency is reflected in various encounters. One character who features prominently in the opening chapter is the narrator's late colleague, the French lecturer Janine Rosalind Dakyns, whose apparently chaotic research method mirrors the narrator's own explorations. The piles of paper covering her office form "eine richtige Papierlandschaft mit Bergen und Tälern" (a virtual paper landscape . . . with mountains and valleys; *RS*, 17/8), but Dakyns, a traveler in this landscape, does not get lost in its maze. Indeed, her focus on obscure details is by no means random; thus she points out to the narrator, "daß die scheinbare Unordnung in ihren Dingen in Wahrheit eine vollendete oder doch der Vollendung zustrebende Ordnung darstelle" (that the apparent chaos surrounding her represented in reality a perfect kind of order, or an order which at least tended towards perfection; *RS*, 19/9).

Janine Dakyns's eschewal of the obvious in favor of the obscure resembles the narrator's own outlook. Like her, he traces underlying patterns — the aforementioned "traces of destruction" (*RS*, 11/3) — which guide his attention. This capacity to impose order onto apparent chaos is a vital strategy of orientation, spatial as well as textual. The narrator, however, associates this skill with a particular emotional disposition; observing Dakyns in her office, "entweder vornübergebeugt kritzelnd . . . oder zurückgelehnt und in Gedanken verloren" (bent almost double scribbling on a pad on her knees or sometimes just lost in thought), he comments that she resembles "dem bewegungslos unter den Werkzeugen der Zerstörung verharrenden Engel der Dürerschen Melancholie" (the angel in Dürer's *Melancholia*, motionless among the instruments of destruction; *RS*, 18–19/9; trans. modified). Sebald's portrayal of Dakyns, like his text more generally, echoes Walter Benjamin's *Ursprung des deutschen Trauerspiels* (*The Origin of German Tragic Drama*, 1928), which explores the impact of melancholy on the individual's engagement with the world.[47] Benjamin's argument, like Sebald's narrative, revolves around a tension between mobility and stasis. On the one hand, he comments on "die Neigung des Melancholischen zu weiten Reisen" (the melancholic's inclination for long journeys),[48] a tendency also displayed by Sebald's protagonists, whose travels are often triggered by depression or crisis, by the urge to escape from an oppressive situation.[49] On the other hand, however, melancholy also produces a sense of rigidity, enabling the melancholic to focus in on particular objects with specific persistence (*UT*, 318/*OGD*, 139). As Benjamin argues, such objects are dissociated from their everyday context and turned into objects of contemplation, in a process that "rescues" them from pervading indifference and oblivion (*UT*, 334/*OGD*, 157).

This strategy of focalization informs Sebald's writing in *Die Ringe des Saturn* as elsewhere. Repeatedly the narrative "zooms in" on seemingly marginal topics, unearthing their history and significance. In this respect his texts do indeed have a preserving effect, in that their evocative descriptions anchor in our memory the objects, people, or stories thus explored. This engagement, however, has a second dimension. Benjamin describes melancholy as a "pathologische Verfassung" (pathological state; *UT*, 319/*OGD*, 140) whose pondering can take on excessive, (self-) destructive dimensions; ultimately, melancholy contemplation does not create new meaning but merely projects its emotional disposition onto the encountered world, thereby perpetuating "die Trostlosigkeit der irdischen Verfassung" (the hopelessness of the earthly condition; *UT*, 260/*OGD*, 81).

Benjamin's diagnosis has many resonances within *Die Ringe des Saturn*, whose very title casts this travelogue under the sign of Saturn, the planet traditionally associated with melancholy. Not only does the narrator display unmistakable signs of this disposition, but *Die Ringe des Saturn* contains its own etiology of melancholy as the result of an excessively focused, unwavering attention. In the final chapter the narrator traces the history of silk production. This story eventually leads him back to Norwich, the starting point of his journey, which in the eighteenth century became a center of European silk manufacturing, producing fabrics of breathtaking beauty. This, however, comes at a cost, for the concentration required of the silk weavers takes on excessive, pathological dimensions:

> Daß darum besonders die Weber und die mit ihnen in manchem ver-gleichbaren Gelehrten und sonstigen Schreiber, wie man in dem etwa zu jener Zeit in Deutschland veröffentlichten *Magazin für Erfahrungs-seelenkunde* nachlesen kann, zur Melancholie und zu allen aus ihr entspringenden Übeln neigten, das versteht sich bei einer Arbeit, die einen zwingt zu beständigem krummem Sitzen, zu andauernd schar-fem Nachdenken und zu endlosem Überrechnen weitläufiger künst-licher Muster. Man macht sich, glaube ich, nicht leicht einen Begriff davon, in welche Auswegslosigkeiten und Abgründe das ewige, auch am sogenannten Feierabend nicht aufhörende Nachsinnen, das bis in die Träume hineindringende Gefühl, den falschen Faden erwischt zu haben, einen bisweilen treiben kann.

> [That weavers in particular, together with scholars and writers with whom they had much in common, tended to suffer from melancholy and all the evils associated with it, is understandable given the nature of their work, which forces them to sit bent over, day after day, strain-ing to keep their eye on the complex patterns they created. It is dif-ficult to imagine the depths of despair into which those can be driven who, even after the end of the working day, are engrossed in their intricate designs and who are pursued, into their dreams, by the feel-ing that they have got hold of the wrong thread. (*RS*, 334–35/283)]

The affinities between weaving and similarly taxing intellectual activities such as writing and reflection connect this episode to the larger theme of attention. Weaving, a common metaphor for the process of writing, is particularly applicable to Sebald's texts, in which narrative threads are intertwined to form a densely woven fabric of images and motifs. In this respect the mental stance of the weavers reflects the disposition of Sebald's narrator. The mobile yet detailed attention needed to interlink apparently disparate episodes is reminiscent of, but ultimately exceeds, Freud's "gleichschwebende Aufmerksamkeit," which is designed precisely to prevent mental exhaustion.[50] The self-reflexive significance of the above passage for Sebald's narrative is underlined by its identificatory perspective — by the pronoun "einen," which tentatively includes the narrator among this afflicted group, and even more so by the inserted "glaube ich," through which the narrator turns the last sentence into a personal statement about the difficulties associated with the writing process.[51]

Melancholy, therefore, is a prominent theme in *Die Ringe des Saturn*, and its prominence manifests itself in the realm of attention, where mobile alertness increasingly gives way to rigid contemplation. The implications of this disposition are illustrated *ex negativo* by the text's subtitle, *Eine englische Wallfahrt*. Contemplation is a central aspect of religious devotion and pilgrimage; the pilgrim contemplates objects — such as religious images or relics — as a stepping stone toward the encounter with God. Melancholy contemplation, in contrast, lacks this transcendental horizon. Benjamin discerns the roots of this nihilism in the Lutheran doctrine of *sola gratia* — the emphasis on God's grace as the sole means of salvation, which in turn devalues human (good) deeds: "Jeder Wert war den menschlichen Handlungen genommen. Etwas Neues entstand: eine leere Welt" (Human actions were deprived of all value. Something new arose: an empty world; *UT*, 317/*OGD*, 138–39).

This notion of an empty world devoid of transcendental meaning resonates with Sebald's text. In the penultimate chapter the narrator recounts how during the great storm of 1987 he had gazed out of the window toward a neighboring park. Where there had previously been trees, all he could see now was "den fahlleuchtenden, leeren Horizont. . . . Es schien mir, als hätte jemand einen Vorhang beiseite gezogen und als starrte ich nun hinein in eine gestaltlose, in die Unterwelt übergehende Szene" (the paleness of the empty horizon. It seemed as if someone had pulled a curtain to one side to reveal a formless scene that bordered upon the underworld; *RS*, 316/266). In the cycle of destruction that is at the heart of Sebald's narrative, nature is both the victim of human greed and ignorance and a destructive force in its own right. What the narrator beholds with horror is a world that has lost any transcendental meaning and that has thereby become infernal. The sight of the horizon after the storm recalls the various images of the sea that are inserted into the narrative. As the above passage implies, these sights do not offer an outlook into another world but reflect a *horror vacui* at the sight of nature devoid of higher meaning.

The text contains one illustration, however, in which the horizon is not empty. Walking along the cliffs of Covehithe, the narrator is struck by an uncanny sight: "Draußen auf dem bleifarbenen Meer begleitete mich ein Segelboot, genauer gesagt schien es mir, als stünde es still und als käme ich selber, Schritt für Schritt, so wenig vom Fleck wie der unsichtbare Geisterfahrer mit seiner bewegungslosen Barke" (Out on the leaden-colored sea a sailing boat kept me company, or rather, it seemed to me as if it were motionless and I myself, step by step, were making as little progress as that invisible spirit aboard his unmoving barque; *RS*, 84/65–66). This description of the motionless boat, which is accompanied by a photographic illustration, acts as yet another reference to the unredeemed traveler Gracchus, who haunts *Schwindel. Gefühle*. While in Kafka's text the boat is an (all too) mobile vehicle that can be taken off course even by a momentary distracted attention, in *Die Ringe des Saturn* this risk is allayed; here the vessel is no longer the vehicle of a mobile, endlessly meandering narrative but embodies the sense of stasis and repetition that counteracts the narrator's (mental) movements.[52]

Highlighting the importance of tracing the shifts and developments within Sebald's work, Richard Sheppard describes one crucial difference between the earlier and the later texts. When writing *Schwindel. Gefühle.*, Sebald was, as he argues, "still open to epiphanic moments and the possibility that chance events might be moments of significant revelation";[53] sights such as the beautiful Alpine landscape, which the narrator of *Schwindel. Gefühle.* views from the bus, and which he describes as "eine Offenbarung" underline this essential openness to experiences that disrupt the veil of *Gewohnheit*. In later texts such as *Die Ringe des Saturn*, however, this receptivity is increasingly foreclosed. Although the narrative's digressive structure contains vestiges of the earlier, spontaneous form of attention, its underlying melancholy curbs any genuine moments of epiphany.

The difference between Sebald's two travelogues is nowhere more apparent than in the closing section of *Die Ringe des Saturn*, which replays a core scene from Sebald's earlier text:

> Thomas Browne . . . vermerkt an irgendeiner, von mir nicht mehr auffindbaren Stelle seiner Schrift *Pseudodoxia Epidemica*, in Holland sei es zu seiner Zeit Sitte gewesen, im Hause eines Verstorbenen alle Spiegel und alle Bilder, auf denen Landschaften, Menschen oder die Früchte der Felder zu sehen waren, mit seidenem Trauerflor zu verhängen, damit nicht die den Körper verlassende Seele auf ihrer letzten Reise abgelenkt würde, sei es durch ihren eigenen Anblick, sei es durch den ihrer bald auf immer verlorenen Heimat.

> [Sir Thomas Browne . . . remarks in a passage in the *Pseudodoxia Epidemica* that I can no longer find that in the Holland of his time it was customary, in a home where there had been a death, to drape

black mourning ribbons over all the mirrors and all canvasses depicting landscapes or people or the fruits of the field, so that the soul, as it left the body, would not be distracted on its final journey, either by a reflection of itself or by a last glimpse of the land now being lost for ever. (*RS*, 350/296)]

As befits the (quasi-)religious framework of his "English Pilgrimage," Sebald closes his travelogue with the one journey that must be undertaken even by the most reluctant traveler. In Thomas Browne's account of Dutch mourning rituals, the journey from life to death unfolds without the diversions that turn Gracchus's boat off course. Significantly, however, the diversions that are counteracted in Browne's Holland are the same ones that lead Gracchus astray. While both his helmsman and Sebald's earlier narrator are spellbound by the sight of a beautiful *Heimat*, the Dutch mourning ribbons, cast over pictures and mirrors, dull their beauty until it no longer offers a temptation for the meandering attention of the departing soul. Ultimately, of course, the Dutch practice is not aimed at the dead but at the living; it ensures that during times of mourning they remain focused on the commemoration of the dead and on their own impending fate.

Sebald's texts emulate this practice in their melancholy focus on suffering and destruction, enacting what could be described as a literary mourning ritual. Yet while in Browne's Holland the ribbons covering the beauty of landscapes and of nature more generally are a temporary measure designed to foster inward-looking contemplation, this melancholy veil becomes an increasingly prominent and near-permanent feature in Sebald's literary oeuvre. This is nowhere more apparent than in relation to the beauty of nature, and in particular to the beauty of *Heimat*. In *Schwindel. Gefühle.*, beauty can still be experienced, albeit only in a momentary and displaced manner. Thus the beautiful panorama that unfolds beneath the narrator on his bus journey through Austria gives way to a more hostile environment as soon as he has arrived in his native Germany. The Black Forest that so spellbinds Kafka's helmsman, in contrast, is a German landscape, yet it is only with the — albeit extended — words of his Austro-Jewish predecessor that Sebald's narrator can describe this scene as a "wunderschöne dunkelgrüne Heimat" (the beauty of the huntsman's dark green country; *SG*, 180/*V*, 165). In later texts such moments become increasingly rare, to the point where in *Luftkrieg und Literatur* the picture of a blossoming Bavarian meadow is rejected as inauthentic by Sebald, who stresses that only images of bombed German cities produce a "Heimatgefühl" (a feeling of being at home; *LL*, 78/*NH*, 71; trans. modified) in him.

Ultimately, then, it would appear that it is Gracchus — a character content to leave his *Heimat* behind, indifferent to its beauty — who is the true model of Sebald's travelers. Then again, Gracchus's eagerness to cross the threshold between life and death is only partially shared by them. Although Sebald's texts are melancholically and at times almost obsessively drawn to traces of suffering and destruction, they also betray a sense of horror in response to these findings — and to the sense of uniformity and repetition that stalls the narrative. In this respect, the Dutch mourning rituals described by Browne act as both a parable of Sebald's travelogues and a warning example. By seeing the world through a gaze veiled by melancholy, the narrators, particularly of his later works, foreclose the insights and narrative openings facilitated by a more mobile, unpremeditated attention. Ultimately, then, it is their capacity to be spellbound and diverted by unexpected encounters that anchors Sebald's travelers in the here and now, preventing their "Dahinwandern" from turning into a rigid journey toward death.

Notes

¹ Psychological theories have repeatedly focused on this issue. For Sigmund Freud, for instance, one of the primary tasks of the psychological apparatus is to avert external stimuli: "Für den lebenden Organismus ist der Reizschutz eine beinahe wichtigere Aufgabe als die Reizaufnahme" (for the living organism, the process *protecting* it against stimuli is almost more important than the process whereby it *receives* stimuli). Sigmund Freud, "Jenseits des Lustprinzips," in *Gesammelte Werke*, ed. Anna Freud et al., vol. 13 (1952–68; repr., Frankfurt am Main: Fischer, 1999), 1–69; here 27; in English, "Beyond the Pleasure Principle," in *Beyond the Pleasure Principle and Other Writings*, trans. John Reddick (London: Penguin, 2003), 43–102; here 66.
² "Seine Arbeit ist gegen Erfahrung abgedichtet" (His work has been sealed off from experience). Walter Benjamin, "Über einige Motive bei Baudelaire," in *Gesammelte Schriften*, ed. Rolf Tiedemann and Hermann Schweppenhäuser, vol. 1 (Frankfurt am Main: Suhrkamp, 1991), 605–53; here 632; in English, "On Some Motifs in Baudelaire," in *Selected Writings, Vol. 4: 1938–1940,* ed. Howard Eiland and Michael W. Jennings, trans. Edmund Jephcott and others (Cambridge, MA: Belknap Press, 2003), 314–55; here 329.
³ Max Horkheimer and Theodor W. Adorno, "Kulturindustrie: Aufklärung als Massenbetrug," in *Dialektik der Aufklärung: Philosophische Fragmente* (Frankfurt am Main: Suhrkamp, 1997), 140–91; in English, "The Culture Industry: Enlightenment as Mass Deception," in *Dialectic of Enlightenment;* trans. John Cumming (London: Verso, 1979), 120–67.
⁴ Thomas Mann, *Der Zauberberg: Roman*, ed. Michael Neumann (Frankfurt am Main: Fischer, 2002), 159; in English, *The Magic Mountain*, trans. H. T. Lowe-Porter (London: Vintage, 1999), 101; trans. modified.
⁵ Mann, *Zauberberg*, 162; *Magic Mountain*, 104; trans. modified.

[6] J. J. Long describes maps such as the ordnance survey map reprinted in Sebald's *Die Ringe des Saturn* as instruments of power, disciplinary tools designed to homogenize space and stabilize (capitalist) power relations. Long, *W. G. Sebald: Image, Archive, Modernity* (New York: Columbia UP, 2007), 130–32.

[7] Wolfgang Schivelbusch, *The Railway Journey: The Industrialization of Time and Space in the 19th Century* (Berkeley and Los Angeles, CA: U of California P, 1986), 124.

[8] As Mann's narrator argues, the life of the traveler can quickly become a routine in its own right. Mann, *Zauberberg*, 160–61; *Magic Mountain*, 102.

[9] On Sebald's reception of *Minima Moralia* and his correspondence with Adorno, see Marcel Atze and Sven Mayer "'Unsere Korrespondenz': Zum Briefwechsel zwischen W. G. Sebald und Theodor W. Adorno," in *Sebald: Lektüren,* ed. Marcel Atze and Franz Loquai (Eggingen, Germany: Edition Isele, 2005), 17–38.

[10] Theodor W. Adorno, *Minima Moralia: Reflexionen aus dem beschädigten Leben*, in *Gesammelte Schriften*, vol. 4, ed. Rolf Tiedemann (Frankfurt am Main: Suhrkamp, 1997), 53–54; in English, *Minima Moralia: Reflections from Damaged Life*, trans. by E. F. N. Jephcott (London: Verso, 1974), 48.

[11] Long, *Image, Archive, Modernity*, 136.

[12] John Zilcosky singles out the inability of Sebald's narrators to get lost, that is, to escape from an uncanny network of familiar sites, details, and memories, as one of the defining features of his travelogues. Zilcosky, "Sebald's Uncanny Travels: The Impossibility of Getting Lost," in *W. G. Sebald: A Critical Companion,* ed. J. J. Long and Anne Whitehead (Edinburgh: Edinburgh UP, 2004), 102–20.

[13] Franz Kafka, *Nachgelassene Schriften und Fragmente I,* ed. Malcolm Pasley (Frankfurt am Main: Fischer, 2002), 306; and "The Hunter Gracchus: Four Fragments," in *The Great Wall of China and Other Short Works,* trans. and ed. Malcolm Pasley (London: Penguin, 2002), 47–55; here 47. Further references to the German and English editions of this text are cited in the text using the abbreviation *Gr* and page numbers.

[14] In Sebald's edition of the "Gracchus" story this passage is both underlined and highlighted in the margins.

[15] As it turns out, however, this *Heimat* is not an entirely self-contained space. Gracchus dies pursuing a chamois, an Alpine animal not native to the Black Forest. While this detail might have simply been a slip on Kafka's part, it is more likely to be a deliberate incongruity. This non-native animal marks the intrusion of the unknown into the hunter's world; its pursuit in turn leads to the hunter's death and turns him into a traveler.

[16] Gracchus lies motionless in his cabin, but on the cabin wall facing him is the picture of a bushman pointing a spear at him (*Gr,* 312/51). Following the non-native chamois, this image is yet another example of the foreign and exotic intruding into the hunter's surroundings.

[17] Nineteenth-century commentators in particular picked up on the passenger's objectification as a result of train travel; thus Marx argues that railroad travel assimilated the traveler into a "system for moving goods," while John Ruskin

remarks that the train passenger is treated like a "living parcel." Schivelbusch, *The Railway Journey*, xiv and 54.

[18] Martin Klebes, in his otherwise insightful cross-readings of Kafka and Sebald, fails to pick up on this crucial aspect of the story, claiming that the helmsman takes the wrong turn "for an unknown reason." Klebes, "Infinite Journey: From Kafka to Sebald," in Long and Whitehead, *A Critical Companion*, 124.

[19] Despite this drive, however, Gracchus's own concentration is by no means flawless. He falls to his death ignoring the perils of the mountains when chasing the chamois. While the helmsman is excessively alert to his surroundings, causing him to lose sight of his destination, the hunter in turn falls to his death because he is too fixated on his goal at the expense of his immediate context.

[20] Alexander Honold, "Erzählen," in *Benjamins Begriffe*, ed. Martin Opitz and Erdmut Wizisla (Frankfurt am Main: Suhrkamp, 2000), 363–98; here 386.

[21] Walter Benjamin, "Franz Kafka: Zur zehnten Wiederkehr seines Todestages," in *Gesammelte Schriften*, ed. Rolf Tiedemann and Hermann Schweppenhäuser (Frankfurt am Main: Suhrkamp, 1991), 2:410–38; here 427; in English, "Franz Kafka: On the Tenth Anniversary of His Death," in *Selected Writings, Volume 2*, ed. Michael W. Jennings, Howard Eiland, and Gary Smith, trans. Rodney Livingstone and others (Cambridge, MA: Belknap, 1999), 794–818; here 807.

[22] To enforce the impact of Kafka's story, which is recounted with subtle alterations, this passage is accompanied by a grainy photograph of a sailing ship, whose sinister appearance is, as Jo Catling argues, "suggestive . . . of the fateful vessel in Murnau's *Nosferatu*." Catling, "Gratwanderungen bis an den Rand der Natur: W. G. Sebald's Landscapes of Memory," in *The Anatomist of Melancholy: Essays in Memory of W. G. Sebald*, ed. Rüdiger Görner (Munich: iudicium, 2003), 19–50; here 39.

[23] As Mark R. McCulloh points out, the outmoded character of the "170er Diesel" used for the childhood trip highlights the transience of human inventions, memory, and experience, which contrasts with the enduring beauty of nature. McCulloh, "Destruction and Transcendence in W. G. Sebald," *Philosophy and Literature*, 30.2 (2006): 395–409; here 396.

[24] Moreover, the term "wunderschön" is taken up again in the landscape's "Schönheit" as it was experienced by the child.

[25] The intensity with which the narrator experiences this panorama is anticipated by his view of a waterfall, which appears to him in a "schleierhafte Zeitlupenhaftigkeit" (mysterious slow motion quality; *SG*, 192/*V*, 176).

[26] As Jo Catling points out, those landscapes that are dreamed or remembered are often more vivid than those in which Sebald's narrators find themselves in the present. Catling, "Gratwanderungen," 30.

[27] Only the first part of this sentence, up to "field," is included in the English translation.

[28] Kafka is once again evoked in the scene of the narrator's arrival in W.; standing on the bridge that leads into the town, he listened to the sound of the river "und schaute in die nun alles umgebende Finsternis hinein" (looking into the blackness which now enveloped everything; *SG*, 200/*V*, 183), a scenario that echoes the

opening lines of Kafka's last novel, *Das Schloß* (*The Castle*, 1922), where K. is likewise standing on a bridge "die von der Landstraße zum Dorf führt und blickte in die scheinbare Leere empor" (that led from the main road to the village, gazing up into the seeming emptiness). Kafka, *Das Schloß*, ed. Malcolm Pasley (Frankfurt am Main: Fischer, 2002), 7; in English, *The Castle*, trans. Idris Parry (London: Penguin, 2000), 3.

[29] Christina Kraenzle, "Picturing Place: Travel, Photography, and Imaginative Geography in W. G. Sebald's *Rings of Saturn*," in *Searching for Sebald: Photography after W. G. Sebald*, ed. Lise Patt with Christel Dillbohner (Los Angeles: The Institute of Cultural Inquiry, 2007), 126–45; here 126.

[30] Eric Santner, *On Creaturely Life: Rilke — Benjamin — Sebald* (Chicago: U of Chicago P, 2006), 57. As J. J. Long rightly points out, however, Santner's term, which refers to the persistence of past *suffering* in the present, is "too narrow a definition of the presence of the past" in Sebald's texts and should be extended to include other, non-traumatic, events and experiences. Long, *Image, Archive, Modernity*, 147n16.

[31] Rebecca Solnit describes the pilgrimage as a liminal state "outside the established order, . . . a state of possibility" disconnected from normative social structures. Solnit, *Wanderlust: A History of Walking* (London: Verso, 2001), 51.

[32] Cf. *RS*, 59, 67, 89, 187/44, 51, 69, 155.

[33] Kraenzle, "Picturing Place," 142.

[34] As the exhibition at the Literaturarchiv in Marbach has shown, Sebald collected pictures of water — of lakes and oceans that are often but not always depicted as seen from the land. See the section "Wasser" in the exhibition catalogue *Wandernde Schatten: W. G. Sebalds Unterwelt*, ed. Ulrich von Bülow, Heike Gfrereis, and Ellen Strittmatter (Marbach: Deutsche Schillergesellschaft, 2008) [no page numbers].

[35] Derek Tidball, "The Pilgrim and the Tourist: Zygmunt Baumann and Postmodern Identity," in *Explorations in a Christian Theology of Pilgrimage*, ed. Craig Bartholomew and Fred Hughes (Aldershot, UK: Ashgate, 2004), 184–200; here 191.

[36] In this respect the narrator's meandering journey bears a certain resemblance to what Zygmunt Baumann describes as the characteristics of the tourist, whom he regards as an embodiment of the postmodern condition. These include a reluctance to put down roots or make any fixed commitments; "the point of the tourist life is to be on the move, not to arrive." Cited in Tidball, "Pilgrim," 188.

[37] This phrase is not included in the English translation.

[38] As he comments, "Folgte man seinem Instinkt, dann stellte es sich über kurz oder lang unweigerlich heraus, daß der Weg von dem Ziel, auf das man zuhalten wollte, immer weiter abwich" (If one obeyed one's instincts, the path would sooner or later diverge further and further from the goal one was aiming to reach; *RS*, 205/172).

[39] Long describes Sebald's narrative technique in *Die Ringe des Saturn* as a "poetics of digression." Long, *Image, Archive, Modernity*, 137.

[40] My translation. This sentence is not included in the English edition.

[41] *Das Schloß* is a recurring reference point particularly in Sebald's academic writings; indeed, Kafka's novel is the subject of his very first article, "Thanatos: Zur Motivstruktur in Kafka's *Schloss*," *Literatur und Kritik* 66/67 (1972): 399–411.

[42] Thus he remembers verbatim a description of Casement setting off into the jungle and a second, equally detailed passage about him emerging again from the wilderness a few months later, "so unbeschadet, als kehrte er gerade von einem Nachmittagsspaziergang im Hyde Park zurück" (quietly serene as if he had been for a stroll in the park; *RS*, 126/104).

[43] Sigmund Freud, "Ratschläge für den Arzt bei der psychoanalytischen Behandlung," in *Gesammelte Werke*, ed. Anna Freud et al., vol. 8 (Frankfurt am Main: Fischer, 1999), 375–87: here 377; in English, "Recommendations to Physicians Practicing Psycho-Analysis," in *The Standard Edition of the Complete Psychological Works of Sigmund Freud*, vol. 12, ed. and trans. James Strachey (London: Hogarth, 1958), 109–20; here 112.

[44] Indeed, the two are closely connected: walking in Sebald's text "leads to reading, as all experience becomes freighted with intertwined significances that invite interpretation. Reading, likewise, becomes for Sebald a kind of walking, a wandering into the thicket of writing." John Beck, "Reading Room: Erosion and Sedimentation in Sebald's Suffolk," in Long and Whitehead, *A Critical Companion*, 75–88; here 78.

[45] Long, *Image, Archive, Modernity*, 140.

[46] Long, *Image, Archive, Modernity*, 75.

[47] As Richard Sheppard argues, Sebald's "increasingly dark view of the present, his growing, self-confessed disposition to melancholy . . . was almost certainly reinforced by his reading of Benjamin's book on baroque tragedy." Sheppard, "Dexter–sinister: Some Observations on Decrypting the Mors Code in the Work of W. G. Sebald," *Journal of European Studies* 35 (2005): 419–63; here 425.

[48] Walter Benjamin, *Ursprung des deutschen Trauerspiels*, in *Gesammelte Schriften* 1:203–330; here 326; in English, *The Origin of German Tragic Drama*, trans. John Osborne (London: Verso, 2003), 149. Further references to the German and English editions of Benjamin's text are cited in the text using the abbreviations *UT* (German) and *OGD* (English) and page numbers.

[49] This desire motivates the narrator's travels in *Schwindel. Gefühle.*, *Die Ringe des Saturn*, and *Austerlitz*, and also underpins the movements of various minor characters. As Sebald's texts demonstrate, travel is both a symptom of melancholia and a potential remedy; while it can lead to numbness and trance, it can also yield sudden insights as a result of a heightened sensitivity.

[50] As Freud notes, "Man erspart sich auf diese Weise eine Anstrengung der Aufmerksamkeit, die man doch nicht durch viele Stunden täglich festhalten könnte" (In this way we spare ourselves a strain in our attention which could not in any case be kept up for several hours daily; Freud, "Ratschläge," 377/"Recommendations," 112).

[51] The autobiographical resonances of this passage are underlined by Richard Sheppard, Sebald's former colleague at the University of East Anglia, who writes

that "the more Max [Sebald's nickname] wrote and the more successful he became as a writer, the more demands the act of writing made on his imaginative resources and physical well-being" (Sheppard, "Dexter–sinister," 424).

[52] The difference between the Gracchus motif in the two texts is underlined by the two illustrations. *Schwindel. Gefühle.* contains a grainy photo of a sailing boat recorded at mid-distance, its shady outline cropped by the frame (*SG,* 178/*V,* 163) — a perspective that lends the vessel a sense of dynamism and uncontainability. In *Die Ringe des Saturn,* in contrast, the vessel is one of many images of the sea; although here the horizon is not empty, the ship is visible only in the far distance, doubly separated from the observer by the vegetation in the foreground and the sea beyond (*RS,* 84/65).

[53] Sheppard, "Dexter–sinister," 424.

II: Textual Excursions, Expeditions, and Adventures

4: If You Come to a Spa: Displacing the Cure in *Schwindel. Gefühle.* and *Austerlitz*

Martin Klebes

IT WOULD SEEM TO BE A less than controversial assumption that the impetus for spa travel should first and foremost be provided by the recuperative function — anticipated or achieved, real or imagined — of the movement it involves across geographic space and in leisure time. Those who are ill, it might thus be surmised, are prompted to go the distance in order to seek relief or even permanent cure for their affliction, while those who are still healthy — at least for the moment — presumably travel to take the waters in pursuit of preventive care or the mere enjoyment of physical well-being in a pleasant environment.[1] As cultural historians have demonstrated, however, many aspects of the immense popularity of spas among members of the higher social strata from the late eighteenth through the twentieth century were at considerable remove from medical considerations of this sort. In fact, political deal-making, social and sexual adventure afforded through anonymity, gambling, and exotic shopping opportunities all became defining parts of the spa experience, bearing little direct relation to any notion of restoring or maintaining bodily health.[2]

The two Sebaldian protagonists whose spa travels I will be examining here — Dr. K. in "Dr. K.s Badereise nach Riva" (Dr. K. Takes the Waters at Riva), the third part of *Schwindel. Gefühle.* (published in English under the title *Vertigo*), and the character Austerlitz in the book of the same name — could be said to be part of this counter-history insofar as the narratives of their respective sojourns at Riva and Marienbad each recount something other than their outright return to health, and show little evidence that either patient so much as believes in the possibility of such recuperation. Dr. K., Sebald's narrator relates, seeks the utmost possible silence "zwischen den verschiedenen kalten Gußbädern und der ihm verordneten elektrischen Behandlung" (in the intervals between the various cold douches and electrical treatments prescribed for him; *SG,* 170–71/*V,* 155) in order to banish the thought of his troubled relationship with Felice. Even though he does submit to the therapeutic routine of the well-regarded institution directed by Dr. Christoph von Hartungen, the precise nature of his case history ("Krankengeschichte") remains undisclosed, referenced in the narrative only as a fitting subject of conversation with the young Swiss girl. Likewise, the end — if such it can be called — of his stay at Riva is marked, not by any comment on the effectiveness of the treatment Dr. K. received there, but by the succession of the girl's departure, the suicide and subsequent funeral of his dining companion, and the eventual arrival — visual and textual — of the barque of the hunter Gracchus, one of the main intertexts of this part of Sebald's book, as well as of the book as a whole.[3]

Austerlitz's travel to Marienbad with his companion Marie de Verneuil in August of 1972 is prompted by her research interest in its architectural history, as well as what Austerlitz in retrospect identifies as her attempt, "mich aus meiner Vereinzelung zu befreien" (to liberate me from my self-inflicted isolation; *A*, 298/206) — a project that does not appear to come to fruition. Appropriately, the therapeutic benefits of Marienbad appear only as a historiographical quotation, delivered by Marie in a "mit dem ihr eigenen Sinn für alles Komische überzogene . . . medizinisch-diagnostische Wortkoloratur" (verbal coloratura of medical and diagnostic terms, with her strong sense of everything comical; *A*, 303/210) as she details that the spa treatments were historically considered effective

> bei der in der Bürgerklasse damals weit verbreiteten Fettleibigkeit, bei Unreinigkeiten des Magens, Trägheit des Darmkanals und anderen Stockungen des Unterleibs, bei Unregelmäßigkeiten der Menstruation, Verhärtungen der Leber, Störungen der Gallenabsonderung, gichtischen Leiden, Milzhypochondrie, Krankheiten der Nieren, Blase und der Urinwerkzeuge, Drüsengeschwüren und Verformungen skrofulöser Art, aber auch bei Schwächen des Nerven- und Muskelsystems, Abspannung, Zittern der Glieder, Lähmungen, Schleim- und Blutflüssen, langwierigen Hautausschlägen und beinahe jeder anderen nur denkbaren krankhaften Affektion.[4]

> [for curing the obesity then so common among the middle classes, as well as digestive disturbances, sluggishness of the intestinal canal and other stoppages of the lower abdomen, irregular menstruation, cirrhosis of the liver, disorders of bile secretion, gout, hypochondriacal spleen, diseases of the kidneys, the bladder, and the urinary system, glandular swellings and scrofulous deformities, not to mention weakness of the nervous and muscular systems, fatigue, trembling of the limbs, paralysis, mucous and bloody fluxes, persistent eruptions of the skin, and practically every other medical disorder known to the human race. (*A*, 303–4/210, trans. modified)]

She follows up this comical interlude with the comment that it evokes images of the sort of paradoxical culinary indulgences that testify to the manifest disconnect — routinely borne out by the historical record —

between the medical and social dimensions of the spa experience. It is not until Marie has thus evoked the cultural history of Marienbad, designating it as a sphere evidently at cross-purposes with itself, that Austerlitz, "paradoxically," begins to think "daß auch ich, nicht anders als die vor hundert Jahren in Marienbad sich aufhaltenden Gäste, von einer schleichenden Krankheit befallen war, ein Gedanke, der sich verband mit der Hoffnung, ich stünde nun am Beginn meiner Genesung" (that I myself, like the guests staying at Marienbad a hundred years ago, had contracted an insidious illness, and together with that idea came the hope that I was now beginning to be cured; *A*, 304/211). The stay at Marienbad, in other words, is not intended to address a preexisting condition but is capable of producing, in Austerlitz's imagination, both the (undiagnosed) symptom and the hope for its cure at the same time. The indication of the "insidious illness" — as it will occur to Austerlitz only after Vera Ryšanová tells him of the Marienbad vacation of 1938 of which Austerlitz, then four years old, does not have any recollection — consists in the unrecognized but palpable after-effects that the disappearance of his parents exercises on Austerlitz.[5] The "bessere Wendung" (better turn; *A*, 298/206) that Austerlitz's life might be said to take in the wake of the return to Marienbad — which is, in and of itself, an utterly terrible experience — leads to his subsequent attempts to clear up this family history; we will consider below to what extent this pursuit of the past in fact constitutes the cure that occurs to Austerlitz as a hopeful thought in the quotation above.

Both for Dr. K. and for Austerlitz, then, any transformation occasioned by their spa travels is due not to any direct impact of a medical regimen on the body but rather to the peculiar effect of each place on their conception of self. In this respect their double-edged experiences call to mind György Sebestyén's characterization of the spa environment as a fundamentally theatrical space in which prior notions of identity seem suspended:

> Die Kur als Ausnahmezustand schafft Distanz zur eigenen Persönlichkeit, weckt Zweifel, drängt zur Selbsterneuerung. Der Mensch ist nun nicht mehr er selbst; er hat sich gespalten; er ist als Erneuerer seiner selbst in eine ganz bestimmte Rolle geschlüpft. Er spielt.[6]

> [The stay at the spa as a state of exception creates a distance to one's own personality, it nourishes doubt, it urges renewal of the self. Here and now the person is no longer himself; he has split himself in two; he has adopted the particular role of one who is renewing himself. He plays/acts.[7]]

To be sure, the "plays" in which Dr. K. and Austerlitz find themselves cast are anything but comedies performed for the audience of fellow patients with the glee inspired by a sense of newfound liberation. Rather, the "state of exception" in this case calls into question the very notion of self-identity that might otherwise have appeared to be more or less stable. The "renewal" to be observed, in turn, does not amount to a fundamental overhaul of any deep structure of one's personality effected by a cure. Rather, Sebald's narrative strategy is to "renew" his protagonists at the spas of Riva and Marienbad through intertextual references that reveal the split within each of them not as a feature of their psychological constitution but rather as a division visible on the textual surface itself. In an ironic reversal, the novelty that results from this narrative operation consists precisely in the fact that it is an effect of role-playing, not the certifiable achievement of a new self. As John Zilcosky has compellingly argued, in Sebald's texts "disorientations never lead to new discoveries, only to a series of uncanny, intertextual returns."[8] The new is hence always the return of the old (text), though never without an ineradicable difference. Freud considered that which is *unheimlich* to be at the same time "irgendwie eine Art von heimlich" (in some way or other a kind of heimlich)[9] because it always remained subject to an eventual "Zurückführung auf altvertrautes Verdrängtes" (tracing back to something familiar that has been repressed; 12:261/17:247). The "tracing back" of a path to other textual layers in Sebald's works, while it demonstrates the impossibility of the radically new (or: of the perfect cure), does not therefore rest on these layers as though on secure, familiar ground. The effects of textual displacement, in fact, routinely inspire uncertainty as to the identification of characters and narrative voices. For example, Dr. K. both is and is not "Franz Kafka," just as Austerlitz and Marie are and are not the characters X, A, and M in *L'année dernière à Marienbad*. "Playing" at the spa as described by Sebestyén is, in this way, inseparable from playing with the text, and the doubling of the personages that results indeed prompts the reader to resort to distance and doubt with respect to the notion of a unified self. What happens on the stage constituted by Sebald's spas neither originates there nor stays there as the object of a final *Zurückführung*. Rather, it is inscribed as a trace in the sort of dynamic that Samuel Weber characterizes in his remarks on the concept of theatricality:

> When an event or series of events takes place without reducing the place it [has] "taken" to a purely neutral site, that place reveals itself to be a "stage," and those events become theatrical happenings. As the gerund here suggests . . . such happenings never take place once and for all but are ongoing. This in turn suggests that they can neither be contained within the place where they unfold nor entirely separated from it. They can be said, then, in a quite literal sense, to come to pass. They take place, which means in a particular place, and yet simultaneously also pass away — not simply to disappear but to happen somewhere else.[10]

The spa marks the place of just such a theatrical happening that spreads uncontained between the texts we will be considering here.

In "Dr. K.s Badereise nach Riva," the instability of intertextual reference announces itself immediately, in the title, in which Sebald alludes to Jean Paul's novel *Dr. Katzenbergers Badereise*[11] and grafts the reference to Kafka onto the latter by abbreviating the name of Jean Paul's protagonist to its first letter only. As incongruous as the conjunction of Sebald's melancholy and Jean Paul's humor may initially appear, even a brief glance at *Dr. Katzenbergers Badereise* reveals the keen eye its author casts on the play of identities that forms a key element of the spa trope. The novel describes the travels of anatomist Dr. Amandus Katzenberger, not to Riva but to the spa at Maulbronn in Swabia, his intent being neither cure nor amusement but rather business, "um da nämlich einen Rezensenten beträchtlich auszu-prügeln und ihn dabei mit Schmähungen an der Ehre anzugreifen" (in order there to dole out a considerable beating to a reviewer and to attack his honor with insults at the same time; *KB*, 91–92). The resident spa doctor at Maulbronn, Strykius, had written a number of apparently dismissive reviews of Katzenberger's previous three main publications, as well as counter-replies to Katzenberger's own replies to these reviews. Katzenberger now aims to continue the discourse in a more tangible, pugilistic manner and decides to take his daughter Theoda along to Maulbronn, where he hopes to get even with Strykius. Theoda's interest in taking the trip, meanwhile, is due not to her father's business but rather to the anticipated presence of the famed poet Theudobach — "der bekanntlich mit Schiller und Kotzebue die drei deutschen Horatier ausmacht, die wir den drei tragischen Kuratiern Frankreichs und Griechenlands entgegensetzen" (who, as is well known, is one of the three German Horatians, along with Schiller and Kotzebue, whom we regard as counterparts to the three tragic Curatians hailing from France and Greece; *KB*, 94) — whom she idolizes. Father and daughter are joined by another travel companion, the poet von Nieß, who, as it will turn out, is actually identical with the (fictional) Theudobach whose friend he claims to be. Nieß, for his part, is on the way to Maulbronn because he fully recognizes the potential for additional exposure at the spa,

> den schicklichsten Ort, den ein Autor voll Lorbeeren, der gern ein lebendiges Pantheon um sich aufführte, zu erwählen hat, besonders wegen des vornehmen Morgen-Trinkgelags und der Maskenfreiheiten und des Kongresses des Reichtums und der Bildung solcher Örter.

> [the most fitting place of choice for a laurelled author who likes to surround himself with a living pantheon, given especially the distinguished morning banquets, the freedoms afforded by masks, and the congregation of wealth and *Bildung* found in such places. (*KB*, 97)]

His ploy in traveling incognito is to heighten the dramatic effect of "Theudobach's" entrance, to be delayed until he, under his non-poetic identity of Nieß, has properly worked the spa crowd in preparation. Nieß's project collapses when an army captain actually named Theudobach takes a detour to Maulbronn after coming across a notice Nieß planted in a newspaper that announced "Theudobach's" anticipated arrival at the spa. Katzenberger's daughter, initially devastated by the discovery that the theatrical works she idolized were actually written by the less than imposing Nieß, ends up falling in love and eventually marrying the real Theudobach — a happy ending of ironically tinged quality that retains to the last sentence Jean Paul's customarily dim view of marriage.[12]

This narrative setup enables Jean Paul to offer biting assessments — his own preface fittingly invokes the parallel qualities of Swift's "satirisches Schlammbad" (satirical mud-bath; *KB*, 83) — of the questionable status both of the aspiration to literary "Bildung" on the part of spa guests, and — by way of their conspicuous omission — the medical benefits of spas like Maulbronn, which are barely mentioned in this account of Katzenberger's so-called business trip. Nieß appears to have no doubts regarding his own identity:

> Nieß wußte also recht gut, was er war, nämlich eine Bravour-Arie in der dichterischen Sphärenmusik, ein geistiger Kaisertee, wenn andere (z.B. viele unschuldige Leser dieses) nur braunen Tee vorstellen.

> [Nieß thus knew very well who he was, namely a glamorous aria in the poetic music of the spheres, an emperor's tea of the spiritual sort, compared to others (such as many innocent readers of his works) who only amounted to brown tea. (*KB*, 98)][13]

This certainty, however, is in effect built on his theatrical representation of himself as Theudobach, glamorous and popular only in virtue of his plays. This identity split in the name of literary fame points Jean Paul's reader to the disjunction between biological and textual identity, a division that the latter would be wise to keep in mind, given the circumstances surrounding the text he himself is reading:

> Nämlich Nieß hieß Nieß, hatte aber als auftretender Bühnen-Dichter um seinen dünnen Alltagnamen den Festnamen Theudobach wie einen Königmantel umgeworfen und war daher in vielen Gegenden Deutschlands weit mehr unter dem angenommenen Namen als unter dem eignen bekannt, so wie von dem hier schreibenden Verfasser vielleicht ganze Städte, wenn nicht Weltteile, es nicht wissen, daß er sich Richter schreibt, obgleich es freilich auch andre gibt, die wieder seinen Paradenamen nicht kennen.

> [For although Nieß was named Nieß, he had, as a playwright in the public sphere, wrapped his thin common name in the celebratory name Theudobach as if in a royal robe; he was thus known in many parts of Germany under his assumed name rather than his own, just as whole

towns if not continents do not know of the author writing these lines
that he writes his name as Richter, although there are, to be sure, others who in turn do not know the name he uses for show. (*KB*, 97)]

Perhaps it would be asking too much of Nieß's readers to pay sufficient
heed to the distinction however, given that Nieß's own knowledge of his
"true" identity is as liquid as any. The confusion surrounding his name
seems fully compatible with Jean Paul's general démarche to suspend the
(certain) declaration of particular realities in favor of focusing on the
deceptive nature of the declarative mode itself. As Michael Schaer writes in
reference to Jean Paul's text: "Es geht primär nicht mehr um Handlung,
Personen, Verhältnisse; sondern jetzt ist das Spiel mit der Wirklichkeit
bedeutsamer als deren Reproduktion" (It is no longer primarily a matter
of plot, characters, relationships; rather, the playing with reality is now
more significant than its reproduction).[14] In other words, Nieß's self-
"knowledge" can no more reach beyond the comedy of names that he
himself has set in motion[15] than Theoda could prevent her inevitable marriage to someone named "Theudobach," given that the "zufällige
Hochzeit der Namen Theoda und Theudobach" (accidental marriage of
the names Theoda and Theudobach; *KB*, 99) has suggested itself from the
very beginning. As products of language, Theoda and Theudobach are
quite literally made for each other,[16] and the fact that in order to make the
accidental marriage of names into a reality Theoda has to marry a different
person than the one by whom she was originally star-struck is just part of
the (narrative) game.

Katzenberger himself is implicated in other cross-referencing of names
in the novel: his first name ("Amandus") is duplicated in the baptism of the
newborn child of Theoda's best friend, Bona, from whose impending birth
Katzenberger implicitly flees to Maulbronn, showing little love for the
reproduction of life in his role as the prototypical anatomist, dissector of
dead bodies. Elsewhere Katzenberger is caught in the act, as "ein wahrer,
abscheulicher Katzen-Berger und -Würger" (a true, abominable cat-grab-
ber and cat-choker; *KB*, 111), when he attempts — apparently not for the
first time — to abduct kittens for anatomical purposes from an innkeeper
along the way to Maulbronn. Jean Paul's intricate narrative detours,
designed never to hit their target along the shortest possible route, offer
such onomatic twists in an explicit refusal to advance the story as straight-
forwardly as possible; although the narrator concedes that he could well
finish the book in virtually no time by resorting to narrative fireworks
instead of the drawn-out, slow burn of a "steppe fire," he defiantly vows:
"Ich will aber Katzenberger heißen, entzünd ich's nicht zu einem" (My
name shall be Katzenberger if I should fail to light such a fire; *KB*, 104).

Considering the thirty-seven chapters that follow this resolution, the
narrator seems fully within his rights not to be called Katzenberger. He

dutifully reminds himself that "wir wollen auf der Bad-Reise die Einheit des Ortes beobachten" (we aim to maintain the unity of space during our journey to the spa; *KB;* 105). We, the readers, are invited to conceive of the transient locality that Jean Paul's prose puts before us as a theatrical one. A space, that is, that opens up under a pseudo-Aristotelian constraint, claimed both by the dubious playwright Nieß/"Theudobach" and by the sphere of the spa as theater in which the narrative unfolds. Clearly, the "unity of space" of this travel narrative does not — and could not possibly — live up to Castelvetro's strict neoclassical interpretation of Aristotelian dramatic unity that first introduced the notion of space into the equation.[17] After all, the narration of the departure takes up a full eight chapters, anticipating difficulties of prompt leave-taking not unfamiliar to readers of Kafka.[18] "Unity of space," then, can be said to refer to nothing more, nor less, than the sustained theatricality of Jean Paul's prose itself as it plays with its overabundance of objects.

Sebald's protagonist in "Dr. K.s Badereise nach Riva" bears the name "Katzenberger" no more than does Jean Paul's narrator. We need to be clear: the intertextual reference embodied by the title does not identify "Dr. K." with Jean Paul's belligerent and disagreeable anatomist. Michael Schaer's characterization of Jean Paul's novel that was cited earlier applies in equal measure to its intertextual transposition onto Sebald's narrative: to repeat, it is no longer primarily a matter of plot, characters, relationships. What travels over into Sebald's account of Dr. K.'s stay at the spa in Riva is not the character features of a man called "Katzenberger" but rather the trope of travel itself, "unified" as a theatrical event of language. The tropical dynamic at issue here corresponds to that invoked by Jacques Derrida in his discussion of public transportation in the opening moments of "The *Retrait* of Metaphor." A contemplation of even our most quotidian movement through space, Derrida points out, may well collapse the traveling of people (the "contents" of a city bus, as we might say) onto the level of a metaphorical travel of linguistic form. As fellow passengers on a so-called "bus" (abbreviated from the Latin term "omnibus," meaning "all") or a "metaphorikos" (Greek for "transport vehicle"), we are "in a certain way . . . the content and tenor of this vehicle: passengers, comprehended and displaced by metaphor."[19] Katzenberger and "Kafka" may be — metaphorically — considered part of this group of passengers, and it is also worth recalling that earlier in *Schwindel. Gefühle.* the narrator of "All'estero" is confronted with a pair of twins who bear an uncanny resemblance to the young Kafka — on a bus from Desenzano to Riva (*SG,* 101–4/*V,* 88–90).

At its point of arrival, the transmigration of Katzenberger from Jean Paul's text into Sebald's connects with the second major intertext of this part of the book, Kafka's letters to Felice Bauer and his diary entries, a few of which make reference to the Riva episode. As I have argued elsewhere, this referential layer is not to be taken as providing for the truth about "Dr. K.," not least because it is Kafka himself who notes the evident construct-edness of his own diary in relation to what one might be tempted to call "experience."[20] Dr. K. goes to Riva neither in search of settling scores with a critic nor to bathe himself in the adoration of a crowd versed in contemporary drama, but he becomes, at the hands of Sebald's narrator, a figure at whose core the reader will not succeed in finding either "Katzenberger" or "Kafka," but only that which we tend to call, for lack of a better name, "literature." A few days before his departure for Vienna and points south, Kafka wrote to Felice: "mein Schlechtsein geht auf jenen Kern zurück, den Du Literatur nennen kannst oder wie Du willst" (my abjectness goes back to that core which you may call literature or whatever you like).[21] To the extent that Sebald's "Dr. K." partakes of these self-directed bad feelings, they are indeed literary in character — and they do not constitute a condition likely to be cured at the spa. Even the seemingly positive turn of events for Dr. K. at Riva — the encounter with the girl later designated "Seejungfer" (mermaid; *SG*, 175/*V*, 160) and "Undine" (*SG*, 175/*V*, 160)[22] — takes place against the backdrop of scenery, appearing as if drawn by hand, that Sebald imports from Robert Walser's prose piece "Kleist in Thun" (*SG*, 172–73/*V*, 158).[23]

In his book on Kafka and the cinema, which was well known to Sebald,[24] Hanns Zischler describes Kafka's rediscovery, during a business trip in 1911 to Friedland in northern Bohemia, of the diorama, a spherical stereoscopic apparatus that presents to the viewer spatially realized scenes that appear as if frozen in time. Among the landscapes pictured are the northern Italian vistas that Kafka would have seen on his later trip toward Riva. Given that, as Zischler writes, the images are "im Grunde theaterhaft nachgestellte Szenen, Bilder, die von außen nach innen gehen, von der 'befestigten' Figur zu den Kulissen" (fundamentally . . . theatrically simulated scenes, images that proceed from the outside in, from the "fixed" figure to the background scenery),[25] it comes as less of a surprise that the apparatus — in an improbable differential repetition of Nieß's self-conception as an imperial beverage — came to be known as the *Kaiserpanorama*. In Zischler's reading the diorama presents an image of Kafka's Italian travels, and it does so not in the mode of the time-bound cinema image — which conveys "eine mechanische Wirklichkeit, eine automatisierte Unruhe" (a mechanical reality, an automated unease; 45/28) — but rather from the imperial perspective, within the constraints of a mediated unity of space:

> In einem übertragenen Sinn ist das zyklisch aufgebaute Kaiserpanorama ein Bild der Italienreisen Kafkas. . . . Das Panorama Oberitaliens, das sich von Venedig bis Verona erstreckt, kannte er bereits — wie im Falle Brescias und Rivas — oder sollte es in den Jahren bis zum

Ausbruch des Weltkriegs kennenlernen. Tatsächlich blickt und reist
er, wenn er in den Süden aufbricht, stets entlang der Grenzen des bis
1859 weit nach Oberitalien vorgeschobenen Habsburgischen Reiches.
Über diese südliche Grenze, deren äußerste Stationen das
Kaiserpanorama ihm vor Augen führt, wird er nie hinausgehen.

[In a metaphorical sense, the cyclically constructed Kaiser Panorama
is an image of Kafka's Italian journey. [. . .] The panorama of northern Italy, stretching from Venice to Verona, was either already familiar
to Kafka — as in the case of Brescia and Riva — or he would come to
know it during the years leading up to the outbreak of the world war.
In fact, when he heads south, his eye and he himself always skirt the
boundaries of the Habsburg Empire, which until 1859 extended deep
into the northern Italian peninsula. He will never transgress this
southern border, whose most distant points the Kaiser Panorama lets
pass before his eyes.[26]]

The dioramatic space, as Kafka notes in his diary, facilitates a fixed gaze
altogether unlike the frantic movement of cinematography. It thus fosters
the illusion that the expanse of the Habsburgian Empire, down to its one-
time Italian parts, could be traversed while sitting in place and be captured
from the fixed perspective as an image more "lebendig" (alive) than the
mechanical theater of the cinema.[27]

This impression, however, hardly corresponds to what Dr. K. will
encounter on his trip, during which his troubles with Felice, though they
indeed appear "wie zu etwas Lebendigem geballt ([to] continually come
over him, like a living thing; *SG,* 171/*V,* 155), keep attacking him rather
than remaining in place where they might calmly be surveyed. During
their stopovers in Verona on the way to Riva, Kafka and Dr. K. also vol-
untarily submit to be assaulted by cinematic images; as Zischler and
Sebald's narrator report, it is impossible to ascertain which movie either
may have seen there, and Sebald's narrator fastens on this lacuna to substitute an alternative for one of the materially documented options, the
alpine drama *La lezione dell'abiso,* which appears to be lost to history,
though Zischler manages to include at least a French promotional poster
and a bit of descriptive advertising copy. In Sebald's text the altogether
speculative possibility is suggested that Dr. K. may have watched a different film, one that was shown concurrently in Austrian cinemas, though
there is no record of any showings in Verona at the time of Dr. K.'s travels: Paul Wegener's *The Student of Prague.* Wegener's film tells the story
of an abyss of a quite different sort: this Faustian tale of the student
Balduin and his doppelgänger introduces once again the notion of a split
self, and the narrator claims, perhaps not implausibly, that Dr. K., had he
actually seen the film, would have recognized in Balduin "seinen
Doppelgänger . . ., wie dieser ihn erkennt in dem unabweisbaren Bruder
im dunklen Kleid, dem er niemals und nirgends entkommen kann" (a

kind of *doppelgänger*, just as Balduin recognizes his other self in the dark-coated brother whom he could never and nowhere escape; *SG*, 166–67/ *V*, 151). Thus the static certainty of the *Kaiserpanorama* — its imperial message, so to speak — is undermined by a media transfer that is speculative in more than one sense. Balduin, we should recall, fights with his mirror image; this is documented by Sebald with the inclusion of a still image from the film. The narrator's tenuous conjecture removes Dr. K.'s journey to Riva one more step from its availability as a portrait of a split personality potentially amenable to the spa cure, and instead traces the split squarely across the intermedial distance that Dr. K. must travel before he could ever hope to reach us as readers.

The second Sebaldian spa episode that we will consider, Jacques Austerlitz's stay at Marienbad, picks up where "Dr. K.s Badereise nach Riva" leaves off — with a Kafka connection that points to an absence rather than a certifiable presence. The hotel where Austerlitz and his parents stayed in the summer of 1938, according to Vera, was the Osborne-Balmoral (*A*, 298/206), the same Marienbad establishment that hosted Kafka in 1916.[28] Austerlitz, as we remarked at the outset, retains no recollection of this vacation, and his remark that "die Marienbader Erinnerung" (the Marienbad memory) kept him awake all night after departing from Vera (*A*, 313–14/217)[29] is indeterminate in its reference — it could be referring either to his extant memory of visiting the Palace Hotel with Marie in 1972, or else to the recollection reported by Vera that he does *not* have of the Osborne-Balmoral — which Kafka called "der Palast Balmoral"[30] — in 1938. If the imperial lodging of 1972 thus casts an impenetrable shadow on the Osborne-Balmoral that is "gleich hinter" (immediately behind; *A*, 298/206) it, this is not least because — as in "Dr. K.s Badereise nach Riva" — the intertextual reference does not point toward a resolution of the riddle that would present itself within the imperial sphere — or within the Palace. Russell Kilbourn has characterized Austerlitz's second trip to Marienbad, which may be said to reveal the first one as an irretrievable ideal, as an ironically transmuted *katabasis* that sends the protagonist on a descent into a hell primarily constituted not by other people but rather by his own history.[31] Austerlitz does not gain access to any presumably lost memory of the Osborne-Balmoral, but what is projected as a "better turn" at Marienbad in 1972 initiates his archival search for traces of his mother, Agáta, that culminates in his painstaking analysis of the Theresienstadt propaganda film and his research in the theater archive in Prague. Neither the dissimulative cinematic portrayal of the ghetto as "angenehmen böhmischen Luftkurort namens Theresienbad" (pleasant resort in Bohemia called Theresienbad; *A*, 342–43/239) nor the copy of an uncaptioned newspaper photograph manages to reveal, despite Austerlitz's greatest efforts, any clear and incontrovertible visual evidence of his mother. J. J. Long rightly reminds us that although "Vera is the authority to whom final appeal is made in order to verify Agáta's identity," she emerges as an unreliable witness to the extent that "she foregrounds the tendency of her own memory images to merge with childhood recollections of visual spectacle."[32] The spectacle in question, it turns out, is of the very same kind as the one Kafka re-encountered in 1911 — a diorama (*A*, 231–32/158).

The trace that leads Austerlitz from Marienbad to "Theresienbad" and beyond, in other words, ultimately makes it impossible to decide whether, factually, his life has taken a turn for the better or not. Kilbourn proposes to read Austerlitz's post-Marienbad journey as a modern, fractured variant of the path of subjectivity toward "a new, more deeply negative and therefore ironic, self-awareness through memory."[33] If, in whatever negative iteration, this mnemonic journey were to enable a more thorough awareness of self, it would constitute the achievement of a cure from the splitting of the self that Sebestyén identified as the inevitable by-product of inhabiting the world of the spa. Does Sebald's primary intertextual reference beyond Kafka in the Marienbad episode — *L'année dernière à Marienbad* by director Alain Resnais and writer Alain Robbe-Grillet[34] — function as the trigger of this sort of eventual cure ex negativo?

The sentence immediately following the very first mention of the name "Marienbad" in *Austerlitz* already forges a link to the film and opens up the question that will prompt Austerlitz's eventual quest for certainty about his mother:

> Da kam [Vera] auf einmal wieder in den Sinn, wie Agáta am Tag meiner Abreise vom Wilson-Bahnhof, als der Zug uns aus den Augen entschwunden war, sich ihr zugewandt und gesagt hatte: Noch im vergangenen Sommer sind wir von hier nach Marienbad gefahren. Und jetzt, wohin fahren wir jetzt?

> [She suddenly remembered how, on the day of my departure from the Wilsonova Station, Agáta had turned to her when the train had disappeared from our view, and said: We left from here for Marienbad only last summer. And now — where will we be going now? (*A*, 297/205–6)]

Her traveling, at this juncture to points unknown, will lead Agáta to Terezín and ultimately to a death the circumstances of which will resist all attempts at reconstruction. Agáta's lack of certainty regarding her future corresponds to Austerlitz's later inability to reconstruct that future in the mode of the past. The tempting promise of certainty is held out with an equally indeterminate outcome in Resnais's film, in which the male spa guest X repeatedly confronts the female character A with his alleged recollection of having spent time with her at Marienbad the previous year. He claims that she agreed to meet again this year in order to elope with him:

X: Mais vous savez bien que c'est possible, que vous êtes prête, que
nous allons partir.
A: Qu'est-ce qui vous donne cette certitude? (Un temps.) Partir pour
aller où?
X (voix douce): N'importe où . . . Je ne sais pas.

[X: But you know very well that it is possible, that you are ready, that
we're going to leave
A: What makes you so sure? (A pause.) Leave for where?
X (very gently): Anywhere . . . I don't know. (*AD*, 131/*LY*, 120)]

As X attempts to persuade A of the possibility — or perhaps even the *fait
accompli* — of leaving the spa together with him, a particular destination
is never discussed.[35] A's hesitancy to give in to X's entreaties throughout
the entire film constitutes a refusal to subscribe to the notion that the past
— last year — may be reconstructed with certainty as X suggests it can be,
and that this reconstruction would inevitably make possible, and would
justify, his plan for the future: to elope with A, removing her from the
grasp of her companion M. The scene immediately continues with the following exchange:

A: Vous voyez bien. Il vaut mieux nous séparer, pour toujours . . .
L'année dernière . . . mais non, c'est impossible. Vous allez partir seul
. . . et nous serons, pour toujours,
X (plus violent, la coupant): Ce n'est pas vrai! Ce n'est pas vrai que
nous ayons besoin de l'absence, de la solitude, de l'eternelle attente.
Ce n'est pas vrai. Mais vous avez peur!

[A: You see. We'd better not see each other any more . . . ever . . .
Last year . . . Oh no, it's impossible. You're going to leave by yourself
. . . and then we'll be . . . forever,
X (more violently as he interrupts her): That's not true! It's not true
that we need absence, loneliness, waiting forever. It's not true. But
you're afraid! (*AD*, 131/*LY*, 121)]

For A, the future remains open, as an unfinished sentence beyond the
comma, despite — or because of — X's interruption that insists on the
truth of an achieved future, an end to the deferral brought about by uncertainty. Sebald's narrator borrows X's emphatic insistence on the possibility
of truth when he lets Marie plead for Austerlitz to alter his withdrawn
demeanor: "Es ist nicht wahr, sagte Marie, daß wir die Abwesenheit und
die Einsamkeit brauchen. Es ist nicht wahr. Nur du bist es, der sich äng-
stigt" (It isn't true, said Marie, that we need absence and loneliness. It isn't
true. It's only you who is afraid; *A*, 312/216). In a structural approximation of the circular repetition of linguistic and visual elements throughout
Robbe-Grillet's text and Resnais's film that removes these elements from
an attachment to any particular subject, Sebald rotates the quotations

transferred into *Austerlitz* in such a way that they sometimes match up with the names in Sebald's narrative and might be taken as extensions of these abbreviations, and sometimes not. Thus Marie's appeal above channels X, not M,[36] while a variation of A's earlier question is attributed to Agáta. This strategy suggests, as we found with respect to the transfer between *Dr. Katzenbergers Badereise* and "Dr. K.s Badereise nach Riva," that what travels between source and target is language, not the subjectivity of characters. Even in the source text, as its critical reception shows, it cannot be ruled out that X, A, and M might perhaps be holographs or specters rather than people,[37] and this effect is only heightened through Sebald's intertextual transfer. On the one hand, Marie may play the role of X to the extent that she beseeches Austerlitz to drop his guard, while the "Vereinzelung" (isolation; *A*, 298/206) from which she tries to liberate him ties Austerlitz to A, insisting on her separation from X. As the last spoken line of the film makes clear, however, A's earlier declaration that X will have to depart "alone" is irremediably ambiguated by X's repetition of this adjective when he glosses the closing panorama of the spa grounds as a place "où vous étiez maintenant déjà en train de vous perdre, pour toujours, dans la nuit tranquille, seul avec moi" (where you were now already getting lost, forever, in the calm night, alone with me; *AD*, 172/*LY*, 165). This affirmation of detachment cancels any clear separation between separation and unity, leaving A and her determination "lost" both spatially and temporally. Her earlier sentence, stunted by his interruption, which offered no concrete object or mode of being for the infinite future of the "pour toujours," is now grammatically completed but remains semantically as indeterminate as before.

If X and A indeed leave Marienbad together (like most questions in the film, this remains an open one), they would ultimately do so not to escape the isolation that X himself had branded an untruth but to remain alone and together at the same time. The liminal space of the spa grounds on the way to that outside — a rationally constructed space where "il semblait, au premier abord, impossible de s'y perdre" (it seemed, at first glance, impossible to get lost; *AD*, 172/*LY*, 165) — does not allow for the safe projection of a return to normalcy, a break from the state of exception that the spa denotes. The loss of self is furthered, not mitigated, by the formal unity of the spatial arrangement of Marienbad within which time does not, in the end, function as a liberating *kairos*.

This unachieved promise of a relief through being in the right place at the right time — if only in successful recollection — is picked up in *Austerlitz* to indicate the main character's thwarted hope of anchoring his life by means of memory work. X arrives punctually at midnight, "à l'heure dite" (at the time we set; *AD*, 170/*LY*, 161), for the (possible) departure pictured at the end of the film, while M arrives past the stroke of midnight to find X and A gone. Upon their arrival at the Palace Hotel, Austerlitz

Fig. 3. A opens the drawer. Video still from Alain Resnais, L'année dernière à Marienbad *(1961). Courtesy of StudioCanal.*

and Marie enter "das durch eine Reihe hoher Wandspiegel gewissermaßen verdoppelte Foyer, das so verlassen und so still war, daß man meinen konnte, es sei längst nach Mitternacht" (the foyer, which was made to look double its size, so to speak, by a row of tall mirrors along the walls, and which was so deathly still and deserted that you might have thought the time long after midnight; *A,* 296/208). Sebald's narrator carefully places his two characters in the same trompe-l'oeuil surroundings that Resnais captures on film, and thus lets Austerlitz's entire second stay at Marienbad unfold within the bracket of the *too late.* The time of Austerlitz's conscious life begins past midnight, too late to embark on a reconstruction of the past to arrive at certainty. The architecture "aus einer vergangenen Zeit" (from a past time; *A,* 302/209) — "cette construction — d'un autre siè-cle" (this structure — of another century; *AD,* 24/*LY,* 18) — lets Austerlitz set out on a path from Marienbad forward in time that dangles the promise in front of him that the certain visual identification of Agáta will provide for a certain closure regarding his clouded past. But just as the photograph of A that X presents as proof of her presence "last year" refers back neither to the reality of the photographed object nor to the situation it captures, so the cinematic and photographic images that Austerlitz unearths do not, ultimately, serve to connect him reliably to the past. In Resnais's film, A is eventually shown kneeling before the desk in her room, opening the central drawer to find it filled with identical prints of the pho-tograph X gave to her earlier to support his contention that, indeed, both he and A stayed at Marienbad last year (fig. 3).[38]

    As Austerlitz, too, will find, the photographic image refers back to the event of which it is supposed to provide evidence no more than the cine-matic or the dioramatic one. Instead, it makes reference only to its own status as the object of potentially unlimited mechanical reproduction; it may be reinscribed within the moving image as it is in this scene, but it will not thereby surrender the truth about the time or place of last year. The medium of the still image can, in the end, make no more claim to be "alive" (as Kafka had claimed of the diorama in comparison to the cinema) than moving images, of which Deleuze remarks that they "are substituted for my own thoughts."[39] Sebald effects this substitution not just for Austerlitz, whose "own" thoughts must forever — *pour toujours* — revolve around their own displacement by the media that are supposed to validate them, but across the vast majority of his literary texts. Like the architecture at Marienbad, they present the reader with "surfaces sans mystères" (surfaces without mystery; *AD*, 172/*LY*, 165) in which one will yet get lost, and in which every facade and every staircase retains the capacity to appear "zugleich bekannt und vollkommen fremd" (both familiar and utterly alien at the same time; *A*, 306/212).

Notes

[1] Herbert Zeman, "Vom Badereisen und vom Dichten — Goethe," in *Zwischen Aufklärung und Restauration: Sozialer Wandel in der deutschen Literatur (1700–1848)*, ed. Wolfgang Frühwald and Alberto Martino (Tübingen: Niemeyer, 1989), 263–81; here 264.

[2] Karin Wurst, *Fabricating Pleasure: Fashion, Entertainment, and Cultural Consumption in Germany, 1780–1830* (Detroit, MI: Wayne State UP, 2005), 256–58; David Blackbourn, "Fashionable Spa Towns in Nineteenth-Century Europe," in *Water, Leisure and Culture: European Historical Perspectives*, ed. Susan C. Anderson and Bruce H. Tabb (Oxford: Berg, 2002), 9–21.

[3] See Martin Klebes, "Infinite Journey: From Kafka to Sebald," in *W. G. Sebald: A Critical Companion*, ed. Jonathan Long and Anne Whitehead (Edinburgh: U of Edinburgh P, 2004), 123–39; here 133–34.

[4] Marie's performance provides a fitting example of Sebaldian humor and shows clear affinities with the way in which Jean Paul's character Katzenberger, whose presence in a different spa location we will discuss below, is likewise comically obsessed with human infirmities and aberrations. Paul Fleming's account of Jean Paul's humor as a "truly modern aesthetic category" that reappropriates a despised life in the mode of enjoyment rather than to attempt to overcome that life seems to capture the spirit of certain humorous passages in Sebald quite accurately, even if such paeans to human finitude are modulated rather differently in Sebald compared with the register of Jean Paul's prose. See Paul Fleming, *The Pleasures of Abandonment: Jean Paul and the Life of Humor* (Würzburg: Königshausen & Neumann, 2006), 21 and 47.

[5] In her analysis of *L'année dernière à Marienbad* — a film routinely thought to have no historical undertones whatsoever — Lynn Higgins notes that Marienbad, in particular, was popular among well-to-do Jews until the German invasion in March 1939, when Jews who remained there were arrested and executed. The

desertedness of the hotel grounds throughout much of the film — also echoed in Marie de Verneuil's remark "von den armen Liebenden qui se promenaient dans les allées désertes du parc" (about the poor lovers *qui se promenaient dans les allées désertes du parc; A,* 309/216) — could therefore be read as a figuration of this violent imposition of "order." See Lynn A. Higgins, *New Novel, New Wave, New Politics: Fiction and the Representation of History in Postwar France* (Lincoln: U of Nebraska P, 1996), 103.

[6] György Sebestyén, "Die Kurpromenade oder die Erfindung der Kunstnatur," in *Große Welt reist ins Bad, 1800–1914: Baden bei Wien, Badgastein, Bad Ischl, Franzensbad, Karlsbad, Marienbad, Teplitz.* Catalogue of an Exhibition by the Adalbert Stifter Association, Munich, in Cooperation with the Austrian Museum of the Applied Arts, Vienna (Passau, Germany: Passavia, 1980), 36.

[7] All translations are my own unless otherwise credited.

[8] John Zilcosky, "Sebald's Uncanny Travels: The Impossibility of Getting Lost," in Long and Whitehead, *A Critical Companion,* 102–20; here 102.

[9] Sigmund Freud, "Das Unheimliche," in *Gesammelte Werke,* ed. Anna Freud et al. (London: Imago, 1940–52), 12:227–68; here 237. In English, "The 'Uncanny,'" in *The Standard Edition of the Complete Psychological Works of Sigmund Freud,* ed. and trans. James Strachey (London: Hogarth, 1953–), 17: 217–56; here 226. For the sake of clarity, I have modified the translation.

[10] Samuel Weber, *Theatricality as Medium* (New York: Fordham UP, 2004), 7.

[11] Jean Paul, *Dr. Katzenbergers Badereise,* in *Werke,* ed. Norbert Miller (Munich: Hanser, 1963), 6:77–309. Further references to this work are given in the text using the abbreviation *KB.*

[12] Paul Fleming aptly explains this attitude with reference to Jean Paul's penchant for expecting the unexpected, a stance that would reveal any notion of marriage conceived as ultimate fulfillment to be illusory: "Fullness always demands a lack for fantasy to fill with images and expectations of infinite pleasures. Satiation is a mixed state of being empty and savoring the bliss of imagining what true satiation may be like. Therefore, Jean Paul rarely has a good word to say about marriage" (Fleming, *The Pleasures of Abandonment,* 149). Similar considerations may well have been at stake in Kafka's well-documented ongoing struggle with the question of marriage.

[13] The term "Kaisertee" is variously used for exclusively harvested batches of either green tea (in Japan) or white tea (in China), as opposed to regular black tea, which Jean Paul here dubs "brown."

[14] Michael Schaer, *Ex negativo: "Dr. Katzenbergers Badereise" als Beitrag Jean Pauls zur ästhetischen Theorie* (Göttingen: Vandenhoeck & Ruprecht, 1983), 11.

[15] In another context the narrator succinctly characterizes Nieß as someone who desires to be known "zugleich als Münzer und als Münze" (as coiner and coin in one; *KB,* 118); indeed, Nieß initiates an economy of semiotic circulation of his own assumed name ("Theudobach") that he ultimately cannot contain.

[16] See Schaer, *Ex Negativo,* 16.

[17] See Manfred Pfister, *The Theory and Analysis of Drama* (Cambridge: Cambridge UP, 1991), 249–50.

[18] Consider, for example, the short prose fragment, posthumously titled "Der Aufbruch" in some editions, in Franz Kafka, *Nachgelassene Schriften und Fragmente II*, ed. Jost Schillemeit (Frankfurt am Main: Fischer, 1992), 374–75.

[19] Jacques Derrida, "The *Retrait* of Metaphor," in *Psyche: Inventions of the Other*, ed. Peggy Kamuf and Elizabeth Rottenberg (Stanford, CA: Stanford UP, 2007), 1:48.

[20] See Klebes, "Infinite Journey: From Kafka to Sebald," 131–33.

[21] Franz Kafka, *Briefe 1913–März 1914*, ed. Hans-Gerd Koch (Frankfurt am Main: Fischer, 1999), 273 (30 Aug. 1913).

[22] In Kafka's retrospective diary entry of 15 Oct. 1913 she appears not in the guise of an elementary spirit but rather as "ein christliches Mädchen" (a Christian girl). Franz Kafka, *Tagebücher*, ed. Hans-Gerd Koch, Michael Müller, and Malcolm Pasley (Frankfurt am Main: Fischer, 1990), 582.

[23] Interestingly enough — in light of the theatricality of the spa context at issue here — Walser's main clause immediately preceding the passage that Sebald lifts from this story reads: "Die Berge sind wie die Mache eines geschickten Theatermalers" (The mountains are like the fabrication of a skillful theater painter). Robert Walser, "Kleist in Thun," in *Sämtliche Werke in Einzelausgaben*, ed. Jochen Greven (Frankfurt am Main: Suhrkamp, 1985–86), 2:70–81; here 71.

[24] Sebald's review of Zischler's book for the *Frankfurter Rundschau* was reprinted in *Campo Santo* under the title "Kafka im Kino" ("Kafka Goes to the Movies"; *CS*, 193–209/151–67).

[25] Hanns Zischler, *Kafka geht ins Kino* (Reinbek: Rowohlt, 1996), 39. In English, *Kafka Goes to the Movies*, trans. Susan H. Gillespie (Chicago: U of Chicago P, 2003), 26.

[26] Zischler, *Kafka geht ins Kino*, 46; *Kafka Goes to the Movies*, 30–31.

[27] In her discussion of Kafka's relationship to this apparatus, Carolin Duttlinger points out that for all its attempts to animate lifeless photographs, the *Kaiserpanorama* ends up underlining the uncanny hovering between life and death of many of the images (such as those of tomb monuments, which were routinely featured); that ambiguity, she argues, also extends to the mechanical nature of the display technology by means of which the sense of "life" is induced in the viewer. See Carolin Duttlinger, *Kafka and Photography* (Oxford: Oxford UP, 2007), 51–61.

[28] Franz Kafka, *Briefe, April 1914–1917*, ed. Hans-Gerd Koch (Frankfurt am Main: Fischer, 2005), 168 (5 Jul. 1916).

[29] Trans. modified. Note that Anthea Bell here translates as "my memories of Marienbad."

[30] Kafka, *Briefe, April 1914–1917*, 168.

[31] Russell J. A. Kilbourn, "Architecture and Cinema: The Representation of Memory in W. G. Sebald's *Austerlitz*," in Long and Whitehead, *W. G. Sebald: A Critical Companion*, 140–54; here 148. See also Alan Itkin's chapter in the present volume, 163–87.

[32] J. J. Long, *W. G. Sebald: Image, Archive, Modernity* (New York: Columbia UP, 2007), 162.

[33] Kilbourn, "Architecture and Cinema," 152.

[34] Alain Resnais, *L'année dernière à Marienbad* (France/Italy, 1961). Alain Robbe-Grillet, *L'année dernière à Marienbad: Ciné-roman* (Paris: Éditions de Minuit, 1961); in English, Alain Robbe-Grillet, *Last Year at Marienbad,* trans. Richard Howard (New York: Grove Press, 1962). Further references to this work are given in the text using the abbreviation *AD* (French edition) and *LY* (English edition), with page numbers for the German and English versions. With critical reference to Kilbourn's discussion of Resnais's film in the context of the Marienbad episode in *Austerlitz,* Klaus Bonn insists on pointing out that the film should not be considered an "explicit" reference because it is not "marked" in Sebald's text. While it is true that neither Resnais's name nor the title of the film are mentioned outright in this passage, several unmistakable references — *unmarked,* if that is what we choose to call them — may be discerned, and will be discussed below. This underhanded form of intertextual reference is pervasive throughout Sebald's work; unfortunately, Bonn does not proceed to tell the reader in what way the particular taxonomical distinction he urges would help to illuminate that work. See Klaus Bonn, "W. G. Sebalds laufende Bilder: Der Film und die Worte,"*Arcadia* 42.1 [2007]: 166–84; here 181–82.

[35] It should be noted, of course, that the point of departure is hardly more determinate than that unknown destination, since the location in which the narrative of the film unfolds is connected to the name "Marienbad" only through the ruminations on what happened there "last year" — it is never directly called "Marienbad." This is a literal reflection of the visual surface of the film, insofar as the footage was shot at several different chateaux in Germany and in a Paris studio, not in the actual geographical location of Marienbad. See Laura Rascaroli, "'L'année dernière à Marienbad'" in *The Cinema of France,* ed. Phil Powrie (London: Wallflower, 2006), 101–10; here 102.

[36] M, in pointed contrast to X, repeatedly refrains from challenging A directly about the *truth* of some of her assertions, such as her claims that she told him to come in when he knocked on the door (M claims that her words were inaudible), that the photograph given to her by X may have been taken by "Frank" (who, according to M, was not at Marienbad the previous year), and that she had spent time in the green room earlier in the afternoon (where M would have had to come across her; *AD,* 143/*LY,* 132–33).

[37] Matthias Frey, "Theorizing Cinema in Sebald and Sebald with Cinema," in *Searching for Sebald: Photography after W. G. Sebald,* ed. Lise Patt (Los Angeles: The Institute of Cultural Inquiry, 2007), 226–41; here 229.

[38] In Robbe-Grillet's text, the drawer instead contains photographs showing A and X in different situations, all of them stills from the film seen up to this point (*AD,* 152/*LY,* 142).

[39] Gilles Deleuze, *Cinema 2: The Time-Image,* trans. Hugh Tomlinson and Robert Galeta (Minneapolis: U of Minnesota P, 1989), 166.

5: *Campi deserti:* Polar Landscapes and the Limits of Knowledge in Sebald and Ransmayr

James Martin

> *Und so kannte es John Franklin von allen langsamen Katastrophen:*
> *wenn die ersten zugrunde gingen, war die Bequemlichkeit der*
> *übrigen noch stärker als das Begriffsvermögen.*
> — Sten Nadolny, *Die Entdeckung der Langsamkeit*

> *Die "Beherrschung der Natur" kommt als Wunschziel nicht vor, die*
> *"Beherrschung" der Laborspülmaschine ist weit wichtiger.*
> — Wolfgang Burgstaller, "Der Mensch in
> naturwissenschaftlicher Forschung und Theorie"

WHILE IT IS NO LONGER TRUE that W. G. Sebald's 1988 prose elegy, *Nach der Natur: Ein Elementargedicht*, has been largely ignored by the world of literary criticism, it remains one of his least known works.[1] The lengthy prose poem is divided into three sections, each presenting a mixture of biographical facts and fictionalized episodes from the lives of the master of the Isenheim altar, Matthias Grünewald, the eighteenth century botanist, Georg Wilhelm Steller, and a semi-autobiographical version of Sebald's own childhood. Although the author published numerous prose poems in literary magazines, newspapers, and anthologies from the seventies until his death in 2001, he is still better known for his longer prose works and his literary criticism.[2] The relative obscurity of *Nach der Natur* also derives in part from its unusual subtitle, *Ein Elementargedicht* (an elemental poem), which does not allow for easy categorization. Those expecting lyric poetry are perplexed by the unrhymed prose that is merely typeset with line and section breaks and stylized with an elegiac tone that approximates poetry.[3] Those expecting nature writing are confronted with descriptions of artworks, intertextual literary allusions, biographies of historical figures, and uncanny autobiographical coincidences, which are all inflected by man's relationship to nature if not actually directly about nature itself. Also, simply considering the length of *Nach der Natur,* a little over a hundred pages, the later prose works seem to stand apart as lengthy collected stories or even, in the case of *Austerlitz,* something approaching a novel. It is thus clear, given the belated and still limited attention to Sebald's poetry, how *Nach der Natur* might appear at first glance to be an anomaly or an unpolished prototype among Sebald's prose writing.

However, in its basic form *Nach der Natur* contains the essential or elemental narrative forms of Sebald's writing that also hold true for his later work: the semi-autobiographic, first-person narrator, the melancholic perspective, and the direct or indirect representations of other images and texts within the text itself.[4] Like *Schwindel. Gefühle.*, and to some extent *Die Ausgewanderten,* the form is based on a series of real and fictional portraits. Like all of the author's works, travel forms the impetus and guiding motion behind each of the stories; this catapults the reader beyond the physical journeys described in the text, along pathways of the imaginary that transcend space and time.[5] Yet my intent is neither to dispel the myth of *Nach der Natur*'s obscurity nor to offer an analysis that situates and understands the prose elegy in the context of the author's other works.[6] As a critic I have chosen to respond to what may be the least commented-upon section of Sebald's prose poem, the account of the naturalist Wilhelm Georg Steller's participation in the polar expedition led by Vitus Bering, entitled "Und blieb ich am äussersten Meer."[7]

David C. Ward, in a brief but interesting comparison of Sebald's use of photographs with Gerhard Richter's "Grey Paintings," singles out this section of *Nach der Natur* as comparatively less compelling. "The flatness of this middle section (which may also be due to the uncompelling figure of Steller) is due to Sebald having had to include it for chronological and structural reasons; he is not sympathetic enough about the Enlightenment to be passionate about it; the Enlightenment was something to be gotten through."[8] In contrast, I would argue that this flatness is an effect of Sebald's deliberate evocation of the blankness and emptiness of the polar landscape as a metaphor for the limits of the Enlightenment's quest for knowledge, a strategy shared by Austrian author Christoph Ransmayr in his 1984 novel *Die Schrecken des Eises und der Finsternis (The Terrors of Ice and Darkness),* in which an Italian named Josef Mazzini disappears in 1981 in the glaciers of Spitzbergen, Norway, during a failed voyage to retrace the journey of the 1872 Austro-Hungarian expedition that discovered Franz Josef Land.[9]

This is not the only instance in which a resemblance between these two authors has been noted. Without directly naming the author, Thomas von Steinacker makes an overt allusion to Ransmayr's most famous novel, *Die letzte Welt,* in his discussion of the double-page black-and-white photographs by Thomas Becker that accompanied the original 1988 edition of *Nach der Natur:*

So wie die Grisaille-Töne auf Heironymus Boschs Rückseite des Triptychons "Der Garten der Lüste" die vorparadiesische Welt des ersten Schöpfungstages zeigen, auf der Adam und Eva noch fehlen, verweist das Grau der Landschaftsaufnahmen Sebalds auf eine Zeit, in der der Mensch als temporäres Phänomen verschwindet und die "letzte Welt" im Begriff steht, wieder zurück ins Chaos zu stürzen.[10]

[Just as the grisaille [monochromatic gray] tones on the back of Heironymus Bosch's *The Garden of Earthly Delights* depict a pre-paradise world where Adam and Eve are absent, the gray of Sebald's landscape shots points to a world in which humanity disappears as a temporary phenomenon and the "last world" is in the process of falling back into chaos again.]

Sebald had several of Ransmayr's novels, including *Die Schrecken des Eises und der Finsternis,* in his personal library, now housed at the Literaturarchiv Marbach.[11] Kurt Foster observes that Sebald had corresponded with Ransmayr about *Die Schrecken des Eises und der Finsternis,* praising the novel's clarity and vision.[12] Although the different length of Ransmayr's novel and Sebald's prose poem makes a comparison seem somewhat unlikely, the themes and techniques employed in both correspond greatly.

The first characteristic that they share is an intertextual quality, which begins with an interest in the historical accounts documenting, in the case of Sebald, the Great Northern Expedition of 1741 sponsored by the Russian Tsar and led by the Dane Vitus Bering, and, in the case of Ransmayr, the Austro-Hungarian North Pole Expedition of 1872 led by Carl Weyprecht and Julius von Payer. Both authors' intertextual strategies quickly expand to include a breadth of scientific, sacred, and literary works. Sebald weaves various allusions, references, and even quotations into his prose poem without directly marking them as such, including adaptations from Steller's journal.[13] Ransmayr employs a similar range of intertexts in a more overt manner, by citing titles, attributing quotations, and directly inserting cursive-printed entries from the journals of the members of the Austro-Hungarian expedition, Carl Weyprecht (commander at sea and on ice), Julius von Payer (commander on land), Johann Haller (hunter and dogsled driver), and Otto Krisch (machinist). Second, there is a shared preoccupation with the intersection of the text with visual images. Although *Nach der Natur* does not include photos or illustrations within the text, descriptions of artworks play a central role in the structure and meaning of the text.[14] Ransmayr's novel is one of the rare examples where the Austrian author proceeds in a manner typical of what Sebald would come to do in the rest of his works, reproducing copious visual images directly in the text, including photographs of the ship and crew as well as engravings created by Julius von Payer after the expedition. Above all, Sebald's and Ransmayr's texts share the theme of polar exploration and travel to the extreme limits of the knowable world, where a hostile, empty landscape threatens not only humanity's capacity for physical survival but also the mental ability to encompass and describe such an experience within a system of knowledge, whether scientific or aesthetic.

The initial section of *Nach der Natur,* concerning the medieval painter Matthias Grünewald, ends with the image of ice, snow, and blindness:

> Späh scharf voran, dort siehst du im Grauen des Abends die fernen Windmühlen sich drehen. Der Wald weicht zurück, wahrlich, in solcher Weite, daß man nicht kennt, wo er einmal gelegen, und das Eishaus geht auf, und der Reif zeichnet ins Feld ein farbloses Bild der Erde. So wird, wenn der Sehnerv zerreißt, im stillen Luftraum es weiß wie der Schnee auf den Alpen.

> [Peer ahead sharply, there you see in the graying of nightfall the distant windmills turn. The forest recedes, truly, so far that one cannot tell where it once lay, and the ice-house opens, and rime, on to the field, traces a colorless image of the earth. So, when the optic nerve tears, in the still space of the air all turns as white as the snow on the Alps. (*NN,* 33/*AN,* 37)]

The first line betrays the passage as an adaptation from Dante's *Inferno,* from the 34th canto, in which Vergil leads Dante to confront ultimate evil in the form of Beelzebub ensconced from the waist in a house of ice upon a frozen sea. Dante bemoans his inability to represent the massive proportions and horrific nature of the devil to his audience, yet crawling across the devil's back to escape hell, he lingers in order to ask about the peculiar landscape. Vergil explains that the sea was created when Lucifer fell from the heavens, parting the land and throwing up the mountain of purgatory, toward which they are headed. Sebald superimposes the blinding white of the snow on the Alps over the icy landscape of hell, indicating the elision of the metaphysical boundaries that separated hell from purgatory for Dante and held out the possibility of redemption in the form of travel between these realms. For the painter Grünewald, despair threatens to become blindness when trying to represent a natural world, constantly on the brink of its own dissolution into chaos, decay, and death, which still makes sense within a transcendental order.

This image marks the transition to the central section of *Nach der Natur,* entitled "Und blieb ich am äussersten Meer." The title comes from Psalm 139, which praises God's omnipresent and omniscient nature:

> Herr, Du erforschest mich und kennest mich. Ich sitze oder stehe auf, so weißt du es; du verstehst meine Gedanken von ferne. Ich gehe oder liege, so bist du um mich und siehst alle meine Wege. Denn siehe, es ist kein Wort auf meiner Zunge, das du, Herr nicht alles wissest. Von allen Seiten umgibst du mich und hältst deine Hand über mir. Solche Erkenntnis ist mir zu wunderbar und zu hoch; ich kann sie nicht begreifen. Wo soll ich hin gehen vor deinem Geist, und wo soll ich hin fliehen vor deinem Angesicht? Führe ich gen Himmel, so bist du da.

Bettete ich mir in die Hölle, siehe, so bist du auch da. Nähme ich
Flügel der Morgenröte und bliebe am äussersten Meer, so würde mich
doch deine Hand daselbst führen und deine Rechte mich halten.

[O Lord, you have searched me and you know me. You know when
I sit and when I rise; you perceive my thoughts from afar. You discern
my going out and my lying down; you are familiar with all my ways.
Before a word is on my tongue you know it completely, O Lord. You
hem me in — behind and before; you have laid your hand upon me.
Such knowledge is too wonderful for me, too lofty for me to attain.
Where can I go from your Spirit? Where can I flee from your presence? If I go up to the heavens, you are there; if I make my bed in the
depths, you are there. If I rise on the wings of the dawn, if I settle on
the far side of the sea, even there your hand will guide me, your right
hand will hold me fast. (Psalm 139, 1–10)][15]

However, Sebald omits the second half of the psalm's final sentence, which
refers to God's guidance, and eliminates the obvious indication of the
subjunctive mood in the remaining fragment (*Und blieb ich am äussersten
Meer*), which he uses as the title of this central section. The resulting possibility of reading the fragment in the more fatalistic preterite seems to
indicate that redemption may no longer be available in this world.[16]
Whereas travel between distinctly bounded realms for Dante indicated, at
least didactically, the possibility of progressing from hell through purgatory to heaven, the erasure of that boundary in Sebald's work prefigures
Steller's travel in the polar landscape as movement without transcendence,
giving new intertextual heft to the stereotype of the Arctic as hell on earth.
Instead of facing the awful maw of Beelzebub, humanity has taken the
devil's place enclosed in the ice and is confronted instead by the realization
that the horror of this experience cannot be encompassed in any human
system of knowledge.

Anja K. Maier describes Sebald's use of ice and snowscapes as a yearn-
ing for an unambivalent wholeness of nature beyond history and human
society, similar to Stifter's predilection for the inorganic, ahistorical quality
of the Alpine landscape.[17] Heinrich Detering also points to the description
of the snowy mountaintops in Altdorfer's "Alexanderschlacht" painting,
which ends the final section of *Nach der Natur,* entitled "Die dunckle
Nacht fahrt aus," as a vision of transcendence towering above the ruinous
fields of human conflict.[18] However, I would argue that Sebald's treatment
of these frozen landscapes is inherently ambivalent. The author already
acknowledges the presence of a religious duality in the images of icy mountains in Grünewald's Isenheim altar:

. . . wonach kommt die Berglandschaft der Beweinung, in der
Grünewald mit pathetischem Blick auf die Zukunft einen wildfremden Planeten vorgebildet hat, kalkfarben hinter dem schwarzblauen

Strom. Hier ist gemalt in schlimmer Erodiertheit und Öde das Erbteil der Zerschleißung, die zuletzt noch die Steine zerfrißt. In Anbetracht dessen dünkt mich die Eiszeit, das hellweiße Turmgebäude der Gipfel im oberen Bereich der Versuchung, die Konstruktion einer Metaphysik, und ein Schneewunder.

[. . . after which comes the mountain landscape of weeping in which Grünewald with a pathetic gaze into the future has prefigured a planet utterly strange, chalk-colored behind the blackish-blue river. Here in an evil state of erosion and desolation the heritage of the ruining of life that in the end will consume even the stones has been depicted. In view of this it seems to me that the ice age, the glaringly white towering of the summits in the upper realm of the *Temptation*, is the construction of a metaphysic and a miracle. (*NN*, 27–28/*AN*, 31)]¹⁹

The utterly barren desolation of the chalk-colored mountains depicted in the *Lamentation of Christ* (on the predella) are transposed into an alien future, while the gleaming, icy mountains from *St. Anthony's Temptation* (right, inner wing) represent a present hope for salvation through the pious abnegation of earthly temptations. Thus the ice and snowscape can embody both the inevitability of earthly death and destruction, as well as the hope of otherworldly redemption. However, the promise of transcendence is prefigured as unattainable in this world, despite the longings of Sebald's protagonists. Immediately following the description of the Isenheim altar the author recounts the slaughter of thousands of passively resisting peasants at Frankenhausen in 1525, the horrific culmination of the Peasant's Revolt led by the visionary and radical theologian Thomas Müntzer, who sought to overthrow the existing social order and install an egalitarian divine order on earth.

For Georg Wilhelm Steller the religious world order of the Middle Ages is replaced by the scientific discourse of the Enlightenment, "perscrutamini scripturas, soll das nicht heißen, perscrutamini naturas rerum?" (*perscrutamini scripturas*, shouldn't that read, *perscrutamini naturas rerum? NN*, 40/*AN*, 47). In this respect he diverges from his forebear, the sixteenth-century physician and botanist Paracelsus, who sought to supplement Christ's injunction to study the scriptures with the addition of the study of natural things, "*dan so Christus spricht, perscrutamini scripturas, warumb wolt ich nicht auch sagen darvon: perscrutamini naturas rerum?*" (As Christ says, study the scriptures, why shouldn't I also say, study natural things?).²⁰ Sebald's intertextual adaptations throughout the text bear crucial differences, and here the exclusion of the word "also" marks the transition from a premodern mysticism that integrates nature study into a Christian cosmology to an Enlightenment perspective that replaces religious worldviews from the late Middle Ages with a belief in the primacy of rationality and scientific observation in the pursuit of knowledge.

Upon arriving in St. Petersburg Steller retreats from the chaos of the
city in the botanical garden of the marine hospital, reveling in the encyclopedic drive of botany to name, catalogue, and thus systematize an otherwise unruly nature. "Säuberlich wandelt er über die Wege zwischen den
Beeten, bestaunt die gläsernen Treibhäuser, die exotischen Pflanzen, lernt
in einem fort neue Namen und weiß sich vor Hoffnung kaum zu helfen"
(Neatly he walks the paths between the flowerbeds, marvels at the hot-
houses, filled with tropical plants, learns one name after another and is
almost beside himself with so much hope; *NN,* 42/*AN,* 50). The patriarch
of Novgorod, Archbishop Theophon, who employs Steller as his private
doctor, warns him of the false totality of knowledge that rationalized science promises:

> Alles aber, sagt Theophon, alles mein Sohn, ändert sich in das Alter,
> weniger wird das Leben, alles nimmt ab, die Proliferation der Arten
> ist bloß eine Illusion, und niemand weiß, wo es hinausgeht.

> [But all things, Theophon says, all things, my son, transmute into old
> age, life diminishes, everything declines, the proliferation of kinds is a
> mere illusion, and no one knows to what end. (*NN,* 43/*AN,* 51)].

For the patriarch, the experience of decline and impending death reveal the
limitations of humanity's ability to fully know and comprehend existence,
in stark contrast with Steller's enthusiasm for the unbounded potential of
scientific discovery. Science in the Enlightenment takes on a totalizing
character as a system for understanding the world under the banner of an
unwavering belief in progress and rationality. It claims to be able to
describe the entirety of existence and replace the Alpha and Omega of God
with a scientific order.

The move from a religious to a scientific fantasy of absolute knowledge
is already connected with polar travel in Sebald's account of Steller's early
biography:

> Bilder von dieser Entdeckungsreise verdichteten sich in der Phantasie
> Stellers, der, als Sohn eines Kantors mit einer schönen Tenorstimme
> begabt und einem christlichen Stipendium versehen, zunächst in
> Wittenberg gewesen, dann aber der Theologie abtrünnig geworden
> und zur Naturwissenschaft übergelaufen war, allmählich derart, daß
> er während der Disputationen, die er auf das glänzendste absolvierte,
> an nichts anderes zu denken vermochte als an die Formen der Fauna
> und Flora jener Weltgegend, in der Osten und Westen und Norden
> zusammentreffen, und an die Kunst ihrer Beschreibung.

> [Visions of this voyage of discovery, Steller later recorded, had so seized
> his imagination that he, the son of a cantor, gifted with a fine tenor
> voice and furnished with a bursary for true Christians, having aban-
> doned Wittenberg and theology for natural science, could now, during

his doctoral disputations, which he passed with the highest distinction, think of nothing other than the shapes of the fauna and flora of that distant region where East and West and North converge, and the art and skill required for their description. (*NN*, 38/*AN*, 44)]

The pole represents an exemplary or ideal space that scientific description has merely to fill in. Yet even before Steller sets out on his journey there are signs that science is not fully capable of conveying the extreme experiences of mental deprivation, physical dissolution, and death that accompany polar travel:

> Dem Akademiemitglied Daniel Messerschmidt waren die langen arktischen Reisen auf die Nerven geschlagen. Steller, der Messerschmidt in dem Gartenhaus, das er mit einer Bäckerstochter aus Sesslach bewohnte, noch lebend antraf, hat aus dem schwer melancholischen Menschen nichts mehr herausbringen können.

> [The long Arctic journeys had frayed the nerves of the Academy member Daniel Messerschmidt. Steller, who found Messerschmidt still living in the summerhouse he occupied with a baker's daughter from Sesslach, came too late to get anything out of the deeply melancholic man. (*NN*, 44/*AN*, 52)].

The harsh conditions of the polar landscape result not only in the body's physical decline but also in an emotional state of melancholy, which disrupts the communicative imperative of scientific exploration to translate that experience into knowledge.

In the section on Matthias Grünewald the icy landscape is associated with blindness, and in the middle section on Georg Wilhelm Steller the Arctic is connected with muteness. These tropes express a breakdown in the ability of humanity to perceive and communicate experience. In the context of contemporary Austrian travel literature, Heinz-Peter Preußer notes that experience bound to a subject, especially in the case of the explorer, has become epistemologically problematic.[21] This is a central concern of Christoph Ransmayr's *Die Schrecken des Eises und der Finsternis*, in which the narrator attempts to communicate the experience of polar exploration but must admit the limitations of such a project:

> Ich habe mir vorzustellen versucht, was ein Einfältiger empfinden muß, der, auf einem festgefrorenen Schiff dahindriftend, umgeben von allen Schrecken des Eises und der Finsternis, plötzlich erkennt, daß sein Ziel ohnedies unsichtbar ist, ein wertloser Punkt, ein Nichts. Es blieb beim Versuch; ich konnte eine solche schmerzliche Enttäuschung nicht nachempfinden.

> [I have attempted to imagine what an innocent must feel when he suddenly realizes — on a ship frozen fast and drifting, surrounded by all the terrors of ice and darkness — that his goal is invisible in any

case, a worthless point, a cipher. I got no further in this attempt; I could not recreate that feeling of painful disappointment. (*SEF*, 43/ *TID*, 31)]

In order to approach an adequate description of the polar landscape and its place within the realm of human knowledge, the narrator relies on the partial accounts provided by the members of the ship's crew but simultaneously notes the limitations of these accounts.

Carl Weyprecht, the ship's captain and expedition leader, embodies the Enlightenment perspective, which subjugates experience to the rational ordering of scientific observation and reduces nature to numbers, laws, and probabilities:

> Nächtelang sitzt er allein in einem Beobachtungszelt, das er auf dem Eis hat errichten lassen, führt seine meteorologischen, astronomischen und ozeanographischen Journale, mißt die Schwankungen des Erdmagnetismus, zeichnet lange Zahlenkolonnen auf, berechnet den wirren Kurs ihrer Drift, lotet Meerestiefen, beschreibt, kalkuliert, stellt Zusammenhänge her.

> [He spends his nights sitting alone in an observation tent he has built out on the ice; he keeps meteorological, astronomical, and oceanographic journals, measures variations in the earth's magnetic force, records long columns of numbers, reckons the course of their drift, sounds the sea's depths, describes, calculates, establishes connections. (*SEF*, 106–7/*TID*, 85)].

The scientific method's reliance on measurable phenomena and inductive reasoning necessarily presents a reductive view of the world that is subsumed within a totalizing myth of never-ending progress and limitless rationality. "In der Erforschung der Räthsel, mit welchen sie [die Natur] uns umgiebt, kommt das Streben des denkenden Menschen nach Fortschritt zum vollsten Ausdrucke" (By examining the riddles with which nature surrounds us, we give fullest expression to thinking mankind's aspirations for progress; *SEF*, 107/*TID*, 85). However, the limitations of the Enlightenment myth become abundantly clear when the narrator attempts to describe the suffering of the human explorers trying to survive in the extreme conditions of the polar landscape.

The scientific observation of facts is inadequate to encompass the horrifying experience of isolation and physical decline that the crew of the Austro-Hungarian expedition must undergo when they are trapped for months in a sea of ice and the darkness of the Arctic midnight. Their ship, the *Admiral Tegetthoff*, is surrounded by a shifting ice mass, and attempts to break channels in the ice are fruitless, as they quickly freeze over again, leaving the crew marooned to wait for next year's thaw (*SEF*, 102–3/*TID*, 82). The ship is tossed up at an angle upon a hill of broken ice that itself threatens to crush the ship at any given moment so that the crew has to be on constant alert to flee catastrophe (*SEF*, 113–14/*TID*, 91). The temperature falls to minus forty Celsius and the cabin walls, berths, and blankets are covered in ice from the sailors' own breath (*SEF*, 117–18/*TID*, 93). The freezing temperatures, continual darkness, insufficient nourishment, and loneliness leave most of the crew in varying degrees of lethargic infirmity, trapped not only by the Arctic ice but also by the dissolution of their own bodies.

Ransmayr draws upon another myth, the biblical tale of Job, to provide at least a schema of misery that might flesh out the experience, which is missed in the list of physical illnesses that plague the expedition:

> Jänner. Das Eismeer gleicht doch dem Lande Uz. Und jeder hier dem Hiob.
> Jäger Klotz leidet an Melancholie und *Lungenschwindsucht*;
> Matrose Fallesich an Skorbut;
> Zimmermann Vecerina an Skorbut und *Gliederreißen*;
> Matrose Stiglich an Skorbut;
> Jäger Haller an Gliederreißen;
> Matrose Scarpa an Skorbut und Krämpfen;
> Maschinist Krisch an Lungenschwindsucht.

> [January. The sea of ice is truly the land of Uz. And everyone here is Job.
> Hunter Klotz is ill with melancholy and consumption;
> Able seaman Fallesich with scurvy;
> Carpenter Vecerina with scurvy and rheumatism;
> Hunter Haller with rheumatism;
> Able seaman Scarpa with scurvy and cramps;
> Machinist Krisch with consumption. (*SEF*, 138/*TID*, 112)]

Yet the story of Job is just one more discursive layer that also remains mute in relation to the sea of ice. "Die Weisheit aber — wo findet man sie, und wo ist die Stätte der Einsicht? . . . Das Urmeer spricht: 'In mir ist sie nicht' und der Ozean sagt: 'Ich bin leer'" (But where shall wisdom be found? And where is the place of understanding? . . . The deep says, "It is not in me," and the sea says, "It is not with me"; *SEF*, 188/*TID*, 153). As the ice continues to shift, a chasm opens up and the sea swallows up Weyprecht's observation tent, a portion of the expedition's coal rations, and one of the sled dogs (*SEF*, 139/*TID*, 113).

The primary contrast to the Enlightenment discourse of rationality in the text is Julius Payer's diary, which is in line with a Romantic tradition including Caspar David Friedrich, Shelley, and Byron, that depicts the rugged landscape of ice and snow as combining both horror and the sublime.[22] Payer's entries seek to express the beauty and desolation of the

Arctic as a coherent whole, in terms that place the sufferings of the heroic subject and the Promethean drive of the explorer to discover new lands at its center. Unfortunately, the inexactness of his cartography and the bold gestures of his Romantic prose are suspect to the members of the academies and learned societies, leading them to judge his sufferings as, "doch wohl ein bißchen sehr fabelhaft, pure Literatur" (that really is somewhat fantastical, purest literature; *SEF, 267/TID, 220*). Neither his writings nor the paintings that he later makes can convey the reality of his experiences, and his images of a land of ice and darkness are taken as fantasy.[23]

The question arises then, of whether an author can convey experiences that approach the extremes of horror or the sublime. This is especially relevant for a contemporary author writing after the conditions of postmodernity, in which experience, as well as texts and images, have been taken to be emptied of aura and affect. If Weyprecht and Payer could not translate the horrors of the ice and darkness into an adequate form to communicate that experience, then it seems impossible for a writer one hundred years afterward to be able to do so either. Yet Ransmayr and Sebald develop effective literary strategies for dealing with this conundrum. Given the postmodern surplus of literary images and horror's loss of affect, literature can recycle past images that have been forgotten so that they appear revitalized, as if new again.[24] Both Gerda Elisabeth Moser and Markus Oliver Spitz maintain that the archive of literary and visual images can be plundered to create a "mosaic" or "montage" of historical and fictional sources that, even though it reveals its own artifice and constructedness, can still convey a sense of reality and authentic emotional intensity.[25] Sebald and Ransmayr suture together different texts and images to create literary accounts that necessarily remain fragmented, all the while exposing the limits of literary representation and systems of knowledge. They deliberately take a peripheral approach that relies on intertextuality and metonymic substitution to indicate the beauty and horror, the positive and negative sublime, of the polar landscape, which cannot be communicated in any single, authoritative account. Both authors use polar exploration as a means of critiquing the totalizing claims of modern scientific discourse, offering instead an evocative pastiche of intertexts that moves toward but can never entirely encompass an understanding of the incommensurable experience of survival in the extreme conditions of polar landscapes.

Part of the authors' strategy is to reveal the pervasive mediation of experience through preexisting texts, a key aspect of postmodern intertextuality. Bianca Theisen notes that Sebald's traveling personas are never really in search of the authentic or an unmarked territory because these quests, "can only lead to what is already marked, to what is historically inscribed, culturally framed, and geographically mapped."[26] This is a particularly interesting stance, given that voyages of discovery to uncharted territories, especially the polar regions, are often posited as an attempt to discursively fill in the blank spaces through cartography and scientific description. However, at the beginning of every expedition, part of the necessary preparation is an investigation into the maps, charts, logbooks, scientific treatises, travelogues, diaries, and various other texts that document previous voyages. Sebald describes Georg Wilhelm Steller starting his preparation to join the Bering expedition by studying the notes of his deceased predecessor, the naturalist Daniel Messerschmidt, in St. Petersburg. "Einen ganzen Sommer verbringt er über die Zettelwirtschaft gebeugt (He spends the whole summer bent over the jumble of cards; *NN*, 44/*AN*, 52). Ransmayr takes this strategy a step further by including his own "Formblatt aus der Chronik des Scheiterns" (A Table from the Chronicle of Failure; *SEF*, 92–93/*TID*, 71). The table chronicles the failed voyages that preceded the Austro-Hungarian expedition, listing the name of the expedition commander, years in the ice, unachieved goals, and notes on the demise of the commanders and the failed route. Sebald and Ransmayr depict polar travel as fully embedded in an intertextual world that prefigures catastrophe and death. Although Theisen's assumption that Sebald's protagonists always encounter what is already culturally inscribed is indeed correct, it does not account for the overpowering drive that motivates Steller (and Ransmayr's protagonist Josef Mazzini) to undertake such dangerous travel given the documented risk of failure. I would argue that both characters ignore the physical (and in both cases fatal) realities of the Arctic because they are obsessed with recreating the "triumph" of the exemplary experiences modeled in the written accounts of their predecessors.

Travel throughout the centuries has had an intimate relation with the process of documenting the journey and places seen for posterity. Within the early culture of European travel, the archive, the library, and the cabinet became repositories for the documents and objects that bore witness to the intellectual benefits of travel and thus themselves became influential in the shaping of future trips.[27] The growing importance of documenting travel quickly expanded as improvements in the means and conditions of transportation allowed more types of journeys to be undertaken by members of different social classes. By the eighteenth century, travel literature had taken on a multitude of functions beyond being a travel guide, including scientific, economic, pedagogical, religious, political, literary, and not least of all touristic purposes.[28] Writing about exploration was often couched in religious and secular discourses of spreading civilization, even though the primary motivation for most exploration was the desire to increase political and economic power. Under the influence of the Enlightenment, the subjugation of nature masked the subjugation of foreign territories and peoples as science replaced the civilizing mission concealing the expansionist objectives of even polar exploration.[29] Sebald's and Ransmayr's protagonists are deluded by the modern myth of man's mastery over nature and thus ignore the dangers and inconsistencies present in the existing records documenting the Pole.

Ransmayr presents a selection of quotes from various texts about the Arctic from ancient times to the twentieth century in a subsection entitled, "Der Große Nagel — Fragmente des Mythos und der Aufklärung" (The Great Nail — Fragments of Myth and Enlightenment; *SEF*, 187/ *TID*, 152). The myths of the frozen North that came from the ancients and indigenous tribes are replaced by supposedly rational scientific and geographic texts, each making a claim to represent the truth about the Arctic. However, the claims made in these documents are so contradictory that past statements of posited knowledge become the new myths as competing truth claims emerge, a process outlined in the *Dialectic of Enlightenment* by Max Horkheimer and Theodor Adorno, which critiqued the Enlightenment's false promise of rational progress leading to limitless knowledge and mastery over nature.[30] Not only does the presence of these competing claims cast doubt on the historical documents and texts created by polar explorers, but it also forces the reader to question the veracity of Sebald's and Ransmayr's texts. By mixing fiction with facts and directly citing historical intertexts, the literary works also make a claim to representing the realities of polar exploration. However, Sebald and Ransmayr adopt postmodern literary strategies that point out the text's own artifice and constructedness as an admission of the limits of representation and, I would argue, the limits of knowledge under the conditions of postmodernity.

Ransmayr narrates a New Year's celebration, in which the crew circles the ship by torchlight and the Italian sailors sing for the officers:

> Sole e pensoso I più deserti campi
> Vo mesurando a passi tardi e lenti,
> E gli occhi porto per fuggire intenti,
> Ove vestigio uman l'arena stampi . . . (*SEF*, 120)

> [Alone and pensive I measure the deserted fields
> with slow and lingering steps,
> and turn my eyes ready to flee
> any human trace imprinted in the sand]

The reader's first reaction is that the text, presented in stanza form, is the actual song that the sailors sang, but Ransmayr immediately negates that assumption. "Aber nein, *was* sie gesungen haben, ist nicht überliefert" (But no, *what* they sang has not been passed down to us; *SEF*, 120/*TID*, 95). The author points out the gap between fiction and reality in representing the experience of being alone in the polar ice, which he is filling in for the reader. However, what is filled in is always based on intertextual precursors. The song is actually Petrarca's Sonnet 35 and in the next chapter, entitled *Campi deserti*, Josef Mazzini lies in the safety of a house in Longyearben, Norway, reciting the sonnet and dreaming that he is being crushed by the ice (*SEF*, 122/*TID*, 98). Not only does Mazzini imagine himself reliving the terror of the crew of the Tegetthoff, but he also calls out for the woman he left behind in Vienna, Anna Koreth, mirroring Petrarca's longing for Laura expressed in the sonnet and the posture of the tortured soul seeking out a no-man's-land to flee heartache.

Throughout Ransmayr's novel there are gestures of repetition and intertextual modeling, but always marked by the failure to recapitulate authentic experience. Josef Mazzini attempts to recreate the journey of the Austro-Hungarian expedition but is sidelined when the research vessel heading to Franz-Josef Land must turn around because of bad weather. The narrator retraces Mazzini's travels in order to figure out how and why he disappeared in the glaciers of Norway shortly thereafter, but ultimately has to fill in the multiple gaps and questionable motives with conjecture. The narrator's study and even memorization of Mazzini's notes and journals leads to an uncomfortable realization that he has become a sort of odd *doppelgänger* inhabiting Mazzini's experience:

> Noch immer ist mir die Erinnerung an jenen Märztag unbequem und lästig, an dem mir auf dem Weg in eine geographische Bibliothek plötzlich bewußt wurde, daß ich längst in die Welt eines anderen hinübergewechselt war; es war die beschämende, lächerliche Entdeckung, daß ich gewissermaßen Mazzinis Platz eingenommen habe.

> [It still perturbs me to recall that day in March — I was on my way to a geography library — when I suddenly realized that I had taken up residence in another man's world. It was an embarrassing, absurd discovery — I had more or less taken Mazzini's place. (*SEF*, 25/*TID*, 15)]

In Sebald's *Nach der Natur* Georg Steller also becomes an odd double of Daniel Messerschmidt, marrying his wife, taking up his research on the Siberian coastal territory, and his interest in the fossils of the wooly mammoth discovered there, which purportedly appears in Steller's dreams upon his death (*NN*, 68/*AN*, 78).[31] When Messerschmidt's wife eventually refuses to accompany Steller to Siberia, he takes on two ravens, "die ihm des Abends ominöse Sprüche diktieren" (which in the evenings dictated ominous sayings to him; *NN*, 47/*AN*, 55). Again, not only does he inhabit the world of his predecessor, but he also takes on an intertextual character, resembling Odin (Wotan) with the two ravens Huginn and Muninn (Thought and Memory). The authors' use of *doppelgänger* figures thus does not refer to Romantic notions of a split soul or psychoanalytic embodiments of the uncanny or unconscious; rather it is a technique of overt repetition that denotes the waning of affect and increasing mediation of experience in postmodern literature.

Nach der Natur and *Die Schrecken des Eises und der Finsternis* represent a different type of travel literature, which reacts to the changes of postmodernity. As Ulla Biernat observes, "Die Reiseliteratur der neunziger Jahre antwortet auf die Globalisierung und auf die neue Semantisierung des Raumes durch simulierte Erlebniswelten und inszenierte Geschichte mit geographischen Grenzgängen" (The travel literature of the '90s responds to globalization and the semanticization of space through simulated experience-worlds and staged history with geographic frontier travels).[32] The effects of globalization seem to bring distant places closer, and the spread of media makes knowledge seem infinitely accessible. However, the modern problems of communicating experience and the dialectic of the Enlightenment were not resolved with the advent of the postmodern; it is simply that artists and writers developed strategies to allow them to recognize the limitations that these problems create and yet still get on with the task of creating art. Thus, when speaking about *Nach der Natur*, Colin Riordan can maintain that the "modern crisis of nature" is also for Sebald a crisis of representation, and Gregory Bond can declare Sebald a "modernist melancholic" based on his critique of the history of progress, which presupposes the Enlightenment and the negative dialectic.[33] Both of these critics are right; however, Sebald and Ransmayr employ postmodern literary techniques, such as repetitions, intertextuality, and the recycling of images, as well as the use of polar landscapes as markers of the limits of knowledge, to address these modern dilemmas.

Notes

The first epigraph to this chapter is from Sten Nadolny, *Die Entdeckung der Langsamkeit,* 39th ed. (Munich: Piper, 1983), 349; in English, Sten Nadolny, *The Discovery of Slowness,* trans. Ralph Freedman (Philadelphia: Paul Dry Books, 2005): "And as Franklin knew from all catastrophes that came on slowly, when the first few perished, the insouciance of the survivors was greater than their understanding" (316). The second epigraph is from Wolfgang Burgstaller, "Der Mensch in naturwissenschaftlicher Forschung und Theorie," in *Menschenbilder,* ed. Hans Czuma (Vienna: Verlag für Gesellschaftskritik, 1988), 117–28: "The 'mastery' of nature' doesn't occur as a desired result. The 'mastery' of the laboratory washing machine is far more important" (122). All translations in this chapter are my own, unless otherwise indicated.

[1] Sven Meyer explains that critical notice for *Nach der Natur* was largely absent early on and only increased as Sebald became more famous, lagging in comparison with the multitude of analyses of his longer prose works. Sven Meyer, "Der Kopf,

der auftaucht: Zu W. G. Sebald's *Nach der Natur,*" in *Sebald: Lektüren,* ed. Marcel Atze and Franz Loquai (Eggingen, Germany: Edition Isele, 2005), 67–77; here 67. A number of recent analyses by critics such as Claudia Albes, Gregory Bond, Anja K. Maier, Sven Meyer, and Colin O'Riordan are a sign of renewed interest in this early prose poem.

[2] Versions of each of the sections of *Nach der Natur* initially appeared as long, stand-alone, poems in the Austrian literary periodical *manuskripte* in the following chronological order: "Und blieb ich am äussersten Meer," *manuskripte* 85 (1984): 23–27; "Wie der Schnee auf den Alpen," *manuskripte* 92 (1986): 26–31; "Die dunckle Nacht fahrt aus," *manuskripte* 95 (1987): 12–18. See Meyer, "Der Kopf, der auftaucht," 71–72. Sebald was quite productive as a poet and several collections of his poetry have been released posthumously. The volumes *For Years Now: Poems* (London: Short Books, 2001) with illustrations from Tess Jaray (presumably translated into English by Sebald himself) and *Unerzählt: 33 Texte und 33 Radierungen* (Munich: Hanser, 2003), with etchings by Jan Peter Tripp, were planned before Sebald's death. Most recently Sven Meyer has collected and edited a broad range of Sebald's poems in *Über das Land und das Wasser: Ausgewählte Gedichte, 1964–2001* (Munich: Hanser, 2008).

[3] Claudia Öhlschläger, *Beschädigtes Leben. Erzählte Risse: W. G. Sebalds poetische Ordnung des Unglücks* (Freiburg: Rombach, 2006), 211.

[4] Claudia Albes, "Porträt ohne Modell: Bildbeschreibung und autobiographische Reflexion in W. G. Sebald's 'Elementargedicht' *Nach der Natur,*" in *Politische Archäologie und melancholische Bastelei,* ed. Michael Niehaus und Claudia Öhlschläger (Berlin: Erich Schmidt, 2006), 47–76; here 48.

[5] Richard Bales, "The Loneliness of the Long-Distance Narrator: The Inscription of Travel in Proust and W. G. Sebald," in *Cross-Cultural Travel: Papers from the Royal Irish Academy Symposium on Literature and Travel,* ed. Jane Conroy (New York: Lang, 2003), 507–12; here 507–8.

[6] Both Claudia Albes in "Porträt ohne Modell" and Claudia Öhlschläger in the respective chapter of her book *Beschädigtes Leben. Erzählte Risse* present detailed analyses of the overall structure and content of *Nach der Natur* in relation to Sebald's central themes. In particular, both critics note the importance of Albrecht Dürer's engraving *Melencolia,* concealed in the literary portrait of Vitus Bering, and other intertextual references for understanding Sebald's work.

[7] Although readers and critics alike seem more intrigued by the more colorful accounts of the medieval painter Matthias Grünewald and the semi-autobiographical narrator's childhood, the importance of the Steller episode as the central part of the "triptych" form is evident. Sven Meyer argues for the importance of "Und blieb ich am äussersten Meer" as the germ of *Nach der Natur* and the start of Sebald's literary career, based upon the author's chance reading of Konrad Bayer's *Der Kopf des Vitus Bering* (1970) and the coincidence of his shared initials with the botanist Steller ("Der Kopf, der auftaucht," 70–71).

[8] David C. Ward, "Ghost Worlds of the Ordinary: W. G. Sebald and Gerhard Richter," *PN Review* 29.6 (2003): 32–36; here 35–36.

[9] Christoph Ransmayr, *Die Schrecken des Eises und der Finsternis* (Frankfurt am Main: Fischer, 1987). Further references to this work are given in the text using the abbreviation *SEF* to refer to this edition and *TID* to refer to the English translation, *The Terrors of Ice and Darkness*, trans. John E. Woods (New York: Grove, 1991). The icy landscape reappears most prominently in the first section of *Die Ausgewanderten* in the form of a glacier that expels the body of a hiker who had been missing for decades. The emphasis of this episode has shifted away from exploration and the limits of knowledge to the persistence of trauma and the return of the repressed. The move toward connecting European, Alpine settings with the return of memory is already indicated in the final section of *Nach der Natur*, a reminiscence from the narrator's childhood in the Allgäu of a hunter falling into a ravine and freezing to death. The peculiar emptiness of the polar landscape, which makes it a surface for intertextual projections and a trope for the limits of knowledge, is ascribed to ruins in later works such as *Die Ringe des Saturn: Eine englische Wallfahrt*, in which the narrator visits a strange, abandoned military site on the isle of Orfordness.

[10] Thomas von Steinacker, "Zwischen schwarzem Tod und weißer Ewigkeit: Zum Grau auf den Abbildungen W. G. Sebalds," in *Verschiebebahnhöfe der Erinnnerung: Zum Werk W. G. Sebalds*, ed. Sigurd Martin and Ingo Wintermeyer (Würzburg: Königshausen & Neumann, 2004), 135.

[11] Works by Ransmayr that were in Sebald's personal library are *Die Schrecken des Eises und der Finsternis* (Frankfurt am Main: Fischer, 1987); *Die letzte Welt* (Nördlingen: Greno, 1988); *Morbus Kitahara* (Frankfurt am Main: Fischer, 1995); and *Das Labyrinth: Drei Prosastücke* (Frankfurt am Main: Fischer, 1997).

[12] Kurt Foster, "Bausteine I: Bilder geistern durch Sebalds Erzählungen, Geister bewohnen ihre Zeilen," in *Wandernde Schatten: W. G. Sebalds Unterwelt*, ed. Ulrich von Bülow, Heike Gfrereis, and Ellen Strittmaier (Marbach: Deutsche Schillergesellschaft, 2008), 87–100; here 98.

[13] Meyer provides examples of Sebald's direct textual borrowings from Steller's travel journals of the polar expedition. For example, he notes items listed in Steller's manifest that Sebald's fictionalized character silently exchanges for indigenous artifacts in an abandoned hut, an episode that is mentioned but not detailed in Steller's journals ("Der Kopf, der auftaucht," 74–75).

[14] Later editions of *Nach der Natur* do not include Thomas Becker's black-and-white landscape photographs. Most of Sebald's works were initially released with smaller publishing houses and then widely reprinted by large-scale commercial publishers as the author's reputation grew. As a result, there are often changes to cover and jacket illustrations, as well as shifts in pagination and the layout of images and text, with significant consequences for interpretation.

[15] Psalm 139, *Lutherbibel (1912)*, 2004, http://l12.bibeltext.com/psalms/139.htm (accessed 9 Jun. 2009); in English, Psalm 139, *New International Version*, 1995, http://www.biblegateway.com/passage/?search=Psalm%20139 (accessed 9 Jun. 2009).

[16] Meyer, "Der Kopf, der auftaucht," 75.

[17] Anja K. Maier, "'Der panische Halsknick': Organisches und Anorganisches in W. G. Sebalds Prosa," in Niehaus and Öhlschläger, 111–26; here 124.

[18] Heinrich Detering, "Schnee und Asche, Flut und Feuer: Über den Elementardichter W. G. Sebald," *Neue Rundschau* 109.2 (1998): 147–58; here 154–55.

[19] The *Schneewunder* (snow miracle) refers to another painting by Grünewald from 1519 depicting the legend of the founding of the St. Maria Maggiore church in Rome. Supposedly, after Pope Liberius had visions of the Virgin Mary, snow fell on the Esquiline Hill in the summer of 352, indicating the location to build a church in her honor.

[20] Quoted in Andrew Weeks, *Paracelsus: Speculative Theory and the Crisis of the Early Reformation* (Albany: SUNY Press, 1997), 169.

[21] Heinz-Peter Preußer, "Reisen ans Ende der Welt: Bilder des Katastrophismus in der neueren österreichischen Literatur. Bachmann — Handke — Ransmayr," in *1945–1995: Fünfzig Jahre deutschsprachige Literatur in Aspekten* ed. Gerhard Knapp and Gerd Labroisse. Amsterdamer Beiträge zur neueren Germanistik 38/39 (Amsterdam: Rodopi, 1995), 369–407; here 389.

[22] Reingard Nethersole, "Marginal Topologies: Space in Christoph Ransmayr's *Die Schrecken des Eises und der Finsternis,*" *Modern Austrian Literature* 23.3 (1990): 135–53; here 140.

[23] Margarete Lamb-Faffelberger, "Christoph Ransmayr's *Die Schrecken des Eises und der Finsternis*: Interweaving Fact and Fiction into a Postmodern Narrative," in *Modern Austrian Prose: Interpretations and Insights*, ed. Paul F. Dvorak (Riverside, CA: Ariadne, 2001), 269–85; here 279.

[24] Gerda Elisabeth Moser, "Das postmoderne ästhetische Tableau und seine Beziehungen zu Leben und Denken," in *Postmoderne Literatur in deutscher Sprache: Eine Ästhetik des Widerstands?* Amsterdamer Beiträge zur neueren Germanistik 49, ed. Henk Harbers. (Amsterdam: Rodopi, 2000), 35–58; here 47.

[25] Gerda Moser, "Das postmoderne ästhetische Tableau," 46; Markus Oliver Spitz, "Traveling Borderline Territories: *Die Schrecken des Eises und der Finsternis* by Christoph Ransmayr," in Conroy, *Cross-cultural Travel*, 453.

[26] Bianca Theisen, "Prose of the World: W. G. Sebald's Literary Travels," *Germanic Review* 79.3 (2004): 163–79; here 172.

[27] Jill Bepler, "Traveling and Posterity: The Archive, the Library and the Cabinet," in *Grand Tour: Adliges Reisen und europäische Kultur vom 14. bis zum 18. Jahrhundert. Akten der internationalen Kolloquien in der Villa Vigoni 1999 und im Deutschen Historischen Institut Paris 2000,* ed. Rainer Babel and Werner Paravicini (Ostfildern, Germany: Jan Thorbecke, 2005), 191–204; here 191.

[28] Gerhard Sauder, "Formen gegenwärtiger Reiseliteratur," in *Reisen im Diskurs: Modelle der literarischen Fremderfahrung von den Pilgerberichten bis zur Postmoderne,* ed. Anne Fuchs and Theo Harden (Heidelberg: Winter, 1995), 552–73; here 552.

[29] Lisa Bloom, in her book *Gender on Ice: American Ideologies of Polar Expeditions* (Minneapolis: U of Minnesota, 1993), draws attention to the way in which the

presumed neutrality of scientific discourse that accompanies polar exploration often masks longings for empire and the need to define masculinity on a national level.

[30] See Max Horkheimer and Theodor Adorno, *Dialektik der Aufklärung: Philosophische Fragmente* (Frankfurt am Main: Fischer, 1969), especially the first chapter, "Begriff der Aufklärung" (The Concept of Enlightenment).

[31] For a description of Daniel Messerschmidt's contribution to the study of the woolly mammoth see the website of the Academy of Natural Sciences, http://www.ansp.org/museum/jefferson/otherFossils/mammuthus.php (accessed 9 Jun. 2009).

[32] Ulla Biernat, *"Ich bin nicht der erste Fremde hier": Zur deutschsprachigen Reiseliteratur nach 1945* (Würzburg: Königshausen & Neumann, 2004), 185.

[33] Colin Riordan, "Ecocentrism in Sebald's *After Nature*," in *W. G. Sebald: A Critical Companion,* ed. J. J. Long and Anne Whitehead (Seattle: U of Washington, 2004), 45–57; here 48. Gregory Bond, "On the Misery of Nature and the Nature of Misery: W. G. Sebald's Landscapes," in Long and Whitehead, *A Critical Companion,* 31–44; here 42.

6: "Eine Art Eingang zur Unterwelt": *Katabasis* in *Austerlitz*

Alan Itkin

IN W. G. SEBALD'S NOVEL *Austerlitz*, at the beginning of his journey to discover his buried past, the eponymous main character finds himself in an antiquarian bookshop, whose proprietor bears the unusual but suggestive name, "Penelope Peacefull." This Penelope, although she is just as welcoming and worldly-wise as the "circumspect Penelope" who is Odysseus's faithful wife, to whom Odysseus returns at the end of his own wearisome travails in the *Odyssey*, is not cross-stitching the shroud of Laertes but instead working on what is perhaps the modern equivalent, the crossword puzzle in the *Telegraph*. There is, nevertheless, a certain parallel between the two episodes, suggesting a larger parallel between the voyage of the proto-hero of Western literature and the post-hero of Sebald's novel.[1] Penelope, for Homer's Odysseus, is one of the anchors of his identity. It is only she who can positively identify him as her husband, lost for twenty years, and the rightful ruler of Ithaca. In reclaiming her from the suitors who seek to usurp his place, he reclaims his home and even himself. Penelope, in fact, grounds Odysseus's identity in memory by testing his knowledge of something that only her husband would know, that their marriage-bed, made out of an old stump, is literally rooted to the ground of Ithaca.[2]

Likewise, in Penelope Peacefull's shop, Jacques Austerlitz begins to remember his past, and by remembering it to reclaim his identity. It is here that he listens with rapt attention to a story about the *Kindertransporte* over the radio playing in the background, finally coming to terms with the fact that he himself was one of the children rescued from the fate of their parents by these transports. The effacement of this past, he realizes, lies at the core of his emotional problems and may, in fact, be the motivation for his entire academic career as an architectural historian "des bürgerlichen Zeitalters" (of the bourgeois age; *A*, 205/140) which preceded the rise of National Socialism.

This is not the only allusion to the *Odyssey* in *Austerlitz*, either. As it is Odysseus's nursemaid, for example, who first recognizes him in Ithaca and helps him take his bloody revenge on the suitors occupying his home, so it is Austerlitz's nursemaid whom he finds in Prague and who helps him discover his parents' fate. There is an echo, as well, in the ghostly image of his mother that Austerlitz finds in a Prague theater archive, of the shade of Odysseus's mother the Greek hero encounters in the land of the dead. Odysseus journeys across the world to his home in Ithaca. At the same time, though, by encountering the traces of the past and coming to terms with them along the way, he finds his own place in history and establishes his own identity. As such, the *Odyssey* establishes conventions that will guide much of later travel writing. Austerlitz, in his journey across Europe, has a history behind him that is radically different from that of Odysseus. By constantly referring back to the *Odyssey*, Sebald highlights both the similarities and the differences in Austerlitz's search for his own identity among the traces of the past he encounters in his travels across modern Europe.

It is, of course, well established that Sebald's literary prose works borrow heavily from the genre of travel writing. Bianca Theisen argues that Sebald finds in travelogues a "hybrid genre" upon which he partially models his own literary peregrinations.[3] It is by using this model that Sebald articulates his own peripatetic brand of engaging with the historical past.[4] John Zilcosky argues that Sebald's literary works, far from repeating the game of lost and found of Romantic travel writing, where the traveler gets lost only to find his way again, instead demonstrate that it is the uncanny position of the modern subject never to be sufficiently lost.[5] In "Lost and Found: Disorientation, Nostalgia, and Holocaust Melodrama in Sebald's *Austerlitz*," Zilcosky revises this thesis: *Austerlitz*, he claims, is different. Here Sebald returns to a model of travel writing based on the idea of losing one's way and finding it again. He also, as Zilcosky points out, returns to the *Odyssey* and the tradition of epic journeys it initiates. The question, then, is why in *Austerlitz*, the last of his completed works, Sebald returns to this most originary form of travel writing, the classical epic journey, as one of his primary models.[6] How Sebald follows this generic model and, more importantly, how he pointedly deviates from it, will reveal unique dimensions of the peripatetic engagement with the historical past that *Austerlitz* enacts. More particularly, the analysis of *Austerlitz*'s relationship to the classical epic model will show how Sebald finds new currency for the relationship to the past embodied by epic, while simultaneously resisting the epic model of coming to terms with the past.

We have already discussed the similarities between the episode in Penelope's shop and its classical model. The differences between that episode and Odysseus's return to his wife, though, are just as striking as the similarities. Odysseus reaches Penelope at the end of the *Odyssey*, even if all of the loose ends are not quite wrapped up — the gods still have to stop the cycle of violence by preventing the families of the suitors Odysseus has slain from taking vengeance. Austerlitz's encounter with his past in Penelope Peacefull's shop, however, is hardly the beginning of his journey. In Sebald's novel there can be no true *nostos*, or homecoming.[7] Austerlitz finds his childhood home, in Prague, but his search for his roots does not end there. There is always more to find of his parent's fate, the fate he has been spared, and the novel ends with a strong hint that this journey may never be over.[8] Homer's epic, on the other hand, is all homecoming; Odysseus's return to Ithaca is the engine of the plot, what everything is building toward. It is the constant hope of the protagonists, the bane of their enemies.[9] If the novel, *Austerlitz*, then, is a sort of latter-day *Odyssey*, it is one whose time sequence, the archetypal order of the episodes, has been completely scrambled, even if Austerlitz's narration of his story (as well as the narrator's narration of his encounters with Austerlitz) follows a more or less chronological order. Time, as Hamlet would say, is out of joint.

In fact, there is a different archetypal epic episode, besides *nostos*, that seems to be repeated in *Austerlitz* time and again. Just prior to his "breakthrough" in Penelope's shop, Austerlitz makes a trip to the Liverpool Street train station, the very place where, as a child, he first met his adoptive parents, the Reverend Elias and his wife, Gwendolyn, and thus began to lose his connection to his own past. Now, in the dim light of the train station, the past begins to surface for him in hallucinatory but at first indecipherable images. In telling this story to the narrator, he describes the station as "eine Art Eingang zur Unterwelt" (a kind of entrance to the underworld; *A*, 188/127–28). This is not just a figure of speech, however. Over and over again, in *Austerlitz*, the entrance to such "places of memory" will be described, both explicitly and implicitly, as journeys to the land of the dead.

The journey to the land of the dead is a common motif in classical epic. It is usually referred to as *nekuia* in Homer's *Odyssey*, but in the rest of the classical tradition, such as Virgil's *Aeneid*, as *katabasis*. In classical epic, *katabasis* is a means of representing the continued influence of the past in the present, a spatial and architectonic trope for the workings of memory.[10] However, it is also more than this. As I will argue, *katabasis* is also linked to classical philosophies of history and, more importantly, to Austerlitz's own "Metaphysik der Geschichte" (historical metaphysic; *A*, 23/13). When Odysseus journeys, literally, to the ends of the earth, where the border between this world and the next becomes permeable, he encounters not only faces from the past — historical, memorial, mythological — but also those who have succumbed entirely to their destinies and become, in fact, mere emblems of that destiny.

Destiny, *moira* in Greek, *fatum* in Latin, is a central concept of the epic worldview. It is often, in fact, a driving force in the plot of the classical epics.[11] Both the Greek and Latin terms, however, are used metonymically to mean "death" as well. This connection between death, as one's ultimate fate, and the concept of destiny carries over into depictions of the land of the dead. The dead appear only in the form of their final destiny. Nor are they dynamic characters — they remain both *how* and *who* they were at the moment of their death. Or rather, they are mere images of who they were.[12] The dead, in Homer's world, still wear the bloody armor in which they were cut down, and they cannot even speak; they need the still-warm blood Odysseus spills out upon the earth for them if they are to regain this capacity.[13] The land of the dead, in other words, is not just a spatial representation of history, a place where historical events and their representative figures are categorized and these categories put into spatial relationships to one another — heroes here, villains there; innocents up above, sinners down below; it is, in the *Odyssey*, the place where a rudimentary theory of history is articulated. The theory, in this case, is history *as* destiny, history as an implacable, divine force, which wears its heroes down and ultimately reduces them to mere emblems of their final defeat. Odysseus must circumvent this, or at least put it behind him and move on to meet his destiny. However, other classical journeys to the land of the dead, Aeneas's in Virgil's *Aeneid*, or the Pilgrim's in Dante's *Divine Comedy*, bear this out as well — the confrontation with the dead is a confrontation with the past, but it also contains a theory of how the past, how history operates, or at least how it appears to operate in the present.[14]

Austerlitz takes his place among the ranks of these heroes and heroic adventurers of the nether realm. Not only does he appear to the author like a modern-day Siegfried, but his spell-binding art of historical narration is described as a sort of communion with the dead, a "schrittweise Annäherung an eine Art Metaphysik der Geschichte . . . in der das Erinnerte noch einmal lebendig wurde" (a gradual approach to a kind of historical metaphysic, bringing remembered events back to life; *A*, 22–23/13). Here the dichotomy between the dead past and the living present, and the permeable border between the two (which will be major themes of the rest of the novel) are described as an implicit part of Austerlitz's mode of historical representation. This is a very Odyssean model of the engagement with the historical past,[15] one that Frederic Jameson, himself borrowing the terms of the *Odyssey*, might call "existential historicism," in which

> the historicist act revives the dead and reenacts the essential mystery of the cultural past which, like Tiresias drinking the blood, is momentarily returned to life and warmth and allowed once more to speak its mortal speech and to deliver its long-forgotten message in surroundings unfamiliar to it.[16]

This is, in other words, history-writing as *nekuia* and *katabasis*, but also an invitation to turn the equation around as well, to read *katabasis* as a form of history-writing.

It is my claim, then, that Sebald, making classical *katabasis* modern, also takes the opportunity to articulate a historical thesis, or philosophy of history: that the historical traumas of National Socialism and the Holocaust cannot be entirely separated from the era of bourgeois expansionism and colonialism (whose architecture the character Austerlitz has made a living of studying) that directly preceded them. Instead, these traumas were the apotheosis of the logic of this previous era — and even more disturbing, this legacy of destruction may not entirely have run its course in the present but instead lies unrecognized everywhere around us.[17] As Austerlitz tells the narrator in a programmatic passage, "die ganze Bau- und Zivilisationsgeschichte des bürgerlichen Zeitalters, die ich erforschte, [drängte] in die Richtung der damals bereits sich abzeichnenden Katastrophe" (the whole history of the architecture and civilization of the bourgeois age, the subject of my research, pointed in the direction of the catastrophic events already casting their shadows before them at the time; A, 205/140).

What is encapsulated in this statement is not, of course, as in the *Odyssey*, an idea of history as destiny, but instead a historical engagement with the question of what has taken the place of destiny in the modern world. This question is part of a larger concern with how we represent and relate to the traumatic past of the twentieth century in the present, which is at its most intense where *Austerlitz* most clearly draws on the classical epic tradition of journeys to the land of the dead. In each of the *katabasis* episodes in *Austerlitz*, Austerlitz or the narrator enters not only a "place of memory" but a place that bears witness to the compulsive expansion of the bourgeois age, "weit über jede Vernunftgrenze hinaus" (far beyond any reasonable bounds; A, 31/18), *in addition to* the horrors of the Holocaust.[18] Over and over again in *Austerlitz*, the confrontation with this uncanny coincidence, in which the same places that bear the partially effaced marks of the violence of the bourgeois age are seen to have taken on a new and even more horrifying significance during the era of National Socialism, is articulated in the terms of a classical journey to the land of the dead. This is not to say, however, that the spirits of the dead literally manifest themselves in Sebald's underworlds of history. Instead, Austerlitz and the narrator illustrate Sebald's theory of history by bringing the dead and forgotten objects left behind in these places, which are the only remaining witnesses to the past entombed there, back to life. By allowing these objects to evoke the "remembered events" of which they were once a part, in other words, they give them an active role in recreating the historical past and thus new life. Just as the classical epic poets, in *katabasis*, offer us a vision of the past seen through the lens of their particular philosophy of history, we see, in the engagement with the objects in these otherworldly places of memory in *Austerlitz*, the history of these two eras through the lens of the logic that connects them. It is then also our relationship, as historically conscious individuals in the present, to this specific legacy of destruction that the journey to the land of the dead thematizes in *Austerlitz*.

The Overture

Although it has no chapters, *Austerlitz* begins with what I will call an "overture." In this section, which focuses on the narrator's first encounters with Austerlitz, during his more or less aimless wanderings around Antwerp, Sebald establishes the themes that will be prevalent throughout Austerlitz's story. And from the very beginning of this section we find ourselves in a sort of annex of the underworld. The narrator wanders down "die Jeruzalemstraat, die Nachtegaalstraat, die Pelikaanstraat, die Paradijsstraat, die Immerseelstraat" (*A*, 9/3), streets named after biblical images of redemption in the afterlife. He then ends up in the Nocturama in the Antwerp Zoo, another nether realm, where day is night and night day, and where the animals, like the shades in Homer's or Dante's underworlds, enact the same futile gestures over and over in hopes of escape. In this overture, however, we do not emerge from the underworld into the light of day — instead, the narrator brings us with him to yet another underworld, the *Salle des pas perdus* in Antwerp's Centraal Station, which he describes as "ein zweites Nocturama" (another Nocturama; *A*, 13/6), and where Austerlitz emerges like a specter from the gloom, prepared, like Achilles's or Agamemnon's ghost, to tell the narrator what's what.[19] Here, we are given, for the first time, an indication of one of the major themes of the novel and of Austerlitz's life-work — the senseless expansion of the bourgeois age and the "Schmerzensspuren" (the marks of pain; *A*, 24/14) that lurk behind it. The station, as Austerlitz begins to tell the narrator, was built not only by expropriating slave labor abroad, in Belgium's colonies under Leopold II, but also by exploiting workers at home (*A*, 23/13); it was modeled on the Pantheon at Rome, turned into a profane temple to "die Gottheiten des 19. Jahrhunderts . . . der Bergbau, die Industrie, der Verkehr, der Handel, und das Kapital" (the deities of the nineteenth century — mining, industry, transport, trade, and capital; *A*, 21/10–12). The classical worldview with its heroes and divinities, it seems, has not died out; it has been transformed into something new and profane.

From this second underworld, in turn, where the focus sharpens on the transgressions of the more distant past of the nineteenth century, we move to a third, the fort of Breendonk, where the second and more urgent point of focus of the novel begins to appear, the horrors of the era of National Socialism. Breendonk, however, is really the perfect emblem of both of these eras. As Austerlitz informs the narrator in his impromptu history lesson in the train station waiting room, it was "Das letzte Glied in der Kette" (the last link in the chain; *A*, 31/18) of the ever-expanding and entirely pointless ring of fortifications surrounding the city of Antwerp. Only later was it turned into an internment camp and torture chamber by the occupying Nazis, where, in fact, the author Jean Améry was tortured.[20]

Memory, its distortions and aporias, is, of course, an ever-present theme in *Austerlitz*, but the underworld he enters in Breendonk, which is a "für immer vom Licht der Natur getrennte[.] Welt" (world . . . cut off forever from the light of nature; *A*, 38/23–24), offers the narrator the chance to consider more pointedly the dialectic of memory and forgetting. Like Dante's Pilgrim, who is constantly disturbed by the horrible sights of the Inferno, he is not sure that he is equipped to *see* what there is to see — "ich [wollte] nicht wirklich sehen, was man dort sah" (I did not really want to see what it had to show; *A*, 38/23); like the Pilgrim, he suffers a fainting spell at the end of the episode, which effectively brings the over- ture section of the novel to a close. However, more important than this failure of vision is the failure of memory. Breendonk forces the narrator to realize, "was alles und wieviel ständig in Vergessenheit gerät" (how every- thing is constantly lapsing into oblivion; *A*, 39/24). There is a certain urgency here in the confrontation with "den ungezählten Orten und Gegenständen . . ., welche selbst keine Fähigkeit zur Erinnerung haben" (countless places and objects which themselves have no power of memory; *A*, 39/24). The question that haunts the narrator and that is posed to us is whether we can allow their stories simply to fade away, especially when they are connected to such a crucial chapter in history.

These "countless places and objects" are, of course, mute, and, in a metaphorical sense, they have died: their life in the present and their voice in history have been eclipsed. Here, however, like Frederic Jameson's Odyssean "existential historian," the narrator himself (and of course, on a more "meta" level, the author, Sebald) enacts a sort of *nekuia*. He attempts, like Odysseus, to give these objects a voice, to allow them to tell their stories, which would otherwise be forgotten. It is through the stories of these objects that he comes closer to the memories of the inmates, whose presence he feels haunting this place, like the ghostly shades of Odysseus's *nekuia*, who strive to tell their own stories of victimization. There are two main examples of this evocation of the dead past in the Breendonk episode. First, in the anteroom of the fort the narrator encounters the wheelbarrows that the prisoners of the SS used to perform their forced labor. He describes these wheelbarrows in detail, comparing them to those he remembers seeing the farmers use in his home town — they are twice as big and must be unbelievably heavy (*A*, 36/22). He begins to imagine how they were used by the prisoners, the effort and pain that would have required, but he stops himself. He cannot imagine what that labor was like. The suffering of the victims is beyond his ability to comprehend:

> Es war mir undenkbar, wie die Häftlinge, die wohl in den seltensten Fällen nur vor ihrer Verhaftung und Internierung je eine körperliche Arbeit geleistet hatten, diesen Karren, angefüllt mit dem schweren

Abraum, über den von der Sonne verbrannten, von steinharten Furchen durchzogenen Lehmboden schieben konnten oder durch den nach einem Regentag bereits sich bildenden Morast, undenkbar, wie sie gegen die Last sich stemmten, bis ihnen beinah das Herz zersprang, oder wie ihnen, wenn sie nicht vorankamen, der Schaufelstiel über den Kopf geschlagen wurde von einem der Aufseher.

[I could not imagine how the prisoners, very few of whom had probably ever done hard physical labor before their arrest and internment, could have pushed these barrows full of heavy detritus over the sun-baked clay of the ground, furrowed by ruts as hard as stone, or through the mire that was churned up after a single day's rain; it was impossible to picture them bracing themselves against the weight until their hearts nearly burst, or think of the overseer beating them about the head with the handle of a shovel when they could not move forward. (*A, 37/22*)]

Here he begins to paint a vivid picture of the suffering endured at Breendonk, while at the same time claiming that he cannot imagine what the victims of the SS endured. It is in fact, he quickly admits, only the lives of the perpetrators, the SS guards, who must have been like "die Familienväter und die guten Söhne" (the good fathers and dutiful sons; *A*, 37/23) among whom he grew up, that he can truly imagine.

The second example is the straw-mattresses in the cells of Breendonk. As the wheelbarrows were the mementoes of those forced into slave labor in Breendonk, so these "Strohsäcke" are the stand-ins, or metonyms, for the victims interned and tortured there, "als seien sie die sterblichen Hüllen derjenigen, so erinnere ich mich jetzt, dachte ich damals, die hier einst gelegen hatten in dieser Finsternis" (and now, in writing this, I do remember that such an idea occurred to me at the time — as if they were the mortal frames of those who lay there in the darkness; *A*, 39/24). Once again, though, the narrator draws back from engaging with these objects out of the past. He claims to want to tell their story, but he only tells us that they have fallen apart over time and hints at the larger story of imprisonment and torture of which they were a part.

Nevertheless, this history and the question of how it may or may not be remembered are a large part of what is at stake here. This episode addresses, in its elliptical way, the suffering not just of the inmates of Breendonk but of all of the victims of National Socialism. The wheelbarrows are not simply those that the victims of Breendonk were forced to haul back and forth, but open up insights, albeit of an extremely tentative kind, into the forced labor of all of the concentration camps. As the narrator tells us, he can imagine the lives of the SS guards "im Gegensatz zu dieser in Breendonk ebenso wie in all den anderen Haupt- und Nebenlagern Tag für Tag und jahrelang fortgesetzten Schinderei" ([in contrast to] the drudgery performed day after day, year after year, at Breendonk and all the other main and branch camps; *A*, 37/22–23). And the mattresses and plank beds upon which they are laid might as well be those of any of the concentration camps that offered such primitive accommodations to their inmates. Breendonk, in other words, was not just the "last link in the chain" of the fortifications around Antwerp; it was also a link in the chain of concentration camps stretched across Europe by the Nazis. As we have said, it is this specific historical thesis, the inextricability of the horrors of National Socialism from the bourgeois expansion that preceded it that we will find thematized time and again in these *katabasis* episodes.

However, the narrator's attempt to bring back to life the past embodied in the objects that inhabit Breendonk seems to dissolve almost immediately into a meditation on the impossibility of doing so. Almost as soon as he has started discussing the straw mattresses he begins musing on the "countless places and objects" whose stories will never be fully explored. There is, then, a delicate balancing act here, in the engagement with the history of the places and objects that cannot speak for themselves, a tension preserved between the possibilities for memory and memorialization, and the aporias that will forever remain. This goes, of course, not only for the wheelbarrows and mattresses but for all that they represent. Similarly, there are things we both can and cannot say about the victims of National Socialism whom these objects represent, as well as things that we will never know. The sordid details of Breendonk's history of torture and violence under the Nazis and the larger history of which it is a part are left in twilight, only hinted at and half-explicated. The closer we come to the traces of the past entombed in Breendonk and brought to light by the narrator, the more we feel, like the specters Odysseus encounters in the land of the dead, that something is essentially receding from us.

And indeed there is once again something otherworldly in the choice of words and images with which the narrator describes this scene. The mattresses are "schattenhaft" (shadow-like), that is, like the ghostly spirits of the underworld, who are often described in classical literature as "shadows" or "shades"; the darkness "verdichtet sich bei dem Gedanken, wie wenig wir festhalten können" (becomes yet heavier as I think how little we can hold in mind), becomes thicker in thinking on what remains and what does not in memory; and the mattresses have become "schmäler und kürzer" (thinner and shorter; *A*, 39/24). The key to understanding the significance of this last detail is a passage that appears later in the novel where the blacksmith, Evan, tells the young Austerlitz that the dead are "verkürzt" (diminished) by the "Erfahrung des Todes" (the experience of death; *A*, 83/54). It is worth noting, as well, that both the animals in the Nocturama and the inhabitants of the *Salle des pas perdus* appear miniaturized to the narrator — this seems to be one of the signs of a spectral presence in *Austerlitz*.

This *Schattenspiel*, though, between revelation and effacement, must come to an end. The narrator, as impersonal observer of a history to which he is only tenuously connected, can only go so far. Eventually, he retreats into the more familiar realms of personal memory and literature. The "Schrecken der Kindheit" (childhood terrors; *A*, 41/25) arise for him out of the abyss of memory in the torture chamber, culminating in his Dantesque fainting spell, and this section of the overture effectively comes to a close with an extended reverie on the story of Jean Améry. Even here, though, the narrator does not address the whole story head-on. He claims not to have read Améry's account of his torture at the time of his journey to Breendonk, and even in retrospect he approaches it, so to speak, from an angle, by way of the story of the character Gastone Novelli in Claude Simon's novel *Le jardin des plantes*, who endured the same torture as Améry at Dachau. The real exploration of this underworld of history and memory, then, will be left to the adventurer-hero, Austerlitz, whose narration of his journey of self-discovery will take up the rest of the novel. This is only a prelude, a hint of things to come in the novel, the groundwork for a far more personal engagement with the legacy of the Holocaust, enacted by a character who was himself profoundly impacted by this history. This makes this section, the "overture" as I have called it, analogous to the so-called *Telemacheia* that occupies the first four of the twenty-four books of the *Odyssey*, focusing not on Odysseus but on his son, Telemachos, in his quest to learn the fate of his father and to become a man in his own right. The narrator is not Austerlitz's son (although he will become, in a sense, his heir, inheriting the stock of photographs Austerlitz has taken in his journey), but his more distant engagement with this past sets the stage for Austerlitz's story.

What remains, though, from this *katabasis* episode in Breendonk is the sense of an engagement and sympathy with the victims of National Socialism, a desire to allow them to speak, even though they can speak no more, by telling the stories of the relics they have left behind. Equally important, however, is the backdrop of this encounter. One must not forget why the narrator has journeyed here in the first place: it is because of what Austerlitz has told him about how Breendonk fits into the story of the "bourgeois era," with its undergirding ideology of progress, which turns out to mask an equally strong compulsion to destruction. This darker side of progress, as Austerlitz will later hint to the narrator, has been exposed in all of its horrifying dimensions by the Holocaust (*A*, 205/140). The dialectic of these quasi-deterministic concepts, of progress and its shadow, is what takes the place of destiny in the *katabases* of *Austerlitz*.

Encapsulated in this episode, then, is an engagement not only with the victims of National Socialism but also with a fatalistic and mechanistic conception of the events leading up to their victimization. In the Centraal Station, the gods of Virgil's Rome, themselves the descendants of the gods of Homer's Greece, are transformed into the monolithic symbols of a mechanistic world order run according to the logic of capital. Likewise, the victim-shades of Breendonk find themselves enmeshed in the milieu of this clockwork logic, like Homer's shades in their ignominious destinies. Breendonk, the "last link in the chain" of bourgeois military progress, fulfills its ultimate and hidden purpose as a stunningly cruel "document of barbarism" — something that seems to have been built into its very structure, its "Schema irgendeines krebsartigen Wesens" (the anatomical blueprint of some alien and crab-like creature or cancer-like life-form; *A*, 36/22) and its gloomy interior, from the very beginning. This verdict on progress is, of course, well known. Benjamin's famous thesis on the "documents of civilization" perhaps puts it most succinctly, but what emerges here is not merely a generalized historical thesis.[21] What the narrator cannot give us is exactly what the framed narration of the character Austerlitz throughout the rest of the novel will provide — a *personal* engagement with the history of destruction, culminating in the Holocaust. It is this personal story (based, as Sebald has said, partially on the stories of real people)[22] that moves *Austerlitz* away from the highly mediated peripatetic historicism of *Die Ringe des Saturn* (where the particular history the book tells is mediated by the ruins the narrator encounters in the landscape of East Anglia and the books he reads in its libraries) and into the range of the testimonials of *Die Ausgewanderten*. Or rather, like the *Odyssey* and the other classical epic journeys modeled on it, *Austerlitz* combines these two impulses, the peripatetic and the testimonial, into one single literary form.[23]

Liverpool Street Station

Everywhere Austerlitz goes and every key juncture of his life-story is a sort of *katabasis*, but there are two key episodes in which this classical motif plays a particularly important role: the one in Liverpool Street Station, where his suppressed memories begin to surface, and another, later, when he journeys to Theresienstadt, the concentration camp where his mother was interned, in an attempt to learn her fate. As Austerlitz tells the narrator, the first of these episodes begins in a period of decreased mental stability in his life. Unable to work or to think clearly as the repressed past begins to intrude on his daily life, he takes to wandering the streets of London by night. Like in T. S. Eliot's "Wasteland," this London is itself a sort of gloomy nether realm.[24] Austerlitz leaves the city precisely at the time of morning when the "armen Seelen . . . von der Peripherie zurückfluten in die Mitte" (poor souls . . . flow from the suburbs towards the center; *A*, 187/126). However, the spectral forms that appear to Austerlitz amongst this throng are, rather than merely the regular working stiffs, emanations of his own repressed memories. "Dabei ist es mir in den Bahnhöfen wiederholt passiert, daß ich . . . ein mir von viel früher her vertrautes Gesicht zu erkennen. . . . vermeinte. Immer hatten diese bekannten Gesichter etwas von allen anderen Verschiedenes, etwas Verwischtes" (As I passed through the stations, I thought several times that . . . I saw a face known to me from some much earlier part of my life, but I could never say whose it was. These familiar faces always had something different from the rest about them, something . . . indistinct; *A*, 187/127).

We are meant, once more, to think back to Evan's excursus on the ghosts who walk among us. Not only are they smaller than in life, as we have said, but: "Auf den ersten Blick sähen sie aus wie normale Leute, aber wenn man sie genauer anschaute, verwischten sich ihre Gesichter oder flackerten ein wenig an den Rändern" (At first glance they seemed to be normal people, but when you looked more closely their faces would blur or flicker slightly at the edges; *A*, 83/54). There is, in other words, something "indistinct" about the faces of these ghosts. Indistinctness and diminution are thus two signs that herald the intrusion of the otherworldly into our own world. There is, though, even a third sign about which Evan tells Austerlitz. It is, he says, nothing but a "schwarze[r] Schleier" (black veil; *A*, 83/54) or a "Seidentuch" (piece of silk; *A*, 84/54), which separates us from the next world. And indeed, in his own spectral encounters in London, it is exactly through this sort of "veil" that Austerlitz sees these apparitions: "Tatsächlich begann ich damals . . . durch eine Art von treibendem Rauch oder Schleier hindurch Farben und Formen von einer sozusagen verminderten Körperlichkeit zu sehen, Bilder aus einer verblichenen Welt" (I began seeing what might be described as shapes and colors of diminished corporeality through a drifting veil or cloud of smoke, images from a faded world; *A*, 188–89/127). This "faded world" of "diminished corporeality" that Austerlitz sees through a veil, then, is strongly meant to evoke the spirit world, into which Evan is his first guide.

Immediately after this description of his nightly wanderings, Austerlitz's discussion begins to focus on the "entrance to the underworld" in Liverpool Street Station, to which, he says, he found himself unavoidably drawn (*A*, 188/127) and which, on one particular night, was the site of another revelatory moment in the recovery of his past. As the focus narrows spatially, though, the historical focus simultaneously expands. Like in the overture, the "marks of pain" left over from the oppression and exploitation of the bourgeois age, "das Leid und die Schmerzen, die sich dort über die Jahrhunderte angesammelt haben" (the pain and suffering accumulated on this site over the centuries; *A*, 191/129–30), from the famous insane asylum Bedlam to the graves literally dug up to make room for progress, are brought to light (a full-page photograph here shows a collection of ghastly skeletons — even the dead do not escape the violence of modernization). Unlike in Breendonk, however, the connection between this place and the horrors of National Socialism, for Austerlitz, are personal, memorial rather than merely historical, for it is here that he first met his adoptive parents, the Reverend Elias and his wife, Gwendolyn. In fact, this very scene, the first encounter with these strange, sad people who are to be his adoptive family, is played out before Austerlitz's eyes, in a sort of hallucinatory vision, immediately after an encounter with a shabby porter whose repeated, purposeless, pathetic work, "in seiner Zwecklosigkeit an die ewigen Strafen gemahnte, die wir, sagte Austerlitz, wie es heißt, nach unserem Leben erdulden müssen" (in its pointlessness reminded me of the eternal punishments that we are told, said Austerlitz, we must endure after death; *A*, 196/132). This porter, in other words, would himself be just as much at home in Dante's or Homer's underworlds. He leads Austerlitz into the station and then promptly disappears (as ghosts are wont to do).

The underworld into which this ghostly spirit leads him is certainly an example of architecture as spatial metaphor for memory, as well. Vast and impossible vistas open up to Austerlitz, here, in the Ladies' Waiting Room (which was being remodeled), where "mitten in dieser Gefängnis- und Befreiungsvision die Frage mich quälte, ob ich in das Innere einer Ruine oder in das eines erst im Entstehen begriffenen Rohbaus geraten war" (in the middle of this vision of imprisonment and liberation I could not stop wondering whether it was a ruin or a building in the process of construction that I had entered; *A*, 199/135–36). This space is populated, once again, by "winzige Figuren" (tiny figures; *A*, 198/135). It is, however, equal parts cultural and personal memories that are being thematized here. For it is not only Austerlitz's partially effaced, ruined, and rebuilt past that surfaces here, his personal, childhood traumas that bind him in the "prison-house of memory" and whose realization simultaneously sets him free, but also his past as a victim of National Socialism, as one of those rescued from the fate of their parents by the *Kindertransporte*; and it is not only the architectural history of the building that comes to the fore but also the "marks of pain" of the bourgeois age.

Here, however, Austerlitz does not stand on one side while the traces of the traumatic past stand on the other. His childhood fears are not separate from the vision that appears before his eyes. It is *himself* as child and as victim that he sees, there, before his eyes. This is not the sort of engagement with the past we saw the narrator enact in the Breendonk episode, mediated, as it was, through the literature he had read and the unrelated memories of his childhood, but a desperate attempt, on Austerlitz's part, to reclaim his own past and his own identity, a past and identity that can only speak in the hushed tones of the dead and that threaten to disappear in the next moment. The ghostliness of the images Austerlitz sees, though, is also more than just a trite trope for the ineffability of memory. It is also, as in the overture, the sign of an implacable historical logic at work in the events that have left their trace in the train station, as, indeed, in all of the monuments of modernity in *Austerlitz*. This logic is the logic of "progress," which, as we have said, fills the role of classical destiny in *Austerlitz*. It is a logic to which the porter, the gray figures streaming through the city at dawn, and the "tiny figures" that appear in the hallucinatory architectural cityscape within the train station all seem to have succumbed, and of which they appear as emblems. It is the absence and purposelessness of their eternally repeated gestures that, like in the classical visions of the underworld, demonstrate their submission to the forces enshrined all around them. That this logic leads, implacably, to the events that placed Austerlitz and the Eliases here together in 1939, via whatever circuitous route, and that it was adopted and distorted by the Nazis as agents of the so-called "Endlösung" (final solution), are only hinted at in this episode, through the constant interweaving of the two frames of reference, the era of bourgeois progress and that of the rising threat of National Socialism. After this episode, however, Austerlitz will confront this history head-on. From here, emboldened by what he has recovered of his past in this underworld and in the relative peace of Penelope's shop, he travels to Prague, where he had lived as a young child with his parents, and from there to the former concentration camp at Terezín, where, he learns, his mother was interned by the Nazis.

Terezín

In the empty concentration camp museum in Terezín, Austerlitz comes face to face with the historical realities, which, incredibly, despite his historical erudition, he had avoided confronting his entire life, realities that he both begins to understand and finds beyond the means of comprehension: "Das alles begriff ich nun und begriff es auch nicht, denn jede Einzelheit . . . überstieg bei weitem mein Fassungsvermögen" (I understood it all now, yet I did not understand it, for every detail . . . far exceeded my comprehension; *A*, 287/199). Curiously, though, in retrospect, it is not on this particular historical reality and the mute relics of this period that he reflects, but rather on the period of the construction of what was, like Breendonk, an impressively elaborate military outpost, leading up to its later appropriation as a concentration camp by the Nazis:

> Und jedesmal, wenn ich jetzt an das Museum von Terezín zurückdenke, sagte Austerlitz, sehe ich das gerahmte Grundschema der sternförmigen Festung . . . das Modell einer von der Vernunft erschlossenen, bis ins geringste geregelten Welt.

> [And whenever I think of the museum in Terezín now, said Austerlitz, I see the framed ground plan of the star-shaped fortifications . . . the model of a world made by reason and regulated in all conceivable respects. (*A*, 288/199)]

What is stressed here is not the *difference* between the period of European military architectural expansion during which the fort was constructed and later used, partially, as a military and civilian prison, but the congruence between this purpose, as well as the worldview that enabled it, and that of the Nazis who appropriated it for their own purposes, the fine gradient between the military architects' "world made by reason and regulated in all conceivable respects" and that of the architects of *l'univers concentrationnaire*.

And it is once again as a journey to the underworld that Austerlitz describes his trip to the town of Terezín, once the concentration camp Theresienstadt. What strikes him, first of all, is the ramshackle town's emptiness. It is a sort of ghost town. The only figure he sees is a solitary man on the street who promptly, like the porter in Liverpool Street Station, disappears (*A*, 274/189). The photographs accompanying this episode are also uncannily otherworldly — several pages are filled with pictures of decrepit doorways. As Austerlitz tells us: "Am unheimlichsten aber schienen mir die Türen und Tore von Terezín, die sämtlich, wie ich zu spüren meinte, den Zugang versperrten zu einem nie noch durchdrungenen Dunkel" (What I found most uncanny of all, however, were the gates and doorways of Terezín, all of them, as I thought I sensed, obstructing access to a darkness never yet penetrated; *A*, 276–80/190). These doorways, then, are, like the entrance to Liverpool Street Station, another form of entrance to the underworld. Like Dante's gateway in the *Inferno*, in their ominous decrepitude, they seem to convey the message "Lasciate ogne speranza, voi ch'intrate" (III.9; Abandon all hope, ye who enter here). One even seems to have a sort of pit in front of it (*A*, 277/191).[25] Another photograph shows trash cans lined up against a decrepit wall, each with a faded number painted on it — metonymic stand-ins, like the mattresses in Breendonk, perhaps, for the very image that is not shown here but remains the undeniable subtext, that of concentration camp inmates with their numbered uniforms or the numbers tattooed into their flesh (*A*, 276/190; fig. 4).

It is not merely these enigmatic and gloomy traces of a town gone under that interest Austerlitz but the past that lies, partially obscured, behind them. To connect with this past, however, he requires an act of imagination. He imagines, in vivid detail, that the inhabitants of the ghetto at Theresienstadt (sixty thousand of whom, he tells us, were housed in at most a one kilometer area) are still there, all around him:

> [es schien] mir auf einmal mit der größten Deutlichkeit so, als wären sie nicht fortgebracht worden, sondern lebten, nach wie vor, dichtgedrängt in den Häusern, in den Souterrains und auf den Dachböden, als gingen sie pausenlos die Stiegen auf und ab, schauten bei den Fenstern heraus, bewegten sich in großer Zahl durch die Straßen und Gassen und erfüllten sogar in stummer Versammlung den gesamten, grau von dem feinen Regen schraffierten Raum der Luft.

Fig. 4. W. G. Sebald, Austerlitz *(Munich: Hanser, 2001), 272. Copyright © by W. G. Sebald, used with permission of the Wylie Agency LLC.*

[it suddenly seemed to me, with the greatest clarity, that they had never been taken away after all, but were still living crammed into those buildings and basements and attics, as if they were incessantly going up and down the stairs, looking out of the windows, moving in vast numbers through the streets and alleys, and even, a silent assembly, filling the entire space occupied by the air, hatched with gray as it was by the fine rain. (*A,* 289/200)]

Here, as in the narrator's descent into the fort of Breendonk, there is a sense of incompletion, something unsatisfying and provisional. Imagination has to step in precisely where memory and historical understanding end. Likewise, when Austerlitz stands before an antique shop window in Terezín, expecting the mementoes assembled there, like dead spirits, to speak their fates to him: "als müßte aus irgendeinem von ihnen, oder aus ihrem Bezug zueinander, eine eindeutige Antwort sich ableiten lassen auf die vielen, nicht auszudenkenden Fragen, die mich bewegten" (as if one of them or their relationship with each other must provide an unequivocal answer to the many questions I found it impossible to ask in my mind; *A*, 283/195). In fact, all he sees here (as we can see in one of the photographs included at this point; *A*, 284/197) is his own shadow, amid the various objects "die aufgrund unerforschlicher Zusammenhänge ihre ehemaligen Besitzer überlebt und den Prozeß der Zerstörung überdauert hatten" (that for reasons one could never know had outlived their former owners and survived the process of destruction; *A*, 285/197). Peter Weiss (one of Sebald's enduring influences) states in his short literary-prose piece, "Meine Ortschaft,"[26] that this is his place, the place to which he, a German Jew, was doomed by the Nazi bureaucratic mechanisms that, ordering and ruling the world, would take the place of classical destiny. Weiss, like Austerlitz, only escaped the concentration camp by a twist of fate, and both Austerlitz and Weiss have the sense that it is where they belong, where, in a sense, they were destined to be. Austerlitz tells the narrator as much, later, when he sees a photograph of the records room at Terezín (*A*, 401/283), and he is already, as his shadow-image in the mirrored glass shows, in a way, one of the "shades" entombed here.

There is, however, something missing here, something that has necessitated the same backward step into the purely imaginative that the narrator has undertaken in the overture. What is missing is precisely the image Austerlitz has been searching for all along — that of his mother, who presumably died here in the camp at Theresienstadt. This, then, is another connection between Odysseus's journey in the *Odyssey*, and that of Austerlitz. It is, in the *Odyssey*, the sentimental climax of the *nekuia* when Odysseus speaks to the shade of his mother, who has died (of heartbreak and, up to this point, unbeknownst to Odysseus) during his long absence. He has been forced, while he communes with the seer Teiresias, to keep her, along with the other shades, at bay, and when he finally gets the opportunity to speak to her, he attempts to embrace her three times, only to find that she slips through his hands three times:

> Three times
> I started toward her, and my heart was urgent to hold her,
> and three times she fluttered out of my hands like a shadow
> or a dream, and the sorrow sharpened at the heart within me.
> (11.205–8)

This, of course, in the *Odyssey*, may already be read as a thematization of the distance between the living and the dead, between presence and remembrance. Austerlitz's journey, however, and his engagement with this particular personal history do not end when he leaves the underworld of Terezín. What becomes increasingly clear is that what he is really searching for here is the *image* of his mother.[27] The shades of the dead in classical literature are frequently described as "images" (*imagines*, in

Latin), and what the character Austerlitz (and the author Sebald) is interested in is the photographic image in particular, which is, for him, the expression par excellence of this difficult dialectic of memory and forgetting.[28] As Austerlitz explains to the narrator in a particularly programmatic passage:

> Besonders in den Bann gezogen hat mich bei der photographischen Arbeit stets der Augenblick, in dem man auf dem belichteten Papier die Schatten der Wirklichkeit sozusagen aus dem Nichts hervorkommen sieht, genau wie Erinnerungen, sagte Austerlitz, die ja auch inmitten der Nacht in uns auftauchen und die sich dem, der sie festhalten will, so schnell wieder verdunkeln, nichts anders als ein photographischer Abzug, den man zu lang im Entwicklungsbad liegenläßt.

> [In my photographic work I was always especially entranced, said Austerlitz, by the moment when the shadows of reality, so to speak, emerge out of nothing on the exposed paper, as memories do in the middle of the night, darkening again if you try to cling to them, just like a photographic print left in the developing bath too long. (*A*, 117/77)]

Once again, the key word, "shadows," clues us in to the otherworldly aspect of this relationship, and the delicate play of appearance and disappearance, light and dark, as Austerlitz tells us, is the perfect analogue and companion of memories, which simultaneously obscure and reveal the so-called realities of the past.[29]

This play of light and dark, though, is itself a kind of revision of the aesthetic of the classical land of the dead. It is no accident that Milton describes the hell of *Paradise Lost* as a "darkness visible."[30] This is just as apt a description of the underworld Aeneas visits in Book 6 of Virgil's *Aeneid*, where words related to darkness and shadow crowd the page as the dead souls crowd around the epic hero — words such as *umbra* (shadow), *tenebra* (gloom), *obscurus* (dark), and *atrus* (black). It is equally true, though, of the land of the dead in Homer's *Odyssey*, where the spirits are described as "shadows," *skiai* (10.495), even that of Odysseus's own mother (11.207). This is the peculiar magic of the past embodied by the classical land of the dead, which it is both visible and dark, all around the epic hero yet intangible. There is certainly something paradoxical about this idea of "darkness visible." At the same time, however, it captures perfectly the dialectic of memory and forgetting, the demand to know the past and the impossibility of truly doing so, embodied by the encounter with the spirits of the underworld in classical epic. For the character Austerlitz in Sebald's novel this dialectic is thematized by the development of photographs.

Fig. 5. W. G. Sebald, Austerlitz *(Munich: Hanser, 2001), 357. Copyright © by W. G. Sebald, used with permission of the Wylie Agency LLC.*

Austerlitz, like Odysseus, whose attempts to embrace his mother are three, encounters three images that may or may not be of his mother — only the last of which is verified, by his childhood nursemaid, whom he encounters again in Prague. The first of these (*A,* 265/182) is a photograph that materializes mysteriously (along with one of himself as a child) between the pages of Balzac's *Le colonel Chabert* and shows a couple on a stage (Austerlitz's mother was a professional actress), who, at first glance, appear to be Austerlitz's parents, but turn out not to be. The second (*A,* 358/251) is from a Nazi propaganda film made at Theresienstadt and meant to hide the reality of the inmates' lives there, which Austerlitz slows down to the point where it is almost a slide show of still images. It is only then, when it has been, so to speak, turned into a series of static photographic images that this one image appears, which Austerlitz thinks may show his mother; but Vera, the nursemaid, denies this.

The final image, which Vera confirms is actually of Austerlitz's mother (*A,* 361/253; fig. 5), is worth a closer look, so to speak. Austerlitz finds the photograph, which is included in the text, in a theater's archives in Prague. It is almost completely black. Only in the right half of the picture is the face of a young woman, itself half-covered in shadow. The face in the photograph seems to be in the process either of appearing or disappearing, either of emerging out of the shadow and into the light or retreating, disappearing again into the shadows. The expression, which one can only just make out, since the right side of the face, and part of the left cheek as well, is almost entirely swathed in darkness, is almost blank, illegible. Is this a happier moment, or is the figure already burdened by the troubles just appearing on the horizon? It is impossible to tell.

This photograph, if anything, is a particularly spectral image. It thematizes perfectly the play of light and dark that has so fascinated Austerlitz in photography, and that seems to translate into the realm of the photographic image the entire metaphoric of shadow and ghostliness that has gone hand-in-hand with the engagement with the past of the Holocaust throughout the novel. This metaphorics, in turn, builds upon the shadowy aesthetics of historical representation embodied by classical *katabasis*. It highlights the fact that there is as much that we will never know about this person as what we, along with Austerlitz, are able to find out. As in Breendonk, what seems to be thematized here is the limits of Austerlitz's engagement with the traumatic past — his mother has been turned into smoke and shadow by the Nazis, and she can only be allowed to speak again in the limited sense in which the few traces of her presence constitute a message out of the past.

This, however, the mere authentication of her presence, the undeniable proof of her existence that the photograph represents, seems, to a certain extent, to satisfy Austerlitz. With this, he is off to seek any traces of his father, whose fate is slightly less clear than that of his mother, a journey on which, unlike in the *Odyssey*, we do not follow him. Odysseus comes home, puts the past behind him, and reclaims his own identity. In Sebald's late-twentieth-century re-envisioning of the epic, there can be no such conclusion. What, then, does it say that the narrative of *Austerlitz* is structured on a continuous repetition of this central epic motif of *katabasis* without a proper conclusion? In a spatial sense, perhaps that anywhere in Europe, anywhere Austerlitz or the narrator goes, contains traces of the unspeakable violence of the era of National Socialism and its roots in the colonialist, capitalist, bourgeois expansion that preceded it — "There is no document of civilization which is not at the same time a document of barbarism."[31] In a temporal sense, however, it perhaps rather suggests that the engagement with this past, with the creeping forces that would take the place of destiny, with the partially effaced and irrecoverable memories and histories of this violence, can only ever be tentative and incomplete, and thus needs to be repeated again and again. The past refuses to stay past, and we cannot simply put it aside or get over it. Nor can we ever be sure that we have entirely escaped from its legacy of violence; after all, what separates Austerlitz (or indeed us) from the ghostly figures haunting the train-station waiting rooms and other forgotten way stations of this world? Sebald's *Austerlitz*, then, draws on classical epic to highlight not merely a similarity between the epic mode of storytelling and the epic worldview and its own in dealing with the traumatic past of the twentieth century, but also a difference, a fundamental incongruence, in how they relate to the past. It is one of the laments of literature "after Auschwitz," that the classical tradition no longer seems relevant when faced with the utter failure of its ideals of humanity and dignity in the horrors of National Socialism. It is, however, precisely by virtue of, not in spite of, its failures and aporias that Sebald's epic technique manages to bridge this gap and give new relevance to the classical tradition in the wake of the Holocaust.

Notes

[1] I refer to *Austerlitz,* here, as a novel, although further study of Sebald's reception of classical literature might call that generic classification into question. It is the general critical consensus that *Austerlitz* is the most novelistic of Sebald's literary works. Andreas Huyssen, for example, in *Present Pasts: Urban Palimpsests and the Politics of Memory* (Stanford, CA: Stanford UP, 2003), calls *Austerlitz* Sebald's "first 'real' novel" (177 n. 40). For an excellent discussion of this question, see John Zilcosky, "Lost and Found: Disorientation, Nostalgia, and Holocaust Melodrama in Sebald's *Austerlitz, MLN* 121.3 (Apr. 2006): 679–98; here 684–87.

[2] Homer, *Odyssey,* 23.173–206. All translations from Richmond Lattimore, *The Odyssey of Homer* (New York: Harper Collins, 1999). Froma I. Zeitlin argues, in her analysis of the marriage-bed scene, that Homer depicts Penelope as a woman with a remarkable amount of power in certifying Odysseus's claim to his rights as husband and king of Ithaca: "In her role as the custodian of his rights to exclusive possession of her and hence as the mainstay of the social system in which both spouses are awarded their respective positions, Penelope is faced with a situation that gives her unaccustomed power . . . to grant or withhold from her errant husband the stability of a safe anchorage at home." Zeitlin, "Figuring Fidelity in Homer's *Odyssey,*" in *Playing the Other: Gender and Society in Classical Greek Literature* (Chicago: U of Chicago P, 1996), 19–52; here 27.

[3] Bianca Theisen, "Prose of the World: W. G. Sebald's Literary Travels," *Germanic Review* 79.3 (Summer 2004): 163–79; here 165.

[4] "For Sebald, the dark history of oppression has left a deep trace in our physical and psychological make-up. . . . Using recourse to genres and media invested in the indexical and bordering on the documentary or factual — such as travelogue, autobiography, detective fiction . . ., and photography — Sebald follows such traces." Theisen, "Prose of the World," 175.

[5] John Zilcosky, "Sebald's Uncanny Travels: The Impossibility of Getting Lost," in *W. G. Sebald: A Critical Companion,* ed. J. J. Long and Anne Whitehead (Seattle: U of Washington P, 2004), 102–20.

[6] *Austerlitz* is a complex text with a number of different intertextual layers. I emphasize its connection to the classical epic tradition, because it allows us access

to questions pertaining to the type of historical representation the text both proposes and enacts. It is worth noting, as well, that it is not only the epic tradition of Homer, Virgil, Dante, Milton, etc. upon which Sebald draws in *Austerlitz*.; it is also the Germanic tradition of the *Nibelungenlied*. When Austerlitz first appears to the narrator, it is as a modern-day Siegfried — albeit the version of Siegfried from Fritz Lang's Nibelungen film, something Russell J. A. Kilbourn has pointed out in his essay "Architecture and Cinema: The Representation of Memory in W. G. Sebald's *Austerlitz*," in Long and Whitehead, *A Critical Companion*, 140–54; here 141.

[7] "And unlike the epitome of the Western world's traveler, Ulysses (i.e. Odysseus), the journeys of Sebald's protagonists never end in a return home, even if their travels take them to Ithaca (New York)." Theisen, "Prose of the World," 171.

[8] "*Austerlitz*'s final sentence gives the story another turn of the screw, suggesting that the narrator has not come to any closure at all: he keeps reading Jacobson's book *Heshel's Kingdom* — he was only on chapter 15! — and heads back toward the town, probably to get on yet another train, headed perhaps for Austerlitz's home in Alderney Street or perhaps in some unforeseen direction, toward yet another set of characters and stories. This final motion, however, does not differ significantly from Austerlitz's earlier journey toward the south of France: the apparent nomadism of both characters is contained in the preexisting nostalgic structure of lost and found." Zilcosky, "Lost and Found," 697.

[9] This is one of the central arguments William B. Thalman makes about the *Odyssey*, tying it to the tradition of *nostoi*, or poems about the Greek heroes' homecoming, now lost, which once filled out the epic cycle about the Trojan War. According to Thalman, the *Odyssey* is "the story not only of the longest and most difficult of the Returns but also of the most successful one because of the suppleness, intelligence, and dedication to the purpose of its hero and heroine." William B. Thalman, *The* Odyssey: *An Epic of Return* (New York: Twayne, 1992), 45–46.

[10] This is the argument that Russell J. A. Kilbourn makes about Sebald's use of *katabasis*, that it is the locus of "the conflation of different architectural metaphors for memory — memory as both labyrinth and city of the dead." Kilbourn, "Architecture and Cinema," 141.

[11] In discussing the *Aeneid*, for example, David Quint tells us that "The hero's individual agency is illusory, at best greatly diminished, even when he appears to promote his destiny." David Quint, "Repetition and Ideology in the *Aeneid*," in *Epic and Empire: Politics and Generic Form from Virgil to Milton* (Princeton, NJ: Princeton UP, 1993), 50–96; here 91–92.

[12] In the land of the dead, "Odysseus can observe how the pattern of a person's life is fixed, once and for all, at the moment of death. Nothing now can be changed, and all the possibilities for development and achievement that life holds out are gone. A life is now viewed as a whole, a finished story, and judged for better or worse from the perspective of its ending." Thalman, *The* Odyssey, 89–90.

[13] Among the dead are "many fighting men killed in battle, stabbed with brazen / spears, still carrying their bloody armor upon them" (*Odyssey* 11.40–41). "This

is the physical consequence of death: parted from the body, the soul lives a shadowy existence as a faint copy of its former self that can be revived to speak only temporarily by a taste of blood." Thalman, *The* Odyssey, 89.

[14] In Virgil's *Aeneid* the spirit of Aeneas's father, Anchises, not only gives Aeneas a quick lesson in a quasi-Platonic metaphysics but shows him, as well, the dead spirits of heroes, who, when a thousand years are up, will return to the world above to fill their allotted slots as the new heroes of the Roman state — their dance card, it seems, is already full. In the *Divine Comedy* this same Virgil, himself now turned into a literary figure, guides the Pilgrim through an after-life where he must come to terms with the divine providence according to which God's love moves the world, and of which the figures in the *Inferno* and in the *Paradiso* (excluding those in the *Purgatorio*, who are slowly transforming from one to the other) are emblems. It is not only biblical and mythical figures that he encounters, however, but also the historical figures of the Europe of his age that are each put in their place, so to speak.

[15] One might also read this in relation to the myth of the musician Orpheus's journey to the underworld to bring his wife back to the world of the living. Julia Hell has discussed this Orphic angle, in relation, specifically, to Sebald's essay *Luftkrieg und Literatur*, in her essay "The Angel's Enigmatic Eyes, or The Gothic Beauty of Catastrophic History in W. G. Sebald's 'Air War and Literature,'" *Criticism* 46.3 (Summer 2004): 361–92.

[16] Fredric Jameson, "Marxism and Historicism," *New Literary History* 11 (Autumn 1979): 41–73; here 51–52.

[17] Sebald's historical thesis, then, is similar to that of Giorgio Agamben, who also sees the concentration camp as the apotheosis of the impulses of the modern era: "In this light, the birth of the camp in our time appears as an event that decisively signals the political space of modernity itself. It is produced at the point at which the political system of the modern nation-state, which was founded on the functional nexus between a determinate localization (land) and a determinate order (the State) and mediated by automatic rules for the inscription of life (birth or the nation), enters into a lasting crisis, and the State decides to assume directly the care of the nation's biological life as one of its proper tasks." Agamben, *Homo Sacer: Sovereign Power and Bare Life*, trans. Daniel Heller-Roazen (Stanford, CA: Stanford UP, 1998), 174–75.

[18] Apropos of the rings of fortifications around cities like Antwerp, which turned out ultimately to be futile, but extremely expensive, gestures, Austerlitz tells the narrator: "könne man gut sehen, wie wir, im Gegensatz etwa zu den Vögeln, die Jahrtausende hindurch immer dasselbe Nest bauten, dazu neigten, unsere Unternehmungen voranzutreiben weit über jede Vernunftgrenze hinaus" (unlike birds, for instance, who keep building the same nest over thousands of years, we tend to forge ahead with our projects far beyond any reasonable bounds; *A*, 31/18).

[19] Achilles and Agamemnon are the two heroes of the Trojan War to whom Odysseus speaks in the land of the dead (11.385–540). Their stories, ending in

death on the battlefield for Achilles and death by ambush upon coming home for Agamemnon, provide a contrast to Odysseus's own successful homecoming.

[20] Améry is a constant companion of Sebald's, as attested by the two critical essays Sebald wrote about him: "Verlorenes Land: Jean Améry und Österreich." *Text + Kritik* 99 (1988): 20–29; and "Mit den Augen des Nachtvogels: Über Jean Améry," in *Campo Santo* (Frankfurt am Main: Fischer, 2006), 149–70. Irene Heidelberger-Leonard argues that Améry's character Lefeu, from the literary prose work *Lefeu oder der Abbruch* (Stuttgart: Klett, 1974), is one of the models for the character Austerlitz. More to the point, however, is what she says about Améry's role in the Breendonk episode: "So wird ihm, dem skrupulösesten Empathiker, die Durchquerung des früheren Straflagers zu einem veritablen Passionsweg durch den ihn der Nachtvogel Améry führt, wie Virgil Dante durch das Inferno." Améry, in other words, is not the subject of the Breendonk episode, but his spirit guides the narrator through his recollection of this episode. Irene Heidelberger-Leonard, "Jean Amérys Werk — Urtext zu W. G. Sebalds Austerlitz?" in *W. G. Sebald: Mémoire, Transferts, Images — Erinnerung, Übertragungen, Bilder,* ed. Ruth Vogel-Klein, Recherches germaniques 2 (Strasbourg: Université Marc Bloch, 2005), 127.

[21] "There is no document of civilization which is not at the same time a document of barbarism." Walter Benjamin, "Theses on the Philosophy of History," in *Illuminations,* 253–64; here 256. One might also mention, in this context, the *Dialectic of Enlightenment* of Max Horkheimer and Theodor W. Adorno, at whose heart lies the insight encapsulated in Benjamin's famous thesis. Horkheimer and Adorno, *Dialectic of Enlightenment,* ed. Gunzelin Schmid Noerr, trans. Edmund Jephcott (Stanford, CA: Stanford UP, 2002).

[22] Sebald has said that there are "zweieinhalb Lebensgeschichten" (two and a half life stories) behind the character of Austerlitz. Martin Doerry and Volker Hage, "Ich fürchte das Melodramatische: Gespräch mit W. G. Sebald," *Der Spiegel* (3 Dec. 2001): 228–34; here 230.

[23] In none of Sebald's books is what Bianca Theisen says more true than in *Die Ringe des Saturn:* "For Sebald, the return home or the return to an origin, that super-semantic moment of reappropriation or of coming into one's own, is a highly staged event that only ever leads to museums, libraries, or maps." Theisen, "Prose of the World," 172.

[24] "Unreal city, / Under the brown fog of a winter dawn, / A crowd flowed over London Bridge, so many, / I had not thought death had undone so many." T. S. Eliot, *The Annotated Wasteland with Eliot's Contemporary Prose (Second Edition),* ed. Lawrence Rainey (New Haven, CT: Yale UP, 2006), lines 60–63.

[25] It is worth noting, as well, that such images are common in cultural responses to the Holocaust. Two images of the gates of Auschwitz — one with the ironic inversion of Dante's motto, "Arbeit macht frei," the other the spectral railway entrance, which, it does not take a large act of imagination to feel, may as well be the entrance to the land of the dead — are, as Marianne Hirsch points out, staples of Holocaust scholarship and memorialization. Hirsch, "Surviving Images:

Holocaust Photographs and the Work of Postmemory," *Yale Journal of Criticism* 14.1 (2001]: 5–37.

[26] Peter Weiss, "Meine Ortschaft," in *Rapporte* (Frankfurt am Main: Suhrkamp, 1968), 113–24.

[27] That this "pursuit of the mother-image" is one of the main structuring elements of *Austerlitz*'s narrative has been demonstrated by Avi Kempinski. Kempinski claims that Austerlitz, in fact, never finds a true image of his mother and instead must be satisfied with a photograph he finds of himself as a young boy, during the last months he spent with his mother. Avi Kempinksi, "'Quel Roman!' Sebald, Barthes, and the Pursuit of the Mother-Image," in *Searching for Sebald: Photography after W. G. Sebald*, ed. Lise Patt (Los Angeles: Institute of Cultural Inquiry, 2007), 456–71; here 469.

[28] There has been a significant amount of research on the connection between photography and memory in *Austerlitz*. See, for example, Carolin Duttlinger, "Traumatic Photographs: Remembrance and the Technical Media in W. G. Sebald's *Austerlitz*," in Long and Whitehead, *A Critical Companion*, 155–71; Alexandra Tischel, "Aus der Dunkelkammer der Geschichte: Zum Zusammenhang von Photographie und Erinnerung in W. G. Sebalds *Austerlitz*," in *W. G. Sebald: Archäologie und melancholische Bastelei*, ed. Michael Niehaus and Claudia Öhlschläger (Berlin: Erich Schmidt Verlag, 2006), 31–45.

[29] This connection, between the dialectic of memory and forgetting encapsulated in the photograph and the otherworldly is confirmed by Sebald's own discussion, in an interview with Christian Scholz, of the photographs in his books: "I believe that the black-and-white photograph, or rather the gray zones in the black-and-white photograph, stand for the territory that is located between death and life." Scholz, "'But the Written Word Is Not a True Document': A Conversation with W. G. Sebald on Literature and Photography," trans. Markus Zisselsberger, in Patt, *Searching for Sebald*, 104–9; here 108. Stefanie Harris has explored this connection in *Die Ausgewanderten*, in "The Return of the Dead: Memory and Photography in W. G. Sebald's *Die Ausgewanderten*," *German Quarterly* 74.4 (Autumn, 2001): 379–91.

[30] John Milton, *Paradise Lost*, ed. David Scott Kastan (Indianapolis: Hackett, 2005), 1.62.

[31] Walter Benjamin, "Theses on the Philosophy of History," 256.

III: Traveling Companions and Convergences

7: Convergence Insufficiency: On Seeing Passages between W. G. Sebald and the "Travel Writer" Bruce Chatwin

Brad Prager

IN A EULOGIZING REVIEW ESSAY that W. G. Sebald referred to as an *Annäherung* — a word that refers to an "approach," but one that also suggests a "convergence" — occasioned by the publication of Nicholas Shakespeare's authoritative biography of the English author Bruce Chatwin, Sebald observes that it is not easy to think of a contemporary German writer with whom Chatwin compares.[1] In his negative construction, Sebald gives himself away: he may have been all-too aware of the considerable proximity between his work and Chatwin's. In trying to think of an author who was a "rastlose[r] Wanderer" (tireless traveler) and whose works, as Sebald writes, "mit keinem bekannten Genre übereinstimmen" (correspond to no known genre; *CS*, 215/173; trans. modified), he could have taken himself as a clear example of a comparable contemporary.

Those interested in these authors' biographies will note that both are sometimes referred to as "travel writers," that both elected not to use their given names (disposing of Georg and Charles, their fathers' names, Winfried Georg Sebald generally went by "Max," and Charles Bruce Chatwin went only by Bruce), and, although Sebald could not have foreseen his own death at the time he wrote his essay, that both of them died too young — Chatwin died of an AIDS related illness at 48, and Sebald in an auto accident at 57.[2] They each left behind a handful of books that may or may not be categorized as fiction alongside a relatively large body of writings that evince interest in, yet a certain disdain for, the conventional methods of scholarly study. Perhaps more important is that both were known for how they represented others' stories in their own work. Sebald's former colleague Richard Sheppard describes this tendency as the author's "desire for polyphony" (though he notes that distinctions in the works between the writer, his narrators, and his figures frequently become blurred).[3] Critics have observed similar tendencies in Chatwin. Hans Magnus Enzensberger writes that Chatwin's tales "always admit, and even embrace, the voice of others," and David Estes similarly remarks: "Chatwin's activity of literary creation depends . . . on frequent silences

about his experiences so that readers can hear the voices of others."[4] There
are, of course, major stylistic divergences — Chatwin, for example, relies
on dialogue, where Sebald tends to employ indirect speech — however,
both faithfully relate others' stories and, with varying degrees of success,
attempt to inscribe the part they themselves play into the background.

The question of genre is a vexing one when applied to these writers.
Most of their "true" stories take up positions in the gray area defined by
terms such as creative non-fiction, "docufiction," or "fiction with a basis
in fact," and both attempt to challenge generic boundaries, writing works
that are properly neither novels, memoirs, or travel narratives. Ian Buruma,
in an essay that takes Chatwin's work as a starting point for a discussion of
Werner Herzog's films, describes the tendency to cross boundaries
between documenting and poeticizing the world as a "sharpening" of reality, whereby real circumstances serve, more here than in the cases of other
artists, as an inspiration for poetic creation.[5] Nicholas Shakespeare explains
in his biography of Chatwin that at Sotheby's auction house, where
Chatwin was employed for many years, where he expanded on his interests
in art and archeology, and where he found inspiration for his writing, the
phrase "doing a Bruce," meant "wrapping up something in a bit of myth
and making a story of it."[6] This describes Chatwin's authorial approach.
Enzensberger remarks: "His very first book shows a sublime disregard for
the categories of fiction and non-fiction. *In Patagonia* has been called a
'documentary' and a 'travelogue,' but neither of those odious terms will
fit."[7] Likewise, Michael Dirda begins his review of Chatwin's *Utz* (1988)
noting, "Librarians must have a nightmare in categorizing Bruce Chatwin."[8]
And, when it came to *The Songlines* (1987), Chatwin himself voiced a
consciousness of the dilemma: "[*The Songlines*] has to be called a novel
because I've invented huge chunks of it in order to tell the story that I
wanted to tell. . . . To write it as fiction gives you a greater flexibility; otherwise, if you were laying down the law on these subjects, and indeed I had
a go at laying down the law, I can't tell you how pretentious you sound."[9]
In writing that Chatwin's work corresponds to "no known genre," Sebald,
who constantly crossed similar boundaries, who drew upon others' biographies in writing *Die Ausgewanderten*, *Die Ringe des Saturn*, and
Austerlitz, and who resisted referring to those works as novels,[10] implicitly
avows their authorial kinship.

Examining the question with respect to generic expectations brings
certain common features of their writing into light. Why are these two
poetic rewriters of history, biography, and memory not "travel writers"?
Chatwin was a notorious traveler, championing movement as an essential
human need, and in his essay, "It's a Nomad *Nomad* world," he laments:
"We spend far too much time in shuttered rooms," adding: "Movement is
the best cure for melancholy." Comparing us with migrating geese,
Chatwin refers to our "involuntary compulsion to wander."[11] The author's

obituary in *The Washington Post* refers to him as a "travel writer,"[12] but he rejected that term. Speaking of his book *On the Black Hill* (1982), which deals with twins living on an isolated farm near the Welsh-English border, Chatwin said, "It's always irritated me to be called a travel writer. So I decided to write something about people who never went out."[13] But because of *The Songlines,* as well as his earlier *In Patagonia* (1977), Chatwin was taken for a travel writer. The former work concerns the "songlines" that are the basis for some Australian aboriginal belief systems. Chatwin's largely fictional work starts with some facts and poeticizes around them. He was interested in the beliefs of aboriginals and fabricated a story about their creation myths. According to aboriginal lore we exist eternally in the space of the "dreaming," or in an original age of creation prior to the emergence of individual selves. These creation stories take the form of songlines, which correspond to the construction of the landscape through language and songs, all of which are connected to a collection of myths. The terrain is formed by language; external landscape is thus predicated on a collective text. Chatwin's protagonist, Arkady, explains: "Each totemic ancestor, while traveling through the country, was thought to have scattered a trail of words and musical notes along the line of his footprints. . . . These Dreaming-tracks lay over the land as 'ways' of communication between the most far-flung tribes."[14] The concept of the songline is an aural expression of collective memory and takes the form of an archive spread across the landscape.

Sebald also conceived of the landscape as an archive: it is an aural — and sometimes oral — site of memory, and the songline is an apt metaphor for the movement across the land that takes place throughout his work.[15] During the story of Paul Bereyter in *Die Ausgewanderten*, the protagonist, who at first appears to be a typical European hiker, seems to walk along a songline informed by his cultural history and directly connected with the landscape. The narrator informs us:

[Paul ging] mit leicht aufwärts gekehrtem Gesicht und mit den für ihn so charakteristischen, weit ausgreifenden und federnden Schritten vor uns her, ein wahres Inbild, wie ich jetzt erst in der Rückschau erkenne, der deutschen Wandervogelbewegung, die ihn zeit seiner Jugend geprägt haben mußte. Es gehörte zu den Gewohnheiten Pauls, auf dem Weg durch die Felder in einem fort zu pfeifen. Er hatte im Pfeifen eine wirklich seltene Fertigkeit; wunderbar voll war der Ton, genau wie der einer Flöte, den er hervorbrachte, und er konnte, sogar beim Bergaufgehen, mit anscheinender Leichtigkeit, die längsten Bögen und Läufe aneinanderreihen, und zwar nicht einfach etwas Beliebiges, sondern auskomponierte, schöne Passagen und Melodien, die keiner von uns zuvor je gehört hatte und die mir, wenn ich sie Jahre später in einer Bellini-Oper oder in einer Brahms-Sonate wiederentdeckte, jedesmal das Herz umdrehten.

[[Paul] would walk ahead of us with his face slightly upturned, taking those long and springy steps that were so characteristic, the very image (as I realize only now as I look back) of the German *Wandervogel* hiking movement, which must have had a lasting influence on him from his youth. Paul was in the habit of whistling continuously as he walked across the fields. He was an amazingly good whistler; the sound he produced was marvelously rich, exactly like a flute's. And even when he was climbing a mountain, he would with apparent ease whistle whole runs and ties in connected sequence, not just anything, but fine, thoroughly composed passages and melodies that none of us had ever heard before, and which infallibly gave a wrench to my heart whenever, years later, I rediscovered them in a Bellini opera or a Brahms sonata. (*DA*, 61/*E*, 40–41)]

Here, but also on the pilgrimage through Suffolk that comprises *Die Ringe des Saturn*, one finds a multiplicity of songlines, many of which are meant as starting points for a critique of those specific cultural histories that line European paths.[16] Throughout Sebald's writings, though with particular emphasis in *Die Ringe des Saturn*, the author's melancholy wanderers move one after the next through psychologically inflected spaces defined less by any particular geography than by their memories, the memories of those they encounter, and the prose and paintings that form an eclectic collection of touchstones taken from the archives of the Western world — texts and events chosen in connection with its creative and destructive heights, from Homer and Alexander through to Joseph Conrad, Sir Arthur Harris, and beyond.[17] For Sebald, language and literary history provide the contours of the landscape, and the figures constitute the staffage. As yet another example, one might look to *Schwindel. Gefühle.*, where the narrator traverses paths marked by the writings of Stendhal and Kafka. His work wanders equally through its protagonist's outer and inner spaces, and Sebald uniformly de-differentiates the act of losing oneself in the streets — of Venice, Manchester or anywhere else — from losing oneself in thought.

But the fact that the label "travel writer" fits neither of these two authors bespeaks their ambivalence about travel itself. In the case of Chatwin, two hearts beat inside his breast: that of the wanderer, who travels light and believes that nomadry is the essential human condition, and that of the collector, who accumulates souvenirs of distant places and earlier times, perhaps in the hope that he might stop the motion of the world. Shakespeare cites Chatwin's own avowal of this contradiction, one found throughout his writings: "In one of his many attempts to make sense of a book on nomads, which dogged him for 20 years and which he never published, Bruce wrote 'This book is written in answer to a need to explain my own restlessness — coupled with a morbid preoccupation with roots'" (*BC*, 15).[18] Shakespeare quotes a series of tortured rhetorical questions from Chatwin's unfinished work *The Nomadic Alternative*: "*Where* does happiness lie? Why is Here so unbearable? Why is There so inviting? But why is There more unbearable than Here?" (*BC*, 278). In Sebald's work one also finds evidence of a double-edged urge. His over-arching contention is that we are seized by the need to wander (a need Chatwin took to be instinctive or innate) but can never really get away from our origins.

Issues of this sort pertain specifically to Sebald's much scrutinized relationship to the concept of *Heimat*.[19] It is not something we ever truly leave behind; as far as he was concerned, German identity was not something he could shed.[20] Along these lines and "against the grain of what has already become a recurring argument in Sebald criticism; that Sebald's heroes are postmodern nomads, figures of disorientation desperately lost at the turn of our twenty-first century,"[21] John Zilcosky writes: "Sebald tells stories in which subjects can never become sufficiently disoriented, can never really lose their way. . . . The traveler, no matter how far away he journeys, can never leave his home."[22] Zilcosky adds: "We find ourselves in the same hotel in a city we have already visited . . . we become disoriented only to keep circling back to the same spot. . . . It is this persistence of the familiar, this *unheimlich* (uncanny) inability to lose one's way that haunts Sebald's travel narratives."[23] For Zilcosky, the many mazes in Sebald's work suggest the opposite of travel; one moves constantly yet gains no ground. Where Chatwin was torn between two desires (that one wants both to travel and to make a home; that one longs to be both "here" and "there"), Sebald posited that travel is an illusion (that one wants to travel yet inevitably goes nowhere; that one longs to be "there" yet invariably finds oneself "here"). As though on a permanently taut leash, we move in circles, never closing in on the center. This familiar image, bound to the idea of going nowhere, assumes its place among Sebald's most consistent tropes. Referencing images of rings, windmills, and sandstorms, David Darby points out that in *Die Ringe des Saturn* "nothing will run on and on all the way to anywhere."[24] Perhaps the most poignant invocation of this eternal circle is the moment when the narrator of that work emerges from Somerleyton Hall, the country house in Suffolk, and is saddened to see, in an otherwise deserted aviary,

eine einsame chinesische Wachtel . . ., die — offenbar in einem Zustand der Demenz — in einem fort am rechten Seitengitter ihres Käfigs auf und ab lief und jedesmal, bevor sie kehrtmachte, den Kopf schüttelte, als begreife sie nicht, wie sie in diese aussichtslose Lage geraten sei.

[a solitary Chinese quail, evidently in a state of dementia, running to and fro along the edge of the cage and shaking its head every time it was about to turn, as if it could not comprehend how it had got into this hopeless fix. (*RS*, 50/36)]

In both writers' works, then, one sees similar hallmarks of tension. We want to get away, yet cannot; the gravity of the world to which we are bound is too great. It is hardly surprising, then, that Sebald took up the concept of vertigo, which comes from the Latin *vertere* (to turn or revolve). Vertigo may make us feel as though we are moving, spinning, or swaying, despite the fact that we are stationary.[25] At the climax of Sebald's *Schwindel. Gefühle.* the narrator experiences this sensation while riding on a train — while he feels himself to be sitting still and imagines the world moving around him. Though the word *Schwindel* in the German title of Sebald's book is different from its English translation *Vertigo*, it differs primarily in its additional connotations, those associated with "swindling" or deception, both of which invoke the games his book plays with the reader. Sebald would surely have been aware of the implications of his English language title, likely even the inaccurate ones that bind the concept to Hitchcock's film about acrophobia.[26] While aboard a train that has just left Liverpool Station, Sebald's narrator falls asleep reading Samuel Pepys's account of the great fire of London (*SG*, 285/*V*, 261). He then has a dream in which he imagines himself standing above a vertigo-inducing gorge and imagines: "Zu meiner Linken ging es in eine wahrhaft schwindelerregende Tiefe hinab" (To my left there was a drop into truly vertiginous depths; *SG*, 286/*V*, 262).[27] Envisioned descents of this sort awaken vertiginous sensations because when one looks into such depths, the "there" vanishes into a bottomless nothingness: how can one be "here" without the comforting thought that there is a certain "there" in the distance with which one might converge? For Chatwin, feeling either "here" or "there" produces anxiety because each one recalls the absence of the other. By contrast, in Sebald's circular works, the anxiety comes from depriving the reader of one of the terms in this equation, or from starting with the abyssal supposition that there is no "there" out there.

A Feeling of *Vertiko*

For both Sebald and Chatwin, however, the image of the traveler, or that of the man set reluctantly in motion, may be offset by the image of the collector, who stays in one place and accumulates. The collector's collection is presented as a refuge from the vertiginous motion of the world. As Massimo Leone has noted, cabinets of curiosities can be juxtaposed with the traveler's sometimes burdensome *Wanderlust*.[28] In Sebald's essay on Chatwin one finds an unusual term for the collector's cabinet: he refers to the storage unit as a *Vertiko*, or an upright chest, closely connecting the image with Chatwin's work.[29] Sebald likely took note of this recurring motif, one that makes appearances throughout Chatwin's biography, because related images appear in his own writings, where collectors are ubiquitous. One thinks of the multiple entrances of the butterfly collector onto the scene of *Die Ausgewanderten*, of Thomas Browne's fantasized *Museum Clausum* or *Biblioteca Abscondita* in *Die Ringe des Saturn*, as well as of Austerlitz's over-crowded study and his collection of cameras. The trope of the collector has, in turn, been described as a central metaphor for Sebald's work. Philip Schlesinger notes: "As those who have read Sebald's work will know, the method of *Austerlitz* is precisely that of the case study, a *Vitrine* that illuminates a life and the wider processes that have made it what it is."[30] Without saying it explicitly, Sebald aligns his method with Chatwin's. When writing about Chatwin and his collectors, he refers to the English writer's days at Sotheby's, when he had access to the "Schatzkammern der Vergangenheit" (the treasure chambers of the past; *CS*, 218/176). Citing the importance of such images in Shakespeare's biography, and in terms closely related to those Schlesinger would later use, Sebald writes: "Das verschlossene Glasvertiko mit seinen rätselvollen Dingen wurde . . . zur zentralen Metapher sowohl für den Inhalt als auch für die Form von Chatwins Arbeit" (The locked glass-fronted cupboard with its mysterious contents became . . . a central metaphor for both the content and the style of Chatwin's work; *CS*, 219/177).

In his biography of Chatwin, Shakespeare highlights the concept of the *Wunderkammer*, or the cabinet of curiosities (*BC*, 37). He recounts the story of Charles Milward, a cousin of Chatwin's grandmother Isobel, who had

> befriended a German gold-panner who was blowing up a cave near Puerto Natales to obtain specimens of a prehistoric animal. The discovery, in perfect condition, of a Giant Sloth, or mylodon, excited European scientists into believing the animal must recently have been alive. Scraps of mylodon were sought by natural history museums and Charles Milward was in a position to supply them.
>
> Sometime in 1902 or 1903, he sent a piece of this mylodon to his cousin Isobel as a wedding present. The skin, a good-sized tuft, was a fragment of reddening coarse hair attached to a card with a pin. It was wrapped in paper and kept in a pillbox. (*BC*, 36)

Shakespeare adds: "The hairy remnant became Bruce's favorite object. 'Never in my life have I wanted anything as I wanted that piece of skin.'"[31] Throughout Chatwin's childhood the red-brown skin — after which Sebald titled his Chatwin essay — was kept in a vitrine, and there, in this *Vertiko*, lay his fetish object.

Directly related to the object in the *Vertiko* is the feeling of vertigo. Sebald certainly had Freud's concept in mind when he wrote, with reference to the red-brown skin, "Der Fetischcharakter des Faultierrelikts ist unübersehbar" (There is no mistaking the fetishistic character of the sloth relic; *CS*, 220/177). Freud's explanation is predicated on a fear of castration, or on the trauma induced by a male child's realization that his mother has no penis, which is a traumatic revelation because if he perceives that the mother has been "castrated," then he too is a candidate for castration. In Freud's schema, rather than re-experience the trauma, children will block out the memory of the traumatic experience by investing another object, often the last one seen before the traumatic sight, such as a foot or a shoe, with special meaning. Following his observation that, "the foot or shoe owes its preference as a fetish — or part of it — to the circumstance that the inquisitive boy peered at the woman's genitals from below," Freud then refers directly to fur, writing: "fur and velvet — as has long been suspected — are a fixation of the sight of the pubic hair, which should have been followed by the longed-for sight of the female member."[32] In considering the furry red-brown skin Sebald likely recognized that Freud's fetishism has a vertiginous quality; though we stand in one place our minds spin and sway, both "here" and "there," between traumatic memories and the substitute objects that serve as their screen.

Drawing on the example of a man whose fetish was "an athletic support belt," Freud writes: "This piece of clothing covered up the genitals entirely and concealed the distinction between them. Analysis showed that it signified that women were castrated, and that they were not castrated; and it also allowed the hypothesis that men were castrated, for all these possibilities could equally well be concealed under the belt."[33] It is thus the indeterminacy of the object that draws our gaze — that there is no certain "there" upon which the mind may rest. As Giorgio Agamben explains: "the fetish is a negation and the sign of an absence, it is not an unrepeatable unique object; on the contrary, it is something infinitely capable of substitution, without any of its successive incarnations ever succeeding in exhausting the nullity of which it is the symbol."[34] The red-brown skin, which Sebald describes as an "an sich völlig wertlose[s] Ding" (a thing "entirely without value in itself"; CS, 220/177), represents, in this case, something both right in front of Chatwin yet also something far away; the pleasure is derived from its role as an arbitrary marker of an absence. It is a dearly held souvenir that screens a "nullity," a "there" that is permanently out of reach. No coincidence, then, that this red-brown piece of fur stands for an extinct animal, something all the more fascinating because it is forever lost in the abyss of time.

The most prominent collector — one might say the most notable fetishist — in Chatwin's oeuvre is the predominantly fictional protagonist Kaspar Joachim Utz.[35] The character's name resonates: Kaspar recalls the ways the writers are linked through the figure of Kaspar Hauser,[36] and we are informed by the narrator of *Utz* that the character's last name carries a series of negative connotations, including, drunk, dimwit, card-sharp, or dealer in horses. Utz is a diminutive of Ulrich, and St. Ulrich, a patron saint of happy deaths, may be understood to oversee the happy death that ultimately befalls

Chatwin's main character, who, at the novel's ambiguous end, may have surrendered his treasured collection (of porcelain) in the name of love.[37] Sebald asserts that one should see this porcelain fetishist as an alter ego of Chatwin, noting that the writer moves between his own partly real and partly imagined characters "wie der Porzellansammler Utz zwischen seinen Meißener Figurinen" (as his china collector Utz moves among his Meissen figurines; *CS*, 217/175). Shakespeare makes a similar connection, noting that the slothskin with which Chatwin had once been absorbed — the one he had fetishized as a child — takes the form of the Meissen harlequin figure central to the novel. He summarizes: "In his last novel, Bruce reaches back to his four-year-old self, to the young Utz visiting his grandmother's castle outside Prague and standing on tiptoe before her vitrine of antique porcelain and saying 'I want him.'" Shakespeare concludes: "The slothskin has been recast as a Meissen harlequin with a leering orange mask" (38).[38]

Though Chatwin's novel hardly shares Sebald's elegiac tone, relying on short scenes and short paragraphs, and including a good deal of dialogue instead of the reported speech toward which Sebald tends, there is no shortage of convergent motifs. As with any number of characters in Sebald's world, Utz is not relaxed when he is at home in Prague, nor is he at home abroad, and, as in Sebald's works, the narrator is to some degree a surrogate for the author himself. This quasi-Chatwinian narrator begins by explaining to the reader that he had intended his article on Utz, the one he had set out to write, to be part of a larger work on the psychology — or psychopathology — of the compulsive collector. He then explains that this plan came to nothing.[39] His remark evokes memories of Chatwin's never-completed study of nomadry,[40] yet it is also meant ironically: this "nothing" is actually the book we have before us. To reinforce the author's own connection to his mostly fictional collector, Chatwin's narrator tells us that he stopped on the way to Czechoslovakia to see the *Kunstkammer* (which he translates as "cabinet of curiosities"), assembled by Rudolf's uncle, the Archduke Ferdinand of Tyrol. Here the narrator shares a fascination with his protagonist, and we are later provided with an excerpt from Utz's own writings on the subject of collecting. In "The Private Collector," an apocryphal text that seems to voice some of Chatwin's own views, Utz defends the idea of individual collections, ones kept beyond public purview. He writes:

> An object in a museum case . . . must suffer the de-natured existence of an animal in the zoo. In any museum the object dies — of suffocation and the public gaze — whereas private ownership confers on the owner the right and the need to touch. As a young child will reach out to handle the thing it names, so the passionate collector, his eye in harmony with his hand, restores to the object the life-giving touch of its maker. The collector's enemy is the museum curator. Ideally, museums should be looted every fifty years, and their collections returned to circulation. (20)

In the book's best-known sentences Utz finally confronts his own fixation. Reflecting on his porcelain figurines, which never grow old, he offers a formulation reminiscent of Oscar Wilde: "Things are tougher than people. Things are the changeless mirror in which we watch ourselves disintegrate. Nothing is more ageing than a collection of works of art" (13; also *BC*, 168). This changelessness corresponds to the feeling of stasis afforded the collector. Collections appear to stop time; though a collector continues to age, his or her collection stands still.

Collecting is the flash point for Utz's vertigo, as it was in the life of the traveler Chatwin. His collection both haunts him like the Medusa and allows him the freedom to retreat inwardly, or to disappear from his Eastern Bloc home into a fantasy world. The narrator eventually recounts his conclusions:

> I realized, as Utz pivoted the figure [of the harlequin in the orange mask] in the candlelight, that I had misjudged him; that he, too, was dancing; that, for him, this world of little figures was the real world. And that, compared to them, the Gestapo, the Secret Police and other hooligans were creatures of tinsel. And the events of this somber century — the bombardments, blitzkriegs, putsches, purges — were, so far as he was concerned, so many "noises off." (114)

Along lines that recall central figures in *Die Ausgewanderten*, published only four years later, Utz, who is one-fourth Jewish, who feels as though he has been a bystander to Europe's mid-century atrocities, and who wonders about his own guilt and complicity for having survived the Second World War, flees into a private world. Though Chatwin does not explore these themes with the same intense scrutiny that Sebald would have, the relationship of certain modes of Jewish iconoclasm to collecting (not to mention the image of the Golem) is explicitly evoked. Sebald would certainly have seen that Utz, the fetishist who plays the role of Chatwin's alter ego, could have been a character in his own works. Likewise, the many affinities Chatwin himself shares with Sebald's characters would have been plain to him as he read Shakespeare's biography; Chatwin would have been a credible subject had he been among those residing in the pages of Sebald's prose. He collected butterflies in his youth,[41] which is a hallmark of Sebald's protagonists, and he was a traveler, one who appeared to be in permanent exile from nowhere in particular.

Double Blind

Still more striking, however, as one reads through Shakespeare's biography, is Chatwin's experience with temporary blindness. As though it were lifted straight out of *Austerlitz*, Chatwin's persistent eye complaint has the look of a literary conceit.[42] Shakespeare explains that following two important sales at Sotheby's in 1964 Chatwin went blind, or rather, as he tells it: "I manufactured a nervous eye complaint, which I came to believe in and then suffered from. This was interpreted in many ways." Shakespeare adds: "On 31 December, Bruce visited the eye specialist Patrick Trevor-Roper. By now, the problem was not confined to his eyesight. 'He described a multiplicity of symptoms,' says Trevor-Roper. 'He had feelings of fatigue, discomfort and vague subjective unease.'"[43] Chatwin explains: "The eye specialist who looked at me said, 'You've been looking too closely at pictures. Why don't you swap them for some long horizons?' So I said, 'Why not?' He said, 'Where would you like to go?' I said, 'Africa.' And so instead of writing a prescription for new spectacles, he wrote a prescription saying that he recommended travel to Africa."[44]

But what was amiss with Chatwin's eyes? For what problem was "travel" the cure? According to his editor Susannah Clapp: "Throughout his life, after reading or writing for any length of time, he would say that he couldn't see." She adds, "The eye specialist whom he consulted on the occasion of his sudden loss of sight was a friend, Patrick Trevor-Roper, who diagnosed Chatwin's trouble as 'convergence insufficiency'; he had a latent squint which showed itself under stress."[45] Down to the details, this resembles the disorder described in *Austerlitz*. In that work, the narrator, a quasi-Sebaldian figure, tells us that after not seeing Austerlitz for a long time he saw him again shortly after a period in which he had been "in einiger Unruhe" (in some anxiety):

weil ich beim Heraussuchen einer Anschrift aus dem Telephonbuch bemerkt hatte, daß, sozusagen über Nacht, die Sehkraft meines rechten Auges fast gänzlich geschwunden war. . . . [Es war] mir ständig, als sähe ich am Rand des Gesichtsfeldes mit unverminderter Deutlichkeit, als müßte ich mein Augenmerk nur ins Abseits lenken, um die, wie ich zunächst meinte, hysterische Sehschwäche zum Verschwinden zu bringen. Gelungen ist mir dies allerdings nicht, trotzdem ich es mehrfach probierte. Vielmehr schienen die grauen Felder sich auszudehnen, und bisweilen, wenn ich die Augen abwechslungsweise auf- und zumachte, um den Grad der Sehschärfe vergleichen zu können, kam es mir vor, als sei auch linksseitig eine gewisse Beeinträchtigung des Blicks eingetreten.

[because I had noticed, looking up an address in the telephone book, that the sight in my right eye had almost entirely disappeared overnight, so to speak. . . . I kept feeling as if I could see as clearly as ever on the edge of my field of vision, and had only to look sideways to rid myself of what I took at first for a merely hysterical weakness in my eyesight. Although I tried several times, I did not succeed. Instead, the gray areas seemed to be spreading, and now and then, opening and closing my eyes alternately to compare their degrees of clarity, I thought that I had suffered some impairment on the left as well. (*A*, 54–55/34–35)]

The description of the disorder — a possibly hysterical occlusion of vision — recalls Shakespeare's biography (which Sebald likely already encountered while working on *Austerlitz*). In *Austerlitz* the narrator adds:

> Über die Ursachen dieser in der einschlägigen Literatur als zentral-seröse Chorioretinopathie beschriebenen Störung herrsche weitgehend Unklarheit. . . . Man wisse eigentlich nur, daß sie fast ausschließlich auftrete bei Männern mittleren Alters, die zuviel mit Schreiben und Lesen beschäftigt seien.

> [There was considerable uncertainty . . . about the causes of the disorder, described by the literature on the subject as central serous chorioretinopathy. All that was really known was that it occurred almost exclusively in middle-aged men who spent too much time reading and writing. (*A*, 59/38)]

Though retinopathy is not the same as convergence insufficiency, they are both forms of temporary blindness, conditions that may be caused by too much reading or stress. Like Chatwin, Sebald appears to have actually suffered from one or another of these disorders. His friend Richard Sheppard explains: "Max really was afflicted by a blindness in his right eye in late 1996 for a reason that the Norwich doctors could not initially diagnose."[46]

Considering the metaphorical meanings of Sebald's eye problem, Sheppard adds: "I cannot help wondering whether this could have been a psychosomatic condition brought about by Max's 'increasingly' painful memories of the 'sinister,' 'blinding' side of his psychic ancestry and everything with which this had become associated over the years" (432). What might these disorders mean, the ones that, even according to the authors' friends, have no proper causes, and that most assume are psychological in origin? In the case of Chatwin, as Clapp informs us, it was a "convergence insufficiency," or a neuromuscular eye problem, characterized by the inability to converge one's eyes or to maintain their convergence. It is, then, the inability to reconcile what is near with what is far away, or, taken metaphorically, the inability to reconcile "here" and "there." The condition, with its implied confusion of proximity and distance, recalls Chatwin's tortured complaint: "*Where* does happiness lie? Why is Here so unbearable? Why is There so inviting? But why is There more unbearable than Here?" (*BC*, 278).

In the stories of *Die Ausgewanderten* the inability to reconcile near and far plays a key role. We are told, in the book's second story, about Paul Bereyter's myopia, but as J. J. Long points out, the photograph that introduces both this section and its discussion of the detail about myopia shows the opposite of a myopic effect. Of the picture of the railway lines at the beginning of the narrative Long observes: "The focus of the image is the very inverse of the effects of myopia: the foreground is blurred, while objects in the middle and far distance are in focus."[47] Perhaps Sebald is being ironic, suggesting that neither we readers nor Paul Bereyter have properly understood his disorder. Bereyter had considered himself German yet learned he was one-fourth Jewish when he was forbidden to teach German children. His family members died more or less as a consequence of anti-Semitism and his subsequent blindness seems psychosomatic — the result of having both survived and having died along with his parents, of feeling both connected to his German origins and thoroughly unwelcome in his homeland.[48]

A similarly emblematic image appears in *Die Ringe des Saturn* during the narrator's encounter with Thomas Abrams. Abrams is constructing an exact scale model of the Temple in Jerusalem, which, we are told, includes more than 2,000 figurines no more than a quarter of an inch high and covers an expanse of nearly ten square yards (*RS*, 243).[49] Abrams reflects rhapsodically:

> Jetzt, wo es allmählich dunkel zu werden beginnt an den Rändern meines Gesichtsfelds, frage ich mich manchmal, ob ich den Bau jemals zu Ende führen werde und ob nicht alles, was ich bislang geschaffen habe, bloß ein elendes Machwerk ist. Aber an anderen Tagen wieder, wenn das Abendlicht seitwärts hier durch das Fenster dringt und wenn ich die Gesamtansicht auf mich wirken lasse, dann sehe ich den Tempel . . . als sei alles bereits vollendet und als schaute ich hinein in die Gefilde der Ewigkeit.

> [Now, as the edges of my field of vision are beginning to darken, I sometimes wonder if I will ever finish the Temple and whether all I have done so far has not been a wretched waste of time. But on other days, when the evening light streams in through this window and I allow myself to be taken in by the overall view, then I see for a moment the Temple . . . as if everything were already completed and as if I were gazing into eternity. (*RS*, 291, 294/245, 248)]

The image that accompanies his remark, indeed, the one that interrupts this passage, serves as an apt metaphor for vision that either cannot focus on things both near and far, or does not know how to. The pillars in the photo's foreground are out of focus and obscure, as is the image's distant vanishing point — deliberately one assumes — insofar as it is located in the crease between the pages of the book. There is, in this instance, neither a properly clear "here" on which one can focus nor a "there" at the far end of the temple aisle. One can see neither near nor far properly. The connection to the speaker's obscured vision is articulated in the accompanying text, much as it was in the case of Bereyter, whose suicide dominates the second chapter of *Die Ausgewanderten*, who develops serious cataracts decades after the war, and about whom we learn that he could see only "zerbrochene oder zersprungene Bilder" (fragmented or shattered images; *DA*, 88/*E*, 59).

Backpacking (Into the Dark)

The obstruction of sight — myopia, retinopathy, and other problems — is a point of convergence between Sebald and Chatwin. It is a literalization of the frustration associated with their travel narratives and of the inability to reconcile proximity with distance. Along the same lines, the recurring image of the rucksack functions as a point at which traveling and collecting meet; it can be described as a *vitrine* of sorts, in which things are accumulated, and it serves as the traveler's surrogate home while he is on the road. Chatwin was consistently linked with his rucksack, and as an inveterate traveler he was rarely seen without it. The first sentence of Shakespeare's biography ties him to it, opening with a description of, "an Englishman with a rucksack and walking-boots," who "strides into a bungalow in the Irene district of Pretoria" (*BC*, 1). The regular appearance of this traveler with his rucksack recalls the direct, metonymic connection Sebald's Austerlitz shares with his rucksack.[50] At one point in that work the narrator, having not seen Austerlitz for a long time, lists the rucksack as one of the key constituent elements of his appearance (*A*, 62/39) and shortly thereafter realizes that he associates Austerlitz with Wittgenstein because both were said to have always carried a bag of this sort (*A*, 63–64/40–41). Later we are informed that Austerlitz would rather live out of his backpack than with his lover Marie, who accuses him of never properly unpacking (*A*, 311/216).[51]

The meaningful metonymy is associated as much with Sebald as it is with Chatwin. For Sebald, the rucksack is the source of a multiplicity of meanings. When, for example, he speaks of the aftereffects of the Holocaust, in an evocation of the major themes of *Austerlitz*, Sebald explains to one interviewer: "It happened almost throughout Europe, and the calamitous dimensions of it are something that, even though I left Germany when I was twenty-one, I still have in my backpack and I just can't put it down."[52] As far back as his early writings on Kafka, Sebald concerns himself with the image of the land-surveyor in Kafka's *Castle*, identifying him by his iconic rucksack and walking stick.[53] And, as the narrator of *Schwindel. Gefühle.*, the one frequently taken to stand in for Sebald himself, wanders the gorge near his hometown of W., in the section entitled "Il ritorno in patria," he sets off "bloß mit dem kleinen ledernen Rucksack über der Schulter" (carrying nothing but my small leather rucksack over my shoulder; *SG,* 193/*V,* 177), and notes that the gorge into which he is walking is strangely abyssal ("Der Tobel war erfüllt von einer Dunkelheit, wie ich sie mitten am Tag nicht für möglich gehalten hätte"; The gorge was sunk in a darkness that I would not have thought possible in the middle of the day; *SG,* 194/*V,* 177). The image of the solitary wanderer journeying into a dark gorge with nothing but a rucksack links him to Schlag, the spectral hunter of *Schwindel. Gefühle.,* a figure who lurks within the narrator's childhood memories, who has a rucksack of his own, and who dies virtually alone (*SG,* 268/*V,* 245).[54] As a child, the narrator hears of Schlag's death and sees the fallen hunter in his mind's eye, lying dead at the bottom of a ravine, only to encounter the corpse later on his way home (*SG,* 268–70/*V,* 246–47). Here again, as in *Die Ausgewanderten,* the traveler is confronted at once with both the gorge and the grave; the man in motion is confronted with a dark abyssal absence in place of a "there."

This association between the author and his rucksack is so close that the photographer Axel Forrester, in a series of photographs entitled "Max," presents the viewer with images of a traveler and his rucksack, whom he declares to be Sebald on the basis of the rucksack alone. This gesture recalls the one by which Sebald's narrator had identified Austerlitz.[55] The exchange of rucksack-wearing travelers — from Wittgenstein to Austerlitz and from Austerlitz to Sebald — is hardly surprising.[56] To this list one might add Chatwin, who was identified with his knapsack as well. Speaking of his first meeting with Chatwin, the director Werner Herzog recounts: "How would I recognize him? 'Look for a man with a leather rucksack' he told me."[57] Even after the author's death the rucksack was treated as a fetish, or a passage through which to access the dead author. To his story Herzog adds: "I still carry the leather rucksack he used all his life. He gave it to me saying, 'You are the one who has to carry it on now.' I still carry it, and I had it with me in the snow storm in Patagonia, sitting on it for fifty hours dug into the snow. It is much more than just a tool to carry things. If my house were on fire I would first grab my children and throw them from the window. But of all my belongings it would be the rucksack that I would save" (283).

As a souvenir of an absent traveler, the rucksack is a means to retrieve Chatwin. Whether a traveler can be retrieved from the abyss is the central question of "Dr. Henry Selwyn," the first story in *Die Ausgewanderten,* the one in which a body emerges from the glacial ice after seventy years, prompting the narrator to reflect: "So also kehren sie wieder, die Toten" (And so they are ever returning to us, the dead; *DA,* 36/*E,* 23). Sebald's story is concerned with Henry Selwyn, who, as a young man, lost his friend and close companion Johannes Naegeli in a hiking accident. Selwyn's older companion's name is, in part, a pun inspired by the "genagelte Schuhe" (hobnailed boots),[58] which are, along with his bones, all that rises to the surface decades later, yet the name also links the character phonetically to Sebald's maternal grandfather, Josef Egelhofer, to whom he was extremely close, and who introduced Sebald to the literature that remained important to him throughout his life.[59] The story is, of course, about mourning. Naegeli, who died from a fall into a crevasse — into an abyss, like the hunter Schlag — seems to have taken the melancholy main character, Selwyn, down with him as he fell. Selwyn cannot get over the loss, and the word "fall" in his own description of the event — his use of the participle "schwergefallen" to denote the hard fall associated with his strong feeling of loss and express his reaction to this death — tells the story (*DA*, 24). When the news reached him that Naegeli had fallen into a glacier, he says, it was "als sei ich begraben unter Schnee und Eis" (as if I was buried under snow and ice; *DA*, 25/*E*, 15). Even his separation from his wife, he adds, was not as painful for him as the loss of Naegeli. He not only feels as though he died in that same glacier, but it appears that he may hold himself responsible for Naegeli's death.[60]

All of these details — the fall into a crevasse and the fascination with mourning — link Sebald's story to one written years earlier by Chatwin. Published in 1979, "The Estate of Maximilian Tod" deals with an obsessive collector and his relationship to a researcher named Estelle Neumann. Neumann, a glaciologist at Harvard and a friend of the narrator, makes a discovery concerning the Belgrano Glacier in Chilean Patagonia. Her insight into a lost valley connected to the glacier leads the narrator to the hidden home of the collector Maximilian Tod. Despite informing us that "inventories make tiresome reading,"[61] Chatwin's narrator shares with us long lists of objects in Tod's collection. Finally, after the items have been lovingly enumerated, the narrator reveals the truth: "it should be clear even to the most unobservant reader that I am Maximilian Tod" (65). Here again, as in *Utz*, Chatwin offers a study of the psychology of the collector, a jealous, protective keeper of his things, who describes himself as having "with Bedouin rigor abolished the human form from my possessions" (69). In the story's final line, Tod tells us that Neumann has died in the glacier and that he is now tormented. He then confesses that he is her murderer, a secret we have long since suspected: "one particular color continues to torment me: the orange of Estelle Neumann's anorak the second before I pushed her" (69).

Tod's name, which means "death," is clearly playful: Chatwin has given us a story about an obsessive who has killed in the name of protecting his precious wares. He pushed his friend and colleague into a glacier, yet he cannot quite get over her death. Despite his desire to protect his possessions, his guilt torments him, and Sebald's famous sentence — "It is as if I was buried under snow and ice" — would have fitted Chatwin's conclusion as well. According to Shakespeare, Chatwin maintained that archeologists, and presumably others who share a similarly thanatophilic absorption with the study of physical remains, desire to die in the trenches they dig; they would like to be buried among the dead, through whose eyes they hope to see. Shakespeare explains: "Suicide lodged in Bruce's mind as a metaphor for [archeology]. He began to collect stories about archaeologists who had died in their own trenches, the result of a secret desire to be buried. 'Most archaeologists interpret the things of the remote past in terms of their own projected suicide,' he wrote in his notebook. And: 'If an archaeologist has faith in his method he must use that method to its logical conclusion — and bury himself'" (*BC*, 223).

Death by fall into a glacier is among the most obvious convergences, yet perhaps more striking is the next coincidence, the appearance of a painting of the Battle of Alexandria. At the onset of one of his essays on *The Castle*, Sebald inscribes the following epigram from Kafka: "Der Tod ist vor uns, etwa wie im Schulzimmer an der Wand ein Bild der Alexanderschlacht" (Death is before us, much like a painting of the battle of Alexandria on a schoolroom wall).[62] In his story "The Estate of Maximilian Tod" Chatwin makes reference to Albrecht Altdorfer's painting *The Battle of Alexander at Issus* (*Die Alexanderschlacht*, 1528–29), which was, the reader is informed, the subject of Tod's first art historical essay at age sixteen. Eros and Thanatos collide in Tod's description: "My theme was the expression in the eye of Darius, horrified yet amorous, as he sees the tip of Alexander's lance aimed at him through the furious mêlée of the battle" (66). Altdorfer's painting is best known for its impossible standpoint: it communicates detail in the foreground, as though the artist had been standing near the fighting soldiers on the ground, while it also presents a view from the skies, as our gaze is directed into the distant background. The painting's sublimity comes from its inclusion of both the near and the far; death is seen from the standpoint of those thousands of infantrymen who died, and from the redemptive perspective of heaven.

In Sebald's story "Dr. Henry Selwyn," following the revelation that Naegeli died in a glacier, Sebald makes a suggestive mention of Dr. Selwyn's Meissen figurines — an invocation that could certainly lead readers of both Sebald and Chatwin to think of *Utz* (*DA*, 26/*E*, 15).[63] Perhaps this was meant as a wink, a way to connect his writing to that of Chatwin, not a "travel writer" but a traveler, with whom he shared a relationship to the concepts of "here" and "there," as well as to those of blindness and darkness. In this way one can perhaps understand why he wrote in his review essay that he remembers seeing Chatwin wasted to skin and bone in a final television interview, and he describes this vision as "die erschütterndste Epiphanie einer Schriftstellerperson, die ich kenne" (the most shattering epiphany of a writer that I know; *CS*, 222/179). The Catholic connotations of the word "epiphany" suggest both a presence and an absence, or the possibility that one has, like a ghost, returned from the abysses of the past. In the same essay Sebald also asserts that one of

Chatwin's favorite stories was Flaubert's "Saint Julien l'hospitalier" (1877), in which the eponymous saint atones for his many sins through horrible punishments until, at the end of the story he is taken up to heaven, face to face with Christ. His own reading of the story allows him to conjure up Chatwin, to make him present, Sebald continues, adding that he cannot read a single page of this story "ohne Chatwin zu sehen, so wie er gewesen ist" (without seeing Chatwin as he was; *CS*, 216/174).

In "Die Alpen im Meer" ("The Alps in the Sea"), part of Sebald's last, unfinished work, he details his own fascination with that same story — or at least the fascination that is experienced by his unnamed narrator. While on the island of Corsica, the narrator accidentally (in the drawer of a bedside table) happens across Flaubert's version of the legend. He describes the end of the tale, where Julian is generous to a leper, and closely attends to the profoundly homoerotic imagery. Sebald writes that Julian

> nach viel Drangsal und Pein von einem Aussätzigen über das Wasser gerudert wird am Ende der Welt. Drüben auf der anderen Seite muß Julian das Lager des Fährmanns teilen, und dann, indem er das von Schrunden und Schwären bedeckte, teils knotig verhärtete, teils schmierige Fleisch umarmt und Brust an Brust und Mund an Mund mit diesem ekelhaftesten aller Menschen die Nacht verbringt, wird er aus seiner Qual erlöst und darf aufsteigen in die blaue Weite des Firmaments.

> [at last, after much hardship and suffering, . . . is rowed by a leper across the water to the end of the world. On the opposite bank, Julian must share the ferryman's bed, and then, as he embraces the man's fissured and ulcerated flesh, partly hard and gnarled, partly deliquescent, spending the night breast to breast and mouth to mouth with that most repellent of all human beings, he is released from his torment and may rise into the blue expanses of the firmament.]

He then adds, "Erst der Gnadenakt der Transfiguration auf der letzten Seite ließ mich wieder aufschauen" (Only the act of grace when the saint is transfigured on the last page let me look up again).[64] One can understand this return to the story, in the review essay and in the prose text, as a doubled attempt to see both life and literature as Chatwin did. He repeatedly strove to see, as if prosthetically, with the eyes of his predecessors, to ask what they would say to us from beyond, if they could, and he implicitly or explicitly expressed the wish that writers such as Robert Walser, Kafka, or Nabokov could speak to him from the grave. In that sense he travels, as a "travel writer," over to the other side and, like Chatwin's archeologists, places himself in deathly proximity to his subjects. Thus, here as elsewhere, his eulogic review essay — in this case, an *Annäherung* — serves as a series of signposts that suggest to the reader the possibility of a posthumous convergence.

Notes

[1] Sebald writes, "Man kann sich nicht leicht einen zeitgenössischen deutschen Schriftsteller denken, der von Anfang an so viel aufs Spiel gesetzt hätte wie Bruce Chatwin, dieser rastlose Wanderer, von dessen fünf, nach jedem Maß außergewöhnlichen Büchern jedes einen anderen Weltteil zum Schauplatz hat" (It is not easy to think of a contemporary German writer who would have ventured as much from the first as that tireless traveler Bruce Chatwin, each of whose five books, remarkable by any standards, is set in a different part of the world. Sebald, "Das Geheimnis des rotbraunen Fells: Annäherung an Bruce Chatwin"; in English, "The Mystery of the Red-Brown Skin: An Approach to Bruce Chatwin," in *CS*, 215–22/173–80; here *CS*, 215/173). The German version of the review essay was originally published under the extended title "Das Geheimnis des rotbraunen Fells: Annäherung an Bruce Chatwin aus Anlass von Nicholas Shakespeares Biographie" in *Literaturen* 11 (2000): 72–75.

[2] Richard Sheppard in "Dexter–sinister: Some Observations on Decrypting the Mors Code in the Work of W. G. Sebald," *Journal of European Studies* 35.4 (2005): 419–63, indicates that the cause of Sebald's death was more ill health than the car crash, writing that during the 1990s Sebald's health got worse and his "state of mind grew darker." He writes: "We were all deeply shocked when Max died from an aneurysm that precipitated a car crash on 14 December 2001" (420).

[3] See Sheppard, "Dexter–sinister," 426.

[4] See Hans Magnus Enzensberger, "Much Left Unsaid," *Times Literary Supplement*, 16–22 Jun 1989, 657, and David C Estes, "Bruce Chatwin's *In Patagonia*: Traveling in Textualized Terrain," *New Orleans Review* 18.2 (1991): 67–77; here 68.

[5] See Ian Buruma, "Herzog and His Heroes," *New York Review of Books*, 19 Jul. 2007.

[6] Nicholas Shakespeare, *Bruce Chatwin: A Biography* (1999; repr., New York: Anchor Books, 2001), 96. Further references to this work are given using the abbreviation *BC*.

[7] Enzensberger, "Much Left Unsaid," 657.

[8] Michael Dirda, "Bruce Chatwin and the Collector of Prague," *Washington Post*, 22 Jan. 1989, Book World, X1.

[9] Michael Ignatieff, "An Interview with Bruce Chatwin," *Granta* 21 (1987): 23–37; here 23–24. When Chatwin says, "I had a go at laying down the law," he is likely referring to his incomplete scholarly study, *The Nomadic Alternative*.

[10] Sheppard cites a number of interviews in which Sebald voiced this resistance ("Dexter–sinister," 433).

[11] Bruce Chatwin, "It's a Nomad *Nomad* World" in *Anatomy of Restlessness: Selected Writings, 1969–1989*, ed. Jan Borm and Matthew Graves (New York: Penguin Books, 1997), 100–106; here 100 and 103 respectively. The essay was originally published in the magazine *Vogue* in December 1970.

[12] Richard Pearson, "Travel Writer, Novelist Bruce Chatwin Dies," *Washington Post*, 23 Jan. 1989, B7.

[13] Quoted in John Lanchester, "A Pom by the name of Bruce," *London Review of Books*, 29 Sept. 1988, 10.

[14] Bruce Chatwin, *The Songlines* (New York: Penguin Books, 1988), 13.

[15] The concept of the archive is key in J. J. Long's study of Sebald. See *W. G. Sebald: Image, Archive, Modernity* (New York: Columbia UP, 2007). On movement across the landscape see especially chapter 7, "The Ambulatory Narrative: *The Rings of Saturn*," 130–48.

[16] Deane Blackler also makes this connection, pointing out that in Sebald's texts, "the narrator is a restless traveler . . . a note-taking, photograph-collecting restless *Wandersmann* who seems like a *revenant* pursuing traces of the past, constructing his own European 'songlines' . . . out of the traces of literary and historical culture with which his memory engages." See Blackler, *Reading W. G. Sebald: Adventure and Disobedience* (Camden House: Rochester, NY, 2007), 94.

[17] On this tendency, see David Darby, "Landscape and Memory: Sebald's Redemption of History," in *W. G. Sebald: History — Memory — Trauma*, ed. Scott Denham and Mark McCulloh (Berlin: De Gruyter, 2006), 265–77. Darby notes: "Movement through landscape is essential to the process of memory enacted in Sebald's writing" (265).

[18] The ambivalence is referred to elsewhere in Shakespeare as well: "The textile dealer Jonathan Hope had never seen anyone with two natures at such odds. 'Half of Bruce despised being European and longed to be a Mauritanian nomad, renouncing everything; the other half was a worldly acquisitive collector with an eagle's eye for the unusual.'" He adds: "Hugh Honour wrote, 'He was a split personality, at any rate in this respect, and his extraordinary vitality and sharpness of perception owed much to the inner conflict of his two obsessive urges, the one sparking off the other'" (*BC*, 117–18).

[19] On the concept of *Heimat* in Sebald, see Markus Zisselsberger, "Stories of *Heimat* and Calamity," *Modern Austrian Literature* 40.4 (2007): 1–27, esp. 7–10.

[20] Sebald says: "I could have had a British passport years ago. But I was born into a particular historical context, and I really don't have an option." See Carole Angier, "Who Is W. G. Sebald?" *Jewish Quarterly* 164 (1996/97): 10–14; here 13.

[21] John Zilcosky, "Sebald's Uncanny Travels: The Impossibility of Getting Lost," in *W. G. Sebald: A Critical Companion*, ed. J. J. Long and Anne Whitehead (U of Washington P: Seattle, 2004), 102–20; here 102.

[22] Zilcosky, "Sebald's Uncanny Travels," 103.

[23] Zilcosky, "Sebald's Uncanny Travels," 104.

[24] Darby, "Landscape and Memory," 272.

[25] Massimo Leone remarks: "None of Sebald's works provides a better occasion for an inquiry into the writer's poetics of travel-dizziness than *Vertigo*. This is immediately evident in the title itself (notwithstanding the considerable semantic slip

between the German title *Schwindel. Gefühle.* and the English *Vertigo*). It is confirmed by the frequency with which Sebald's prose dwells on the description of dizziness, giddiness and vertigo as emotional states. At the same time, it is undeniable that the narrative structure of *Vertigo* can be seen as an exploration of, and a challenge to, the traditional patterns of travel literature." See "Textual Wanderings: A Vertiginous Reading of W. G. Sebald," in Long and Whitehead, *A Critical Companion*, 89–101; here 91.

[26] Lise Patt asks: "For what are we to make of his English book title which directly links Sebald to Alfred Hitchcock's most surrealist film? Especially since we know that by the end of the 1990s Sebald was teaching film at UEA and had more than a passing knowledge of the medium?" See "Introduction: Searching for Sebald: What I Know for Sure," in *Searching for Sebald: Photography after W. G. Sebald*, ed. Lise Patt (Los Angeles: Institute of Cultural Inquiry, 2007), 17–101; here 69.

[27] The term, of course, appears elsewhere in the text. See, for example, *SG*, 42/*V*, 35.

[28] Massimo Leone writes: "The semantics of confusion is counterbalanced by what I should like to call the rhetoric of the collector . . . . Components of reality that commonly either go unnamed or are subsumed beneath broad generic labels here receive a specific denomination, as in a collector's cabinet of curiosities." See Leone, "Textual Wanderings," 97.

[29] Sebald also uses the term in a title inserted in the German version of the review, not similarly highlighted in the translation. The heading that separates the section reads: "Das verschlossene Glasvertiko als Metapher." See "Das Geheimnis des rotbraunen Fells," *Literaturen* 11:73. On other cabinets of curiosities in Sebald's work, especially *Naturalienkabinette*, see Long, *Image, Archive, Modernity*, 39–44.

[30] Philip Schlesinger "W. G. Sebald and the Condition of Exile," *Theory, Culture & Society* 21.2 (2004): 43–67; here 44.

[31] See *BC*, 37. Shakespeare here is drawing on Chatwin's *In Patagonia*.

[32] See "Fetishism (1927)" in Sigmund Freud, *The Standard Edition of the Complete Psychological Works of Sigmund Freud*, trans. and ed. James Strachey (London: Hogarth, 1961), vol 21 (1927–1931), 148–57: here 155.

[33] Freud, "Fetishism," 156.

[34] Giorgio Agamben, *Stanzas: Word and Phantasm in Western Culture*, trans. Ronald L. Martinez (Minneapolis: U of Minnesota P, 1993), 33.

[35] Shakespeare explains that the character is based somewhat on a Dr. Rudolf Just. See *BC*, 500–502.

[36] On the name, see *BC*, 504–5. Kaspar Hauser is invoked in Sebald's Chatwin review ("Das Geheimnis des rotbraunen Fells," *Literaturen* 11:74; in *CS*, 221/178) as well as in *Die Ausgewanderten* (*DA*, 29/*E*, 17) in connection with the story of Dr. Henry Selwyn.

[37] The connection with Ulrich is made by Patrick Meanor. See *Bruce Chatwin* (New York: Twayne, 1997), 132. St. Ulrich is symbolized as a fish in Christian

iconography, which is no minor matter as far as Sebald studies are concerned. See W. G. Sebald, "Scomber scombrus, or the Common Mackerel: On Pictures by Jan Peter Tripp," in CS, 210–14/169–72. In that essay Sebald writes: "Perhaps it is no coincidence that to dream of fish is said to mean death" (170). The essay was originally published as "Scomber scombrus oder die gemeine Makrele: Zu Bildern von Jan Peter Tripp," in the *Neue Zürcher Zeitung*, 23 and 24 Sept. 2000.

[38] Shakespeare is referring to Chatwin's *Utz* (New York: Viking, 1989), 18–19.

[39] Chatwin, *Utz*, 12.

[40] The book was never quite finished, though the manuscript, such as it is, was rescued from the dustbin. See *BC*, 277.

[41] On Chatwin as a collector of butterflies, Shakespeare explains that Chatwin spent the summer with a Swedish boy his own age, Thomas Bratt, to whom he was supposed to teach English. There were problems: "According to Thomas's younger brother Peter, the fault lay with Bruce. 'I remember an extremely dull boy running around with a net,' says Peter Bratt. 'It's a strange thing, a boy of 14 mostly interested in collecting butterflies and putting needles through them.'" See *BC*, 78–79.

[42] About Chatwin's ailment and its "cure," Kenneth S. Calhoon is also suspicious. He writes: "This sounds apocryphal and has a familiar ring." He cites as an antecedent Richard Henry Dana Jr.'s two-year voyage around Cape Horn, undertaken "to cure, if possible . . . a weakness of the eyes." See Calhoon, "Charming the Carnivore: Bruce Chatwin's Australian Odyssey," in *Writing Travel: The Poetics and Politics of the Modern Journey*, ed. John Zilcosky (Toronto: U of Toronto P, 2008), 173–94; here 192.

[43] See *BC*, 167. One suspects that Patrick Trevor-Roper was predisposed toward such a diagnosis. In *The World through Blunted Sight* (New York: Bobbs-Merrill, 1970), Trevor-Roper identifies a number of great creative writers with eye ailments. For example, his long list of myopic geniuses includes Keats, Tennyson, Pope, Milton, and Yeats. See esp. 28–29.

[44] Ignatieff, "An Interview with Bruce Chatwin," 25. A version of this dialogue also appears in Chatwin's *The Songlines*, 17.

[45] See Susannah Clapp, *With Chatwin: Portrait of a Writer* (New York: Alfred A. Knopf, 1997), 115.

[46] See Sheppard, "Dexter–sinister," 432.

[47] J. J. Long, "History, Narrative, and Photography in W. G. Sebald's *Die Ausgewanderten*," *Modern Language Review* 98 (2003): 117–37; here 133.

[48] For background on the story and on the real Paul Bereyter, see Mark M. Anderson, "Documents, Photography, Postmemory: Alexander Kluge, W. G. Sebald, and the German Family," *Poetics Today* 29.1 (2008): 129–53; esp. 146.

[49] In the German original this character's name is Alec Garrard (*RS*, 286).

[50] See Mona Körte, "'Un petit sac': W. G. Sebalds Figuren zwischen Sammeln und Vernichten," in *Sebald: Lektüren*, ed. Marcel Atze and Franz Loquai (Eggingen, Germany: Edition Isele, 2005), 176–94 on how the rucksack functions

as part of the body (178) and on how it becomes a material repository of memory (186).

51 This characteristic recalls a description of Chatwin quoted in Shakespeare. Miranda Rothschild "found him an immensely talented but detached person whose emotional luggage had to be honed down to the single perfect accoutrement of a rucksack" (*BC*, 259).

52 See W.G. Sebald and Gordon Turner, "Introduction and Transcript of an Interview Given by Max Sebald," in Denham and McCulloh, *History — Memory — Trauma*, 21–29; here 28.

53 See W.G. Sebald, "Thanatos: Zur Motivstruktur in Kafkas *Schloss*," *Literatur und Kritik* 66/67 (1972): 399–411; here 399, and "The Undiscover'd Country: The Death Motif in Kafka's *Castle*," *Journal of European Studies* 2 (1972): 22–34; here 23. The latter essay begins with a relevant epigram drawn from Samuel Beckett's *Molloy* (1951): "And in the end, or almost, to be abroad alone, by unknown ways, in the gathering of the night, with a stick. It was a stout stick, he used it to thrust himself onward, or as a defence, when the time came, against dogs and marauders. Yes, night was gathering, but the man was innocent, greatly innocent, he had nothing to fear, though he went in fear, he had nothing to fear, there was nothing they could do to him, or very little." The connection is also pointed out in Sheppard ("Dexter–sinister," 437).

54 Schlag's rucksack is mentioned in *Schwindel. Gefühle.*, 271, and in *Vertigo*, 248. For background on Schlag the hunter and his link to Kafka, see Markus Zisselsberger, "Melancholy Longings: Sebald, Benjamin, and the Image of Kafka," in Patt, *Searching for Sebald*, 280–301; here 295–96.

55 This refers to the selection of Axel Forrester's photos as reproduced in Lise Patt's *Searching for Sebald*, 512–13.

56 The rucksack Sebald chose to depict in *Austerlitz* belonged to his close friend, the poet Stephen Watts. Sheppard, however, provides an alternative account. See "Dexter–sinister," 452n13: "The real rucksack definitely belonged to Max."

57 See Paul Cronin, ed., *Herzog on Herzog* (London: Faber & Faber, 2002), 283.

58 Also noted by Carol Jacobs in "What Does It Mean to Count? W. G. Sebald's *The Emigrants*," *Modern Language Notes* 119.5 (2004): 905–29; here 916.

59 For more on this, see Sheppard, "Dexter–sinister," 429–33; also Sebald's essay on Robert Walser entitled "Le promeneur solitaire: Zur Erinnerung an Robert Walser," in *LG*, 127–68; esp. 135–37; and also Mark M. Anderson, "Fathers and Son: W. G. Sebald," *Bookforum*, Dec-Jan (2007): 28–31.

60 Following the revelations about Naegeli, Selwyn tells Sebald's narrator that he still experiences homesickness, and the narrator notes suggestively that he perceives this as a "confession," pointing out that no other word would do (see *DA*, 30/*E*, 18).

61 Bruce Chatwin, "The Estate of Maximilian Tod" (1979), in *Anatomy of Restlessness*, 63.

[62] See W. G. Sebald, "Das unentdeckte Land: Zur Motivstruktur in Kafkas *Schloß*," in *BU*, 78–92; here 78.

[63] Porcelain figures make an appearance in *Austerlitz* as well (see *A*, 284/197).

[64] W. G. Sebald, "Die Alpen im Meer" / "The Alps in the Sea," *CS*, 39–50/35–46; here 48/44. Sebald originally published this story under the same title in *Literaturen* 1 (2001): 30–33, the same publication for which he wrote his Chatwin essay.

8: Tripping: On Sebald's "Stifter"

Neil Christian Pages

> Apart from a few writers who don't make up in anything else for
> their lack of inner life — ... — I have enjoyed everything of impor-
> tance I've ever read.
> > — Nuala O'Faolain, *Are You Somebody?*
> > *The Accidental Memoir of a Dublin Woman*

> *Zuweilen muß man auch einen Blick in sich selbst tun. Doch soll
> man nicht stetig mit sich allein auch in dem schönsten Lande sein;
> man muß zu Zeiten wieder zu seiner Gesellschaft zurückkehren,
> wäre es nur, um sich an mancher glänzenden Menschentrümmer,
> die aus unsrer Jugend noch übrig ist, zu erquicken, oder an man-
> chem festen Turm von einem Menschen empor zu schauen, der sich
> gerettet hat.*
> > — Adalbert Stifter, *Der Nachsommer*

> *Der Blick von der Milchstraße herab auf die öde und schwarz im
> Weltall sich drehende, ausgebrannte Ruine der Erde könnte fremder
> nicht sein, und doch liegt die Kindheit, die wir auf ihr verbrachten
> und die aus den Worten des Hausfreunds herausklingt, kaum
> weiter zurück als der gestrige Tag.*
> > — W. G. Sebald, "Es steht ein Komet am Himmel:
> > Kalenderbeitrag zu Ehren des rheinischen Hausfreunds"

> *Ja, es scheine, als hätten im Kunstwerk
> die Männer einander verehrt wie Brüder,
> einander dort oft ein Denkmal gesetzt,
> wo ihre Wege sich kreuzten.*
> > — W. G. Sebald, *Nach der Natur: Ein Elementargedicht*

Indifferent Landscapes

TWO ESSAYS ON ADALBERT STIFTER (1805–68) frame W. G. Sebald's first
book on Austrian literature, *Die Beschreibung des Unglücks: Zur österreichischen Literatur von Stifter bis Handke* (1985), which opens with "Bis
an den Rand der Natur: Versuch über Stifter" and closes with "Helle Bilder
und dunkle: Zur Dialektik der Eschatologie bei Stifter und Handke."[1]

In the final essay of the anthology Sebald begins his investigations by per-
forating the surface of the object with an ekphrastic excursion into a
Biedermeier landscape etching ("Stich") he claims to have acquired in an
antiquarian bookshop. The image, the critic remembers, had always seemed
to him like an illustration taken from a work by Stifter (*HB*, 165). Such
associations are unsurprising for readers who know Stifter well, since the
Austrian writer was also a talented amateur painter, an avid collector, a
restorer of antique furniture, and a professional *Denkmalpfleger*.[2] Sebald's
picture, however, has little to do with the idyllic landscapes associated with
the decorative *Vedutenmalerei* from which Stifter's paintings and drawings
emerged, not least of all because the image is populated by human figures,
a rarity in Stifter's visual oeuvre. Sebald's reexperiencing of the image represents part of an imaginative relation that transforms the work into a
metaphysical object of curious significance. Leading the reader into the
depth of the (re)collected work of art, Sebald first describes a kind of
Landpartie set in a sunny upland landscape, with four human figures and a
dog, but then remarks of the scene that "alle schauen sie, etwas vornübergebeugt, in einen anscheinend bodenlosen Abgrund hinunter, der da unmittelbar vor ihren Füßen sich auftut" (*HB*, 165; and all of them, bending
slightly forward, seem to be gazing down into what is apparently a bottomless chasm that opens itself there at their feet).[3]

The wording here is striking, not least of all because Sebald's prose is
known for its exacting craftsmanship. Here the imaginative operation the
critic performs in guiding the reader into the essay doubles the image
described and opens up a chasm of its own. Indeed, Sebald's reader joins
the assembled figures and gazes into an abyss that is at once the absence
of the etching itself (uncharacteristically for both Sebald's fictional and
essayistic works, the image is not reproduced on the page) and the absence
of what lies in the chasm into which the represented figures seem to peer.
This absence is reinforced in the narration by Sebald's recollection of having "read" the visual image somewhere else, namely in Stifter's written
corpus, adding to a series of *dislocations* that offers up a picture that has
now traveled from text to image to memory to text (description), and that
suggests the difficulty of definitively locating Stifter, an author who carefully camouflaged his life story in the thicket of his prose.[4]

Sebald unpacks Stifter's formidable body of work as a series of perspec-
tival layers that remind us of the dizzying possibilities of perceiving — at
once — very different levels of signification.[5] Having produced a sense of
vertigo in describing the image and the memory of the image — *Schwindel.
Gefühle.*, as it were — the critic recalls reassuringly, "Daß die Stifterische
Prosa den Leser immer wieder an solchen Plätzen vorbeiführt, ist oft
bemerkt worden" (*HB*, 165; It has often been noted that Stifter's prose
leads the reader past such places again and again). Moving away from the
generalization about the repetitions in Stifter's work, Sebald's second essay

— as *Versuch* — takes on another kind of abyss by attempting to compensate for what is not there, and by focusing on that which has indeed *not* "often been remarked" about Adalbert Stifter. With no reference to the presumed sources of his broad generalization about the ubiquitous dead ends to which Stifter scholarship leads — the "fast schon ins Aschgraue gediehende Sekundärliteratur" (*VS*, 17; the secondary literature, which has almost faded into an ashen gray) — the essayist instead provides a series of idiosyncratic references from his own readings on painting as taken from Stifter's mammoth novel *Der Nachsommer* (itself a kind of *Künstlerroman*). These citations unravel downward on the page, landing appropriately enough at the recapitulation of the larger theme of the volume of which the essay is a part, namely the search for what remains of the latent pathologies that constitute "das Unglück des schreibenden Subjekts," in this case, Stifter (*BU*, 11; the calamity of the writing subject).

Sebald localizes the residue of Stifter's *Unglück* as his unhappiness, his calamity, his pathology in a particular text, "einem einzigartigen autobiographischen Fragment" (*HB*, 166; in a singular autobiographical fragment), namely the posthumously published "Nachgelassenes Blatt," which Sebald refers to by its alternate title "Mein Leben." Stifter wrote the fragment — "zunächst für mich allein" (for now for me alone) — during a visit to his birthplace at Oberplan in Bohemia one year before taking his own life.[6] Remarkable in the oeuvre of a writer who recorded so few of his own memories and who seems to have been wholly uninterested in one of the central concerns of Sebald's prose fiction, namely memory and the commemoration of traumatic experiences and historical catastrophes, the fragment provides the stuff for Sebald's attempts to unpack Stifter as a personality. The text, the only extant piece of autobiographical "evidence" in Stifter's corpus, is hardly typical, a fact Sebald does not emphasize. It serves nonetheless as a means to link the work and life of a subject whose stubborn attention to a project of scrupulous self-fashioning — despite contemporary revisions of that image and the fascination with his grisly suicide[7] — left few clues to the pathological nature of "das abgründige Innenleben Stifters" (*HB*, 169; abyssal inner life of Stifter).[8] While Sebald's approach is speculative, it does work because of the fact that in many ways Stifter's historical persona lends itself to the critic's method of weaving together fact, fiction, fictionalization, and affect to produce what Sven Meyer has called "imaginierte Konjekturen," imagined conjectures and convergences.[9]

On the one hand, what Sebald describes as the image of Stifter as a "Biedermeier Käfer und Blumenpoet" has endured because Stifter's public persona can well be seen as prosaic (*VS*, 15; as the Biedermeier poet of ladybugs and flowers). That traditional view is supported not only by surface readings of Stifter's literary works, but also by the author's biography, his "selfless" devotional practice as tutor, pedagogue, civil servant,

Landeskonservator, and foster father. In turn, that public image was received and cemented by the commemorative practices of the early scholarship and by the institutions and monuments that were dedicated to Stifter's writings and to his memory. On the other hand, Stifter's self-described artistic practice, particularly as he represented it in his extensive correspondence, lives up to such an ideal only superficially, leading to impressions that contradict the view of Stifter as Austrian *Heimatdichter*. As one scholar observes, Stifter believed that the artist

> hat sich im Dienst seiner Sache so weit zurückzunehmen, bis er zur *bloßen Durchgangsstation, zum transparenten Medium* geworden ist, in dessen vermittelnder Hervorbringung sich *der Gegenstand* ohne alle Beimischung von Subjektivität als er selber zeigen kann.[10]

> [The task of the artist is to withdraw himself in the service of his object to the point at which he has become a mere way station, a transparent medium in whose mediating creative activity the object can reveal itself as itself without any admixture of subjectivity.]

But Stifter's self-effacement in theory, which would make him typical of his era, collides with the conspicuous characteristics of his prose style in practice, which makes him remarkably "modern." What sounds like a recapitulation of the infamous *sanftes Gesetz* (the gentle law) as self-sacrifice to the "natural" order of things is, on the contrary, quite similar to the abyss that opens itself upon the reader in Sebald's essay when faced with the etching. Indeed, even though Stifter withdraws as a biographical person from his textual landscapes, it seems that his works remain nonetheless shadowed by an indistinct though ever-present corpse.[11]

Sebald's approaches to Stifter are thus very much attempts to describe a kind of disappearing act and thus to give an account of the artist's life through his writing in the face of the conspicuous lack of overt autobiographical material.[12] At the same time, this representation of the convergence of life and work relies on the depiction of an image that occupies a particular imagination, namely that of the reader Sebald. The composite image of Stifter as Sebald imagines him emerges from a critical turn to the kind of literary biography that readers familiar with Sebald's scholarly essays will recognize. The unsaid in Stifter's prose, then, is evidenced by the writer's documented pathological behaviors — his eating disorders, apparent misogyny, latent pedophilic tendencies, alcoholism, hypochondria, and mania for collecting everything from ecclesiastical ephemera to exotic cacti — and is set against what the critic senses was his subject's reluctance to tell the true story of his own life, essentially his resistance to memory. In the supposed sacrifice to his *Sache* or *Gegenstand*, then, Sebald will see a connection to an inner life that went consciously unrecorded but that nonetheless resisted its complete effacement.[13] In mining this repressed past and the voids and traces it has left behind, Sebald's restitutive project insists that the single autobiographical fragment in Stifter's corpus, "Mein Leben," is the manifest key to understanding the latent presence of death and destruction in Stifter's writing, in which the demonic is at one with the beautiful and in which the natural world is necessarily connected to horror and disaster as the *sublime*. In a turn that suggests the kind of writing Sebald will pursue later in his prose fiction, the critic here focuses on the autobiographical fragment and its relation to his own imagination. From it he reconstructs an image of a writing subject whose "truth" is also determined by the subjective impressions of a reading experience that is now recalled under the guise of a critical essay. This, then, is Sebald's "Stifter."[14]

The present essay aims to describe the figuration of "Stifter" in Sebald's work in order to illuminate how Sebald read and to see how those readings inform and reverberate in his prose fiction. In locating some of the key elements of the critic's approach to Stifter and their reappearance elsewhere, my investigation will suggest that while Sebald's two essays fail to capture Stifter in adequate scholarly argumentation, they do succeed in sketching out the bases for another kind of storytelling that becomes operative elsewhere in Sebald's work. From his reading of Stifter's absent (and apparently absented) autobiographical project, the critic fashions a kind of literary character and therewith redeems "Stifter" for that later work. Where Stifter is the historical figure for scholarly investigation, "Stifter" becomes the figuration that Sebald constructs from his own impressions as a reader who mobilizes this composite figure to tell the story of an experience that emerges at the "Indifferenzpunkt" at which the difference between the two "Stifters" no longer matters. At that point the critical essays become literary in their "Versuch der Restitution," in an attempt at restitution that Sebald insisted could only be enacted in literature and that functions here to restore to the (reader's) image of Stifter a sense of the writer's inner life, of the world that is only intimated in the autobiographical fragment (*CS*, 248/205).

Of course, to understand the critical process at work in Sebald's thinking about Stifter we must examine his primary scholarly source, "Mein Leben." It is there that we glimpse those traces of what Sebald calls the "kaum überdachten psychischen und sozialen Vorprägung" of Stifter's personality, a prelinguistic, presocialized "self" that has both barely been considered by Stifter scholars (*überdenken*) and is only barely covered (*überdachen*) by Stifter's formidable "Kunstwillen," his will to create as an artist (*VS*, 18; *HB*, 167; the psychic and social preformation of Stifter's personality). "Mein Leben" comprises three eidetic memories from Stifter's earliest childhood, all recounted in an at-times-almost-hallucinatory parataxis.[15] Each recounted episode is then interrupted by frame-narrative references to *das Entsetzliche, das Zugrunderichtende*, the

abysmal and the destructive, through which Stifter contrasts the presence
of "Wunder" and "Verwunderung" (wonder and wonderment), which are
again unsettled by the appearance of a spatial abyss, a below, "Nichts,"
"ein Unten." Here Stifter, who, as Benjamin noted in a rare piece of praise,
"von dem menschlichen Leben, wo es noch nicht als Schicksal entfaltet
ruht, also von den Kindern wunderbar gesprochen hat" (spoke wonder-
fully of human life where it was not yet unfolded as fate, namely of children), conjures himself as a child whose bizarre experience of the world
contrasts markedly with the adult's placid and carefully maintained self-
image.[16]

In the fugue of memory Stifter depicts in "Mein Leben," the child
"Stifter" is no longer able to "see" clear boundaries, defined limits, and
presumed differences, but rather senses in the return to a preindividuated
state (a Kafkan turn to be sure) that which — and here Sebald intervenes
pathographically — "der Verdrängung verfiel mit dem Erlernen der
Sprache," that which succumbed to repression with the acquisition of language (*HB*, 167). Stifter's uncharacteristic turn to the story of his own
childhood thus reveals those remnants of what was not elided by what
Novotny describes as Stifter's "Gestaltungsdrang," his drive to model and
to form and therewith to eliminate the fragmented and formless in an
aesthetic program.[17] Nonetheless, in the writer's recording of sensations
and impressions from his own life, the reader Sebald identifies an
"Indifferenzpunkt" at which *helle Bilder* merge with *dunkle Bilder* to
reveal the inner identity ("Innenleben") of a subject *durchdrungen* (permeated, penetrated) by a sense of (and a sense for) what Stifter recalls,
from his memories of earliest childhood, as *das Entsetzliche* and *das
Zugrunderichtende*, the abysmal and the destructive that he cannot quite
eliminate from memory (*HB*, 166; *NB*, 680).[18] The disturbing ambivalence of so many of the images in Stifter's prose now becomes comprehensible at a crucial "Indifferenzpunkt," Sebald contends, at which "in der
Sensation des Schwindels, in der wiederum das aus lauter jähen Abstürzen
bestehende frühkindliche Gefühlsleben des erzählenden Subjekts erinner-
lich wird" (*HB*, 166; point of indifference at which, in the sensation of
vertigo, the emotional life of the storytelling subject's early childhood,
which comprises a series of sheer, precipitous, and plummeting crashes,
becomes "rememberable"). With this act of recuperation "Mein Leben"
provides an epiphanic moment at which the manic tendencies of Stifter's
descriptive prose become comprehensible in the present.

In tripping over the inexorable traces of this unprocessed preconscious
("Vorbewußtsein"), Stifter becomes afflicted ("heimgesucht") by involuntary memories that overwhelm his attempts at self-control and self-presentation.[19] What is more, the experience of vertigo disturbs the strict
aesthetic binaries (*helle Bilder* emptied of *dunkle Bilder*) of Stifter's prose,
which now dissolve into a single, nebulous image that grows from eidetic

memories whose representation defies the aesthetic and poetic limits of Stifter's method (*HB*, 167). As a result, the laws of genre that regulate Sebald's own text, the demand for a strict division between life and work required of conventional scholarly writing, is rendered inoperable at a point of indifference at which the storytelling subject (*das erzählende Subjekt*) becomes haunted by a memory of having read Stifter and of having seen "Stifter" in an etching the reader ("Sebald") coincidentally purchased at a Freiburg bookshop. The experience of *Schwindel*, then, generates true *Gefühle*, sensations from a time prior to the reflection and abstract reason of the language, training, and aesthetic sensibilities of an adult.[20] Sebald's subjective impression, informed also by visual evidence, is that "Mein Leben," like Stifter's visual art, shows how that *sanfte Gesetz* only camouflages the demonic that is part and parcel of its grounding. Stifter's recording of his earliest sensations — itself an act of *Gestalten* that requires the structuring hand of an adult *Erinnerung* — relates these bizarre and uncannily vivid sensations of the external, finite world to an infinite cosmos whose celestial bodies, Stifter writes, can be captured empirically but whose true proportions remain unimaginable and imperceptible, essentially beyond recall (*NB*, 583). Thus perception proves to be "so wie die ungemeine Größe der Körper selbst, [die] wir wohl durch Zahlen ausdrücken, aber in unserem Vorstellungsvermögen nicht vergegenwärtigen können" (*NB*, 583; like the immense size of the bodies themselves, which we can express in empirical terms, but which we cannot envision in our imagination).

Sebald's own *Indifferenzpunkt*[21] reveals the extent of Stifter's influence on both his critical and his literary work. It suggests further that in overcoming the indifferent, "objective" detachment demanded by the conventions of academic writing, Sebald's engagements with Stifter catalyze the *Gestaltungsdrang* of a reader whose own *eidetic* memories require both the telling of the story of a reading experience and the correction of a critical tradition that simply does not confirm that experience.[22] Here the secondary literature on Stifter is dismissed *tout court*: "Über Adalbert Stifter," Sebald observes boldly, "ist viel geschrieben worden, Hagiographisches, und Abfälliges, ohne daß deshalb die schwierige Schönheit seines Werks zugänglicher geworden wäre" (*VS*, 17 and 15; Much has been written about Adalbert Stifter — some of it hagiographic, some of it disparaging — but all without having made the difficult beauty of his work more accessible).[23] As a response to this lack, Sebald proposes that we abandon the *Abfall* of Stifter's reception and establish a readerly *Zugang* as a point of access to life and work that is reinstaurated through the telling of the story of a reading experience that belongs to the critic himself. As he would do elsewhere in his work as a kind of public intellectual in the controversies surrounding the literature of the air war — to name just one example of Sebald's provocations — the critic packages his approach as an urgent attending to a glaring deficiency, here the "längst überfällige pathographische Darstellung Stifters" (*VS*, 21; the long overdue pathographic representation of Stifter) that must lie beneath an "Anschein der Selbstbeherrschtheit," the appearance of self-control at the surface of his work.

In assigning himself this task, or rather in discovering it in an image (that "Stich"), Sebald functions as a structuring instance, assuming several different rhetorical roles simultaneously: reader, memoirist, essayist, critic, and storyteller. The resulting tension (*Spannung*) between these positions allows Sebald to cast a net (*spannen*) over the slippery "object" Stifter and to appropriate his style, that "mit allen Mitteln verdeckte und gebändigte Maßlosigkeit," as a means to tell stories.[24] It is thus appropriate that Sebald's own prose fiction provides the operative term for characterizing this relation between reading Stifter and writing about him, for understanding how "Stifter" makes his way into the textual landscapes of works like *Nach der Natur* and *Die Ringe des Saturn*. Building upon a body of scholarship on the connections between Sebald and Stifter (Bond, Fuchs, Huyssen, McCulloh, Öhlschläger, and Zisselsberger, for example),[25] I seek to discern how the experience of reading Stifter, framed by the categories of *Lehre* and *Lernen* (teaching and learning) that Sebald identifies as central to the Austrian literary tradition (*BU*, 13), determines a very particular, "Sebaldian" poetics of reading in which influence and appropriation become, in turn, illumination and transmigration.

Transmigrations

Unlike the prose of Adalbert Stifter, of course, Sebald's writing enjoys a wide and enthusiastic readership, particularly in the English-speaking world. In addition, the number of scholarly works on Sebald continues to grow at a rate that is remarkable for the work of a contemporary author.[26] His essays on Austrian literature, perhaps unsurprisingly, remain largely untranslated, a fact that underscores the marginal position his interest in Austrian authors occupies in Sebald's broader reception as a writer and literary critic.[27] Sebald's commitment to Stifter has, however, increased the circulation of the name "Stifter," at least in terms of mentions in the blogosphere and in the popular press, where Sebald aficionados (at least in the English-speaking world) are eager to track down the myriad references in his fictional works.[28] The writing of those texts was also the focus of the many interviews Sebald gave before his death, where he cited Stifter as a direct influence. In a radio interview with Michael Silverblatt in December 2001, for example, Sebald described his own literary patrimony and the influence of Stifter specifically:

They [Gottfried Keller and Adalbert Stifter] are both absolutely wonderful writers who achieved a very, very high intensity in their prose. One can see that for them it's never a question of getting to the next phase of the plot, but that they devote a great deal of care and attention to each individual page, very much the way a poet has to do. What they all have in common is this precedence of the carefully composed page of prose over the mechanisms of the novel."[29]

Emphasizing the style and craftsmanship of Stifter's prose and its static "intensity" as a contrast to the advancing plot trajectory of the novel in its isolation, Sebald confirms the connections scholars have since noted between his own vaguely "nineteenth century" writing style and that of Stifter (and, concomitantly, of Thomas Bernhard). More important is the fact that Sebald's comments speak to the extent to which he was, in the words of Hugo Dittberner, "ein Autor der Lektüren," an author of readings whose prose was deeply affected by the affinities he established with the texts and authors he read.[30]

Conscious of the extent to which the process of reading is itself generative of writing, Sebald seems to have transcribed an experience of reading Stifter onto his own "carefully composed page." That process was also informed by his scholarly practice and philological and literary-historical research, as well as his academic training as a *Germanist*. Seen in retrospect, then, the essays on Stifter bear the marks of a preparatory exercise for that withdrawal from scholarly criticism to the fiction writing Sebald did later, the works whose focus on the process of composition and the autofictional makes their genre classification nearly impossible and probably unnecessary.[31] The same could be said of Sebald's essays, which, while "scholarly" in their packaging, exhibit a "subjective" kind of narration that prioritizes storytelling over argument, that seeks less to convince and more to attract.[32] As Markus Zisselsberger notes, though, Stifter thwarts Sebald's very project in *Die Beschreibung des Unglücks* because he provides no "way for the subject to translate, recode, and potentially work through his pathological affliction and personal misfortune."[33] Stifter is "pathological" not only because of the image formed by the hearsay about his neurotic behaviors and strange proclivities but also because his writing fails to offer up the stuff that would suit Sebald's argument about the writing subject. Nonetheless, while the "historical" Stifter stymies the critic's attempt at writing a "scholarly" pathography based on reliable documentation from the author's life, he ironically does provide — in *not* remembering — a necessary void for the kind of storytelling for which Sebald is renowned and for an imagined, creative reconstruction of "Stifter" for the critic's purposes.

What the essays on Stifter tell us about the relation between Sebald and his subject, then, is that Sebald's focus on Stifter's *Unglück* is also an interest in the calamities and unhappiness at the core of his own writing.

222 ◆ NEIL CHRISTIAN PAGES

There the abysses of that which has been effaced through historical trauma and collective amnesia seem just as ubiquitous as the natural and unnatural chasms in Stifter's landscapes. Whereas Stifter works to fill these gaps through the mobilization of a descriptive sanitation detail, Sebald seeks to uncover the traces of effaced pasts that can still be rescued and whose presence is ironically marked as a void. What Stifter kills *qua* description and overwriting[34] now becomes the stuff for the writing of another, who empathizes with a subject who reminds him, as Sebald remarks in an essay on the contemporary Austrian writer Peter Handke, of that which "in den Kindern zugrunde gerichtet wird" (that which is destroyed in children).[35] What Stifter feared, repressed, and elided (also from his childhood) becomes for Sebald the material for his prose fiction, where the static images of Stifter's works become mobile and multivalent, circulating with some freedom.[36] As Claudia Öhlschläger observes,

> Es scheint, als ob Sebald das Schwinden der Dinge, das Stifter so vehement bekämpft, umgekehrt ästhetisch fruchtbar machen wolle, um sich in ein anderes Geschichts- und Gedächtnismodell einzuschreiben. Dieses zielt eben nicht auf eine enzyklopädische Verfügbarkeit, sondern auf eine Konzeption von Geschichte und Erinnerung, die dem zufälligen Augenblick entspringt[37]

> [It seems as if Sebald wants conversely to make the disappearance of things, which Stifter combats so vehemently, aesthetically productive in order to write himself into a different model of history and remembrance. His approach seeks not an encyclopedic availability of things, but rather a conception of history and memory that emerges in the chance moment, in coincidence].

Such a chance moment is catalyzed by a process of reading and recognition that cannot be tethered to argument or evidence but is only at home in a singular imagination.

While the accessibility provided for by an encyclopedic organization of knowledge that Stifter pursued with such vehemence could itself be seen as ironically *zufällig*, this possibility seems not to have occurred to him. What seems to have terrified him, though, namely that fragmentation of a modernity that encroached upon the conventions and practices of his time, becomes now for Sebald an opportunity to grasp experiences that cannot be captured in a presumed historical or "objective" reality. Such experiences can only be perceived as sensation and affect, in subjective perception. In making Stifter's anxieties "fruchtbar," Sebald thus converts Stifter's concern for "das Schwinden der Dinge" (the passing away of things and their form, their very *Gegenständlichkeit*) into an attention to a modern atrophy of memories and the loss of experiences that could be shared in storytelling. Where Stifter's controlled composition of representations seeks to capture objects so that they will remain "as they are" (for

Stifter this means as "Nature" intended, or in the Rankean sense as what and how they actually were), Sebald's writing grasps coincidental convergences that acknowledge the ineluctable traces of "what was" and mourn in a commemorative practice that which has been lost.

That process is enacted and crafted into a sensory experience through *transmigration*, a term that figures prominently in Sebald's *Die Ringe des Saturn*, specifically in a meditation on the life of the seventeenth-century physician Sir Thomas Browne, from whom Sebald's narrator learns how to see. Indeed, in that work the narrator stumbles upon a metaphor — not a model — for seeing the world and for transcribing that experience into writing. In the first section of this "englische Wallfahrt" (English pilgrimage, a detail omitted from the English translation), he describes how Browne, during "eines gefahrvollen Höhenfluges der Sprache" (a parlous loftiness in his language), sought to understand the "Unsichtbarkeit und Unfaßbarkeit dessen, was uns bewegt" (the invisibility and the intangibility of that which moves us; *RS*, 29 and 30/18 and 19) and, at the same time, to uncover a means of survival through the study of objects and creatures. Similarly concerned with those anxieties about the accelerating destruction of the natural world that plagued Stifter, Browne aims to intervene in his own (prognosed) melancholy by searching for the key to the strange ability of certain things and creatures to escape annihilation: "Und weil der schwerste Stein der Melancholie die Angst ist vor dem aussichtslosen Ende unserer Natur, sucht Browne unter dem, was der Vernichtung entging, nach den Spuren der geheimnisvollen Fähigkeit zur *Transmigration*, die er an den Raupen und Faltern so oft studiert hat" (And since the heaviest stone that melancholy can throw at a man is to tell him he is at the end of his nature, Browne scrutinizes that which escaped annihilation for any sign of the mysterious capacity for *transmigration* he has so often observed in caterpillars and moths; *RS*, 38/26; emphasis mine). Ironically, Stifter's *Dinge* are rendered immobile via description and are thus unable to transmigrate. They are thus, following Browne's thinking, doomed by the very action meant to save them.[38]

The plural, multiple valences of "transmigration" that appear from this excursion into the life and writerly practice of Browne suggest some possible inroads for an exploration of how "Stifter" reappears or is appropriated in and by Sebald's writing. Transmigration is a physical process, "the migration or passage of cells through a membrane or the wall of a vessel" and also "the spiritual transfer of a soul into another body."[39] Both of these senses of the term indicate an unconscious or unintended migration of one object (here understood also as a text) into another. Transmigration differs from mere influence or sheer copying, for it implies an empathetic connection established through the act of reading a text and the experience of having read that text. At the same time, the resemblance between the object before its transmigration and its present state is, as Browne indicates in his scientific observations, hardly obvious, but can only be discovered through the coincidental observation of a certain perceiving subject. In the present comparison, transmigration is suggestive of an operation described in a footnote in Stifter's first published novella, *Der Condor* (1840), a work Sebald knew well and quoted often in his essays: "Durchscheinende Körper werfen einen Theil Licht zurück, lassen den anderen durch" (Transparent bodies reflect a portion of light, and allow another portion of light to pass through them).[40] Read with this scientific apercu, transmigration could be configured as a means to describe both how Sebald reproduces Stifter's writing in his prose fiction and how he as a reader identifies with Stifter's biography.

There is some evidence to support the impression that Sebald borrowed from Stifter in both senses. As Mark McCulloh discovered, Stifter's *Der Condor* serves as a "literary model" for Sebald's own exercises in levitation in *Die Ringe des Saturn*.[41] Appropriately enough for this case of textual lifting, *Der Condor* is itself modeled on the work of another, namely Jean Paul's fictional journal, *Des Luftschiffers Giannozzos Seebuch*, so that the intertextual labyrinth grows even more complex.[42] Stifter's diegetic narrator adds to the confusion in *Der Condor* by noting that the material inside the frame narrative comes from the diary of a young, budding artist (Gustav), "ein angehender Künstler" whose fetching looks seem to interest him even more than the levitation that begins a harrowing balloon ride (13). In *Die Ringe des Saturn* we trip over Stifter's story in the passage that is woven into the excursion into reading Sir Thomas Browne's "Höhenflüge," his flights of fancy. Hospitalized after a collapse that follows an attempt to escape ("entkommen") a looming emptiness that is described as an "in mir sich ausbreitenden Leere" (emptiness that takes hold of me; *RS*, 11/3), Sebald's medicated narrator depicts a hallucinatory balloon ride that seems to be taken from Stifter's *Der Condor*.[43] Because of the skill with which Sebald weaves Stifter's wording into his own prose, I will quote the passage at length:

> Unter dem *wundervollen* Einfluß der Schmerzmittel, die in mir kreisten, fühlte ich mich in meinem eisernen Gitterbett wie ein *Ballonreisender*, der schwerelos dahingleitet durch das rings um ihn her sich auftürmende Wolkengebirge. Bisweilen teilten sich die *wallenden Tücher*, und ich sah hinaus in die *indigofarbenen Weiten und hinab auf den Grund*, wo ich unentwirrbar und schwarz, die Erde erahnte. Droben aber *am Himmelsgewölbe waren die Sterne, winzige Goldpunkte, in die Öde gestreut.* An mein Ohr drangen durch die dröhnende Leere die Stimmen der beiden Schwestern, die mir den Puls maßen und ab und zu *die Lippen netzten* mit einem kleinen, rosaroten, an einem Stäbchen befestigten Schwamm, der mich an die würfelförmigen Lutscher aus türkischem Honig erinnerte, die man vormals auf dem Jahrmarkt kaufen konnte.

[Under the wonderful influence of the painkillers coursing through me, I felt, in my iron-framed bed, like a balloonist floating weightless amidst the mountainous clouds towering on every side. At times the billowing masses would part and I gazed out at the indigo vastness and down into the depths where I supposed the earth to be, a black and impenetrable maze. But in the firmament above were the stars, tiny points of gold speckling the barren wastes. Through the resounding emptiness my ears caught the voices of the two nurses who took my pulse and from time to time moistened my lips with a small, pink sponge attached to a stick, which reminded me of the Turkish Delight lollipops we used to buy at the fair. (*RS*, 28, my emphases/17–18)]

This remarkable play of *Innenwelt* and *Außenwelt* in the recollection of a hallucination brought on by narcotics — an interplay prominent also in Stifter's "Mein Leben" — transfigures the narrator's body into a cosmos in which the drugs penetrate the body and circulate within it while the narrator, too, circulates, flying around the earth in his iron hospital bed while experiencing the trip within him.[44] Did Sebald, here in the guise of a narrator no longer subject to the laws of gravity, learn to describe a balloon trip by reading Stifter?[45]

Two pertinent passages from Stifter's balloon trip in *Der Condor* suggest as much, however different their valence and tone. Here is Stifter's first description of the balloon rising into the air:

Dann sacht steigend zog er das Schiffchen los vom *mütterlichen Grund der Erde*, und mit jedem Athemzug an Schnelle gewinnend, schoß er endlich pfeilschnell senkrecht in den Morgenstrom des Lichtes empor — und im Momente flogen auch auf seine Wölbung und in das Tauwerk die Flammen der Morgensonne, daß Cornelia erschrak und meinte, der ganze Ballon brenne, denn *wie glühende Stäbe schnitten sich die Linien der Schnüre aus dem indigoblauen Himmel, und seine Rundung flammte wie eine riesenhafte Sonne. Die zurücktretende Erde war noch ganz schwarz und unsichtbar — in Finsterniß verrinnend.* (15, my emphases; Stifter's orthography retained)

[And then gently rising, it pulled the little airship loose from the motherly ground of the earth and, gaining in speed with each breath of air, it shot upward like an arrow into the stream of morning light — and in that moment the flames of the morning sun flew onto the vault of the balloon and into its riggings so that Cornelia became horrified, for she thought it was as though the entire balloon were burning, since the lines of the ropes were cut out of the indigo-blue sky like glowing rods, and the curvature of the balloon had become enflamed like a gigantic sun. The retreating earth was still utterly black and invisible, trickling away in the darkness.]

In the passage from *Die Ringe des Saturn* cited above, the genders are switched and the effect of the scenes is reversed: Katy and Lizzie, the female nurses who attend to Sebald's hallucinating narrator, replace Cornelia's two male traveling companions, seemingly inhuman figures who, like the nurses, busy themselves with scientific measurements and experiments (the purpose of the balloon excursion) and break the silence only "durch monotone Laute" (17; with monotone noises). While the ecstatic, drug-induced visions of Sebald's flying narrator begin with illness and breakdown and move in a *schwereloses Dahingleiten* provided by the "wonderful" influence of the painkillers toward a recuperation, Stifter closes Cornelia's trip upward to the heavens with terror and physical collapse, all brought on by the abrupt transformation of an experience of beauty into something altogether abysmal and demonic:

> Erschrocken wandte die Jungfrau ihr Auge zurück, als hätte sie ein Ungeheuer erblickt, — aber siehe, auch um das Schiff *walleten* weiter weiße, dünne, sich *dehnende und regende Leichentücher* — von der Erde gesehen Silberschäfchen des Himmels; — zu diesem Himmel nun floh der Blick — aber das Himmelsgewölbe, die schöne blaue Glocke unserer Erde, war ein ganz schwarzer Abgrund geworden, ohne Maß und Grenze in die Tiefe gehend — das Labsal, das wir so gedankenlos genießen, war hier oben ganz verschwunden, die Fülle und Flut des Lichtes auf der schönen Erde. Wie zum Hohne wurden alle Sterne sichtbar — *winzige, ohnmächtige Goldpuncte, verloren durch die Öde gestreut* — und endlich die Sonne, ein drohendes Gestirn, ohne Wärme, ohne Strahlen, eine scharf geschnittene Scheibe, aus *wallendem* blähenden, weißgeschmolzenen Metalle glotzte sie mit vernichtendem Glanze aus dem Schlunde — und doch nicht einen Hauch des Lichtes festhaltend in diesen wesenslosen Räumen; nur auf dem Ballon und Schiffe starrte ein gelbes Licht, das sich gespenstig von der umgebenden Nacht abhob, und die Gesichter scharf zeichnete wie *in einer laterna magica.* Und dennoch (die Phantasie begriff es kaum) war es noch unsere zarte liebe Luft, in der sie schifften, dieselbe Luft, die morgen die Wangen *eines Säuglings* fächelt. (18–19; my emphases; Stifter's orthography retained)

> [Horrified, the girl turned her eyes away, as if she had seen a monster — but look, even around the gondola the white, thin, expanding and undulating shrouds continued to undulate — seen from the earth they were like the heavens' silvery feathers, — her glance fled now up toward this sky — but the vault of the heavens, the beautiful blue dome of our earth, had become a completely black abyss, without dimensions and limits and slipping back into the chasm — the succor that we so thoughtlessly enjoy had completely disappeared up here, the fullness and flood of light on our beautiful earth. As if mocking us, all the stars became visible — tiny, barren gold dots, strewn into the wasteland and lost — and finally the sun, a threatening star, without warmth, devoid of rays, a sharply cut disc that glowed from its maw with an annihilating effulgence of distended, white-hot metal

— yet it held not the slightest trace of light in its unsubstantial spaces; only onto the balloon and the gondola did a yellowish light cast its glare, which differentiated itself in a ghostly manner from the surrounding night and sharply circumscribed their faces as in a *laterna magica*. And still (the imagination could hardly grasp it) this was still our tender, beloved air in which they navigated, the same air that tomorrow will fan the cheeks of an infant.]

While McCulloh's claim that Stifter's story is "quoted verbatim" in Sebald's "fiction" is a bit overstated, the similarities in the word choice and, probably more importantly, in the prosody of these passages is striking.[46] The transformation of the earth from material to metaphor and its topsy-turvy conversion into an "Abgrund" in the last passage also suggests a metaphor of separation between infant and mother that returns as a central theme in Stifter's "Mein Leben," where the three eidetic memories merge for the reminiscing author in a "Schleiermeer der Vergangenheit, wie Urerinnerungen eines Volkes (*NB,* 584; a veiled sea of the past, like the *Ur*-memories of a people). This epic return to a pre-individuated state (the self dissolves into an organic *Volk* that now shares the memory that is essentially collectivized, universalized) is described by Stifter as almost *in utero*. It is also accompanied by senses that are beyond the grasp of reason. In the first memory Stifter recalls, "Es war Glanz, es war Gewühl, es war unten" (There was a shimmering light, there was turmoil, it was below). The characteristic of the second memory is aural, "Es waren Klänge" (there were sounds). Finally, movement leads to a "nichts mehr," a nothingness, a nothing more: "Dann schwamm ich in etwas Fächelndem, ich schwamm hin und wieder, es wurde immer weicher und weicher in mir, dann wurde ich wie trunken, dann war nichts mehr" (584; Then I swam in something fan-like, I swam back and forth, it felt softer and softer inside me, and then it was as if I were intoxicated [drowned], and then there was nothing).

Similarly, Stifter's balloon ride in *Der Condor* leads to the scientific observation of natural "Wunder" that is by no means "wundervoll." It leads metonymically only to a kind of terrible ("unnatural") wresting of the human from the mother earth, a process that becomes unimaginable ("die Phantasie begriff es kaum") and thus demonic. In *Der Condor* the memory of the earth's motherly *Grund* is bound to an experience of danger and destruction (*Abgrund*), one in which even the sun becomes a surgical instrument, "eine scharf geschnittene Scheibe." Nature, so often veiled by those Stifterian poetics described in the *sanftes Gesetz*, is present here only in repeated undulations ("wallen") of shrouds behind which lurks a menacing reality, the "wirkliche Wirklichkeit" that Stifter, in a letter to his publisher Gustav Heckenast, maintained would make art "ungenießbar," unpalatable and indigestible, just like "unsere zarte liebe Luft," which is rendered unsuitable for the fanning of an infant, or even for taking a breath.[47] Cornelia's daring balloon ride becomes not only "unenjoyable"; it becomes — if we interpret the scene through its transmigrated form in "Mein Leben" — "inedible," unsuitable for human (and for the reader's) consumption. Only the two footnotes Stifter provides, with their reassuring references to scientific information on the function of light, seem to atone for the thick terror of the passage on the center of the page.[48]

While Stifter's balloonists witness a scene of transformation in which the earth becomes a "Finsternis" beneath their feet, the hallucinatory trip of Sebald's narrator in *Die Ringe des Saturn* ironically catalyzes a return to childhood (and even infancy) and to the care of two doting women. Of this state of incapacitation the narrator remembers, "daß ich nur selten so glücklich gewesen bin wie unter ihrer [the nurses, Katy and Lizzie] Obhut in dieser Nacht (and I think I have rarely been as elated as I was in their care that night; *RS*, 28/18). As if to indicate that the hallucination contains some condensed truth,[49] Sebald's narrator awakens from the stupor of the anesthesia to the sight of an airplane's vapor trail ("Kondensstreifen") in the sky. Read at first as a sign of luck, the omen later comes to symbolize "der Anfang eines Risses, der seither durch mein Leben geht" (the beginning of a fissure that has since riven my life; *RS*, 29/18), a chasm of the type conjured elsewhere in Sebald's writing, where it is often associated with his German childhood and the disturbing manner in which the past returns to the present. What is at first an augury described as "wundervoll" leads to the tearing-apart of a psyche through the recollection of a memory so deep and impenetrable that it offers only a faint sense — as in Kafka's work — that at some time in the past something went horribly awry, something, however, that will remain beyond recall. That error can never be fully reconstructed and cannot be understood in the present, just as the "Finsterniß" experienced by the human desire for knowledge in Stifter's tale — the balloon ride is an occasion for scientific experiments — becomes a reminder of the "invisibility and incomprehensibility of that which moves us," to return to Browne, of those experiences from childhood that have since been effaced.

In Stifter's story the transmigration of the image of light and air into something terrifying — Cornelia faints from altitude sickness later in the passage, a symbolic drop of blood forming on her lips — suggests that the birth (levitation) of the balloon from the "maternal earth" also portends death, symbolized by the ascent into heaven and the harrowing nature of the description of the sky itself, the air of which no longer provides "Labsal" (succor, refreshment) but rather becomes quite literally unbreathable. This depiction of an "indifferente zerstörerische Gewalt" (an indifferent, destructive force in nature in which birth and death are the same), as Sebald notes in his remarks on *Der Condor* in "Bis an den Rand der Natur," occurs here not as an exception but as a rule,: as the critic puts it, part of Stifter's "kaum noch tragfähigen positiven Konvention" (positive convention that is itself hardly sustainable any longer) in which "ein geradezu antinomisches Weltbild geliefert wird" (*VS,* 24; a downright contradictory image of the world is offered up). Through the representation of this contradictory image of a world in which logic, like the physical, human body at high altitudes, no longer functions, Stifter has brought us quite literally — and Sebald comes along on the ride, too, — "bis an den Rand der Natur," to the limits, to the end, of nature.

Patterns (from Childhood)

Sebald seems to have acquired his own ability to bring readers to the edge, at least if we consider the representation of such *Weltbilder* across his oeuvre, in part from reading Stifter's "high intensity" prose. Indeed, beyond merely lifting a passage from Stifter's work, Sebald rides *Der Condor* all the way back into childhood (his *and* Stifter's), where he discovers "Mein Leben," that story left in our inheritance ("Nachgelassenes Blatt"). As the references above imply, this constructed convergence is another site at which we witness the transmigration of words and images between Sebald's prose fiction and Stifter's "schwierige Schönheit," which, the critic insists, is also the product of memories from childhood that went largely unprocessed, that remained *unsichtbar* and *unfassbar* in Stifter's lifetime. These elements are now mobilized in the essays as support mechanisms for Sebald's sometimes questionable speculation about the connections between Stifter's life and work. More importantly, these traces are adapted to represent Sebald's own childhood memories, which return in his prose fiction, where the presentation of evidence gives way to the telling of stories from an imagination that refuses to conform to the demands of scholarly objectivity. Something similar occurs in Stifter's "Mein Leben," for that text suggests a moment at which the facade of "Stifter" cracks, allowing for a registration of a psychology and a depth that are absent in his characteristically strict representational program, which one reader describes as his "naturgesetzliches Erzählen," a narrative strategy determined by the empirical registration of details and events that mimic an imagined natural law.[50]

In his memory fragment Stifter recollects via the senses and not via observation and thus deviates from the "intentional order" of his adult writing in order to describe a body overwhelmed by the sensory (*VS,* 17): "Weit zurück in dem leeren Nichts," he recalls, "ist etwas wie Wonne und Entzücken, das gewaltig fassend, fast vernichtend in mein Wesen drang und dem nichts mehr in meinem künftigen Leben glich" (*NB,* 584; Far back in that empty void is something that approaches bliss and delight, which, grasping powerfully, penetrated into my being in an almost

eviscerating, annihilating manner, something that remained unlike anything else in my future life). Just as *unerhört* as this bizarre penetration of
Stifter's essence and the statement that its intensity remained unparalleled
in his entire life, is the "Begebenheit," the event that will suggest that the
images and memories of childhood in Stifter's text also transmigrated into
Sebald's memory and into his writing (*NB*, 585). Stifter recalls in "Mein
Leben" that he finds himself once again in the realm of horror and
destruction: "Dann war Klingen, Verwirrung, Schmerz in meinen Händen
und Blut daran, die Mutter verband mich" (*NB*, 585; Then came a ring-
ing, confusion, pain in my hands, blood on them, mother bandaged me).
Here it is striking that as narrator Stifter pays no attention to cause and
effect, and only later in the text do we learn the actual nature of the
recalled event, mediated through Stifter's grandmother, whom the writing
adult now cites from memory: "Mit einem Knaben, der die Fenster
zerschlagen hat, redet man nicht" (*NB*, 585; One does not speak with a
boy who breaks windows). What follows confirms the performative aspect
of the words, for Stifter remembers that his mother spoke not a word to
him: "Mutter sprach wirklich kein Wort" (*NB*, 585; And indeed, mother
in fact spoke not a word to me).

From this primal scene of trauma in which Stifter is first pulled from
the demonic state only to be punished — exiled "vom Mütterlichen Grund
der Erde" (from the motherly ground of the earth), as it were — Stifter
lifts off, remembering the uncanny sense that this memory of a motherly
silence left behind: "und ich erinnere mich, daß ein Ungeheures in meiner
Seele lag, das mag der Grund sein, daß jener Vorgang jetzt in meinem
Innern lebt" (*NB*, 585–86; and I remember that something monstrous lay
in my soul; that must be the reason that this episode lives on in me). From
this singular event Stifter recognizes an inner self inextricably bound to
something *ungeheuerlich* that he no longer can recall but that occupies his
interior, his inner life, nonetheless: "Nach dieser Begebenheit ist abermals
Dunkel" (*NB*, 586; After this event there is once again darkness). From
that darkness emerges a descriptive passage far more typical of Stifter's
mature prose. The childhood *Stube* and the family table are rendered in
exacting detail in a passage that takes up a good quarter of the entire text,
one that leads us to the "Fensterbrett" where the child Stifter first begins
to read.

This domestic scene returns in another form in Sebald's prose poem
Nach der Natur: Ein Elementargedicht, his first non-fiction publication
and the beginning of his career as a prose writer. *Nach der Natur* appeared
in 1988, some four years after the essays on Stifter were published. A comparison between that work and Stifter's childhood memories is instructive
in illuminating a final example of the transmigration of the Stifterian text
into Sebald's corpus. In "Mein Leben" Stifter describes the liminal site at
the window, at the interstices of *Innenwelt* and *Außenwelt*:

Die Fenster der Stube hatten sehr breite Fensterbretter und auf dem
Brette dieses Fensters saß ich sehr oft und fühlte den Sonnenschein
und daher mag das Leuchtende der Erinnerung rühren. Auf diesem
Fensterbrette war es auch allein, wenn ich zu lesen anhob. Ich nahm
ein Buch, machte es auf, hielt es vor mir und las: "Burgen, Nagelein,
böhmisch Haidel." Diese Worte las ich jedes Mal, ich weiß es; ob
zuweilen noch andere dabei waren, dessen erinnere ich mich nicht
mehr. Auf diesem Fensterbrette sah ich auch, was draußen vorging,
und ich sagte sehr oft: "Da geht ein Mann nach Schwarzbach, da
fährt ein Mann nach Schwarzbach, da geht ein Weib nach Schwarzbach,
da geht ein Hund nach Schwarzbach, da geht eine Gans nach
Schwarzbach." (*NB*, 586–87)

[The windows of the room had very deep windowsills and on these I
often sat and felt the sunshine and that may be the source of the radi-
ance of this memory. It was also on this windowsill alone that I began
reading. I took a book, opened it and held it up before me and read:
"Castles, nails, Bohemian fields." I know I read these words every
time; whether I read others from time to time, I can no longer recall.
On the sill I also saw what went on outside and I said very often:
"There a man is walking to Schwarzbach, a man is driving to
Schwarzbach, there a woman is walking to Schwarzbach, a dog is
going to Schwarzbach, a goose is going to Schwarzbach."]

In this lucent recollection of a scene of seeing and reading, Stifter seems
to make no connection between his position as a reader, the "illuminations" of memory and the recurrence of "was draußen vorging," what
happened in the world outside the domestic sphere at whose edge he sat
in the windowsill. In the monotonous repetition of memory Stifter confirms the reality beyond the window only to seize it for his own creative
purposes, lining up pieces of kindling in patterns on the sill and concluding
(and here Stifter splits himself, quoting himself as the imagined child
"Stifter"), "Ich mache Schwarzbach" (*NB*, 556; I make Schwarzbach).
Stifter, having recollected this ordering of wooden pieces, leaves the reader
of this intimate vignette to comprehend what *Schwarzbach machen* might,
in fact, instantiate and how it might be connected to what the child's eyes
actually saw while recording that Schwarzbach-bound traffic.

One of those readers, of course, was W. G. Sebald. He cites the passage above at length in an essay on the eschatological in Stifter and
Handke, "Helle Bilder und dunkle." Sebald, too, seems to have found that
the scene's impenetrability made it useful in the context of a scholarly
argument only as a convenient transition to the next part of his trajectory
on the *Unglück* of Austrian writers, here to that of Peter Handke, whose
eschatological *Züge* and rural origins recall those of Stifter. In a more
speculative move, however, Sebald mobilizes the "beschwörende verbale
Geste" (the evocative verbal gesture) of this "Chiffre Schwarzbach" (the

cipher "Schwarzbach") in Stifter's recollection of early childhood as evidence that very early in his life Stifter set about eliminating the unsaid and unwanted through writing, "schreibend." This mode of writing, however dissimilar to Sebald's project later in life, is of course also an option. Thus, while writing would enable the artist's physical and social escape from a meager existence in the hinterlands of Bohemia and make possible his legitimate entry into the realm of bourgeois society, "die ideale Welt der bürgerlichen Zivilisation" (*HB*, 167; the ideal world of bourgeois civilization), its mastery also allowed for the elimination of unwanted memories, for the securing of a persona for the future. In one of those questionable leaps that leave some readers of Sebald's literary essays nonplussed, Sebald concludes that the closing scenes of "Mein Leben" mark the beginning of the evolution of Stifter's desire — which now proves reminiscent of Handke's climb out of his own childhood abyss — to craft a way out of "dem unterpriviligierten Dasein in einer hinteren Provinz" (an underprivileged existence in the backwoods provinces) and therewith to achieve through writing — and only through writing — the possibility of a "Transzendierung eines von unguter Erinnerung beschwerten Lebens" (*HB*, 167–68; to transcend a life burdened by bad memories). Through writing, then, Stifter sought to return to a life unburdened by unpleasant memories, to rediscover the "Labsal" lost by both his own pathological tendencies and by an unwelcome Modernity that encroached on his desired image of an ordered, ideal world of which he had already been robbed in childhood. Whereas Stifter sought to "restore" a world that never was, Sebald's prose fiction attempts to describe that which has been lost or effaced, to describe the losses of historical catastrophe and therewith, in an act of mnemonic restitution, to commemorate the victims of history.

Sebald, however, omits from his reasoning the crucial capstone to Stifter's memory text, which might have contradicted the critic's insistence on Stifter's repressed *Unglück*. Having reconstructed the reader-child "Stifter" at the window, the one who seizes "Schwarzbach" for his own purposes, Stifter concludes the bizarre narrative of "Mein Leben" with a surprisingly reassuring conclusion: "In meiner Erinnerung ist lauter Sommer, den ich durch das Fenster sah, von einem Winter ist von damals gar nichts in meiner Einbildungskraft" (*NB*, 587; In my memory I saw through that window nothing but summers; there is nothing at all of winters from back then left in the power of my imagination). The autobiographer has now led us to the edge, to the abyss that follows the final word of the text, "Einbildungskraft," a point at which we do not know whether he seeks to reassure the reader or himself. The void where the winters might have been echoes back to the chasm Sebald saw in the "Stich" he described at the outset of the essay, the ekphrastic passage that began my own investigations. To be sure, the memory of a life with no "winters" is itself an indication of the elisions and repressions that inform the "truth" about a writing subject whose powers of imagination ("Die Phantasie begriff es kaum," Stifter wrote of the uncanny experience of levitation and alienation from the mother earth in *Der Condor*) fail in the face of any sort of inclement weather. Purged of colder temperatures that might have maintained it, Stifter's memory in this exceptional text did not keep well. The text thus closes by confirming the rule of the writer's approach to description and self-representation, that "absent characteristic" through which Stifter's poetics refuse all psychological depth (*VS*, 17; *HB*, 169). Thus even Stifter's exceptions cannot elude the rules and regulations of his larger poetic program and its chilling attention to excessive objective description as a means to eliminate the unwanted and the inassimilable from his highly crafted narratives.

In reading these absences and repressions, Sebald's essays on Stifter map the possible locations of chasms and abysses as points at which Stifter is on the verge of something, perhaps of submitting to the objects he worked so diligently to seize, approaching the "winters" that he absented from his memory.[51] That is so because the ironic map of what is not there is simultaneously a topography of the lacks and deficiencies to which Sebald attends in both his prose fiction and his literary criticism. There, seeing becomes the transmigration of objects into the writing subject, one who is changed by those objects in profound ways. In a Benjaminian turn to be sure, Sebald wrote in an essay on Gerhard Roth's novel *Landläufiger Tod*, "Im Schauen spüren wir, wie die Dinge uns ansehen, verstehen, daß wir nicht da sind, um das Universum zu durchdringen, sondern um von ihm durchdrungen zu sein" (In looking we sense how things look at us, we understand that we are not here in order to pervade the universe, but rather to be pervaded by it; *UH*, 158/37; trans. modified).[52] Unlike the penetration of Stifter's body by a bliss and delight that are now beyond recall, this penetration of the gazing subject by the object suggests again the vertiginous spiraling evident in Sebald's prose fiction. It enacts not a blind spot at which memory proves inaccessible, but rather what James Martin has described as an "affective phenomenology" in Sebald's writing that "emphasizes the power of poetic images to unleash a potentially limitless process of reflection in the reader through scrupulous perception of details that expose a surreal seam, the presence of fantastic elements normally unobserved in reality."[53]

For Stifter such limitlessness seems to have been so terrifying as to require as a defensive, compensatory mechanism an endless kind of monotonous description that would secure the world as object. For Sebald, though, this disorienting phenomenon, however disturbing, is itself constituent of writing, because it makes experience possible in the first place.[54] Where Stifter would refuse such a project, Sebald embraces it, adjusting and correcting his object's childhood memories as they transmigrate into other contexts. If we read with Sebald, then we must also trip over Stifter, as in *Nach der Natur*, where Sebald recalls himself as a child who

> [. . . bin ich]
> aufgewachsen ohne einen Begriff der Zerstörung.
> Aber daß ich vielfach auf der Straße gestürzt
> und mit einbandagierten Händen oft im Fenster
> bei den Fuchsienstauden gesessen bin,
> auf das Nachlassen der Schmerzen gewartet
> und stundenlang nichts als hinausgeschaut habe,
> brachte mich früh auf die Vorstellung
> von einer lautlosen Katastrophe, die sich
> ohne ein Aufhebens vor dem Betrachter vollzieht.

> [grew up . . . without any
> idea of destruction. But the habit
> of often falling down in the street and
> often sitting with bandaged hands
> by the open window between the potted
> fuchsias, waiting for the
> pain to subside and for hours
> doing nothing but looking out,
> early on induced me to imagine
> a silent catastrophe that occurs
> almost unperceived. (*NN*, 76–77/*AN*, 89)]

The "Stich" provided by the "almost" of Michael Hamburger's English translation inserts into the memory a troubling uncertainty factor that was banished from Stifter's "Mein Leben." Stifter's description of his own "accident" and a similar setting at the window fails to recall or imagine what he *actually* saw through that window in Oberplan. Instead, we are offered the monotone patterns of repetition that represent nothing more than the rhythm of their own utterance as it becomes increasingly meaningless for the recollecting adult and his reader. Stifter's *lautlose Katastrophe*, at least in Sebald's idiosyncratic readings and borrowings, lies somewhere in what he refused to say and to write, and more importantly in the failure of his "Einbildungskraft," the power of his imagination, to allow the experience of what he saw to transmigrate into the imagination of his readers. And while this silence might thwart Sebald's diagnostic program in his scholarly essays, it seems to have generated an empathetic relation in which the writer sensed that something of Stifter had survived in the chasms and abysses of his literary images and in the voids that remain in the story of his life.

In the process, the relation between Sebald and Stifter becomes a liminal, imaginative space with no concrete referent. It is marked most prominently not by those explicit borrowings from Stifter that we can track down in Sebald's prose but rather by the suggestion that the border region between reading and writing is itself a kind of sensory "Schleiermeer." From this unstable ground Sebald's excursions take flight, and in so doing they suggest that Sebald understood what it means to read in the way Georg Brandes, the once renowned literary historian (author of the six-volume *Hovedstrømninger i det nittende Aarhundredes Litteratur, Main Currents in Nineteenth Century Literature*), whose reputation is now far more obscure than even that of Stifter, maintained was to "forøge vor Indsigt, aflægge vore Fordomme og blive I stedse højere Grad Personligheder" (increase our insight, shed our prejudices and become, to an ever greater extent, *personalities*).[55] In a later essay on Gottfried Keller published in *Logis in einem Landhaus* Sebald reverses the equation, writing: "Die Kunst des Schreibens ist der Versuch, das schwarze Gewusel, das überhand zu nehmen droht, zu bannen im Interesse der Erhaltung einer halbwegs praktikablen Persönlichkeit" (*LG,* 125–26; The art of writing is the attempt, in the interest of maintaining a halfway practicable personality, to hold at bay the black seething mass that threatens to get out of hand).[56] In twisting and bending the "Gewusel" of Stifter's corpus into a figure, a "practicable personality" for literary criticism, Sebald retained that dizzying, unwieldy "half" that refused that project, saving it for his prose fiction, where readers still stumble upon those trips that "Stifter" continues to make.

Notes

Sources for the introductory quotations are as follows: Nuala O'Faolain, *Are You Somebody? The Accidental Memoir of a Dublin Woman* (New York: Henry Holt, 1996), 27; Adalbert Stifter, *Der Nachsommer* (Munich: Winkler, 1966), 113 (From time to time one must indeed look into oneself, though one should not always remain alone, not even in the most beautiful of landscapes. At times one must indeed return to the company of others, if only to refresh oneself with one of those splendid ruins of a human being that has remained from our youth or to look upward upon one of those solid towers of a person who has rescued himself). All translations are my own unless stated otherwise. See also the published translation of this massive work, Adalbert Stifter, *Indian Summer,* trans. Wendell Frye (New York: Peter Lang, 1985); W. G. Sebald, *LG,* 40–41 (The view from the Milky Way down onto the barren and black, burned-out ruin of the earth revolving in the galaxy could not be more strange, but nonetheless the childhood that we spent on it, and which resounds from the words of the gallant, is hardly farther away than yesterday). The fourth epigraph is from *NN,* 8/*AN,* 6 (Indeed it seemed as though in such works of art / men had revered each other like brothers, and / often made monuments in each other's / image where their paths had crossed).

¹ W. G. Sebald, "Helle Bilder und dunkle: Zur Dialektik der Eschatologie bei Stifter und Handke," in *BU,* 165–86, and "Bis an den Rand der Natur: Versuch über Stifter," in *BU,* 15–37. Further references to these works are given in the text using the abbreviations *HB* and *VS.* The first essay was published in *manuskripte* in 1984 under a slightly different title, "Helle Bilder und dunkle — Eschatologie und Natur bei Stifter und Handke." The second, "Bis an den Rand der Natur — Versuch über Stifter," appeared first in *Österreichische Porträts: Leben und Werk bedeutender Persönlichkeiten — von Maria Theresia bis Ingeborg Bachmann.* For more on Sebald and Austrian literature see the special issue of *Modern Austrian Literature* 40.4. (Dec. 2007) devoted to W. G. Sebald, edited by Markus Zisselsberger. See also Uwe Schütte's "Der Hüter der Metaphysik — W. G. Sebalds Essays über die österreichische Literatur," *manuskripte* 155 (Mar. 2002): 124–28, and "'In einer wildfremden Gegend' — W. G. Sebalds Essays über die österreichische Literatur," in *The Anatomist of Melancholy: Essays in Memory of W. G. Sebald,* ed. Rüdiger Görner (Munich: iudicium, 2003), 63–74.

² For more on Stifter as a visual artist see Fritz Novotny, *Adalbert Stifter als Maler,* 4th ed. (Vienna: Anton Schroll, 1979), originally published in 1940. Taking up the painterly in Stifter's prose, Hannah Arendt wrote in an unpublished review of the 1945 translation of Stifter's *Bergkristall* that he was "the greatest landscape-painter in literature," and claims that he had an "altogether happy relationship with reality." Hannah Arendt, "Great Friend of Reality: Adalbert Stifter," in *Reflections on Literature and Culture,* ed. Susannah Young-Ah Gottlieb (Stanford, CA: Stanford UP, 2007), 110–11; here 111.

³ There is something of a pattern to what Sebald "sees" in visual images and in his readings of ekphrasis in the writings of others. Sebald's narrators often home in on chasms and abysses in the perspectives of paintings. The depiction of Grünewald's Basel Crucifixion in *Nach der Natur* is just one example: "Auf dem um 1505 entstandenen Basler Kreuzigungsbild / erstreckt sich hinter der Gruppe der Klagenden / eine so weit in die Tiefe hineingehende Landschaft, / daß unser Auge nicht ausreicht, sie zu ergründen" (On the Basel Crucifixion of 1505 / behind the group of mourners / a landscape reaches so far into the depth / that our eyes cannot see its limits; *NN,* 26/*AN,* 29). Sebald and his narrators seem to look continually into the depths to that which lies beyond the image itself.

⁴ See Jean-Luc Nancy, "Uncanny Landscape," in *The Ground of the Image,* trans. Jeff Fort (New York: Fordham UP, 2005), 51–62; here 58–59. Nancy underscores the abyssal nature of the landscape genre generally: "The landscape opens onto the unknown. It is, properly speaking, place as the opening onto a taking place of the unknown. It is not so much the imitative representation of a given location as the presentation of a given absence of presence. If I may force the point a bit, I would say that, instead of depicting a 'land' as a 'location' [*endroit*], it depicts it as a 'dislocation' [*envers*]" (59). The concern of the landscape painting, then, is not the accurate depiction of a "real" place but rather the discourse in which that place is discovered elsewhere. Sebald also suggests the difficulty of accepting the invitation to "enter" a landscape: "Im Landschaftsbild, das zum Betreten einlädt, verschwim-

men die Grenzen zwischen objektiver Wirklichkeit und subjektiver Phantasie, ist Natur nicht mehr nur das, was wildfremd um uns herumsteht, sondern ein größeres Leben, unserem eigenen analog" (*VS*, 24; In the landscape, which invites us to enter it, the boundaries between objective reality and subjective fantasy blur. Nature is no longer that which surrounds us as something wild and strange, but rather is a larger life form that is analogous to our own).

[5] For more on this perspective effect and its functions, see Erwin Panofsky, "Die Perspektive als 'symbolische Form,'" in *Deutschsprachige Aufsätze* II, ed. Karen Michels and Martin Warnke (Berlin: Akademie Verlag, 1998), 664–756.

[6] Adalbert Stifter, "Nachgelassenes Blatt," in *Gesammelte Werke in sechs Bänden*, vol. 6 (Gütersloh: C. Bertelsmann, 1957), 583–84. Further references to this work are given in the text using the abbreviation *NB* followed by the page number. The early Stifter biographer Alois Raimund Hein reproduced the fragment in the first volume of his *Adalbert Stifter: Sein Leben und seine Werke*, 2 vols (Vienna: Walter Krieg, 1952), which was originally published in 1904. Hein claims to have found the handwritten manuscript of this "Nachgelassenes Blatt," which he maintains was the beginning of a planned autobiography, among Stifter's papers at the family home in Oberplan. In both of the essays on Stifter, Sebald refers to the text as "Mein Leben" and quotes from the version published in *Die fürchterliche Wendung der Dinge: Erzählungen,* ed. Hans Joachim Piechotta (Darmstadt: Luchterhand, 1981). Sebald's copy of this edited collection of Stifter's stories (the first two chapters of this edition are "Mein Leben" and the novella "Der Condor") is part of the collection of Sebald's books that has been deposited at the Deutsches Literaturarchiv in Marbach. Sebald's underlinings in this work correspond more or less to the passages he emphasizes in the essays on Stifter. In the margin of page 10 of the version of "Mein Leben" in the anthology, Sebald has written "KASPAR," presumably a reference to Handke's play and the subject of another essay by Sebald that suggests further linkages between the essays and Sebald's prose fiction, connections that cannot be explored adequately here. I would like to thank Markus Zisselsberger for this helpful legwork.

[7] The details of Stifter's death in 1868 were a well-kept secret in the decades that followed and became something of a legend among biographers and scholars alike. Hein provides a dramatic description: Stifter, apparently in agonizing pain from liver cancer and other various ailments, slit his own throat with a razor and then lay unconscious for two days before dying of, as the official death certificate stated, "Zehrfieber infolge chronischer Atrophie," an emaciating fever resulting from chronic atrophy. The attending doctor macabrely remarked on the ailing Stifter's "impatience," the "Ungeduld von seiten des Kranken" (Hein, *Adalbert Stifter,* 789). See also Urban Roedl, *Adalbert Stifter in Selbstzeugnissen und Bilddokumenten* (Reinbek bei Hamburg: Rowohlt, 1965), 146–47.

[8] Stifter's first sensory memory is, tellingly, of an abyss, "ein Unten": "Merkwürdig ist es, daß in der allerersten Empfindung meines Lebens etwas Äußerliches war, und zwar etwas, das meist schwierig und sehr spät in das Vorstellungsvermögen gelangt, etwas Räumliches, ein Unten" (*NB*, 585; It is odd that the very first sensation in

my life was of something external, something that usually reaches our imagination only with difficulty and very late in life, something spatial, a below). Stifter's recollection of this self-described sensory precociousness indicates what Walter Benjamin called his demonic "Doppelnatur," his "two faces, dual nature." Benjamin, "Stifter," in *Gesammelte Schriften* 2.2, ed. Rolf Tiedemann and Hermann Schweppenhäuser (Frankfurt am Main: Suhrkamp, 1989), 610; in English, "Stifter," in *Selected Writings, Volume 1: 1913–1926*, ed. Marcus Bullock, trans. Michael William Jennings (Cambridge, MA: Belknap, 1996), 111–12; here 112, trans. modified.

[9] Sven Meyer, "Fragmente zu Mementos: Imaginierte Konjekturen bei W. G. Sebald," *Text+Kritik* 158.4 (2003): 75.

[10] Christian Begemann, "'Realismus' oder 'Idealismus'? Über einige Schwierigkeiten bei der Rekonstruktion von Stifters Kunstbegriff," in *Adalbert Stifter: Dichter und Maler, Denkmalpfleger und Schulmann; Neue Zugänge zu seinem Werk*, ed. Hartmut Laufhütte and Karl Möseneder (Tübingen: Max Niemeyer, 1996), 5. Emphases mine. Similarly, Eva Geulen notes that "Die Bedingung von Autorenschaft ist der Verlust des Selbst, . . . Die Autoren schreiben sich in Traditionszusammenhänge ein, um dann anderen Autoren kommender Geschlechter als Vorlage bzw. als Vorher-Sage im wörtlichen Sinne zu dienen" (The precondition of authorship is the loss of self, . . . The authors of the period write themselves into traditions and contexts in order to serve then as models or in the literal sense as precursor-prognosticators for other authors of the generations to come). Eva Geulen, *Worthörig wider Willen: Darstellungsproblematik und Sprachreflexion in der Prosa Adalbert Stifters* (Munich: iudicium, 1992), 13.

[11] The similarities in tone and message between the *Vorrede* and the autobiographical fragment "Mein Leben" are striking. In the former, Stifter maintains that one of the goals of his writing is "ihnen allen bekannten wie unbekannten einen Gruß zu schicken" (to send greetings to those [readers] I know and those I do not know). *Bunte Steine* (Stuttgart: Reclam, 2005), 7–8. In "Mein Leben," Stifter addresses his readers in a similar manner, but that readership is limited to his friends and family. Nonetheless, he predicts the wider circulation of the fragment, noting in regard to other, future, addressees, "Finden sie [his words] eine weitere Verbreitung, so mögen Gattin, Geschwister, Freunde, Bekannte einen zarten Gruß erkennen und Fremde nicht etwas Unwürdiges aus ihnen entnehmen" (583–84; Should they find a wider circulation, then may my wife, siblings, friends and acquaintances recognize a tender greeting in them and may strangers not take anything unseemly from them). This is yet another indication of the extent to which Stifter sought to control his image for posterity.

[12] For a comparable perspective see Wolfgang Matz, *Adalbert Stifter oder diese fürchterliche Wendung der Dinge* (Munich: dtv, 2005).

[13] This approach, no matter its inherent problems, is hardly novel in the context of Stifter. Fritz Klatt, writing in *Dichtung und Volkstum* in 1939, posited the demonic, excessive, gluttonous, and even self-indulgent as the central elements of Stifter's being: "Die Grundstruktur von Adalbert Stifters Wesen ist eine mit allen

Mitteln verdeckte und gebändigte Maßlosigkeit" (The basic structure of Adalbert Stifter's personality is an excessiveness that he hid and controlled through any means possible). Fritz Klatt, "Stifter und das Dämonische," *Dichtung und Volkstum* 40 (1939): 276–95; here 276. Klatt does what Sebald contends has not yet been done — he writes a pathographic portrait of Stifter.

[14] Here in Sebald's criticism we stumble upon traces of concerns that he would describe more succinctly in the context of his prose fiction writing. Sebald was aware of the kind of authoritative, and even authoritarian, voice typical of much scholarly writing and sought to avoid and undermine that kind of voice. As he told James Wood, "Any form of authorial writing, where the narrator sets himself up as stagehand and director and judge and executor in a text, I find somehow unacceptable. I cannot bear to read books of this kind." James Wood, "An Interview with W. G. Sebald," *Brick* 59 (1998): 23–29; here 26. Richard Sheppard notes similarly of Sebald's writing that, "as though to subvert the *ex cathedra* voice he inserts deliberate factual errors into his narrative with a completely straight face" and "parodies the same *ex cathedra* voice by making it sound like Stifter, Kafka or Hofmannsthal." Richard Sheppard, "Dexter–sinister: Some Observations on Decrypting the Mors Code in the Work of W. G. Sebald," *Journal of European Studies* 35 (2005): 419–63; here 428.

[15] For a compelling analysis of Stifter's "Mein Leben" see Laurence A. Rickels, "Stifter's Nachkommenschaften: The Problem of the Surname, the Problem of Painting," *MLN* 100, 3 (1985): 577–98.

[16] Benjamin, "Stifter" 1:608/112; trans. modified.

[17] Novotny, *Adalbert Stifter als Maler*, 25.

[18] Novotny notes the tension between the tenets of the famous preface to *Bunte Steine* and Stifter's actual artistic production, in terms of both his paintings and his literary work: "Es decken sich die Grundsätze jener Apologie vor den 'Bunten Steinen' auch in der Dichtung nicht ganz mit der künstlerischen Praxis" (24–25; In Stifter's writing, too, it is apparent that his artistic *praxis* is not entirely consistent with those principles in the *apologia* that prefaces *Bunte Steine*).

[19] Like the single episode in Stifter's fragment, involuntary memory often intrudes on many a character's "reality" in Sebald's prose fiction. In *Austerlitz*, to cite only one example, the German narrator visits the SS torture chambers at Breendonk, which bizarrely trigger a memory of his childhood "in W." He concludes, "Genau kann niemand erklären, was in uns geschieht, wenn die Türe aufgerissen wird, hinter der die Schrecken der Kindheit verborgen sind" (No one can explain exactly what happens within us when the doors behind which our childhood terrors lurk are flung open; *A*, 41/25).

[20] Here Sebald returns the historical context to the ahistoricized world of Stifter's prose, in which the "sanftes Gesetz" — as Theodor Adorno stressed in his remarks on Stifter in *Ästhetische Theorie* — eliminates the unwanted signs of violence and destruction that encroach from the social world onto and into the work of art. For Adorno, Stifter's monotone and monotonous writing reduces itself "zur Graphik" (to a pencil sketch) through the exclusion of anything of the obstreperous or

disturbing that comes from social reality, "durch den Ausschluß des Störenden und Ungebärdigen einer sozialen Realität, die mit der Gesinnung des Dichters so unvereinbar ist wie mit dem epischen Apriori, das er krampfhaft von Goethe übernahm" (by the exclusion of everything unruly and disturbing to the social reality that was as incompatible with the mentality of the poet as with the epic apriori that he took from Goethe and clung to). Adorno, *Ästhetische Theorie*, ed. Gretel Adorno und Rolf Tiedemann (1970; repr., Frankfurt am Main: Suhrkamp, 1972), 346; in English, Adorno, *Aesthetic Theory*, trans. Robert Hullot-Kentor (New York: Continuum, 2004), 305.

[21] Merriam-Webster's Medical Dictionary defines the indifference point as "1: the point in a series of judged magnitudes where there is no constant error of either overestimation or underestimation; 2: a midway point between two opposite sensations." http://medical.merriam-webster.com/medical/indifference%20point. The OED definition includes the following: "7. 'the middle zone of a magnet where the attractive powers of the two ends neutralise each other' (Syd. Soc. Lex. 1886)." At this point the question of whether Sebald's reading is subjective or objective is vacuumed of its relevance, for the critic has demarcated another kind of terrain for recounting how he imagines the experience of reading Stifter.

[22] For more on the autobiographical in Sebald's writing see my "No Place But Home: W. G. Sebald on the Air War and Other Stories," *Crossings* 7 (2005): 91–135.

[23] The fact that Sebald's critical method is problematic has not gone unremarked. See, for example, Ulrich Simon, "Der Provokateur als Literaturhistoriker: Anmerkungen zu Literaturbegriff und Argumentationsverfahren in W. G. Sebalds essayistischen Schriften," in *Sebald: Lektüren*, ed. Marcel Atze and Franz Loquai (Eggingen, Germany: Edition Isele, 2005), 78–104. Simon describes Sebald's readings of Stifter in particular in order to critique the critic's idiosyncratic approach. Sebald's conclusions about the object of his investigations, drawn from Stifter's "Der Hochwald," are, according to Simon, an "als Syllogismus *getarnten* Zirkelschluß" (a piece of circular logic camouflaged as a syllogism). "Es ist bekannt," Sebald concludes quite absurdly after citing a passage from the story, "daß ein prononciertes pädagogisches Talent zumeist Hand in Hand geht mit unausgelebten pädophilen Wünschen" (Simon, "Der Provokateur," 83; *VS*, 29; It is known that a pronounced talent for pedagogy usually goes hand in hand with pedophilic desires that have not been acted upon). Here Simon indeed catches the text in the act. It should nonetheless be noted that exaggeration is one of Sebald's rhetorical techniques: *Der Condor* and *Abdias* are Stifter's "bengalisch ausgeleuchteten Erzählungen" (*VS*, 24; Stifter's multicolored stories); Stifter's "kontinuierliche Einverleibung gewaltiger Mengen tierischer Nahrungsmittel" (*HB*, 172; Stifter's continual incorporation of immense amounts of food [or meat]) is a means by which he sought to secure acceptance by the "better" classes. It is not much of a discovery to state that the first example is hardly, to quote Simon, "außordentlich gut abgesichert" (extremely well supported). These turns of phrase are, to be sure, camp elements of a style that seeks to extricate itself from the

prohibitions of scholarly writing in order to play with the excesses of Stifter's own prose, which, as Simon points out, is itself quite campy (83). I do not dismiss Simon's objections to Sebald's approach, but I wonder whether, as in the premise of Simon's larger argument, any reading of Sebald's work that excludes a priori "die Verflochtenheit und Beziehbarkeit von essayistischem und literarischen Schreiben" (79; the interwoven and intertextual nature of Sebald's essayistic and literary writing) can do much more than note how the text camouflages some of its intentions through stylistic acrobatics that, I would argue, are present in each and every piece of art criticism.

24 Klatt, *Stifter und das Dämonische*, 276.

25 The secondary literature on Sebald has become so vast that I cannot do justice even to what would seem a manageable subfield, the critic's engagement with Stifter. Suffice it to say, the affinities between the two have been noted in the critical literature, but usually as asides in larger arguments. Andreas Huyssen mentions Sebald's first essay on Stifter as one of the sources of persistent attention to questions of catastrophe. Huyssen, *Present Pasts: Urban Palimpsests and the Politics of Memory* (Stanford, CA: Stanford UP, 2003), 176n22. McCulloh refers often to Stifter in the survey *Understanding W. G. Sebald* (Columbia: U of S. Carolina P, 2003). Working from McCulloh, Eric Santner mentions Stifter as one of the authors "critics have named in their efforts to locate Sebald in a literary tradition or genealogy," only to locate him in Rilke's *The Notebooks of Malte Laurids Brigge*. Santner's connection suggests a possible triangulation, particularly given Stifter's importance for Rilke's work, evidenced also by Rilke's famous 1914 "Stifter Brief" to August Sauer. Santner, *On Creaturely Life: Rilke, Benjamin, Sebald* (Chicago: Chicago UP, 2006), 47. More detailed investigations into the intertextual relations between Stifter and Sebald can be found in Anne Fuchs's *Die Schmerzensspuren der Geschichte: Zur Poetik der Erinnerung in W. G. Sebalds Prosa* (Cologne: Böhlau, 2004). Fuchs describes the convergences between descriptions of nature in Stifter and Sebald and their phenomenological dimensions (see the section "Naturautonomie: Stifter als Intertext," 223–31, for example). McCulloh explores the critic's readings of Stifter specifically and mentions Stifter's "Mein Leben," noting that in Sebald's work "the sublime is counterbalanced or accompanied by the destructive process of history," an element that he says is absent in Stifter. McCulloh, "Destruction and Transcendence in W. G. Sebald," *Philosophy and Literature* 30.2 (2006): 395–409; here 398. This view reinforces Adorno's assessment of Stifter in *Ästhetische Theorie*. Greg Bond and Claudia Öhlschläger both mobilize the description of a snowstorm in Stifter's *Aus dem bairischen Walde* to investigate the prevalence of threatening landscapes in Sebald's work. Bond, "On the Misery of Nature and the Nature of Misery: W. G. Sebald's Landscapes," in *W. G. Sebald: A Critical Companion*, 31–44; here 35–36; Öhlschläger, *Beschädigtes Leben. Erzählte Risse: W. G. Sebalds poetische Ordnung des Unglücks* (Freiburg im Breisgau: Rombach, 2006), 226. Öhlschläger sees Sebald's work as indicative of a threatening "Verlust des Gedächtnisses," loss of memory. See her chapter "Weiße Räume: Adalbert Stifter, Thomas Mann, Max Frisch, W. G. Sebald," in *Beschädigtes*

Leben, 217–33; here 226. In "The Stylistics of Stasis: Paradoxical Effects in W. G. Sebald," *Style* 38.1 (2004): 38–49, McCulloh argues that the writing of Stifter and Sebald "is in large measure an act of recovering, through memory and the citing of others' memories, the seemingly intact world of the past" (43–44). Eva Juhl, in "Die Wahrheit über das Üngluck: Zu W. G. Sebald *Die Ausgewanderten*," in *Reisen im Diskurs: Modelle der literarischen Fremdenerfahrung von den Pilgerberichten bis zur Postmoderne*, ed. Anne Fuchs and Theo Harden (Heidelberg: C. Winter, 1995), 640–50, notes the intertextual "Motivreihung und -verdoppelung" in Sebald's fictional and critical work (647). She specifically treats the recurrence of spatial relations in Sebald's readings of Stifter and in *Die Ausgewanderten*, describing Sebald's approach to reading and the connections he establishes between texts and contexts as part of a subjective perception: "Die Zusammenhänge werden als subjektive, durch die Wahrnehmung des jeweiligen Erzählerbewußtseins hergestellte, angedeutet, nicht als der außertextuellen Wirklichkeit per se inhärente behauptet" (648; Connections are asserted as subjective and are signified through the perception of the individual consciousness of each narrator and not as elements inherent to the extratextual reality).

[26] Part of what I have called elsewhere the "Sebald-industrial complex" now also includes pithily titled articles that review the scholarly literature on Sebald, two examples of which are Lynn Wolff, "'Das metaphysische Unterfutter der Realität': Recent Publications and Trends in W. G. Sebald Research," *Monatshefte* 99.1 (2007): 78–101, and Richard Sheppard, "'Woods, trees and the spaces in between': A Report on Work Published on W. G. Sebald, 2005–2008," *Journal of European Studies* 39.1 (2009): 79–128.

[27] One notable exception is W. G. Sebald, "In a Completely Unknown Region: On Gerhard Roth's Novel *Landläufiger Tod*," trans. Markus Zisselsberger, in *Modern Austrian Literature*, ed. Zisselsberger, Special Issue on W. G. Sebald and Austrian Literature 40.4 (2007): 43–60.

[28] The recent republication of a 1945 translation of *Bergkristall* by Elizabeth Mayer and Marianne Moore with an introduction by W. H. Auden (*Rock Crystal* [New York: New York Review of Books, 2008]) is another example of such a resurgence, as is the popularity of a 2008 London production of the avant-garde composer Heiner Goebbels's performance piece "Stifter's Dinge." The work was co-commissioned by Artangel (the organization that commissioned Rachel Whiteread's *House*) and the Théâtre Vidy-Lausanne. Artangel's promotional materials for the performance parachute in Stifter as "an Austrian writer, poet and painter who lived in Vienna and Linz, earning his living from teaching and painting before becoming a writer. Stifter's writing is characterized by his lush, vivid descriptions of landscape and the minutiae within them. His landscapes become subjects in which human interaction is simply a minor detail: objects in space." See http://www.e-flux.com/shows/view/5230 (accessed 16 Dec. 2008).

[29] For a transcription of the interview see Lynne Sharon Schwartz, ed., *The Emergence of Memory: Conversations with W. G. Sebald* (New York: Seven Stories, 2007), 77–86.

[30] Hugo Dittberner, "Der Ausführlichste oder, ein starker Hauch Patina: W. G. Sebalds Schreiben," *Text + Kritik* 158.4 (2003): 6–14; here 7.

[31] With the term "autofiction" I want to indicate, following the work of Roland Barthes, the breakdown of genres and the turn to a kind of "life writing" in which a process of subjectivation renders neutral the difference between fiction writing, autobiography, and even criticism.

[32] Martin Swales emphasizes Sebald's relation to a larger German literary tradition and its "significant theoretical component" (24): "Above all else, what that whole German tradition articulates is a sense of and feel for the complex and ceaseless interplay of materiality and mentality. In my view, precisely that interplay, in shifting configurations, is at the heart of Sebald's creative achievement. His writing constantly has a descriptive force to it." In the place of "materiality and mentality," I would substitute "work and life." Swales mobilizes Hegel ("The key witness is Hegel") to make his argument on the interplay of prose and poetry in Sebald's project. While the use of the term "Indifferenzpunkt" suggests such a link, I see a closer kinship in Kierkegaard's bifurcation of his works into the pseudonymous texts and those he wrote in his own name, as well as his critical stance toward abstract reflection. That is, to be sure, stuff for another essay. Martin Swales, "Theoretical Reflections on the Work of W. G. Sebald," in Long and Whitehead, *A Critical Companion*, 23–30.

[33] Markus Zisselsberger, "Fragments of One's Own Existence: The Reader W. G. Sebald" (PhD diss., Binghamton U, SUNY, 2008), 32. Geulen strongly objects to such an approach: "Das Verdikt des Pathologischen ist moralisch leichtfertig, hermeneutisch problematisch und überhaupt in keiner Hinsicht eine akzeptable, geschweige denn legitime Kategorie der Literaturkritik (*Worthörig wider Willen*, 28; The verdict "pathological" is morally reckless, hermeneutically problematic and generally in no way an acceptable, not to mention legitimate, category of literary criticism).

[34] For Geulen, Stifter's "maßloses Beschreiben" (exorbitant, excessive description) objectifies in order to save objects for eternity, therewith bringing about their very death. Sebald notes similarly of Stifter's *Der Nachsommer*: "Die Prosa des Nachsommers liest sich wie ein Katalog letzter Dinge, denn alles erscheint in ihr unterm Aspekt des Todes beziehungsweise der Ewigkeit" (*VS*, 23; The prose of *Indian Summer* reads like a catalogue of last things, since everything appears in the work under the aspect of death or eternity).

[35] W. G. Sebald, "Unterm Spiegel des Wassers — Peter Handkes Erzählung von der Angst des Tormanns," in *BU*, 115–30; here 130.

[36] Charlotte Schoell-Glass characterizes Sebald's visual method in terms of art historical approaches. She notes that the character Austerlitz is "in a sense, the personification of Sebald's method of literary visuality or visual writing. Austerlitz lends his voice to objects. His descriptions are as detached as they should be when an art historian goes about his business; they are inevitably subjective but corroborated by visual evidence." Charlotte Schoell-Glass, "Fictions of the Art World: Art, Art History and the Art Historian in Literary Space," in *Writing and Seeing: Essays*

on Word and Image, ed. Rui Carvalho Homem and Maria de Fátima Lambert (Amsterdam: Rodopi, 2006), 118.

[37] Öhlschläger, *Beschädigtes Leben,* 228.

[38] The descriptions of Browne's writing by Sebald's narrator take on the conspicuous tone of a literary critic: "Zwar gelingt es ihm, unter anderem wegen dieser enormen Belastung, nicht immer, von der Erde abzuheben, aber wenn er, mitsamt seiner Fracht, auf den Kreisen seiner Prosa höher und höher getragen wird wie ein Segler auf den warmen Strömungen der Luft, dann ergreift selbst den heutigen Leser noch ein Gefühl der Levitation" (Browne's writing can be held back by the force of gravitation, but when he does succeed in rising higher and higher through the circles of his spiraling prose, borne aloft like a glider on warm currents of air, even today the reader is overcome by a sense of levitation; *RS,* 30/19).

[39] OED, http://dictionary.oed.com/cgi/entry/50256373?single=1&query_type =word&queryword=transmigration&first=1&max_to_show=10 (accessed 28 Jan. 2009).

[40] Stifter, *Der Condor,* in *Sämtliche Erzählungen nach den Erstdrucken,* ed. Wolfgang Matz (Munich: Deutscher Taschenbuch Verlag, 2005), 18. The novella was first published in the *Wiener Zeitschrift für Kunst, Literatur, Theater und Mode* in 1840 and later became the first novella in the first of the six volumes of the *Studien,* 1844–50; see Ursula Naumann, *Adalbert Stifter* (Stuttgart: Metzler, 1979) for more on the history of publication.

[41] Mark R. McCulloh, "Destruction and Transcendence in W. G. Sebald," 402 and 408 n.19. McCulloh erroneously attributes Sebald's treatment of *Der Condor* to "Versuch." The novella is mentioned only briefly there. It is analyzed in detail in "Helle Bilder" (173–74). Greg Bond locates similarities between a passage from Stifter's *Aus dem bairischen Walde* and the chapter "Il ritorno in patria" in *Schwindel. Gefühle.* ("On the Misery of Nature," 36–37). Ben Hutchinson sees the trope of levitation as a part of Sebald's supposed "Hang zum Kleinen," his tendency toward the small, in which the reduction of the size of objects through the change in perspective lends them a kind of clarity. Ben Hutchinson, "Die Leichtigkeit der Schwermut: W. G. Sebalds 'Kunst der Levitation,'" *Jahrbuch der Deutschen Schillergesellschaft* 50 (2006): 458–77; here 468.

[42] For a fascinating history of the theme see Guillaume de Syon, *Zeppelin!: Germany and the Airship, 1900–1939* (Baltimore, MD: Johns Hopkins UP, 2007). On the specific connection between Stifter and Jean Paul see the careful detective work done by Friedrich Wilhelm Korff in his book *Diastole und Systole: Zum Thema Jean Paul und Adalbert Stifter* (Bern: Francke, 1969).

[43] In his translation Michael Hulse renders the catalyst for the narrator's trip, "in der Hoffnung, der nach dem Abschluß einer größeren Arbeit in mir sich ausbreitenden Leere entkommen zu können" as "in the hope of dispelling the emptiness that takes hold of me whenever I have completed a long stint of work," which indicates a regularity and repetition that is not as clear in the original (*RS,* 11/3).

[44] This intertextual processing of the experience of levitation relates to the experience of the spiraling, circular, and vertiginous that is characteristic of Sebald's work.

From the dizzying madness of *Vertigo* to Thomas Browne's spiraling prose in *Die Ringe des Saturn* and the various labyrinths of *Austerlitz*, Sebald's writing, itself a kind of spiral prose in terms of style, is seeded with just such experiences of sensory dislocation, in which the prose and its theme seem to spiral around and toward an unknown center. In an interview for Dutch television Sebald linked the experience as described in *Die Ringe des Saturn* to his own biography: "Yes, that's right. It does have a spiraling swirl in it somewhere and I think that in most of my texts it becomes at least obliquely obvious that the dark centre behind it all is the German past between 1925 and 1950 which I came out of." W. G. Sebald and Gordon Turner, "Introduction and Transcript of an Interview Given by Max Sebald (Interviewer Michaël Zeeman)," in *History — Memory — Trauma*, ed. Scott Denham and Mark McCulloh (Berlin: de Gruyter, 2006), 21–29; here 27–28.

[45] Narrator identity is a perennial theme in Sebald criticism. One scholar, for example, explains his use of the term "Sebaldian narrator" as a way to "draw attention to the near-perfect correspondence between the biographical details of the narrator and the author." Christopher C. Gregory-Guider, "The 'Sixth Emigrant': Traveling Places in the Works of W. G. Sebald," *Contemporary Literature* 46 (2005): 422–49; here 424n3.

[46] McCulloh, "Destruction and Transcendence," 402.

[47] Letter of Jan. 1861 from Stifter to Gustav Heckenast. *Adalbert Stifters Sämmtliche Werke*, vol. 19.3 (Reichenberg: Sudentendeutscher Verlag Franz Kraus, 1929), 265–66.

[48] Stifter's footnotes provide information on the properties of light, including the fact that sunlight can be divided into an infinite number of kinds of light, "in unendlich viele Lichtsorten getheilt werden könne" (18). Elsewhere Sebald aptly describes *Der Condor* as one of Stifter's "bengalisch ausgeleuchteten Erzählungen," one of his multicolored stories (*VS*, 24). I have omitted the footnotes in the long citation above for the sake of readability.

[49] In a reading of *Die Ausgewanderten*, Eva Juhl describes the nature of this "truth" in Sebald's writing as a "dialektische Bewegung zwischen Representivität und Individualität, als Wechselwirkung zwischen einem Individuum und seinem Kontext, die aber in der zusammenschauenden Betrachtung mehrerer solcher Schicksale eine Regularität, d.h. einen systematischen Aspekt sichtbar werden läßt, der über einen bloßen Zufall, die bloße Kontingenz hinausweist" (a dialectic movement between representationality and individuality, as a reciprocal interaction between an individual and a context, but one that in the synoptic observation of many such fates allows a regularity, which means a systematic aspect, to become visible, one that goes beyond mere chance, mere contingency). Juhl, "Die Wahrheit über das Unglück, 658.

[50] Hans Esselborn, "Adalbert Stifters 'Turmalin': Die Absage an den Subjektivismus durch das naturgesetzliche Erzählen," *Vierteljahresschrift des Adalbert-Stifter-Instituts* 34.1/2 (1985): 3–26; here 17.

[51] Describing what he sees as Sebald's "stylistics of stasis," McCulloh observes that "the characters and things — indeed, the readers themselves are 'on the verge,' or

'on the brink' of something. But on the verge of what? An experience? A discovery? Ultimately, and fatalistically, the answer is that things are on the brink of destruction and living beings are on the verge of death" (McCulloh, "Stylistics of Stasis," 38–39).

[52] The essay's title is "In einer wildfremden Gegend — Zu Gerhard Roths Romanwerk Landläufiger Tod." "The metaphysical vision and overview derive from a profound fascination in which our relation to the world is temporarily turned upside-down. While looking we sense how things are looking at us, and we understand that we are not here in order to pervade the universe, but to be pervaded by it" (Sebald, "In a Completely Unknown Region," 37).

[53] James P. Martin, "Die bezaubernde Anmut eines chemischen Prozesses — Photography in the Works of Gerhard Roth and W. G. Sebald," in *Modern Austrian Literature* 40.4 (2007): 42–60; here 45 (special issue on W. G. Sebald and Austrian Literature, ed. Zisselsberger).

[54] I describe the importance of this "subjective derangement" in my "Crossing Borders: Sebald, Handke and the Pathological Vision," *Modern Austrian Literature* 40.4 (2007): 61–92.

[55] Georg Brandes, "Om Læsning," in *Samlede Skrifter* 12 (1899; repr., Copenhagen: Gyldendalske Boghandels Forlag, 1902): 29–48; here 47.

[56] Sebald, "Her kommt der Tod, die Zeit geht hin: Anmerkungen zu Gottfried Keller," in *LG*, 125–26. In this passage Sebald reads Keller's graphic "Kritzelwerk," his doodling about his unrequited love, "Betty," whose name he writes "in langen verschlungenen Linien, Spiralen, Kolonnen und Schlaufen in vielhundertfacher Variation (125; in long, ornate lines, spirals, columns and loops in hundreds and hundreds of variations). Keller's doodling on his desk blotter represents the graphic form of Stifter's repetitive naming in "Mein Leben."

9: Adventure, Imprisonment, and Melancholy: *Heart of Darkness* and *Die Ringe des Saturn*

Margaret Bruzelius

> ... *it fascinated me as a snake would a bird*
> — *a silly little bird.*
> — Joseph Conrad, *Heart of Darkness*

CRITICS AND READERS TEND TO ASSUME the happy endings of adventure yarns, perhaps especially in the Robinsonade, where the voyage out results in successful imperial exploitation. But the usual end of the modern form of the romance called the adventure novel is instead deeply tinged with melancholy: once the adventure is over, there is nowhere else to go, neither in the life of the hero, who has finished his journey and returns to the quotidian (or sometimes hovers on the edge of return), nor in the life of the story, which has served its purpose and is now over, nor in the experience of the reader, who must close the book. Even in Sir Walter Scott, where the conclusion of the fiction is one that the author wholeheartedly embraces (life in an adult world of compromise and negotiation), endings are suffused with a sense of a dying fall: Scott's *Waverley* ends with a lengthy enumeration of all the narrator refuses to describe.[1] Ian Duncan has linked Scott's very mannered and ambivalent endings to his recognition that "historical being can only be rationally possessed, recognized, *as romance* — as a private aesthetic property, in the imagination."[2] Yet it is not only "historical" being that must be possessed by the imposition of formal devices, but life-history itself. The formal schema of the voyage out and return is a standard topos through which the achievement of adulthood is described, and it persistently links the accomplishment of maturity with the onset of the non-narratable and un-interesting.

For Joseph Conrad and W. G. Sebald the sense of decay and things passing that marks the end of adventure becomes an overriding obsession as the melancholy inherent in the end suffuses the entire fiction. Both *Heart of Darkness* and *Die Ringe des Saturn* use the standard armature of an adventure plot: a man leaves his everyday world to journey out, encounters vivid characters and places, and eventually returns safe (if sometimes damaged), ready to be reinserted into the workaday. Both fictions are first-person accounts that imply lived experience. But in reusing the well-worn adventure framework both Conrad and Sebald create tales permeated by an acute consciousness of storytelling as a process that leads nowhere. In shaping experience the tale reveals truth, but inevitably and concomitantly produces lies. The narrators' inevitable participation in the plot becomes an account of narrative and its discontents: a formal pattern that must be told and necessarily betrays the experience it is meant to express. Moreover, the close relation between author and narrator (Conrad and Sebald share important life experiences with Marlow and the narrator of *Die Ringe des Saturn*) adds to the sense of unease with which the reader follows these stories. Tale-telling loses whatever redemptive or integrative function it may once have had, as the sense of artifice that distinguishes the ends of adventure yarns now permeates the whole.

In most adventure stories the hero's return, no matter how flat, marks not only the end of his journey but his accession to another kind of being. Waverley becomes an adult and marries; Darsie Latimer becomes Sir Arthur Darsie Redgauntlet (*Redgauntlet*);[3] Alan Quartermain becomes a landholder (*King Solomon's Mines*);[4] Jim Hawkins acquires a fortune (*Treasure Island*).[5] In contrast, for Conrad and Sebald, while the story fulfills its function and returns the hero safely home, the socially integrating purpose of the story disappears and the return leaves the hero retelling a history whose purport is unclear. It is as though the inherited pattern of the voyage out imposes itself and must simply be endured with no reward or resolution.[6] For Conrad, Marlow's voyage out is the tale of a "silly little bird" who has been mesmerized by the idea of the map. His story "seem[s] to throw a kind of light" but is also "sombre" and "not very clear" (*H*, 21). For Sebald, the walk that his narrator takes is the pretext for a series of meditations on death and decay linked to sights he sees as he crosses Suffolk. He begins his story in the hospital, with the hospitalization providing the impetus for writing, but the writing has no recuperative effect, and the book ends with a meditation on the Victorian manufacture of silk for mourning clothes.[7] The gloomy ends of Marlow's trip upriver and Sebald's tour of Suffolk are a result of the dimness of the "kind of light" shed by their peregrinations. Having survived the journey, both tale-tellers find themselves uneasily scrutinizing their travel accounts, the constitutive talismans they have brought back from the exotic elsewhere, able neither to discard them nor to recuperate meaning from them. Both tales are steeped in melancholy as the peripatetic narrator recounts the instances of folly, greed, and waste he encounters as he accomplishes a journey that achieves nothing.

The question of genre haunts criticism of both Conrad and Sebald, although it is expressed in different modes. For Conrad, whose debt to the adventure-romance is obvious, the question for critics has always been how to differentiate him from Haggard, Henty, Marryatt, and others with whom he shares not only plots but an almost distasteful readability. Jameson clearly articulates Conrad's generic "problem": "even after eighty years, [Conrad's] place is still unstable, undecidable, and his work unclassifiable, spilling out of high literature into light reading and romance, reclaiming great areas of diversion and distraction by the most demanding practice of style and écriture alike."[8] Clearly, for Jameson Conrad must be "reclaimed" from the forms of "light reading and romance" that he used as a framework. Critics concerned with issues of post-coloniality, such as Edward Said, Andrea White, and Linda Dryden, focus more narrowly on Conrad's link to the imperial romance. They identify the continuities between Conrad's fictions and those of his contemporaries in order to demonstrate that Conrad destabilizes and subverts the (supposedly) easy categories of imperialist fiction.[9] Said writes: "What makes Conrad different from the other colonial writers who were his contemporaries is that . . . he was so self-conscious about what he did. . . . *Heart of Darkness* cannot just be a straightforward recital of Marlow's adventures."[10] But "self-consciousness" about what one does is a standard trope of the adventure form from Scott on, not a particular quality that characterizes Conrad as a romancer — even glib romancers such as John Buchan display the facticity of their fictions. Marlow's self-consciousness is hardly unique to Conrad, but rather integral to the mechanism of the adventure genre — a standard move in the genre that emphasizes its status as romance — not an exceptional quality that separates Conrad from the realm of trivial literary distraction and distasteful ideological excess.[11]

For Sebald, a critical question is the genre itself. What kind of books are these melancholy journeys told by a narrator whose name is revealed only in passing and illustrated with grainy black and white photographs? A *New York Times Book Review* reviewer asks, "What does one call them? Meditations, elegies, mutations grown from memoir, history, literary biography and prose poetry."[12] *Die Ringe des Saturn* is said to "cross and recross the border between genres, taking up temporary residence in fiction, autobiography, thumbnail biographies of other men, travelers' tales, and a prayerful rumination on the crumbling of livelihoods and lives."[13] As with Conrad, critics have focused on the admittedly astonishing narrative voice Sebald produces and ignored the plot conventions that allow that voice to sound. But as with Conrad, Sebald has adapted the standard adventure trope of the voyage out, with its usual paraphernalia of unfamiliar landscapes populated by overweening males, decaying families, and sinister women, and adapted it to his own fiction. He and Conrad are not melancholy *despite* the fact that they are romancers, they are melancholy *because* they are romancers, and they share the dismaying suspicion that the romance, rather than leading them toward understanding, leads them inevitably, fatally, away from any real comprehension of the world.

Critics of both Conrad and Sebald have either dismissed or failed to recognize the powerful generic continuities between classic adventure novels and both *Heart of Darkness* and *Die Ringe des Saturn*. Both fictions recount a journey out and safe return. Both include all the central elements of the adventure story, although in Sebald's case they are presented in a fragmented and decentered form. Both are stories of transition into an undelineated life fixated on looking backward to a "culminating point of . . . experience" (*H*, 21) shrouded in obscurity. Both are encounters with a strange and exoticized landscape. Sebald's Suffolk may seem too ordinary to represent adventure's exotic landscape, but adventure's elsewheres need not be far away — think of Scott's highlands, *The Count of Monte Cristo*'s Europe,[14] or *Rogue Male*'s Dorset,[15] all nearby places transformed by the plot that inhabits them. Within the larger landscape of adventure's exotic the hero always enters a highly charged space that contains something he must know or understand — this space is usually described in highly feminized terms and is often explicitly depicted as a female body. This space is generative, in that it contains within itself a person or thing that is the source of the adventure; it thus figures as the occluded originating space of the story, and both *Heart of Darkness* and *Die Ringe des Saturn* include such a space. For both narrators, entrance into the exotic is a way of encountering raw and implacable energies that exist only in veiled form in the world at the center. Both novels include demonic males, the fascinating, ambitious, and energetic male figures who are always finally excluded from the world of the frame narrative — figures such as Fergus MacIvor (*Waverley*), Long John Silver (*Treasure Island*), or the Count of Monte Cristo. Both include the stock wild woman of adventure who resists the dominant male order — women like Meg Merrilies in *Guy Mannering*[16] or Ayesha, the *She-who-must-be-obeyed* of Haggard's *She*.[17] *Heart of Darkness* also includes a classic example of the blond, compliant female of Scott's fiction, a woman completely subservient to the masculine order that adventure celebrates. Both take the consciousness of literariness that imbues all adventure and heighten it so that issues of representation become central. And finally, for both, the consciousness of operating in a highly formalized plot structure is experienced as imprisonment, for the narrators share the fundamental traits of the adventure hero willy-nilly: they are lucky, and they come home safe. Adventure, despite its derring-do, is always fundamentally about stasis, and Conrad and Sebald completely conform to this generic imperative. By recognizing and heightening adventure's tradition of parading its facticity, its status as fabulation, as *lie*, Conrad and Sebald "modernize" the Scott narrative only in that they greatly exaggerate the awareness of storytelling that has always characterized the adventure yarn. By emphasizing the self-consciousness of the narrator, both Conrad and Sebald draw from adventure's well-worn instrument a deeply melancholic chord. In both works, despite the continuous motion across a rebarbative and ultimately meaningless landscape, the adventure form can only return us, unchanged, to where we already are. Conrad's and Sebald's awareness of the compulsions of their narratives and their lack of liberating power suffuse their texts with a narratorial consciousness that cannot help recounting, but also recognizes that such accounting does not, and cannot, count.

Marlow and the Compulsions of Adventure

Of all the writers in the modernist canon, Conrad most explicitly represents the problem of adventure and the place of romance forms: he is disreputably readable. Recent scholarship has tended to formulate the question of Conrad and the romance in terms of his relation to the "imperial romance" produced by writers such as Marryat, Henty, Haggard, Kingsley, Kipling, and others. Influenced especially by Said's *Orientalism* and *Culture and Imperialism*, such work has insisted on his superiority to the ruck of imperialist writers (perhaps most especially Haggard, whom Conrad himself despised). For Said, *Heart of Darkness* provides an exemplary instance of a mode of reading that has persistently occulted the generative importance of empire in the institutions of the novel. But adventure, as a form in which a young person, invariably a man, voyages out and returns, is concerned with a geography of exotic elsewheres, not as places that are real in themselves but as places that exist *for* the world at the center. "Elsewhere" subtends the world at the center, the world from which the young man exits, and to which he returns. The tradition to which Conrad is so deeply indebted is the larger adventure tradition of Scott and Dumas, deeply conservative fictions that exist to comfort and console middle-class men in an uncertain world.[18] While the form was useful to the imperial project, in that empire supplied a handy geography, adventure provides no more critique of imperialism in Conrad and Sebald than it does in Henty. Marlow doesn't like Belgian empire, but he thinks that "real work is being done" (*H*, 25) in the English one. In Sebald's miasmatic despair it's not clear that any form of governance is more than exploitation.

In the framing of his story, Conrad's acknowledgment of its status *as* story has always been taken to be an example of a modernist practice that foregrounds narrative facticity. Conrad is described as canny about the ways in which plots engender effects without himself being bound to those effects. Said takes Marlow's "self-consciousness" about his story as an ironic distancing that permits a critical stance toward the enterprise of empire, a distancing that remains possible no matter what Conrad's own attitude toward empire may have been.[19] Brooks's earlier narratological account sees *Heart of Darkness* as a tale in which the author and his readers acknowledge a common, if inscrutable, fate: the tale exists because of the affirmation of experience asserted in its telling. For White, Conrad's early fiction (her discussion ends with *Heart of Darkness*) "subvert[s] generic expectations and disturb[s] hegemonic construction in place, and convincingly insist[s] that the exotic, as a category constructed by the dominant colonial discourse, no longer serve[s] imperial purposes."[20] For Dryden, Conrad "speaks through Marlow, indicating the questioning sensibility of the skeptic. . . . Conrad questions the simple values of the romance genre."[21]

These critics' recuperation of Conrad from distasteful forms of imperial fiction reveals a more general discomfort with the form of romance-adventure itself and its influence on the novel. The novel/romance divide, like the mind/body split we acknowledge to be false and nevertheless believe to be true, persists in shaping expectations of both readers and authors in ways that we are reluctant to recognize. On the most basic level, we want Conrad to rise above his romance-writing peers, because we want to rescue him from the form that he himself adopted. But Conrad employs the romance form self-reflexively in order to illustrate its power — his story is a painful meditation on the lie that is romance and conforms in all its particulars to the adventure paradigm. Marlow repeats the itinerary of every adventure hero — he journeys away from home into an exotic elsewhere entered in a moment of idleness. In that elsewhere he is first seduced by the idea of, and then meets in the flesh, a demonic male whom he must learn to resist. The encounter occurs in a generative space lit by hell fires and marked by water. The hero's entrance and exit from the generative space are marked by moments in which his vision is obscured. Like every adventure hero, his itinerary is marked by coincidence and luck. He meets two female figures, one dark and one fair. What is different is Marlow's understanding of the compulsive power of romance, his self-conscious realization that his tale requires him to lie, despite his professed devotion to truth: he recounts a story he cannot control. The narrator ends the tale with an image of the Thames flowing into what appears to be a black hole, "the tranquil waterway . . . seemed to lead into the heart of an immense darkness" (*H,* 124), a final vision of fluency that generates no light. Both Conrad's multiple frames and the way in which he makes Marlow repeatedly evoke sight illustrate the way in which the exigencies of plot make it impossible to see straight, indeed, to see at all. At its darkest, Marlow's lie is not only his polite fib to the Intended, but his entire narrative, which leads its hearers into the dark.[22]

Marlow's debt to the romance is immediately evident in his opening evocation of maps: "Now when I was a little chap I had a passion for maps. I would . . . lose myself in all the glories of exploration" (*H,* 21). The genre of adventure has already been suggested by the unnamed narrator, in his brief history of the Thames: "It had known and served all the men of whom the nation is proud, from Sir Francis Drake to Sir John Franklin, . . . the great knight-errants of the sea" (*H,* 17). (Compare the opening of

Charles Kingsley's *Westward Ho!*: "It was the men of Devon, the Drakes and Hawkins', Gilberts and Raleighs, Grenviles and Oxenhams, . . . to whom she [England] owes her commerce, her colonies."[23]) The map also suggests other literary territories whose existence is guaranteed by a map, perhaps most famously *Treasure Island*. Marlow's venture into exotic territory is instigated by the same idle curiosity that motivates most heroes. He has been first "loafing about" (*H*, 21) and then fruitlessly trying to get a job. In the course of his unemployment he comes upon a map of the Congo in a shop window, and it is this coincidence that motivates his journey: "And as I looked at the map of it [the 'mighty big river'] in a shop window it fascinated me as a snake would a bird — a silly little bird" (*H*, 22).[24] The boy Marlow had a hankering to go to the North Pole; the man Marlow decides in a moment of idleness, the classic moment of entry into the exotic, to find a job captaining a steamboat in the "biggest, most blank" place (*H*, 22).

Marlow's traversal through the exotic world is a journey through an allegorical landscape whose meaning has been evacuated, a pilgrim's progress with no delectable mountain. The grove of death in the outer station, where Marlow stumbles across the slaves dying of starvation, or the Belgian traders, the "faithless pilgrims" (*H*, 44) of the inner station are terrifying precisely because they completely lack redemptive meaning; they are the signs only of folly and waste. Human wreckage accompanies wrecked machinery: the "boiler wallowing in the grass, . . . an undersized railway truck lying there on its back with its wheels in the air" (*H*, 32), and Marlow's own steam ship, sunk in the mud. Every journey is an endless progress through an undifferentiated landscape: "every day the coast looked the same" (30); "paths, paths, everywhere; a stamped-in network of paths spreading over the empty land" (*H*, 39); "trees, trees, millions of trees, massive, immense, running up high; and at their foot . . . the little begrimed steamboat, like a sluggish beetle" (*H*, 61). The landscape of Africa is described as outside time — like all adventure exotic landscapes, it represents a survival from the past. Marlow imagines that a splashing he hears is "an ichthyosaurus . . . taking a bath of glitter in the great river" (*H*, 54), and as he steams up river he describes the group on the ship as "wanderers on a prehistoric earth, on an earth that wore the aspect of an unknown planet" (*H*, 62).

The outer limit of Marlow's journey is Kurtz's clearing, the generative space within which he discovers his story. Like innumerable other such spaces — the caves inhabited by John Balfour (*Old Mortality*)[25] or the plotters in *Guy Mannering* — it is close to water and is described as hellish: "deep within the forest, red gleams . . . wavered, . . . seemed to sink and rise from the ground" (*H*, 103). When the steamer sets off with Kurtz aboard, Marlow describes the ensuing scene as a conflict between devils. The steamboat is a European demon, a "splashing, thumping fierce river-demon beating the water with its terrible tail and breathing black smoke into the air," while the three Africans on the shore are devils, "plastered with bright red earth from head to foot . . . they stamped their feet, nodded their horned heads, swayed their scarlet bodies" (*H*, 108). The clearing is dominated by Kurtz, Marlow's demonic male, contains forbidden knowledge, and is associated with a wildly resistant woman. Like all heroes, Marlow has trouble both entering and exiting the space. On his way in, his vision is obstructed when the boat is stuck in the fog so that "our eyes were of no more use to us than if we had been buried miles deep in a heap of cotton-wool" (*H*, 73). On the return, Marlow becomes sick and nearly dies in "an impalpable grayness" (*H*, 113). And of course it is here, at the farthest point of his journey, that Marlow discovers what he needs: the tale that constitutes his being in the frame of the novel, the central, unadventurous world — the world of the lawyer, the Director of Companies, the accountant, and the narrator.

Kurtz exemplifies the demonic male; he is overweening, aggressive, and completely self-centered, a figure whose sense of his own importance far exceeds his situation. He arrogates to himself limitless, nearly divine authority. Marlow quotes from his pamphlet for the "International Society for the Suppression of Savage Customs," in which Kurtz writes, "whites . . . must necessarily appear to them [the 'savages'] in the nature of supernatural beings" (*H*, 83). Even the "luminous and terrifying" postscript that Kurtz appends to his document, "Exterminate all the Brutes!" (*H*, 84), demonstrates the unfailing ruthlessness of the demonic, incommensurate even in defeat. Demonic males are distinguished by their ability to cross class boundaries and are closely linked to outlaw or unorthodox systems of knowledge. Kurtz allows himself to be worshipped, "[he] had taken a high seat among the devils of the land — I mean literally" (*H*, 81) and has also permitted human sacrifice, if not in his honor at least in his presence, as testified by the ring of human skulls that surround his hut. Kurtz claims everything about him as his possession: "My Intended, my ivory, my station, my river, my — everything belonged to him" (*H*, 81). Like all demonic males, he is a law unto himself: "a being to whom I [Marlow] could not appeal in the name of anything high or low" (*H*, 107). Kurtz's capacity for indeterminate but vast effort parodies the limitless capacities of the demonic male. Like Captain Nemo (*20,000 Leagues under the Sea*)[26] he is a polymath, a "universal genius" (two characters use this phrase to describe him). When Marlow tries to sum him up, he tells us that he had taken Kurtz for "a painter who wrote for the papers, or else for a journalist who could paint" (*H*, 116). Kurtz's cousin says that he was "essentially a great musician" (*H*, 115), and a former colleague describes him as someone who "would have been a splendid leader of an extreme party. . . . Any party" (*H*, 116). He is described as a "a prodigy, . . . an emissary of pity, and science, and progress, and devil knows what else" (*H*, 47). Of course,

Conrad's story makes these comments about Kurtz's prowess deeply ironic; nevertheless, Kurtz exemplifies the demonic male's protean abilities.

As with all demonic males, Kurtz's claims are incompatible with the restraint of the public world. Indeed, Marlow uses him as the gold standard of lack of self-control. He says of his African helmsman, "he had no restraint, no restraint — just like Kurtz" (H, 85). When Marlow intercepts Kurtz as he tries to escape from his European rescuers, Kurtz insists on his complete self-possession, claiming that he knows "perfectly" what he is doing (H, 106).[27] Like every demonic male, Kurtz overwhelms his hero, and even after Kurtz's death, Marlow remains fascinated by him: "He was a remarkable man. After all, this was the expression of some sort of belief; it had candor, it had conviction, it had a vibrating note of revolt in its whisper, it had the appalling face of a glimpsed truth" (H, 113).[28] Despite his distaste for Kurtz, Marlow cannot deny his power: "I can't choose. He won't be forgotten. Whatever he was, he was not common" (H, 84).

Heart of Darkness also conforms to, and grotesquely exaggerates, the conventions of the feminine that mark adventure. While Marlow does not marry either of the two women in the novel, they are arranged in the usual romance topography: the wild woman is found at the generative space in the exotic world, and Kurtz's "Intended" fills the role of the dutiful maiden (usually blond) wholly identified with the masculine order in the world at the center. The wild woman is clearly the "wild and gorgeous apparition of a woman," Kurtz's African queen, the *ne plus ultra* in willful women.[29] Nothing could be more emphatically unmarriageable and theatrical than this icon of otherness who appears as Kurtz leaves on Marlow's steamboat: "She was savage and superb, wild-eyed and magnificent" (H, 99). Like other wild women of adventure, the African woman shows masculine courage and determination and alone stands her ground when Marlow blows his terrifying steam whistle: "Only the barbarous and superb woman did not so much as flinch, and stretched tragically her bare arms after us" (H, 109). Marlow describes her as a warrior: her hair is "done in the shape of a helmet," and she has "brass leggings to the knee, brass wire gauntlets to the elbow" (H, 99). By "intending" Kurtz to be her partner, she is guilty of the same sin as innumerable defeated women in adventure: she has wished to impose her desire. Conrad's version of this role — she is not only dark-haired but also dark-skinned, speaks a different language, and exists in a different and incomprehensible world — is a fantastic intensification of the standard traits of the wild female in romance.

The wild woman's marriageable counterpart is, of course, the Intended, who fills the role of the dutiful maiden of adventure. Just as Kurtz's African queen is parodic in her exaggeration of the figure of the wild woman, the Intended is a caricature of the role of the maiden. She has no proper name, her name is her role — nothing else about her has any importance. While the words associated with the African queen are all about pattern and color (striped, fringed, brass, crimson, tawny, yellow) the ones associated with the Intended are all white and black (black, pale, fair, pure, ashy); the only hint of color is her hair catching "the remaining light in a glimmer of gold" (*H*, 121). The Intended's whiteness and blankness suggest her complete identification with Kurtz's legacy: because he is dead she will be "unhappy for life" (*H*, 121). Everything about the Intended suggests emptiness and death: Marlow waits for her in a room with a fireplace of "monumental whiteness" and a "polished sarcophagus" (*H*, 118) of a piano in a city that Marlow has described as a "whited sepulcher" (*H*, 24). Without the man for whom she was a purpose, the "Intended" is essentially dead.

Conrad dramatizes the inescapable coercion of the adventure plot in Marlow's meeting with the Intended. Marlow has told us that he hates lies, not because he is a particularly moral person, but because they carry the "flavor of mortality": "There is a taint of death, a flavor of mortality in lies, — which is exactly what I hate and detest in the world — what I want to forget" (*H*, 49–50). He has also told us (apropos his aunt): "It's queer how out of touch with truth women are. They live in a world of their own, and there had never been anything like it, and never can be. If they were to set it up it would go to pieces before the first sunset" (*H*, 28). But when he is faced with the Intended's romantic preconceptions about her fiancé, the generic fiction that she has constructed around him, Marlow is forced to utter the lie that encapsulates the betrayal of experience that is romance: he tells her that Kurtz died with her name on his lips.[30] Even the self-aware are subordinated to the constraints of plot, though they attempt to resist; Marlow, although he knows that the lie betrays his lived experience, finds he must rehearse the expected plot rather than tell the truth. To be seduced by the adventure story as Marlow has been, just like a "silly little bird," is to be condemned to the corruption he most detests.[31]

During his journey Marlow repeatedly refuses the narrative within which he finds himself by clinging to the "surface-truth" of work, "get[ting] the old tin-pot along by hook or by crook" (*H*, 63). Indeed, he distinguishes between the red (British) areas on the map, where "some real work is being done" (*H*, 25), and the yellow (Belgian) area where he eventually goes, entirely on the basis of efficiency, of getting something done. The only people that he mentions with any kind of admiration are the chief accountant at the outer station, a "miracle" in a "high starched collar" (*H*, 36) who manages to keep his shirt cuffs white and "mak[es] correct entries of perfectly correct transactions" (*H*, 38), and his African helmsman, who (despite his Kurtz-like "lack of restraint") had "done something, he had steered" (*H*, 84). For Marlow, physical labor stands for "an honest concern for the right way of going to work" (*H*, 65), a concern metonymically represented by his obsession with rivets, "what I really wanted was rivets, by heaven! Rivets. To get on with the work — to stop the hole" (*H*, 51).

Throughout the novel labor represents an escape from language, as when Marlow escapes from Kurtz's endless babble because he has to help fix the steamship: "I had not much time to give him, because I was helping the engine-driver to take to pieces the leaky cylinders. . . . I lived in an infernal mess of rust, filing, nuts, bolts, spanners, hammers, ratchet-drills — things I abominate, because I don't get on with them" (*H*, 111). Marlow "does not get on with" nuts and bolts, but they offer him a respite from talk, the one thing he does "get on with." But as Marlow tells his story it becomes apparent that there is no "right way of going to work" for the storyteller — no salvation in the mechanics. The story does not work — it does not help the storyteller or his listeners to understand; it does not do anything for them, and they learn nothing from it. Marlow's ghostly voice, rambling on about his encounter with another wraith, expresses his frustration that he cannot make his interlocutors see — "Do you see him? Do you see the story? Do you see anything?" then remarks: "Of course in this you fellows see more than I could then. You see me, whom you know" (*H*, 50). The narrator, however, immediately intervenes to point out that in fact they cannot see: "It had become so pitch dark that we listeners could hardly see one another. For a long time already he . . . had been no more to us than a voice" (*H*, 50).[32] Like Kurtz, Marlow ends as "A voice! A voice!" caught up in a story whose culmination is a lie.

Tzvetan Todorov begins his reading of *Heart of Darkness* by dismissing its similarity to the adventure story as "superficial." He ends by suggesting that "the story of Kurtz symbolizes the act of fiction, a construct based on a hollow center" which is in turn held to represent "all processes of knowledge, of which the knowledge of Kurtz is but one example."[33] From a very different starting point, Mario Vargas Llosa comes to the very similar conclusion that Marlow's final lie represents fictionality itself.[34] J. Hillis Miller suggests that "the narrative of *Heart of Darkness* as a whole is based on the facts of history and on the facts of Conrad's life but uses these to express something transhistorical and transpersonal, the evasive and elusive 'truth' underlying both historical and personal experience."[35] That truth turns out to be the impossibility of revelation, of moving beyond the printed page to vision, and "*Heart of Darkness* is posited on the impossibility of achieving its goal of revelation."[36] But the impossibility of revelation in Conrad, as in Scott and other adventure writers, reflects perhaps the paradoxical condition of writing itself but also, and certainly, the merciless logic of the adventure plot.[37] The adventure's well-worn machinery *intends* to take us back to where we began: it exists to be circular and ultimately meaningless. The outermost narrator says of Marlow's tales in general that "the meaning of an episode was not inside like a kernel but outside, enveloping the tale which brought it out only as a glow brings out a haze, in the likeness of one of these misty halos that sometimes are made visible by the spectral illumination of moonshine" (*H*, 18). Marlow himself refers to "one immense jabber, silly, atrocious, sordid, savage, or simply mean, without any kind of sense. Voices, voices" (*H*, 80). Romance is fabulation, noise, jabber. Its "spectral illumination" is fake, moonshine. The story ends where it began; the meaning is not in the story but in the moonshine, the aura of romance, fabulous and untrue. The group of listeners that was joined at the beginning — "Between us there was . . . the bond of the sea" (*H*, 15) — ends with Marlow sitting "apart, indistinct and silent" (*H*, 39). *Heart of Darkness* asserts that the hero survives but that the tale he tells, following its own heedless logic, keeps him apart and in the dark, telling the lie that brings death in its wake.

Sebald on Conrad — Another Turn of the Screw

Reading *Die Ringe des Saturn* with *Heart of Darkness* suggests that Conrad is a central influence for Sebald's novels of wandering exiles. Both writers imagine a world in which the compulsion to voyage out ends not with reintegration and a renewed sense of belonging, but rather with mere survival and despair. Both share an overwhelming melancholy and a deep distrust of the solace provided by fiction. Sebald most closely mimics the romance forms on which Conrad so deeply meditated in *Die Ringe des Saturn*, but all of his writings share Conrad's awareness of the ways that inherited modes of tale-telling necessarily betray lived experience. The narrative connections that Conrad and Sebald's narrators make are arbitrary, partial, and always insufficient. (On the biographical level, both Conrad and Sebald lived in England, away from their native country, although Conrad, of course, wrote in English while Sebald composed in his native German.) In *Die Ringe des Saturn*, the disassembled machinery of the romance form litters the book — every part of the well-worn engine is there, even though they are strewn about its surface as the bits of a motorcycle might be strewn across a garage floor. But as in Conrad, no matter how far the wanderer strays, he accomplishes nothing.

As Sebald became well known in the Anglo-American world, reviewers puzzling over the question of his seemingly opaque form ignored his debt to Conrad and the conventions of adventure so clearly manifested in *Die Ringe des Saturn* in order to stress that his work is "unclassifiable" or wildly innovative. In a typical review, James Wood cites Benjamin's observation that all "great works either found a new genre or dissolve an old one" to buttress his assertion that Sebald's writing finds "a way to protest the good government of the conventional novel-form and to harass realism into a state of self-examination"[38] (Only the London *Times Literary Supplement* resists swooning over Sebald's generic innovations. It reviewed *Die Ringe des Saturn* under the rubric of "Travel," and its reviewer ends by remarking that it is a "notable addition to the literature of Suffolk."[39])

But the walk Sebald recounts in *Die Ringe des Saturn*, although performed in a much less exotic landscape, repeats adventure's familiar itinerary (and Marlow's trip upriver in *Heart of Darkness*). Both journeys seem "somehow to throw a kind of light on everything" and yet are "sombre . . . and pitiful — not extraordinary in any way — not very clear, either" (*H,* 21). In *Die Ringe des Saturn*, however, the adventure itinerary is no longer the supposed occasion for a narrative (the "fabula" for Sebald's "sjuzet"); rather, like a Joseph Cornell box, the narrative scraps *are* the adventure. "Real" adventure, in the shape of dramatic encounter, is absent as the narrator summarizes the narratives of others, whether fiction or nonfiction, that Sebald has read or researched: Sebald's journey is merely an exiguous armature for reflections on philosophy and literature. The narrator's "adventure" is his linking of these tales to each other and to the sights he sees in his walk across Suffolk, during which nothing happens and adventure (in the sense of an out-of-the-ordinary experience) does not even seem possible. But even this most characteristic effect of Sebald's style derives from the classic adventure yarn's flaunting of itself as *story* and the genre's addiction to literary allusions. Where Scott occasionally allows a hero like Waverley artily to soliloquize, as when in sight of the reiver Benn Lean's cave he thinks of himself as "on a visit to the den of some renowned outlaw, a second Robin Hood, perhaps, or Adam o'Gordon"[40]), Sebald's narrator compulsively connects: everything reminds him of something else and connects him not merely to "Robin Hood or Adam o'Gordon" but to Conrad, the Empress Tz'u-hsi, Kafka, Swinburne, and a seemingly endless series of others. John Beck has asserted that Sebald's "metacommentary" opens a gap "between the 'real' and the monstrous textual reflection of it. . . . As such, the reader is exiled from the text's putative 'truth' and left to wander uncompassed with the narrator along the coastal threshold between the solid and the fluid."[41] But Sebald's *Die Ringe des Saturn* is not an attempt at realism or mimetic representation (Beck's "putative 'truth'"); rather, it is a highly mannered and unconventional romance that appropriates scraps of external narrative in order to construct an "adventure." Like Freud, another purveyor of romance as internal consciousness, Sebald narrates a journey as an interior adventure, although he explores not a personal archeology but rather a miscellany of material gathered in reading. And, like all adventurers, the narrator ends up going home to a dispirited present.

Even for the type of adventure yarn inaugurated by Scott, in which the hero rarely does anything more than stand and stare, the narrator of *Die Ringe des Saturn* does remarkably little: he walks around, eats bad meals in lousy restaurants, and talks to strangers in bars.[42] Sebald transforms the hero's lucky breaks, the chance encounters that turn out to be essential to the hero's eventual success, into the narrator's excursions: random sights give birth to the digressive method that become his story; and after all, adventure is the digressive genre *par excellence* as it both recounts and celebrates digression from the everyday. In spite of his ineptitude, the narrator — adventure hero that he is — finds on the road all he needs. Simply by moving across the English landscape he exposes a web of stories, connections that link provincial England to mainland Europe, China, and Africa. Like Dumas's Monte Cristo, who appears everywhere and knows everything, Sebald's tale-teller connects disparate worlds.[43] At the beginning of his story, for example, the narrator stays in a hospital that at one time contained a collection of artifacts that included Sir Thomas Browne's disinterred skull, which leads to his first extensive discourse on Browne, who recurs throughout the novel. A chance meeting with a Dutchman in a hotel in the eighth chapter leads to a disquisition on the relation between the fortunes made in sugar that are the basis of several great European art galleries (including the Mauritshuis, which the narrator earlier recounts having visited in order to see Rembrandt's *The Anatomy Lesson*) and then segues into a discussion of Edward Fitzgerald, the translator of Omar Khayyam. At the end of his long excursus on Conrad, the narrator remarks that Kafka's uncle had left for the Belgian Congo from the same port as Conrad, and uses that coincidence as a means of describing first the uncle's successful African career and then the persistent ugliness of the Belgian capital.

Sebald's discursive form connects wildly disparate people and events through tangents linked only by the narrator's consciousness in a parodic version of the way in which the negligible hero of adventure fiction becomes the focus of energy that far exceeds him. Each chapter is constructed as a series of meditations loosely linked to the sights the narrator sees, some of which are illustrated by snapshots. A sample chapter description from the Contents page runs: "The Bridge over the Blyth — the Chinese court train — The Taiping rebellion and the opening of China — Destruction of the garden of Yuan Ming Yuan — The end of Emperor Hsien-feng — The Dowager empress Tz'u-hsi — Mysteries of power — The town beneath the sea — Poor Algernon." In this example (and all the chapters are equally discursive), Sebald gets from the bridge over the Blyth to the Chinese court by remarking that the bridge was built for a narrow gauge train thought originally to have been commissioned by the emperor of China. This in turn leads to a description of Chinese court life, a brief review of the lives of the last two Chinese emperors, and a description of the life of the dowager empress. Sebald lingers over her maniacal greed and love of silkworms, whose idiotic industriousness she admired above all things, and her death. Using a reference from Borges's story "Tlön, Uqbar, Orbis Tertius" as a pivot point, Sebald moves on to the medieval town of Dunwich, most of which has been lost under the sea, which leads him to Swinburne, who once visited Dunwich. All of this material is loosely tied together by the narrator's peregrination through the English countryside, his walking anchoring these reflections on silkworms, transience, decay, and death.

As always in adventure, the decay of old families and buildings is central. The hero's journey always takes him through a world whose dilapidation represents fruitless resistance to an inexorable present and loyalty to a moribund history. The narrator perambulates past great estates now in various states of disrepair and coastal towns whose sea-coast industries have disappeared. Just as Scott has Mannering stumble onto the decaying estate of Ellangowan in *Guy Mannering* to inaugurate his adventure, or Axel in Verne's *Journey to the Center of the Earth*[44] sees the decay of an entire lost world in the great dinosaur boneyard, the narrator's trip is punctuated by meditations on the dead or dying past. In the first chapter he visits an estate named Somerleyton, discourses on the FitzOsberts and Jernegans who once controlled it (*RS*, 45/32), only to reveal that the current, much damaged building was built by an industrial age upstart who bought it from its last impoverished, genteel owner (whose name, appropriately enough, was Anguish). When he reaches Woodbridge he visits the deserted estate of Boulge, the home of the FitzGerald family, which then brings to mind the misfortunes of another decayed family in whose house he once stayed on a visit to Ireland. This in turn leads to a description of the mansion of the "shooting domain" of Bawdsey, a Moorish extravaganza that was eventually sold to the crown in order to finance its owner's passion for flying (*RS*, 270/226). In *Die Ringe des Saturn* all families are in the process of dying off. His Suffolk, like Scott's highlands, is populated by those who espouse the values of former times and cannot be reconciled to the present. (Alan Bennett waspishly remarks on Sebald's aggressive depopulation of the English countryside: "The fact is, in Sebald nobody is ever about."[45]) Even a former secret military installation that the narrator visits on the island of Orfordness is described as a funereal monument to departed purpose:

> Die ringsum mit Unmengen von Steinen zugeschütteten Betongehäuse, in denen, während der meisten Zeit meines Lebens, Hundertschaften von Technikern an der Entwicklung neuer Waffensysteme gearbeitet hatten, nahmen sich aus der Entfernung, wahrscheinlich aufgrund ihrer seltsamen Kegelform, wie Hügelgräber aus, in denen in vorgeschichtlicher Zeit große Machthaber beigesetzt worden waren mit all ihren Gerätschaften und all ihrem Silber und Gold.

> [From a distance, the concrete shells, shored up with stones, in which for most of my lifetime hundreds of boffins have been at work devising new weapons systems, looked (probably because of their odd conical shape) like the tumuli in which the mighty and powerful were buried in prehistoric times with all their tools and utensils, silver and gold. (*RS*, 281/235–36)][46]

Every adventure plot brings the hero to a furthermost point in which he finally rejects the seductive energy of the man who dominates the exotic world, a figure possessed by a demonic energy usually dedicated to a lost cause — Kurtz, Fergus MacIvor, Captain Nemo. He must also encounter a wild woman — Kurtz's African lover, Meg Merrilies, or Ayesha, "*She-who-must-be-obeyed.*" At the center of the novel and of his itinerary, at the apogee of his arc of melancholy and despair, Sebald conjures up these two central stock figures of adventure, the demonic male and the wild woman. He makes no attempt to construct imaginary characters; rather, both appear in the guise of historical figures: the role of the demonic male is shared by two figures, Joseph Conrad and Roger Casement, linked through their African experiences, and the figure of the wild woman by the Chinese Empress Tz'u-hsi, scraps of whose biography are recounted by the narrator. Conrad and Casement, like the eternally frustrated demonic male in adventure, are described as possessed, destined by their familial and national inheritances to failed resistance and desolation. The empress represents the unredeemed female will to power that destroys all around it in adventure fiction. Like Lady Ashton in Scott's *Bride of Lammermoor*,[47] she focuses on her own desire and thereby destroys all around her. (Usually in Scott the wild woman repents and helps the hero at the end; Lady Ashton uniquely perseveres in her willfulness and brings about the destruction of her entire family). Having summoned these masterful, yet as always in adventure, ultimately impotent figures, the narrator begins his return to the center. As with *Heart of Darkness*, whose composition is at the heart of Sebald's book, there is no redemption, only itinerary and recounting.

The immediate occasion of the narrator's inclusion of Conrad in his tale is his recollection of falling asleep while watching a TV program about Roger Casement. Sebald connects that memory to two facts: that Conrad saw Casement in Africa and that Conrad took ship on coastal steamers out of Lowestoft (which the narrator also visits). The process of slipping from one main figure to another is a standard effect in Scott and is part of a technique of linkage that characterizes adventure. (For example in *Guy Mannering*, where Mannering appears initially to be the central character, he is superseded by Van Beest Brown, the "real" hero, and then returns to close the circle at the end.) Sebald's chapter on Conrad begins with Casement, who met Conrad in Africa and whom Conrad, according to the narrator, "unter den . . . Europäern, denen er dort begegnete, für den einzigen geradsinnigen Menschen gehalten hat" (considered . . . the only man of integrity among the Europeans whom he had encountered there; *RS*, 126/104). In the first image we have of Casement he is exactly the sort of imperturbable master of the universe that the demonic always appears to be:

> Ich habe ihn einmal, so ein mir seltsamerweise wortwörtlich gegen-
> wärtig gebliebenes Zitat aus dem Kongo-Tagebuch Conrads, nur mit
> einem Stecken bewaffnet und nur in Begleitung eines Loanda-Jungen

und seiner englischen Bulldogen Biddy und Paddy in die gewaltige Wildnis aufbrechen sehen. . . . Und einige Monate darauf sah ich ihn dann, seinen Stecken schwingend, mit dem Jungen, der das Bündel trug, und den Hunden aus der Wildnis wieder hervorkommend, etwas magerer vielleicht, aber sonst so unbeschadet, als kehrte er gerade von einem Nachmittagsspaziergang im Hyde Park zurück.

[I've seen him start off into an unspeakable wilderness (thus the exact words of a quotation from Conrad, which has remained in my head) swinging a crookhandled stick, with two bulldogs: Paddy (white) and Biddy (brindle) at his heels and a Loanda boy carrying a bundle. A few months afterwards it so happened that I saw him come out again, leaner, a little browner, with his stick, dogs, and Loanda boy, and quietly serene as though he had been for a stroll in the park. (*RS*, 126/104)].

The figure of Casement almost immediately dissolves as the narrator rehearses Conrad's life, starting with his family's exile to Vologda, continuing with his mother's death from tuberculosis, his father's death and the immense funeral procession for his interment, his education, early voyages, and love life, and ending with an account of Conrad's voyage up the Congo, in which Marlow and Conrad are blended into one figure, just as Sebald and his narrator merge into one another. The narrator rehearses Marlow's descriptions of his history as though they were Conrad's biography: Marlow's "It [the map] had ceased to be a blank space of delightful mystery — a white patch for a boy to dream gloriously over" (*H*, 22) becomes "Damals war der Kongo nur ein weißer Fleck auf der Afrikakarte gewesen, über die er [Conrad] . . . gebeugt saß oft stundenlang" (At that time the Congo had been but a white patch on the map of Africa over which he [Conrad] had often pored for hours; *RS*, 143/117).[48] The story of Conrad's life dissolves into the narrator's description of Ostend, followed by an excursus on the ugliness of Brussels and the Waterloo monument (that in itself echoes Marlow's distaste for that city from *Heart*) — the narrator seems to view Belgian hideousness as retribution for its rapacity in the Congo); and then moves into an account of Casement's battles to expose the greed and folly of colonial exploitation, his final disastrous engagement with the cause of Irish independence, and his death by hanging.

Like other demonic males of adventure Conrad and Casement represent an unsuccessful struggle to constrain the powers of the world at the center. Both are described as imprisoned by their pasts and unable to accommodate themselves to the present, compelled to repeat the conflict that shaped them. Sebald consistently focuses on Conrad's "lang anhaltende Verzweiflungsanfälle" (protracted bouts of despair; *RS*, 147/121) rather than his success as a writer, and Casement is described as someone whose "bedingsloser Einsatz für die Rechtlosen und Verfolgten" (unconditional partisanship for the victims and those who had no rights) was incompatible with a successful career in the English foreign office (*RS,* 156/128). From the "grünen Winter" (green winter) of Vologda, where "alles ringsum versinkt, verfault und verrotet" (everything round about rots, decays and sinks into the ground; *RS,* 128/105), to Matadi on the Congo, "eine desolate . . . Ansiedlung, die wie ein Geschwür den Schutt überzieht, der seit Jahrtausenden ausgeworfen wird . . . (a desolate settlement . . . like an ulcer . . . fester[ing] on the rubble thrown up over thousands of years; *RS,* 145/119), to the "besondere Häßlichkeit" (distinctive ugliness) of Belgium (*RS,* 149/122), to Casement's "kaum mehr zu identifizierenden Überresten" (scarcely identifiable . . . remains" (*RS,* 162–63/134) dug up from a lime pit in Pentonville prison, Sebald emphasizes the wretchedness of both men's lives and the ineffectiveness of their attempts to expose the inhumanity of colonial exploitation.

In his general disinterest in women Sebald displays the characteristic androcentric worldview of adventure, preeminently a world of male struggle. Sebald's wild woman, and the only woman whom he describes at any length, is the Empress Tz'u-hsi, who is evoked when the narrator sees a railway bridge built for a narrow-gauge train that was supposedly ordered by the Chinese court but never delivered (*RS,* 166/138). In the narrator's account, the Empress Tz'u-hsi poisoned her dead son's pregnant wife and installed her two-year-old nephew on the throne in order to preserve the power she had gained on the death of her husband. When she suspected her nephew of betrayal, she jailed him until his death. Tz'u-hsi completely disregards the masculine order of succession in pursuit of her ambitions: "die Art, in welcher sich die ansonsten äußerst konservativ eingestellte Kaiserinwitwe nötigenfalls hinwegzusetzen vermochte über die ehrwürdigsten Traditionen, war eines der Anzeichen ihres von Jahr zu Jahr rücksichtsloser werdenden Anspruchs auf unumschränkte Ausübung der Macht" (The way the Dowager Empress, in other respects extremely conservative in her views, contrived to flout the most venerable precepts when it became necessary, was one sign of her craving for absolute power, which grew more ruthless with every year that passed; *RS,* 179–80/149). As with other wild women, her unbending will to power destroys her family, since her ambition makes the orderly descent of inheritance impossible. Sebald's account of the immense expenditure necessary to maintain her household contrasts with the description of the massive drought that killed millions during her reign. The empress, who devoured all around her through her maniacal will to rule and lavish display of power, loved only silk worms, who struck her as "das ideale Volk, dienstfertig, todesbereit, in kurzer Frist beliebig vermehrbar, ausgerichtet nur auf den einzigen ihnen vorbestimmten Zweck" (ideal subjects, diligent in service, ready to die, capable of multiplying vastly within a short space of time, and fixed on their one sole preordained aim; *RS*, 183/151). Insanely focused on power and untamed by familial loyalty, Tz'u-hsi represents adventure's nightmarish fantasy of feral female voracity: she eats ground pearls to prolong her life while all around her die. The only thing that stops her is her own death, one that results directly from her habit of excess: she dies when she insists, despite her doctor's warning, on eating two helpings of dessert.

Sebald also conforms to adventure's generic imperatives in his version of the generative space, in an episode in which he gets lost on a heath between Dunwich and Middleton. In adventure, the hero's entry into this highly charged space is linked to an essential bit of information about his past that he must know to free himself of the trammels of his plot. In *Die Ringe des Saturn*, as one would expect from its pervasive melancholy, the moment is one of déjà vu and misery, and forcefully illustrates the circular and meaningless structure of the romance. The narrator's entry into the space begins with the requisite moment of inattention:

> In die unablässig in meinem Kopf sich drehenden Gedanken verloren . . ., wanderte ich auf der hellen Sandbahn dahin, bis ich zu meinem Erstaunen, um nicht zu sagen zu meinem Entsetzen, mich wiederfand vor demselben verwilderten Wäldchen, aus dem ich vor etwa einer Stunde oder, wie es mir jetzt schien, in irgendeiner fernen Vergangenheit hervorgetreten war.

> [Lost in the thoughts that went round in my head incessantly . . . I stuck to the sandy path until to my astonishment, not to say horror, I found myself back again at the same tangled thicket from which I had emerged about an hour before, or, as it now seemed to me, in some distant past. (*RS*, 204/171)]

Having finally escaped from the maze of paths, the narrator then reports dreaming months later of how "[ich] wieder über die unendlich verschlungenen Wege gegangen [bin] und habe wieder nicht aus dem, wie ich glaubte, eigens für mich angelegten Irrgarten herausgefunden" (walking the endlessly winding paths again, and again I could not find my way out of the maze which I was convinced had been created solely for me; *RS*, 205–6/173). In his dream the heath on which he wandered transforms into a yew maze with a pattern "von dem ich im Traum mit absoluter Sicherheit wußte, daß es einen Querschnitt darstellte durch mein Gehirn" (I knew in my dream, with absolute certainty, represented a cross-section of my brain; *RS*, 206/173). In this reverie the narrator experiences the generative space as a place of disorientation (he's wandering in circles) and solipsism (he sees a slice of his own brain) and, of course, as yet another occasion for a literary reference: in the dream he perceives "die Figur eines einzelnen greisen Mannes mit wirrem Haupthaar neben seiner toten Tochter, beide winzig wie auf einer meilenweit entfernten Bühne" (a solitary old man with a wild mane of hair [who] was kneeling beside his dead daughter, both of them so tiny, as if on a stage a mile off; *RS, 208/174*), clearly a reference to Lear. The narrator recounts Lear's final plea at second hand and characteristically adds, "Kein letzter Seufzer, kein letztes Wort zu hören" (no last sigh, no last words were to be heard); Lear's pathetic words can only be rehearsed without any immediacy — they fail to resound (*RS, 208/174*). This moment of intense disorientation, alienation, and despair marks the furthest point of the narrator's journey. Like all heroes, he can neither explain how he got in nor how he came out: "Ich kann nicht sagen, . . . auf welche Weise ich zuletzt einen Ausweg gefunden habe" (I cannot say how . . . I found a way out; *RS, 205/172*). Having experienced the generative space he begins the return that finally ends with his call to Clara.

Readers of Sebald's work regularly mention the series of deliberately inept photographs that illustrate *Die Ringe des Saturn* and are a feature in all of his fictions. The inclusion of these images is seen by critics as integral to the baffling generic status of his work and are taken to be a token of his postmodern amorphousness, a display of arbitrary yet evocative detritus. But when his work is aligned with the adventure genre, the photographs' "documentary" purpose, their faux realism, evokes instead the map, a classic motif of romance fiction. (Indeed, one of the images in *Die Ringe des Saturn* is a map of the area around Orford [*RS, 277/232*].) Adventure's cartography — Tolkien's map of Middle Earth,[49] Le Guin's map of Earthsea,[50] Herbert's map of Arrakis (*Dune*)[51] — with its specious exactness about purely imaginary spaces — shores up the supposed realness of the fictional and serves to situate the reader in a mapped, hence real (or at least "realistic") universe.[52] Sebald's photographs may be of "real" things, but they function within *Die Ringe des Saturn* as the map on the frontispiece of an adventure novel does: they create the illusion of real space and time in a literary universe that exists only as text.

In *Die Ringe des Saturn* the highly mannered consciousness of the narrative as fiction that is endemic to adventure becomes an exaggerated mode of being: the narrator's walk is only important as a pretext for artful musing. The narrative illusion of "real happenings" is so little fleshed out as to be skeletal, and so little adventurous as to be trivial. In an article that discusses *Die Ringe des Saturn* as a "book about the erosion of confidence in the power of representation,"[53] John Beck asserts that the novel is a "document that consistently and visibly repeats the crimes it also exposes: *Die Ringe des Saturn* . . . is the carrier of catastrophe and also its historian."[54] But the consciousness of writing as fantasy, as wholly factitious, is constitutive of adventure, which is one of the reasons that Conrad reverts to it as a form. Its horizon of expectation is precisely the horizon of the conventionally not-real. From the opening passage of *Die Ringe des Saturn*, when the narrator painfully creeps to his window and compares himself to Gregor Samsa of Kafka's *Metamorphosis*,[55] unable to recall the sense of liberation that looking out the window once gave him (*RS*, 13/5), the intense artificiality and literariness of *Die Ringe des Saturn*'s narrative links Sebald to other writers of adventure who allow the exotic and untamable to erupt, if not quite at home, then at least right next door. Sebald uses the adventure plot to explore the impact of the form detached from any semblance of regenerative meaning (reinsertion into the world at the center in Scott; a dream of autarchy in Dumas; instruction and amusement in Verne). *Die Ringe des Saturn*, like Conrad's *Heart of Darkness* to which it is an unstinting homage, is a sustained meditation on a form that goes nowhere and means nothing.

Sebald's ornate last sentence reiterates his recurring theme of death and decay:

> Und Thomas Browne, der als Sohn eines Seidenhändlers dafür ein Auge gehabt haben mochte, vermerkt an irgendeiner, von mir nicht mehr auffindbaren Stelle seiner Schrift *Pseudodoxia Epidemica*, in Holland sei es zu seiner Zeit Sitte gewesen, im Hause eines Verstorbenen alle Spiegel und alle Bilder, auf denen Landschaften, Menschen oder die Früchte der Felder zu sehen waren, mit seidenem Trauerflor zu verhängen, damit nicht die den Körper verlassende Seele auf ihrer letzten Reise abgelenkt würde, sei es durch ihren eigenen Anblick, sei es durch den ihrer bald auf immer verlorenenen Heimat.

> [And Sir Thomas Browne, who was the son of a silk merchant and may well have had an eye for these things, remarks in a passage of the *Pseudodoxia Epidemica* that I can no longer find that in the Holland of his time it was customary, in a home where there had been a death, to drape black mourning ribbons over all the mirrors and all canvasses depicting landscapes or people or the fruits of the field, so that the soul, as it left the body, would not be distracted on its final journey, either by a reflection of itself or by a last glimpse of the land now being lost for ever. (*RS*, 350/296)]

As a hero, the narrator ends where he began, seemingly with a meditation on the "land now being lost forever." But his focus is not on the lost landscape, but rather on the silk that covers it. His evocation of the mourning ribbons is immediately preceded by a description of the Duchess of Tieck's attire at Queen Victoria's funeral, "einem wahrhaft atemberaubenden . . . Kleid aus schwarzer Mantuaseide, von der die Seidenweberei Willett & Nephew in Norwich . . . zu diesem einzigen Zweck und zur Demonstration ihrer auf dem Gebiet der Trauerseide nach wie vor unübertroffenen Kunstfertigkeit eine sechzig Schritt lange Bahn herstellte" (a breathtaking gown . . . all of black Mantua silk of which the Norwich silk weavers Willett & Nephew . . . had created, uniquely for this occasion and in order to demonstrate their unsurpassed skills in the manufacture of mourning silks, a length of some sixty paces; *RS*, 350/296). Like the Duchess who flaunts her extravagant mourning, the narrator is fixated on flaunting his despair, the despair of one who reflects on a story that has nothing "inside like a kernel," but conveys only its self-reflective facticity, Conrad's "immense jabber . . . without any kind of sense" (*H*, 80). And Sebald's insistence on melancholy should not obscure for us the sustaining certainties he shares with every adventure hero: a place to return to, food to eat, a "Clara" to call for a ride home.

Mark McCulloh has pointed out that *Die Ringe des Saturn* has many connections to the dream/nightmare itinerary described by Freud in his essay "The Uncanny."[56] Freud's essay is itself a highly condensed adventure narrative, and in this sense the feeling of "Auswegslosigkeit" or "exit-less-ness," that "most modern of conditions in which one is both helpless . . . and hopeless"[57] is a reaction not so much to the world as to a narrative universe driven by the romance plot. For Sebald and his narrator everything decays and nothing changes. The end of his journey is the beginning of his recounting of it, which brings him again to the end in a recursive structure. Adventure presents the world as immutable while distracting the reader by endless fabulation. No matter how much froth it kicks up, adventure is always, finally, about stasis. While it ostensibly celebrates the wild and unusual, it persistently enacts the return to the ordinary. Marlow and Sebald's narrator enliven the humdrum space of England by their evocations of elsewhere; both begin their journeys in a place the reader will recognize, even if the latter's acquaintance with this place is purely literary, and both end where they began — in the public world that remains unchanged at the center.

In his discussion of genre in "The Soul and the Harpy," Moretti proposes a "slower" literary history, one that is more inclusive of fictions that have not survived the time of their production and that would emphasize continuities of form rather than innovative discontinuities.[58] For Moretti, a focus on continuity rather than rupture allows a fuller literary history to be achieved, one more able to confront a wider range of texts and less susceptible to the vagaries of taste. To place Scott, Conrad, and Sebald side by side, ignoring the differences of their fictions, is perhaps to indulge too ruthlessly in such a recuperation of generic norms, but the formal similarities of these authors' plots reveal the continuing force of the adventure/romance form.[59]

Loosened from an allegorical framework, the romancer continues endlessly to fabulate — just look at the shelves of science fiction and fantasy in any book store. As literary readers we have relegated adventure to the beach. But Conrad's trip up the river and Sebald's walk along the shore suggest that adventure, fabulation empty of regenerative meaning and chasing endlessly after its own tale, continues to generate its effects not merely in light reading but also where it is least expected. Conrad ends his story at the beginning of the ebb; Sebald "[bringt] [s]eine Aufzeichnungen zum Abschluß" (brings [his] notes to a conclusion; *RS,* 348/294) on a Maundy Thursday with a characteristic recital of the disasters that have happened on that day. For both, the unsatisfactory form of adventure and its discontents is literalized in a figure of decay, Marlow's ebb, the narrator's mysterious, paralyzing illness. And yet, for both, the romance also offers resolution — they are, after all, home. For the reader, the idle hour has been whiled away and nothing has changed, and that, of course, is the whole point.

Notes

This essay is a modified version of a chapter that was previously published in my book, *Romancing the Novel: Adventure from Scott to Sebald* (Lewisburg: Bucknell UP, 2007); it is reproduced here with the permission of Bucknell University Press. The epigraph at the start of this chapter is from Joseph Conrad, *Heart of Darkness with The Congo Diary,* ed. Robert Hampson (New York: Penguin, 1995), 22. Further references to this work are given in the text, using the abbreviation *H* followed by the page number(s). All translations in this chapter are my own unless otherwise credited.

[1] Sir Walter, Scott, *Waverley,* ed. Andrew Hook (New York: Penguin, 1988).

[2] Ian Duncan, *Modern Romance and Transformations of the Novel* (Cambridge: Cambridge UP, 1992), 61–62. Duncan ends this passage by writing that Scott represents a "troublesome kind of artistic greatness, whereby the powerful pleasures and important truths offered by fictions are precisely those of its inauthenticity" (62).

[3] Sir Walter Scott, *Redgauntlet* (New York: The Waverley Book Co. 1898).

[4] H. Rider Haggard, *King Solomon's Mines* (New York: Oxford UP, 1989).

[5] Robert Louis Stevenson, *Treasure Island,* ed. Emma Letley (New York: Oxford UP, 1985).

[6] J. Hillis Miller sees this as not a generic problem but one central to writing itself: "By unveiling the lack of unveiling in *Heart of Darkness,* I have become another witness in my turn, as much guilty as any other in the line of witnesses of covering over while claiming to illuminate. My *Aufklärung* too has been of the continuing impenetrability of Conrad's *Heart of Darkness.*" J. Hillis Miller, "*Heart of Darkness* Revisited," in *Conrad Revisited: Essays for the Eighties,* ed. Ross C. Murfin (Tuscaloosa: U of Alabama P, 1985), 31–50; here 50.

[7] Sebald's narrator begins the account of his walk by recounting a subsequent hospitalization: "auf den Tag genau ein Jahr nach dem Beginn meiner Reise [wurde] ich. . . in das Spital der Provinzhauptstadt Norwich [eingeliefert], wo ich dann, in Gedanken zumindest, begonnen habe mit der Niederschrift der nachstehenden Seiten" (a year to the day after I began my tour, I was taken to the hospital in Norwich. . . . It was then that I began in my thoughts to write these pages;

RS, 11–12/3–4). While the illness may be a deferred result of the walk, it is thus certainly the occasion for his account of it.

[8] Fredric Jameson, *The Political Unconscious: Narrative as a Socially Symbolic Act* (Ithaca, NY: Cornell UP, 1981), 206.

[9] Linda Dryden, *Joseph Conrad and the Imperial Romance* (New York: St. Martin's, 2000); Edward Said, *Culture and Imperialism* (New York: Vintage, 1993) and *Orientalism* (New York: Pantheon, 1978); Andrea White, *Joseph Conrad and the Adventure Tradition* (Cambridge and New York: Cambridge UP, 1993).

[10] Said, *Culture and Imperialism*, 23.

[11] By limiting their comparisons to Haggard, Henty, et al., critics have neglected Conrad's strongest forerunner, Scott, who shares with Conrad a wary and deeply ambiguous relation to the form they both so artfully manipulate. On Scott's complex relation to the romance see Ian Duncan, *Modern Romance*. For Conrad's relation to Scott see Robert Caserio, "*The Rescue* and the Ring of Meaning," in *Conrad Revisited: Essays for the Eighties*, ed. Ross C. Murfin, 125–50.

[12] Margo Jefferson, "Writing in the Shadows," the *New York Times Book Review*, 18 Mar. 2001.

[13] Anthony Lane, "Higher Ground," *New Yorker*, 29 May 2000, 128.

[14] Alexandre Dumas, *Le comte de Monte Cristo* (Paris: Gallimard, 1981).

[15] Geoffrey Household, *Rogue Male* (New York: Penguin, 1977).

[16] Sir Walter Scott, *Guy Mannering* (New York, Penguin, 2003).

[17] H. Rider Haggard, *She* (New York: Oxford UP, 1992).

[18] Robert Caserio's discussion of Conrad's link to Scott in "*The Rescue* and the Ring of Meaning" focuses on the act of rescue as an echo of the code of individual aristocratic generosity that he sees as central to Scott's fiction, in which characters who live in a bureaucratized, democratic world arrogate to themselves the power of action formerly associated with a king's right to forgive. For Caserio the question is how Conrad, a modernist, can use a plot derived from Scott. His answer, although he applies it to Conrad's later fiction and explicitly excludes *Heart*, is that "Conrad could . . . dramatize the romance of the rescue event as . . . the story of representation in art transcending art so as to stand for life" (136). In this way Conrad manages to avoid the "aestheticization" of romance that Caserio associates with Stevenson.

[19] See Said, *Culture*, 23–31, esp. 24. Conrad's complex relation to empire-making and storytelling as related enterprises can also be linked to Scott's elaborate prefatory material. The narrative frameworks provided by Peter Pattieson for the series *Tales of My Landlord* emphasize the stories as artifacts. The self-consciousness that Said ascribes to Conrad's Polish background can also be linked to Scott, an author at the heart of the English novel tradition.

[20] White, *Conrad and Adventure*, 203.

[21] Dryden, *Imperial Romance*, 193.

[22] In contrast, Peter Brooks focuses on *Heart* as an example of a Freudian compulsion to repeat as an affirmation of community. Brooks cites Benjamin's "The

Storyteller" in order to read *Heart* as a novel that illustrates the imperative to narrate: "The effort to narrate one's life story as it relates to their [the dead's] numinous and baleful presence is never done. One must tell and tell again." Brooks, *Reading for the Plot: Design and Intention in Narrative* (New York: Vintage, 1984), 263. My argument runs parallel to that of Brooks but suggests that the problem of irrecuperable meaning is a structural effect of the genre.

[23] Charles Kingsley, *Westward Ho!* (New York: Dutton: Everyman's Library, 1967), 10.

[24] For a straight Freudian reading of Marlow's relation to the map that both conflates Marlow with Conrad and also illustrates the literalization of literary tropes as psychic realities, see Richard F. Sterba's "Remarks on Joseph Conrad's *Heart of Darkness,*" *Journal of the American Psychoanalytic Association* 13.3 (1965): 570–83; here 574: "The blank space on the map must be understood in terms of 'anatomical geography' — it presents the unknown territory of the female genital, which Marlow as a little boy intended to contact and explore when he grew up."

[25] Sir Walter Scott, *Old Mortality* (New York: Penguin, 1985).

[26] Jules Verne, *20,000 Leagues under the Sea*, trans. William Butcher (Oxford: Oxford UP, 1998).

[27] In "Three Ways of Going Wrong: Kipling, Conrad, Coetzee," *Modern Language Review* 95.1 (Jan. 2000): 18–27, Douglas Kerr links Marlow to other fictional Europeans who "go wrong" by obtaining too much information about the natives: "each of these outlaws . . . is treated as suspicious, at the least, by his own people, because each has gone beyond the pale, known and seen too much, and betrayed the public codes of his kind" (24).

[28] Although Marlow judges Kurtz's ambition "to have kings meet him at railway-stations" as "contemptibly childish" (110).

[29] Feminist criticism has linked the African queen and the Intended as two faces of the coin of Conrad's patriarchal preconceptions about women. See Johanna M. Smith, "'Too Beautiful Altogether': Patriarchal Ideology in *Heart of Darkness,*" in Murfin, *Joseph Conrad: Heart of Darkness* (New York: St Martin's, 1989), 169–84; Nina Pelikan Straus, "The Exclusion of the Intended from Secret Sharing in Conrad's *Heart of Darkness,*" *Novel: A Forum on Fiction* 20.2 (Winter 1987): 123–37; Rita Bode, "'They . . . should be well out of it': The Women in *Heart of Darkness,*" *Conradiana* 26.1 (1994): 20–34.

[30] In a lovely example of unreflective gender positioning, Addison Bross writes: "In his awe of woman's absurd, irrational belief, Marlow represses his *rational nature*" (emphasis mine); notice how the Intended has become generalized to "woman." Bross, "The Unextinguishable Light of Belief: Conrad's Attitude towards Women," *Conradiana* 2 (1969–70): 39–46; here 43.

[31] In Bruce Stark's view Marlow does not tell a lie but rather states the truth, because the Intended and the Horror are actually different names for the same thing: "If Kurtz cried out 'The horror! The horror!' at some image of the Intended, the question then arises did Marlow in fact lie . . ." (553). On the next

page he answers his own question: "The answer is an ironic 'yes and no' . . . from Conrad's point of view . . . one of the Intended's names is the 'The Horror'" (555). Stark, "Kurtz's Intended: The Heart of the *Heart of Darkness*," *Texas Studies in Literature and Language* 16.3 (1974): 535–55. In a different context Herbert Klein repeats the same observation: "Kurtz's last words ('The Horror! The Horror!') and the Intended's name have become interchangeable." Klein, "Charting the Unknown: Conrad, Marlow, and the World of Women," *Conradiana*, 20.2 (1988): 147–57; here 149–50.

[32] As Marlow speaks, the unnamed narrator twice mentions the fact that he, at least, is not asleep: "The others might have been asleep, but I was awake" (*H*, 50); "I knew there was at least one listener awake besides myself" (*H*, 60), thereby suggesting that Marlow may be discoursing to a largely indifferent audience.

[33] Tzvetan Todorov, "Knowledge in the Void: *Heart of Darkness*," *Conradiana* 21.3 (1989): 161–72; here 172.

[34] "Fue una mentira piadosa para consolar a una mujer que sufría? Sí, tambien. Pero fue, sobre todo, la aceptación de que hay verdades tan intolerables en la vida que justifican las mentiras. Es decir, las ficciones; es decir, la literatura." Mario Vargas-Llosa, "Extemporáneos: Las raíces de lo humano," *Letras Libres* (Dec. 2001): 18–22; here 22. (Was it a pious lie in order to console a suffering woman? Yes, of course. But it was, above all, the acceptance of the idea that there are truths so intolerable that lies are justified. That is, fictions, that is, literature.). The dismissal of adventure as the genre of Marlow's story overgeneralizes its effect and turns it into an unsolvable epistemological conundrum, rather than a more limited, and therefore more pointed, story about the compulsions of one very seductive form of story.

[35] Hillis Miller, "*Heart of Darkness* Revisited," 36.

[36] Hillis Miller, "*Heart of Darkness* Revisited," 39.

[37] Bette London makes a parallel argument in a different vein: "The narrative registers the lies that support cultural authority — that promote the illusion of an autonomous identity. It registers the lie of voice itself." London, "Reading Race and Gender in Conrad's Dark Continent," *Criticism* 31.3 (1989): 235–52; here 249.

[38] James Wood, "The Right Thread," *The New Republic* 6 (July 1998): 38–42; here 38.

[39] Alan Bennett, "2002 Diary," *London Review of Books*, 2 Jan. 2003, 5.

[40] Sir Walter Scott, *Waverley*, 139.

[41] John Beck, "Reading Room: Erosion and Sedimentation in Sebald's Suffolk," in *W. G. Sebald: A Critical Companion*, ed. J. J. Long and Anne Whitehead (Seattle: U of Washington P, 2004), 75–88; here 82.

[42] Greg Bond remarks of the passage where Sebald dilates at length on what sounds like a truly dreadful meal, "this kind of stylistic faux pas is what happens when the melancholy gaze has to be upheld at all costs, even when there is nothing for it to fix itself upon." Bond, "On the Misery of Nature and the Nature of Misery," in Long and Whitehead, *A Critical Companion*, 31–44; here 41.

[43] McCulloh remarks, "Astonishingly, a Suffolk walking tour with Sebald can connect one with not just Africa but the Orient as well. He is intent on uncovering yet

more astonishing facts buried just below the surface of contemporary life." Mark R. McCulloh, *Understanding W. G. Sebald* (Columbia: U of South Carolina P, 2003), 71.

[44] Jules Verne, *Journey to the Center of the Earth,* trans. Lowell Blair (New York: Bantam Classics, 1991).

[45] Bennett, "2002 Diary."

[46] And ". . . war es auch mir ein Rätsel, was für Wesen hier einstmals gelebt und gearbeitet hatten und wozu die primitiven Anlagen im Innern der Bunker, die Eisenschienen unter den Decken . . . gedient haben mochten" (the beings who had once worked and lived here were an enigma, as was the purpose of the primitive contraptions and fittings inside the bunkers, the iron rails under the ceilings" (*RS,* 282–83/237).

[47] Sir Walter Scott, *The Bride of Lammermoor* (Edinburgh: Edinburgh UP, 1995).

[48] Conrad's "there was in it one river . . . resembling an immense snake uncoiled" (*H,* 22) becomes Sebald's "weil die Kartographen in solche Leerräume gern irgendein exotisches Tier . . . hineinmalten, machten sie aus dem Kongo-Fluß . . . eine quer durch das immense Land sich ringelnde Schlange" (as cartographers would often embellish such empty spaces with drawings of exotic beasts . . . they had rendered the Congo . . . as a snake coiling through the blank, uncharted land" (*RS,* 143/117). The description of the grove of death is found on pp. 34–35 in *Heart* and on pp. 119–10 in *Ringe des Saturn.*

[49] J. R. R. Tolkien, *The Lord of the Rings* (Boston, MA: Houghton Mifflin, 2005).

[50] Ursula Le Guin, *A Wizard of Earthsea* (New York: Bantam, 1975).

[51] Frank Herbert, *Dune* (New York: Ace Books, 1999).

[52] In his essay "My First Book" Stevenson remarks on the importance of maps for the writer: "[He] who is faithful to his map . . . and draws from it his inspiration, daily and hourly, gains positive support. . . . The tale has its root there; it grows in that soil" (*Treasure Island,* 200).

[53] Beck, "Erosion," 75.

[54] Beck, "Erosion," 88.

[55] Franz Kafka, *The Metamorphosis and Other Stories,* trans. Willa and Edwin Muir (New York: Schocken Books, 1988).

[56] Sigmund Freud, "The Uncanny" in *The Standard Edition of the Complete Psychological Writings of Sigmund Freud,* vol. 17 (London: Hogarth, 1953–74), 227–68; here 245.

[57] McCulloh, *Understanding W. G. Sebald,* 58.

[58] Franco Moretti, *Signs Taken for Wonders: Essays in the Sociology of Literary Forms* (London: Verso, 1983), 16.

[59] Although perhaps things are changing. J. Jeffrey Franklin has put together Haggard's *She* and Eliot's *Middlemarch* in a very interesting article on memory and Darwinism in Victorian fiction: Franklin, "Memory as the Nexus of Identity, Empire, and Evolution in George Eliot's *Middlemarch* and H. Rider Haggard's *She,*" *Cahiers victoriens et édouardiens* 53.13 (2001): 141–69.

IV: Topographies and Theories

10: Mapping Historical Networks in *Die Ringe des Saturn*

Barbara Hui

I<small>N</small> *D<small>IE</small> R<small>INGE</small> <small>DES</small> S<small>ATURN</small>* the unnamed first-person narrator recounts his 1992 summer walking tour of a thirty-odd mile coastal stretch of the Suffolk region, which lies in the easternmost part of England. From the vantage point of the present, and from his perspective as a pilgrim visiting the region on foot, the narrator contrasts the deserted, decaying towns and empty estates of contemporary Suffolk with tales of the area's rise to prominence during the nineteenth century, when British colonial power was at its height and Suffolk was home to opulent wealth and a place of countless comings and goings. As the narrator works his way along this travel path, he also departs the English coast at various points to tell related stories of more distant places and times. The book thus becomes filled with geography, from England to Western Europe, Eastern Europe, Turkey, Western Africa, and the Caribbean, with additional mentions of Jerusalem, the United States, Argentina, and other locations around the world.

History in this pilgrimage narrative develops along both temporal and spatial axes — space is not merely the inert container in which events take place, but rather a dynamic dimension with a developmental logic of its own. I argue that Sebald adopts the postmodern, late-twentieth-century logic of the network in recounting this trek through the English countryside. At the same time, Sebald wraps the travelogue story structurally and thematically in a secondary narrative with a different spatial logic, namely the historical philosophy of seventeenth-century physician and writer Sir Thomas Browne. Browne's pre-Enlightenment worldview espouses a spatiality of history that is not networked but rather cosmological. These two spatial logics of the narrative — the *networked* and the *cosmological* — are woven together side-by-side throughout the narrative of *Die Ringe des Saturn*, making for a text whose spatial and temporal dimensions are both extraordinarily expansive and complex.

"A Global Sense of the Local, a Global Sense of Place"

In the 1980s and 1990s during the "spatial turn" in critical theory, there occurred the overall recognition that a thorough-going change needs to take place in the way in which thinkers conceive of space and place. Theorists such as Michel Foucault,[1] Henri Lefebvre,[2] Edward Said,[3] and Edward Soja[4] begin in multiple ways to salvage space from its longstanding stepsister[5] definition in Western thought as the negative inverse of time, arguing that far from being the inactive container in which historical events take place, it is instead a dynamic social, political, and historical dimension worthy of rigorous theorization. As a consequence of these arguments, space and spatiality in general begin to play a more central role in critical theory overall. In her 1991 essay "A Global Sense of Place,"[6] British geographer Doreen Massey intervenes in the burgeoning spatial discourse within her own particular field to argue for a reconceptualization of "place." I would like to explore Massey's concept of place in some depth here, as I have found her definition to be extremely useful in understanding the spatial imaginary as it exists in the narrative of *Die Ringe des Saturn*.

Massey poses her essay as a challenge to what she notes is the current tendency among those writing on "space, place and postmodern times" to embrace the notion that post-modernity ushers in a new experience of space, which therefore also requires a new spatial epistemology.[7] Instead of rejecting old concepts, Massey seeks to redefine them in a way that is attuned to the changes that have come about in the postmodern era of globalization. Although Massey does not explicitly name his work in her essay, one of the most influential proponents of a radically new postmodern spatiality is geographer David Harvey. In *The Condition of Postmodernity* (1990), he makes the argument that our experience of time and space in the late twentieth century has changed so fundamentally that we have entered a new stage of human history.[8] Harvey and those who write in his wake observe that the development of new technologies such as transcontinental telephony, airplane travel, satellites, and the internet[9] effectively compress once dauntingly vast distances into manageable, even instantly traversable ones.

Massey begins her essay by noting that in general, postmodern geographers have not only accepted this concept of space-time compression but have as a corollary also begun to reject the concept of "the local" altogether, thinking of it as an outdated, reactionary idea that can only work to the advantage of traditionalists' nostalgia for a myth of unified origins. Massey points out, however, that not everybody in the world experiences postmodern spatiality in the same way: consider the woman who spends hours a day on foot collecting water in sub-Saharan Africa vs. the jet-setting first-world businessman, for example (148–49). We must recognize the fact that space is "socially differentiated": many people still experience space in terms of local places, living lives that are relatively untouched by new technologies. Instead of privileging the experience and perspective of those who experience space-time compression to the fullest and applying it across space in an uncritical manner, Massey argues for a socially attuned understanding of space and place. Thus she redefines "place" in terms of dynamic processes that constantly change over time rather than as fixed physical entities. Localities are not defined by geographically stable boundaries, but rather by their linkage to other places. These other places, moreover, constitute the make-up of that local place. Thus in Massey's way of thinking, one can and should still conceive of the local, albeit as a social, dynamic entity that owes its particularity to its location in a larger global network of places.

Massey elucidates her redefinition of place by way of a vivid visual explanation:

> In this [alternative interpretation] of space, what gives a place its specificity is not some long internalized history but the fact that it is constructed out of a particular constellation of social relations, meeting and weaving together at a particular locus. If one moves in from the satellite towards the globe, holding all those networks of social relations and movements and communications in one's head, then each "place" can be seen as a particular, unique, point of their intersection. It is, indeed, a meeting place. Instead then, of thinking of places as areas with boundaries around, they can be imagined as articulated moments in networks of social relations and understandings, but where a large proportion of those relations, experiences and understandings are constructed on a far larger scale than what we happen to define for that moment as the place itself, whether it be a street, a region, or even a continent. (28)

Massey's worldview in this lucid passage is quintessentially postmodern in the sense that it has its material basis in late-twentieth-century technologies. She can reliably refer to both a "satellite view of the globe" and a "network of social relations" and trust that her readers are familiar with these concepts. While the idea of the network per se is not a new one, in 1991 it is in the process of gaining new currency with the impending explosion of internet technology. While Harvey and others point to travel and communications technologies as having provided the material basis for the new space-time compression of postmodernity, Massey here leverages technological perspectives and paradigms in order to argue for a more socially nuanced understanding of globalization. Her call is truly to cultivate "a global sense of the local, a global sense of place" (156). I will now

280 + ◆ BARBARA HUI

move on to examine how her theories relate to Sebald's travel narrative in *Die Ringe des Saturn*.

Mapping *Die Ringe des Saturn*

The text of *Die Ringe des Saturn* is divided into ten chapters, with chapters II through IX devoted to a retelling of the narrator's walking tour through Suffolk in the summer of 1992. When mapped, this travelogue has a more-or-less simple figure-eight shape, as represented by the pins and dashed line on the map in figure 6. The narrator first walks from north to south along the coast from Lowestoft to Walberswick, then veers inland to visit Woodbridge, next heads briefly back out toward the coast to Ordfordness, and finally walks north through the countryside, ending his journey in Bungay a few miles inland from where his pilgrimage began. The local travelogue narrative — that is, the text via which the narrator retells his walking tour — unfolds in stride with the narrator's journey and is thus temporally and spatially linear. This unity of space and time does not hold for long, however. As the narrator progresses along this route, he often departs this local path to tell tales that are spatially and temporally removed from it. These interstitial narratives — which as discrete stories vary in length from a few sentences to several dozen pages — move around in time and space, adding the elements of narrative complexity and destabilization that are so characteristic of Sebald's novel-length texts in general. In the context of this sometimes Gordian narrative style, the central walking-tour narrative serves as a reorienting mechanism for the text and a reminder that in spite of its global reach, this is ultimately an English pilgrimage. The narrator always eventually returns to this spatio-temporally stable core, and this is the narrative node around which the rest of the sprawling story is structured.

When mapped as a whole, the geography of *Die Ringe des Saturn* that emerges has the shape of a global network, with Suffolk as the northern node in a vast web of intercontinental histories. The map in figure 7 represents several of the major connections between Suffolk and the rest of the world. As one can see, the spatiality of Suffolk as portrayed in *Die Ringe des Saturn* cannot be represented by just one or even a few pins in a regional map — here the area has worldwide dimensions. In other words, Suffolk's relationship with other places is intrinsic to its definition and therefore also part of its spatial scope. Throughout the travelogue the narrator tells tales that show how Suffolk has been significantly affected by a number of major modern events, including British and Dutch colonialism and imperialism, the industrialization of the North Sea fishing industry, the decline of Chinese imperialism, global

Fig. 6. Map of Suffolk, with the narrator's journey indicated by numbered pins. © 2010 Google — map data © 2010 Tele Atlas.

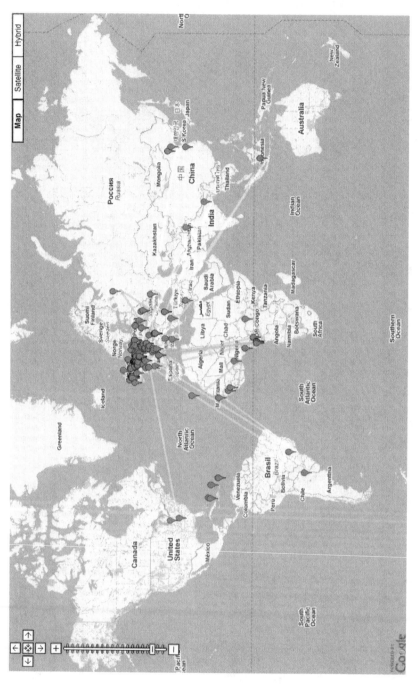

Fig. 7. World map showing locations mentioned in Die Ringe des Saturn. © *2010 Google — map data* © *2010 Tele Atlas.*

deforestation, and the French Revolution. Conversely, Sebald demonstrates the way in which these far-flung places have been affected by events that originated in Suffolk. The travelogue narrative thus builds for the reader a sense of the local that is neither inward-looking nor bounded but rather shows the area's particular character of place to be fundamentally defined and shaped by its location at the intersection of multiple global histories. Sebald's concept of place in this account is very much in line with the "global sense of the local" that Massey advocates. Sebald differs from Massey, however, in that he focuses on what Andreas Huyssen has called "present pasts."[10] As in his other novel-length prose texts, Sebald is interested in investigating and exposing the history that lies within or underneath the ruins and topographies of the present. In *Die Ringe des Saturn*, this historical investigation takes on particularly global, spatial dimensions.

And yet in spite of the worldwide reach of his narrative, the narrator remains remarkably focused on the locale of Suffolk itself. This is not a world history but rather a local history that is global in scope. The narrator takes pains to experience Suffolk from the perspective of an earthbound pilgrim: he goes on foot rather than by car, thereby shunning modern technologies that might compromise his immediate experience of the local. In so doing, he follows in the footsteps of his recently deceased colleague Michael Parkinson who, as the narrator notes in chapter I, believed that walking tours were the truest form of historical research and himself often embarked on long localized treks in connection with his studies of French-speaking Swiss writer Charles Ramuz (*RS*, 15/6).

The text of *Die Ringe des Saturn* quantifiably reflects this focus on the local: roughly a quarter of the place names mentioned in the book are located along the narrator's Suffolk walking path, while the remainder are scattered around the globe. As the stories become further removed from the Suffolk region, the places mentioned become less specific in scope: in Suffolk, the place names tend to be those of individual estates, churches, and other landmarks, or villages and towns, whereas in remote places, most place names are those of cities and entire regions, areas, or countries. And while the narrator describes the landscapes, houses, and views of Suffolk in the kind of detail that is informed and circumscribed by the perspective of experience, his descriptions of far-flung places such as China, western Africa, and South America are far more generalized. In fact, these narratives are written in an encyclopedic register — one that takes a broad summary overview, without giving any experiential detail. For example, Sebald's recounting of Joseph Conrad's and Roger Casement's life travels in chapter V, as well as his description of the Taiping Rebellion in China in chapter VI, read as though they were paraphrased from memoirs, biographies, and encyclopedia articles on each of those histories. Sebald's narrator takes care to point out the particular facts that connect these stories back to the local Suffolk history from which they were spawned but adds no descriptive embellishments or details to the basic events as they are presented in the narrative.

Sebald even makes two minor geographical errors concerning South America, further evidence that he is far more interested in detailing the history of the local than detailing the history of the remote. The first error occurs in regard to the place where Jorge Luis Borges wrote his story "Tlön, Uqbar, Orbis Tertius," which is referred to several times in *Die Ringe des Saturn*. The Sebaldian narrator describes the story as having been written in "1940 in Salto Oriental in Argentinien" (in 1940 at Salto Oriental in Argentina; *RS*, 87/67) and then later as "die im vorigen schon erwähnte argentinische Schrift" (the Argentinian tale I have referred to before; *RS*, 89/69). "Salto Oriental" is in fact the historical name for what is known today as "Salto," a city in northwestern Uruguay on the border with Argentina. Borges's note at the end of the story simply reads, "Salto Oriental, 1940,[11] and does not specify a country. Sebald seems to have made an error in placing Salto Oriental in Borges's home nation. Sebald's second geographical error — also relatively minor — again occurs with regard to a piece of secondary literature, this time Claude Lévi-Strauss's *Tristes Tropiques*. Here, the narrator refers to Levi-Strauss's description of "der Campos Elyseos . . ., einer Straße in São Paulo" (the Campos Elyseos, a street in São Paulo; *RS*, 110–11/89). In fact, Campos Elyseos is a low-income residential *neighborhood* in São Paulo. Ultimately, Sebald is more interested in composing a cogent work of art and gathering compelling examples of the historical cycle of rise and decline than he is in exhaustively researching the basis of his descriptions for strict factual accuracy.

Sebald's project is local and remains stubbornly so; the geographical errors described above attest to the fact that he did not spend time meticulously studying the history of far-off lands, nor did he spend time traveling to them. Indeed, according to Arthur Lubow, Sebald "derided the promiscuity of contemporary travel," saying,

> That is what is so awful about modern life — we never return. . . . One year we go to India and the next year to Peru and the next to Greenland. Because now you can go everywhere. I would much rather have half a dozen places that meant something to me than to say, at the end of my life, "I have been practically everywhere." The first visit doesn't reveal very much at all.[12]

This aversion to the dilettantism of tourism is reflected in the narrator's approach to historical research in *Die Ringe des Saturn*: this is "eine Englische Wallfahrt" (an English pilgrimage) and indeed, like a religious pilgrim, the narrator traverses his chosen locality (which is notably not far from Norwich, where Sebald himself lived) slowly, laboriously, and with a reverential attention to the distinct personalities of the region and its inhabitants. The word "Wallfahrt" does indeed have religious connotations, lending weight to the notion that this is a spiritually inflected, mystical exploration of history. The walking-tour narrative at the core of *Die Ringe des Saturn* is, then, a fiercely local story that is simultaneously and definitively global. To utilize Massey's conceptualization of space, I would argue that Sebald's narrative conveys "a global sense of the local, a global sense of place."[13]

In one of the interstitial passages during which the narrator departs his Suffolk coast walking path to tell a story about the global history of Suffolk, he recalls looking down onto the earth from a plane during a flight from Amsterdam to Norwich, and remarks that

> Gleich ob man über Neufundland fliegt oder bei Einbruch der Nacht über das von Boston bis Philadelphia reichende Lichtergewimmel, über die wie Perlmutt schimmernden Wüsten Arabiens, über das Ruhrgebiet oder den Frankfurter Raum, es ist immer, als gäbe es keine Menschen, als gäbe es nur das, was sie geschaffen haben und worin sie sich verbergen. . . . Und doch sind sie überall anwesend auf dem Antlitz der Erde, breiten sich stündlich weiter aus, bewegen sich durch die Waben hochaufragender Türme und sind in zunehmenden Maße eingespannt in Netzwerke von einer das Vorstellungsvermögen eines jeden einzelnen bei weitem übersteigenden Kompliziertheit, sei es so wie einst in den Diamantenminen Südafrikas zwischen Tausenden von Seilzügen und Winden, sei es wie heute in den Bürohallen der Börsen und Agenturen in den Strom der unablässig um den Erdball flutenden Information. Wenn wir uns aus solcher Höhe betrachten, ist es entsetzlich, wie wenig wir wissen über uns selbst, über unseren Zweck und unser Ende, dachte ich mir, als wir die Küste hinter uns ließen und hinausflogen über das gallertgrüne Meer.
>
> [No matter whether one is flying over Newfoundland or the sea of lights that stretches from Boston to Philadelphia after nightfall, over the Arabian deserts which gleam like mother-of-pearl, over the Ruhr or the city of Frankfurt, it is as though there were no people, only the things they have made and in which they are hiding. . . . And yet they are present everywhere upon the face of the earth, extending their dominion by the hour, moving around the honeycombs of towering buildings and tied into networks of a complexity that goes far beyond the power of any one individual to imagine, from the thousands of hoists and winches that once worked the South African diamond mines to the floors of today's stock and commodity exchanges, through which the global tides of information flow without cease. If we view ourselves from a great height, it is frightening to realize how little we know about our species, our purpose and our end, I thought, as we crossed the coastline and flew out over the jelly-green sea. (*RS*, 113–14/91–92)]

As is true of the passage in which Massey explicates her redefinition of
space via the visualization of the view from a satellite, the point of view in
this passage from *Die Ringe des Saturn* has a quintessentially modern basis.
The perspective represented here — an aerial view of the earth from above
— would be difficult if not impossible to imagine in quite the same way
without the technological advances of the twentieth century. In this case,
the technology in question is airplane flight. Like Massey, the narrator can
assume that his audience is conversant with the bird's eye view presented
in this passage. People living at the turn of the twenty-first century are
familiar with aerial imagery of the earth, whether they have actually
traveled in an airplane or not. Indeed, such views of the globe are at the
time of this writing — and indeed already at the time when *Die Ringe des
Saturn* was published — very much a part of the collective perception of
the material world.[14]

   In the above passage the narrator utilizes the aerial point of view to
consider the attributes of the global networks that exist on the earth
below him. Looking down from the plane, he notes that no people are
visible from such a great height. Unlike Massey, who zooms in on various
parts of the globe in order to get the socially differentiated perspective
that the satellite view does not afford, the narrator remains at a distance,
taking the opportunity to ruminate upon the grand overview — one to
which he definitely does not have access as an earthbound pilgrim. He
notes that from the aerial vantage point one can only see "das, was [die
Menschen] geschaffen haben" (the things [people] have made; *RS*,
113/91) and not the people themselves. It is these visible structures and
the systems of power they represent that he considers as the passage continues.

   The narrator goes on to paint the picture of a vast, complex network
of power that exists on the earth below him. In his estimation, the material
basis for this network is constituted by the various physical structures he
describes: the "hochaufragende Türme" (towering buildings) that often
come into focus throughout Sebald's oeuvre as examples of the ill-fated
grandiosity of human attempts at progress, as well as the "Seilzüge[.] und
Winden" (hoists and winches) of the erstwhile South African diamond
mines and the "Bürohallen der Börsen und Agenturen" (floors of [the]
stock and commodity exchanges). In a nod to late-twentieth-century glo-
balism, Sebald refers to "Information" (information) as an immaterial
commodity that "flute[t]" (flows) through these exchanges "unablässig"
(without cease). People are "eingespannt in" (tied up in) the global finan-
cial network they have built up via these structures, and yet according to
the narrator's imagining, the system takes on a life of its own, outgrowing
the schemes of those who first constructed it both in terms of size and
intricacy. As the narrator puts it, these networks are "von einer das
Vorstellungsvermögen eines jeden einzelnen bei weitem übersteigenden

Kompliziertheit" (of a complexity that goes far beyond the power of any one individual to imagine).

The narrator's final thought as quoted above implies that although people can now view themselves from a great height — for the first time in history we have the godlike perspective that humanity has always imagined — it turns out that we have nevertheless come no further in terms of knowing ourselves. Rationalism does not offer much regarding the answers to the bigger existential questions such as those of "unseren Zweck und unser Ende" (our purpose and our end). Given this lack of insight, the narrator looks to other sources for a way in which to understand the local and global histories that he encounters on his pilgrimage of Suffolk.

Thomas Browne's Cosmological View of History

On his walking tour of Suffolk the narrator sees ample evidence for the failure of post-Enlightenment Western thought: proud faith in progress has resulted in ruin and decay, while disregard for the human body has led to horrific violence and subjugation. Given the failed outcomes of faith in pure rationality, the narrator looks for an alternative philosophy of history through which to view the events of modernity. For this he turns to the writings of Thomas Browne, the English seventeenth-century physician and thinker. The walking-tour narrative of *Die Ringe des Saturn* is wrapped structurally and thematically in this secondary Brownian narrative: in chapter I the narrator discusses his research into Browne's life and ideas, and the tropes and images he introduces here are woven into the rest of the text — indeed through to the very last sentence. In many respects *Die Ringe des Saturn* can be read as homage to Thomas Browne.

Unlike post-Enlightenment rationalist thought, Browne's view is mystical and quasi-astrological: clearly influenced by both Christianity and Hermetic philosophy, as Brownian scholars have noted,[15] he sees the earth as a unified whole, its fate determined by its position in the cosmos. Sebald's narrator describes Browne's philosophy as follows:

> Für Thomas Browne [hat] nichts Bestand. Auf jeder neuen Form liegt schon der Schatten der Zerstörung. Es verläuft nämlich die Geschichte jedes einzelnen, die jedes Gemeinwesens und die der ganzen Welt nicht auf einem stets weiter und schöner sich aufschwingenden Bogen, sondern auf einer Bahn, die, nachdem der Meridian erreicht ist, hinunterführt in die Dunkelheit. Die eigene Wissenschaft vom Verschwinden in der Obskurität ist für Browne untrennbar verbunden mit dem Glauben, daß am Tag der Auferstehung, wenn, so wie auf einem Theater, die letzten Revolutionen vollendet sind, die Schauspieler alle noch einmal auf der Bühne erscheinen, *to complete and make up the catastrophe of this great piece.*

[Nothing endures, in Thomas Browne's view. On every new thing there lies already the shadow of annihilation. For the history of every individual, of every social order, indeed of the whole world, does not describe an ever-widening, more and more wonderful arc, but rather follows a course which, once the meridian is reached, leads without fail down into the dark. Knowledge of that descent into the dark, for Browne, is inseparable from his belief in the day of resurrection, when, as in a theatre, the last revolutions are ended and the actors appear once more on stage, to complete and make up the catastrophe of this great piece. (*RS*, 35–36/24)]

For Browne, then, history describes a cyclical trajectory through time. This stands in stark opposition to the Enlightenment concept of historical progress, in which history describes a steady curve upwards through time in tandem with the development of rationality. For Browne, the repeated cycle of history is one in which every sector of society, both "thing" and human, ascends, reaches a high point, and then necessarily begins its descent once again. In this worldview, the Enlightenment ideal of progress is a false one. Contrary to the quintessentially rationalist Hegelian *Weltgeschichte* (world history), which sees cultural and philosophical progress through time as a positive, forward-moving phenomenon that ends in the consummate rise of the Christian, Germanic world, Sebald's narrator adopts the view — in line with Browne — that progress necessarily heralds its own decline.[16] Progress is an inherently grandiose idea: once the meridian, the apex in a natural cycle of rise and decline, is reached, descent necessarily begins. This is simply the organic flow of things and cannot be controlled or thwarted. In this context, the walking tour narrative of *Die Ringe des Saturn* can be read as a case study of the Brownian concept of history: the narrator focuses on one particular spot on the globe to examine the remaining ruins of the cycles of history that have taken place there until today.[17]

According to Browne's way of thinking, these cycles of history are driven at least in part by cosmological relationships. The history of a local place is determined by the ever changing spatial relationship vis-à-vis its position on the earth and the influence upon that spot of the other heavenly spheres. This is a strongly astrological philosophy of history. In chapter 4, for example, the narrator remarks:

Wie ich an jenem Abend in Southwold so dasaß auf meinem Platz über dem deutschen Ozean, da war es mir auf einmal, als spürte ich ganz deutlich das langsame Sichhineindrehen der Welt in die Dunkelheit. In Amerika, so Thomas Browne in seinem Traktat über das Urnen-Begräbnis, stehen die Jäger auf, wenn die Perser gerade eintauchen in den tiefsten Schlaf. Gleich einer Schleppe wird der Nachtschatten über die Erde gezogen, und da nach Sonnenuntergang

fast alles von einem Weltgürtel zum nächsten sich niederlegt, so fährt
er fort, könnte man, immer der untergehenden Sonne nachfolgend,
die von uns bewohnte Kugel andauernd voller hingestreckter, wie von
der Sense Saturns umgelegter und geernteter Leiber erblicken —
einen endlos langen Kirchhof für eine fallsüchtige Menschheit.

[As I sat there that evening in Southwold overlooking the German
Ocean, I sensed quite clearly the earth's slow turning into the dark.
The huntsmen are up in America, writes Thomas Browne in *The
Garden of Cyrus*, and they are already past their first sleep in Persia.
The shadow of night is drawn like a black veil across the earth, and
since almost all creatures, from one meridian to the next, lie down
after the sun has set, so, he continues, one might, in following the
setting sun, see on our globe nothing but prone bodies, row upon
row, as if levelled by the scythe of Saturn — an endless graveyard for
a humanity struck by a falling sickness. (*RS*, 97/78–79)]

The cheerless view of the earth presented here is decidedly pre-Enlightenment: in this picture the fate of humanity is again determined by cosmic
forces over which it has no control, and the concept of human progress has
no real currency. Sunset — arguably the most familiar cosmic event on
earth — is pictured as an ominous occurrence, a daily reminder that society
is at the mercy of higher powers. People lying down as night falls are
described as "fallsüchtig" (epileptic): even sleep is pictured as a physical
abnormality, a disease. Browne's descriptions of shadows, spherical cycles,
death, and sickness suggest an agrarian, cosmological, and apocalyptic
worldview, and his references to huntsmen and the scythe of Saturn hark
back to pre-industrial cultures whose rhythms of life are profoundly connected to the physical cycles of the earth.

Browne's view of the world here is global in scope in that he makes
reference to America and Persia and to the Earth's revolutions as a whole.
However, his philosophy of history is by no means global in the same sense
as Massey's. The seventeenth-century physician's worldview is clearly
predicated on a very different material reality than the technologies of the
late twentieth century, and his historical philosophy lacks the sense of "the
global in the local" and the complex logic of the network that defines the
spatiality of the travelogue narrative in *Die Ringe des Saturn*. For Browne,
places on the other side of the globe are simply too distant in real terms
(that is, communication and travel time) to be thought of as having any
influence on the history of the local. He looks to the heavens for an explanation of what drives local history, thus having a cosmological, mystical,
and spiritual sense of place. For a deeper explanation of what drives history,
Browne looks upward into the cosmos rather than outward to the rest of
the globe. His view of the earth is vertically networked and God- or crea-
tor-centric.[18]

The vertical orientation of Browne's worldview is captured in the following passage from *Die Ringe des Saturn*:

In einem fort hat er darum denkend und schreibend versucht, das irdische Dasein, die ihm nächsten Dinge ebenso wie die Sphären des Universums vom Standpunkt eines Außenseiters, ja man könnte sagen, mit dem Auge des Schöpfers zu betrachten.

[In his thinking and writing he therefore sought to look upon earthly existence, from the things that were closest to him to the spheres of the universe, with the eye of an outsider, one might even say of the creator. (*RS*, 29/18–19)]

In both Browne's and Massey's (and other postmodern geographers') cases, the (in)ability to see and/or visualize the rest of the world has a fundamental influence on each person's philosophy of history. Both types of thinkers are interested in the grand overview of the whole, but whereas Browne can only imagine this macro perspective in his mind's eye, Massey — and the narrator of *Die Ringe des Saturn* — has actually seen the earth from the sky. Browne's worldview begins at a local, limited point on the earth and expands from there upward and outward into the cosmos. This is not a scientific, rationalist view, but rather an otherworldly, mystical, and religious view of the earth. In Browne's estimation, history is driven by a higher power. The postmodern worldview, on the other hand, begins at a local, limited point on the earth and expands from there in a networked fashion laterally outward around the globe.

In embracing this cosmological approach, Browne can be seen as seeking to return to an earlier, pre-Enlightenment view of historical events, which is during his lifetime being institutionally replaced by faith in pure reason. Whereas astrology is nowadays considered by the academy as an unscientific, superstitious, consummately non-academic practice, until the sixteenth century it was an esteemed field of scholarship, having been studied alongside geography and astronomy as a discipline since ancient times.[19] In the 1600s, when Browne is writing, these cosmological, mythical notions of world history are still in circulation. Even though they are falling out of academic favor, they exert a strong influence on his thinking. As Bianca Theisen points out in her insightful article on Sebald's use of "allegorical indirection" as a literary technique,

The sixteenth and seventeenth centuries witnessed a scientific and philosophical revolution that discarded the closed cosmos determined by a hierarchy of values and saturated by a dense web of meanings for the rationalist and scientific embrace of a devalued world of facts. In *Die Ringe des Saturn*, Sebald rediscovers those sixteenth- and seventeenth-century artists, thinkers, and authors such as Albrecht Dürer,

Thomas Browne, and Hans Jakob Christoffel von Grimmelshausen, who tease the older saturation of meaning out of new rationalist or theoretical approaches, thereby pointing to the lack and insufficiency of mere reason.[20]

Indeed, one of Sebald's core aims in this book (and in his other works) is to question purely rationalist conceptions in general. In invoking the ideas of Thomas Browne and other sixteenth- and seventeenth-century thinkers, Sebald tries to establish, or at least consider, a reconnection to the mystical approaches that have been discarded altogether in favor of purely rational and scientific approaches.

This attempt to reconnect with the mystical is evident throughout the narrative of *Die Ringe des Saturn*, where Sebald's narrator is clearly taken by Browne's otherworldly notion of the earth and its history. From the beginning, the narrative of *Die Ringe des Saturn* is located not only geographically in Suffolk but also *astrologically*, that is, under the dual influences of the Dog Star and Saturn. The title of the book and the last quotation in the epigraph together allude to the classical belief in the malevolent influence of Saturn, which thus sets a tone of foreboding for the book as a whole.[21] Then there is the narrator's reference to Browne's image of sleeping people around the Earth appearing as though they were "von der Sense Saturns umgelegte[.] und geerntete[.] Leiber" (prone bodies . . . levelled by the scythe of Saturn; *RS,* 97/79). Additionally, the very first sentence of the book informs the reader that the narrator's walking tour took place "als die Hundestage ihrem Ende zugingen" (when the dog days were drawing to an end; *RS,* 11/3), thus placing that event under the negative influence of Sirius, or the Dog Star,[22] which immediately gives the text an astrological framework. Sebald thus enlarges the spatial imaginary of *Die Ringe des Saturn* to include the cosmos, at least insofar as the practitioners of classical astrology would have understood it. The "outer space" of the planets and stars that Sebald inserts into his narrative worldview is not the postmodern realm of satellites or men on the moon — all of which can be seen as contributing to the space-time compression of globalization — but rather the celestial sphere of pre-Enlightenment and pre-globalization thinking. This space is viewed by both the ancients and more recent thinkers who like Thomas Browne are influenced by mystical philosophies such as Hermeticism and Kabbala, as being fundamentally linked to the fate of the earth.

Sebald's representation of Suffolk's history in *Die Ringe des Saturn* thus simultaneously reflects postmodern and seventeenth-century worldviews. The spatial imaginary of the travelogue narrative is both global and cosmological, rationalist and mystical. These interwoven layers of rationalism and pre-rationalism make for part of the labyrinthine experience that is reading and making sense of this complex text.

Spatiotemporal Networks

Having concluded the core Suffolk travelogue narrative at the end of chapter IX, the narrator ends *Die Ringe des Saturn* in chapter X with another kind of travel narrative, namely the journey of sericulture from eastern Asia to western Europe, beginning in the sixth century with the smuggling of silkworms out of China by Byzantine monks; followed by its move westwards across the European continent all the way to the British Isles, where by the mid-eighteenth century Norwich stands as one of the great silk-manufacturing centers of Europe; and finally ending in Germany, where a 1939 film and accompanying pamphlet on "Deutscher Seidenbau" (German Sericulture) distributed by the "Reichsfachgruppe Seidenbauer" (Reich Association of Silkworm Breeders) argues for the promulgation of sericulture in Germany as necessary for the "Aufrichtung einer unabhängigen Wehrwirtschaft" (formation of a self-sufficient economy of national defence; *RS*, 347/293) and gives an ominous tutorial on the silkworm-killing process, which is undertaken "zur Vermeidung rassischer Entartung" (to preempt racial degeneration; *RS*, 348/294).

Through the story of the silkworm's westward journey around the globe, Sebald demonstrates once more that the global is in the local — and moreover that it has been so for centuries. Significantly, he chooses a historical example that shows Norwich to have been enmeshed in the global network of sericulture centuries before the emergence of information technology in the late twentieth century, before the Western colonialism and imperialism of the nineteenth century, and even before industrialization. As the narrator points out,

> Wenn damals, so habe ich neulich in einer Geschichte der Seiden-
> manufaktur in England gelesen, ein Wanderer in der einbrechenden
> Winternacht unter einem tintenschwarzen Himmel Norwich von
> fernher sich näherte, dann war es für ihn zum Erstaunen, was für ein
> Glanz über der Stadt war von dem noch zu später Stunde aus den
> Gadenfenstern der Werkstätten dringenden Licht. Die Vermehrung
> des Lichts und die Vermehrung der Arbeit, das sind ja
> Entwicklungslinien, die parallel zueinander verlaufen. Denke ich
> heute, wo unser Blick den fahlen Widerschein, der über der Stadt und
> ihrer Umgebung liegt, nicht mehr zu durchdringen vermag, an das
> achtzehnte Jahrhundert zurück, dann nimmt es mich wunder, in
> welch großer Zahl, zumindest an manchen Orten, die Menschen
> bereits in der Zeit vor der Industrialisierung mit ihren armen Körpern
> fast ein Leben lang eingeschirrt gewesen sind in die aus hölzernen
> Rahmen und Leisten zusammengesetzten, mit Gewichten behangenen
> und an Foltergestelle oder Käfige erinnernden Webstühle in einer
> eigenartigen Symbiose, die vielleicht gerade aufgrund ihrer vergleich-
> weisen Primitivität besser als jede spätere Ausformung unserer

Industrie verdeutlicht, daß wir uns nur eingespannt in die von uns
erfundenen Maschinen auf der Erde zu erhalten vermögen.

[It is said in a history of silk manufacture in England that a traveler
approaching Norwich under the black of a winter night would be
amazed by the glare over the city, caused by light coming from the
windows of the workshops, still busy at this late hour. Increase of
light and increase of labor have always gone hand in hand. If today,
when our gaze is no longer able to penetrate the pale reflected glow
over the city and its environs, we think back to the eighteenth century, it hardly seems possible that even then, before the Industrial
Age, a great number of people, at least in some places, spent their
lives with their wretched bodies strapped to looms made of wooden
frames and rails, hung with weights, and reminiscent of instruments
of torture or cages. It was a peculiar symbiosis which, perhaps because
of its relatively primitive character, makes more apparent than any
later form of factory work that we are able to maintain ourselves on
this earth only by being harnessed to the machines we have invented.
(*RS*, 333–34/282–83)]

In this deeply techno-averse passage, Sebald implicitly argues that
although we who live in the late twentieth century may think the world
has fundamentally changed with the emergence of new information technologies and globalization, things are in actual fact not as different as
they might seem. Whether we labor in the pre-industrialized silk manu-
factories of Norwich or the light-saturated cities of the late twentieth
century, some things remain constant. For example, where there is an
increase of labor, there will be an increase of light, and we always become
beholden to the technology we have ourselves invented. Sebald is essentially distrustful of the kind of thinking that would announce today's
technological developments and resulting human experience as fundamentally new, and therefore detached from history. Although one could
not conceive of networking on a global scale before the technological
advances of modernity, it does not follow that history previously operated
on entirely different principles. The new machinery of the twentieth century merely gives us access to new points of view. Sebald approaches the
present-day region of East Anglia, not by looking at its contemporary
particularities in isolation, but rather by seeking to understand them in
light of the past. He remains committed to a focus on the local and the
familiar, even while he acknowledges and explores the complexly global
nature of place.

In the final lengthy paragraph of *Die Ringe des Saturn*, Sebald takes
what might be thought of as a decidedly temporal turn, using a day of the
year — the thirteenth of April — as the focal point for his narrative.
Instead of taking a journey through geographical space as the primary axis,

and excavating the history of its places, Sebald here uses a particular day of the year as his primary axis. The narrator writes:

> Heute, da ich meine Aufzeichnungen zum Abschluß bringe, schreibt man den 13. April 1995. Es ist Gründonnerstag, der Tag der Fußwaschung und das Namenfest der Heiligen Agathon, Carpus, Papylus und Hermengild. Auf den Tag genau vor dreihundertsieben-undneunzig Jahren wurde von Heinrich IV. das Edikt von Nantes erlassen; wurde in Dublin, vor zweihundertdreiundfünfzig Jahren, das Messias-Oratorium Händels uraufgeführt; Warren Hastings, vor zweihundertdreiundzwanzig Jahren zum Gouverneur von Bengalen ernannt; in Preußen, vor einhundertdreizehn Jahren, die anti-semitische Liga gegründet und ereignete sich, vor vierundsiebzig Jahren, das Massaker von Amritsar, als der General Dyer zur Statuierung eines Exempels das Feuer eröffnen ließ auf eine fünfzehn-tausendköpfige aufständische Menge, die zusammengelaufen war auf dem unter dem Namen Jallinwala Bagh bekannten Platz. Nicht wenige der damaligen Opfer mögen beschäftigt gewesen sein in dem damals in der Gegend von Amritsar wie in Indien überhaupt auf den einfachsten Grundlagen sich entwickelnden Seidenbau. Vor nunmehr fünfzig Jahren auf den Tag wurde in den englischen Zeitungen gemel-det, daß die Stadt Celle gefallen sei und daß die deutschen Truppen vor der unaufhaltsam vordringenden Roten Armee das Donautal hinauf sich im vollsten Rückzug befänden. Ja, und zuletzt, wie wir am Morgen früh noch nicht wußten, ist Gründonnerstag, der 13. April 1995 auch der Tag, an dem Claras Vater, kurz nach seiner Einlieferung in das Coburger Spital, aus dem Leben geholt wurde.

[Today, as I bring these notes to a conclusion, is the 13th of April, 1995. It is Maundy Thursday, the feast day on which Christ's washing of the disciples' feet is remembered, and also the feast day of Saints Agathon, Carpus, Papylus and Hermengild. On this very day three hundred and ninety-seven years ago, Henry IV promulgated the Edict of Nantes; Handel's *Messiah* was first performed two hundred and fifty-three years ago, in Dublin; Warren Hastings was appointed Governor-General of Bengal two hundred and twenty-three years ago; the Anti-Semitic League was founded in Prussia one hundred and thirteen years ago; and, seventy-four years ago, the Amritsar mas-sacre occurred, when General Dyer ordered his troops to fire on a rebellious crowd of fifteen thousand that had gathered in Jallianwala Bagh Square, to set an example. Quite possibly some of the victims were employed in silk cultivation, which was developing at that time, on the simplest of foundations, in the Amritsar region and indeed throughout India. Fifty years ago to the day, British newspapers reported that the city of Celle had been taken and that German forces were in head-long retreat from the Red Army, which was advancing up the Danube Valley. And finally, Maundy Thursday, the 13th of April 1995, was also the day on which Clara's father, shortly after being taken to hospital in Coburg, departed this life. (*RS*, 348–50/295–96)]

Of course, this particular temporal axis has a decidedly spatial quality, in that both year and day are units of time defined by the relationship of the earth to the sun (or the sun to the earth, as the ancients believed). In taking the thirteenth of April as his focal point, Sebald engages in a fundamentally astrological line of thinking; indeed, it would not be too far-fetched to suggest that the narrator is pondering whether or not that day of the year, like the dog days under which he set out on his walking tour of Suffolk, portends some particular fate with regard to the influence of the heavens on the earth. The enumeration of events as quoted above also serves to recapitulate the notion that the global has been in the local for a long time: the reader remembers that the Edict of Nantes links France to East Anglia via the flight of the Huguenots to Britain, where many settled in Norwich; the work of German/English composer Handel links England to Ireland; the Indian subcontinent is linked to Britain via the latter's colonial exploits; and the establishment of formal anti-Semitism links the former Prussia to a future France. Additionally, the list of events serves to remember once again the victims of the violent modern histories of colonialism and war, and allows the Sebaldian narrator to memorialize the passing away of Clara's, his wife's, father, placing the event of this more personal death into a larger web of global histories.

After narrating this list, Sebald goes on to end the book on a decidedly melancholy note, stating that our history is "beinahe nur aus Kalamitäten [bestehend]" (but a long account of calamities; *RS*, 349/295), and reintroducing, one final time, the image of silk. This time the narrator points to the fact that black silk fabrics have been used as a part of traditional mourning rituals; upper-class women used to wear black silk fabric clothing when grieving, and according to Thomas Browne,

> In Holland sei es zu seiner Zeit Sitte gewesen, im Hause eines Verstorbenen alle Spiegel und alle Bilder, auf denen Landschaften, Menschen oder die Früchte der Felder zu sehen waren, mit seidenem Trauerflor zu verhängen, damit nicht die den Körper verlassende Seele auf ihrer letzten Reise abgelenkt würde, sei es durch ihren eigenen Anblick, sei es durch den ihrer bald auf immer verlorenen Heimat.

> [In the Holland of his time it was customary, in a home when there had been a death, to drape black mourning ribbons over all the mirrors and all canvases depicting landscapes or people or the fruits of the field, so that the soul, as it left the body, would not be distracted on its final journey, either by a reflection of itself or by a last glimpse of the land now being lost forever. (*RS*, 350/296)]

This last mournful sentence of the book thus echoes the narrator's earlier Brownian ruminations in chapter I on burial, silkworms, and the transmigration of the soul, reminding us, in case we had forgotten, that this is a mystically inflected portrayal of history, one that is cyclical and filled with uncanny repetitions. In this and other ways, the spatial imaginary of the *Die Ringe des Saturn* expands to include a cosmological view of the earth, and in investigating the multiple, complex networks that fill these layers of space, we can better understand Sebald's commitment to an investigation of place that is inextricably linked to its multiple, global pasts.

Notes

[1] Foucault makes the oft-quoted statement about Western philosophy that "Space was treated as the dead, the fixed, the undialectical, the immobile. Time, on the contrary, was richness, fecundity, life, dialectic." See Foucault, "Questions on Geography," trans. Colin Gordon, in *Space, Knowledge and Power: Foucault and Geography*, ed. Jeremy W. Crampton and Stuart Elden (Burlington, VT: Ashgate, 2007), 173–82; here 178.

[2] See Henri Lefebvre, *The Production of Space*, 1974, trans. Donald Nicholson-Smith (Oxford: Blackwell, 1991).

[3] Arguing that orientalist and imperialist thinking are inherent to the practice of Western comparative literature scholarship until the 1970s, and asserting the need for uncovering the geographical realities that are obscured by that Western-centric perspective, Said writes in *Culture and Imperialism* that "most cultural historians, and certainly all literary scholars, have failed to remark the *geographical* notation, the theoretical mapping and charting of territory that underlies Western fiction, historical writing, and philosophical discourse of the ["age of empire"]." Edward Said, *Culture and Imperialism* (New York: Vintage Books, 1993), 58.

[4] Writing in the field of urban geography, Soja argues that even while thinkers like Sartre and Heidegger were instrumental in pushing philosophy toward considering spatiality as well as temporality vis-à-vis history and social relations, they nevertheless still valued time as the ontological given, privileging it over space. Edward Soja, "Reassertions: Towards a Spatialized Ontology," in *Postmodern Geographies: The Reassertion of Space in Critical Social Theory* (London: Verso, 1989), 118–37.

[5] Theorists attuned to issues of gender (including Lefebvre in *The Production of Space*) point out that the definition of time as active/strong and space as inactive/weak is itself a gendered definition; thus my use of a gendered designation here.

[6] Doreen Massey, "A Global Sense of Place," in *Space, Place, and Gender* (Minneapolis: U of Minnesota P, 1994), 146–56.

[7] Massey, "A Global Sense of Place," 146.

[8] David Harvey, *The Condition of Postmodernity* (Oxford: Blackwell, 1990).

[9] Opinion regarding whether or not to capitalize the noun "internet" is at the time of this writing (March 2009) undergoing a shift towards the lower case. My decision

not to capitalize the word in this essay is based on my agreement with the arguments summed up in Wired online's article "It's just the 'internet' now" (Tony Long, "It's just the 'internet' now," 2004, *Wired*, http://www.wired.com/culture/lifestyle/news/2004/08/64596 [accessed 20 Mar. 2009]). Although "Internet" was originally used to designate a proper name, it is now most often used to refer to a distributed communications medium, in much the same way as "radio" or "television."

[10] Andreas Huyssen, *Present Pasts: Urban Palimpsests and the Politics of Memory* (Stanford, CA: Stanford UP, 2003).

[11] Jorge Luis Borges, "Tlön, Uqbar, Orbis Tertius," trans. Andrew Hurley, in *Collected Fictions* (New York: Penguin Books, 1998), 68–81; here 78.

[12] Arthur Lubow, "Crossing Boundaries," in *The Emergence of Memory: Conversations with W. G. Sebald*, ed. Lynne Sharon Schwartz (New York: Seven Stories, 2007), 159–73; here 167.

[13] Massey, "A Global Sense of Place," 156.

[14] For those who have access to a personal computer and a high-speed internet connection, satellite imagery of the globe has become all the more available since the release of the *Google Earth* application in 2005. *Google Earth* is a free virtual globe/map program which, as Google currently puts it, "lets you fly anywhere on Earth to view satellite imagery, maps, terrain, 3D buildings, from galaxies in outer space to the canyons of the ocean." "Google Earth," http://earth.google.com (accessed 20 Mar. 2009).

[15] *The Garden of Cyrus*, in which Browne discusses the mystical symbolism of the quincunx, is considered to be particularly exemplary of Hermetic and Kabalistic philosophies, both of which are centrally invested in discovering mathematical patterns in the (natural) world. Browne, *Religio Medici, Hydrotaphia and the Gardens of Cyrus*, ed. R. H. A. Robbins (Oxford: Oxford UP, 1982). See *RS*, 30–32/19–21 for the narrator's discussion of this Brownian text.

[16] As Todd Presner points out in his Saidian-inspired "contrapuntal" reading of Sebald and Hegel, Sebald's works present a world in which human progress is defined as existing in a necessarily dialectical relationship with decline; every ostentatious building and monument constructed by the colonial empire therefore is seen to contain the seeds of its own eventual decay and ruin. Presner argues that Sebald, in contrast to Hegel, who in his *Weltgeschichte* (philosophy of world history) sees cultural and philosophical progress through time as a positive, forward-moving phenomenon that ends in the consummate rise of the Christian, Germanic world, adopts the view — in line with Browne and others — that progress necessarily heralds its own decline. Todd Presner, "Hegel's Philosophy of World History via Sebald's Imaginary of Ruins: A Contrapuntal Critique of the 'New Space' of Modernity," in *Ruins of Modernity*, ed. Julia Hell and Andreas Schönle (Durham, NC: Duke UP, 2010), 193–211.

[17] Indeed, this narrative project of exposing the false grandiosity of progress is a recurring one throughout Sebald's oeuvre. What is distinct about *Die Ringe des Saturn* is that this particular examination of the cycles of history takes on such globally networked and cosmological dimensions.

[18] Although Browne consistently professed his Christian faith, his status as a Christian was the subject of a good deal of controversy during his lifetime, mainly due to the unorthodox religious beliefs expressed in his writings, particularly in the *Religio Medici* (1643), which became a European bestseller. See for example Frank Livingstone Huntley, "'Well Sir Thomas?' Oration to Commemorate the Tercentenary of the Death of Sir Thomas Browne," *BMJ: British Medical Journal* 285.6334 (1982): 43–47.

[19] For an illuminating article on the changing role of astrology as an academic field of study in seventeenth-century England, and the relationship of astrology to "science" in the Western academy in general, see Peter Wright, "Astrology and Science in Seventeenth-Century England," *Social Studies of Science* 5.4 (1975): 399–422. Wright points to the fact that the scientific establishment has taken great pains to naturalize the division between scientific and non-scientific "systems of knowledge" such as astrology, but in fact the demarcation is constructed and often unclear.

[20] Bianca Theisen, "A Natural History of Destruction: W. G. Sebald's *The Rings of Saturn*," *Modern Language Notes* 121.3 (2006): 563–81; here 563.

[21] In the epigraph to *Die Ringe des Saturn*, Sebald includes an excerpt from the *Brockhaus Encyclopedia* entry on Saturn. In the quotation, the provenance of the rings of Saturn is explained thus: "Wahrscheinlich handelt es sich um die Bruchstücke eines früheren Mondes, der, dem Planeten zu nahe, von dessen Gezeitenwirkung zerstört wurde (→ Roch'sche Grenze)" (In all likelihood these are fragments of a former moon that was too close to the planet and was destroyed by its tidal effect [→ Roche Limit]). This is indeed one theory commonly accepted by the scientific establishment as an explanation for the origin of Saturn's rings; the current online edition of the Oxford English Dictionary defines the Roche Limit as "the closest distance to which a self-gravitating body . . . can approach a more massive body without being pulled apart by the gravitational field of the latter body." What interests us here is that even in this scientific narrative Saturn is characterized as an ominously destructive force. Sebald thus rounds out the epigraph with a quotation that sets an aura of uneasiness for the reader at the outset.

[22] The current online edition of the Oxford English Dictionary defines "dog days" as follows: "The days about the time of the heliacal rising of the Dog-star; noted from ancient times as the hottest and most unwholesome period of the year. . . . The name . . . arose from the pernicious qualities of the season being attributed to the 'influence' of the Dog-star; but it has long been popularly associated with the belief that at this season dogs are most apt to run mad . . . fig. An evil time; a period in which malignant influences prevail."

11: Topographical Anxiety and Dysfunctional Systems: *Die Ausgewanderten* and Freud's *Little Hans*

Dora Osborne

Introduction

W. G. SEBALD'S *DIE AUSGEWANDERTEN* uses the reconstructive research of the narrator to compose four emigrant portraits. The protagonists are all afflicted by an overwhelming feeling of displacement, at once a compulsion and refusal to disassociate themselves from their place of origin. The reader is led to understand their sense of dispossession through the instability of cultural identity that they experience in their various relations to Jewishness and the National Socialist regime. The protagonist of the first story, Henry Selwyn, is a Lithuanian Jew who moves to England as a boy. In the second, the teacher Paul Bereyter, is described as a "Dreiviertelarier" (three-quarters an Aryan) and circles uneasily around his Alpine homeland (*DA*, 74/*E*, 50). The third describes the narrator's great uncle, Ambrose Adelwarth, who serves a wealthy Jewish emigrant family, and who seems to experience vicariously the homesickness of their son, Cosmo. And the final story tells how the painter Max Aurach moved from Nazi Germany to Manchester ahead of his family to escape the persecution of the Jews.[1] The narrator's investigations are mobilized through topographical and transportational networks, which inform the structures of Sebald's prose more generally. The movements of Sebald's narrator produce a sense of uneasiness that seems to replicate the spatial and topographical uncertainty experienced by the four emigrants. As Stuart Taberner notes, in *Die Ausgewanderten*, "it seems that everybody is an exile."[2]

The loss or destabilization of identity bound to place has formed the core of many critical readings of *Die Ausgewanderten*, not least in terms of *Heimat*, understood as a peculiarly German conception of topographically and culturally determined identity.[3] Where familiar spaces are experienced as irrecuperably foreign, the home is rendered uncanny, in its Freudian sense. John Zilcosky identifies in Sebald's writing an "uncanny paradigm, in which the subject is always, against his will, returning to familiar places."[4] Moreover, as J. J. Long notes, for the emigrants, the desire to return to an originary place can only lead to renewed departure.[5] The emigrants' experiences of disorientation and displacement are bound in particular to the effects of encroaching urbanization and industrialization, that is, to the traumatic impact of modernity as described by urban theorists such as Walter Benjamin and Georg Simmel. The emigrants' lives and reminiscences span a broad section of these technological developments, exemplified in the reader's encounter with different vehicles, such as horses and carts, aeroplanes and trains. The narrative movement between, and via, these vehicles refuses fixed spatial and temporal coordinates.

Where spatial systems exceed the control of the modern subject, modes of representation are subject to certain kinds of distortion, or warping, as Anthony Vidler has shown. Departing from the conceptualization of different phobias, which were used at the end of the nineteenth century to diagnose the neuroses of city dwellers, Vidler cites Freud's 1909 case history of Little Hans. The case not only shows the impact of the rapidly changing urban environment on the subject but also exposes the sort of domestication implied in these diagnostics: Freud deconstructs the topographical elements of Hans's phobia in order to reveal the oedipal scenario they supposedly screen.[6] The boy's fear extends to the urban systems of early twentieth century Vienna, but Freud brings the phobia back to the pre-industrial figure of a horse which, in this case, is visible from the home and thus remains bound to it. Freud describes the development of Hans's phobia "im Zeichen des Verkehres" (under the sign of traffic),[7] but the boy's castration complex causes him to withdraw from these more extended and extensive spaces of social and urban traffic, where he fears the accident of a horse falling, to the home. For Vidler, the case of Little Hans functions as an exemplary model for the "anxious visions of the modern subject . . . attempting to make representational and architectural sense of its predicament."[8] Sebald's emigrants are drawn to the technologies and structures of "mobile modernity," to quote Todd Presner,[9] but their fascination is ultimately overwhelmed by the topographical anxieties which emerge as a symptom of their modern urban experience.

The resonance with Freud is not insignificant, and as the intertextual element of Sebald's writing has produced a complex network of comparative criticism, so the link to Freud seems to merit investigation. Notably, Sebald's working library at the Literature Archive in Marbach includes the Freud *Studienausgabe* with marginalia in key texts such as the Schreber case.[10] The relation between Freudian psychoanalysis and Sebald's postwar writing has been understood primarily in terms of memory and trauma.[11] Martin Klebes has drawn on the nineteenth-century empiricist tradition, out of which Freud's project develops, to show how Sebald produces his own pathographies. Klebes argues that in his literary criticism Sebald uses a certain kind of diagnostic, the "text as manifestation of clinical symptoms," which his literary texts, through the impenetrable interiors of his elusive protagonists, then refuse.[12]

This essay turns to Freud's *Analyse der Phobie eines fünfjährigen Knaben* (Analysis of the Phobia of a Five-Year-Old Boy), the Little Hans case, in order to read the spatial relations in *Die Ausgewanderten*, both inter- and intratextually. It argues for affiliations between the modeling of topographical and genealogical elements in Freud's case history and Sebald's narratives. In the case of the emigrants, these elements are subject to distortion or displacement by the over-freighted and ambivalent significance of transportation systems and networks after 1945. The use and abuse of particularly the railway system to transport victims of National Socialism to death camps has shaped the legacy of industrialization retrospectively and inflects any evocation of such technologies after Auschwitz. The obsessive recurrence of and return to railway stations in Sebald's work offers a particularly complex example of this inflection and is a key mode for the oblique referencing of the Holocaust that characterizes his writing. Todd Presner has described how a combined legacy of psychoanalysis and modernism informs Sebald's contingent and mobile mode of representing the past. Drawing on a German-Jewish tradition, Presner argues that "the dialectical history of modernity [is] a problem of mobility," a relationship schematized by Freud and Sebald through the extended metaphor of the railway system, which embodies at once "emancipating freedom" and "coordinated destruction."[13]

Freud makes his analysis of Little Hans's anxieties via the observations made by the patient's father. His conversations with his son describe how Hans's movement around Vienna comes to be restricted by his fear of horses and laden vehicles. The case history describes the demarcation and transgression of the boundaries between the domestic and the urban. The horse, as phobic object, moves between the home and the industrialized transportation network that lies beyond. Freud's analysis draws Hans back to a familiar, familial locus, seeing his fear of horses and travel as a belated response to his fear of castration. Following an oedipal model, this threat of separation or mutilation comes from the father, who wants to punish the boy's desire for the mother. Hans's phobia marks the intrusion of another element into the dyadic relationship with the mother, but one that is uncanny, since it is always already located in the home. For Freud, Hans's fear that the horse might be found in the room makes visible the links and shifts between the different elements of his phobia, between the domestic and the urban, the familiar and the undiscovered (*LH*, 260/24).

The uncanny threat that underlies Little Hans's phobia and Freud's analysis emerges symptomatically in the topographical anxieties and cultural dispossession that characterize the experiences of the protagonists in

Die Ausgewanderten. Arguably the emigrants' discontent is produced where the familiar elements that structure space have been lost through their displacement by other overwhelming systems. Where Little Hans feels threatened by his father, understood psychoanalytically to embody the imperative of the Law, the growth of National Socialism represents an overwhelming symbolic power that distorts and exceeds domestic relations for Sebald's emigrants. They find that their condition of displacement intensifies upon their confrontation with Nazi ideology, which emerges from within the familiarity of their everyday lives and threatens their very existence in an ostensibly safe space. Paul Bereyter tries to understand how his hometown of S. turns a blind eye to the anti-Semitic crimes perpetrated against local residents as the Nazis came to power (*DA,* 80–81/*E,* 54–55). In the final story, Max Aurach recalls how the confiscation of the family's property by the Nazis is initially disavowed but ultimately forces them from their home (*DA,* 277/*E,* 185). Freud's and Sebald's texts have a mutual interest in the topographical and genealogical structures, that is, in questions of space and origins, and it is the places at which these organizing principles become warped, displaced, or even obliterated that will form the focus of the following reading of *Die Ausgewanderten.*

Topographical Anxieties

Freud's case history, as mapped via the analysand's fascination with and fear of his Viennese topography, and Sebald's short stories reveal similarly ambivalent responses to spaces of movement and habitation. Little Hans strays from the domestic space but is forced back there because he is afraid. Sebald's protagonists are plagued by a sense of not belonging, of homelessness, but their attempts to escape these spaces of anxiety produce stalled movements. Once a keen motorist who toured Europe, Henry Selwyn owns a valuable collection of cars, which stand unused in various garages (*DA,* 34/*E,* 21), Paul Bereyter's belatedly developed "Platzangst" (claustrophobia) prevents him from teaching (*DA,* 65/*E,* 43),[14] Max Aurach suffers from "Reiseangst" (fear of travelling; *DA,* 252/*E,* 170), and describes travelling as "eine einzige Pein" (all of it is torture; *DA,* 252/*E,* 169), while Ambrose Adelwarth writes that each walk taken abroad with Cosmo is "voller Überraschungen, ja Schrecken" (full of surprises, and indeed of alarm; *DA,* 192/*E,* 130). Sebald's protagonists are found on the borders of their respective worlds. Henry Selwyn lives as a "kind of ornamental hermit" (in English in the original; *DA,* 11/*E,* 5); Ambros Adelwarth, overwhelmed by a melancholic fixation on the past, dies in an asylum. Their eccentricity excludes them from familial relations: Paul Bereyter's lover is presumed to have been deported to Theresienstadt (*DA,* 73/*E,* 50), and Max Aurach's portraiture produces a lineage that compulsively erases its forefathers (*DA, 239–40/ E, 162*).

The uneasy trajectories of Sebald's emigrants produce complex spatial networks that diverge and intersect repeatedly, often via a later encounter with a place as it has been imaged or photographed. Pictographic representations and narrative topographies are condensed most concretely in the scale drawing and plan found in "Paul Bereyter" (*DA, 50 and 91/E, 166 and 170*), which bear an uncanny resemblance to the schematizations reproduced in Freud's case history (*LH, 281 and 282/46 and 48*). Both texts are concerned with movements between strange and familiar spaces and the traumatic displacements implicated in these transitions, and in both cases these diagrams map spaces of transition. Freud illustrates the movement that Little Hans attempts between his house and the street, while in "Paul Bereyter" Sebald includes a plan of a railway station and the surrounding warehouses, as well as of the narrator's classroom, which functions as a space for social initiation.

Whilst the likenesses between the pictorial diagrams in *Little Hans* and "Paul Bereyter" offer an explicit link between Freud's text and that of Sebald, other textual examples might represent a more diffuse system of references, or a distorted and displaced sort of similarity. This essay departs from the graphical schematisations of space that supplement both texts, and moves to spatial representations conceived more broadly, in order to understand how topographical anxieties are inscribed in the narrative. The fears that find oblique expression in these terms are always about loss and separation. In Freud's account of the case of Little Hans this fear is about the loss of the mother and of the phallus, and in the case of the emigrants, of homeland and of identity. To what extent does the slippery movement between networks serve to displace our attention from the trauma of loss and separation?

Likeness, distortion, and displacement are key terms in this reading, and the shifts they produce are symptomatic of Sebald's writing. Where Sebald's narratives are so concerned with questions of *Ähnlichkeit*, it is important to consider the kinds of organizing principles he employs, not least because of the ethical issues of appropriation and misappropriation that are necessarily bound to his project. To what extent does Sebald suggest equivalence between his four emigrants?[15] The claims of affiliation, *Brüderlichkeit*, with others, through coincidence of history and location (*DA, 248 and 253/E, 166 and 170*), might work to develop family likenesses, that is, Wittgensteinian *Familienähnlichkeiten*. This would expose a sort of Galtonian composite image, where the narrator forms the principle subject and the four protagonists recede from view.[16] In identifying certain likenesses between the emigrants, singular characteristics are subject to displacement, rendering the portrait of the individual distorted.

Perhaps more so than Sebald's other works, *Die Ausgewanderten* is a highly visual text, incorporating and citing photographs, sketches, postcards, and old masters.[17] In its reconstructive work, the text is concerned with collecting visual evidence, which is often found in distorted or displaced form. The spatial relations in both Little Hans and *Die Ausgewanderten* are informed by and bear the marks of Freudian *Entstellung,* that is, distortion that functions through literal dis-placement. Freud emphasizes the double function of *Entstellung,* which means that a body of evidence is found in another place and form: "Es sollte nicht nur bedeuten: in seiner Erscheinung verändern, sondern auch: an eine andere Stelle bringen, anderswohin verschieben" (It should mean not only "to change the appearance of something" but also "to put something in another place, to displace").[18] It is the double sense of corporeal distortion and topographical displacement that is fundamental to Sebald's project. In the case of *Die Ausgewanderten,* the portraits Sebald produced refuse fixed location and identity.

The sorts of change in form and place that Freud identifies in his case history are further developed in the work of Jacques Lacan, and Gilles Deleuze and Félix Guattari. Their responses to the Little Hans case provide useful approaches for thinking about the kinds of system and systemic dysfunction operating and failing to operate in Freud's and Sebald's texts. Lacan's psychoanalytic project constructs a system of orders, the imaginary, symbolic, and real, which the subject must negotiate and move between in order to situate himself in relation to the object. Deleuze and Guattari oppose Freud's return to unitary, familial structures, and instead map the desire of the subject via imperceptible shifts in state, where the subject becomes animal and machine.

As with his integration of textual supplements more generally, Sebald's use of schematizations and construction of networks does not serve to elucidate spatial relations; rather, the replication of schematized topographies puts at a remove the originary spaces that at once repel and attract the emigrants. The diagrams used by Freud to show the trajectories of his patient's desire also function ambiguously. In his analysis of *Little Hans,* Lacan thus deems them in need of additional mapping. However, Lacan is forced to supplement his supplement with a correction when he realizes he has overlooked a particular element in the analysand's topography.[19] This omission represents a blind spot, but one that is symptomatic for a case where Lacan finds the signifying elements to be obscured or in flux. For Lacan the black around the horse's eyes and mouth are paradigmatic for the kinds of stains that mark the analysis. They are constitutive of the phobic image for Hans but also constitute a blind spot in Freud's analysis, which, Lacan argues, covers over a traumatic abyss that even the analyst is not prepared to uncover (*RO,* 245).

Lacan is particularly interested in the significance of the horse for Hans's anxieties. It ostensibly provides a suitable object onto which the meaning of the phobia can be transferred and around which Freud can

construct his oedipal explanation. However, Lacan shows how the temptation to work through analogy, that is, to find elements in the case that
resemble the phobic object, masks the horse's real function as an obscuring
signifier. The horse functions as a signifier that negotiates the chasm
opened upon the loss of the object of desire. Emerging from Hans's picture book, but being identified with the father, the horse works as a mobile
object that moves between the imaginary and symbolic orders, and as such
is emblematic for the rupture produced by this differentiation in the realm
of the subject's experience.

Die Ausgewanderten contains elements that, like the horse, are to be
detached, moved, and reattached. Tin plates, horses, fish, ice-skaters, and
wagons are exemplary for the objects which are found again in other stories, serving a different function, but connected via an associative network.
In what ways are these mobile elements being used in Sebald's narratives
either to obscure or to move between the traumatic losses thematized? The
mobility inherent in these objects shows how the similarities and associations that are constructed between them are themselves subject to literal
dis-placement, that is, *Entstellung*. The kinds of *Ähnlichkeiten* that emerge
are displaced and encoded.

Resisting Psychoanalysis

The inter- and intratextual similarities and correspondences in *Die
Ausgewanderten* produce shifting, hybrid identities that oppose the unitary logic of Freud's oedipal project. Freud posits a link between the
child's oedipal development and the totemism of primitive societies via
the ambivalent identificatory and phobic relationship to the totem animal
and the father. He has a particular interest in the animal phobias of his
young analysands and claims, in *Totem und Tabu*, that Little Hans's case
history has shown the kind of displacement that takes place in such phobias: "Das Kind [verschiebt] unter solchen Bedingungen einen Anteil
seiner Gefühle von dem Vater weg auf ein Tier" (in such circumstances
children displace some of their feelings from their father onto an animal).[20]

Freud's psychoanalysis works toward the resolution of this oedipal
complex through the domestication of the animal. However, the centrism
and unitarity of Freud's model has been rejected by Gilles Deleuze and
Félix Guattari, who argue for a becoming animal that preserves the hybrid
condition of the subject. Their anti-oedipal project suggests how the sorts
of mobility and networks found in Little Hans's case history carry the
potential for animal and machinic becomings. Such becomings describe
the proximity to identity boundaries where the subject enters into a space
beyond a centralized, unified understanding of self. Their critique of the

Little Hans case emphasizes the potential of the horse as vehicle for the boy's desires: Hans drives toward a becoming horse that his father resists.[21]

Deleuze and Guattari's becoming animal constitutes a revision of the particular tendency in early psychoanalysis to give analysands a hybrid, animal identity, which analysis then resolves (Freud's Wolf Man and Rat Man, Ferenczi's Little Chanticleer). In a significant gesture of *Entstellung* as corporeal distortion, Sebald creates his own hybrid figures, the recurrence of the Butterfly Man being a key example in *Die Ausgewanderten* (*DA*, 26, 170, 259, and 260/*E*, 15–16, 115, and 174). However, his position is ambivalent, situated between a Freudian animal composite in the logic of the case history and a more deconstructive movement into zones beyond the human, following Deleuze and Guattari. Sebald's unresolved relationship to psychoanalysis is illustrated in the link to Little Hans, a case that is exemplary for the shifts and instabilities of Freud's own project.

Deleuze and Guattari read the case of Little Hans as exemplary for the way the family, both real and analytic "barred him from the rhizome of the street, they rooted him in his parents' bed, they radicaled him to his own body, they fixated him on Professor Freud."[22] Their anti-oedipal project proposes mapping desire rather than fixing it in the image of the family. They acknowledge how Freud does undertake a kind of cartographical work by including pictographic supplements, but always in the service of a kind of transposition to a mimetic, visual mode: "Freud explicitly takes Little Hans's cartography into account, but always and only in order to project it back onto the family photo."[23] Sebald's well-documented and not unproblematic use of photographs seems to reflect this mimetic, genealogical drive of psychoanalysis, but considered alongside his use of plans and maps, perhaps more accurately reflects upon the family resemblances between psychoanalysis and narrative structures.

The proposed intertextual links between *Die Ausgewanderten* and the case history of Little Hans expose the non-viability for Sebald's postwar writing of narrative structures that insist on the demarcation of the domestic and the unfamiliar, the proper and foreign. Elsewhere I have used Freud's case history of the Wolf Man for a reading and viewing of *Austerlitz* in order to show how Sebald's return to a psychoanalytical model after 1945 exposes both the limits and persistence of Freud's genealogical fantasy.[24] Freud's interpretative model, for Deleuze, "consists in recovering persons and possessions,"[25] a work that, after the catastrophic erasure of families, communities, and properties in the Second World War, is rendered deeply problematic. For Sebald's narrator and protagonists it is the futility of such recovery that provokes its obsessive pursuit where the influence of National Socialism has overwhelmed domestic and family relations.

Dysfunctional Systems

Sebald's writing is characterized by an obsession with groups and lists that can be understood in terms of the construction of systems. His taxonomic strategies work associatively, generating networks, the elements of which are linked by finding similarities between them. The meaning of his narratives is mobilized through different systems that operate as, and through, language: that is, as a system of signification that generates meaning via the movement between signifiers. Both Freud's and Sebald's texts are thus bound by different kinds of systems, spatial, vehicular, and animal, which are linked to each other. The horse's potential for movement fascinates Hans, but since its identification with sexual desire and its prohibition by the father, it has become an object of fear: "Das Pferd war für den Knaben immer das Vorbild der Bewegungslust . . ., aber da diese Bewegungslust den Koitusimpuls einschließt, wird die Bewegungslust von der Neurose eingeschränkt und das Pferd zum Sinnbild des Schreckens erhoben" (For Hans horses had always typified pleasure in movement . . .; but since this pleasure in movement included the impulse to copulate, the neurosis imposed a restriction on it and exalted the horse into an emblem of terror; *LH,* 370/139). Despite the anxiety he experiences, Little Hans is fascinated by the industrial, urban mechanisms that surround him: "Ein Rest ist noch jetzt da, der sich nicht mehr in Furcht, sondern in normalem Fragetrieb äußert. Die Fragen beziehen sich meist darauf, woraus die Dinge verfertigt sind (Tramways, Maschinen usw.), wer die Dinge macht usw" (A trace of his disorder still persists, though it is no longer in the shape of fear but only in that of the normal instinct for answering questions. The questions are mostly concerned with what things are made of (trams, machines, etc.), who makes things etc.; *LH,* 334/99).

Little Hans describes a machinic system that is harnessed to an animal system. As Freud notes, Hans's fantasy is formed "under the sign of traffic," which allows him to shift from horse to train, from animal to machine: "und [Hansens Phantasie schreitet] konsequenterweise vom Pferde, das den Wagen zieht, zur Eisenbahn fort" (logically from the horse that pulls the cart, to the railway; *LH,* 319/84). In his analysis, Freud works to bring Hans back to the familial and familiar, but the boy's fantasies take him beyond this limit. The case describes a dual system of animal and machine, but one where, as Deleuze and Guattari would have it, the system makes the body become machine. The metonymic logic of the system works according to a principle of displacement where the body of the little boy is harnessed first to a horse, then a cart, then a train. Conventional serial structures are overturned, however, and there is a sense in which, in harnessing the machinic system to the animal system, the cart is put before the horse. The kinds of system found in *Die Ausgewanderten* are harnessed in similar ways. Sebald's protagonists show signs of becoming animal and becoming machine. However, these systems are subject to breakdown or dysfunction. The meaning transported from one object to the next in these metonymic shifts threatens to be lost when an accident or incident arrests the system's movement. After 1945 systems of signification carry a different freight and are arguably over-burdened. The abuse of modern technology in the Second World War and the Holocaust makes the railway in particular monstrous. The metonymic logic of these systems displaces Sebald's protagonists so radically that they cannot be brought back to any kind of home or family.

Paul Bereyter's obsession with different types of system, specifically the railway, displaces language as a system of signification. The meaning it transports for Paul proves fatal — it is on the railway that he takes his own life: "Die Eisenbahn hatte für Paul eine tiefere Bedeutung. Wahrscheinlich schien es ihm immer, als führe sie in den Tod" (Railways had always meant a great deal to him — perhaps he felt they were headed for death; *DA*, 90/*E*, 61). It is not a productive system and only finds expression in infinite, schematized reproductions and replications. Even Lucy Landau's use of language to describe Paul's "Eisenbahnmanie" (railway obsession; *DA*, 91/*E*, 61) feeds into a network of further schematizations: "Mir fielen bei diesen Worten Mme. Landaus die Bahnhöfe, Gleisanlagen, Stellwerke, Güterhallen und Signale ein, die Paul so oft an die Tafel gemalt hatte und die wir mit möglichster Genauigkeit in unsere Schulhefte übertragen mußten" (When Mme Landau said this, I thought of the stations, tracks, goods depots and signal boxes that Paul had so often drawn on the blackboard and which we had to copy into our exercise books as carefully as we could; *DA*, 91/*E*, 61).

In Paul's case the significance of language is given an additional load, belatedly, both in terms of the collective and the personal, that is, in the abuse of technological systems by the Nazis and in Paul's suicide on the railway. Lucy Landau remembers the sense of veiled foreboding she felt when Paul's uncle said his nephew "werde noch einmal bei der Eisenbahn enden" (he would end up on the railways; *DA*, 92/*E*, 62): "Wahrscheinlich weil ich den Ausdruck *bei der Eisenbahn enden* in der von dem Onkel gemeinten landläufigen Bedeutung nicht sogleich begriff, hatte er auf mich die dunkle Wirkung eines Orakelspruchs" (I suppose I did not immediately see the innocent meaning of Paul's uncle's expression *end up on the railways*, and it struck me as darkly foreboding; *DA*, 92–93/*E*, 63). The failure of language as system to reach beyond spatial boundaries — *landläufig* describes something common or accepted, but in relation to place — induces an uneasiness in Lucy Landau. She understands this retrospectively in visual terms: "Die von meinem momentanen Fehlverständnis ausgelöste Beunruhigung — heute ist mir manchmal als hätte ich damals wirklich ein Todesbild gesehen" (The disquiet I experienced because of that momentary failure to see what was meant — I now sometimes feel that at that moment I beheld an image of death; *DA,* 93/*E,* 63).

Where the symbolic order, that is, language as a system of signs used for collective communication, is required to express something that exceeds human experience, the system is subject to breakdown. The persistence of the black round the horse's mouth, the remainder or reminder of a traumatic abyss, which reduces the otherwise precocious Hans to silence (*RO,* 244), works symptomatically for the failure of signification found in Freud's analysis. Sebald's writing, on the other hand, reflects the symptoms of the over-freighting of a system of signification that characterizes the dysfunction of language after 1945 more generally and is symptomatic of postwar writing. The implications of this breakdown for modes of mourning and remembering after 1945 have been described by Eric Santner as "disorientations and decenteredness" in the face of "an inability to remember a past dismembered under the sign of Auschwitz."[26] In their attempts to remember experiences of displacement Sebald's otherwise eloquent protagonists are sometimes reduced to silence (*DA,* 28, 73, 149, and 273/*E,* 17, 49, 103, and 183).[27] Where language fails them, they have recourse to images. However, these are marked by blind spots that resist the integrity of what is represented, or else are subject to reduction and replication in schemata that attempt to master the precarious burden of meaning they carry.

In "Max Aurach," the shadow cast belatedly over memories marks Luisa Lanzberg's childhood reminiscences. They are written both as an attempted diversion from the oppression of the encroaching Nazi regime and as a correspondence with her son, who has already been sent to England (*DA,* 288/*E,* 192–93). While Luisa seems to move through her everyday life with ease and familiarity, a sense of fear or uncertainty underlies her narrative. She describes the weekly trip to the fishmonger's, which involves a confrontation with the fish as it lives and then as a revenant at mealtime and into the night:

> Übrigens malt uns die Mama am Donnerstagmorgen immer einen Fisch auf das pergamentene Einwickelpapier, damit wir nicht daran vergessen, auf dem Heimweg von der Bewahranstalt beim Fischer ein halbes Dutzend Barben zu holen. . . . Wenn wir sie zum Nachtmahl dann essen, dürfen wir, wegen der Gräten, nicht sprechen und müssen selber so stumm sein wie Fische. Mir ist bei diesem Essen nie besonders wohl gewesen, und die verdrehten Fischaugen haben mir oft nachgesehen bis in den Schlaf.

> [And then every Thursday morning Mama draws a fish on the waxed paper she wraps the sandwiches in, so that we won't forget to buy half a dozen barbels from the fish man on our way home from the kindergarten. . . . When we eat them for supper we are not allowed to speak

because of the bones, and have to keep as quiet as fish ourselves. I never felt particularly comfortable about those meals, and the skewed fish-eyes often went on watching me even in my sleep. (*DA*, 295–96/ *E*, 197–98)]

This episode marks the ritual inscription of an image that serves as mnemonic before language can. The children imitate the silent fish because of a hidden danger that they ostensibly embody. Where an inexpressible element remains, language is withdrawn. Here the fish eye figures this enigmatic residue that refuses symbolization, reminiscent of the black around the horses mouth about which the otherwise precocious Little Hans (and analyst-in-the-making) can or will not speak in Freud's case (*RO*, 244). Years later, when Luisa reads the telegram bringing the news of her lover's death, the "verdrehten Augen" of the fish have been reconfigured in the words that swim in front of her eyes: "dessen Wörter und Buchstabenfolgen in andauernd wechselnder Zusammensetzung wochenlang vor meinen Augen sich drehten" (and for weeks the words and letters danced before my eyes in all sorts of new combinations; *DA*, 322/*E*, 215). Her idyllic childhood ends with the outbreak of war, and language, failing to communicate or make sense, bears a mark of this rupture.

"Wegen dem Pferd"

The condition of the emigrants expresses, in topographical terms, how the subject is defined always in relation to, and through displacement by, an other. For Lacan, the case history of Little Hans describes the subject's entrance into the symbolic order, that is, language as a system of signification. In grammatical systems the conjunction of two clauses through the causal link "because" shows how one element is given meaning through its relation to another element. However, there is syntactic ambiguity in Freud's case history when his analysand repeats the construction "wegen dem Pferde" ('cos of the horse). In a footnote, Freud sees Hans moving between "wegen" and the Viennese vernacular "Wägen" for the plural form "Wagen" (*LH*, 293 and 59). For Lacan, this slippage shows how the function of the horse as signifier is bound to a signified, but, following the mobilization of transportation mechanisms, always subject to uncoupling and reattachment to a different object: "Hans articule lui-même que le cheval est d'abord et avant tout un élément fait pour être attelé, amovible, attachable" (Hans says himself that the horse is first and foremost an element to be harnessed, mobile, attachable; *RO*, 316; my translation).

The figure of the "Wagen" or "Wägelchen" seems to work in Sebald's text as an object to which the protagonists are always attached and by which they are at once burdened and defined. These detachable objects want to bridge the gap opened up upon the loss of or separation from that which was once proper to the subject. However, where the emigrants have been displaced from the familiar and familial, the objects that are supposed to transport meaning across temporal and spatial boundaries become foreign and defunct. In "Max Aurach" the narrator stumbles across a boy on a Manchester street "der in einem Wägelchen eine aus ausgestopften alten Sachen gemachte Gestalt bei sich hatte und der mich, also wohl den einzigen Menschen, der damals in dieser Umgegend unterwegs gewesen ist, um einen Penny bat für seinen stummen Gesellen" (with a Guy stuffed with old rags on a hand-cart:[28] the only person out and about in the whole area, wanting a penny for his silent companion; *DA*, 233/*E*, 158).

The various vehicles or containers for luggage also function as carriers of memories and seem to ask to be opened after a time, to be viewed again belatedly, as in the case of Henry Selwyn, whose memories of his family's emigration are centered around shifting topographies, spaces of transition and transportation:

> Im Spätherbst des Jahres 1899 sei es gewesen, als sie . . . auf dem Wägelchen des Kutschers Aaron Wald nach Grodno gefahren seien. . . . Ich sehe mich zuoberst auf dem Wägelchen sitzen, sehe die Kruppe des Pferdes, . . . den Wartesaal des Bahnhofs mit seinem frei im Raum stehenden, von einem Gitter umgebenen überheizten Ofen und den um ihn herumgelagerten Auswandererfamilien.

> [In the late autumn of 1899 they had ridden to Grodno on a cart that belonged to Aaron Wald the coachman. . . . I can see myself sitting topmost on the cart, see the horse's crupper . . . the waiting room at Grodno station, overheated by a freestanding, railed-off stove, the families of emigrants lying round it. (*DA*, 30–31/*E*, 19)]

The fireplace is displaced to a railway station, rendering the domestic hearth strange. Surrounded by a fence, it is a space of restricted access. Moreover, the retroactive significance of this belching oven carries the connotation of the Holocaust's killing machinery, shifting the fireplace into a monstrously industrialized context that exceeds anything familiar or homely.

When Henry Selwyn makes a semi-public spectacle of his memories in a sort of slide show, it is his servant, Aileen, who brings the apparatus for this projection on a little "Wägelchen" (trolley; *DA*, 26/*E*, 15). She is an uncanny, infantilized figure seen playing with dolls and laughing like a horse (*DA*, 17–18/*E*, 10). However, Aileen's neighing in her room is completely dislocated from any family context, and she is a strange remnant of Selwyn's mysterious past. Her likeness to an asylum patient means, in the postwar context, that she figures as a displaced reminder and remainder of the inhumane treatment shown in recent history: "Aileen, so hieß sie, hatte das Haar nach Art von Anstaltsinsassen bis in den Nacken hinauf geschoren"

(Elaine, as she was called, wore her hair shorn high up to the nape, as the inmates of asylums do; *DA*, 16/*E*, 9). This association is strengthened by a link to the final story, when, after his internment at Dachau, Max Aurach's father returns "um einiges magerer und mit kurzgeschorenem Haar wieder nach Hause" (he came home, distinctly thinner, and with his hair cropped short; *DA*, 277/*E*, 186). The father comes back to the home but bearing the marks of a threat that overwhelms the domestic.

Uncanny Spatiality

Freud's case history is marked by his analysand's desire at once to depart from and return to the family, and the impossible trajectories that structure the case might be used to understand the spatial relations in *Die Ausgewanderten*. Little Hans strains at the confines of his domestic scene but, through his fear of his father as it manifests itself in his horse phobia, is forced back to the home; paradoxically, it is the thing he fears most that draws him back. The impossibility of departure is traced and retraced in a train journey Hans makes with his father and grandmother. Hans explains how his father misses the train that he travels on — Hans can see him waiting on the platform — but then finds his father is with him and his grandmother on the same train (*LH*, 317/81–82). Lacan sees this impossible trajectory as constituting another blind spot in the case: "Comment le petit Hans qui était déjà parti, est-il revenu? C'est bien là l'impasse, et à la vérité, une impasse que personne ne réussit à élucider" (How has Little Hans, who has already left, come back ? This is indeed the impasse and, to be truthful, an impasse that no one succeeds in explaining; *RO*, 315; my translation). The trajectories of the case history map the desire for and fear of the departure from the domestic.

The experiences of the emigrants are marked by uncanny returns and displacements that collapse the boundaries between homely and threatening spaces. Recounting Ambrose Adelwarth's departure, Fini tells the narrator how she returns one day to find "eine seiner Visitenkarten mit einer Nachricht für mich, die ich seither stets bei mir getragen habe. . . . Have gone to Ithaca" (a visiting card with a message for me, and I have carried it with me ever since. Have gone to Ithaca; *DA*, 150/*E*, 103). Both the visiting card and the journey away to the Odyssean *locus classicus* of origin and return indicate the instability of any notion of permanence or belonging. The violence of the treatment Ambrose receives in the asylum, at Ithaca, stands for the sort of threatening presence that haunts the various (dis)locations of the emigrants. The return to familiar space is accompanied by either a feeling of horror: "Einen furchtbaren Herzschlag lang glaube ich mich in der Schweiz oder wieder daheim" (For one awful heartbeat I imagine myself in Switzerland or at home again; *DA*, 193/*E*, 131), or a momentary failure of recognition: "ein tief verstaubtes . . . Kabinett, das ich nach einigem Zögern erkannte als das Wohnzimmer meiner Eltern" (a gallery covered in layers of dust . . . that, after some hesitation, I recognized as my parents' drawing room; *DA, 261–622/E*, 176). The different topographies are linked back to originary spaces via their arrangement in a network, rendering departure impossible.[29]

The uneasiness Paul Bereyter feels in relation to any notion of home is carried over into the classroom, where he adopts a liminal position at the window. He is anxious to escape its confines and frequently conducts his lessons out of doors. Paul feels restricted by the prescriptive pedagogy in which he has been trained and finds an alternative voice and space in which to teach:

> In seiner Windjacke . . . ging er . . . mit den für ihn so charakteristischen, weit ausgreifenden und federnden Schritten vor uns her, ein wahres Inbild, wie ich jetzt erst in der Rückschau erkenne, der deutschen Wandervogelbewegung, die ihn zeit seiner Jugend geprägt haben mußte.

> [Wearing his windcheater . . . he would walk . . . taking those long and springy steps that were so characteristic, the very image (as I realize only now as I look back) of the German *Wandervogel* movement, which must have had a lasting influence on him from his youth. (*DA, 60–61/E*, 40)]

This description produces a kind of caricature, and the image of Paul as bird seems to demand a psychoanalytic reading where his jaunty steps are understood more literally as feathered. His compulsion to teach outside the confines of the classroom induces his own becoming bird, but one that is always bound to a certain historical load. The (mis)appropriation of the bird by National Socialism directs the trajectory of youth movements from *Wandervogel* to *Hitlerjugend*. Paul feels persecuted by these sorts of historical associations and it is not for nothing that he performs his becoming bird in the same windbreaker worn on his final journey to the railway tracks (*DA, 90/E*, 61).

The different systems at work in the text harness the animal and the machinic: Paul not only moves toward a becoming bird, following Deleuze and Guattari, but also performs a sort of becoming machine. However, the alternative system this gestures toward is always threatened by dysfunction. Paul is described as a metal man who might be thrown off course at any moment: "der ganze Paul sei ein künstlicher, aus Blech- und anderen Metallteilen zusammengesetzter Mensch, den die geringste Funktionsstörung für immer aus der Bahn werfen konnte" (Paul in his entirety was a mechanical human made of tin and other metal parts, and might be put out of operation for ever by the smallest functional hitch; *DA, 52/E*, 35).

The tin from which Paul seems to be partially constructed returns elsewhere in Sebald's text, and in this sense, functions like the detachable elements in the Little Hans case that transport meaning, negotiating the gaps opened up by loss or separation. On their nomadic journey Ambrose and Cosmo put their horses to rest under a sort of metallic tree "dessen Blätter wie Blechplättchen leise rascheln" (the leaves of which rustle softly like tiny sheets of metal; *DA*, 190/*E*, 129, and Luisa Lanzberg recalls that the tinsmith's roof was covered with "Blechplättchen" (green tin shingle cladding; *DA*, 291/*E*, 194).[30] In her childhood idyll they are an integral part of the domestic structure, but the craft of the tinsmith is threatened by decline. Kasimir replaces the synagogue roof in Augsburg that was taken down to help the war effort (*DA*, 117/*E*, 80) and in the United States he continues with his work as *Spengler* until a fall while he is ice-skating forces him to stop (*DA*, 124/*E*, 86).

Fall of the Family

The significance of this accident might be understood in terms of the psychoanalytic case history, that is, as *Fall*. Psychoanalysis is concerned with accidents, as John Forrester has pointed out.[31] It is structured around a practice of retrospective understanding as opposed to a formulation of constitutive developmental stages in the formation of the subject. Psychoanalysis works back, conferring meaning onto traumatic experience retrospectively. Through its repetition, trauma is brought into the symbolic order, and meaning is conferred after the event. This transfer between orders, however, leaves a mark or stain of the real, which, in the case of Little Hans, would be the black around the horse's mouth and eyes.

Freud creates a field of signification surrounding the fall, including the accident (*Unfall*) that restricts the boy's locus of movement (*LH*, 281/46). Together with Hans's father, Freud understands the analysand's vision of a horse that falls down in the street in terms of the father's struggle to exert his power in the domestic scene and the boy's desire to see him fall and die (*LH*, 358/126). For Lacan, Freud's use of the figure of the accident has to do with coincidence (*Zufall*), that is, the potentially shifting relationship between signifier and signified. The points of resonance in *Die Ausgewanderten* with the figure of the fall also relate to a coincidence of signifiers that gain retrospective significance, and, in the context of war, often try to carry an unbearable load that leads to renewed collapse.

In "Max Aurach," Luisa Lanzberg describes ice-skating with her lover on a frozen lake in winter. Her memoirs overwrite a locus of a potential fall with liberated movements experienced in a moment of relief: "und auf der Theresienwiese war, erstmals seit Kriegsbeginn, wieder eine Eisbahn angelegt, auf der der Fritz . . . und ich . . . die schönsten und weitesten Bögen miteinander gefahren sind" (and on the Theresienwiese they opened up an ice rink for the first time since the outbreak of war, where Fritz and I would skate in wonderful, sweeping curves; *DA*, 327/*E*, 217). While the threat of accident seems remote, the temporary ice rink forms a precarious cover over the fact of war. The Theresienwiese resonates with Theresienstadt (the final destination for Paul Bereyter's lover, whose point of departure is, notably, a Viennese railway station (*DA*, 73/*E*, 50) and where the ice is "durchschnitten von den Spuren verschwundener Schlittschuhläufer" (crisscrossed by the tracks of ice-skaters long vanished; *DA*, 327/*E*, 218), and the trajectory of the couple is always implicated in a network with those who vanished there. The power and influence of the Nazi regime is always already inscribed in a network linking spaces of fall, accident, and coincidence. Katja Garloff's work on Sebald has emphasised the significance of "missed encounters" for his protagonists, and the traces of vanished skaters in the ice offers a further example.[32] The resonance of the "missed encounter" for psychoanalysis shows how Sebald's use of this notion is bound to the impossibility of witnessing the traumatic encounter and the work of analysis in producing a return, albeit belated, to the site of the accident.[33]

The figure of the skater is also found in the narrator's imagined scenes of Paul Bereyter, but coupled directly to his fall, to his prostrate position on the railway lines: "Ich sah ihn eislaufen im Winter, allein auf dem Moosbacher Fischweiher, und sah ihn hingestreckt auf dem Geleis" (I imagined him skating in the winter, alone on the fish ponds at Moosbach; and I imagined him stretched out on the track; *DA*, 44/*E*, 29).[34] Sebald's conspicuous use of "Geleis" instead of "Gleis" disrupts the flow of the narrative and draws attention to the "Eis" in "Gleis," reinforcing the links in his topographical networks. While Little Hans's father explains his son's enthusiasm for ice-skating through his encounters with other children (*LH*, 251–52/15), Sebald's vision juxtaposes an ostensibly social scenario with a scene of complete isolation.

In the course of his analysis of Little Hans, Freud comes to understand the falling horses in the context of birth (*niederkommen*): "Er [kann] im Umfallen der schweren oder schwer belasteten Pferde nichts anderes gesehen haben als eine — Entbindung, ein Niederkommen. Das fallende Pferd war also nicht nur der sterbende Vater, sondern auch die Mutter in der Niederkunft" (and that when a heavy or heavily loaded horse fell down he can have seen in it only one thing — a childbirth, a delivery. Thus the falling horse was not only his dying father but also his mother in childbirth; *LH*, 360–61/128). In the case of a young homosexual woman, Freud uses this lexical association to explain his patient's suicide attempt, her fall onto a railway line: "Als letztere bedeutete er die Durchsetzung jenes Wunsches, dessen Enttäuschung sie in die Homosexualität getrieben hatte, nämlich vom Vater ein Kind zu bekommen, denn nun kam sie durch die Schuld des Vaters nieder" (As the latter it meant the attainment of the very wish which, when frustrated, had driven her into homosexuality — namely, the wish to have a child by her father, for now she "fell" through her father's fault).[35] Here the breakdown of traditional genealogy is shown in the displacement of the domestic, since the patient's illicit desire for her father's child can only be born on the train tracks.

Sebald's emigrants are ostensibly childless and the associative networks via which their narratives are modeled contrast with the arboreal familial structure that forms the root of Freud's project. In "Ambrose Adelwarth" we learn that Cosmo Solomon lives a life of excess, indulging in gambling and moving in affluent polo circles that take him away from his family legacy. The narrator's research takes him on a journey to Deauville, which produces oneiric scenes of racing day. In his dream the narrator witnesses a kind of becoming animal, but one destined to fall, following Little Hans: "It actually seems as though people have learnt to sleep on the hoof. It's their glazed look that gives them away. Touch them, and they keel over" (in English in the original; *DA,* 182/*E,* 123).

Sebald is interested in genealogies that find themselves at the limit of the familiar and the human. As well as anti-oedipal, Deleuzean animal-becomings, he writes about hybrid identities in an oedipal, totemic sense. Following Freud, he explores the significance of totemic animals for patrilinear tradition. In an article on the Austrian poet Ernst Herbeck, Sebald describes how the figure of a hare becomes over-burdened with meaning. Referring to what he describes as the "Identitätsmerkmal" (distinguishing mark of identity) of Herbeck's harelip, thought in folklore to represent an incomplete twin birth, Sebald refers to a slip in Herbeck's biography where he describes his mother "getting" a hare: "Herbecks kürzere Wendung suggeriert jedoch, daß die Mutter den Hasen bekam, so wie man ein Kind bekommt" (The brief phrase used by Herbeck, however, suggests that his mother 'had a hare' as a woman might have a baby).[36] In addition to the resonance with the *Niederkommen* of Freud's case studies, the title of Sebald's article, "Des Häschens Kind, der kleine Has" with its echo of "der kleine Hans," might gesture toward the sort of syntactic slippage that occurs in Freud's case study, particularly *Wägen/wegen* (*LH,* 293/59). Herbeck's childhood trauma reaches its climax in the totem meal shared with his parents, where the boy becomes party to this "Familienverbrechen" (family crime) in the "Verspeisung seines Ebenbildes und Namensvetters" (having helped to consume his likeness and namesake; *CS,* 178/133).

In "Max Aurach," Luisa Lanzberg's memory of a mysterious household and its putative domestic secret resonates with Freud's cases of Hans and the young homosexual woman, and carries the threat of some kind of "Familienverbrechen":

> Die Pferde, die das alles die längste Zeit schon gewohnt sind, bleiben brav neben dem umgeworfenen Wagen stehen. . . . Anderntags

bleiben die grünen Läden ihrer Wohnung geschlossen, und wir Kinder . . . fragen uns, was dort drinnen wohl vorgefallen sein mag.

[The horses have long been used to all this and stay patiently by the up-ended waggon. . . . The next day, the green shutters at their windows remain shut, and . . . we wonder what can have happened in there. (*DA*, 295/*E*, 197, trans. modified)]

The green blinds screen what is happening in the home, deflecting the gaze of the children like the mysterious markings around the horse's eyes for Little Hans. The green blind appears elsewhere in the narrative, variously as green awnings and the green visor worn by casino croupiers, functioning to deflect the gaze of others (*DA*, 58, 169, and 177/*E*, 38, 115, and 120). The accident, either imminent or complete, is a figure of visual fascination that distracts from the domestic scene proper and from the primal scene of loss and separation that takes place there.

Conclusion

In *Die Ausgewanderten* Sebald constructs different sorts of systems that function according to the principles of *Ähnlichkeit*, similarity, and *Entstellung*, distortion or displacement. The associative networks that emerge between texts and protagonists produce blurred, hybrid identities rather than four discrete emigrant figures. The animal and machinic systems that are harnessed to each other function ambivalently; they can be understood according to an oedipal, totemic logic that wants to stabilize the subject in relation to the familiar and familial, or in terms of anti-oedipal, Deleuzean becomings. The dual functioning of these systems resonates usefully with Freud's case study of Little Hans to show how the experience of the modern subject in a mechanized, industrialized environment radically warps spatial and genealogical relations.

Looking for and locating origins in *Die Ausgewanderten* produces disorientation, not least because the traces have been erased by the systems and mechanisms mobilized by National Socialism. The search for origins is made always at a remove, as the narrator's memory of America schematized in his school atlas shows: "Ich weiß noch, wie ich damals mit dem Vergrößerungsglas nach dem Ursprung des immer kleiner werdenden Hudson-Flusses gesucht und mich dabei verloren habe in einem Planquadrat mit sehr vielen Berggipfeln und Seen" (I still remember searching the map with a magnifying glass for the source of the Hudson River and getting lost in a map square with a great many mountains and lakes; *DA*, 155/*E*, 106). The topographical schematizations used by both Freud and Sebald to supplement their texts are exemplary for the kinds of distortions and displacements that mark geneaological and spatial structures and that resist the desire to recover a unified subject and fixed meaning through narrative.

The networks developed in *Die Ausgewanderten* work in ultimately unresolved ways, and Sebald's project is found caught between the lure of origin and a deconstructive impulse. Sebald shows an attachment to a fantasy of family and to the kinds of domestication found in Freud's case histories, and paradigmatically in *Little Hans*. *Die Ausgewanderten* moves across topographical networks, linking the memory work of its protagonists, but the text seems drawn back to the home and the desire for the putatively reparative logic of Freud's familial, oedipal model. The mobility of Little Hans's case and its affiliation with *Die Ausgewanderten* show the relationship in suspension that informs Sebald's writing. However, his attachment to the principle of origin and the desire to adopt the emigrant into a family structure can only produce an encounter with the fallacy of this fantasy after 1945.

Notes

[1] The first edition of *Die Ausgewanderten* used the name Max Aurach, but, following the objections of Frank Auerbach, the artist whose biography and work forms the basis for Sebald's fictional creation, the English translation and subsequent German editions tell the story of Max Ferber.

[2] Stuart Taberner, "German Nostalgia? Remembering German-Jewish Life in W. G. Sebald's *Die Ausgewanderten* and *Austerlitz*," *German Quarterly* 79.3 (2004): 181–202; here 184.

[3] Gisela Ecker, "'Heimat' oder Die Grenzen der Bastelei," in *W. G. Sebald: Politische Archäologie und melancholische Bastelei*, ed. Michael Niehaus and Claudia Öhlschläger (Berlin: Schmidt, 2006), 77–88; and "'Ein auffallend geschichtsblindes und traditionsloses Volk': Heimatdiskurs und Ruinenästhetik in W. G. Sebalds Prosa," in Niehaus and Öhlschläger, 89–110.

[4] John Zilcosky, "Sebald's Uncanny Travels: The Impossibility of Getting Lost," in *W. G. Sebald: A Critical Companion*, ed. J. J. Long and Anne Whitehead (Edinburgh: Edinburgh UP, 2004), 102–20; here 106.

[5] J. J. Long, "Intercultural Identities in W. G. Sebald's *The Emigrants* and Norbert Gstrein's *Die englischen Jahre*," *Journal of Multilingual and Multicultural Development* 25.5–6 (2004): 512–28; here 517.

[6] Anthony Vidler, *Warped Spaces: Art, Architecture, and Anxiety in Modern Culture* (Cambridge, MA: MIT Press, 2000), 41–42.

[7] Sigmund Freud, *Analyse der Phobie eines fünfjährigen Knaben*, in *GW* 7:241–377; here 319; in English, *Analysis of a Phobia in a Five-Year-Old Boy*, trans. and ed. James Strachey in *SE* 10:3–149; here 84. The *Standard Edition* translates this as "coloured by traffic," but I have used my own translation, since it is the Lacanian notion of movement in a system of signification that I want to emphasize here. Further refer-

ences to this work are cited in the text using the abbreviation *LH* followed by the page number from the German original and the standard English translation.

[8] Vidler, *Warped Spaces*, 1.

[9] Todd Samuel Presner, *Mobile Modernity: Germans, Jews, Trains* (New York: Columbia UP, 2007).

[10] Freud, *Psychoanalytische Bemerkungen über einen autobiographisch beschriebenen Fall von Paranoia (Dementia Paranoides)* (1911), in *GW* 8:239–320; in English, *Psycho-Analytic Notes on an Autobiographical Account of a Case of Paranoia (dementia paranoides)*, in *SE* 12:3–80.

[11] Carolin Duttlinger, "Traumatic Photographs: Remembrance and the Technical Media in W. G. Sebald's *Austerlitz*," in Long and Whitehead, *A Critical Companion*, 155–71; Jan Henrik Witthaus, "Fehlleistung und Fiktion: Sebaldsche Gedächtnismodelle zwischen Freud und Borges," in Niehaus and Öhlschläger, 157–72.

[12] Martin Klebes, "Sebald's Pathographies," in *W. G. Sebald: History — Memory — Trauma*, ed. Scott Denham and Mark McCulloh (Berlin: de Gruyter, 2006), 65–75; here 70.

[13] Presner, *Mobile Modernity*, 278 and 239.

[14] The German *Platzangst* can be translated as both claustrophobia and agoraphobia, as Vidler's argument in *Warped Spaces* explains, and it is perhaps in this dual relation of topographical anxiety that Paul Bereyter's pathology is to be understood (Vidler, *Warped Spaces*, 33).

[15] Quoting Thomas Kastura's "Geheimnisvolle Fähigkeit zur Transmigration: W. G. Sebalds interkulturelle Wallfahrten in die Leere," *Arcadia: Internationale Zeitschrift für Literaturwissenschaft* 31.1/2 (1996): 197–216, Ana-Isabel Aliaga-Buchenau considers the implications of the narrator's emergence over the four stories, but her analysis does not go much beyond identifying his reluctance to tell his own story: "His own story of exile remains 'a fifth story of exile kept quiet' (Kastura 197)." Ana-Isabel Aliaga-Buchenau "'A Time He Could Not Bear to Say Any More About': Presence and Absence of the Narrator in W. G. Sebald's *The Emigrants*," in Denham and McCulloh, *History — Memory — Trauma*, 142–55; here 153.

[16] In an essay on the ethical problem of identification in Sebald's writing, Jan Ceuppens has posited a Galtonian composite photograph as the final image of *The Emigrants*, but suggests the resulting portrait would be "neutral and vague," allowing Sebald a means of distancing himself and his reader from the lives he recounts (Jan Ceuppens, "Transcripts: An Ethics of Representation in *The Emigrants*," in Denham and McCulloh, *History — Memory — Trauma*, 251–63; here 256–57). Elsewhere I have shown how Wittgenstein's mobilization of the composite image to illustrate his notion of *Familienähnlichkeiten* forms a key exchange with Sebald's prose and questions the kinds of loss that might occur in the attempt to find similarities and emergent groups; see Dora Osborne, "Blind Spots: Viewing Trauma in W. G. Sebald's *Austerlitz*," *Seminar* 43.3 (2007): 517–33. Martin Klebes, in his book *Wittgenstein's Novels* (New York: Routledge, 2006) has also drawn on Sebald's use of Wittgenstein's

Familienähnlichkeiten, but it is the problematic use of this concept via the illustration of Galton's composite image as it is found in Wittgenstein's 1929 *Lecture on Ethics* that I see as informing Sebald's use of photography and taxonomic modes.

[17] Anne Fuchs provides an inventory of the visual elements of Sebald's prose in her article "W. G. Sebald's Painters: The Function of Fine Art in His Prose Works," *Modern Languages Review* 101 (2006): 167–83.

[18] Freud, *Der Mann Moses und die monotheistische Religion,* in *GW* 16:144; in English, *Moses and Monotheism,* in *SE* 23:43.

[19] Jacques Lacan, *Le séminaire: Livre IV. La relation d'objet,* ed. Jacques-Alain Miller (Paris: Seuil, 1994), 326. Further references to this work are cited in the text using the abbreviation *RO* followed by the page number.

[20] Freud, *Totem und Tabu,* vol. 9 of *GW,* here 157; in English, *Standard Edition,* vol. 13, *Totem and Taboo,* in *SE* 13:1–163; here 129.

[21] Gilles Deleuze, *Essays Critical and Clinical,* trans. Daniel W. Smith and Michael A. Greco (London: Verso, 1998), 64.

[22] Gilles Deleuze and Félix Guattari, *A Thousand Plateaus: Capitalism and Schizophrenia,* trans. Brian Massumi (London: Continuum, 2004), 15.

[23] Deleuze and Guattari, *A Thousand Plateaus,* 15.

[24] Osborne, "Blind Spots," 517–33.

[25] Deleuze, *Essays Critical and Clinical,* 65.

[26] Eric Santner, *Stranded Objects: Mourning, Memory and Film in Postwar Germany* (Ithaca, NY: Cornell UP, 1990), 8.

[27] Jan Ceuppens has noted how instances of "Sprachlosigkeit" are often bound to Germany in *Die Ausgewanderten.* Ceuppens, "Realia: Konstellationen bei Benjamin, Barthes, Lacan — und Sebald," in Niehaus and Öhlschläger, 241–58; here 248.

[28] A reference to Guy Fawkes Night, or Bonfire Night, 5 November. Fireworks are set off and an effigy of Guy Fawkes burned in memory of the Gunpowder Plot of 1605, when a small group of Catholic extremists planned to blow up James I and his parliament. In preparation for this event, children used to beg on the streets so they can buy fireworks. The traditional cry is "Penny for the Guy!"

[29] John Zilcosky has identified the ambiguous topographical relationships that inform the trajectories of Sebald's protagonists and ultimately prevent them from losing their way, that is, from moving away from these sites of unstable identity and memory (Zilcosky, "Sebald's Uncanny Travels, 111–16). Katja Garloff's article on *Die Ausgewanderten* uses specifically "Max Aurach" to discuss the problematic notion of witness. She writes that "the text can be read as a series of impossible returns and missed encounters." Katja Garloff, "The Emigrant as Witness: W. G. Sebald's *Die Ausgewanderten,*" *German Quarterly* 77.1 (2004): 76–93; here 77.

[30] In the English translation, Michael Hulse renders "Spengler" as plumber (194), but the South German context of Luisa Lanzberg's memoirs suggest that tinsmith might be meant here.

[31] John Forrester, *The Seductions of Psychoanalysis: Freud, Lacan and Derrida* (Cambridge: Cambridge UP, 1994), 205.

[32] Garloff, "The Emigrant as Witness," 77.

[33] Jan Ceuppens makes an intertextual link between Sebald's missing skaters and those invoked by Paul Celan's poem *Heimkehr*. Questions of absence and trace are discussed in the context of Derrida's preoccupation with date, that is, with the impossible coincidence of events and their witness, and the inevitability of a date's return. Ceuppens, "Tracing the Witness in W. G. Sebald," in *W. G. Sebald and the Writing of History*, ed. Anne Fuchs and J. J. Long (Würzburg: Königshausen und Neumann, 2007), 59–72; here 70.

[34] In *Austerlitz*, the narrator draws attention to the falling figure of a woman ice-skating on the periphery of Lucas van Valckenborch's *Ansicht von Antwerpen* (*A*, 19/13).

[35] Freud, *Über die Psychogenese eines Falles von weiblicher Homosexualität*, in *GW* 12:269–302; here 289–90; in English, *The Psychogenesis of a Case of Homosexuality in a Woman*, in *SE* 18:145–72; here 162.

[36] W. G. Sebald, "Des Häschens Kind, der kleine Has: Über das Totemtier des Lyrikers Ernst Herbeck" / "Des Häschens Kind, der kleine Has (The Little Hare, Child of the Hare). On the Poet Ernst Herbeck's Totem Animal," in *CS*, 171–78; here 178/125–33; here 133.

12: While the Hidden Horrors of History are Briefly Illuminated: The Poetics of Wandering in *Austerlitz* and *Die Ringe des Saturn*

Peter Arnds

WHEN THE NARRATOR IN SEBALD'S *Austerlitz* first meets the protagonist Austerlitz in the *Salle des pas perdus* of the Central Train Station in Antwerp, he is immediately reminded of the animals of the zoological nocturama he has just visited and thinks of the occupants of the waiting room as members of a reduced, "aus seiner Heimat ausgewiesenen oder untergegangenen Volks" (race that had perished or had been expelled from its homeland; *A*, 14/7). This moment reveals key themes in the Sebaldian landscape: memory and forgetting, the proximity between man and animal, the gulf between reason and myth, between dwelling and wandering, between the bourgeois, sedentary citizen and the rootless wanderer and nomad. The paradigms of wandering in Sebald's work extend to the urban and rural landscape through which his characters roam, the architectural constructs with which they engage emotionally and intellectually, and their homelessness in labyrinthine places, reflecting their aimless wandering, imprisonment, even insanity. A mapping of place and space in any of Sebald's texts may elucidate his unique stance toward dwelling and wandering, his vision of humanity's *Dasein* (being) as a *Verlorensein* (being lost) on a planet that witnesses multiple forms of increasing destruction.

Sebald's work showcases modernity's central rift dividing unreason and migration on the one hand from reason, bourgeois roots, and the search of dwelling on the other, a chasm that his work shares with a host of cultural theories that critically take on the Enlightenment project. Mikhail Bakhtin opposes his transgressive and subversive carnival with the constraints and officialdom of the two power institutions, the church and the state, Michel Foucault discusses madness (as a form of migration) in the Age of Confinement, and Friedrich Nietzsche offers Dionysian excess and intoxication as an alternative to Apollonian repression of suffering through the semblance of beauty and orderliness.[1] In seconding Foucault, Said argues in *Culture and Imperialism* that this age's mass movement and migration challenges "something very basic to every art and theory of government, the principle of confinement . . ., whose ultimate extension is represented at its most simple and severe by the prison or mental hospital."[2] Another central dichotomy in Sebald's work, which seems to be related to the dyad of dwelling versus wandering, is that between forgetting and the concealment of destruction on the one hand, and memory and the revelation of destruction on the other. While sedentariness or immobility in Sebald is often associated with the forgetting of destruction, the mode of wandering, of travel, triggers the revelation of that destruction. These poetics of wandering in Sebald's work have the potential of triggering memory and of unearthing history's various forms of destruction of species, whether man or animal, of uncovering and briefly illuminating the hidden horrors of history. The wandering of many of Sebald's characters is a wandering through a landscape marked by concealment, destruction, and oblivion, and can be understood at a deeper level via a set of cultural theories that complement each other in their concern with the binaries of wandering and dwelling, memory and forgetting, revelation and concealment. In these binaries wandering is tied to revelation and memory as dwelling is tied to forgetting and concealment. The cultural theorists that may best aid our understanding of these dichotomies in the context of two texts I want to discuss here, Sebald's *Austerlitz* (2001) and *Die Ringe des Saturn* (1995), are Gilles Deleuze and Felix Guattari, Friedrich Nietzsche, and Martin Heidegger. Specifically, this essay will engage with Deleuze/Guattari's dyad in *Mille Plateaux* (*A Thousand Plateaus*) of the image of *arborescence* for sedentariness versus the nomadic *rhizome*; Friedrich Nietzsche's discussion in his *Die Geburt der Tragödie* (*The Birth of Tragedy*) of the Apollonian as a figure denoting semblance and concealment versus the Dionysian as the revelation of what is concealed and as the surfacing of more deeply situated truths; and Martin Heidegger's thoughts in his Parmenides lectures from 1942/43 on *lethe* as concealment, forgetting, and destruction, versus *aletheia*, as the disclosure of the concealed, forgotten, and destroyed. This article will show that travel or wandering occurs within a field of tension in Sebald's two texts, tension between arborescence, the Apollonian, and *lethe* as tropes of non-movement, concealment, and forgetting on the one hand, and, on the other hand, the rhizome, Dionysus, and *aletheia*. This tension is inscribed into concrete textual moments that reflect how wandering triggers memory and the revelation of concealed truths. At the same time these illuminated moments in the wanderings of Sebald's characters will reveal the absurdity of life and history, very much in the Nietzschean mode of a complete pessimism regarding any progress and historical teleology and in the eternal return of terror and suffering. The Deleuzian rhizome expresses this absurdity of wandering as much as Nietzsche's Dionysus and Heidegger's *aletheia*, which is why I propose to read these concepts in close proximity to each other and to wandering.

Deleuze and Guattari, Nietzsche, Heidegger, and the Literature of Travel

Despite the skepticism one might harbor toward the philosophy of Deleuze and Guattari, their thinking promotes a deeper understanding of Sebald's fictional landscape and the relationship this landscape unfolds between wandering, dwelling, and the destruction of the planet. Their concepts of the rhizome and arborescence in particular lend themselves to an interpretation of the clash between Sebald's typically postmodern focus on the uncanniness and aimlessness of wandering and modernity's persistent concern with finding roots. The rhizome is characterized by a lack of linearity and is ambivalent in its capacity to offer lines of flight. As an image of entanglement, it is open-ended, anti-genealogical, anti-hierarchical, and anti-teleological.[3] Its subterranean but easily eradicable roots of tubers and bulbs make it the classical image of nomadic wandering.[4] Arborescence, on the other hand, indicates structure, organization, teleology, purpose, the deep roots of trees, and genealogies. It is an image for the rationality of the sedentary bourgeois class and its creed of progress, in its obsession with roots an image even for the search for racial purity, while the rhizome's transgressiveness is anarchic, carnivalesque in the Bakhtinian sense, a trope also for mental aberrancy. Rather than offering a clear-cut dialectic, however, the rhizome and arborescence often also supplement each other ("There are knots of arborescence in rhizomes. . . . The important point is that the root-tree and canal-rhizome are not two opposed models"; *MP*, 20).

Deleuze and Guattari's arborescence of Western societies, the deep roots of their teleologies and their territorialism, has the potential of being subverted through the rhizome, the shallow roots associated with deterritorialization, nomadism, and homelessness. This discussion is significant for a number of literary genres in which wandering and travel are central moments. In the magical realist novel of the twentieth century, for example, the archetype of the wandering trickster on the margins of society manifests himself as the picaro, a literary representation of the rhizome and as such in constant conflict with the arborescent, sedentary world, for which the nineteenth-century *Bildungsroman* once was the representative genre. We encounter this dichotomy in authors like Günter Grass, John Irving, Salman Rushdie, Michel Tournier, and Gabriel García Márquez, but also in pure travel literature like Bruce Chatwin's *The Songlines* (1987) or William Least Heat-Moon's *Blue Highways* (1983).[5] In these two texts the rhizomatic world of the indigenous peoples clashes with Western racism, with the latter, in its obsession with blood lines and genealogy, constituting a form of Deleuzian arborescence (*MP*, 20–21). As jazz and blues are part of the rhizomatic world, giving tragicomic hope to African

Americans, so are Australia's songlines, that intricate web of dreaming paths as the manifestation of an ancient nomadic culture, and Heat-Moon's journey across America through the labyrinth of its blue highways, its rarely traveled roads, as a reflection of Hopi visions of totality.

In so-called contemporary German migrant literature the Deleuzian dichotomy can enrich the reading and interpretation of novels such as Rafik Schami's *Die Sehnsucht der Schwalbe* (2000),[6] the story of a series of unsuccessful migrations of the protagonist Lutfi from Syria to Germany. Schami's literary treatment of migration parallels that of Deleuze and Guattari, in that he recognizes the potential of what the two philosophers call the re-territorialization of culture for changing other cultures. Migration's inherent processes of de-territorialization and re-territorialization are the chief causes of cultural exchange in this world. In Schami's elaborations on Oriental versus Western cultures, specifically music and migratory birds become part of the rhizomatic, Orientalist dimension in this novel. The Deleuzian dichotomy becomes apparent specifically in migrant literature's geography. In Schami's emphasis of the labryrinthine, rhizomatic features of the city map of Frankfurt, for example — specifically with its flea market and prison at its core — one can see to what extent the Bakhtinian notion of the carnivalesque marketplace, the Foucauldian distinction between medieval cities, where zanies of all kinds were allowed to roam free, and institutions of confinement, and the Deleuzian theory of rhizomatics complement each other.

Other contemporary German-speaking writers have subconsciously played with the rhizome for the wanderings of their characters: Robert Menasse in *Selige Zeiten, brüchige Welt* (arborescent Vienna versus rhizomatic, carnivalesque Sao Paolo) and *Die Vertreibung aus der Hölle* (Inquisition Spain with its racism and insistence on blood lines versus the tolerance and multiculturalism of Amsterdam, whose city map reflects the rhizome in its web of canals, an image to which Sebald also refers), Robert Schindel in *Gebürtig* (Vienna vis-à-vis the canal city Venice), Emine Sevgi Özdamar in *Die Brücke vom Goldenen Horn* (Berlin versus Istanbul), and Barbara Frischmuth in *Das Verschwinden des Schattens in der Sonne* (Vienna and Istanbul).[7] All these authors are voicing their concern with multiculturalism, orientalism, and immigration today. The cultural theory of Deleuze and Guattari allows for an interpretation of this literary oeuvre in a comparative context that reflects specifically to what extent a paradigm like arborescence can point to racism and the horrors of the Nazi period, while the figure of the rhizome in this literature of migration may also reflect Said's notion of Orientalism and offer mechanisms for resisting racism and coping with traumatic memory.

In Sebald's texts the rhizome functions as a trope of wandering, that of the narrator but also those of others, both man and animal, from Jews to herrings to desert caravans; and yet here the potential of liberation and resistance offered by the rhizome is as temporary and questionable as that of the Bakhtinian carnival, which Deleuze and Guattari would argue offers a typically rhizomatic line of flight from power structures. Ultimately, rhizomatic wandering may result from a loss of memory, as in the case of Austerlitz, from confusion, homelessness and despair in the world, and it tends to lead Sebald's characters toward images of imprisonment, concealment, and destruction. It coincides with the kind of lethargy that Nietzsche associated with Dionysus, which "outweighs every motive for action"[8] and instills sensations of a complete "Verstoßen-und Ausgelöschtseins" (rejection and annihilation; *A*, 330/228) in many of Sebald's characters and results in their incapacity to connect with other human beings. Many of them experience a Dionysian breakdown of their *principium individuationis* that may temporarily deprive them of their speech (Austerlitz, or Max Aurach in *Die Ausgewanderten*) or mobility (Ambros Adelwarth in *Die Ausgewanderten*), submerge all memory of the past, and even lead to institutionalization in a mental clinic.

Deleuze and Guattari closely associate the rhizome with smooth space, nomadic, usually non-civic space, with landscapes like the desert, sea, sky, or sweep of forest. Striated space, on the other hand, is arborescent and tends to be civic, urban space that has lost its smooth surface and is striated by straight vertical and horizontal lines. Striated space is space that has unnatural boundaries, borders, the space of the nation-state. While the smooth space tolerates the rhizome as web, it is the straight lines of the fabric that striate space: for example, Penelope Peacefull's crossword puzzle or the checkerboard streets of Theresienstadt in *Austerlitz*, a hospital window in *Die Ringe des Saturn* (*RS*, 12/4) or Thomas Browne's geometric structure of the Quincunx (*RS*, 31/20). Striated space contains territorial boundaries that invade, structure, and conquer smooth space.[9] In connection with time and memory, smooth space and the shallow roots of the rhizome can be images of short-term memory, which "includes forgetting as a process" (*MP*, 16), whereas long-term memory corresponds to striated space and the deep roots of arborescence. If we contend with Deleuze and Guattari that the rhizome obscures because its labyrinthine web of roots is an image of confusion, and arborescence reveals because it is one root leading into depth, then we can align this dichotomy with Heidegger's *lethe*, which obscures, and *aletheia* which reveals. We can also align these two dichotomies with Nietzsche's distinction between the Apollonian as semblance, beauty that conceals human suffering, and the Dionysian that reveals human suffering. This distinction then leads us to myth. Myth is the additional glue that holds our three philosophical constructs together.

Smooth space and the rhizome relate to a mythological subtextuality in Sebald's work, to myth's aspects of wandering, irrationality, its connection with beginnings, the primordial, but also its sinister side, its thematic concern with atrocities. Wandering along rhizomatic lines in Sebald's land-scapes leads to the revelation of atrocities often hidden just under the surface, their eradication as close at hand as the rhizomatic tubers dis-cussed by Deleuze and Guattari. This is where Sebald's work touches with the genre of magical realism. In the novel of magical realism, or mythical realism, as I prefer to call it, the grotesque, the mythical, is closely con-nected to the remembrance of atrocities, if we think, for example, of Grass's *Die Blechtrommel* (*The Tin Drum*),[10] a literary reaction against the rational climate and politics of oblivion during the Adenauer period, or García Márquez's grotesque unearthing of the hidden moments of Columbia's history in *One Hundred Years of Solitude* (1967),[11] where offi-cial history and Miguel Abadía Mendez's denial of the 1928 massacre of thousands of strikers at the United Fruit Company are rewritten or "debunked."[12] The retrieval of lost memories is a perpetual concern in this book.

We said that the rhizome is anti-hierarchical and anti-teleological. In these qualities it resembles Nietzsche's understanding of the Dionysian principle as a social equalizer, a phenomenon we see reflected for example in Euripides' play *The Bacchae*, where Pentheus, the King of Thebes, is torn to pieces by the bacchae, the women of Thebes gone mad under the influence of Dionysus.[13] Pentheus's corporal fragmentation is initiated by his own mother because he refuses to pay tribute to Dionysus but still wishes to catch a glimpse of Dionysian ecstasy by spying on it from a dis-tance, an act that is interpreted as mockery of Dionysus. In Dionysian madness everyone becomes the same, boundaries between personalities are suspended, and unlike the Apollonian, which tends to cover over human suffering, the Dionysian reveals it in all its absurdity. In its location between joy and terror, between ecstatic orgies and the fragmentation of bodies the Dionysian reveals the absurdity of life and history, history's anti-Hegelian nature, its circularity and the idea of an eternal return of suffering, rather than historical progress and teleology. Such a denial of progress and teleol-ogy establishes a connection between the Dionysian and the Deleuzian rhizome. By providing lines of flight the latter leads away from the teleol-ogy of arborescence inasmuch as the Dionysian breaks through — frag-ments — the semblance and make-believe of Apollo. Dionysus's transgression of boundaries, his power to challenge liminality, also recalls the rhizome's association with the transgression of territorial boundaries. By ignoring territorial boundaries the rhizome is a postmodern figure of migration *par excellence*, while arborescence, the deep-rootedness in the home soil, reflects the concerns of modernity, its obsession with the build-ing of nation-states, in the wake of the Enlightenment.

It is this anti-Enlightenment stance that the rhizome shares with the Dionysian as this principle was conceived both by Euripides and Nietzsche. Nietzsche understood the disenchantment that came from the

Enlightenment of the eighteenth century with its inherent suppression of myth as something irrational, and he offered Dionysian excess as an alternative to Apollonian *ratio* and semblance. In comparison, in Greek antiquity the Dionysian was pre-Socratic and disappeared with the turn to the Apollonian after Socrates, whose philosophy of reason makes him the chief representative of this early form of Enlightenment in that era. Rediscovering Dionysus in the music of Wagner was for Nietzsche a reaction against the Apollonian atmosphere of the nineteenth century, with its tendency to cover over or oust anything that smacked of irrationalism in the arts, especially in architecture. The Dionysian promised a re-enchantment of life, while at the same time Nietzsche was aware that it gave expression to humanity's suffering and life's, history's, absurdity, of which the bourgeois world of the nineteenth century was in denial. I would argue that this absurdity is expressed in the Dionysian as much as in the rhizome, while arborescence and the Apollonian are in denial of an absurdity of life and human suffering and try to cover it over. The rhizome and the Dionysian contain a moment of subversion, but that too remains absurd, absurd in the face of history and the teleological minds who reassert a semblance of order in life. As figures for nomadism and madness the rhizome and the Dionysian are closely connected to myth, to the instinctual, the beginnings and the primordial. Pentheus's repression of Dionysus in Euripides' *Bacchae* is a suppression of the power of myth in a society that is adopting the principles of reason, a society in denial of the absurdity and insanities of life and history. Myth is often seen as the opposite of history. In fact, myth expresses the absurdity of history primarily in its use of circular time and of archetypes, as both express the idea of non-progress, of an eternal return. We encounter this denial of the linearity of time, of historical progress, in the persistent use of circular time in the novel of magical realism, a tradition deeply steeped in myth. In Sebald's work, too, the linearity of time is often dissolved, which reflects the non-linearity of travel, the aimless drifting of his characters.[14] For Austerlitz, for example, time itself has become the smooth space of *lethe*. Convinced that "sämtliche Zeitmomente gleichzeitig nebeneinander existier[]en" (all moments of time have co-existed simultaneously; *A*, 152/101), he is in permanent denial of the linearity of time, of a *Nacheinander* (one-after-another) of past, present, and future. *Lethe* as oblivion, Heidegger argues, "is the concealment that lets the past, the present, and the future fall into the path of a self-absenting absence. And with that it sets man himself away into concealedness."[15]

Rhizomatic wandering in Sebald may be aimless, absurd, circular, and not lead to any clear destination, but it is also directly linked to the idea of the concealment and revelation of painful memories and of atrocities. This is where the philosophies of Deleuze and Guattari and of Nietzsche resonate with that of Heidegger. If the rhizome and the Apollonian conceal destruction and painful memories, then these two categories correspond to what in his Parmenides lectures Heidegger described as *lethe* in its three-fold meaning of concealment, forgetting, and destruction.[16] Its purported opposite, *aletheia*, as an emergence from these would then correspond to the Dionysian as a moment that breaks through Apollonian semblance and reveals the truth, and it would correspond to arborescence in its capacity of revealing long-term memory. Yet how problematic these dichotomies really are in the sense of being pseudo-dichotomies will become clear if we look at Sebald's texts more closely. The rhizome conceals in its faculty of being labyrinthine, but without following the rhizome a revelation of the truth would not be possible. In the same way, the Dionysian may reveal atrocities and human suffering but the state of intoxication also hides something. Madness may have a rapport with the truth but it is also a self-enclosed world that shuts itself off from reality. In the same way, *aletheia* denotes a brief surfacing from *lethe*, but this is only temporary since *aletheia* always leads back to *lethe*. Travel in Sebald ties these three pseudo-dichotomies together, and it takes place between their polarities, leads from one to the other and back again.

Austerlitz

Sebald's texts are filled with images of repose and violence, liberation and horror, escape and imprisonment, reflecting the protagonist's "erstarrte Unruhe,"[17] his vacillation between immobility and unrest. Austerlitz is caught not only between aimless rhizomatic wandering and his arborescent search for home but also between the smooth space of short-term memory and the striation of his long-term memory that, once uncovered, eventually leads him to the concentration camp of Theresienstadt. Before that happens, however, his aimless London night walks in particular fill him with a temporary, and therefore illusory, sense of liberation from his troubled past. In line with Michel de Certeau's theory of walking, to Austerlitz walking is a sort of pedestrian speech act, "a spatial acting-out of the place just as the speech act is an acoustic acting-out of language,"[18] which is supported by the fact that Austerlitz starts his night walks through London precisely at the moment when his language and writing fail (*A*, 180/120–21). For Austerlitz walking, traveling, thus becomes an act of communication with his fellow human beings from whom he feels excluded, an act that confirms his humanness, since to the animal "the word is denied."[19] He tries to express himself through his aimless wandering, as it were, through his walking rhetorics.[20] De Certeau further argues that to walk is "to lack a place. It is the indefinite process of being absent, reflected for instance in Austerlitz's feeling of "Geistesabwesenheit" (mental absence; *A*, 332/230) and "Abgetrenntsein" (sense of disjunction; *A*, 161/109).

> The moving about that the city multiplies and concentrates makes the city itself an immense social experience of lacking a place — an experience that is, to be sure, broken up into countless tiny deportations (displacements and walks), compensated for by the relationships and intersections of these exoduses that intertwine and create an urban fabric.[21]

In this sense the rhizome of Austerlitz's web of walks functions for him as a way of coping with his traumatic early childhood. As one substantial component of working through trauma is its being acted out, Austerlitz is reenacting his childhood experience, which at this point he is still repressing, of being deported on the *Kindertransport.*

In *Austerlitz,* however, mobility is not confined to the gravity of walking and flaneurism across rhizomatic city landscapes; it is also expressed in the grace of flying. Austerlitz has a school-friend, Gerald Fitzpatrick, who like him yearns to escape from the troubles of striated space and its inherent lack of healthy dwelling. Gerald's obsession with airplanes and flying stems from his desire for the untroubledness of the celestial smooth space and to escape from the desolation of the world[22] in which nihilism, the abandonment of the divinities, has resulted in a loss of "an essential connection to the earth, the soil, the ground, and the homeland."[23] The sky remains the one largely unconquered smooth space that may still promise good dwelling, as is indicated also by the bird's nest Austerlitz mentions (*A,* 31/18) as an ideal form of all *Bauen* (building). Gerald's escape from the earth into the sky — "je weiter man von der Erde abhebe, desto besser" (the further you can rise above the earth the better; *A,* 164/111) — is as nomadic as Austerlitz's urban perambulations, reflecting the elusiveness of their rhizomatic tracks in view of the oppressiveness of dwelling, the destruction of the earth's surface, and the nation-state's arborescent gravity.[24] Although Sebald would concur with Heidegger about the destitute status of this planet, Heidegger's perception of good dwelling, a vision deeply rooted in the ideology of blood and soil, which was much influenced by his Black Forest background, differs widely from Sebald's view.[25] Heidegger's much idealized Black Forest peasants are sedentaries who have taken possession of the ground, which they occupy through their immobility, whereas nomadism knows that it cannot occupy and possess space (the desert, the steppe). In *Austerlitz,* too, the only form of dwelling seems to be nomadic wandering with its reluctance to possess the earth and conquer the sky, a belief that Sebald shares with Bruce Chatwin,[26] Native Americans, and other nomadic people. Ultimately, nomadic dwelling extends beyond the confines of life itself. That Gerald does not return from one of his flights may attest to the absurdity of his escape and the Nietzschean thought that to escape the absurdity and cruelty of life and nature it is best to die young.[27]

One of the principal mythological manifestations for the Deleuzian rhizome is the labyrinth. It occurs in various shapes in *Austerlitz*, most ominously as the web of railway tracks, which lead in two directions, to Auschwitz and to England, thus reiterating the two functions of the rhizome, imprisonment and liberation.[28] We encounter the rhizome as labyrinth in descriptions of London with its "immer verwinkelter werdenden Gewirr fauliger Gassen" (warren of putrid streets; *A, 194/130*), the Parisian Metro, and in the memories that assail Austerlitz in the Ladies' Waiting Room of Liverpool Station, which "immer das eine im andern verschachtelt" (all interlocking) accompany the image of the "labyrinthischen Gewölbe" (labyrinthine vaults; *A, 200/136*) he finds himself in.

The rhizomatic labyrinth offers a link to Nietzsche's Dionysus, in that like this god of the underworld it contains much of what the Age of Reason tried to suppress: wandering, madness, that is, aberrancy of the mind as a form of wandering, and the devil. The latter appears in the image of the bull in Knossos, that white bull from the sea, Poseidon's gift to Minos that was intended to be offered back in sacrifice. It had a silver circle on its forehead, and horns like a crescent moon. The silver circle stands symbolically for the sun, the horns for the moon, thus expressing a cosmic harmony that repeats itself in the union of Apollo and Dionysus, of reason and unreason. The horns as a crescent moon and Dionysus, Bull-God and god of the underworld, both show this connection with unreason as lunacy, which came to be increasingly institutionalized from the eighteenth century on. The word "labyrinth" itself expresses this idea of the two-pronged moon/horns, *labrys* being the double-axe, a motif that resurfaces throughout European cultural history in various characters on this side of lunacy, the harlequin, the fool, *Eulenspiegel*, and is ultimately associated with the devil, that undesirable *par excellence*, whom the Enlightenment tries to chase off the world stage and whom Christianity tries to suppress. Dionysus himself is represented as a bearded satyr "whose name and attributes were borrowed from the goat" and whom, unlike the "calmly-sitting" Apollo, Nietzsche identifies with the migration of the St. Vitus dancers, "ever-growing throngs" roaming "from place to place."[29]

While Austerlitz's wanderings are in themselves rhizomatically labyrinthine, the places he visits often display these qualities too: libraries, cities, but above all the camp at the heart of this novel — Terezin. It combines the rhizomatics of the labyrinth with the arborescence of its perfidious organization and the striation of its territory, the checkerboard structure of its streets and the star-like shape of its fortification, a reference to the yellow star with which the Nazis imprinted their stamp of striation onto Jewish wandering.[30] It also combines the notions of concealment and revelation as inherent features of the mythological labyrinth. The Cretan labyrinth partakes of concealment as long as wandering takes place in it (*lethe*), but once the center is reached the monster reveals itself in a moment of *aletheia*. The Minotaur in particular finds itself in permanent suspension between concealment and un-concealment, *lethe* and *aletheia*, Apollo and Dionysus. The same holds for Terezin in *Austerlitz*. Austerlitz walks in the field of *lethe* as long as he walks the rhizomatic lines of the labyrinth along which his life takes him, but when he visits the camp it reveals to him a glimpse of the sheer immensity of human suffering.

Concealment and revelation are central motifs for Terezin, where killing and torture are disguised behind the facade of a place of healing, Theresien*bad*, and a place for sedentary citizens, a home, Theresien*stadt*. This facade is briefly penetrated as Austerlitz watches the documentary *Der Führer schenkt den Juden eine Stadt* and turns it into slow motion. Playing this film in slow motion reveals the camp inmates as prisoners in pain, reduced to the level of animals, and shows their complete loss of home and dwelling. This is a pivotal moment in the text: as the *lethe* of Theresien*stadt* yields to the *aletheia* of Terezin as a concentration camp and gives the onlooker an idea of what Giorgio Agamben called *nuda vita*, bare life,[31] the *lethe* in Austerlitz's own life (as the repression of his deep memory) yields to *aletheia*, the truth about his Jewish origins and collective identity. But Austerlitz's descent into the underworld of the camps can be read in even more concrete mythological terms, mythological in the sense of Nietzsche's discussion of Apollonian semblance and a Dionysian revelation of the truth. As argued, this distinction of Apollonian semblance, of the way things seem to be upon the surface, versus the revelation of a Dionysian underworld is closely tied to the Heideggerian distinction into *lethe* and *aletheia*. Revealing the *aletheia* of the camps Austerlitz's Dionysian experience is one that brings him into close contact with the camp's *nuda vita*. While the documentary *Der Führer schenkt den Juden eine Stadt* sounds cheerful at normal speed, in slow motion the film's musical soundtrack is transformed into sounds that seem to emerge from a "subterranen Welt, in schreckensvollen Tiefen . . ., in die keine menschliche Stimme jemals hinabgestiegen ist" (subterranean world, through the most nightmarish depths, . . . to which no human voice has ever descended; *A*, 356/250). Austerlitz associates these sounds with the menacing growls of lions and tigers driven mad in captivity. I would argue that the soundtrack played at regular speed conveys what Nietzsche has described as Apollonian semblance, that is, superficial appearance (Theresien*stadt* as a city), while the slow-motion version reveals it to be what it is: a concentration camp, with its Dionysian proximity to bare, creaturely life, to the demonic, and to wandering.[32] Especially the mentioning of "growls of tigers" seems to point to Dionysus, whose origins are in the Ganges delta and whom the myth frequently associates with tigers.

Yet Austerlitz's moment of *aletheia* is only very brief, as it leads him right back into the realm of *lethe* and what Nietzsche described as lethargy induced by the Dionysian experience, the glimpse of horror that leads to the complete breakdown of the *principium individuationis*. The moment of truth about his mother triggers Austerlitz's ultimate crisis, in which a three-week-long mental absence paralyzes all thought processes and emotions, leads to a complete breakdown of his language, and makes a sojourn in a psychiatric clinic necessary.

We can observe a definite connection here between Nietzsche's Dionysian moment, with its breakdown of the *principium individuationis*, and Agamben's *nuda vita*. This *nuda vita* reveals itself primarily in the Muselmann of the camps, that figure between life and death who in Muslim fashion has surrendered completely to fate. One could argue that Austerlitz's own breakdown mirrors that of the Muselmann, albeit in much muted form, as the Muselmann's lethargy, his suspension between life and death, is directly related to having witnessed the deepest layers of life's horror. The Muselmann reflects *ad extremis* Nietzsche's view of the cruelty of all life and nature, the complete absurdity of all suffering. In arguably muted form Austerlitz's breakdown also has parallels with the Germans' initial reactions to their own suffering after the war, their non-expressive, stereotypical language in the face of complete destruction and this language's "Funktion . . ., die über das Fassungsvermögen gehenden Erlebnisse zu *verdecken* [my italics in reference to Heidegger's *lethe*] und zu neutralisieren, . . . in Wahrheit nichts als eine Geste zur Abwehr der Erinnerung" (function . . . to cover up and neutralize experiences beyond our ability to comprehend . . ., . . . in truth nothing but a gesture of self-defense against remembering; *LL*, 32/*NH*, 25; trans. modified).

This moment in which human suffering leads to its immediate concealment in the minds of the onlookers for their own self-protection shows how close Heidegger's *lethe* and *aletheia* really are, that they are not opposites. Heidegger discusses *lethe* as *Abwehr* (defense) of the *verum* (truth), etymologically equating the *Wehr* and *verum*,[33] an idea that also refers to Theresienstadt as *Wehr*, as a fortified town, concealing the truth about suffering in its camp. It refers to Austerlitz's as well as the Germans' "Abwehr der Erinnerung" (self-defense against remembering). *Lethe*'s brief breaking up into *aletheia*, where extreme suffering reveals itself, captured in the image of fragmentation in Austerlitz's breakdown so reminiscent of the Muselmann's self-abandonment — "[ich] sah mich . . . von innen zerspringen und Teile meines Körpers über eine finstere und ferne Gegend verstreut" (I visualized myself being broken up from within, so that parts of my body were scattered over a dark and distant terrain; *A*, 331/229–30) — is the motif most closely connected to the Dionysian myth (if we think for example of Pentheus being torn apart by the bacchae, the followers of Dionysus) and seems to be necessary for the shattering of *lethe* for the sake of allowing a moment of *aletheia* to surface. Austerlitz's reaction to the camps reflects to what extent in final analysis *lethe* and *aletheia*, Apollo and Dionysus, the rhizome and arborescence, are really pseudo-dichotomies.

Heidegger's *aletheia*, Nietzsche's Dionysus, an arborescent homecoming that reveals the dark secret about Austerlitz's past, may be moments of unconcealment, but as we can see these moments of unconcealment lead to immediate paralysis, to Austerlitz's shattering, the breakdown of his *principium individuationis*, that is, they ultimately lead back to *lethe*, to immobility, speechlessness, and lethargy. It may consequently not surprise us that Nietzsche's overall pessimism concerns both the Apollonian and the Dionysian, as one just conceals suffering, while the other reveals it, but both lead to despair, whether as a result of repressing the truth or of facing it directly. Neither can detract from the absurdity of nature's cruelty. The melancholia that arises from this awareness is possibly best rendered in Sebald's aimless wanderings under the Rings of Saturn.

Die Ringe des Saturn

In *Die Ringe des Saturn* wandering happens entirely under the sign of Saturn through a landscape that bears all the signs of an apocalypse, a hell on earth. In his act of pedestrian perambulation and narrative speech act the narrator is at times eyed suspiciously by the local population, a mistrust very much in line with the old fear of nomads and itinerants as being some-how in cahoots with the underworld: "Schließlich zieht jeder Fußreisende, auch heute noch, ja gerade heute und vor allem, wenn er nicht dem gän-gigen Bild des Freizeitwanderers entspricht, sogleich den Verdacht der Ortsansässigen auf sich" (After all, every foot traveler incurs the suspicion of the locals, expecially nowadays, and particularly if he does not fit the image of a local rambler; *RS,* 209/175).[34] In *Die Ringe des Saturn* the rhizome occurs in a variety of forms and images, many of which are recy-cled throughout Sebald's travels: in the form of tracks, the narrator's own wanderings, crisscrossing railway lines, intersecting *Lebensbahnen* (life-stories), the tracks of certain species — Deleuze defines these as the pack rhizome — the swallows (*RS,* 87/67), or herrings (*RS,* 72/55). We encounter the rhizome in the threads spun by silk worms, in a caravan cut-ting across the smooth space of the desert (*RS,* 100/80), the canals of Holland (*RS,* 104/84), or as projects that never end, like the figments of the imagination of the farmer Alec Garrard, who has been trying for years to construct a model of Jerusalem instead of looking after his farmland: rhizomatic flights of the imagination instead of the arborescent farmer's work on his soil, grace versus gravity.

The memory of his foot journey ultimately liberates the narrator from the constraints experienced a year later when "in einem Zustand nahezu gänzlicher Unbeweglichkeit (in a state of almost total immobility; *RS,* 12/3) he ends up in a hospital in Norwich. This contrast of immobility and mobility once again permeates the entire text, as it does in *Austerlitz.*

Central to the act of walking is also the contrastive experience of joy and terror — the joy of escaping urban gravity and being liberated by the smooth space, and the terror this smooth space reveals in its landscape of destruction. Here the "unendlich verschlungene[n] Wege" (endlessly winding paths; *RS*, 206/173) of the Dunwich Heath entangle the wanderer and lead him around in circles, preventing him from moving in any direction. This immobility within his circular mobility marks him as a nomad in the classical sense, for the "nomad is he who does not move" (*MP*, 381), who "clings to the smooth space left by the receding forest" (*MP*, 381), remains deterritorialized, without a real home, unlike the migrant who becomes reterritorialized. This is precisely the narrator's experience on the Dunwich Heath: the related phenomena of treelessness and homelessness, where "going native" is impossible as the natives do not understand him, although he speaks their language well (*RS*, 175–76/209) — a complete lack of arborescence in the concrete sense of having deep roots, where only "die gelben Wurzeln der Brennesseln kriechen unter der Erde fort" (the yellow roots of nettles creep onwards in the soil; *RS*, 216/181). This is an apt image for the Deleuzian rhizome as tubers, and here the vertiginous wanderer is surrounded not only by the ubiquitous destruction of plant and animal life but also by the horrors of the war machine — one of the principal features of the Deleuzian nomadology — and by images of colonialism. These three key domains, the destruction of plants and animals, the horrors of war, and those of colonialism partake extensively of the rhizomatic mode. The idea of a fabric or web recurs in the narrator's discovery of the "ins Meer hinausreichenden Rohrlei-tungssystem[s] . . . vermittels dessen bei einer Invasion mit explosionsarti-ger Geschwindigkeit ein Petroleumbrand sich entfachen ließe" (a system of pipes extending far out to sea by means of which a petroleum inferno could be unleashed with such explosive rapidity in the event of an invasion; *RS*, 275–76/231), in the "Wege, auf denen [der Hering] wandert" (the routes the herring take; *RS*, 72/55) before these fish experience their yearly mass destruction, and in the discussion of Joseph Conrad and the Congo brand of colonialism. The geography of the web-like river land-scape makes Conrad's *Heart of Darkness* a central subtext of Sebald's *Die Ringe des Saturn*, especially in view of the thematic approximation of the rhizome, human atrocities, and smooth space (although in Conrad it is the vast carpet of forests, that is, arborescent smooth space, that shows that the rhizome and arborescence do not necessarily antagonize each other).[35]

Perhaps nowhere does the side of torture within the joy/terror ambiv-alence of rhizomatic travel ("ich wußte wohl weder damals, noch weiß ich es heute, ob ich das einsame Gehen als eine Wohltat empfand oder als eine Qual" / I knew then as little as I know now whether walking in this soli-tary way was more of a pleasure than a pain; *RS*, 285/241) surface as much as in the book's final image of the weavers, who experience the

Benjaminian melancholia *ad extremis* as their work drives them into insanity. The title of the book thus refers not only to the narrator's melancholic circular wanderings but quite literally also to the image of the rings of silk spun by a certain type of moth, the *Saturnia carpini* (in the English translation, *Saturnia pavonia*; *RS*, 324/274), the progenitors of the weavers' saturnine spirit of lethargy, their heightened sensation of torture and *Qual* ("an Foltergestelle . . . erinnernde Webstühle," / looms . . . reminiscent of instruments of torture; *RS*, 334/282). Rhizomatic *travel* reveals its inherent *trouble* and *travail*, or *travaglio*, as both labor and anguish, even as madness: for the weavers and a host of other characters in Sebald's texts, including literary figures like Hölderlin. The cause for Hölderlin's mental breakdown was the impossibility of his search for the "ultimate etymological root (or *logos*) that lay buried [*lethe*] beneath all the divisions of language," his failure "to disclose the unity of the divine word [*aletheia*]."[36] The poet's search for the deep root of words and its aberrance into madness demonstrates how the Deleuzian deep (arborescent) versus shallow (rhizomatic) roots can be related to Hölderlin and Heidegger. Their shared passion with the deep root of the *logos* is literally arborescent, while Hölderlin's failure in breaking through the covers of *lethe* sent his mind to rhizomatic wandering. In this sense madness has a close relationship with wandering, the madman's mind that travels too much but also the traveler who can be driven mad, as in the case of Kurtz in Conrad's *Heart of Darkness*.

In cultural theory, madness not only connects Foucault's and Bakhtin's celebrations of unreason with Deleuze's rhizome but also evokes Nietzsche's Dionysian underworld. This underworld appears in different forms in Sebald's work. Sebald's wanderers traverse it in similar fashion to the mythical hero of Greek antiquity who had to descend into Hades.[37] Sebald's fascination with moths, for example, which according to many indigenous beliefs (of Australia, for example) are messengers of death, points to this hellish scenario, as does the weaver's work at the loom, a kind of hell on earth. The associations the moths and weavers open up are manifold, from Ariadne's thread in the labyrinth of Knossos to the novels of magical realism — the moth buzzing around the lamp at the birth of Oskar Matzerath, Grass's anti-hero who is deeply rooted in the sati(y)rical, Dionysian domain. In the context of aimless wandering, of which both Austerlitz and the narrator in *Die Ringe des Saturn* partake, *The Odyssey* as a lesser subtext is also of interest, in particular Odysseus's *Irrfahrten* as well as the image of Penelope weaving and unweaving the burial shroud for Odysseus's father Laertes to keep her suitors at bay. Her weaving, which does not move forward with linearity but stays on the spot to avoid the trouble of having to choose a suitor as bridegroom while still waiting for Odysseus, corresponds to the narrator's own travel in circles that reveal the troubles of humanity as well as his technique of dissolving the linearity of time into a *Nebeneinander* of temporal layers, especially of moments of historical horror and collective violence.

As mentioned above, Nietzsche has pointed out that Dionysian intoxication is linked to feelings of lethargy.[38] It is precisely in this phenomenon and term *lethargy* that I think Nietzsche is very close to Heidegger's discussion in his Parmenides lectures of *lethe* as forgetting, deliberate concealment, and destruction, and connected to this, *aletheia* as the un-concealment of the concealed, forgotten, or destroyed, as a moment of truth. In Sebald's text, walking leads to intoxication in the sense of allowing brief moments of truth to be illuminated — to use an image from the text where the freshly killed herrings glow for a few days — and thus surface from the darkness of forgetting. As the Greek a-privative signals, this Heideggerian *aletheia* emerges from the field of *lethe* — *lethe* here in the sense of immobility, non-walking, forgetting, and concretely the flats of East Anglia, that forgotten and often ignored corner of England — and falls back into *lethe*, as the narrator's walk is followed by immobility and hospitalization. Even during the walk, as we have seen, *aletheia* as an emergence from the prison house of forgetting, an emergence from darkness (Sebald uses countless images of light and dark, white and black), always threatens to revert back to *lethe* in the form of an entanglement within the rhizome of the labyrinthine paths. In similarity to Austerlitz's gradual descent into the Dionysian underworld of Theresienstadt, *lethe* and the rhizome repeatedly occur as the figure of the labyrinth, a location where the philosophy of Deleuze resonates with Nietzsche and Heidegger, one that implies the impossibility of remembering anything over time. As the rhizome thickens and clouds long-term memory, the Apollonian and *lethe* are the norm, the Dionysian and *aletheia* the exception.

> Immer wenn aufgrund irgendeiner im Seelenleben vor sich gegangenen Verschiebung ein solches Bruchstück in einem auftaucht, dann glaubt man, man könne sich erinnern. Aber in Wirklichkeit erinnert man sich natürlich nicht. Zu viele Bauwerke sind eingestürzt, zuviel Schutt ist aufgehäuft, unüberwindlich sind die Ablagerungen und Moränen.[39]

> [Whenever a shift in our spiritual life occurs and fragments such as these surface, we believe we can remember. But in reality, of course, memory fails us. Too many buildings have fallen down, too much rubble has been heaped up, the moraines and deposits are insuperable. (*RS*, 211/177)]

Through the loss of dwelling, the rubble, and the natural world of sediments and moraines this passage lexically links forgetting to the atrocities of war and to the destruction of nature. In his narrative journey with the objective to unearth the forgotten, Sebald carefully interweaves the fates of individuals like the Irish revolutionary Roger Casement with other temporal layers of oppression: the horrors of the Holocaust, colonialism, and the destruction of a species like the herring. This careful structural arrangement of semantic fields that uses lexical keywords as beacons of remembrance is reminiscent of Heidegger's own esoteric comments on the Holocaust.[40]

> Zuletzt das Löschen der Ladung, die Arbeit in den Hallen, wo die Heringe von Frauenhänden ausgenommen, der Größe nach sortiert und in Fässer verpackt warden. Dann nehmen die Güterwagen der Eisenbahn (so heißt es in dem Beiheft zu dem 1936 gedrehten Film, das ich unlängst habe auftreiben können) den ruhelosen Wanderer des Meeres auf, um ihn an die Stätten zu bringen, wo sich sein Schicksal auf dieser Erde endgültig erfüllen wird.

> [At last the catch is unloaded and we see the work in the halls where women's hands gut the herring, sort them according to size, and pack them in barrels. Then (so says the booklet accompanying the 1936 film), the railway goods wagons take in the restless wanderer of the seas and transport it to those places where its fate on this earth will at last be fulfilled. (RS, 71/54)]

One can safely leave it to most readers of this problematic passage to determine which terms tie the extermination of herrings to the Holocaust. This linkage is even further emphasized through the photo on page 71 of the German version showing mountains of dead herrings, an image that stands in direct relation to the one of the camp victims of Bergen Belsen on page 78–79. This proximity of the slaughter of herrings and the genocide of Jews is further supported by the experiments conducted on herrings in order to investigate their ability to survive (RS, 74/56–57).

In the case of the herrings the moment of *aletheia* as an emergence from the depths of darkness happens when "der Hering während der Frühlings- und Sommermonate in ungeahnten Millionen aus den dunklen Tiefen steige" (millions of herring rise from the lightless depths in the spring and summer months; RS, 71/55), a moment that recalls the emergence of corpses during excavations in London in *Austerlitz*. Here the corpses meant to be silenced in deep space are like the rhizomatic flat roots just under the surface, the dead still being alive in spirit, not dwelling but walking and easily rising to the surface. As *lethe* gives way to *aletheia*, the Freudian *Heimliche*, the dark secret, rises to the surface as the *Unheimliche*, the uncanny.[41] The *Heimliche* (in Freud's translation as the home-like and the hidden secret) of the herrings, their *Dasein* (existence) in the sea, turns into the *Unheimliche*, the uncanny of their mass extermination just after they rise to the surface.

Another image that ties together Sebald's individual works and different forms of genocide, the horrors of fascism and colonialism, is the forest.

Unlike Sebald, who laments the loss of trees, Deleuze and Guattari claim that "arborification destroys desire" (*MP*, 9) and that "we're tired of trees" (*MP*, 15). In Sebald's landscape the lack of forests, like in East Anglia, is a sign of destruction, but so also can be their presence. When Austerlitz retraces his childhood steps through Germany by train, his reaction to the German forest, where the trees blur into smooth space ("kahle Eichen- und Buchenstände . . . einem grenzen- und namenlosen, gänzlich von finsteren Waldungen überwachsenen Land" / leafless stands of oak and beech trees . . . a nameless land without borders and entirely overgrown by dark forests; *A*, 324/224; see also the photo on p. 325 of the German edition), also conjures up Freud's conjunction of the *Unheimliche* and the *Heimliche*. This forest is the original of all "heimsuchend[en]" (haunting [literally home-seeking]; *A*, 324/224) images that once pervaded Austerlitz's childhood dreams in Wales. As such it is *unheimlich* and *heimlich* at the same time. It is both haunting and "not like home," since not only is Wales not his real home, but the forest is also literally "home-seeking" in that this landscape drives home to him his personal connection with the history of the persecution of Jews. Both the *Mäuseturm* in Bingen (*A*, 325/225) and the "Mordstadt" Bacharach (the murderous town of Bacharach; *A*, 327/227), which are surrounded by the huge expanse of German forests, remind him of this persecution, the former through the image of burning mice (Jews as vermin in Nazi ideology), the latter more concretely through the execution of Jews in Bacharach in the thirteenth century. This landscape points beyond legend and medieval atrocities to the Holocaust (*Buchen*wald, "drei riesige Schlote" / three gigantic chimneys; *A*, 326/226) as well as to Heidegger, whose vision of autochthony was deeply connected to the German forest, specifically the Allemannic one with its peasant culture.

This conflation of *lethe/aletheia*, and correspondingly Freud's *heimlich/unheimlich* of the forest landscape and its reference to genocide then repeats itself in Sebald's discussion, in *Die Ringe des Saturn*, of the atrocities of colonialism in the context of Joseph Conrad's *Heart of Darkness*. And this is where we once again encounter Nietzsche's Apollo and Dionysus. Joseph Conrad himself is viewed as a messenger of the underworld, the hell of colonialism with its human suffering, à la Nietzsche. For it is Conrad's father, *Apollo* Korzeniowski, whom the Russians banished to Vologda, the heart of darkness of their empire, and who translated "Victor Hugos *Les travailleurs de la mer*. Dieses unendlich langweilige Buch kommt ihm vor wie der Spiegel des eigenen Lebens" (Victor Hugo's *Les travailleurs de la mer*. That prodigiously boring book seemed to him to mirror his own life; *RS*, 130/107). This book contrasts with the Dionysian world of his son's book and his own biography (if the father is Apollo, Joseph is Dionysus, if you will). The intertextuality between Sebald's *Die Ringe des Saturn* and Conrad's *Heart of Darkness* is intense

in their shared theme of wandering through the smooth space of a superficially empty landscape:

> Fast nichts war im Inneren dieses Weltteils eingezeichnet, keine
> Bahnlinie, keine Straße, keine Stadt, und weil die Kartographen in
> solche Leerräume gern irgendein exotisches Tier . . . hineinmalten,
> machten sie aus dem Kongofluß . . . eine quer durch das immense
> Land sich ringelnde Schlange.

> [Little was marked in the interior of this part of the world, no railway
> lines, no roads, no towns, and as cartographers would often embellish
> such empty spaces with drawings of exotic beasts, . . . they had ren-
> dered the Congo . . . as a snake coiling through the blank, uncharted
> land. (*RS*, 143/117)]

The biblical reference to this primordial and still undisclosed place (again
lethe and *aletheia* come to mind, this time in the context of colonialism's
violent "Erschließung" [disclosure, discovery, unlocking] and
"Durchbrechen" [disruption] of this place of darkness) is hard to miss, and
yet the snake also represents one rhizome line in the labyrinth of the river
landscape whose center, very much in parallel to the mythical labyrinth of
Knossos, is occupied by demons. As Kurtz, who represents the worst of
colonialism, is, as it were, the Minotaur at the center of Conrad's text, this
text in turn then fills the demonic center of Sebald's text (chapter V of X),
from where it is linked thematically and linguistically to other moments of
historical horror. The keywords in this palette of atrocities are *Finsternis,
Schatten, Schattenwesen* (darkness, shadows, shadowy figures) as part of the
realm of *lethe* and their contrast, the light that penetrates this darkness in
a moment of *aletheia*. "Alles spielte sich ab in wüster Finsternis" (everything happened as if in a black void; *RS*, 70/53), says the narrator of the
yearly killing of sixty billion fish, a figure that may remind us of the six
million Jews killed during the Nazi years. But after they die the herrings
begin to glow for days with their scales the color of snow or *ash* (my italics;
RS, 73/56), thus revealing the secret of their slaughter. Their glimmering
is linked to the shadow figures of the Congo — "allmählich, berichtet
Marlow, dringt aus dem Dunkel der Glanz einiger aus dem Jenseits auf
mich gerichteten Augen" (gradually, emerging from the dark, Marlowe
reports, the glimmer of a pair of eyes is directed upon me from beyond;
RS, 146/120, my translation)[42] — who in turn evoke the Muselmann of
the Nazi camps, that figure between life and death, not really alive any
more but also not quite dead yet:[43] "Offenbar hält man diese Schattenwesen
nicht auf, wenn sie sich davonschleichen in den Busch. Sie sind jetzt frei,
frei wie die Luft, die sie umgibt und in die sie sich nach und nach auflösen
werden" (Evidently no one cared to stop these black shadows when they
crept off into the bush. They are free now, as free as the air that surrounds

them and into which they will slowly dissolve; *RS,* 146/120 and my translation).[44] It is keywords like *Schattenwesen, aus dem Jenseits, Asche,* or *in Luft auflösen* (shadowy beings, from beyond, ash, dissolve in air) that are the linking points, the *Knotenpunkte,* of the different lines along which Sebald's walk around East Anglia opens up glimpses of the various atrocities in the gradual destruction of the planet. Travel proves to be trouble along the seams between the semantic fields of these atrocities.

To conclude: travel in Sebald occurs in a field of tension between the polarities of *lethe* and *aletheia,* Apollo and Dionysus, the rhizome and arborescence. Within this field of tension the characters' movement repeatedly seems to favor and, in the end, return to the forms of concealment within these polarities, to *lethe,* Apolline semblance, and the rhizome. Coming full circle these polarities point to the idea that any notion of truth, however briefly it may surface, is fragile and fleeting, that it always resorts to hiding under the cloak of secrecy, of the *Heimliche,* which appears at the same time *unheimlich.* This ultimate secrecy to all historical representation may lead us to confirm that all historiography is fictional, never objective. The aimlessness and non-linearity of travel in Sebald's two texts thus supports the Nietzschean thought that history is a constant flux without any teleology and that it implies the eternal return of useless suffering. The Dionysian dimension in Sebald's texts may have the potential to briefly reveal hidden historical moments of creaturely suffering, but ultimately the Dionysian's inherent connection with lethargy results in a form of *lethe* that obscures again. Travel in *Austerlitz* and *Die Ringe des Saturn* implies the descent into a Dionysian domain that is both revelatory and obscuring and therefore absurd. The very notion of a permanent repetition of horror and suffering at various levels of the creaturely points to this absurdity of life and nature. Travel in Sebald is obsessive but deeply pessimistic, and very much in line with Schopenhauer's outlook on life and that of Nietzsche in his early years. It reflects the idea of historical repetition and non-progress, and although it may stir a temporary remembrance, a surfacing of what resembles the truth about the past and its repetition in other forms in the present, an awareness of these contexts always coincides with their sinking back again into concealment, their being clouded again by non-travel, lethargy, and immobility, leaving mankind trapped in a *Salle des pas perdus.*

Notes

[1] Mikhail Bakhtin, *Rabelais and His World,* trans. Hélène Iswolsky (Bloomington: Indiana UP, 1984); Michel Foucault, *Madness and Civilization,* trans. Richard Howard (New York: Random House, 1988); Friedrich Nietzsche, *The Birth of Tragedy and Other Writings,* ed. Raymond Geuss and Ronald Speirs (Cambridge, Cambridge UP, 1999).

[2] Edward Said, *Culture and Imperialism* (New York: Vintage, 1993), 327.

[3] In a discussion of narrative genre, one might argue that the nineteenth-century *Bildungsroman* is arborescent, while the picaresque novel, with its aimlessly wandering protagonist and its lack of a teleology, contains features of the rhizome.

[4] Gilles Deleuze and Félix Guattari, *A Thousand Plateaus: Capitalism and Schizophrenia*, trans. Brian Massumi (U of Minnesota P, 1987), 6. Further references to this work are cited in the text using the abbreviation *MP* and the page number.

[5] Bruce Chatwin, *The Songlines* (New York: Viking, 1987); William Least Heat-Moon, *Blue Highways: A Journey into America* (Boston, MA: Little, Brown, 1983).

[6] Rafik Schami, *Die Sehnsucht der Schwalbe* (Munich: Hanser, 2000).

[7] Robert Menasse, *Selige Zeiten, brüchige Welt* (Salzburg: Residenz Verlag, 1992) and *Die Vertreibung aus der Hölle* (Frankfurt am Main: Suhrkamp, 2001); Robert Schindel, *Gebürtig* (Frankfurt am Main: Suhrkamp, 1992); Emine Sevgi Özdamar, *Die Brücke vom Goldenen Horn* (Cologne: Kiepenheuer & Witsch, 1998); Barbara Frischmuth, *Das Verschwinden des Schattens in der Sonne* (Salzburg: Residenz Verlag, 1996).

[8] Nietzsche, *The Birth of Tragedy and Other Writings*, ed. Raymond Geuss and Ronald Speirs (Cambridge: Cambridge UP, 1999), 40.

[9] Certain landscapes may demonstrate an ambivalence of smooth and striated space, such as the forest. Despite the verticality of arborescence and its relation to the deep roots of trees, the forest is a smooth space if the trees are seen as blending together.

[10] Günter Grass, *The Tin Drum*, trans. Ralph Manheim (New York, Vintage, 1964).

[11] Gabriel García Márquez, *One Hundred Years of Solitude* (London: Penguin, 1972).

[12] Mendez governed from 1926–30.

[13] Euripides, *Bacchae and Other Plays* trans. and ed. James Morwood (Oxford: Oxford UP, 2008).

[14] See also Carsten Strathausen's article, "Going Nowhere: Sebald's Rhizomatic Travels," in Patt, *Searching for Sebald: Photography after W. G. Sebald* (Los Angeles: Institute of Cultural Inquiry, 2007), 472–92; here 472: "In fact, they [Sebald's narratives] never really arrive anywhere, but continue to wander aimlessly in an infinitely expanding, labyrinthine space that defies traditional topography."

[15] Heidegger, *Parmenides* (Bloomington: Indiana UP, 1992), 83. For a closer reading of time in *Austerlitz* see Amir Eshel, "Against the Power of Time: The Poetics of Suspension in W. G. Sebald's *Austerlitz*," *New German Critique* 88 (Winter 2003): 71–96.

[16] Cf. Heidegger, *Parmenides*. In *Parmenides*, based on his lectures in the winter of 1942–1943, Heidegger exoterically speaks about Greece, but, given the time frame, these lectures esoterically point to the more essential context of Auschwitz.

[17] Eric Santner, *On Creaturely Life: Rilke, Benjamin, Sebald* (Chicago: Chicago UP, 2006), 81.

[18] Michel de Certeau, *The Practice of Everyday Life*, trans. Steven Rendall (Berkeley: U of California P, 1984), 98.

[19] Heidegger, *Parmenides*, 155.

[20] de Certeau, *The Practice of Everyday Life*, 100.

[21] de Certeau, *The Practice of Everyday Life*, 103.

[22] Karsten Harries, *The Ethical Function of Architecture* (Cambridge, MA: MIT Press, 1997), 164: "the modern world represents a refusal of the fourfold . . . and is thus a verwahrloste Welt (a neglected world)."

[23] Charles Bambach, *Heidegger's Roots: Nietzsche, National Socialism, and the Greeks* (Ithaca, NY: Cornell UP, 2003), 38.

[24] On gravity and the state, see Deleuze and Guattari, *MP*, 370–71.

[25] Cf. also Neil Christian Pages's discussion of Sebald and Heidegger in "No Place but Home: W. G. Sebald on the Air War and Other Stories," *Crossings 7* (2004/5): 91–137.

[26] Sebald obviously appreciated Chatwin as a writer; cf. his essay "Das Geheimnis des rotbraunen Fells: Annäherung an Bruce Chatwin; in English, "The Mystery of the Red-Brown Skin: An Approach to Bruce Chatwin," in *CS*, 215–22/173–80. For a comparative approach to Sebald and Chatwin see also Brad Prager's excellent article in this volume (191–214). Especially in view of the rhizome there are clear parallels between the wandering of Sebald's characters and Chatwin's concept of songlines crisscrossing the Australian landscape. Prager indirectly refers to this in his discussion of the landscape as an archive.

[27] See Julian Young, *Nietzsche's Philosophy of Art* (Cambridge: Cambridge UP, 1992): "The terror and horror of the Dionysian experience brings one to the brink of an affirmation of pessimism: an affirmation of the wisdom of Silenus, 'best of all is not to be born, not to *be*, to be nothing. But the second best for you is — to die soon' which leads to action-paralyzing nausea" (39).

[28] de Certeau, *The Practice of Everyday Life*, 113: "There is something at once incarcerational and navigational about railroad travel."

[29] Nietzsche, *The Birth of Tragedy*, 20 and 17.

[30] Cf. Deleuze and Guattari's discussion of star-shaped forms and fractals in *MP*, 486–88.

[31] See Giorgio Agamben, *Homo sacer: Sovereign Power and Bare Life*, trans. Daniel Heller-Roazen (Stanford, CA: Stanford UP, 1998).

[32] Dionysus himself is represented as a bearded satyr "whose name and attributes were borrowed from the goat" (Nietzsche, *Birth of Tragedy*, 20) and whom, unlike the "calmly-sitting" Apollo, Nietzsche identifies with the migration of the St. Vitus dancers, "ever-growing throngs" roaming "from place to place" (17).

[33] Heidegger, *Parmenides*, 47.

[34] As I was writing this article in Florence, Italy, I chanced upon the following passage in *The Florentine.net*, 4.82, 26 Jun. 2008, 4: "To keep its beaches *pristine* (my italics) the municipality of Marina di Campo on Elba has approved a motion to ban *itinerant vendors* (my italics) from island beaches," which shows clearly how the fear of wanderers paired with ruthless uncontrollable capitalism has the poten-

tial to increase under rightwing governments. Note that the Nazis also fostered these fears in addition to their obsession with genetic hygiene.

[35] For an examination of the relationship between *Heart of Darkness* and *Die Ringe des Saturn*, see also Margaret Bruzelius's article in this volume (249–75).

[36] Robert Wechsler, *Performing without a Stage: The Art of Literary Translation* (North Haven, CT: Catbird, 1998), 63.

[37] Cf. also Alan Itkin's article in this volume, 163–87.

[38] "The Dionysiac state, in which the usual barriers and limits of existence are destroyed, contains, for as long as it lasts, a lethargic element in which all personal experiences from the past are submerged" (Nietzsche, *Birth of Tragedy*, 40).

[39] Nietzsche has identified the state of intoxication as a breakdown of the *principium individuationis* in which "subjectivity vanishes to the point of complete self-forgetting" (Nietzsche, *Birth of Tragedy*, 17). Fragmentation, the *Bruchstücke*, is thus closely associated with forgetting.

[40] Cf. eg. Johannes Fritsche, "On Brinks and Bridges in Heidegger," in *Graduate Faculty Philosophical Journal*, vol. 18.1 (1995): 111–86.

[41] Sigmund Freud, *Das Unheimliche: Aufsätze zur Literatur* (Hamburg: Fischer doppelpunkt, 1963).

[42] Hulse's translation shows little fidelity to the original here: "I began to distinguish the gleam of the eyes under the trees, says Marlowe" (*RS*, 120).

[43] Giorgio Agamben, *Remnants of Auschwitz: The Witness and the Archive*, trans. Daniel Heller-Roazen (New York: Zone Books, 2002), 44–45: "The Muselmänner were the living dead in the camps, who had given up on life but were not yet dead; the term is derived from 'the Arabic word muslim: the one who submits unconditionally to the will of God.'"

[44] The second sentence was omitted from the English translation.

Works Cited

Adorno, Theodor W. *Ästhetische Theorie*. Edited by Gretel Adorno and Rolf Tiedemann. Frankfurt am Main: Suhrkamp, 1972. In English, *Aesthetic Theory*. Translated by Robert Hullot-Kentor. New York: Continuum, 2004.

———. *Minima Moralia: Reflexionen aus dem beschädigten Leben*. In *Gesammelte Schriften*, vol. 4, edited by Rolf Tiedemann. Frankfurt am Main: Suhrkamp, 1997. In English, *Minima Moralia: Reflections from Damaged Life*. Translated by E. F. N. Jephcott. London: Verso, 1974.

Agamben, Giorgio. *Homo Sacer: Sovereign Power and Bare Life*. Translated by Daniel Heller-Roazen. Stanford, CA: Stanford UP, 1998.

———. *Remnants of Auschwitz: The Witness and the Archive*. Translated by Daniel Heller-Roazen. New York: Zone Books, 2002.

———. *Stanzas: Word and Phantasm in Western Culture*. Translated by Ronald L. Martinez. Minneapolis: U of Minnesota P, 1993.

Albes, Claudia. "Die Erkundung der Leere: Anmerkungen zu W. G. Sebalds 'englischer Wallfahrt' *Die Ringe des Saturn*." *Jahrbuch der Deutschen Schillergesellschaft* 46 (2002): 279–305.

———. "Porträt ohne Modell: Bildbeschreibung und autobiographische Reflexion in W. G. Sebald's 'Elementargedicht' *Nach der Natur*." In Niehaus and Öhlschläger, *W. G. Sebald: Politische Archäologie und melancholische Bastelei*, 47–76.

Aliaga-Buchenau, Ana-Isabel. "'A Time He Could Not Bear to Say Any More About': Presence and Absence of the Narrator in W. G. Sebald's *The Emigrants*." In Denham and McCulloh, *W. G. Sebald: History, Memory, Trauma*, 142–55.

Anderson, Mark M. "Documents, Photography, Postmemory: Alexander Kluge, W. G. Sebald, and the German Family." *Poetics Today* 29.1 (2008): 129–53.

———. "Fathers and Son: W. G. Sebald." *Bookforum* (December/January 2007): 28–31.

Angier, Carole. "Who Is W. G. Sebald?" *Jewish Quarterly* 164 (Winter 1996/97): 10–14.

Arendt, Hannah. "Great Friend of Reality: Adalbert Stifter." In *Reflections on Literature and Culture*, edited by Susannah Young-Ah Gottlieb, 110–11. Stanford, CA: Stanford UP, 2007.

Artangel. Promotional materials for Heiner Goebbels's performance piece "Stifter's Dinge." http://www.e-flux.com/shows/view/5230. Accessed 16 December 2008.

Atze, Marcel, and Franz Loquai, eds. *Sebald: Lektüren*. Eggingen, Germany: Edition Isele, 2005.

Atze, Marcel, and Sven Mayer. "'Unsere Korrespondenz': Zum Briefwechsel zwischen W. G. Sebald und Theodor W. Adorno." In Atze and Loquai, *Sebald: Lektüren*, 17–38.

Bakhtin, Mikhail. *Rabelais and His World*. Translated by Hélène Iswolsky. Bloomington: Indiana UP, 1984.

Bales, Richard. "The Loneliness of the Long-Distance Narrator: The Inscription of Travel in Proust and W. G. Sebald." In Conroy, *Cross-Cultural Travel: Papers from the Royal Irish Academy Symposium on Literature and Travel*, 507–12.

Balm, Roger, and Briavel Holcomb. "Unlosing Lost Places: Image Making, Tourism, and the Return to Terra Cognita." In *Visual Culture and Tourism*, edited by David Crouch and Nina Lübbren, 157–74. Oxford: Berg, 2003.

Bambach, Charles. *Heidegger's Roots: Nietzsche, National Socialism, and the Greeks*. Ithaca, NY: Cornell UP, 2003.

Barker, Francis. *The Tremulous Private Body: Essays on Subjection*. London: Methuen, 1984.

Beck, John. "Reading Room: Erosion and Sedimentation in Sebald's Suffolk." In Long and Whitehead, *W. G. Sebald: A Critical Companion*, 75–88.

Begemann, Christian. "'Realismus' oder 'Idealismus'? Über einige Schwierigkeiten bei der Rekonstruktion von Stifters Kunstbegriff." In *Adalbert Stifter: Dichter und Maler, Denkmalpfleger und Schulmann. Neue Zugänge zu seinem Werk*, edited by Hartmut Laufhütte and Karl Möseneder, 3–17. Tübingen: Max Niemeyer, 1996.

Benjamin, Walter. *Charles Baudelaire: Ein Lyriker im Zeitalter des Hochkapitalismus*. Frankfurt am Main: Suhrkamp, 1980.

———. "Der Erzähler: Betrachtungen zum Werk Nikolai Lesskows." In *Illuminationen*, 385–410.

———. "Franz Kafka: Zur zehnten Wiederkehr seines Todestages." In *Gesammelte Schriften*, vol. 2, ed. Rolf Tiedemann and Hermann Schweppenhäuser, 410–38. Frankfurt am Main: Suhrkamp, 1991. In English, "Franz Kafka: On the Tenth Anniversary of His Death." In *Selected Writings, Volume 2*, edited by Michael W. Jennings, Howard Eiland, and Gary Smith, translated by Rodney Livingstone and others, 794–818. Cambridge, MA: Belknap, 1999.

———. *Illuminationen*. Edited by Hannah Arendt. Frankfurt am Main: Suhrkamp, 1977. In English, *Illuminations*. Edited by Hannah Arendt. Translated by Harry Zohn. New York: Schocken, 1969.

———. "Das Kunstwerk im Zeitalter seiner technischen Reproduzierbarkeit (zweite Fassung)." In *Gesammelte Schriften,* vol. 1.2, edited by Rolf Tiedemann and Hermann Schweppenhäuser, 471–508. Frankfurt am Main: Suhrkamp, 1980.

———. "Stifter." In *Gesammelte Schriften,* vol. 2.2, edited by Rolf Tiedemann and Hermann Schweppenhäuser, 609–10. Frankfurt am Main: Suhrkamp, 1989. In English, "Stifter." In *Selected Writings, Volume 1: 1913–1926,* translated by Michael William Jennings, edited by Marcus Bullock, 111–12. Cambridge, MA: Belknap, 1996.

———. "The Storyteller: Reflections on the Works of Nikolai Leskov." In *Illuminations,* 83–110.

———. "Theses on the Philosophy of History." In *Illuminations,* 253–64.

———. "Über einige Motive bei Baudelaire." In *Gesammelte Schriften,* vol 1, edited by Rolf Tiedemann and Hermann Schweppenhäuser, 605–53. Frankfurt am Main: Suhrkamp, 1991. In English, "On Some Motifs in Baudelaire." In *Selected Writings, Volume 4,* edited by Howard Eiland and Michael W. Jennings, translated by Edmund Jephcott and others, 314–55. Cambridge, MA: Belknap, 2003.

———. *Ursprung des deutschen Trauerspiels.* In *Gesammelte Schriften,* vol. 1, edited by Rolf Tiedemann and Hermann Schweppenhäuser, 203–430. Frankfurt am Main: Suhrkamp, 1991. In English, *The Origin of German Tragic Drama.* Translated by John Osborne. London: Verso, 2003.

Bennett, Alan. "2002 Diary." *London Review of Books,* 2 January 2003.

Bennett, Tony. *The Birth of the Museum: History, Theory, Politics.* London: Routledge, 1995.

Bepler, Jill. "Travelling and Posterity: The Archive, the Library and the Cabinet." In *Grand Tour: Adliges Reisen und europäische Kultur vom 14. bis zum 18. Jahrhundert. Akten der internationalen Kolloquien in der Villa Vigoni 1999 und im Deutschen Historischen Institut Paris 2000,* edited by Rainer Babel and Werner Paravicini, 191–204. Ostfildern, Germany: Jan Thorbecke, 2005.

Biernat, Ulla. *"Ich bin nicht der erste Fremde hier": Zur deutschsprachigen Reiseliteratur nach 1945.* Würzburg: Königshausen & Neumann, 2004.

Blackbourn, David. "Fashionable Spa Towns in Nineteenth-Century Europe." In *Water, Leisure and Culture: European Historical Perspectives,* edited by Susan C. Anderson and Bruce H. Tabb, 9–21. Oxford: Berg, 2002.

Blackler, Deane. *Reading W. G. Sebald: Adventure and Disobedience.* Rochester, NY: Camden House, 2007.

Bloom, Lisa. *Gender on Ice: American Ideologies of Polar Expeditions.* Minneapolis: U of Minnesota P, 1993.

Bode, Rita. "'They . . . should be well out of it': The Women in *Heart of Darkness.*" *Conradiana* 26.1 (1994): 20–34.

Bond, Gregory. "On the Misery of Nature and the Nature of Misery: W. G. Sebald's Landscapes." In Long and Whitehead, *W. G. Sebald: A Critical Companion,* 31–44.

Bonn, Klaus. "W. G. Sebalds laufende Bilder: Der Film und die Worte." *Arcadia* 42.1 (2007): 166–84.

Borges, Jorge Luis. "Tlön, Uqbar, Orbis Tertius." Translated by Andrew Hurley. In *Collected Fictions,* 68–81. New York: Penguin Books, 1998.

Boyer, M. Christine. *The City of Collective Memory: Its Historical Imagery and Architectural Entertainments.* Cambridge, MA: MIT Press, 1994.

Brandes, Georg. "Om Læsning." In *Samlede Skrifter* 12:29–48. Copenhagen: Gyldendalske Boghandels Forlag, 1902.

Brooks, Peter. *Reading for the Plot: Design and Intention in Narrative.* New York: Vintage, 1984.

Bross, Addison. "The Unextinguishable Light of Belief: Conrad's Attitude towards Women." *Conradiana* 2 (1969–70): 39–46.

Browne, Sir Thomas. *Religio Medici, Hydrotaphia and the Gardens of Cyrus.* Edited by R. H. A. Robbins. Oxford: Oxford UP, 1982.

Burgstaller, Wolfgang. "Der Mensch in naturwissenschaftlicher Forschung und Theorie." In *Menschenbilder,* edited by Hans Czuma, 117–28. Vienna: Verlag für Gesellschaftskritik, 1988.

Burton, Robert. *The Anatomy of Melancholy.* Edited by Holbrook Jackson. London: Dent, 1972.

Buruma, Ian. "Herzog and His Heroes." *New York Review of Books,* 19 July 2007.

Buzard, James. *The Beaten Track: European Tourism, Literature, and the Ways to "Culture," 1800–1918.* Oxford: Oxford UP, 1993.

Calhoon, Kenneth S. "Charming the Carnivore: Bruce Chatwin's Australian Odyssey." In *Writing Travel: The Poetics and Politics of the Modern Journey,* edited by John Zilcosky, 173–94. Toronto: U of Toronto P, 2009.

———. "Der virtuelle Bogen: Abgrund und Brücke in Friedrich Schillers *Der Spaziergang.*" In *Kopflandschaften – Landschaftsgänge: Kulturgeschichte und Poetik des Spaziergangs,* edited by Axel Gellhaus, Christian Moser, and Helmut J. Schneider, 147–60. Cologne: Böhlau, 2007.

Carline, Richard. *Pictures in the Post: The Story of the Picture Postcard and Its Place in the History of Popular Art.* London: Gordon Fraser, 1971.

Caserio, Robert. "*The Rescue* and the Ring of Meaning." In *Conrad Revisited: Essays for the Eighties,* edited by Ross C. Murfin, 125–50. Tuscaloosa: U of Alabama P, 1985.

Catling, Jo. "Gratwanderungen bis an den Rand der Natur: W. G. Sebald's Landscapes of Memory." In *The Anatomist of Melancholy: Essays in Memory of W. G. Sebald,* edited by Rüdiger Görner, 19–50. Munich: iudicium, 2003.

Catling, Jo, and Richard Hibbitt, eds. *Saturn's Moons: A W. G. Sebald Handbook.* Oxford: Legenda, forthcoming 2010.

Ceuppens, Jan. "Realia: Konstellationen bei Benjamin, Barthes, Lacan — und Sebald." In Niehaus and Öhlschläger, *W. G. Sebald: Politische Archäologie und Melancholische Bastelei,* 241–58.

———. "Tracing the Witness in W. G. Sebald." In Fuchs and Long, *W. G. Sebald and the Writing of History,* 59–72.

———. "Transcripts: An Ethics of Representation in *The Emigrants.*" In Denham and McCulloh, *W. G. Sebald: History — Memory — Trauma,* 251–63.

Chatwin, Bruce. *Anatomy of Restlessness: Selected Writings, 1969–1989.* Edited by Jan Borm and Matthew Graves, 54–69. New York: Penguin Books, 1997.

———. "The Estate of Maximilian Tod." In *Anatomy of Restlessness,* 54–69.

———. "It's a Nomad *Nomad* World." In *Anatomy of Restlessness,* 100–106.

———. *The Songlines.* New York: Viking, 1987.

———. *The Songlines.* New York: Penguin Books, 1988.

———. *Utz.* New York: Viking, 1989.

Clapp, Susannah. *With Chatwin: Portrait of a Writer.* New York: Alfred A. Knopf, 1997.

Conrad, Joseph. *Heart of Darkness with The Congo Diary.* Edited by Robert Hampson. New York: Penguin, 1995.

Conroy, Jane, ed. *Cross-Cultural Travel: Papers from the Royal Irish Academy Symposium on Literature and Travel.* New York: Lang, 2003.

Cronin, Paul, ed. *Herzog on Herzog.* London: Faber & Faber, 2002.

Crouch, David, and Nina Lübbren. "Introduction." In *Visual Culture and Tourism,* edited by David Crouch and Nina Lübbren, 1–20. Oxford: Berg, 2003.

Culler, Jonathan. "The Semiotics of Tourism." In *Framing the Sign: Criticism and Its Institutions,* 153–67. Oxford: Oxford UP, 1988.

Cuomo, Joe. "A Conversation with W. G. Sebald." In Schwartz, *The Emergence of Memory,* 93–118. Originally published as "The Meaning of Coincidence. An Interview with the Writer W. G. Sebald." *New Yorker* (online edition), 3 September 2001.

Darby, David. "Landscape and Memory: Sebald's Redemption of History." In Denham and McCulloh, *W. G. Sebald: History — Memory — Trauma,* 265–77.

De Certeau, Michel. *Kunst des Handelns.* Translated by Ronald Vouillé. Berlin: Merve, 1988.

———. *The Practice of Everyday Life.* Translated by Steven Rendall. Berkeley: U of California P, 1984.

Deleuze, Gilles. *Cinema 2: The Time-Image*. Translated by Hugh Tomlinson and Robert Galeta. Minneapolis: U of Minnesota P, 1989.

———. *Essays Critical and Clinical*. Translated by Daniel W. Smith and Michael A. Greco. London: Verso, 1998.

Deleuze, Gilles, and Félix Guattari. *A Thousand Plateaus: Capitalism and Schizophrenia*. Translated by Brian Massumi. Minneapolis: U of Minnesota P, 1987.

———. *A Thousand Plateaus: Capitalism and Schizophrenia*. Translated by Brian Massumi. London: Continuum, 2004.

Denham, Scott, and Mark McCulloh, eds. *W. G. Sebald: History — Memory — Trauma*. Berlin: de Gruyter, 2006.

De Quincey, Thomas. *Autobiography from 1785–1803*. Vol. 1 of *Collected Works*, edited by David Masson. Edinburgh: Adam and Charles Black, 1889.

Derrida, Jacques. "The *Retrait* of Metaphor." In *Psyche: Inventions of the Other*, edited by Peggy Kamuf and Elizabeth Rottenberg, 1–48. Stanford, CA: Stanford UP, 2007.

De Syon, Guillaume. *Zeppelin!: Germany and the Airship, 1900–1939*. Baltimore, MD: The Johns Hopkins UP, 2007.

Detering, Heinrich. "Schnee und Asche, Flut und Feuer: Über den Elementardichter W. G. Sebald." *Neue Rundschau* 109.2 (1998): 147–58.

Dittberner, Hugo. "Der Ausführlichste oder: Ein starker Hauch Patina. W. G. Sebalds Schreiben." *Text+Kritik* 158.4 (2003): 6–14.

Doerry, Martin, and Volker Hage. "Ich fürchte das Melodramatische: Gespräch mit W. G. Sebald." *Der Spiegel*, 12 March 2001, 228–34.

Dryden, Linda. *Joseph Conrad and the Imperial Romance*. New York: St. Martin's, 2000.

Dumas, Alexandre. *Le comte de Monte Cristo*. Paris: Gallimard, 1981.

Duncan, Ian. *Modern Romance and Transformations of the Novel*. Cambridge: Cambridge UP, 1992.

Dünne, Jörg. "Kartographische Meditation: Mediendispositiv und Selbstpraxis in der Frühen Neuzeit." In *Automedialität: Subjektkonstitution in Schrift, Bild und neuen Medien*, edited by Jörg Dünne and Christian Moser, 331–51. Munich: Fink, 2008.

Duttlinger, Carolin. *Kafka and Photography*. Oxford: Oxford UP, 2007.

———. "Traumatic Photographs: Remembrance and the Technical Media in W. G. Sebald's *Austerlitz*." In Long and Whitehead, *W. G. Sebald: A Critical Companion*, 155–71.

Ecker, Gisela. "'Heimat' oder Die Grenzen der Bastelei." In Niehaus and Öhlschläger, *W. G. Sebald: Politische Archäologie und melancholische Bastelei*, 77–88.

Eliot, T. S. *The Annotated Wasteland with Eliot's Contemporary Prose*. 2nd ed. Edited by Lawrence Rainey. New Haven, CT: Yale UP, 2006.

Enzensberger, Hans Magnus. "Much Left Unsaid." *Times Literary Supplement*, 16–22 June 1989, 657.

———. "Eine Theorie des Tourismus." In *Einzelheiten I*, 179–205. Frankfurt am Main: Suhrkamp, 1962.

Eshel, Amir. "Against the Power of Time: The Poetics of Suspension in W. G. Sebald's *Austerlitz*." *New German Critique* 88 (Winter 2003): 71–96.

Esselborn, Hans. "Adalbert Stifters 'Turmalin': Die Absage an den Subjektivismus durch das naturgesetzliche Erzählen." *Vierteljahresschrift des Adalbert-Stifter-Instituts* 34.1/2 (1985): 3–26.

Estes, David C. "Bruce Chatwin's *In Patagonia*: Traveling in Textualized Terrain." *New Orleans Review* 18.2 (1991): 67–77.

Euripides. *Bacchae and Other Plays*. Translated and edited by James Morwood. Oxford: Oxford UP, 2008.

Ficino, Marsilio. *Three Books on Life*. A critical edition and translation with introduction and notes by Carol V. Kaske and John R. Clark. Binghamton, NY: Center for Medieval and Early Renaissance Studies, 1989.

Fischer, Gerhard. "W. G. Sebald's Expatriate Experience and His Literary Beginnings." Introduction to *W. G. Sebald: Schreiben ex patria*, edited by Gerhard Fischer, 15–25. Amsterdam: Rodopi, 2009.

Fleming, Paul. *The Pleasures of Abandonment: Jean Paul and the Life of Humor*. Würzburg: Königshausen & Neumann, 2006.

Flusser, Vilém. "Ansichtskarten." In *Standpunkte: Texte zur Fotografie*, 195–97. Göttingen: European Photography, 1998.

Forrester, John. *The Seductions of Psychoanalysis: Freud, Lacan, and Derrida*. Cambridge: Cambridge UP, 1994.

Foster, Kurt. "Bausteine I: Bilder geistern durch Sebalds Erzählungen, Geister bewohnen ihre Zeilen." In von Bülow, Gfrereis, and Strittmatter, *Wandernde Schatten*, 87–100.

Foucault, Michel. *Madness and Civilization*. Translated by Richard Howard. New York: Random House, 1988.

———. "Questions on Geography." Translated by Colin Gordon. In *Space, Knowledge and Power: Foucault and Geography*, edited by Jeremy W. Crampton and Stuart Elden, 173–82. Burlington, VT: Ashgate, 2007.

Franklin, J. Jeffrey. "Memory as the Nexus of Identity, Empire, and Evolution in George Eliot's *Middlemarch* and H. Rider Haggard's *She*." *Cahiers victoriens et édouardiens* 53.13 (2001): 141–69.

Freud, Sigmund. *Analyse der Phobie eines fünfjährigen Knaben*. In Freud, *Gesammelte Werke* 7:241–377. In English, *Analysis of a Phobia in a Five-Year-Old Boy*. In Freud, *The Standard Edition* 10:3–149.

———. "Fetishism." In Freud, *The Standard Edition* 21:148–57.

———. *Gesammelte Werke.* Edited by Anna Freud, E. Bibring, W. Hoffer, E. Kris, and O. Isakower. 18 vols. 1952–68. Reprint, Frankfurt am Main: Fischer, 1999.

———. "Jenseits des Lustprinzips." In Freud, *Gesammelte Werke* 13:1–69. In English, "Beyond the Pleasure Principle." In *Beyond the Pleasure Principle and Other Writings,* 43–102. London: Penguin, 2003.

———. *Der Mann Moses und die monotheistische Religion.* In *Gesammelte Werke* 16:103–246. In English, *Moses and Monotheism.* In *The Standard Edition* 23:7–137.

———. *Psychoanalytische Bemerkungen über einen autobiographisch beschriebenen Fall von Paranoia (Dementia Paranoides)* (1911). In *Gesammelte Werke* 8:239–320. In English, *Psycho-Analytic Notes on an Autobiographical Account of a Case of Paranoia (dementia paranoides).* In *The Standard Edition* 12:3–80.

———. "Ratschläge für den Arzt bei der psychoanalytischen Behandlung." In *Gesammelte Werke* 8:375–87. In English, "Recommendations to Physicians Practicing Psycho-Analysis." In *The Standard Edition* 12:109–20.

———. *The Standard Edition of the Complete Psychological Works of Sigmund Freud.* Translated and edited by James Strachey. 24 vols. London: Hogarth, 1953–74.

———. *Totem und Tabu.* Vol. 9 of *Gesammelte Werke.* In English, *Totem and Taboo.* In *The Standard Edition* 13:1–63.

———. "Über die Psychogenese eines Falles von weiblicher Homosexualität." In *Gesammelte Werke* 12:269–302. In English, "The Psychogenesis of a Case of Homosexuality in a Woman." In *The Standard Edition* 18:145–72.

———. "Das Unheimliche." In *Gesammelte Werke* 12:227–68. In English, "The Uncanny." In *The Standard Edition* 17:217–56.

———. *Das Unheimliche: Aufsätze zur Literatur.* Hamburg: Fischer doppelpunkt, 1963.

Frey, Matthias. "Theorizing Cinema in Sebald and Sebald with Cinema." In Patt, *Searching for Sebald,* 226–41.

Frischmuth, Barbara. *Das Verschwinden des Schattens in der Sonne.* Salzburg: Residenz Verlag, 1996.

Fritsche, Johannes. "On Brinks and Bridges in Heidegger." *Graduate Faculty Philosophical Journal* 18.1 (1995): 111–86.

Fuchs, Anne. *Die Schmerzensspuren der Geschichte: Zur Poetik der Erinnerung in W. G. Sebalds Prosa.* Cologne: Böhlau, 2004.

———. "'Ein auffallend geschichtsblindes und traditionsloses Volk': Heimatdiskurs und Ruinenästhetik in W. G. Sebalds Prosa." In Niehaus and

Öhlschläger, *W. G. Sebald: Politische Archäologie und melancholische Bastelei,* 89–110.

———. "W. G. Sebald's Painters: The Function of Fine Art in His Prose Works." *Modern Language Review* 101 (2006): 167–83.

Fuchs, Anne, and Theo Harden, eds. *Reisen im Diskurs: Modelle der literarischen Fremdenerfahrung von den Pilgerberichten bis zur Postmoderne.* Heidelberg: C. Winter, 1995.

Fuchs, Anne, and J. J. Long, eds. *W. G. Sebald and the Writing of History.* Würzburg: Königshausen & Neumann, 2007.

Garloff, Katja. "The Emigrant as Witness: W. G. Sebald's *Die Ausgewanderten.*" *German Quarterly* 77.1 (2004): 76–93.

Geary, Christraud M., and Virginia-Lee Webb. "Introduction: Views on Postcards." In *Delivering Views: Distant Cultures in Early Postcards,* 1–12.

———, eds. *Delivering Views: Distant Cultures in Early Postcards.* Washington: Smithsonian Institution P, 1998.

Geulen, Eva. *Worthörig wider Willen: Darstellungsproblematik und Sprachreflexion in der Prosa Adalbert Stifters.* Munich: iudicium, 1992.

Gide, André. *Urien's Voyage.* Translated by Wade Baskin. New York: Philosophical Library, 1964.

Gilpin, William. *Three Essays: On Picturesque Beauty, On Picturesque Travel, and On Sketching Landscape. To Which Is Added a Poem, on Landscape Painting.* London: R. Blamire, 1794.

Grass, Günter. *The Tin Drum.* Translated by Ralph Manheim. New York: Vintage, 1964.

Greenblatt, Stephen. *Marvelous Possessions: The Wonder of the New World.* Chicago: U of Chicago P, 1991.

Gregory-Guider, Christopher C. "Memorial Sights/Sites: Sebald, Photography, and the Art of Autobiogeography in *The Emigrants.*" In Patt, *Searching for Sebald,* 516–41.

———. "The 'Sixth Emigrant': Traveling Places in the Works of W. G. Sebald." *Contemporary Literature* 46.3 (2005): 422–49.

Grillparzer, Franz. *Tagebuch auf der Reise nach Italien.* In *Sämtliche Werke: Ausgewählte Briefe, Gespräche, Berichte,* vol. 4, edited by Peter Frank and Karl Pörnbacher, 275–349. Munich: Hanser, 1965.

Haggard, H. Rider. *King Solomon's Mines.* New York: Oxford UP, 1989.

———. *She.* New York: Oxford UP, 1992.

Harries, Karsten. *The Ethical Function of Architecture.* Cambridge, MA: MIT Press, 1997.

Harris, Stefanie. "The Return of the Dead: Memory and Photography in W. G. Sebald's *Die Ausgewanderten.*" *German Quarterly* 74.4 (Autumn, 2001): 379–91.

Harvey, David. *The Condition of Postmodernity*. Oxford: Blackwell, 1990.

Heckscher, William S. *Rembrandt's Anatomy of Dr. Nicolaas Tulp: An Iconological Study*. New York: New York UP, 1958.

Heidegger, Martin. *Parmenides*. Bloomington: Indiana UP, 1992.

Heidelberger-Leonard, Irene. "Jean Amérys Werk — Urtext zu W. G. Sebalds *Austerlitz?*" In *W. G. Sebald: Mémoire, Transferts, Images — Erinnerung, Übertragungen, Bilder*, edited by Ruth Vogel-Klein, 117–28. Recherches germaniques 2. Strasbourg: Université Marc Bloch, 2005.

Hein, Raimund Alois. *Adalbert Stifter: Sein Leben und seine Werke*. 2nd ed. 2 vols. Vienna: Walter Krieg, 1952.

Hell, Julia. "The Angel's Enigmatic Eyes, or The Gothic Beauty of Catastrophic History in W. G. Sebald's 'Air War and Literature.'" *Criticism* 46.3 (Summer 2004): 361–92.

Herbert, Frank. *Dune*. New York: Ace Books, 1999.

Higgins, Lynn A. *New Novel, New Wave, New Politics: Fiction and the Representation of History in Postwar France*. Lincoln and London: U of Nebraska P, 1996.

Hillis Miller, J. "Heart of Darkness Revisited." In *Conrad Revisited: Essays for the Eighties*, edited by Ross C. Murfin, 31–50. Tuscaloosa: U of Alabama P, 1985.

Hirsch, Marianne. "Surviving Images: Holocaust Photographs and the Work of Postmemory." *Yale Journal of Criticism* 14.1 (2001): 5–37.

Homer. *The Odyssey*. Translated by Richmond Lattimore. New York: Harper Collins, 1999.

Honold, Alexander. "Erzählen." In *Benjamins Begriffe*, edited by Martin Opitz and Ermut Wizisla, 363–98. Frankfurt am Main: Suhrkamp, 2000.

Horkheimer, Max, and Theodor W. Adorno. *Dialectic of Enlightenment*. Edited by Gunzelin Schmid Noerr. Translated by Edmund Jephcott. Stanford, CA: Stanford UP, 2002.

———. *Dialektik der Aufklärung: Philosophische Fragmente*. Frankfurt am Main: Fischer, 1969.

———. "Kulturindustrie: Aufklärung als Massenbetrug." In *Dialektik der Aufklärung: Philosophische Fragmente*, 140–91. Frankfurt am Main: Suhr-kamp, 1997. In English, "The Culture Industry: Enlightenment as Mass Deception." In *Dialectic of Enlightenment*, 120–67. London: Verso, 1979.

Horstkotte, Silke. "Nachbilder: Zur Funktion von Fotografien in der deutschen Gedächtnisliteratur." Habilitationsschrift, University of Leipzig, 2007.

Household, Geoffrey. *Rogue Male*. New York: Penguin, 1977.

Huntley, Frank Livingstone. "'Well Sir Thomas?': Oration to Commemorate the Tercentenary of the Death of Sir Thomas Browne." *BMJ: British Medical Journal* 285.6334 (1982): 43–47.

Hutchinson, Ben. "Die Leichtigkeit der Schwermut: W. G. Sebalds 'Kunst der Levitation.'" *Jahrbuch der Deutschen Schillergesellschaft* 50 (2006): 458–77.

———. *W. G. Sebald — Die dialektische Imagination.* Berlin: de Gruyter, 2009.

Huyssen, Andreas. *Present Pasts: Urban Palimpsests and the Politics of Memory.* Stanford, CA: Stanford UP, 2003.

ICI Research Team. "A Truth That Lies Elsewhere." In Patt, *Searching for Sebald,* 492–509.

Ignatieff, Michael. "An Interview with Bruce Chatwin." *Granta* 21 (1987): 23–37.

Jacobs, Carol. "What Does It Mean to Count? W. G. Sebald's *The Emigrants.*" *Modern Language Notes* 119.5 (2004): 905–29.

Jameson, Fredric. "Marxism and Historicism." *New Literary History* 11 (Autumn 1979): 41–73.

———. *The Political Unconscious: Narrative as a Socially Symbolic Act.* Ithaca, NY: Cornell UP, 1981.

Jarvis, Robin. *Romantic Writing and Pedestrian Travel.* London: Macmillan, 1997.

Jean Paul. *Dr. Katzenbergers Badereise.* In *Werke,* vol. 6, edited by Norbert Miller, 77–309. Munich: Hanser, 1963.

Jefferson, Margo. "Writing in the Shadows." The *New York Times Book Review,* 18 March 2001.

Juhl, Eva. "Die Wahrheit über das Unglück: Zu W. G. Sebald *Die Ausgewanderten.*" In Fuchs and Harden, *Reisen im Diskurs,* 640–50.

Kafka, Franz. "Der Aufbruch." In *Nachgelassene Schriften und Fragmente II,* 374–75.

———. *Briefe, 1913–März 1914.* Edited by Hans-Gerd Koch. Frankfurt am Main: Fischer, 1999.

———. *Briefe, April 1914–1917.* Edited by Hans-Gerd Koch. Frankfurt am Main: Fischer, 2005.

———. "The Hunter Gracchus: Four Fragments." In *The Great Wall of China and Other Short Works,* translated and edited by Malcolm Pasley, 47–55. London: Penguin, 2002.

———. *The Metamorphosis and Other Stories.* Translated by Willa and Edwin Muir. New York: Schocken Books, 1988.

———. *Nachgelassene Schriften und Fragmente I.* Edited by Malcolm Pasley. Frankfurt am Main: Fischer, 2002.

———. *Nachgelassene Schriften und Fragmente II.* Edited by Jost Schillemeit. Frankfurt am Main: Fischer, 1992.

————. *Das Schloß.* Edited by Malcolm Pasley. Frankfurt am Main: Fischer, 2002. In English, *The Castle.* Translated by Idris Parry. London: Penguin, 2000.

————. *Tagebücher.* Edited by Hans-Gerd Koch, Michael Müller, and Malcolm Pasley. Frankfurt am Main: Fischer, 1990.

Kant, Immanuel. "Beantwortung der Frage: Was ist Aufklärung?" In *Werke in zehn Bänden,* edited by Wilhelm Weischedel, 9:51–61. Darmstadt: Wissenschaftliche Buchgesellschaft, 1964.

Kaplan, Caren. *Questions of Travel: Postmodern Discourses of Displacement.* Durham, NC: Duke UP, 1996.

Kastura, Thomas. "Geheimnisvolle Fähigkeit zur Transmigration: W. G. Sebalds interkulturelle Wallfahrten in die Leere." *Arcadia: Internationale Zeitschrift für Literaturwissenschaft* 31.1/2 (1996): 197–216.

Keck, Michaela. *Walking in the Wilderness: The Peripatetic Tradition in Nineteenth-Century American Literature and Painting.* Heidelberg: Winter, 2006.

Kempinksi, Avi. "'Quel Roman!': Sebald, Barthes, and the Pursuit of the Mother-Image." In Patt, *Searching for Sebald,* 456–71.

Kerr, Douglas. "Three Ways of Going Wrong: Kipling, Conrad, Coetzee." *Modern Language Review* 95.1 (2000): 18–27.

Kilbourn, Russell J. A. "Architecture and Cinema: The Representation of Memory in W. G. Sebald's *Austerlitz.*" In Long and Whitehead, *W. G. Sebald: A Critical Companion,* 140–54.

Kingsley, Charles. *Westward, Ho!* New York: Dutton Everyman's Library, 1967.

Klatt, Fritz. "Stifter und das Dämonische." *Dichtung und Volkstum* 40 (1939): 276–95.

Klebes, Martin. "Infinite Journey: From Kafka to Sebald." In Long and Whitehead, *W. G. Sebald: A Critical Companion,* 123–39.

————. "Sebald's Pathographies." In Denham and McCulloh, *W. G. Sebald: History — Memory — Trauma,* 65–75.

————. *Wittgenstein's Novels.* New York: Routledge, 2006.

Klein, Herbert. "Charting the Unknown: Conrad, Marlow, and the World of Women." *Conradiana* 20.2 (1988): 147–57.

König, Gudrun M. *Eine Kulturgeschichte des Spazierganges: Spuren einer bürgerlichen Praktik, 1780–1850.* Cologne: Böhlau, 1996.

Korff, Friedrich Wilhelm. *Diastole und Systole: Zum Thema Jean Paul und Adalbert Stifter.* Bern: Francke, 1969.

Körte, Mona. "'Un petit sac': W. G. Sebalds Figuren zwischen Sammeln und Vernichten." In Atze and Loquai, *Sebald: Lektüren,* 176–94.

Koschorke, Albrecht. *Die Geschichte des Horizonts: Grenze und Grenzüberschreitung in literarischen Landschaftsbildern*. Frankfurt am Main: Suhrkamp 1990.

Kraenzle, Christina. "Picturing Place: Travel, Photography, and Imaginative Geography in W. G. Sebald's *Rings of Saturn*." In Patt, *Searching for Sebald*, 126–45.

Lacan, Jacques. *Le séminaire: Livre IV. La relation d'objet*. Edited by Jacques-Alain Miller. Paris: Seuil, 1994.

Lamb-Faffelberger, Margarete. "Christoph Ransmayr's *Die Schrecken des Eises und der Finsternis*: Interweaving Fact and Fiction into a Postmodern Narrative." In *Modern Austrian Prose: Interpretations and Insight*, edited by Paul F. Dvorak, 269–85. Riverside, CA: Ariadne, 2001.

Lanchester, John. "A Pom by the Name of Bruce." *London Review of Books*, 29 September 1988, 10.

Lane, Anthony. "Higher Ground." *New Yorker*, 29 May 2000, 28.

Least Heat-Moon, William. *Blue Highways: A Journey into America*. Boston, MA: Little, Brown, 1983.

Lefebvre, Henri. *The Production of Space*. Translated by Donald Nicholson-Smith. Oxford: Blackwell, 1991.

Le Guin, Ursula. *A Wizard of Earthsea*. New York: Bantam, 1975.

Leone, Massimo. "Literature, Travel, and Vertigo." In Conroy, *Cross-Cultural Travel: Papers from the Royal Irish Academy Symposium on Literature and Travel*, 513–22.

———. "Textual Wanderings: A Vertiginous Reading of W. G. Sebald." In Long and Whitehead, *W. G. Sebald: A Critical Companion*, 89–101.

Lévi-Strauss, Claude. *Tristes tropiques*. Translated by Doreen Weightman and John Weightman. New York: Penguin Books, 1992.

London, Bette. "Reading Race and Gender in Conrad's Dark Continent." *Criticism* 31.3 (1989): 235–52.

Long, J. J. "A Bibliographical Essay on Current Research." In Fuchs and Long, *W. G. Sebald and the Writing of History*, 11–30.

———. "History, Narrative, and Photography in W. G. Sebald's *Die Ausgewanderten*." *Modern Language Review* 98 (2003): 117–37.

———. "Intercultural Identities in W. G. Sebald's *The Emigrants* and Norbert Gstrein's *Die englischen Jahre*." *Journal of Multilingual and Multicultural Development* 25.5/6 (2004): 512–28.

———. *W. G. Sebald: Image, Archive, Modernity*. New York: Columbia UP, 2007.

Long, J. J., and Anne Whitehead, eds. *W. G. Sebald: A Critical Companion*. Seattle: U of Washington P, 2004.

Long, Tony. "It's just the 'internet' now." 2004. *Wired*. http://www.wired. com/culture/lifestyle/news/2004/08/64596. Accessed 20 March 2009.

Lubow, Arthur. "Crossing Boundaries." In Schwartz, *The Emergence of Memory*, 159–73.

MacCannell, Dean. *The Tourist: A New Theory of the Leisure Class*. 1976. Reprint, New York: Schocken, 1989.

Magris, Claudio. *Danubio*. Milan: Garzanti, 1986.

Maier, Anja K. "'Der panische Halsknick': Organisches und Anorganisches in W. G. Sebalds Prosa." In Niehaus and Öhlschläger, *W. G. Sebald: Politische Archäologie und melancholische Bastelei*, 111–26.

Mann, Thomas. *Der Zauberberg. Roman*. Edited by Michael Neumann. Frankfurt am Main: Fischer, 2002. In English, *The Magic Mountain*. Translated by Helen Tracy Lowe-Porter. London: Vintage, 1999.

Márquez, Gabriel García. *One Hundred Years of Solitude*. London: Penguin, 1972.

Martin, James P. "Die bezaubernde Anmut eines chemischen Prozesses — Photography in the Works of Gerhard Roth and W. G. Sebald." In Zisselsberger, *Modern Austrian Literature*, 42–60.

Massey, Doreen. "A Global Sense of Place." In *Space, Place, and Gender*, 146–56. Minneapolis: U of Minnesota P, 1994.

Matz, Wolfgang. *Adalbert Stifter oder diese fürchterliche Wendung der Dinge*. Munich: dtv, 2005.

McCulloh, Mark R. "Destruction and Transcendence in W. G. Sebald." *Philosophy and Literature* 30.2 (2006): 395–409.

———. "The Stylistics of Stasis: Paradoxical Effects in W. G. Sebald." *Style* 38.1 (2004): 38–49.

———. *Understanding W. G. Sebald*. Columbia: U of South Carolina P, 2003.

Meanor, Patrick. *Bruce Chatwin*. New York: Twayne, 1997.

Menasse, Robert. *Selige Zeiten, brüchige Welt*. Salzburg: Residenz Verlag, 1992.

———. *Die Vertreibung aus der Hölle*. Frankfurt am Main: Suhrkamp, 2001.

Merriam-Webster's Medical Dictionary. http://medical.merriam-webster. com/medical/indifference%20point. Accessed 15 June 2009.

Meyer, Sven. "Fragmente zu Mementos: Imaginierte Konjekturen bei W. G. Sebald." *Text+Kritik* 158.4 (2003): 75–81.

———. "Der Kopf, der auftaucht: Zu W. G. Sebald's *Nach der Natur*." In Atze and Loquai, *Sebald: Lektüren*, 67–77.

———. "Portrait ohne Absicht: Der Lyriker W. G. Sebald. Nachwort." In *Über das Land und das Wasser: Ausgewählte Gedichte, 1964–2001*, by W. G. Sebald, edited by Sven Meyer, 105–12.

Milton, John. *Paradise Lost.* Edited by David Scott Kastan. Indianapolis: Hackett, 2005.

Moretti, Franco. *Signs Taken for Wonders: Essays in the Sociology of Literary Forms.* London: Verso, 1983.

Mosbach, Bettina. *Figurationen der Katastrophe: Ästhetische Verfahren in W. G. Sebalds* Die Ringe des Saturn *und* Austerlitz. Bielefeld: Aisthesis Verlag, 2008.

Moser, Christian. "Anatomie der Folter: Zur Darstellung des gepeinigten Leibes in den Texten W. G. Sebalds." In *Marter — Martyrium: Ethische und ästhetische Aspekte der Folter,* edited by Volker Dörr, Jürgen Nelles, and Hans-Joachim Pieper, 207–26. Bonn: Denkmal, 2009.

———. "'The humour of my irregular self': Sir Thomas Brownes *Religio Medici* — ein Bekenntnis unter Vorbehalt." In *Autobiographisches Schreiben und philosophische Selbstsorge,* edited by Maria Moog-Grünewald, 73–94. Heidelberg: Winter, 2004.

———. "Map vs. Picture: Techniken der Visualisierung in der englischen Großstadtliteratur des frühen 19. Jahrhunderts." In *Visual Culture,* edited by Monika Schmitz-Emans and Gertrud Lehnert, 151–65. Heidelberg: Synchron, 2008.

Moser, Christian, and Helmut J. Schneider. "Einleitung: Zur Kulturgeschichte und Poetik des Spaziergangs." In *Kopflandschaften–Landschaftsgänge: Kulturgeschichte und Poetik des Spaziergangs,* edited by Axel Gellhaus, Christian Moser, and Helmut J. Schneider, 7–27. Cologne: Böhlau, 2007.

Moser, Gerda Elisabeth. "Das postmoderne ästhetische Tableau und seine Beziehungen zu Leben und Denken." In *Postmoderne Literatur in deutscher Sprache: Eine Ästhetik des Widerstands,* edited by Henk Harbers, 35–58. Amsterdamer Beiträge zur neueren Germanistik 49. Amsterdam: Rodopi, 2000.

Murfin, Ross, ed. *Conrad Revisited: Essays for the Eighties.* Tuscaloosa: U of Alabama P, 1985.

———, ed. *Joseph Conrad: Heart of Darkness.* New York: St Martin's, 1989.

Nadolny, Sten. *Die Entdeckung der Langsamkeit.* 39th ed. Munich: Piper, 1983. In English, *The Discovery of Slowness.* Translated by Ralph Freedman. Philadelphia: Paul Dry Books, 2005.

Nancy, Jean-Luc. "Uncanny Landscape." In *The Ground of the Image,* translated by Jeff Fort, 51–62. New York: Fordham UP, 2005.

Naumann, Ursula. *Adalbert Stifter.* Stuttgart: Metzler, 1979.

Nethersole, Reingard. "Marginal Topologies: Space in Christoph Ransmayr's *Die Schrecken des Eises und der Finsternis.*" *Modern Austrian Literature* 23.3 (1990): 135–53.

Neumann, Gerhard. "'lange bis zum Zerspringen festgehaltene Augenblicke': W. G. Sebald liest aus seinem Buch *Die Ringe des Saturn*." *Jahrbuch der Bayerischen Akademie der Schönen Künste* 13 (1999): 553–67.

Niehaus, Michael, and Claudia Öhlschläger, eds. *W. G. Sebald: Politische Archäologie und melancholische Bastelei*. Berlin: Erich Schmidt, 2006.

Nietzsche, Friedrich. *The Birth of Tragedy and Other Writings*. Edited by Raymond Geuss and Ronald Speirs. Cambridge: Cambridge UP, 1999.

Novotny, Fritz. *Adalbert Stifter als Maler*. 4th ed. Vienna: Anton Schroll, 1979.

O'Faolain, Nuala. *Are You Somebody? The Accidental Memoir of a Dublin Woman*. New York: Henry Holt, 1996.

Öhlschäger, Claudia. "'Die Bahn des korsischen Kometen': Zur Dimension 'Napoleon' in W. G. Sebalds literarischem Netzwerk." In *Topographien der Literatur: Deutsche Literatur im transnationalen Kontext*, edited by Hartmut Böhme, 536–58. Stuttgart: Metzler, 2005.

———. *Beschädigtes Leben. Erzählte Risse: W. G. Sebalds poetische Ordnung des Unglücks*. Freiburg: Rombach, 2006.

Osborne, Dora. "Blind Spots: Viewing Trauma in W. G. Sebald's *Austerlitz*." *Seminar* 43.3 (2007): 517–33.

Ousby, Ian. *The Englishman's England: Taste, Travel, and the Rise of Tourism*. Cambridge: Cambridge UP, 1990.

Oxenius, Katharina. *Vom Promenieren zum Spazieren: Zur Kulturgeschichte des Pariser Parks*. Tübingen: Tübinger Vereinigung für Volkskunde, 1992.

Özdamar, Emine Sevgi. *Die Brücke vom Goldenen Horn*. Cologne: Kiepenheuer & Witsch, 1998.

Pages, Neil Christian. "Crossing Borders: Sebald, Handke, and the Pathological Vision." *Modern Austrian Literature* 40.4 (2007): 61–92.

———. "No Place but Home: W. G. Sebald on the Air War and Other Stories." *Crossings* 7 (2004/5): 91–137.

Panofsky, Erwin. "Die Perspektive als 'symbolische Form.'" In *Deutschsprachige Aufsätze II*, edited by Karen Michels and Martin Warnke, 664–756. Berlin: Akademie Verlag, 1998. In English, *Perspective as Symbolic Form*. Translated by Christopher S. Wood. New York: Zone Books, 1991.

Patt, Lise. "Introduction: Searching for Sebald: What I Know for Sure." In Patt, *Searching for Sebald*, 17–101.

———, ed. *Searching for Sebald: Photography after W. G. Sebald*. Los Angeles: Institute of Cultural Inquiry, 2007.

Pfister, Manfred. *The Theory and Analysis of Drama*. Cambridge: Cambridge UP, 1991.

Pic, Muriel. "Sebald's Anatomy Lesson: About Three Images — Documents from *On the Natural History of Destruction, The Rings of Saturn* and *Austerlitz.*" *Colloquy: text theory critique* 9 (May 2005): 6–15.

Polster, Heike. *The Aesthetics of Passage: The Imag(in)ed Experience of Time in Thomas Lehr, W. G. Sebald, and Peter Handke.* Würzburg: Königshausen & Neumann, 2009.

Prager, Brad. "Sebald's Kafka." In Denham and McCulloh, *W. G. Sebald: History — Memory — Trauma,* 105–26.

Pratt, Mary Louise. *Imperial Eyes: Travel Writing and Transculturation.* New York: Routledge, 1992.

Presner, Todd S. *Mobile Modernity: Germans, Jews, Trains.* New York: Columbia UP, 2007.

———. "Hegel's Philosophy of World History via Sebald's Imaginary of Ruins: A Contrapuntal Critique of the 'New Space' of Modernity." In *Ruins of Modernity,* edited by Julia Hell and Andreas Schönle, 193–211. Durham: Duke UP, 2010.

Preußer, Heinz-Peter. "Reisen ans Ende der Welt: Bilder des Katastrophismus in der neueren österreichischen Literatur. Bachmann — Handke — Ransmayr." In *1945–1995: Fünfzig Jahre deutschsprachige Literatur in Aspekten,* edited by Gerhard Knapp and Gerd Labroisse, 369–407. Amsterdamer Beiträge zur neueren Germanistik 38/39. Amsterdam: Rodopi, 1995.

Psalm 139, *Lutherbibel* (1912). 2004. http://l12.bibeltext.com/psalms/139. htm. Accessed 9 June 2009.

Psalm 139, *New International Version.* 1995. http://www.biblegateway.com/ passage/?search=Psalm%20139. Accessed 9 June 2009.

Quint, David. "Repetition and Ideology in the *Aeneid.*" In *Epic and Empire: Politics and Generic Form from Virgil to Milton,* 50–96. Princeton, NJ: Princeton UP, 1993.

Ransmayr, Christoph. *Die Schrecken des Eises und der Finsternis.* Frankfurt am Main: Fischer, 1987. In English, *The Terrors of Ice and Darkness.* Translated by John E. Woods. New York: Grove, 1991.

Rascaroli, Laura. "*L'année dernière à Marienbad.*" In *The Cinema of France,* edited by Phil Powie, 101–10. New York: Wallflower, 2006.

Resnais, Alain, dir. *L'année dernière à Marienbad.* France and Italy, 1961. In English, *Last Year at Marienbad.* Translated by Richard Howard. New York: Grove, 1962.

Rickels, Laurence A. "Stifter's *Nachkommenschaften*: The Problem of the Surname, the Problem of Painting." *Modern Language Notes* 100.3 (1985): 590–91.

Riordan, Colin. "Ecocentrism in Sebald's *Nach der Natur.*" In Long and Whitehead, *W. G. Sebald: A Critical Companion,* 45–57.

Robbe-Grillet, Alain. *L'année dernière à Marienbad: Ciné-roman*. Paris: Éditions de Minuit, 1961.

Roedl, Urban. *Adalbert Stifter in Selbstzeugnissen und Bilddokumenten*. Reinbek bei Hamburg: Rowohlt 1965.

Romm, James S. *The Edges of the Earth in Ancient Thought: Geography, Exploration, and Fiction*. Princeton, NJ: Princeton UP, 1992.

Rondas, Jean-Pierre. "'So wie ein Hund, der den Löffel vergisst': Ein Gespräch mit W. G. Sebald über *Austerlitz*." In *Literatur im Krebsgang: Totenbeschwörung und memoria in der deutschsprachigen Literatur nach 1989*, edited by Arne De Winde and Anke Gilleir, 351–63. Amsterdam: Rodopi, 2008.

Rousseau, Jean-Jacques. *Les confessions*. In *Œuvres complètes* 1:163.

———. *Emile ou de l'éducation*. In *Œuvres complètes* 4:771–72.

———. *Œuvres complètes*. Edited by Bernard Gagnebin and Marcel Raymond. 4 vols. Paris: Gallimard, 1961–69.

Said, Edward. *Culture and Imperialism*. New York: Vintage, 1993.

———. *Orientalism*. New York: Pantheon, 1978.

Santner, Eric, L. *On Creaturely Life: Rilke, Benjamin, Sebald*. Chicago: Chicago UP, 2006.

———. *Stranded Objects: Mourning, Memory and Film in Postwar Germany*. Ithaca, NY: Cornell UP, 1990.

Sauder, Gerhard. "Formen gegenwärtiger Reiseliteratur." In Fuchs and Harden, *Reisen im Diskurs*, 552–73.

Schaer, Michael. *Ex negativo: "Dr. Katzenbergers Badereise" als Beitrag Jean Pauls zur ästhetischen Theorie*. Göttingen: Vandenhoeck & Ruprecht, 1983.

Schami, Rafik. *Die Sehnsucht der Schwalbe*. Munich: Hanser, 2000.

Schelle, Karl Gottlob. *Die Spaziergänge oder die Kunst spazieren zu gehen*. Edited by Markus Fauser. Leipzig: 1802. Reprint, Hildesheim: Olms, 1990.

Schiller, Friedrich. "Der Spaziergang." In *Sämtliche Werke*, edited by Gerhard Fricke and Herbert G. Göpfert, 1:228–34. 8th ed. Munich: Hanser, 1987.

Schindel, Robert. *Gebürtig*. Frankfurt am Main: Suhrkamp, 1992.

Schivelbusch, Wolfgang. *The Railway Journey: Trains and Travel in the 19th Century*. Oxford: Blackwell, 1980.

Schlesinger, Philip. "W. G. Sebald and the Condition of Exile." *Theory, Culture & Society* 21.2 (2004): 43–67.

Schneider, Helmut J. "Selbsterfahrung zu Fuß: Spaziergang und Wanderung als poetische und geschichtsphilosophische Reflexionsfigur im Zeitalter Rousseaus." In *Rousseauismus: Naturevangelium und Literatur*, edited by Jürgen Söring and Peter Gasser, 133–54. Frankfurt am Main: Lang, 1999.

Schoell-Glass, Charlotte. "Fictions of the Art World: Art, Art History, and the Art Historian in Literary Space." In *Writing and Seeing: Essays on Word and Image*, edited by Rui Carvalho Homem and Maria de Fátima Lambert, 107–18. Amsterdam: Rodopi, 2006.

Scholz, Christian. "'But the Written Word Is Not a True Document': A Conversation with W. G. Sebald on Literature and Photography." Translated by Markus Zisselsberger. In Patt, *Searching for Sebald*, 104–9.

Schütte, Uwe. "Der Hüter der Metaphysik — W. G. Sebalds Essays über die österreichische Literatur." *manuskripte* 155 (March 2002): 124–28.

———. "'In einer wildfremden Gegend' — W. G. Sebalds Essays über die österreichische Literatur." In Görner, *The Anatomist of Melancholy*, 63–74.

Schwartz, Lynne Sharon, ed. *The Emergence of Memory: Conversations with W. G. Sebald*. New York: Seven Stories, 2007.

Scott, Sir Walter. *The Bride of Lammermoor*. Edinburgh: Edinburgh UP, 1995.

———. *Guy Mannering*. New York, Penguin, 2003.

———. *Old Mortality*. New York: Penguin, 1985.

———. *Redgauntlet*. New York: The Waverley Book Company, 1898.

———. *Waverley*. Edited by Andrew Hook. New York: Penguin, 1988.

Sebald, W. G. *After Nature*. Translated by Michael Hamburger. New York: The Modern Library, 2003.

———. "Die Alpen im Meer." In English, "The Alps in the Sea." In *Campo Santo* 39–50/35–46.

———. "'Aufzeichnungen aus Korsika: Zur Natur- & Menschenkunde,' von W. G. Sebald." Edited by von Bülow. In von Bülow, Gfrereis, and Strittmatter, *Wandernde Schatten*, 129–58 (first version); 159–210 (second version).

———. *Die Ausgewanderten*. Frankfurt am Main: Fischer, 1992. In English, *The Emigrants*. Translated by Michael Hulse. New York: New Directions, 1997.

———. *Austerlitz*. Frankfurt am Main: Fischer, 2003. In English, *Austerlitz*. Translated by Anthea Bell. New York: The Modern Library, 2001.

———. *Die Beschreibung des Unglücks: Zur österreichischen Literatur von Stifter bis Handke*. Frankfurt am Main: Fischer, 1994.

———. "Bis an den Rand der Natur: Versuch über Stifter." In *Die Beschreibung des Unglücks*, 15–37.

———. *Campo Santo*. Edited by Sven Meyer. Frankfurt am Main: Fischer, 2006. In English, *Campo Santo*. Translated by Anthea Bell. New York: Random House, 2005.

———. "Die dunckle Nacht fahrt aus." *manuskripte* 95 (1987): 12–18.

———. "Es steht ein Komet am Himmel: Kalenderbeitrag zu Ehren des rheinischen Hausfreunds." In *Logis in einem Landhaus*, 20.

———. *For Years Now: Poems.* London: Short Books, 2001.

———. "Das Geheimnis des rotbraunen Fells: Annäherung an Bruce Chatwin." In English, "The Secret of the Red-Brown Skin: An Approach to Bruce Chatwin. In *Campo Santo,* 215–22/173–80.

———. "Des Häschens Kind, der kleine Has: Über das Totemtier des Lyrikers Ernst Herbeck." In English, "Des Häschens Kind, der kleine Has [The Little Hare, Child of the Hare]: On the Poet Ernst Herbeck's Totem Animal." In *Campo Santo,* 171–78/125–33.

———. "Helle Bilder und dunkle: Zur Dialektik der Eschatologie bei Stifter und Handke." In *Die Beschreibung des Unglücks,* 165–86.

———. "Her kommt der Tod, die Zeit geht hin: Anmerkungen zu Gottfried Keller." In *Logis in einem Landhaus: Über Gottfried Keller, Johann Peter Hebel, Robert Walser und andere,* 125–26.

———. "In a Completely Unknown Region: On Gerhard Roth's Novel *Landläufiger Tod.*" Translated by Markus Zisselsberger. In Zisselsberger, *Modern Austrian Literature,* 43–60.

———. "J'aurais voulu que ce lac eût été l'Océan: Anläßlich eines Besuchs auf der St. Petersinsel." In *Logis in einem Landhaus,* 43–74.

———. "Die Kunst des Fliegens." In *Träume: Literaturalmanach, 1987,* edited by Jochen Jung, 134–38. Salzburg: Residenz Verlag, 1987.

———. *Logis in einem Landhaus: Über Gottfried Keller, Johann Peter Hebel, Robert Walser und andere.* Frankfurt am Main: Fischer, 2003.

———. *Luftkrieg und Literatur.* Frankfurt am Main: Fischer, 2001.

———. "Mit den Augen des Nachtvogels: Über Jean Améry." In *Campo Santo,* 149–70.

———. *Nach der Natur: Ein Elementargedicht.* Frankfurt am Main: Fischer, 1995.

———. *On the Natural History of Destruction.* Translated by Anthea Bell. New York: The Modern Library, 2004.

———. "Le promeneur solitaire: Zur Erinnerung an Robert Walser." In *Logis in einem Landhaus,* 127–68.

———. Review of *Donau — Biographie eines Flusses,* by Claudio Magris, translated by Heinz-Georg Held. *Austrian Studies* 1 (1990): 183–84.

———. *Die Ringe des Saturn: Eine englische Wallfahrt.* Frankfurt am Main: Fischer, 2002. In English, *The Rings of Saturn.* Translated by Michael Hulse. New York: New Directions, 1998.

———. *Schwindel. Gefühle.* Frankfurt am Main: Fischer, 1994. In English, *Vertigo.* Translated by Michael Hulse. New York: New Directions, 2000.

———. "Scomber scombrus, or the Common Mackerel: On Pictures by Jan Peter Tripp." In *Campo Santo,* 169–72.

———. "Thanatos: Zur Motivstruktur in Kafka's *Schloss.*" *Literatur und Kritik* 66/67 (1972): 399–411.

———. *Über das Land und das Wasser: Ausgewählte Gedichte, 1964–2001.* Edited by Sven Meyer. Munich: Hanser, 2008.

———. "Und blieb ich am äussersten Meer." *manuskripte* 85 (1984): 23–27.

———. "Das unentdeckte Land: Zur Motivstruktur in Kafkas *Schloß.*" In *Die Beschreibung des Unglücks,* 78–92. In English, "The Undiscover'd Country: The Death Motif in Kafka's *Castle.*" *Journal of European Studies* 2 (1972): 22–34.

———. *Unerzählt: 33 Texte und 33 Radierungen.* Munich: Hanser, 2003.

———. *Unheimliche Heimat: Essays zur österreichischen Literatur.* Frankfurt am Main: Fischer, 1995.

———. "Unterm Spiegel des Wassers: Peter Handkes Erzählung von der Angst des Tormanns." In *Die Beschreibung des Unglücks,* 115–30.

———. "Verlorenes Land: Jean Améry und Österreich." *Text + Kritik* 99 (1988): 20–29.

———. "Wie der Schnee auf den Alpen." *manuskripte* 92 (1986): 26–31.

———. "Die Zerknirschung des Herzens: Über Erinnerung und Grausamkeit im Werk von Peter Weiss." In *Campo Santo,* 128–48. In English, "The Remorse of the Heart: On Memory and Cruelty in the Work of Peter Weiss." In *On the Natural History of Destruction,* 169–91.

———. "Zwischen Geschichte und Naturgeschichte: Über die literarische Beschreibung totaler Zerstörung." In English, "Between History and Natural History: On the Literary Description of Total Destruction." In *Campo Santo,* 69–100/65–95.

Sebald, W. G., and Gordon Turner. "Introduction and Transcript of an Interview given by Max Sebald." In Denham and McCulloh, *W. G. Sebald: History — Memory — Trauma,* 21–29.

Sebestyén, György. *"Die Kurpromenade oder die Erfindung der Kunstnatur."* In *Große Welt reist ins Bad, 1800–1914: Baden bei Wien, Badgastein, Bad Ischl, Franzensbad, Karlsbad, Marienbad, Teplitz.* Catalogue of an exhibition by the Adalbert Stifter Association, Munich, in cooperation with the Austrian Museum of the Applied Arts, Vienna, 36–42. Passau, Germany: Passavia, 1980.

Seume, Johann Gottfried. *Mein Sommer 1805: Reisejournal.* In *Prosaschriften,* 638–858.

———. *Prosaschriften.* Mit einer Einleitung von Werner Kraft. Darmstadt: Wissenschaftliche Buchgesellschaft, 1974.

Shakespeare, Nicholas. *Bruce Chatwin: A Biography.* New York: Anchor Books, 2001.

Sheppard, Richard. "Dexter — Sinister: Some Observations on Decrypting the Mors Code in the Work of W. G. Sebald." *Journal of European Studies* 35 (2005): 419–63.

———. "'Woods, trees and the spaces in between': A Report on Work Published on W. G. Sebald, 2005–2008." *Journal of European Studies* 39.1 (2009): 79–128.

Silverblatt, Michael. "A Poem of an Invisible Subject" (interview). In Schwartz, *The Emergence of Memory*, 77–86.

Simon, Ulrich. "Der Provokateur als Literaturhistoriker: Anmerkungen zu Literaturbegriff und Argumentationsverfahren in W. G. Sebalds essayistischen Schriften." In Atze and Loquai, *Sebald: Lektüren*, 78–104.

Smith, Johanna M. "'Too Beautiful Altogether': Patriarchal Ideology in *Heart of Darkness*." In *Joseph Conrad: Heart of Darkness*, edited by Ross C. Murfin, 169–84. New York: St. Martin's, 1989.

Soja, Edward. "Reassertions: Towards a Spatialized Ontology." In *Postmodern Geographies: The Reassertion of Space in Critical Social Theory*, 118–37. London: Verso, 1989.

Solnit, Rebecca. *Wanderlust: A History of Walking*. London: Verso, 2001.

Sontag, Susan. *Where the Stress Falls*. London: Cape, 2002.

Spitz, Markus Oliver. "Traveling Borderline Territories: *Die Schrecken des Eises und der Finsternis*, by Christoph Ransmayr." In Conroy, *Cross-Cultural Travel: Papers from the Royal Irish Academy International Symposium on Literature and Travel, National University of Ireland, Galway, November 2002*, 449–58.

Staff, Frank. *The Picture Postcard and Its Origins*. 2nd ed. London: Lutterworth, 1979.

Stark, Bruce. "Kurtz's Intended: The Heart of the *Heart of Darkness*." *Texas Studies in Literature and Language* 16.3 (1974): 535–55.

Steinaecker, Thomas von. *Literarische Foto-Texte: Zur Funktion der Fotografien in den Texten Rolf Dieter Brinkmanns, Alexander Kluges und W. G. Sebalds*. Bielefeld: transcript, 2007.

———. "Zwischen schwarzem Tod und weißer Ewigkeit: Zum Grau auf den Abbildungen W. G. Sebalds." In *Verschiebebahnhöfe der Erinnerung: Zum Werk W. G. Sebalds*, edited by Sigurd Martin and Ingo Wintermeyer, 119–36. Würzburg: Königshausen & Neumann, 2004.

Sterba, Richard F. "Remarks on Joseph Conrad's *Heart of Darkness*." *Journal of the American Psychoanalytic Association* 13.3 (1965): 570–83.

Stevenson, Robert Louis. *Treasure Island*. Edited by Emma Letley. Oxford: Oxford UP, 1985.

Stifter, Adalbert. *Bunte Steine*. Stuttgart: Reclam, 2005.

———. "Der Condor." In *Sämtliche Erzählungen nach den Erstdrucken*, 9–28.

———. *Die fürchterliche Wendung der Dinge: Erzählungen.* Edited by Hans Joachim Piechotta. Darmstadt: Luchterhand, 1981.

———. *Indian Summer.* Translated by Wendell Frye. New York: Peter Lang, 1985.

———. "Mein Leben." In *Die fürchterliche Wendung der Dinge.*

———. "Nachgelassenes Blatt." In *Gesammelte Werke in sechs Bänden* 6:583–87. Gütersloh: C. Bertelsmann, 1957.

———. *Der Nachsommer.* Munich: Winkler, 1966.

———. *Rock Crystal.* Translated by Elizabeth Mayer and Marianne Moore. With an introduction by W. H. Auden. New York: New York Review Books, 2008.

———. *Sämtliche Erzählungen nach den Erstdrucken.* Edited by Wolfgang Matz. Munich: Deutscher Taschenbuch Verlag, 2005.

———. *Sämmtliche Werke.* Vol. 19.3. Reichenberg: Sudetendeutscher Verlag Franz Kraus, 1929.

Stone, Will. "At Risk of Interment: W. G. Sebald in Terezin and Breendonk." *Vertigo* 40.3 (Summer 2009): 67.

Strathausen, Carsten. "Going Nowhere: Sebald's Rhizomatic Travels." In Patt, *Searching for Sebald,* 472–92.

Straus, Nina Pelikan. "The Exclusion of the Intended from Secret Sharing in Conrad's *Heart of Darkness*." *Novel: A Forum on Fiction* 20.2 (1987): 123–37.

Summers-Bremner, Eluned. "Reading, Walking, Mourning: W. G. Sebald's Peripatetic Fictions." *Journal of Narrative Theory* 34 (2004): 304–34.

Swales, Martin. "Theoretical Reflections on the Work of W. G. Sebald." In Long and Whitehead, *W. G. Sebald: A Critical Companion,* 23–30.

Taberner, Stuart. "German Nostalgia? Remembering German-Jewish Life in W. G. Sebald's *Die Ausgewanderten* and *Austerlitz*." *German Quarterly* 79.3 (2004): 181–202.

Taylor, John. *A Dream of England: Landscape, Photography and the Tourist's Imagination.* Manchester, UK: Manchester UP, 1994.

The Academy of Natural Sciences. "Woolly Mammoth." http://www.ansp. org/museum/jefferson/otherFossils/mammuthus.php. Accessed 9 June 2009.

Thalman, William B. *The* Odyssey: *An Epic of Return.* New York: Twayne, 1992.

Theisen, Bianca. "A Natural History of Destruction: W. G. Sebald's *The Rings of Saturn*." *Modern Language Notes* 121.3 (2006): 563–81.

———. "Prose of the World: W. G. Sebald's Literary Travels." *Germanic Review* 79.3 (Summer 2004): 163–79.

Tidball, Derek. "The Pilgrim and the Tourist: Zygmunt Baumann and Postmodern Identity." In *Explorations in a Christian Theology of Pilgrimage*, edited by Craig Bartholomew and Fred Hughes, 184–200. Aldershot, UK: Ashgate, 2004.

Tischel, Alexandra. "Aus der Dunkelkammer der Geschichte: Zum Zusammenhang von Photographie und Erinnerung in W. G. Sebalds *Austerlitz*." In Niehaus and Öhlschläger, *W. G. Sebald: Politische Archäologie und melancholische Bastelei*, 31–45.

Todorov, Tzvetan. "Knowledge in the Void: *Heart of Darkness*." *Conradiana* 21.3 (1989): 161–72.

Tolkien, J. R. R. *The Lord of the Rings*. Boston, MA: Houghton Mifflin, 2005.

Trevor-Roper, Patrick. *The World through Blunted Sight*. New York: Bobbs-Merrill, 1970.

Tripp, Jan Peter. "Die Waldauer Begegnung." In *Centrales & Occasionelles*, 98–106. Offenburg: Schwarzwaldverlag, 2001.

Turner, Victor. *The Ritual Process: Structure and Anti-Structure*. New York: Aldine de Gruyter, 1969.

Urry, John. *The Tourist Gaze*. 2nd ed. London: Sage, 2002.

Vargas-Llosa, Mario. "Extemporáneos: Las raíces de lo humano." *Letras Libres* (Dec. 2001): 18–22.

Verne, Jules. *20,000 Leagues under the Sea*. Translated by William Butcher. Oxford: Oxford UP, 1998.

——. *Journey to the Center of the Earth*. Translated by Lowell Blair. New York: Bantam Classics, 1991.

Vidler, Anthony. *Warped Spaces: Art, Architecture, and Anxiety in Modern Culture*. Cambridge, MA: MIT Press, 2000.

Von Bülow, Ulrich. "Sebalds Korsika-Projekt." In von Bülow, Gfrereis, and Strittmatter, *Wandernde Schatten: W. G. Sebalds Unterwelt*, 211–26.

Von Bülow, Ulrich, Heike Gfrereis, and Ellen Strittmatter, eds. *Wandernde Schatten: W. G. Sebalds Unterwelt*. Marbach: Deutsche Schillergesellschaft, 2008.

Wachtel, Eleanor. "Ghost Hunter (interview)." In Schwartz, *The Emergence of Memory*, 37–62.

Wallace, Anne D. *Walking, Literature, and English Culture: The Origins and Uses of the Peripatetic in the Nineteenth Century*. Oxford: Oxford UP, 1993.

Walser, Robert. "Kleist in Thun." In *Sämtliche Werke in Einzelausgaben*, vol. 2, edited by Jochen Greven, 70–81. Frankfurt am Main: Suhrkamp, 1985.

Ward, David C. "Ghost Worlds of the Ordinary: W. G. Sebald and Gerhard Richter." *PN Review* 29.6 (2003): 32–36.

Watson, Nicola J. *Literary Tourism: Readers and Places in Romantic and Victorian Britain.* Basingstoke, UK: Palgrave, 2006.

Weber, Markus R. "W. G. Sebald." In *Kritisches Lexikon zur deutschsprachigen Gegenwartsliteratur,* edited by Heinz Ludwig Arnold, 10:54. 1978–. Reprint, Munich: Text + Kritik, 1996.

Weber, Samuel. *Theatricality as Medium.* New York: Fordham UP, 2004.

Wechsler, Robert. *Performing without a Stage: The Art of Literary Translation.* North Haven, CT: Catbird, 1998.

Weeks, Andrew. *Paracelsus: Speculative Theory and the Crisis of the Early Reformation.* Albany: SUNY Press, 1997.

Weiss, Peter. "Meine Ortschaft." In *Rapporte,* 113–24. Frankfurt am Main: Suhrkamp, 1968.

White, Andrea. *Joseph Conrad and the Adventure Tradition.* Cambridge: Cambridge UP, 1993.

Williams, Raymond. *Keywords: A Vocabulary of Culture and Society.* New York: Oxford UP, 1976.

Witthaus, Jan Henrik. "Fehlleistung und Fiktion: Sebaldsche Gedächtnismodelle zwischen Freud und Borges." In Niehaus and Öhlschläger, *W. G. Sebald: Politische Archäologie und Melancholische Bastelei,* 157–72.

Wolff, Lynn. "'Das metaphysische Unterfutter der Realität': Recent Publications and Trends in W. G. Sebald Research." *Monatshefte* 99.1 (2007): 78–101.

Wood, James. "An Interview with W. G. Sebald." *Brick* 59 (1998): 23–29.

———. "The Right Thread," *The New Republic* 6 (July 1998): 38–42.

Woody, Howard, "International Postcards: Their History, Production and Distribution (circa 1895–1915)." In Geary and Webb, *Delivering Views: Distant Cultures in Early Postcards,* 13–45.

Wright, Peter. "Astrology and Science in Seventeenth-Century England." *Social Studies of Science* 5.4 (1975): 399–422.

Wurst, Karin. *Fabricating Pleasure: Fashion, Entertainment, and Cultural Consumption in Germany, 1780–1830.* Detroit, MI: Wayne State UP, 2005.

Wylie, John. "The Spectral Geographies of W. G. Sebald." *Cultural Geographies* 14 (2007): 171–88.

Young, Julian. *Nietzsche's Philosophy of Art.* Cambridge: Cambridge UP, 1992.

Zeitlin, Froma I. "Figuring Fidelity in Homer's *Odyssey.*" In *Playing the Other: Gender and Society in Classical Greek Literature,* 19–52. Chicago: U of Chicago P, 1996.

Zeman, Herbert. "Vom Badereisen und vom Dichten — Goethe." In *Zwischen Aufklärung und Restauration: Sozialer Wandel in der deutschen Literatur*

(1700–1848), edited by Wolfgang Frühwald and Alberto Martino, 263–81. Tübingen: Niemeyer, 1989.

Zilcosky, John. "Lost and Found: Disorientation, Nostalgia, and Holocaust Melodrama in Sebald's *Austerlitz.*" *Modern Language Notes* 121.3 (April 2006): 679–98.

———. "Sebald's Uncanny Travels: The Impossibility of Getting Lost." In Long and Whitehead, *W. G. Sebald: A Critical Companion*, 102–20.

———. "Writing Travel." In *Writing Travel: The Poetics and Politics of the Modern Journey*, edited by John Zilcosky, 3–24. Toronto: U of Toronto P, 2008.

Zischler, Hanns. *Kafka geht ins Kino*. Reinbek: Rowohlt, 1996. In English, *Kafka Goes to the Movies*. Translated by Susan H. Gillespie. Chicago: U of Chicago P, 2003.

Zisselsberger, Markus. "Fragments of One's Own Existence: The Reader W. G. Sebald." PhD diss., Binghamton University, SUNY, 2008.

———. "Melancholy Longings: Sebald, Benjamin, and the Image of Kafka." In Patt, *Searching for Sebald*, 280–301.

———, ed. *Modern Austrian Literature* 40.4 (2007). Special issue on W. G. Sebald and Austrian Literature.

———. "A Persistent Fascination: Recent Scholarship on the Work of W. G. Sebald." *Monatshefte* 101.1 (Spring 2009): 88–105.

———. "Stories of *Heimat* and Calamity." In Zisselsberger, *Modern Austrian Literature*, 1–27.

———. "Towards an Extension of Memory: W. G. Sebald Reads Jean Améry." In *Trajectories of Memory: Representations of the Holocaust in History and the Arts*, edited by Christina Guenther and Beth Griech-Polelle, 191–223. Newcastle-upon-Tyne: Cambridge Scholars, 2008.

Contributors

PETER ARNDS is Professor of German and Italian at Kansas State University. He currently teaches at Trinity College, Dublin, where he serves as the Director of Comparative Literature and Literary Translation. He is the author of *Wilhelm Raabe's* Der Hungerpastor *and Charles Dickens's* David Copperfield: *Intertextuality of two "Bildungsromane"* (1997); *Representation, Subversion, and Eugenics in Günter Grass's* The Tin Drum (2004); and numerous articles on German literature and culture from the 18th to 21st centuries, as well as of some poetry and prose. He is presently working on a book entitled "Günter Grass and the Tradition of Magic Realism."

MARGARET BRUZELIUS teaches in the Comparative Literature program at Smith College, where she also serves as the Dean of the Sophomore Class. She earned a PhD in Comparative Literature at Yale University in 1994 and subsequently taught in the Literature program at Harvard University. Her book *Romancing the Novel, Adventure from Scott to Sebald* (2007) explores the literary and ethical consequences of the compulsions of romance plot structures in nineteenth- and twentieth-century European fictions. She has also published articles on twentieth-century women poets and on Sir Walter Scott in *Twentieth Century Literature, Revista Hispánica Moderna* and the *Modern Language Quarterly*.

CAROLIN DUTTLINGER is University Lecturer in German at Oxford University and Fellow and Tutor of Wadham College, Oxford. She is the author of *Kafka and Photography* (2007) and coeditor of *Performance and Performativity in German Cultural Studies* (2004). In addition, she has worked on authors such as Mörike, Freud, Benjamin, Adorno, Canetti, Ruth Klüger, and Thomas Kling, and has published several articles on W. G. Sebald. Sebald is also part of her current project, "Dialectics of Attention: Absorption and Autonomy in Twentieth-Century German Literature, Thought and Culture."

BARBARA HUI is a doctoral candidate in Comparative Literature at the University of California, Los Angeles. Her dissertation, "Narrative Networks: Mapping Literature at the Turn of the 21st Century," explores the social production of spatial networks in contemporary German- and

English-language literature. In conjunction with her dissertation, she has developed *Litmap*, a Web-based platform for digitally mapping literature, which she has used alongside traditional methods of close reading in order to critically examine narratives in terms of their geospatiality. As a former full-time computer programmer, she is generally interested in intersections between technology and the humanities.

ALAN ITKIN is a PhD candidate in the Department of Comparative Literature at the University of Michigan, and currently a fellow of the Institute for the Humanities. He holds an MA in Humanities and Social Thought from New York University. His dissertation, "'Bringing the Past Back to Life': Classical Motifs and the Representation of History in the Works of W. G. Sebald," explores the ways in which Sebald and other post-Holocaust authors draw on classical epic poetry to frame new modes of historical representation attuned to the traumatic historical events of the twentieth century.

MARTIN KLEBES received his PhD in Comparative Literary Studies from Northwestern University and is currently Associate Professor of German at the University of Oregon. He is the author of *Wittgenstein's Novels* (2006) and the translator of Ernst-Wilhelm Händler's debut collection of stories, *City with Houses* (2002). His publications include contributions to the collections *W. G. Sebald: A Critical Companion* (2004); *W. G. Sebald: History — Memory — Trauma* (2006), and *W. G. Sebald: Schreiben ex patria / Expatriate Writing* (2009).

J. J. LONG is a Professor in the School of Modern Languages and Cultures at Durham University, UK. He is the author of *W. G. Sebald: Image, Archive, Modernity* (2008) and *The Novels of Thomas Bernhard: Form and its Function* (2001). He has also coedited several books, including *W. G. Sebald: A Critical Companion* (2004) and *W. G. Sebald and the Writing of History* (2007).

JAMES MARTIN is Assistant Professor of German Studies at Washington College, located on the eastern shore of Maryland. His primary research interests are contemporary Austrian literature and colonialism in eighteenth- and nineteenth-century German literature. He has written articles on authors such as W. G. Sebald, Christoph Ransmayr, and Heinrich von Kleist. Other interests include cross-cultural exchange in German-Jewish, German-Turkish, and world cinema.

CHRISTIAN MOSER is Professor of Comparative Literature at the University of Bonn. He was Max Kade Distinguished Visiting Professor at Columbia University, New York, in 2007. From February 2008 until July 2009 he was Professor of German Literature at the Universiteit van Amsterdam. His numerous publications include *Buchgestützte Subjektivität: Literarische Formen der Selbstsorge und der Selbsthermeneutik von Platon bis Montaigne* (2006) and *Kannibalische Katharsis: Literarische und filmische Inszenierungen der Anthropophagie von James Cook bis Bret Easton Ellis* (2005).

DORA OSBORNE completed her PhD thesis on Sebald and Christoph Ransmayr at the University of Cambridge in 2008. She is particularly interested in questions of memory, trauma, and intermediality. She is currently working on a project about the use of archive material in postwar literature and visual culture at the Freie Universität, Berlin.

NEIL CHRISTIAN PAGES teaches at Binghamton University SUNY. His research interests include Austrian, German, and Scandinavian cultural productions, commemorative practices, architectural history and theory, and translation. He has published articles on Kierkegaard, Nietzsche, Rachel Whiteread's Shoah memorial in Vienna, and W. G. Sebald. He is the coeditor (with Mary Rhiel and Ingeborg Majer-O'Sickey) of *Riefenstahl Screened: An Anthology of New Criticism* (2008).

BRAD PRAGER is Associate Professor of German and an active member of the Program in Film Studies at the University of Missouri. He is the author of *The Cinema of Werner Herzog: Aesthetic Ecstasy and Truth* (2007) and *Aesthetic Vision and German Romanticism: Writing Images* (2007). He is the coeditor of a new volume on Visual Studies and the Holocaust entitled *Visualizing the Holocaust: Documents, Aesthetics, Memory* (2008), and of a forthcoming volume on contemporary German cinema entitled *The Collapse of the Conventional: German Film and Its Politics at the Turn of the Twenty-First Century* (2010).

MARKUS ZISSELSBERGER is Assistant Professor of German at the University of Miami, Florida. He has published articles on Musil, Heidegger, Sebald, and Kafka, and has guest-edited a special issue of *Modern Austrian Literature* on the topic, "W. G. Sebald and Austrian Literature." With Gisela Brinker-Gabler, he is the coeditor of *"If we had the word": Ingeborg Bachmann. Views and Reviews* (2004). He is currently working on a book that examines the relationship between reading, literary criticism, and literature in the work of W. G. Sebald.

Index

"n" refers to notes; "f" to figures

Abrams, Thomas, 201
acculturation, 64–66, 68, 74, 85
Adelwarth, Ambrose, 66, 70, 90n57,
  299, 302, 312, 316, 326
Admiral Tegetthoff (ship), 150
Adorno, Theodor W., 20, 92, 94–95,
  116nn9–10, 239n20
Adorno, Theodor W., works by:
  Ästhetische Theorie, 240n20,
  241n25; *Dialektik der Aufklärung*,
  115n3, 160n30, 154, 160n30,
  184n21; "Kulturindustrie:
  Aufklärung als Massenbetrug,"
  115n3; *Minima Moralia*, 94–95,
  116nn9–10
adventure, 19, 22, 28n36, 28n49,
  121, 123, 164, 170, 208n16; and
  romance novel, 247–73
Aeneid (Virgil), 163–64, 178, 182n11,
  183n14
Agamben, Giorgio, 183n17, 196,
  209n34, 332–33, 343n31,
  344n43
Agáta, 133–37
Ähnlichkeit, 303, 305, 317,
  319–20n16
aletheia, 23, 323, 326, 329, 332–34,
  336–41
"All'estero" from *Schwindel. Gefühle.*
  (Sebald), 39, 47–48, 61n43, 66, 68,
  73, 80, 90n57, 95, 99, 130
Altamura, Salvatore, 72
Altdorfer, Albrecht, 146, 205
Améry, Jean, 12–14, 27n30, 166, 170,
  184n20
*Analyse der Phobie eines fünfjährigen
  Knaben* (Freud), 301, 318n7
Anatomy Lesson, The (Rembrandt),
  51–53, 55, 60nn35–36, 72, 260

Anatomy of Melancholy (Burton), 39,
  58n5
Annäherung, 22, 164, 189, 206,
  207n1, 343n26
anti-tourism, 12, 16, 20, 37, 57n2,
  63–91, 284. *See also* tourism
Antwerp Zoo, Nocturama in, 166
Antwerp's Centraal Station, 322; *Salle
  des pas perdus* in, 166, 169, 322,
  341
arborescence, 23, 323–29, 331, 333,
  335, 341, 342n9
Arctic: expedition led by Vitus Bering,
  5, 143–44, 153, 157nn6–7; landscapes, 21, 143–44, 146, 149–52,
  156
Arnds, Peter, 23, 322–44, 371
Ästhetische Theorie (Adorno),
  239–40n20, 241n25
attentiveness. See *Aufmerksamkeit*
Aufmerksamkeit, 20, 21, 92–93,
  95–96, 105, 107, 112; and
  Unaufmerksamkeit, 93, 96, 98,
  105
"Aufzeichnungen aus Korsika: Zur
  Natur & Menschenkunde" (Sebald),
  9–10
Aurach, Max, 66, 84, 90n57, 299,
  302, 309, 311–12, 314, 316,
  318n1, 320n29, 326
Auschwitz, 13–14, 16, 181, 184n25,
  301, 309, 331, 342, 344n43
Austerlitz (Sebald), 3, 7, 9, 12,
  14–15, 18–19, 21, 124–26, 134,
  136–38, 141n34, 161–63,
  165–67, 169–71, 176f4, 179f5,
  180, 181n1, 182n6, 322–23,
  326, 330–31, 334, 338, 341,
  342n15, 363

Austerlitz, Jacques, 39–40, 124–26, 133–38, 161–67, 169–81, 182n6, 182n8, 183n18, 184n20, 184n22, 185n27, 201–3, 322, 326, 328–34, 336–39 176
Austro-Hungarian North Pole Expedition of 1872, 143–44, 150, 153, 155
authenticity, 1, 16, 18, 20, 64–66, 68, 70, 72, 75–77, 84–86, 92, 114, 152, 155, 269

Bad Kissingen, 79; Jewish cemetery at, 84, 86, 88n24; salina at, 69
Badereise, 21, 123, 127, 130, 133, 136, 139n11
Baedeker, 67
Bakhtin, Mikhail, 322, 324–26, 336, 341n1
Balzac, Honoré de, 179
Bates, Richard, 17, 28n38
Beck, John, 119n44, 259, 266, 272n41, 273nn53–54
Becker, Thomas, 143
Benjamin, Walter, 11, 26n21, 60n37, 75–76, 88n31, 89n32, 92, 99, 110–12, 115n2, 117nn20–21, 118n30, 119nn47–48, 171, 184n21, 185n31, 211n54, 218, 233, 238n8, 239n16, 241n25, 258, 270n22, 300, 320n27, 336, 342n17
Bennett, Alan, 261, 272n39, 273n45
Bennett, Tony, 74, 88n28
Bereyter, Paul, 40, 191, 200–202, 210n48, 299, 302–3, 308, 313, 315, 319n14
Bergen Belsen, 338
Bering, Vitus, 5, 143–44, 153, 157nn6–7
Bernhard, Thomas, 221
Beyle, Marie-Henri. See Stendhal
Biernat, Ulla, 156, 160n32
"Bis an den Rand der Natur: Versuch über Stifter" (Sebald), 213, 215, 228–29, 236n1, 244n41
Blackler, Deane, 18–19, 28n36, 28n49, 208n16

Blue Highways (Least Heat-Moon), 324–25, 342n5
Bond, Gregory, 156, 157n1, 160n33, 220, 241n25, 244n41, 272n42
border-crossings, 4, 6–8, 11
Borges, Jorge Luis, 260, 284, 297n11, 319n11
Brandes, Georg, 235, 246n55
Breendonk, 12–15, 29n53, 40, 166–76, 180, 184n20, 239n19, 260, 267; Jean Améry and, 12–14, 27n30, 166, 170, 184n20
Bride of Lammermoor (Scott), 262, 273n47
Browne, Sir Thomas, 7, 22, 40, 48–49, 53, 57, 59–60n30, 61n38, 114, 223, 277, 287–88, 295; cosmological view of history of, 287–91; mystical and quasi-astrological views of, 287–90; *Religio medici*, 57, 60n30, 62nn44–46, 297n15, 298n18
Bruce Chatwin: A Biography (Shakespeare), 189, 190, 192, 195, 197–98, 199–200, 202, 204–5, 207n1, 207n6
Bruzelius, Margaret, 22, 247–73, 371
Bülow, Ulrich von, 10, 16, 25nn16–17, 27n34, 118n34, 158n12
Burgstaller, Wolfgang, 142, 156
Burton, Robert, 39, 58n5
Buruma, Ian, 190, 207n5
bus travel, 40, 100–101, 103, 113–14, 130
butterfly, 195, 198, 210n41, 306
Buzard, James, 64–65, 67, 85, 86n1, 87n4, 87n6, 87nn8–9, 87nn18–19, 88n26

Campo Santo (Sebald), 25n16, 140n24, 184n20, 363
Carline, Richard, 77, 89nn34–36, 89n38, 89n40
Casement, Roger, 7, 105–9, 119n41, 262–64, 283, 337–38
Catling, Jo, 3, 24n5, 28n36, 91n59, 117n22

Chatwin, Charles Bruce, 8, 22, 189–212; childhood, 195–96, 207n1, 343n26; as collector, 192, 194–98, 202, 204–5, 207n8, 208n18, 210n41; experience of blindness, 198–200, 202; as travel writer, 22, 191–92, 205–6, 208n12

Chatwin, Charles Bruce, works by: "The Estate of Maximilian Tod," 204–5, 211n61; *On the Black Hill,* 191; "It's a Nomad *Nomad* world," 190, 207n11; *The Nomadic Alternative,* 193, 207n9; *In Patagonia,* 190–91, 203, 209n31; "The Private Collector," 197; *The Songlines,* 190–91, 208n14, 210n44, 324, 342n5; *Utz,* 190, 196–97, 204–5, 210nn38–39

Clapp, Susannah, 199–200, 210n45

collector, 64, 192, 194–98, 204–5, 207n8, 208n18, 209n28, 210n41, 214

collecting, act of, 22, 75–76, 79, 202, 208n16, 216, 279, 304

colonel Chabert, Le (Balzac), 179

colonialism, 7, 21, 165, 280, 292, 295, 335, 338–40

Conrad, Joseph, 7, 18, 192, 247–73

Conrad, Joseph, works by: *Heart of Darkness,* 22, 247, 249–52, 255, 257–59, 262, 267, 269n, 269n6, 271n24, 271n29, 272n31, 272n33, 272nn35–36, 335–36, 339, 344n35

convergence, 189, 199–200, 202, 206, 216, 229

Corsica, 9–10, 25nn16–17, 27n34, 206

The Count of Monte Cristo (Dumas), 250, 260

Covehithe, 53, 55, 113

Crouch, David, 79, 89n47, 91n64

Cuomo, Joe, 11, 26n23

Dakyns, Janine Rosalind, 110

Dante, 47, 68, 145–46, 166–67, 173, 182n6, 184n20, 184n25; Pilgrim in *Divine Comedy,* 164, 167, 183n14; underworld, 173, 175

Dante, works by: *Divine Comedy,* 164, 167, 183n14; *Inferno,* 145, 175

Darby, David, 17, 24n5, 28n39, 193, 208n17, 208n24

"Das Geheimnis des rotbraunen Fells: Annäherung an Bruce Chatwin" (Sebald), 207n1, 343n26, 364

Das Land des Lächelns, 8–9

Das Schloß (Kafka), 24, 105, 118n28, 119n41, 212n62

"Das unentdeckte Land: Zur Motivstruktur in Kafka's *Schloss*" (Sebald), 4, 212n62

"Das Unheimliche" (Freud), 139n9, 268, 273n56, 344n41

Das Verschwinden des Schattens in der Sonne (Frischmuth), 325, 342n7

De Certeau, Michel, 43–44, 48, 59n23, 60n33, 329, 343n18, 343nn20–21, 343n28

De vita (Ficino), 39, 58n5

Deleuze, Gilles, 23, 138, 141n39, 304–7, 313, 316–17, 320nn21–23, 320n25, 323–28, 334, 336–37, 339, 342n4, 343n24, 343n30

Der Condor (Stifter), 224–25, 227–29, 233, 237n6, 240n23, 244nn40–41, 245n48

"Der Jäger Gracchus" (Kafka), 95–99, 102, 104

Der Nachsommer (Stifter), 213, 215, 235n, 243n34

Der Spaziergang (Schiller), 43, 59n19

Der Zauberberg (Mann), 92, 115nn4–5, 116n8

Derrida, Jacques, 130, 140n19, 321n33

"Des Häschens Kind, der kleine Has: Über das Totemtier des Lyrikers Ernst Herbeck" (Sebald), 62n43, 316, 321n36

Des Luftschiffers Giannozzos Seebuch (Jean Paul), 224

Detering, Heinrich, 146, 159n18

Dialektik der Aufklärung (Adorno, Horkheimer), 115n3, 154, 160n30, 184n21

Die Alexanderschlacht (Altdorfer), 146, 205
"Die Alpen im Meer" (Sebald), 25n16, 206, 212n64
Die Angst des Tormanns beim Elfmeter (Handke), 4
Die Ausgewanderten: Vier lange Erzählungen (The Emigrants) (Sebald), 3, 7, 11–12, 23, 40, 69, 72, 86, 88n24, 90n50, 143, 158n9, 171, 185, 190–91, 195, 198, 200, 202–3, 210n47, 242n25, 245n49, 299, 301–7, 312, 314, 317, 318, 318n2, 318n5, 319n15, 320n27, 320n29, 326
Die Beschreibung des Unglücks: Zur österreichischen Literatur von Stifter bis Handke (Sebald), 4, 8, 213, 221, 363
Die Blechtrommel (Grass), 324, 327, 342n10
Die Brücke vom Goldenen Horn (Özdamar), 325, 342n7
"Die dunckle Nacht fahrt aus" (Sebald), 5, 25n9, 146, 157n2
Die Entdeckung der Langsamkeit (Nadolny), 142, 156
Die Geburt der Tragödie (Nietzsche), 323, 341n1
"Die Kunst des Fliegens" (Sebald), 1, 3–4, 7, 9, 20, 24n2, 31–34
Die letzte Welt (Ransmayr), 143, 158n11
Die Ringe des Saturn: Eine englische Wallfahrt (The Rings of Saturn) (Sebald), 3, 7, 9, 19–20, 22, 25n10, 37, 39–40, 45, 47–49, 52–53, 57nn3–4, 63, 66, 70–74, 81–82, 84, 86, 88n22, 90n57, 91n59, 95, 103–14, 116n6, 118n39, 119n49, 120n52, 171, 184n23, 190, 192–93, 195, 201, 220, 223–25, 228, 245n44, 247–50, 258–59, 261, 265–68, 277–78, 280, 282f7, 283–93, 296, 323, 326, 334–41, 344n35; mapping of, 280–87, 281f6, 282f7

Die Schrecken des Eises und der Finsternis (Ransmayr), 21, 143–44, 149, 154–56, 158n9, 158n11, 159nn22–23
Die Sehnsucht der Schwalbe (Schami), 325, 342n6
Die Spatziergänge oder Die Kunst spatzieren zu gehen (Schelle), 44–46, 59nn25–26
Die Vertreibung aus der Hölle (Menasse), 325, 342n7
"Die Waldauer Begegnung" (Tripp), 29n54, 30f1, 34f2
"Die Zerknirschung des Herzens: Über Erinnerung und Grausamkeit im Werk von Peter Weiss" (Sebald), 60n35
Dionysus, 23, 322–23, 326–29, 331–34, 336–37, 339, 341, 343n27, 343n32, 344n38
Dirda, Michael, 190, 207n8
displacement, 4, 7, 11, 23, 63, 87n11, 91n61, 99, 102–3, 126, 138, 299–305, 307, 309–10, 312, 316–17, 330
Dittberner, Hugo, 221, 243n30
Divine Comedy (Dante), 164, 183n14
Douglas, James, 75, 77, 89n41
Dr. K., 123–27, 130–33, 136
Dr. Katzenbergers Badereise (Jean Paul), 127, 139n11
"Dr. K.s Badereise nach Riva" from *Schwindel. Gefühle.* (Sebald), 96, 123, 127–30, 133, 136
Dumas, Alexandre: 251, 267; *The Count of Monte Cristo*, 250, 260, 270n14
Duncan, Ian, 247, 269n2, 270n11
Dunwich, 53, 82, 104–5, 131, 260, 265, 335
Dürer, Albrecht, 110, 157n6, 290
Duttlinger, Carolin, 20–21, 92–120, 140n27, 185n28, 319n11

East Anglia, 10, 37–39, 47, 49, 53, 86, 171, 293, 295, 337, 339, 341
Edict of Nantes, 294–95
Egelhofer, Josef, 204

"Ein Walzertraum" (Sebald), 8–9,
25n15
Elias, Gwendolyn, 163, 173
Elias, Reverend, 163, 173
Eliot, George, 273n59
Eliot, T. S., 171, 184n24
emigrants, 23, 299–300, 302–4,
310–12, 316
Emile ou de l'éducation (Rousseau),
41–42, 58n10, 58n13
Enzensberger, Hans Magnus, 64,
87nn2–3, 87n17, 189–90, 207n4,
207n7
"Es steht ein Komet am Himmel:
Kalenderbeitrag zu Ehren des
rheinischen Hausfreunds" (Sebald),
60n31, 213
"The Estate of Maximilian Tod"
(Chatwin), 204–5, 211n61
Estes, David, 189–90, 207n4

Familienähnlichkeiten (Wittgenstein),
303, 319–20n16
"Fetishism" (Freud), 209n33
Ficino, Marsilio, 39, 58n5
Fitzgerald, Edward, 260
Fluchttraum, 1, 3, 9
Flusser, Vilém, 78, 82, 89nn44–45
flying, 1–2, 7, 39, 225–27, 261,
285, 330; dream of, 2; drug-
induced visions of, 226–27;
Gerald's obsession with, 330;
"Die Kunst des Fliegens" (Sebald),
31–34; learning, 20, 30f1, 34f2;
Robert Walser and Adolf Wölfli,
30f1, 34f2; and walking, 20,
45–53
Forrester, Axel, 203, 211n55
Forrester, John, 314, 321n31
For Years Now: Poems (Sebald), 157n2,
364
Foster, Kurt, 144, 158n12
Foucault, Michel, 278, 296n1, 322,
336, 341n1
"Franz Kafka: Zur zehnten Wiederkehr
seines Todestages" (Benjamin),
117n21
French Revolution, 43, 283

Freud, Sigmund, 126, 139n9, 195–96,
209n32, 259, 268; case history of
Little Hans, 23, 300–307, 310, 312,
314–18; fear of castration, 195–96;
and psychoanalysis, 300–301,
305–6, 314–15
Freud, Sigmund, works by: *Analyse der
Phobie eines fünfjährigen Knaben*,
301, 318n7; "Fetishism," 209n33;
heimlich/unheimlich, 126, 193,
338–39, 341; "Ratschläge für den
Arzt bei der psychoanalytischen
Behandlung," 107, 119n43;
Totem und Tabu, 305, 320n20;
"Das Unheimliche," 139n9, 268,
273n56, 344n41
Friedrich, Caspar David, 151
Frischmuth, Barbara, 325, 342n7
Fuchs, Anne, 28n35, 74, 88n27,
90nn58–59, 159n28, 220,
241–42n25, 320n17, 321n33

Garrard, Alec, 334
Geary, Christraud, 79, 89n46, 89n48
Gebürtig (Schindel), 325, 342n7
Gide, André, 1, 23n1
Gilpin, William, 43, 48, 54, 59n21
Gracchus, 21, 100–101, 106, 115, 124
Grass, Günter, 324, 327, 336,
342n10
Great Northern Expedition (1741),
144, 151
Gregory-Guider, Christopher C., 3,
24n6, 26–27n25, 87n11, 91n59,
245n45
"Grenzübergänge." *See* border-
crossings
Grillparzer, Franz, 68, 88n21
Grimmelshausen, Hans Jakob
Christoffel von, 291
Grünewald, Matthias, 5, 142, 145–47,
149, 157n7, 159n19, 236n3
Guattari, Félix, 23, 304–7, 313,
320nn22–23, 323–28, 339, 342n4,
343n24, 343n30
Guide des Voyageurs (Reichard), 67
Guy Mannering (Scott), 250, 253,
261–62, 270n16

Haggard, H. Rider, 249–51, 269n4, 270n11, 270n17, 273n59
Halbleib, Friederike, 84
Haller, Johann, 144, 151
Hamburger, Michael, 63, 74, 234
Hamlet (Shakespeare), 4, 163
Handke, Peter, 4, 24n4, 24n7, 159n21, 213, 222, 231–32, 236n1, 237n6, 243n35, 246n54
Harris, Sir Arthur, 192
Hartungen, Dr. Christoph von, 123
Harvey, David, 278–79, 296n8
Hazel, William, 72
Heart of Darkness (Conrad), 22, 247, 249–52, 255, 257–59, 262, 267, 269n, 269n6, 271n24, 271n29, 272n31, 272n33, 272nn35–36, 335–36, 339, 344n35
Hebel, Johann Peter, 48–49, 53, 60n31, 213
Heckenast, Gustav, 227–28, 245n47
Heidegger, Martin, 23, 296n4, 323–24, 326, 328–30, 332–34, 336–39, 342nn15–16, 343n19, 343n24, 343n33, 344n40
Heimat, 8, 10, 25n12, 29n51, 98, 100–103, 113–14, 116n15, 193, 208n19, 216, 267, 295, 299, 318n3, 322
heimlich, 126, 175, 193, 338–39, 341. See also *unheimlich*
"Helle Bilder und dunkle: Zur Dialektik der Eschatologie bei Stifter und Handke" (Sebald), 213, 231, 236n1, 244n41
"Her kommt der Tod, die Zeit geht hin: Anmerkungen zu Gottfried Keller" (Sebald), 235, 246n56
Herzog, Werner, 190, 203, 207n5, 211n57
Hirsch, Marianne, 184–185n25
history: of destruction, 2, 6, 171; and *katabasis*, 21, 133, 161, 163–65, 169–71, 180, 182n10; literary, 58n9, 192, 268; local vs. global, 278, 283–85, 289; and memory, 83, 170, 222, 232; natural, 6, 16, 195;

as network, 277–98; philosophy of history, 21, 163–65, 290, 297n16; and place, 13–15, 169, 294; as progress, 23, 37, 40, 156, 327; Thomas Browne's view of, 22–23, 287–92; of travel writing, 17, 20, 66–67, 85
Hitchcock, Alfred, 194, 209n26
Hölderlin, 336
Holocaust, 21, 26n19, 27n30, 28n45, 162, 165, 170–71, 180–81, 181n1, 184–85n25, 202, 301, 308, 311, 338–39
Homer, 166, 173, 192; *The Odyssey*, 21, 161–65, 170–71, 177–78, 180, 181n2, 182n6, 182n9, 339
Honold, Alexander, 99, 117n20
Horkheimer, Max, 92, 115n3, 154, 160n30, 184n21
horses, 41, 196, 300–301, 304–7, 309–12, 314–17
Hugo, Victor, 339
Hui, Barbara, 22, 277–98, 371–72
Huyssen, Andreas, 181n1, 220, 241n25, 283, 297n10

illumination, 22, 81, 220, 231, 257–58
Institute of Cultural Inquiry (ICI) Research Team, 19, 28n50, 81, 86, 90n52, 90nn54–55
"Il ritorno in patria" from *Schwindel. Gefühle.* (Sebald), 19, 39–40, 79, 95, 100, 202, 244n41
"In a Completely Unknown Region: On Gerhard Roth's Novel *Landläufiger Tod*" (Sebald), 242n27, 246n52
In Patagonia (Chatwin), 190–91, 203, 207n4, 209n31
Inferno (Dante), 145, 175
"Introduction and Transcript of an Interview given by Max Sebald," (Sebald), 211n52, 245n44
Irving, John, 324
Itkin, Alan, 21, 161–85, 372
"It's a Nomad *Nomad* world" (Chatwin), 190, 207n11

Jameson, Frederic, 164, 167, 183n16, 249, 270n8

jardin des plantes, Le (Simon), 170

"J'aurais voulu que ce lac eût été l'Océan: Anläßlich eines Besuchs auf der St. Petersinsel" (Sebald), 58n7

Job (biblical tale of), 151

Jong, Cornelis de, 72

journey to land of the dead, 162–65, 169, 178, 182n12, 183n19, 185n25. *See also katabasis*

Journey to the Center of the Earth (Verne), 261, 273n44

Kafka, Franz, 10, 21; Gracchus, 96–103, 113; letters to Felice Bauer and diary entries, 130–31; Italian travels, 131; travel writings, 95

Kafka, Franz, works by: *Das Schloß*, 24, 105, 118n28, 119n41, 202, 212n62; "Der Jäger Gracchus," 95–99, 102, 104; *The Metamorphosis and Other Stories*, 266–67, 273n55; *Nachgelassene Schriften und Fragmente I*, 116n13; *Nachgelassene Schriften und Fragmente II*, 140n18

Kant, Immanuel, 42, 58n15

Kaplan, Caren, 84, 91n61

katabasis, 21, 133, 163–65, 169–71, 180, 182n10

Katzenberger, Dr. Amandus, 127, 129–31, 138n4

Kehlmann, Daniel, 10–11, 26nn19–20

Kilbourn, Russell, 133–34, 140n31, 141nn33–34, 182n6, 182n10

Kindertransporte, 7, 161, 173, 330

King Solomon's Mines (Haggard), 269n4

Kingsley, Charles, 253, 271n23

Klebes, Martin, 21, 28n37, 117n18, 123–41, 300–301, 319n12, 319n16, 372

"Kleist in Thun" (Walser), 131, 140n23

Korzeniowski, Konrad, 105. *See also* Conrad, Joseph

Koschorke, Albrecht, 54, 61n42

Krisch, Otto, 144, 151

"Kulturindustrie: Aufklärung als Massenbetrug" (Adorno), 115n3

Kurtz, 253–57, 262, 271n28, 271–72n31, 336, 340

La chartreuse de Parme (Stendhal), 50

La lezione dell'abiso, 132

labyrinth, 158n11, 182n10, 224, 245, 291, 322, 325; as characteristic of rhizome, 326, 329, 331–32, 336–37, 340; and space, 27n34, 342n14

Lacan, Jacques, 23, 304–5, 310, 312, 314, 318n7, 320n19, 320n27, 321n31

Lamentation of Christ, 147

Landau, Lucy, 308

Landläufiger Tod (Roth), 233, 242n27, 246n52

landscapes, 1, 20, 39, 41, 48, 50, 59n21, 73, 83, 85, 88n23, 91n59, 93–95, 100–102, 110, 114, 117n22, 117n24, 117n26, 131, 160n33, 192, 208n15, 208n17, 208n24, 213–14, 235n, 236nn2–4, 241n25, 242n28, 249–51, 253, 259–60, 267, 283, 295, 322–24, 326–27, 330, 334–35, 339, 342n9, 343n26; Alpine, 113, 145–46; as an archive, 191; of destruction, 2, 6, 10, 16, 23; of East Anglia, 171; indifferent, 213–20; of Kafka's story, 101; and memory, 4, 17, 24n5, 28n39, 191; photographs, 86, 158n14; polar, 143–44, 146, 149–52, 156, 158n9; as products of the imagination, 3, 9, 24n5, 42–43; as songlines, 191; textual, 19, 216, 220; as "undiscover'd country," 3

L'année dernière à Marienbad (Resnais), 21, 126, 134, 137f3, 138–39n5, 141nn34–n35

Lanzberg, Luisa, 314–15

Latimer, Darsie, 248

Le colonel Chabert (Balzac), 179

Le comte de Monte Cristo (Dumas), 270n14

"Le promeneur solitaire: Zur Erinnerung an Robert Walser" (Sebald), 58n7, 211n59
Le voyage d'Urien (Gide), 1, 23n1
Least Heat-Moon, William, 324–25, 342n5
Lecture on Ethics (Wittgenstein), 320n16
Lefebvre, Henri, 278, 296n2, 296n5
Lehár, Franz, 9
Leone, Massimo, 18–19, 24n4, 28nn47–48, 29n55, 64, 87n11, 194, 208–9n25, 209n28
Les Confessions (Rousseau), 42, 44, 59n18, 59n24
Les rêveries du promeneur solitaire (Rousseau), 44–45
Les travailleurs de la mer (Hugo), 339
Lévi-Strauss, Claude, 62n43, 284
liminality, 20, 118n31, 327; of experience (*Schwellenerfahrungen*), 4; peripatetic, 37–62; and place, 13, 15, 230, 313; and space, 38, 44–46, 49, 54–55, 136, 234
Little Hans, 23, 300–307, 310, 312, 314–18
Liverpool Street Station, 7, 163, 171–75, 180, 331
Llosa, Mario Vargas, 257, 272n34
Logis in einem Landhaus (Sebald), 8, 40, 235
London, 7, 11, 40, 94, 171–75, 184, 258, 329, 331, 338; Samuel Pepys's account of the great fire of, 194
Long, J. J., 20, 24n5, 28nn35–28n36, 63–91, 133–34, 138n3, 200–201, 372
Lübbren, Nina, 79, 89n47, 91n64
Lubow, Arthur, 16, 27n33, 284, 297n12
Luciana, 72
Luftkrieg und Literatur (Sebald), 10, 114, 183n15

MacCannell, Dean, 65, 75, 78, 87n5, 87n10, 88n29, 89n43
Maier, Anja K., 146, 157n1, 159n17
males, demonic, 250, 254–55, 263–64

Mann, Thomas, 10, 92, 115nn4–5, 116n8
maps: of Suffolk showing narrator's journey, 281f6; of world showing locations in *Die Ringe des Saturn,* 280–87, 282f7
Marienbad spa, 123–26, 133–34, 136, 137f3, 138, 138n5, 140n29, 141nn34–36
Marlow, 248–49, 251–59, 263, 268–69, 271–72n31, 271n24, 271nn27–28, 271n30, 272n32, 272n34
Márquez, Gabriel García, 324, 327, 342n11
Martin, James, 21, 142–60, 233, 246n53, 372
Massey, Doreen, 278–80, 283, 285–86, 289–90, 296n6, 297n13
Maulbronn spa, 127–29
McCulloh, Mark, 24n5, 25n8, 25n10, 117n23, 208n17, 211n52, 220, 224, 227, 241–42n25, 244n41, 245–46n51, 245n44, 245n46, 268, 272–73n43, 273n57, 319n12, 319n15
"Mein Leben" (Stifter), 215, 217–19, 227, 229, 234, 238n11, 241n25, 246n56. *See also* "Nachgelassenes Blatt"
"Meine Ortschaft" (Weiss), 60n35, 177, 185n26
Melancholia (Dürer), 110, 157n6
melancholy, 111–12, 114–15; and destruction of nature, 2; distrust of solace and, 258; of main character, 204, 211n54; pedestrian tour as therapy against, 39; perspective, 143, 149, 151, 156; wanderers who are characterized by, 192
memories of childhood: narrators', 203, 228; Sebald's, 142, 157n6, 158n9, 229, 234; Stifter's, 230–32; in Wales, 7
Menasse, Robert: *Die Vertreibung aus der Hölle,* 325, 342n7; *Selige Zeiten, brüchige Welt,* 325, 342n7
Messerschmidt, Daniel, 149, 153, 155, 160n31

The Metamorphosis and Other Stories (Kafka), 266–67, 273n55
Meyer, Sven, 8, 25nn13–14, 156n1, 157n2, 157n7, 215, 238n9
Middlemarch (Eliot), 273n59
Milton, John, 178, 185n30
Minima Moralia (Adorno), 94–95, 116nn9–10
"Mit den Augen des Nachtvogels: Über Jean Améry" (Sebald), 184n20
Moretti, Franco, 268, 273n58
Moser, Christian, 20, 37–62, 58n9, 59n22, 60n30, 60n35, 152, 159n24, 372–73
mourning, 57n4, 87n11, 91n63, 114–15, 204, 248, 267–68, 309, 320n26; rituals, 114–15, 295
Murray, 67
Muselmann, 333, 340, 344n43

Nach der Natur: Ein Elementargedicht (After Nature) (Sebald), 3, 5–6, 21, 142–46, 155–56, 156n1, 157n2, 157n4, 157nn6–7, 158n9, 158n14, 213, 220, 230, 234, 236n3
Nachgelassene Schriften und Fragmente I (Kafka), 116n13
Nachgelassene Schriften und Fragmente II (Kafka), 140n18
"Nachgelassenes Blatt" (Stifter), 215, 229, 231, 237n6. *See also* "Mein Leben"
Nadolny, Sten, 142, 156
Naegeli, Johannes, 203–5
Nancy, Jean-Luc, 236n4
narrators: on bus journey, 113–14; experience of exile and dislocation, 7; on island of Orfordness, 261–62; as quasi-Sebaldian figure, 199; as surrogate for the author, 197; on train, 194; visions of flying, 226–27; on walking tour along Suffolk coast, 7, 104–5, 108–9, 277, 280, 283, 285, 287, 295; worldview of, 6
National Socialism, 21, 161, 165–66, 168–70, 173–74, 180–81, 301–2, 306, 313, 317, 343n23

National Socialist regime, 299, 309, 315
Nazis, 7, 40, 109, 166, 169, 174, 177, 179–80, 299, 308, 325, 331, 340, 344n34; as agents of "Endlösung," 174; ideology of, 302, 339; internment camp and torture chamber, 166, 170, 239n19; propaganda film made at Theresienstadt, 179
networks, 3, 22–23, 95, 116n12, 253; global, 279–80, 286, 292; historical, 277–95; paradigm of, 39; of railway connections, 41; of social obligation, 79; of spatiotemporal, 292–96; of traffic and communication, 46
Neumann, Estelle, 204
Nietzsche, Friedrich, 23, 322–24, 326–28, 330–34, 336–37, 339, 341, 341n1, 342n8, 343n23, 343n27, 343n29, 343n32, 344nn38–39
The Nomadic Alternative (Chatwin), 193, 207n9
nomadism, 84, 182n8, 324, 328, 330
nomadology, Deleuzian, 335
Novotny, Fritz, 218, 236n1, 239nn17–18

Odysseus, 161–64, 167, 169–70, 177–80, 181n2, 182n7, 182n12, 183–84n19
Odyssey, The (Homer), 21, 161–62, 164–65, 170–71, 177, 180, 181n2, 182n9, 182n12, 183n13, 336
O'Faolain, Nuala, 213, 235n
Öhlschläger, Claudia, 25n12, 28n36, 39, 58n6, 60n32, 157nn3–4, 157n6, 159n17, 185n28, 220, 222, 241n25, 244n37, 318n3, 319n11, 320n27
Old Mortality (Scott), 253, 271n25
"Om Læsning" (Brandes), 246n55
Omar Khayyam, 260
On the Black Hill (Chatwin), 191
On the Natural History of Destruction (Sebald), 60n35
One Hundred Years of Solitude (Márquez), 327, 342n11

Orfordness, 47, 55–56, 84, 86, 158n9, 261
Orientalism (Said), 251, 270n9, 325
Osborne, Dora, 23, 299–321, 373
Ousby, Ian, 85, 86n1, 87n2, 87n15, 88n23, 90n53, 91n62
Özdamar, Emine Sevgi, 325, 342n7

Pages, Neil Christian, 22, 213–46, 373
Paracelsus, 147, 159n20
Paradise Lost (Milton), 178, 185n30
Parisian Exposition Universelle of 1889, 76
Patt, Lise, 19, 25n8, 25n11, 27n25, 27n29, 28n50, 80–82, 88n30, 90nn51–52, 91n59, 118n29, 141n37, 185n27, 185n29, 209n26, 211nn54–55, 342n14
Paul, Jean, 21, 127–30, 138n4, 139nn11–14, 224, 244n42
Payer, Julius von, 144, 151–52
Penelope Peacefull, 161–62, 326
Pentheus, 327–28, 333
peripateticism, 37–62; liminality of, 53–57; as mode of traveling, 37–41; as tracing of destruction, 20
photographs, 17, 27n29, 61n43, 75, 79–80, 82–85, 90n57, 91n59, 104, 109, 117n22, 133, 137, 141n36, 141n38, 143–44, 158n14, 170, 172, 175, 176f4, 177–80, 179f5, 185n25, 185nn27–29, 200, 203, 208n16, 249, 266, 303, 306, 319n11, 319n16; tourist, 20, 76, 79–80, 84
photography, 19, 25n8, 27n25, 27n29, 88n23, 88n30, 89n44, 90n49, 91n59, 118n29, 140n27, 141n37, 180, 181n4, 185nn27–29, 209n26, 210n47, 246n53, 320n17, 342n14; as anti-tourist strategy, 82–85; and topography, 75–85, 90n57, 91n59; tourist, 20, 76, 79–80, 84
postcards, 75–82, 85, 89nn34–35, 89n37, 89n41, 89n46, 89n48, 90n50, 90n52
Prager, Brad, 21–22, 189–212, 373

Pratt, Mary Louise, 66–67, 87n16
Presner, Todd, 39, 58n6, 297n16, 300–301, 319n9, 319n13
promenades, 41–42, 45, 56, 58n11, 69, 139n6
promeneur, 41–44, 58n7, 211n59
"Le promeneur solitaire: Zur Erinnerung an Robert Walser" (Sebald), 58n7, 211n59
Psalm, 139, 145–46
psychoanalysis, Freudian, 300–301, 305–6, 314–15, 321n31

railways, 41, 68, 71, 116n7, 117n17, 184n25, 201, 253, 264, 301, 307–8, 313; Paul Bereyter's suicide on, 308, 313, 315; stations, 77, 271n28, 301, 303, 311, 315, 331, 334, 338, 340; system and Holocaust, 301, 308
Ramuz, Charles, 283
Ransmayr, Christoph, 143–44, 149, 151–56, 158n11; works in Sebald's personal library, 158n11
Ransmayr, Christoph, works by: *Die letzte Welt*, 143, 158n11; *Die Schrecken des Eises und der Finsternis*, 21, 143–44, 149, 154–56, 158n9, 158n11, 159nn21–23
"Ratschläge für den Arzt bei der psychoanalytischen Behandlung" (Freud), 107, 119n43, 119n50
Redgauntlet (Scott), 248, 269n3
Reichard, Heinrich August Ottokar, 67
Reiseführer (travel guide), 19, 67, 78, 89n45, 93, 153
Religio medici (Browne), 57, 60n30, 62n44–45, 297n15, 298n18
Rembrandt, 51–53, 55, 60nn35–36, 72, 260
Resnais, Alain, 21, 126, 134–35, 137, 137f3, 138–39n5, 141nn34–35
"The *Retrait* of Metaphor" (Derrida), 130, 140n19
rhizome, 23, 306, 323–31, 333–37, 340–41, 342n3, 343n26
Richter, Gerhard, 143, 157n8
Riordan, Colin, 156, 157n1, 160n33

rituals, Dutch mourning, 114–15, 295
Riva spa, 96–98, 123–24, 126–27,
130–33, 136
Robbe-Grillet, Alain, 134–35, 141n34,
141n38
Roth, Gerhard, 233, 242n27,
246nn52–53
Roth, Joseph, 10
Rousseau, Jean-Jacques, 40–42,
44–45, 56, 67
Rousseau, Jean-Jacques, works by:
Emile ou de l'éducation, 41–42,
58n10, 58n13; *Les Confessions,* 42,
44, 59n18, 59n24; *Les rêveries du
promeneur solitaire,* 44–45
Rushdie, Salman, 324

Said, Edward, 249, 270, 278, 297n16,
325
Said, Edward, works by: *Culture and
Imperialism,* 251, 270nn9–10,
270n19, 296n3, 322, 342n2;
Orientalism, 251
Salle des pas perdus (Antwerp's
Centraal Station), 166, 169, 322,
341
Santner, Eric, 104, 118n30, 241n25,
309, 320n26, 342n17
Schaer, Michael, 129–30, 139n14,
139n16
Schami, Rafik, 325, 342n6
Schawalder, Peter, 2–3
Scheherazade in the *Arabian Nights,*
99
Schelle, Karl Gottlob, 44–46,
59nn25–26
Schiller, Friedrich, 43, 59n19
Schindel, Robert, 325, 342n7
Schivelbusch, Wolfgang, 93, 116n7,
117n17
schizophrenia, 4, 320n22, 342n4
Schlesinger, Philip, 195, 209n30
Scholz, Christian, 75, 27n29, 88n30,
90n56, 185n29
Schreber case, 300, 319n10
Schwellenerfahrungen. See liminality
Schwindel. Gefühle. (Vertigo) (Sebald),
7, 20–21, 68, 72, 74, 80, 95–96,

99–100, 102–3, 105–6, 108,
113–14, 119n49, 120n52, 123,
130, 143, 192, 194, 202–3,
209n25, 211n54
"Scomber scombrus or the Common
Mackerel: On Pictures by Jan Peter
Tripp" (Sebald), 210n37
Scott, Sir Walter, 247, 249–51, 257,
259, 261–62, 267–68, 270n11,
270nn18–19
Scott, Sir Walter, works by: *Bride of
Lammermoor,* 262, 273n47; *Guy
Mannering,* 250, 253, 261–62,
270n16; *Old Mortality,* 253,
271n25; *Redgauntlet,* 248, 269n3;
Waverley, 247, 250, 269n1, 272n40
Sebald, W. G.: academic life, 10; and
Jean Améry, 12–14, 27n30, 166,
170, 184n20; birth, 10–11; and
Bruce Chatwin, 8, 22, 189–212,
330, 343n26; and Joseph Conrad,
7, 18, 22, 105, 192, 247–73, 283,
335–36, 339–40; exhibition at
Deutsches Literaturarchiv in
Marbach, 9; exhibition at the
Literaturhaus in Stuttgart, 10;
and flying, 1–2, 7, 30f1, 31–34,
34f2, 39, 45–53, 225–27, 261, 285,
330; and Franz Kafka, 4, 7–8, 10,
18, 21, 24–25n8, 28n37, 68, 72,
95–108, 113–14, 117n18, 117n22,
117–18n28, 119n41, 126–27,
130–34, 138n3, 140nn24–26, 192,
202, 205–206, 211nn53–54,
212n62, 239n14, 259–60, 266; and
Jean Paul, 21, 127–30, 138n4, 224;
and Christoph Ransmayr, 21,
142–60; "Sebald-Weg" for visitors
to Wertach, 19; and Adalbert
Stifter, 22, 146, 213–46; tour of
Suffolk, 7, 104–5, 108–9, 277, 280,
283, 285, 287, 295; and travel
narratives, 17, 20, 65, 85, 193,
202; and travelogues, 3, 10, 17–18,
20, 24n5, 93, 95, 99, 106, 113,
115, 116n12; and Robert Walser,
8, 40, 58n7, 131, 140n23, 206,
211n59

Sebald, W. G., works by: "All'estero" from *Schwindel. Gefühle.*, 38–39, 47–48, 61n43, 66, 68, 73, 80, 90n57, 99, 103; "Ambros Adelwarth" from *Die Ausgewanderten* (*The Emigrants*) 66, 90n57, 302, 326; "Aufzeichnungen aus Korsika: Zur Natur & Menschenkunde," 9–10, 363; *Austerlitz*, 3, 7, 9, 12, 14–15, 18–19, 21, 124–26, 134, 136–38, 141n34, 161–63, 165–67, 169–71, 176f4, 179f5, 180, 181n1, 182n6, 322–23, 326, 330–31, 334, 338, 341, 342n15; "Bis an den Rand der Natur: Versuch über Stifter," 213, 215, 228–29, 236n1, 244n41; *Campo Santo*, 25n16, 140n24, 184n20; "Das Geheimnis des rotbraunen Fells: Annäherung an Bruce Chatwin," 207n1, 209n29, 209n36, 343n26; "Das unentdeckte Land: Zur Motivstruktur in Kafka's *Schloss*," 4, 24n8, 211n53, 212n62; "Des Häschens Kind, der kleine Has: Über das Totemtier des Lyrikers Ernst Herbeck," 62n43, 316, 321n36; "Die Alpen im Meer," 25n16, 206, 212n64; *Die Ausgewanderten: Vier lange Erzählungen*, 3, 7, 12, 23, 69, 72, 86, 88n24, 90n50, 143, 158n9, 190–91, 195, 198, 200, 202–3, 210n47, 242n25, 245n49, 299, 301–7, 312, 314, 317, 318n2, 318n5, 319n15, 320n27, 320n29; *Die Beschreibung des Unglücks: Zur österreichischen Literatur von Stifter bis Handke*, 4, 8, 213, 221; "Die dunckle Nacht fahrt aus," 5, 25n9, 146, 157n2; "Die Kunst des Fliegens," 1, 3–4, 7, 9, 20, 31–34; *Die Ringe des Saturn: Eine englische Wallfahrt*, 3, 7, 9, 19–20, 22, 25n10, 37, 39–40, 45, 47–49, 52–53, 57nn3–4, 63, 66, 70–74, 81–82, 84, 86, 88n22, 90n57, 91n59, 95, 103–13, 116n6, 118n39, 119n49, 120n52, 171, 184n23, 190, 192–93, 195, 201, 220, 223–25, 228, 245n44, 247–50, 258–59, 261, 265–68, 277–78, 280–87, 281f6, 282f7, 283–93, 296, 323, 326, 334–41, 344n35; "Die Zerknirschung des Herzens: Über Erinnerung und Grausamkeit im Werk von Peter Weiss," 60n35; "Ein Walzertraum," 8–9, 25n15; "Es steht ein Komet am Himmel: Kalenderbeitrag zu Ehren des rheinischen Hausfreunds," 60n31, 213; *For Years Now: Poems*, 157n2; "Helle Bilder und dunkle: Zur Dialektik der Eschatologie bei Stifter und Handke," 213, 231, 236n1; "Her kommt der Tod, die Zeit geht hin: Anmerkungen zu Gottfried Keller," 246n56; "Il ritorno in patria" from *Schwindel. Gefühle.*, 19, 39–40, 79, 95, 100, 202, 244n41; "In a Completely Unknown Region: On Gerhard Roth's Novel *Landläufiger Tod*," 242n27, 246n52; "J'aurais voulu que ce lac eût été l'Océan: Anläßlich eines Besuchs auf der St. Petersinsel," 58n7; "Le promeneur solitaire: Zur Erinnerung an Robert Walser," 58n7, 211n59; *Logis in einem Landhaus*, 8, 40, 235; *Luftkrieg und Literatur*, 10, 114, 183n15; "Max Aurach," from *Die Ausgewanderten*, 66, 309, 311, 314, 316, 320n29; "Mit den Augen des Nachtvogels: Über Jean Améry," 184n20; *Nach der Natur: Ein Elementargedicht* (*After Nature*), 3, 5–6, 142–46, 155–56, 157n2, 157nn6–7, 158n9, 158n14, 213, 220, 230, 234, 236n3; *On the Natural History of Destruction*, 60n35; *Schwindel. Gefühle.* (*Vertigo*), 7, 20–21, 68, 72, 74, 80, 95–96, 99–100, 102–3, 105–6, 108, 113–14, 119n49, 120n52, 123, 130, 143, 192, 194, 202–3, 209n25, 211n54; "Scomber scombrus, or the Common Mackerel: On Pictures by

Jan Peter Tripp," 210n37; "Thanatos: Zur Motivstruktur in Kafka's *Schloss*," 24n8, 119n41, 211n53; *Über das Land und das Wasser: Ausgewählte Gedichte 1964–2001*, 8, 25nn13–15, 157n2; "Und blieb ich am äussersten Meer," 5, 25n9, 143, 145–46, 157n2, 157n7; *Unerzählt: 33 Texte und 33 Radierungen*, 157n2; *Unheimliche Heimat*, 8, 29n52; "Unterm Spiegel des Wassers: Peter Handkes Erzählung von der Angst des Tormanns," 24n7, 243n35; "Verlorenes Land: Jean Améry und Österreich," 184n20; "Wie der Schnee auf den Alpen," 5, 25n9, 157n2; "Zwischen Geschichte und Naturgeschichte: Über die literarische Beschreibung totaler Zerstörung," 61n39

Sebestyén, György, 125–26, 134, 139n6

Selige Zeiten, brüchige Welt (Menasse), 325, 342n7

Selwyn, Dr. Henry, 40, 90n57, 203, 205, 209n36, 302, 311

Seume, Johann Gottfried, 42–43, 45, 59n17, 365

Shakespeare, Nicholas, 189–90, 192–93, 195, 197–200, 202, 204–5, 207n1, 207n6, 208n18, 209n31, 209n35, 210n38, 210n41, 211n51

Shakespeare, William, 4

She (Haggard), 250, 270n17, 273n59

Sheppard, Richard, 27n35, 113, 119n47, 119n51, 120n51, 120n53, 189, 200, 207nn2–3, 207n10, 207n46, 210n46, 211n53, 211n56, 211n59, 239n14, 242n26

Silverblatt, Michael, 11–12, 26n22, 27n26, 220

Simmel, Georg, 300

Simon, Claude, 170

Sims, G. R., 77, 82

Solnit, Rebecca, 118n31, 194, 366

Somerleyton Hall, 38, 40, 45–46, 70–71, 81–82, 90n52, 193

The Songlines (Chatwin), 190–91, 208n14, 210n44, 324, 342n5

Sontag, Susan, 86, 91n63, 366

spas: Marienbad, 123–26, 133–34, 136, 137f3, 138, 138n5, 140n29, 141nn34–36; Maulbronn, 127–29, 136; Riva, 96–97, 123–24, 126–27, 130–31, 133, 136; travel, 21, 123, 125

spatiality, 22, 277–78, 280, 289, 296n4, 312–14

Spitz, Markus Oliver, 152, 159n25

St. Anthony's Temptation, 147

Staff, Frank, 76, 89nn34–35, 89n37, 89n39, 89n41

stasis, 2, 6, 18, 84, 110, 113, 198, 242n25, 245–46n51, 250, 268

Steinacker, Thomas von, 143, 158n10

Steller, Georg Wilhelm, 5, 142–44, 146–49, 153, 155, 157n7, 158n13

Stendhal, 7, 18, 50, 96, 192

Stevenson, Robert Louis, 248, 250, 253, 269n5, 273n52

Stifter, Adalbert, 22, 213–35; balloon trip in *Der Condor*, 225, 227–28; memories of childhood, 230–32; pathological behavior, 216; transmigration into Sebald's work, 213–46

Stifter, Adalbert, works by: *Der Condor*, 224–25, 227–29, 233, 237n6, 240n23, 244nn40–41, 245n48; *Der Nachsommer*, 213, 215, 235n, 243n34; "Mein Leben," 215, 217–19, 227, 229, 234, 238n11, 241n25, 246n56; "Nachgelassenes Blatt," 215, 229, 231, 237n6

Stone, Will, 19, 29n53

Straus, Oscar, 9

The Student of Prague (film) (Wegener), 132

Suffolk: map of, 281f6; walking tour along coast of, 7, 38, 53, 81, 86, 104–5, 108–9, 119n44, 192–93, 248, 250, 258–59, 261, 272n41, 272n43, 277, 280, 283–85, 287, 291–92, 295

Taberner, Stuart, 299, 318n2
Tagebuch auf der Reise nach Italien
(Grillparzer), 68, 88n21
Terezín. *See* Theresienstadt.
"Thanatos: Zur Motivstruktur in
Kafka's *Schloss*" (Sebald), 24n8,
119n41, 211n53
Theisen, Bianca, 17–18, 28nn41–43,
28n46, 58n8, 66–67, 87nn12–13,
88n26, 152–53, 159n26, 162,
181nn3–4, 182n7, 184n23, 290,
298n20
Theresienstadt, 174–81; concentration
camp, 40, 171, 175–77, 179; Nazi
propaganda film made at, 179;
streets of, 326
"Theses on the Philosophy of History"
(Benjamin), 184n21, 185n31
Theudobach, 127–30, 139n15
Tieck, Duchess of, 267
"Tlön, Uqbar, Orbis Tertius"
(Borges), 260, 284, 297n11
Todorov, Tzvetan, 257, 272n33
topography, 20, 27n34, 233, 255,
302, 304, 342n14; and photography, 75–85
Totem und Tabu (Freud), 305,
320n20
tourism, 16–17, 20, 37–38, 46, 57n2,
63–91, 93, 99, 118nn35–36, 153,
284. *See also* anti-tourism
tourist, 16–17, 20, 37–38, 46, 57n2,
63–65, 67–80, 84–86
Tournier, Michel, 324
trains, travel by, 33, 38–39, 58n6, 71,
73, 77, 93–94, 96, 101, 116–
17n17, 134, 182n8, 194, 260, 264,
300, 307, 312, 316, 319n9, 339;
stations, 7, 163, 166, 173–74, 180,
322. *See also* railways
transmigration, 22, 130, 220–30, 233,
244n39, 296
travel: in adventure or romance novel,
247–73; as antidote to melancholy,
3; and anti-tourism, 16, 20, 37, 57,
63–91, 284; and *Aufmerksamkeit*,
20, 21, 92–93, 95–96, 105, 107,
112; and authenticity, 1, 16, 18, 20,

64–66, 68, 70, 72, 75–77, 84–86,
92, 114, 152, 155, 269; to
Breendonk, 12–15, 19, 29n53, 40,
166–76, 180, 184n20, 239n19; by
bus, 40, 100–101, 103, 113–14,
130; by car, 2, 38, 71, 94, 96, 101,
283; in classical epic journey,
161–85; as flight of the imagination,
1–3, 9, 42–43, 50; and flying, 1–2,
7, 20, 31–34, 30fl, 34f2, 39,
225–27, 261, 285, 330 20, 30fl,
34f2; by foot, 37, 40, 47, 61n40,
63, 95 277, 279, 283, 334; guide,
19, 67, 78, 89n45, 93, 153; Kafka's,
4, 7, 18, 68, 95, 131–33; as
katabasis, 21, 133, 163–65, 169–71,
180, 182n10; as *Nachgehen*, 7,
25n1; peripatetic mode of, 8, 15,
17, 20, 27n29, 37–62, 87n11, 162,
171, 248; by plane, 285–86; as polar
expedition, 144, 146, 148–49; and
postcards, 76–77; rhizomatic,
335–36; solitary, 7, 12, 19, 41, 203,
335; spa, 21, 123, 125; and stasis, 2,
6, 18, 84, 110, 113, 198, 242n25,
245–46n51, 250, 268; textual, 3,
10, 18, 66, 70, 87n11, 96, 106,
124, 209n25, 209n28; and tradition
of literary walk, 37–62; by train, 33,
38–39, 58n6, 71, 73, 77, 93–94,
96, 101, 116–17n17, 134, 182n8,
194, 260, 264, 300, 307, 312, 316,
319n9, 339; as transmigration, 22,
130, 220–30, 233, 244n39, 296; as
trope, 7, 11–12, 18, 21–23, 25n11,
63, 130
travel writing, 9, 17, 20, 28n40,
66–67, 79, 85, 87n16, 162
travelogue, 3, 10, 18, 37–38, 46,
61n40, 95–96, 104, 106, 108–9,
111, 114, 181n4, 190, 277, 280,
283, 289, 291–92; as hybrid genre,
18; *Die Ringe des Saturn* as, 20, 37,
95, 108, 111, 113, 277, 280, 289,
291; *Schwindel. Gefühle.* as, 20,
95–96
Treasure Island (Stevenson), 248, 250,
253, 269n5, 273n52

Treblinka extermination camp, 13–14, 16

Trevor-Roper, Patrick, 199, 368

Tripp, Jan Peter, and Sebald's poem about painting, 8–9, 20

Tripp, Jan Peter, works by: "Das Land des Lächelns," 8–9; "Die Waldauer Begegnung," 29n54, 30f1, 34f2, 368

Tristes Tropiques (Lévi-Strauss), 284

Turner, Gordon, 211n52, 245n44

Tz'u-hsi, Empress, 259–60, 262, 264–65

Über das Land und das Wasser: Ausgewählte Gedichte 1964–2001 (Sebald), 8, 25nn13–15, 157n2

"Über einige Motive bei Baudelaire" (Benjamin), 115n2

Unaufmerksamkeit. See *Aufmerksamkeit*

"The Uncanny" (Freud). *See* "Das Unheimliche"

"Und blieb ich am äussersten Meer" (Sebald), 5, 25n9, 143, 145–46, 157n2, 157n7

underworld, 163, 165–67, 169–70, 172–75, 177–78, 183n15; Dante's, 173, 175; Dionysian, 332, 336–37; entrance to the, 163, 172, 175; Homer's, 173

"undiscover'd country," the, 3–4, 8–9, 17

"The Undiscover'd Country: The Death Motif in Kafka's *Castle*" (Sebald), 4, 24n8, 211

Unerzählt: 33 Texte und 33 Radierungen (Sebald), 157n2

Unglück, 215, 221–22, 232

unheimlich, 8, 29n52, 126, 139n9, 175, 193, 338–39. See also *heimlich*

Unheimliche Heimat (Sebald), 8, 29n52, 365

"Unterm Spiegel des Wassers: Peter Handkes Erzählung von der Angst des Tormanns" (Sebald), 24n7, 243n35

Urry, John, 84, 87n3, 88n20, 88n29, 91n60

Ursprung des deutschen Trauerspiels (Benjamin), 110–11, 119n48

Utz (Chatwin), 190, 196–97, 204–5, 210nn38–39

Utz, Kaspar Joachim, 196–98

"Verlorenes Land: Jean Améry und Österreich" (Sebald), 184n20

Verne, Jules, 261, 273n44

Verneuil, Marie de, 124, 139n5

Victoria, Queen, 267

Vidler, Anthony, 300, 318n6, 319n8, 319n14

Virgil, 163–64, 178, 182n11, 183n14

Wachtel, Eleanor, 11, 26n24, 193

walking, 3, 7, 15, 20, 27n29, 37–62, 73, 87n11, 99, 102–5, 108–9, 113, 118n31, 119n44, 172, 191–92, 202–3, 231, 248, 259–60, 265–66, 268, 269–70n7, 272n43, 277, 280, 283, 285, 287–88, 291, 295, 302, 313, 329–30, 335, 337–38, 341; as basis for unique mode of perception, 20; bourgeois "ideology" of, 42; Michel de Certeau's theory of, 43, 48, 59n23, 60n33, 329; in East Anglia, 37–39, 47, 49, 171, 293, 295, 337, 339, 341; as Enlightenment metaphor, 42; and flying, 20, 45–53; Karl Gottlob Schelle's theory of, 44–46, 59nn25–26; tour along Suffolk coast, 7, 38, 53, 81, 86, 104–5, 108–9, 119n44, 192–93, 248, 250, 258–59, 261, 272n41, 272n43, 277, 280, 283–85, 287, 291–92, 295

Wallace, Anne D., 42, 58n16, 59n20, 368

Walser, Robert, 8, 20, 30f1, 34f2, 40, 58n7, 206; Sebald's literary essay on, 8, 20, 30f1, 34f2, 40, 58n7, 206

Walser, Robert, works by: "Kleist in Thun," 131, 140n23

Ward, David C., 143, 157n8

"Wasteland" (Eliot), 171, 184n24
Watson, Nicola J., 85, 91n62
Waverley, 248, 259
Waverley (Scott), 247, 250, 269n1, 272n40
Webb, Virginia-Lee, 79, 89n46, 89n48
Weber, Samuel, 126, 139n10
Wegener, Paul, 132
Weiss, Peter, 60n35, 177, 185n26
Westward Ho! (Kingsley), 253, 271n23
Weyprecht, Carl, 144, 150–52
White, Andrea, 252, 270n9, 270n20
"Wie der Schnee auf den Alpen," 5, 25n9, 157n2
Wiederholungszwang, 109
Wilde, Oscar, 198
Williams, Raymond, 65, 87n8
Wittgenstein, Ludwig, 202–3, 303, 319n15, 320n16

Wolf Man, the, 306
Wölfli, Adolf, 20, 30f1, 34f2
Wood, James, 258, 272n38

Zilcosky, John, 17–18, 28n40, 28nn44–45, 59n28, 66, 71, 87n11, 88n25, 91n63, 116n12, 126, 139n8, 162, 181n1, 181n5, 182n8, 193, 208nn21–23, 210n42, 300, 318n4, 320n29
Zischler, Hanns, 131–32, 140nn24–26
Zisselsberger, Markus, 1–29, 88n30, 185n29, 208n19, 211n54, 220–21, 236n1, 237n6, 242n27, 243n33, 246n53, 373
Zobel, Rosina, 79
"Zwischen Geschichte und Naturgeschichte: Über die literarische Beschreibung totaler Zerstörung" (Sebald), 61n39